ACCOUNTING THOUGHT AND PRACTICE THROUGH THE YEARS

Edited by Richard P. Brief

A Garland Series

CHAMBERS ON ACCOUNTING
Volume V: Continuously Contemporary Accounting

R. J. Chambers and G. W. Dean, editors

Garland Publishing, Inc.
New York and London
1986

For a complete list of Garland's publications in accounting,
please see the final pages of this volume.

The papers in this volume are reprinted with the permission of the
journals, editors, and publishers listed in the table of contents.

Copyright © 1986 by R. J. Chambers

Library of Congress Cataloging-in-Publication Data

Chambers, R. J. (Raymond J.), 1917–
Continuously contemporary accounting.

(Chambers on accounting ; v. 5) (Accounting thought
and practice through the years)
Reprint of works originally published 1955–1985.
1. Current value accounting. I. Dean, G. W.
II. Title. III. Series: Chambers, R. J. (Raymond J.),
1917–   . Chambers on accounting ; v. 5. IV. Series:
Accounting thought and practice through the years.
HF5603.6.C46   vol. 5   657 s   86-9893
    [HF5657.5]   [657]
    ISBN 0-8240-7862-4

Design by Bonnie Goldsmith
The volumes in this series are printed on
acid-free, 250-year-life paper.
Printed in the United States of America

Contents

"Blueprint for a Theory of Accounting," *Accounting Research*, January 1955. — 1

"A Scientific Pattern for Accounting Theory," *The Australian Accountant*, October 1955. — 10

"Detail for a Blueprint," *The Accounting Review*, April 1957. — 18

"Towards a General Theory of Accounting," Australian Society of Accountants Annual Lecture in The University of Adelaide, August 1961; booklet, 1962. — 29

"The Resolution of Some Paradoxes in Accounting," Australian Society of Accountants Lecture in the University of Tasmania, April 1962; presented in University of Malaya, Singapore, July 1962, University of British Columbia, November 1962; published as *Occasional Paper No. 2* of Faculty of Commerce and Business Administration, University of British Columbia, 1963. — 75

"The Foundations of Financial Accounting," *Berkeley Symposium on The Foundations of Financial Accounting*, University of California, Berkeley, January 1967. — 110

"Continuously Contemporary Accounting—Additivity and Action," *The Accounting Review*, October 1967. — 129

"The Canons of Criticism," on a critique of *Accounting, Evaluation and Economic Behavior*, September 1969. — 137

"Second Thoughts on Continuously Contemporary Accounting," *Abacus*, September 1970. — 147

"The Commercial Foundations of Accounting Theory," in Williard E. Stone (ed.), *Foundations of Accounting Theory*, University of Florida, Gainesville, 1971. — 165

"Evidence for a Market Selling Price Accounting System," in Robert R. Sterling (ed.), *Asset Valuation and Income Determination*, Scholars Book Co., Lawrence, Kansas, 1971.	184
"Historical Cost Accounting," (joint author), *Abacus*, June 1971.	207
"Accounting in an International Economic Community," *Journal UEC*, Dusseldorf, January 1972.	208
"Trial—and Error: A Reply" (response to a review by D. Anderson and R. Leftwich of *Securities and Obscurities*), *Journal of Accounting Research*, Autumn 1974.	217
"Third Thoughts," *Abacus*, December 1974.	227
Accounting for Inflation (Exposure Draft), booklet, Department of Accounting, University of Sydney, September 1975.	236
"Accounting for Changing Prices," presentation to Hearings of a Review Committee, set up by the Australian Accounting Standards Committee of the Australian Accounting Research Foundation, on methods of inflation accounting, March 1976.	269
"Whatever Happened to CCE?" *The Accounting Review*, April 1976.	289
"Continuously Contemporary Accounting: Misunderstandings and Misrepresentations," *Abacus*, December 1976.	295
" 'The Taxi Company' under CoCoA," Accounting Researchers International Association Symposium, Houston, May 1978; Robert R. Sterling and Arthur L. Thomas (eds.), *Accounting for a Simplified Firm Owning Depreciating Assets*, Scholars Book Co., Houston, 1979.	311
"The Use and Abuse of a Notation: A History of an Idea," *Abacus*, December 1978.	332
"Inflation Accounting in the Mining Industry," Silver City Accountants Silver Anniversary Convention, Broken Hill, September 1979.	355
"Groundwork for Accounting Standards—or—30 Reasons for CoCoA," a discussion paper, October 1980.	373

"Financial Statements, Asset Valuation and the Neutrality Principle," *Bilancio di Esercizio e Administrazione della Imprese, Studi in onore di Pietro Onida*, Guiffré Editore, Milan, 1981.   401

"The Development of the Theory of Continuously Contemporary Accounting," written in 1981 for the Japanese translation by Ichiro Shiobara of *Accounting, Evaluation and Economic Behavior*, 1984.   421

"Accounting—'One of the Finest Inventions of the Human Spirit,' " Deloitte Haskins & Sells Distinguished Lecture in the University of Edinburgh, April 1983; *Contemporary Issues in Accounting*, Pitman, Bath, 1984.   451

"Accounting for Foreign Business," *Abacus*, June 1983.   474

"The Functional Utility of Resale Price Accounting," the outcome of a five-country mail-survey inquiry, 1985.   489

PREFACE

There is no clear intimation prior to 1961 that a coherent theory might emerge from the articles, papers, and books of earlier years. In retrospect, however, hints of the prospect may be identified. The association of accounting information with judgement and choice or decision making dates from the late forties. It was developed at length in *Financial Management* (1947), *The Function and Design of Company Annual Reports* (1955), and *Accounting and Action* (1957). In *Function and Design* annual reports and financial statements were represented as communications serving internally as means of coordination and externally as guides to the continuation or variation of contracts between firms and their investors, creditors, and work forces.

"Blueprint for a Theory of Accounting" (1955) advanced four general propositions and some auxiliary ideas as fundamental premises of a theory of accounting. Those propositions, in a few lines, linked accounting with economic behavior. Almost everything done since that time has been an elaboration of those premises or their logical consequences. "Towards a General Theory of Accounting" (1961) was a first attempt to put an augmented set of propositions into the form of a coherent argument, drawing for postulates or assumptions on established knowledge, mainly in the social sciences. In effect, it provided a sketch plan for *Accounting, Evaluation and Economic Behavior* written during 1963-64 and published in 1966.

The principal conclusions of that work were that informed economic action is a derivative of a periodical accounting based on the current cash equivalents of assets from time to time, periodical income calculations in dated real terms, and the authenticity of financial statements established by direct observation of prices from time to time. The conclusions seemed to be warranted in the light of the demonstrated unreliability of traditional accounting information and the conflicting or confused justifications advanced in support of traditional processes and products. Material illustrative of these infelicities had been published in papers reproduced in other volumes of this set. Some of it was brought together in "Evidence for a Market Selling Price Accounting System" (1971). That paper in its turn was the forerunner of *Securities and Obscurities* (1973), reprinted by Garland Publishing in 1982 under the title *Accounting in Disarray*.

The description of the system the theory entailed was chosen deliberately, in 1967. Historical cost accounting and replacement cost accounting are strictly misnomers, for every accounting system makes use of selling prices (if only for revenues and receivables); if the terms are descriptive of asset valuation rules, they are inapt descriptions of cash balances. The descriptions resale price accounting and exit price accounting are sometimes used as convenient shorthand for the style of accounting treated in the papers of this volume. They have the same defect, and they do not hint at the calculation of real income that is an important characteristic of the system. Hence the choice of the more generally descriptive name, continuously contemporary accounting. But that is a polysyllabic mouthful. The contraction CCA was used in some papers prior to 1975. About that time, current cost accounting came to be abbreviated by others to CCA. To avoid confusion, therefore, the acronym COCOA, changed later to CoCoA, has been used. The three forms of abbreviation occur in papers in this volume.

The proposal came under several kinds of criticism, to which some of the papers here reproduced were responses. Evidence and argument supportive of the proposal have continued to emerge. A sketch of the variety of that evidence is given in "Groundwork for Accounting Standards—or—30 Reasons for CoCoA" (1980). "The Development of the Theory of Continuously Contemporary Accounting" (1981) is a version up to 1980 of an essay prepared for an edition of *Accounting, Evaluation and Economic Behavior* some years after first publication of that book. It outlines in more or less chronological order many of the experiences, observations, and literary sources that gave rise to the system and cause for confidence in its practicality and serviceability, linking those things with many of the papers in these volumes and with work published elsewhere.

R. J. Chambers
G. W. Dean
December 1985

BLUEPRINT FOR A THEORY OF ACCOUNTING

It is twenty-five years since Professor J. B. Canning wrote "the accountants have no complete philosophical system of thought about income nor is there any evidence that they have ever felt the need for one." Even today the statement is true. In fact, accountants do not appear to have any complete system of thought about accounting—and this might well be considered a more fundamental lack.

There are unquestionably several systems of thought about the *practice* of accounting: systems which attempt to categorise the kinds of things accountants do in practice. These systems are almost all the subject can boast of in the way of theory, and for this reason accounting lacks the sharpness, the progressiveness and the vitality of other technologies. Other technologies are based on systems of ideas which serve as references or criteria of performance. Their systems of ideas are not simply descriptions of practice; they transcend applications as, indeed, any theory should. Only if a theory deals with the ideal can it serve as a guide to developments and improvements in the practice of the related technology. The conditions under which the practitioner works will inevitably cause his work or his results to fall short of the ideal, for the conditions are never ideal. But if the points at which the conditions fall short are discerned, or if the deficiencies in the technique are known (by reference to the theory), there is hope that the practice will be gradually improved.

Theory and Practice

It is necessary to distinguish between systems of rules relating to the practice of accounting and a theory of accounting. A system of rules is necessary for the consistent practice of any art, and it is useful to attempt to sort out the rules which appear to be followed. Only if the rules are adequately described is it possible to discover inconsistencies in the system. But adequate description does not assist in determining which of two inconsistent rules should be adopted and which should be abandoned. The question must be referred to a more fundamental proposition or set of propositions, to the theory of the subject.

The early analytical writers on accounting appear to have been content to limit themselves to descriptions of practice. *Accounting Concepts of Profit*, by Gilman, *A Statement of Accounting Principles*, by Sanders, Hatfield and Moore, *Introduction to Corporate Accounting Standards*, by Paton and Littleton, are examples of attempts to formulate and describe. Whether these writers deliberately or accidentally avoided the use of the phrase " a theory of accounting" or whether they could not envisage a theory of accounting as distinct from a description of practice is not known. But their works cannot be impeached on the grounds that they do not present a theory of accounting, for there is no expressed intention in them to do so.

It remained to post-war writers to attach the word "theory" to accounting. But these writers seem to have been less discriminating, or more anxious to employ a respectable word, than the writers of the 'thirties. They have given to substantially similar sets of rules as were formulated in the 'thirties the description "accounting theory." Thus we have Norris's *Accounting Theory*, Bray's *Four Essays in Accounting Theory*, Littleton's *Structure of Accounting Theory*, not to mention chapters in recent texts and articles in accounting journals which incorporate "accounting theory" in their titles. This practice is misleading and for several reasons tends to hinder developments in accounting.

The practice is misleading because it implies that there is nothing more fundamental in the study of accounting than formulations of practices. It is misleading because it tends to create the impression that accounting now has a basis similar to the basis of other technologies, whereas no scientist or technologist would be content with such a contradictory set of propositions as those described, for example, by Gilman. It tends to hinder developments because students of accounting are not encouraged to consider the possibility of alternative systems of accounting; because there is so much in the formulations of practice that is doctrinaire; because the real nature of the propositions put forward is not carefully considered; and because the assumptions underlying practice are not critically examined.

But the so-called "theories" of accounting are not even complete descriptions of practice. Accounting on a cash basis was probably useful enough for centuries before the idea of matching costs and revenues was recognised; and wide sectors of the business community today find this form of accounting adequate for their purposes. How, then, is its omission from the "theory" of the subject to be justified? It is dealt with in textbooks describing accounting technique, but the "theorists" seem quietly to ignore it. This can only be because accounting on a cash basis does not conveniently fit into a neat (but in part unrealistic) system.

In some of the more elaborate descriptive studies, attempts are made to justify rules or propositions on historical grounds and this is a common habit among accountants. The protagonists of conventional accounting frequently appeal to the antiquity of widely used practices. But antiquity is no criterion: in fact the history of other arts suggests that antiquity makes a practice suspect from the start.

The environment and the conduct of organised activity has changed vastly since the days when double-entry book-keeping was cradled. It would be fatuous to expect the same propositions to be valid now as were valid then, or to expect that no new propositions now require to be added. The resort to history is, in any case, unnecessary and restrictive. It implies that only tried and accepted rules can take an honoured place in the theory of the subject and it leaves little ground for speculating about more useful forms of accounting.

Let it be admitted that formulations of practice are useful, and that historical studies of practice and developments of practice are interesting and informative. This still leaves accounting short of what may properly be described as theory.

The Form of a Theory

If a theory of accounting is to go beyond practice and if the historical development of the practice is to be disregarded, upon what basis, then, may it proceed? Upon the same basis substantially as any other theory; that is, by building up a series of relevant propositions from a few fundamental assumptions or axioms. The system of Gilman and his followers can in no way be related to this idea of a theory: its structure of conventions and doctrines is artificial, having no counterpart in the theory underlying any other technology. Are there no assumptions, for example? There are; but they are not identified as assumptions. Are there no axioms? Yes, but they sail under different colours.

It is possible to build up a theory of accounting without reference to the practice of accounting. This does not mean that the theory will have no connection with reality. To design a theory which has no relevance to reality is quite feasible: but the theorist in any field which has a practical counterpart can scarcely be as delightfully irresponsible as Lewis Carroll. Theory is not synonymous with remoteness from reality. It is, in fact, one of the greatest pleasures of the theorist to put his hypotheses to the test of reality. If one is confronted with what purports to be a theory of accounting, and finds that it deals with corporate accounting only, the existence in reality of unincorporated ventures will cast doubts on the validity of the propositions put forward. This process of checking back is of the nature of scientific method. It is followed to secure that no unreal or unjustifiable assumptions lie beneath the argument.

Premises

The fundamental premises for a theory of accounting lie outside of the field of accounting proper. There is no such thing as accounting in the abstract: accounts are kept for entities which are recognised in other fields of discourse, chiefly in economics and government. The following propositions therefore seem to be necessary:

(a) Certain organised activities are carried out by entities which exist by the will or with the co-operation of contributing parties;
(b) These entities are managed rationally, that is, with a view to meeting the demands of the contributing parties efficiently;
(c) Statements in monetary terms of the transactions and relationships of the entity are one means of facilitating rational management;
(d) The derivation of such statements is a service function.

The first of these propositions is an observation from the real world. It is general enough to cover every circumstance for which accounts may be required. It embraces incorporated and unincorporated trading ventures;

private non-profit making organisations; government and other public bodies; and a community as a whole. It is thus the foundation of private, public and social accounting.

The second proposition is also an observation from reality. It can be interpreted in the sense of maximising economic returns or in the sense of maximising all returns to the contributors. It is substantially the same proposition as one which underlies a great part of economic theory. The precise demands of the contributing parties are not set down because, for the variety of entities contemplated, ends or purposes will differ materially.

The third proposition simply recognises that, in a money economy, money is a convenient common denominator. If it were desired to make a theory fit any other kind of economy, the proposition could be stated in more general terms. That there may be other means of facilitating rational management is recognised at the outset.

The fourth proposition is a corollary of the former two. But it has itself some significant consequences. It implies that there can be no proposition admitted in accounting theory which interferes with the rights of those whom accounting serves: for example, the right of management to have full information and relevant information on the efficiency with which ends are pursued.

Entities

Some further comments on the first of these propositions may emphasise the difference between the view here suggested and that put forward in other systems. The idea of an accounting entity is now generally accepted in discursive treatments of accounting. Gilman and his followers describe it as a convention: Bray thinks of it as a principle. But the "entity" is an anterior idea to the "accounting entity": an entity becomes an accounting entity because and when accounts are kept about it. In the writer's view the entity is a datum, the particular features of which must be taken into consideration in framing an appropriate information-providing system. Many writers note that the entity may have different forms; but in no case is an attempt made to work out propositions which are appropriate to those different forms.

Now this seems to be the crux of the matter. If entities differ it is highly probable that the kinds of information required by their managers and other participants will differ. It becomes necessary to inquire, for each type of entity, what information is required for its rational management. For purposes of illustration it is useful to set down some of the ways in which entities may differ.

Firstly, entities differ in expectation of existence. The possible alternative assumptions are continuity and liquidation. The kinds of information which enter into a system of accounts will differ according to the assumption adopted. Entities also differ in the nature and variety of their contributors; two of the possible assumptions are tight control over performance of the entity and its management, and a loose form of control: the required end-products of an accounting system may be different according to the assumption made. Thirdly, entities may differ in respect of the criteria of performance by which they are judged. Some are conducted on a "sustenance" basis, some on a break-even basis, some on a profit or dividend basic; and in each case there may or may not be assumed a desire to maintain real, or money, capital. The various combinations of assumptions about the "ends" of contributors will yield different models of accounting processes.

It is not sufficient to pass over these differences in the nature of entities or to assume that the environment, scope and criteria of performance are always the same. Such an assumption can never provide a theoretical basis for the many forms of accounting used in the administration of organised activity; it is unreal; it condemns all entities to lie in the same Procrustean bed. Each of the possible assumptions mentioned in the previous paragraph is entirely feasible, and to every one there is a corresponding set of real circumstances and an appropriate technique. Yet in what now passes for accounting theory, the half of these possibilities is disregarded. And the half that is disregarded has just as much right to consideration as the other half, because it represents certain practical situations. Only if a theory, or even a descriptive system, envisages all these possibilities can it pretend to embrace accounting for sole traders, corporations, clubs, fiduciaries, governments and communities.

The Assumption of Rationality

The second basic proposition is rational management. It would be useful to consider at length the conditions of rational action but it is not intended to do so here. There are many uncertainties which cannot be adequately canvassed before making decisions, but the system of accounts should in no way increase these uncertainties. Rational management entails the consideration of alternative courses of action, the making of decisions, the facilitation of their execution and the examination or review of their consequences.

It is therefore a corollary of the assumption of rational management that there shall be an information-providing system; such a system is required both as a basis for decisions and as a basis for reviewing the consequences of decisions. Part of such a system, in money economies, is the accounting system. Because of its formal nature—formal in the sense that all kinds of transactions are expressed in more or less abstract money equivalents—the fact that real things and real relationships lie behind the figures in accounts may easily be overlooked. To avoid this oversight a formal information-providing system should conform with two general propositions.

The first is a condition of all logical discourse. The system should be logically consistent; no rule or process can be permitted which is contrary to any other rule or process. In particular the symbols used should have a sensibly uniform meaning throughout the system. In accounting this involves that equal things should be represented by equal symbols. In the present practice of accounting this proposition has no place. Equal things are often represented by different symbols and the same symbol may represent quite different quantities of the same thing. This is illogical. It can scarcely lead to the same conclusions (decisions) as a logical system, and it is hard to see how it can lead to rational conclusions. One suspects that on many matters appropriate decisions are made in spite of, rather than because of, the system of accounts.

The second proposition arises from the use of accounting statements as a basis for making decisions of practical consequence. The information yielded by any such system should be relevant to the kinds of decision the making of which it is expected to facilitate. There seems to be nothing indefensible about this proposition. If decisions are to be made now to be carried out in the future it is only reasonable that the present state of affairs, expressed in terms now relevant, should be used as their basis. And if the consequences of past decisions are being reviewed, it is only reasonable that achievements and the costs of those achievements should be expressed in terms which recognise the fundamental criteria of performance for the specific entity in question. This proposition, like the former, is in marked contrast with contemporary accounting practice, as will be shown presently.

The Symbols of the System

The symbols used or to be used in a system of accounts are units of currency. This is a corollary of the proposition just stated: no other unit is as relevant as the unit of domestic currency to the general body of contributors or to the entity itself. But here again alternative assumptions may be made about the nature of the monetary unit: it may be assumed that the monetary unit or unit of account has a stable real value or an unstable real value. Either assumption may be realistic in certain circumstances, and each will result in a different system of accounts. Thus, (a) if an entity is assumed to have a continued existence and (b) if the real value of the unit of account has changed over time and (c) if the test of relevance be admitted, the system to be devised is one which will set off against the current gross income the current costs of services consumed, and will show in current terms the financial position which is the result of past transactions. Such a system differs materially from contemporary accounting practice: but it stems directly from the notions of rationality and relevance. Contemporary practice proceeds on the obviously unrealistic assumption of monetary stability, and it is scarcely to be wondered at that businessmen, themselves the users of accounts, so roundly criticise the relevance of accounting statements. The assumption of monetary stability may have been realistic at one time, but to preserve a time-honoured system only on the ground that it is time-honoured is not consistent with the notion of a service function.

Form

An accounting entity is a thing about which accounts are kept; and monetary symbols are the symbols by which the transactions of an entity are described. The form of a system of accounts may now be considered. For convenience of exposition monetary stability will be assumed; but this assumption in no way jeopardises the generality of what follows. It is convenient, too, to start with the simplest kind of entity: the liquidated venture. In this, the simplest case, inputs equal outputs. In the simplest case of a continuing entity inputs equal outputs plus residues. The model can be extended by introducing inputs of an enduring kind and outputs or outlays for enduring benefits; but always inputs equal outputs plus residues. This is a convenient basis for a system, in that it shows what relationship exists between inputs and outputs and what the residues amount to. The equality may be called the basic identity or axiom of accounting. If it is granted that the relationship between inputs and outputs and the size of residues are matters of importance, double-entry follows. If some aspects of these matters are practically less important single-entry accounting may suffice.

For the purpose of recording inputs and outputs a convention is adopted. Inputs will be shown as credits; outputs and residues as debits. Credits and debits will be shown in adjacent columns, credits on the right hand side and debits on the left. The usual book-keeping paraphernalia could be introduced here but will not be discussed. The reason for discussing form is to indicate that only one kind of convention may be permitted in the system of propositions here put forward: conventions as to formal arrangement. Everything else is too significant to be treated as convention only.

Accounting Statements

A second corollary of the assumption of rationality may now be stated. It is an assumption that relates only to continuing entities. The necessity for making new decisions and reviewing past decisions requires that there shall be periodical statements of changes in the affairs of a continuing entity. It may be shown that in complex entities three kinds of statement are useful for this purpose: a statement of the affairs of an entity at the opening and the close of such periods (for example, balance sheets expressed in values relevant to their dates); a statement of the operating incomes and outlays during the period (for example, an operating or revenue account); and a statement incorporating total net additions to the funds of the entity and total net dispositions of those funds in the period (for example, a funds statement, incorporating both the effects of operations and the effects of long-term financial and other arrangements). In simpler entities, a simpler system of statements may suffice. It is not intended to discuss these statements here; although their general nature is suggested it may be possible to work out other statements which promote rational decision-making.

But one point deserves mention. The statements should adequately describe what has happened in the period. They should relate to the period and to that period alone. Where account must be taken of the unexpired values of durable assets or unliquidated assets, certain problems arise. The simplest model is based on the assumption of certain knowledge, and for the purpose of sorting out the issues involved and of devising ways of meeting them this model is useful. But in reality uncertainties exist and the simplest model must be modified to meet the case of uncertainty. This requires some flexibility in the rules formulated for the system. The point is made here because in the teaching of accountancy some of the rules (for example, with respect to depreciation) tend to be stated in a way which virtually assumes certain knowledge.

A third corollary of rationality is that all material particulars are required to be shown. Material particulars are details which may influence judgment. They will vary according to the real nature of the entity involved and according to the assumptions made regarding criteria of performance. This corollary also justifies the omission of non-material particulars, in as much as non-material details interfere with the process of comparison and contrast which is characteristic of ratiocination.

Having established a system based on the assumption of monetary stability it is then appropriate to modify the model on the assumption of monetary instability. This will require the introduction of additional rules, but in every case the test is required to be: "What is necessary for rational decision-making?" The problem of accounting under conditions of monetary instability has been neglected or deliberately put aside by most writers on the so-called theory of accounting. This was perhaps inevitable if, as is here suggested, the discursive treatment of accounting has been confined to descriptions of practice. There has been no recognition of the possibility that all that is involved is a regrouping of assumptions, or the substitution of a realistic assumption for an unrealistic one. It is not a question of working out entirely new "principles."

Conclusion

In conclusion it is useful to point out some of the features of the system of ideas indicated here. The system is only briefly sketched; many details have not been filled in, because the purpose of this outline is to suggest a procedure for developing a theory of accounting rather than to expound such a theory in detail.

Firstly, the system of propositions suggested hangs together. It proceeds from a few data and a few assumptions to which propositions are added as convenience of exposition or recognition of realities requires. It is thus in marked contrast with other descriptive systems the main propositions of which are not tied to a few unifying ideas but are isolated, sometimes artificial, and often contradictory.

Secondly, the method recognises that there are many different entities which require different models. This prevents the gross over-simplification which is characteristic of some descriptive systems. Every type of accounting can be represented by a theoretical model built along similar lines. No descriptive system yet put forward has contemplated the application of similar (but not identical) basic propositions to the problems of private, public and social accounting.

Thirdly, the theory consists of propositions which are a framework for the development of ideal systems of accounts. It may then become easier to discover the deficiencies of existing accounting methods, to devise means of meeting new requirements—and this not in an *ad hoc* fashion, but as the logical consequence of the basic function of accounting, that is, the provision of information to be used in making rational decisions.

Fourthly, the same framework may be extended to provide a theory of cost accounting. For this purpose the broad functions of entities are considered to be the basis for all minor decisions affecting their operations, and the information required is such as will make it possible to make these minor or contributory decisions rationally.

Fifthly, the system incorporates features which economists have found it useful to adopt in studies of business behaviour and social problems. It seems to be likely that many differences of emphasis in accounting and economics may be resolved if it is recognised that both deal with substantially the same entities, and that both should therefore proceed on the same assumptions. In many respects the assumptions of economics are more realistic than the assumptions of contemporary accounting; but each subject is likely to be more helpful to the other if the assumptions are laid bare for comparison. The unfruitfulness of exchanges between accountants and economists in the past seems to have been due to the neglect to discuss assumptions. A theory of accounting in which the assumptions are disclosed may help in this direction.

Sixthly and finally, the training now offered to accountants consists largely of the routine learning of procedures, often of procedures for which no alternative is countenanced. The habit of rigorous, logical thought is not inculcated and it cannot be expected that the products of this training will, by criticism or construction, contribute to the development of a more relevant and realistic accounting. The outline offered in this paper suggests a form of training in which the real nature of the "conventions," "doctrines," "standards," "principles," which appear in descriptive treatments of accounting, is brought to the notice of students. It may be hoped, then, that an assumption, an axiom, a hypothesis will be recognised for what it is, and will not be accepted as inviolable dogma. Descriptive and analytical studies of practice are necessary: only if there are such studies is it possible to test what is done against what is required. But even more necessary is the development of a theory which provides an ideal system against which expedient and convenient and unsystematic practices may be tested.

Sydney, N.S.W., Australia

A Scientific Pattern for Accounting Theory

LIKE all arts, accounting has become the subject of theorising late in its life; by comparison with some arts, very late in life. The slowness with which concepts and generalisations about the relationships between concepts have been developed is probably due to the fact that accountants have always regarded their work as practical, an art which can be learned to the point of practical utility by applying the seat of the pants to the seat of the high stool. Most of the practical men have seen no need to reconsider, or to attempt to clarify, the methods they have used. Few indeed of the partners in the oldest and largest practices have left any contribution to knowledge about accounting by which they may have been remembered. They have gone about their work, as most practical men do, simply confident of the propriety of their methods and of the value of their services to the community.

Simple confidence is of course, a comfortable state of mind. It allows one to go about his business without any gnawing fear that his technique may not be as efficacious as he has been led to believe. It relieves him of the painful problem of devising and experimenting with alternative techniques; it even saves him from thinking about the purposes for which his technique exists at all. It is natural, therefore, that those who have slipped into technical somnolence should be suspicious of theory, for it is the annoying habit of theorists to question established beliefs and customary procedures.

However, simple confidence is a poor foundation for an art which is practised in a continually changing environment. In the last hundred years, the growth in importance of the business corporation, the spread of private investment, the increase in taxation on incomes, and the fluctuations in the fortunes of business through wars and depressions, have brought under notice the need for some changes in accounting practices. The confidence even of practitioners was shaken, and attention began to be directed to the "principles" on which accounting was believed to be based.

The Search for Standards

One of the more obvious problems arose from the negotiability of security investments. The legislation which created the limited liability company recognised that investors needed information on the financial affairs of companies, by providing that public companies should publish financial statements annually. But of what use would this be if companies were to adopt different methods of computing income, or if they were to use technical terms indiscriminately in statements the recipients of which are mainly lay persons? Uniformity of method and terminology appeared to be such an important objective that many professional associations sponsored the publication of statements on these matters. Whether or not this legitimate and justifiable desire for uniformity led to the search for "accounting standards"—the foundations of "good" contemporary practice—is not clear. But there appears to be some ground for believing that the two movements had similar origins, or that one gave rise to the other, for both arose in the 'thirties in the United States.

Looking back, one is prompted to ask whether the search for accounting standards, and even the use of the term "accounting standards," was not premature. Paton and Littleton used the term in preference to "principles" for the latter "would generally suggest a universality and degree of permanence which cannot exist in a human-service institution such as accounting."[1] But it is doubtful whether such an impression is avoided by the use of "standards"; a standard may well be taken to be something established by authority, accepted, or generally approved, and the suggestion of authoritarian support is as much to be avoided as the suggestion of univerality or permanence. The reason for asking whether the attempt to establish standards was premature, however, lies in the necessity for establishing foundations before worrying about standards. As yet it can scarcely be claimed that the foundations of accounting have been thoroughly examined; there are still large areas in which material differences of opinion exist. In fact, the whole process of conventional accounting should be considered as nothing more than the consequence of an hypothesis. In these circumstances it seems to have been unfortunate that attention was diverted from the development of a theory of the subject to the development of standards for practice.

The student of any other discipline may find it strange that the literature of accounting lacks the familiar signs of scientific discourse. Even though the subject has been rescued from declining into dogma, it is still difficult to trace the elements of logical and methodical enquiry through the writings of its exponents. The general treatment of the subject is lacking in rigour. There are many categorical statements which ought to be recognised as hypotheses only; there are some examples of inductive and deductive reasoning, but few examples of the systematic use of both to test or to support a hypothesis; there are many examples of value-judgments masquerading as reasoned conclusions. Several general types of deficiency are worth noticing.

Adoption of Rules as Theory

It is paradoxical that the literature of a subject, the practical effect of which is to promote knowledge about other things, is lacking in evidence of appreciation of the ways of acquiring knowledge about itself. The labels attached to many propositions and concepts bear no similarity to the categories of scientific methodology. The commonly used classification of "basic" concepts into doctrines and conventions is ideally suited to give notice that the subject matter is not amenable to the same treatment as other studies. The persistence of these terms through sixteen years shows that notice was duly taken.

To be fair to Gilman, it should be pointed out that his *Accounting Concepts of Profit* is concerned with the practice of accounting. It was perhaps proper that he should describe as "doctrines" what were generally laid down as desirable practices, and as "conventions" what were commonly accepted practices, for he was not engaged in a study of the theory of the subject. If the latter had been his purpose, he would have had to take these observed practices as things needing inquiry and investigation. He was aware of the internal inconsistencies between some of the propositions he described, but he was not concerned with the construction of a self-consistent body of rules or principles. His followers have, unfortunately, borrowed his framework, adopted substantially the same concepts, and called the lot "accounting theory," regardless of the lack of precision of some of the concepts, and of the contradictions between them. There has been no attempt to link these concepts, or to set one against the other for the purpose of discovering more

---

1. *An Introduction to Corporate Accounting Standards*, 1940. p.4.

ACCOUNTING THEORY — Continued

general concepts or fundamental propositions. In some cases the order in which the propositions are treated strongly suggests that the connexion between them is quite misunderstood. The study of the subject has not passed the stage of crude observation; it is a pity that rules are based on such an unsubstantial foundation.

Excessive Abstraction

The need for abstract thinking appears to have arisen before the art of meaningful abstraction has been mastered. If abstractions must be used, they should be used with care; to do otherwise is unfruitful and may be misleading.

"Accounting" is an abstraction. When it is used without qualification, it is reasonable to suppose that it is used with reference to the whole of a general class of processes, all of which are called "accounting"—single entry accounting, double entry accounting, business accounting, governmental accounting, etc. Many statements about accounting are invalid, because although they use the universal term they are asserted in contemplation of only one of its particular varieties. Professor Bray writes: "the familiar idea of double-entry is quite fundamental to all accounting theory."[2] There can be no doubt of the universality of the last three words. But is it true that there can be no theory of single entry accounting? Professor Littleton calls his monograph *Structure of Accounting Theory*. But on examination it turns out to be concerned solely with double entry accounting, on an accrual basis, for business enterprises—three distinct limits which make the use of the universal term inappropriate. It may be felt that to quarrel with such usages is splitting hairs, because the context in which the term is used clearly suggests the limitations which have been imposed, and any person is quite at liberty to limit his discourse in any way he pleases. But if the limitations are not explicit, abstraction can lead to confusion and to neglect of the part of the subject which is excluded.

This may be illustrated by reference to the entity concept. "Accounting entity" is an abstraction used to enable general statements to be made about accounting for different organisations with verbal economy. Without qualification the term can only be used validly in connexion with statements which are true of all accounting for whatever entity. There are very few such statements. It was pointed out in a previous paper[3] that organisations differ in material particulars, particulars which determine the type of accounting which is appropriate. These particulars may be derived from observation of different organisations; they do not arise within accounting, and no proposition in accounting can dispose of them.

Let it be assumed that there are four possible differences in entities:—

A, differences in expectation of existence:
  a_1, continuity;
  a_2, liquidation;
B, differences in expectation of income:
  b_1, profit objective;
  b_2, no profit objective;
C, differences in attitude towards capital:
  c_1, real capital to be maintained;
  c_2, money capital to be maintained;
  c_3, maintenance of capital not of prime importance;
D, differences in attitude towards participants:
  d_1, contractual rights enforceable and enforced;
  d_2, contractual rights not rigorously exercised.

The differences listed are not exhaustive, but they will suffice for the purpose of illustration. It will also be sufficient to consider two types of organisation in order to suggest the differ-

---

2. *Four Essays in Acounting Theory*, O.U.P. 1953. p.4.

3. "Blueprint for a Theory of Accounting," *Accounting Research*, Jan. 1955; *Australian Accountant*, Sept. 1955.

ences in accounting method which may arise.

A business corporation may be defined in the above terms as $a_1b_1c_1d_1$; a professional association as $a_1b_2c_3d_2$. What proposition may be formulated for the recognition of gross income in each of these cases? For $a_1b_1c_1d_1$ the results of a year and the financial position at its end will be fairly represented if income is recognised when a claim arises. This, because a business corporation has legal rights to enforce such claims and has usually no hesitation in exercising them. But for $a_1b_2c_3d_2$, the results of a year and the financial position at its end will be fairly represented if income is recognised when cash is received. This, because a professional association usually prefers to remove defaulters from its membership rather than to take legal action for the recovery of subscriptions.

Each feature of the accounting process would require a proposition, formulated in a similar way, and if necessary recognising the differences of result arising from differences in entities. In some cases a proposition expressing a general idea would need to be supplemented with subsidiary propositions. The theory of accounting for each entity *abcd* would thus consist of a series of propositions related to one another and related to the observable or assumed characteristics of the entity.

The method of defining entities used above may appear to be cumbersome, but it is a certain way of ensuring that distinctive characteristics are not overlooked in the process of formulating hypotheses, procedures, rules or whatnot. It is a safeguard against making general statements which purport to be universally true but which are valid only in a limited class of instances.

Unwarranted Limitation of the Field of Study

Errors and omissions appear also to have arisen from failure to look further afield than the processes of accounting. Attention will be confined to business accounting. If accounting is considered to be a service function, its methods and assumptions should be tested by reference to the needs of business and businessmen; and, except for the purpose of dealing with the history of business or accounting, the needs of the contemporary business and businessman. At major points in expositions of accounting this test is avoided.

An opportunity for a penetrating examination of the needs of businessmen seems to have been missed by Professor Littleton. He sets down[4] twenty-three "inductively derived principles." But his description of the inductive process is simply this: "Long ago the basic methods of double entry were worked by trial and error . . . practices were presently verbalized into rules and procedures . . . Methods devised by many different people were used and tested by many others. Over the years, and by common consent after tested use, the most suitable procedures became generally accepted practices. Teachers . . . found it necessary to supplement the accumulated rules and descriptions of procedure by explanations and justifications . . . Hence it is appropriate to say that both the methods of practice and the explanations of theory were inductively derived out of experience." Clearly the study is limited to methods and procedures which have come to be accepted.

Further, the use of the term "inductively derived" appears to be inappropriate. It conveys the impression that the principles which follow have arisen simply from the observation of a number of specific instances, that they are statements of general truths which are demonstrated by particular cases. An inductive proposition is usually stated in a positive form; it can be so stated because it is a statement of fact. But none of Professor Littleton's principles is in the positive form; they are all imperatives! They begin with Define, Make, See that, Recognise, Ignore . . . Statements of this kind cannot be derived by induction. They are rules; they may have some kind of inductive basis, but they necessarily incorporate a (frequently undisclosed) value-judg-

---
4. *op. cit.*, p.185.

ACCOUNTING THEORY — Continued

ment. They may be quite proper in a practical handbook, but they are not theory. What is more, it is apparent from the above quotation that there are some deductive elements in the derivation of the author's principles. "Trial and error" involves a deductive process, and "justification" is often entirely deductive. Nevertheless, it appears that Professor Littleton intended to limit the sources of his propositions to observable phenomena, and to avoid the use of the deductive method.

Besides, there are certainly some assumed limitations of the scope and function of accounting beyond which inquiry is not pursued. To impose limits within the subject seems to be at variance with the view that accounting is a "human-service institution," a view that is recognised by the author in his earlier work in collaboration with Professor Paton.

One other example of failure to extend inquiry backwards to business usage may be noted. Messrs. Yorston, Smyth and Brown observe: "Until recently it was held that a balance sheet showed the financial condition of a concern as at a given date. This view is now untenable."[5] These are reasonable enough observations. But the authors are not prompted to ask whether a statement of financial condition is, in fact, required by businessmen. The limitation of conventional accounting is accepted without question. This is legitimate in a work designed to teach the practice of accounting. But it is inappropriate to leave the matter in the air in a treatment of the theory of the subject; and the chapter from which the quotation is drawn is a chapter on "accounting theory."

Brief Outline of a Method of Acquiring Knowledge

The time seems to be ripe for a thorough re-examination of the nature of the propositions which would constitute a theory of accounting. It appears to be particularly important to recognise the distinction between the art and practice of accounting, and the body of knowledge about accounting. That is to say, the propositions which are put forward as instructions to accountants are to be distinguished clearly and unequivocally from the propositions put forward as a means of increasing knowledge of the accounting function. To confuse the two may lead, as it appears to have done in the past, to an unedifying mixture of theoretical propositions and practical rules.

Within the body of knowledge about accounting there will be no imperatives. This does not mean that writers about accounting are prevented from advocating certain practices or procedures. But when they do so they should be recognised as having, for the purpose in mind, abandoned the status of theorist for that of advocate. The difference is material. The only tests to which theoretical propositions may be subjected are tests of the validity of the premises and tests of the validity of the reasoning. The statements of an advocate may in addition, however, be subjected to tests of the value-judgments which influence him to state his case in the imperative form. The importance of the distinction between these tests lies in the effects which criticism may have on the conclusions reached. One may effectively dispose of a defective theoretical conclusion by demonstrating its premises or its reasoning to be invalid. It is not nearly so easy to destroy a stated case, because value-judgments are subjective and there is no certainty that one's own value system will be acceptable to or accepted by others. On the other hand, it is not usually difficult to identify a stated case; "must" and "should" are sufficient warning of the need to ask: what system of values is invoked here?

Within the body of knowledge about accounting there will be both positive and hypothetical propositions. A positive proposition arises from observation; it is a generalisation about certain characteristics of the instances under observation. Such generalisations are true only of the cases observed, and only in respect of the quali-

5. *Advanced Accounting*, Vol. 1. p.9.

ACCOUNTING THEORY — Continued

ties under observation. They may be interesting of themselves, but their primary function is to provide the foundation for further generalisations about the whole family of instances of which those observed are a part.

These deduced propositions may concern themselves with explanation of the observed facts; or they may use the observed facts for the purpose of deriving dependent propositions. Thus, for example, it is apparent that "accounting statements are a means of communication." This is an inductive generalisation. It may be considered to represent the consequence of certain things—the complex nature of business, the remoteness of management from the points at which events occur, the legal and conventional pattern of relationships between an accounting entity and its supporters. Knowledge about accounting will be increased by discovery of the conditions which give rise to the use of accounting statements as means of communication. There may be many such conditions, all of which may not be identified at any time. The propositions which describe these conditions will therefore be under continuous scrutiny to ensure that none has been overlooked. This process of discovering the conditions underlying certain observed facts will be proceeded with to the point where the subject under study ends and some other science begins; for it is reasonable to take as premises the conclusions of another field of study. The underlying conditions, when discovered, may be taken as premises or assumptions for the development of ideas about—to pursue the example—accounting as a means of communication. It may transpire that these ideas represent quite a different kind of accounting from that about which the original observation was made. But note that these derived propositions are hypothetical. They will be true on the hypothesis that all the premises which have a bearing on the conclusion have been taken into consideration.

On the other hand, the same observation "accounting statements are a means of communication" may be taken as a premise, not as a consequence. It is a broad general idea which, of itself, provides no detail either of the particular kinds of information which may be communicated, or of the ways in which that information may be obtained. To provide this detail, subsidiary propositions will be enunciated; they will usually arise from relating different kinds of facts or from relating facts to prior deductions. Here again, it is necessary to keep the premises under constant scrutiny. The facts may change, new combinations of facts may arise; and even though they do not destroy the validity of the general idea they may necessitate restatement of the subsidiary propositions.

There may thus be developed a system of propositions, a theory of the subject, which will represent certain procedures. At this stage it is necessary to see whether the theory fits the facts as a whole. If the procedures indicated by the theory are found in practice, the premises and the reasoning may be considered to be valid. If the hypothetical procedures are at variance with practice, several kinds of inference may be drawn. The assumptions or premises may be inadequate; the reasoning may be illogical; or there may be temporarily operating factors which prevent the practice from conforming with the theoretical model. The former two possibilities would receive attention first, but if the theory is not inadequate on those grounds the third possibility would be considered. At this point it may be necessary to admit value-judgments as hypothetical causes. But not for the purpose of adopting any particular scale of values; merely for the purpose of discovering what value system explains the adoption in practice of a method which does not conform with the method suggested by the theory. The identification of exogenous factors such as regulation, custom and inertia, and some knowledge of their importance is useful both

ACCOUNTING THEORY — Continued

to the theorist and to the advocate of changes in practice. It provides the one with an explanation, and the other with a point of departure.

A theory worked out on the above lines may be expected to have many advantages over the fragmentary and unconnected generalisations which are now current. Firstly, the development of rules for practice would be recognised as a pursuit distinct from the search for knowledge about accounting. Theory, as such, is not committed to the support of any specific technique, new or old. The theorist is free to ask any question in pursuit of knowledge about his subject, and as theorist, all practices, actual or hypothetical, and all phenomena which may be causes or consequences of accounting practices, are of equal interest to him. Secondly, the scientific method provides the means of linking ideas, of forming a network of ideas, in which each is necessarily related to the others as antecedent to consequent, or as premise to conclusion, or as cause to effect. And thirdly, this method is more likely than the prevailing notion of accounting theory to lead to an extension of knowledge about accounting; for the propositions which would be enunciated could be readily identified as assumptions, inductive generalisations or deductions, and the imminent necessity of testing hypothetical propositions by reference to the facts of the business world would prevent the assertion of unwarranted or unrealistic conclusions.

If the study of the subject proceeds in this way it should be possible to avoid what Roger Bacon described as "four stumbling blocks which hinder well-nigh every scholar: the example of frail and unworthy authority, long established custom, the sense of the ignorant crowd and the pretense of wisdom."

DETAIL FOR A BLUEPRINT[1]

I

READERS of the literature of accounting will often have been treated to a discussion of whether accounting is an art or a science or something else. The present writer has frequently felt that argument of this kind is pointless and that the way accounting is described has nothing to do with the effectiveness with which it is carried out. More recently, however, it has seemed that confusion among writers as to what accounting is has led to confused thinking about many of the commonest features of accounting, and may interfere with its development. An attempt is made here to draw some distinctions which may clear the ground for a more rigorous study of the subject.

KNOWLEDGE AND ART

Analogy may serve as an introduction, but it is not to be taken as argument. Law is both a subject of study and a field of practice. So are surgery, engineering, chemistry. About each there is a body of knowledge, to the testing and development of which scholars and research workers devote themselves. In their inquiries these people are guided by a series of methods commonly known as scientific methods designed and proved to be methods of verifying the correctness of bold guesses or patiently worked out hypotheses, and thus of discovering new knowledge. One of these methods is reasoning, logical reasoning about the relationships between observed phenomena or concepts adopted to describe observed phenomena. Reasoning leads to generalizations, principles and laws, the general body of which constitutes the science.

All this is quite different from the field of practice which attaches to or is based on a science. The practicing lawyer, surgeon, engineer or chemist is not concerned, as practitioner, with testing and developing knowledge; but rather with applying existing knowledge to specific cases or problems. In doing this he is not free to experiment; even if he has time he has no freedom from the restraints common in an organized profession. These restraints may be imposed by the profession itself or by the requirements of the general body of clients of the profession. But to the practitioner they are real and limiting. In short, the practitioner is working, on the basis of some underlying body of knowledge, but in a social environment; and, for his own protection as much as for the protection of his clients, he is obliged to conform with the standards, rules, codes or conventions imposed upon him.

The scientific study of any subject is not limited by the standards and conventions necessary in its dependent field of practice. The student is free to consider many possible modes of action, many possible combinations of facts and many hypothetical propositions in his search for knowledge. He is not constrained by the necessity of making any of his theoretical models work in practice; but if his observations are realistic and his reasoning is rigorous, his theoretical models often suggest to practitioners new and more useful practices than those they have been accustomed to follow.

---

[1] The allusion is to the present writer's "Blueprint for a Theory of Accounting," *Accounting Research* (London) 1955, which was the subject of comment by Professor Littleton in "Choice Among Alternatives," THE ACCOUNTING REVIEW, July, 1956.

The distinction between scientific propositions and rules of practice is evident from the form in which each is stated. Scientific propositions, i.e. the conclusions arising from observation and reasoning, are stated in the indicative mood.[2] On the other hand, rules of practice, standards and conventions, are stated in the form of directives or imperatives.[3] The distinction is not a mere verbal quibble; it represents two quite different approaches, one scientific, the other practical. It also has quite important consequences as far as the development of a science or an art is concerned. For, as I have argued elsewhere,[4] the validity of a scientific proposition can be tested by reference to its premises and its reasoning, whereas the appropriateness of a rule is not subject to the same tests because a rule implies a value judgment, an opinion or a belief—none of which is susceptible to scientific testing.

It is emphasized that criticism is not offered here of standards, rules or conventions, as such. In practice they are essential. But they belong to practice (know how) not to science (knowledge about). A billiards player may learn the rules of the game: he then knows what to do. But unless he knows something about the second and third laws of motion and their corollaries, either by learning from books or from experience and careful observation, he is unlikely to be a player of great skill. There will always, of course, be the additional intangible something that makes the great player, the artist, but just what it is can neither be supplied by, nor be effective without, the rules and the knowledge of the underlying science.

Manifestly, although there is an important distinction between knowledge about a subject and knowledge about the practice of its dependent art, the two are not unrelated. Many critics of theorizing believe there is no such relationship; there are few more satisfying (but less effective) ways of condemning a proposal than to describe it as theoretical. Nevertheless, the principal qualification for entry to most professions is a demonstrable skill based on ample knowledge of the underlying science or sciences, i.e. an ample knowledge of the appropriate theory. This knowledge is expected to inform the judgment of the practitioner, enabling him to recognize particular cases as instances of significant large categories. Without the orderly array of connected generalizations of which the underlying sciences consist, the practitioner of a complex art would be reduced entirely to *ad hoc* solutions of his problems. Knowledge of the subject (theory) gives cohesion and consistency to practice. It cannot eliminate measures which have no other justification than expedience or custom, but as knowledge increases and becomes more widely known among practitioners, *they* may take steps to minimize the dependence of the art on rules and conventions which are inconsistent with reason.

ACCOUNTING KNOWLEDGE AND ART

Accounting is in precisely the same position as any other practical art. The field of practice is apparent. The practitioner is expected to have certain skills. The standards, rules and conventions of practice are well known, and are admitted by the present writer to be essential to practice. It is not so apparent that accounting is also a subject of study and that its study can be pursued in exactly the

---

[2] E.g., The third law of motion: To every action there *is* an equal and opposite reaction.

[3] Imperative is used here in the practical sense, not in the grammatical sense. For examples, see the use of *should* in *A Tentative Statement of Accounting Principles* (American Accounting Association), in the *Recommendations on Accounting Principles* (Institute of Chartered Accountants in England and Wales), and in *An Introduction to Corporate Accounting Standards* (Paton and Littleton); and see the use of straight imperatives in the inductively derived principles of Professor Littleton in his *Structure of Accounting Theory*.

[4] "A Scientific Pattern for Accounting Theory," *The Australian Accountant*, October, 1955.

same manner as other scientific inquiries. The reason why this is not apparent can only be guessed; it is possible that preoccupation with the art and a predilection to lay down rules has inhibited free inquiry: it is possible that the fact that scientific study and practice are two distinct disciplines has not been recognized; and it is possible that the course of preparation for entry to the profession has not included some study of a scientific nature which would awaken the curiosity or provide the logical tools for a rigorous study of the foundations of the art. This is, of course, simply speculation; but it is perhaps the same kind of speculation as caused Mr. Priestley to observe:

Nobody in his senses would expect a born seer to *do*. That much is generally acknowledged. But it is equally ridiculous to suppose that a dashing and triumphant doer can really *see*.[5]

What then is the body of propositions which may be said to be the subject underlying the practice of accounting? It has no name unless "accounting" is used (as it has been hitherto in this article) both of the subject and of practice. And what are its contents? Its contents will comprise a set of statements, in the indicative mood preferably, dealing with the relationships between concepts describing common accounting or business phenomena and operations. In seeking a point of departure it is reasonable to consider other subjects which bear reasonably close relationships with accounting. The closest and most obvious is economics. Some accountants, when confronted with this suggestion, demur on the ground that economics is concerned with national aggregates and not with the individual undertakings with which accountants are concerned. This objection, however, can only arise from misunderstanding of the content of economics. Economists are concerned, it is true, to view economic events and phenomena from the viewpoint of whole communties; but as broad economic changes and major economic developments occur through the myriad contributing acts of individuals, business firms and other organizations, economists are equally interested in the ways in which persons, firms and other organizations act. A considerable part of the theory of economics is devoted to examination of such acts. Professor Robbins' definition[6] is indicative of the breadth of the subject: "Economics is the science which studies human behaviour as a relationship between ends and scarce means which have alternative uses."

It is not unreasonable to expect that economics may throw some light on, or provide some basic concepts which will be useful in the study of, accounting. But it is not the only subject to which accounting may be related. It may transpire that some of the conclusions of psychology, political science and jurisprudence are also necessary and useful. Further examples are not necessary. It is sufficient to stipulate that the scientific study of accounting, as a subject, requires the application of scientific methods to observable phenomena, and that, in carrying out such a study, the student (or theorist) is free to observe and to adopt the conclusions of any other scientific study as he requires them. The study would proceed from observations, from the conclusions of other sciences, or from assumptions, to build up by logical processes, a body of propositions which is self-consistent and consistent with reality. Whenever the deduced propositions lack self-consistency and consistency with reality, this lack will be regarded as indicative of flaws in the original observations or assumptions, or of flaws in the argument.

---

[5] J. B. Priestley, "Thoughts in the Wilderness," *The New Statesman and Nation*, 12 March 1955.

[6] *The Nature and Significance of Economic Science* (Macmillan. London) p. 16.

Further study will be devoted to eliminating these flaws.

The article, "Blueprint for a Theory of Accounting," was an attempt to sketch the form which such a theory would take. It sets out four propositions as a basis from which to proceed. For convenience, and as they will be used later in this article, they are reproduced here:

(a) Certain organized activities are carried out by entities which exist by the will or with the cooperation of contributing parties.
(b) These entities are managed rationally, that is, with a view to meeting the demands of the contributing parties efficiently.
(c) Statements in monetary terms of the transactions and relationships of the entity are one means of facilitating rational management.
(d) The derivation of such statements is a service function.

No claim is made that these propositions are themselves a sufficient basis; however, after considering some others, the conclusion was reached that these are perhaps the most general and the most fruitful.

The general form of these statements is deliberately selected in the belief that some conclusions of wide application could be reached. Two substantial uniformities, observable in the real world, provide the basis for the belief that the subject, accounting, includes a number of general propositions, i.e. some *general* theory. These uniformities are (i) the use of accounting information in organizations having vastly different purposes and legal or social forms, and (ii) the substantial similarity of method in all these cases. The general theory to which these observations point would consist of propositions applicable to all situations in which the art of accounting is found to be practiced, propositions equally pertinent to accounting for private householders, unincorporated and corporate business firms, governments, nations, fiduciaries and eleemosynaries.

Obviously these propositions would only be concerned with the broadest features of accounting, but the mere fact that diverse entities can be treated without distinction for some purposes is suggestive of similarities which would not otherwise be apparent. The general propositions in contemplation provide the foundation for all more specific or elaborative propositions.

The "Blueprint" article proceeded to suggest, however, that there are many critical differences between the organizations which use accounting information, differences so great as to require different sets of concepts and propositions (different theoretical models) for each distinct class of organizations or entities. There will thus be a theory of business accounting, a theory of governmental accounting, etc., each depending on the general theory or including the general propositions, but each dealing also with differences with which obviously no blanket generalization could cope. Further, even within the "entity" categories suggested in the last sentence, there may be alternative propositions to cope with materially different features, not of entities themselves, but of the real world in which entities operate.

ILLUSTRATIVE THEOREM

Point may be given, to this very broad description of the way in which the subject may develop, by an example. Take as the proposition to be proved: *In the case of continuing ventures, periodical accounting is a necessary condition of rational action.* The proposition is limited to continuing ventures; it therefore falls outside, though it depends on, the postulated general theory. And as it alludes to accounting, the kinds of action contemplated are those having measurable financial effects or consequences.

Proof. Let $p, q, r, \cdots$ represent different classes of acts having measurable financial effects or consequences; and let the suffixes $_{1,2,3,\ldots}$ indicate acts at different times.

Every continuing entity operates by means of successive acts

$$\begin{array}{llll} p_1 & p_2 & p_3 & \cdots \\ q_1 & q_2 & q_3 & \cdots \\ r_1 & r_2 & r_3 & \cdots \end{array} \quad \text{(axiom)}$$

Every such act is an action taken in the expectation of promoting the entity's objectives (basic proposition b, stated above).

Every such act changes the entity in some respect (axiom).

Acts of the subject entity and of all other entities change the environment of action (axiom).

Therefore, no act p_1 is necessarily identical with any subsequent act p_2, due to changes in the entity or in its environment or in the relationship between the entity and its environment, the objectives remaining constant.

Now rational action is also action taken with knowledge of the relationship between the entity and its environment at the time of action (by definition of rational action).

Part of this knowledge is knowledge of the financial relationship of the entity with its environment (axiom).

The financial relationship between the entity and its environment may be determined from statements in monetary terms, i.e. from its accounting records (basic proposition c).

Therefore it is a necessary condition of rationality in any act, $p, q, r, \cdots$ that such an act is taken with knowledge of the financial relationship of the entity with its environment at that time.

However, let it be assumed that no single act $p, q, r, \cdots$ is an act having a material effect on the entity, but that the cumulative effect of all acts $p, q, r, \cdots$ over the period y is material (assumption).

It follows that it is a necessary condition of rational action that the actor shall have knowledge of the financial relationship of the entity with its environment at a time not further distant from the time of action than the interval y.

Q.E.D.

A similar theorem may be devised to prove that periodical revenue accounts are also necessary.

This theorem is to be considered only as an illustration. The argument is set out fully and the nature of each statement is indicated in order that its quality may be examined. The conclusion is simply a consequence of the stipulated character of the entity and the observable facts of operation. There is only one assumption, and that appears to be a reasonable one. The conclusion is stated in the positive form. There are no imperatives or directives. The conclusion is thus a piece of knowledge. The scientist, or theorist, as such, is unconcerned whether practitioners use it or ignore it. Neither action on the part of the practitioners can prove or disprove it. But practitioners may well be expected to have learned it.

Now, it may seem that the example chosen is unfortunate. Some may say "Everyone agrees that periodical accounting is necessary, so that the above demonstration adds nothing to practice." But for people to *agree* that something is necessary is one thing; to *prove* that the same thing is necessary is another. That people have *agreed* to prepare accounting summaries periodically is signified by the use of the term "convention" in respect of the period concept.[7] But once the necessity of periodical statements is proved, it is no longer necessary simply to *agree*. A principle is established; the practitioner may then know that his customary or conventional procedure is correct in principle (i.e., in theory), and that seems to the writer to be a clear gain to the practitioner. What he once did by convention, he can now go on doing with conviction.

There was another reason for selecting an accepted part of the practice of accounting as an illustration. The theorem demonstrates that one of the accepted notions can be supported by rigorous argument. Others, many others, may be supported by similar theorems. Using the same procedure, however, it is also possible to prove that some of the accepted practices are illogical, or without logical foundation. In the "Blueprint" article it

[7] E.g., Gilman, *Accounting Concepts of Profit*, Ch. 7; Paton and Littleton, *An Introduction to Corporate Accounting Standards*, p. 22.

was hinted that, given the fact that over time price levels change, it could be proved that for continuing business ventures, accounting statements which incorporate adjustments to reflect the change are a necessary condition of rational action.[8] This conclusion, again, is simply a piece of knowledge unless it can be demonstrated to be erroneous; and as a piece of knowledge it can neither be proved nor disproved by action on the part of practitioners as such. One who seeks to disprove it must have recourse to the same process of inquiry and argument by which the proof was derived.

It is the writer's view that a theory of accounting can be built up along these lines. Such a theory will be internally consistent, since it proceeds by logical steps to reasoned conclusions. It will also be consistent with the characteristics of the entities for which accounts are kept and with the environment in which those entities operate, since its premises will be realistic and its detail will be drawn from observation of the environment of action.

II

Sufficient has been said so far, it is hoped, to make the intention and method clear. Some further points may be made, however, by specific reference to Professor Littleton's comments[9] on the "Blueprint" article. It will be convenient first to dispose of some minor features.

OBSERVATIONS ON "CHOICE AMONG ALTERNATIVES"

(a) Professor Littleton says (p. 369) "the astonishing accomplishments of modern business seem of themselves to be the strongest argument in support of [the

[8] The proof is given in the writer's "The Formal Basis of Business Decisions," *The Australian Accountant*, April 1956, pp. 159–160, though it is not set out as is the above theorem.
[9] Page references in the sequel are references to "Choice Among Alternatives," THE ACCOUNTING REVIEW, July 1956.

historical cost basis of accounting]". This is an excellent example of what is a very common logical fallacy: *post hoc ergo propter hoc*.

(b) Again (p. 369), "It is doubtful . . . whether applying the word 'accounting' to the recording system used in totalitarian countries does anything to make accounting universal in fact. It will not be a record system dedicated to the truthful analysis of exchange-priced transactions and presentation of the distinction between, and interrelations of, capital and income." Three observations may be made:

(i) This passage immediately follows the statement, "Accounting lacks universality, and accountants will not be persuaded otherwise by assertions that it ought to be rested upon principles of universal truth." This appears to be an oblique criticism of my suggestion that an accounting theory should concern itself with a wider variety of entities than business ventures. But what is meant by "universality"? It could mean "of universal (actual) application": in this sense accounting lacks universality only to the extent that some imaginable entities have no control over, or transactions in, money or kind; this limitation is provided for by the first word of basic proposition (a) of the "Blueprint" article. But whatever universality means, the presence or absence of it is a matter of observation, not, as Professor Littleton seems to believe, of persuasion. Furthermore, "assertions that [accounting] ought to be rested on principles of universal truth" may well be disparaged; care was taken to avoid the assertion of any such thing in the "Blueprint" article. It is Professor Littleton, not I, who writes of accounting in such terms.[10]

(ii) If Profesor Littleton's criterion of a system to which the designation "account-

[10] See *Structure of Accounting Theory*, pp. 135, 147, 176.

ing" can be applied is "truthful analysis of exchange-priced transactions etc.," then cost accounting is a misnamed process; it is not even accounting according to his test, for a large part of it consists of more or less arbitrary allocations which cannot be described as "truthful analysis," and a large part of the events with which it deals are notional transactions, not "exchange-priced transactions." It is apparent from his writings that Professor Littleton would not deliberately pronounce cost accounting to be beyond the pale; but he is (presumably unwittingly) committed to this position by the narrowness of his test. It follows that the criterion is false, inasmuch as it results in Professor Littleton contradicting his own position.

(iii) But, further, Professor Littleton's choice of the example of totalitarian[11] countries to demonstrate lack of universality seems to be equally unfortunate. Rational action implies accounting (without accounting how could one "count the cost" before a new act?). Rational action is action taken in expectation of achieving a purpose. Now the mode of operation and the method of selecting purposes is different in, say, the U.S.S.R. and the United States of America, but rational action is expected no less in the one than in the other. Hence accounting of substantially the same kind is necessary in both.

Not only may the necessity of accounting in totalitarian countries be shown as above: there is ample evidence of substantial similarity of eastern and western accounting in the first book on the economic development of the U.S.S.R. which came into mind. Baykov's *The Development of the Soviet Economic System*[12] is liberally spiced with references to "reduction of production costs," "unsatisfactory state of affairs in accountancy," "cost prices," "budgets," "valuation of existing productive capital," "appropriations to sinking funds," "unprofitable enterprises" etc. How, otherwise than against a background of accounting similar to the kind found in business firms of the western world, can these and similar allusions make sense?

In pre-war totalitarian Germany large sectors of industry based their accounting on the *Kontenrahmen*,[13] on which, earlier, Professor Schmalenbach did so much work. This "frame of accounts" was substantially similar to the chart of accounts which would be found in any complex but efficiently managed enterprise in non-totalitarian countries. There is absolutely no room for doubt that it envisages the "presentation of the distinction between, and interrelations of, capital (real accounts) and income (nominal accounts)," notwithstanding Professor Littleton's assertion to the contrary (p. 369).

It is manifest that differences in accounting method are not so great as to justify Professor Littleton's remark. On the other hand, the four basic propositions of the "Blueprint" article are quite consistent with such accounting as totalitarian and non-totalitarian countries may require.

(c) As an exploratory exercise, Professor Littleton sets down (p. 366) a *tentative generalization*, reminiscent of the "principle of irrelevant effects" which he has presented elsewhere.[14] It is followed (spatially) by a *corollary* which does not follow (logically, as a corollary should) but which is simply an additional statement. The purpose of the tentative generalization is to assert the undesirability of modifying cost figures by index number adjustments. At several points he leaves no room for doubt about the uselessness of index

---

[11] The term is of the same hazy quality as "democracy" the multi-valence of which Professor Littleton notices on p. 370.

[12] N.I.E.S.R. Economic and Social Studies, V. (Cambridge 1947).

[13] See *The Frame of Accounts and Factory Analysis*, a translation by R. Webb of *Kontenrahmen und Betriebsabrechnung* (Archive and Chart Publishing Co.) Berlin 1946.

[14] *Structure of Accounting Theory*, Ch. 11.

modified accounts.[15] Adjusted figures are described as "irrelevant," "injecting an unethical element of misrepresentation." If these are the effects, then there is certainly no reason for adopting price level adjustments. Equally certainly there is no justification for Professor Littleton's "corollary" which contemplates "supplementary interpretative disclosures of price change effects"! On the other hand, if the information is necessary it can scarcely be called irrelevant or described as misrepresentation.

(d) Finally, Professor Littleton speaks of the *natural* limitations of accounting. There are of course no natural limitations. Accounting is what it is made. And he speaks of the way in which the preparation of accounting statements can *best* be carried on. But *best* implies a value judgment which is not disclosed. He alludes to "features [of accounting entities] which are in tune with the central and controlling characteristic of accounting" without making clear what this characteristic is; but, at all events, would it not be more appropriate to expect accounting to be in tune with the central characteristics of subject entities?

In addition to these minor points, two major features of Professor Littleton's article require attention. The first is the implicit criticism of the four basic propositions of the "Blueprint" article which are reproduced in an earlier paragraph of the present article.

PREMISES OF THE "BLUEPRINT" RECONSIDERED

The case put forward in the "Blueprint" could have been attacked in one of two ways: either by disputing the reality or reasonableness of the four premises, or by demonstrating that the argument based on those premises is logically invalid. Professor Littleton concentrates on the premises, but his difficulties arise from the construction he places on them rather than from the propositions themselves. It will be convenient to deal with them *seriatim*.

(a) Proposition (a) is simply a statement of fact, a generalization based on observable phenomena. Professor Littleton does not deny that it is a fact. But he says (p. 364) "We may choose to assume either that the various kinds of enterprise . . . are basically alike . . . or that it is their differences which are significant and controlling." There is no such simple choice. Both similarities and differences are important, but in different ways. The similarities provide the ground for general theory; the differences make necessary specific additional theory. This point has already been made.

(b) The second proposition—rational management—is also a statement of fact. Professor Littleton does not deny it this status; rather, he goes to some trouble to demonstrate or illustrate it. Again, however, he offers two possible assumptions; actions are likely to be either rational or intuitive and imitative. How he can imagine (p. 364) that I believe the latter to be the significant assumption in this case when my own words unequivocally assert a believe in the former cannot be understood.

(c) The third proposition sets out the function of statements in monetary terms. This too is a statement of fact in respect of all entities having any transactions in money or kind. Professor Littleton does not deny it is a fact. But again he presents a choice—"accounting symbols . . . should be considered either as representing a stable value of money, or as representing an unstable value of money." Why this question is introduced at this point is not clear: proposition (c) makes no reference to it whatever. The reason why it is not

---

[15] The context of the discussion on pp. 366–367 suggests that "the use of money prices other than those associated with transactions of this enterprise" is the same in kind and effect as, if not identical with, price level adjustments. For the purpose of comment this similarity is assumed.

mentioned in the third proposition is that the basic propositions enable some general conclusions to be reached about accounting, whether price levels vary or not. Variation in price levels is a special circumstance; accounting under such a circumstance is one of the specific subsidiary subjects of study, requiring a piece of theorizing dependent upon the above-mentioned general conclusions. For this reason it is mentioned (and then only very briefly) quite late in the "Blueprint" article. In the light of this, it is hard to understand why Professor Littleton selects a concluding statement on the matter from six such statements and devotes so much attention to it; it is equally hard to understand why he describes this statement as the *principal* generalization deduced from the assumptions.

(d) The fourth proposition is also a statement of fact, a status which Professor Littleton does not deny it.

In short, none of the original propositions has been demonstrated to be unrealistic or unwarranted premises.

THE LIMITATIONS OF PRAGMATISM

The second point is of a more general nature. Professor Littleton's approach to accounting is essentially pragmatic. The frequency with which he uses "should" and more forceful imperatives is ample evidence of this. Pragmatism and imperatives have their place in practice, but their very nature leads to oversimplification. One example was noticed above when dealing with proposition (a); the assertion (p. 369) that similarities among entities are of controlling significance is a severely limiting oversimplification.

Another and more important example occurs in Professor Littleton's article. Twice on p. 365 and again on p. 367 he speaks of the work of practitioners as if accounting (either the study of it or the practice of the art) were limited by what practitioners do. Whatever the professional accountant certifies, and however he confines his professional work, does not limit or exhaust accounting. Both the study of it and the practice of it are wider than the work of the independent public accountant. To suggest that only "objectively derived and convincingly verifiable data" are fit and proper material for the accountant is to impose an unrealistic and unsupportable limit on both practice and theory. Once it is granted that accounting is a service function (and this Professor Littleton grants) there can be no ground for restricting its practice by excluding estimated figures. There are many problems in the administration of business and other organizations for which estimated figures *are* used; the process of deriving these figures is surely part of accounting even though it is not that part of accounting with which independent public accountants are concerned. Further, even in the generally accepted practice of accounting there are necessarily estimates; periodical accounting necessitates estimates of the life span or the unexpired cost of durable assets; and, estimation being a subjective act, no such estimate can legitimately be described as "objectively derived and convincingly verifiable." This phrase is therefore a patent oversimplification of reality.

Of some of the difficulties of making this criterion work, Professor Littleton is aware. Standard costing and Lifo are two clear departures. In an attempt to justify these he avers: " . . . standard costs, and even Lifo, are firmly tied to enterprise actualities in a way not seen in the case of imputed interest and index-modified revenue charges. Lifo is based on actual exchange-priced transactions of this enterprise; accounts for variations from standard cost tie the latter to invested cost" (p. 367).

Now Lifo may be based on, but it does

not reflect, actual exchange-priced transactions; a Lifo valuation does not represent invested cost. Similarly, a standard cost and variations from it may be based on, but they do not reflect, actual exchange priced transactions; invested cost is divided arbitrarily into two parts each of which is given a distinctive quality and effect. Index-modified revenue charges are exactly the same in character. They are based on, but they do not reflect, actual exchange-priced transactions; invested cost is divided arbitrarily (inasmuch as a price index is to some extent arbitrary) into two parts each of which is given a distinctive quality and effect. There is thus no significant difference between standard costs, Lifo and index number adjustments. All are departures from objectivity, and from invested cost.

It will be apparent that whether Professor Littleton's criteria (i) "objectively derived and convincingly verifiable data," (ii) "exchange-priced transactions" and (iii) "invested cost" are the same in essence or different in degree, none of them nor any combination of them is sufficient to cover observable accounting practices. In fact they are over-simplifications and they cannot therefore be used as legitimate bases for challenging price level adjustments.

A final example of the limitations resulting from the pragmatic approach is the common failure to examine any other case than that of the privately owned business venture—the business corporation. Statements which appear to be true enough about entities of this class are quite commonly asserted as if they were generally true. The fact that practice and practitioners are more frequently concerned with corporate affairs than with the affairs of other types of entity may be the reason. But the study of the subject and the practice of the art will be hamstrung unless this preoccupation is tempered with critical and imaginative comparisons of different entities and different accounting methods.

CONCLUSION

The theory contemplated in the "Blueprint" article and in Part I of the present article is significantly different from the body of rules, doctrines and conventions which are commonly described as the theory of accounting. The differences may delay the acceptance of the type of theory envisaged by the writer; but the inherent contradictions and the logical and semantic difficulties which characterize existing expositions of accounting theory provide ample reason for seeking a more closely knit and realistic set of concepts and propositions.

TOWARDS A GENERAL THEORY OF ACCOUNTING *

Introduction.

1. The purpose of this paper is to explore the economic and social foundations of accounting in pursuit of a body of general ideas on which the practice of accounting is or may be based. The methods of accounting have been developed in response to a wide variety of impulses and under a variety of influences. Some have been dictated by the nature of the environment; others have been the invention of practitioners faced with technical problems for which the environment did not appear to offer clear direction. Development has been piecemeal; it could not have been otherwise; and it will no doubt continue to be so. It should not be surprising therefore that there are at present a number of concurrent accounting systems, different in some important senses even though similar in certain of their forms. It is not surprising either that the concepts by which some of these systems are described are contradictory. The variety of methods and the internal inconsistency of systems of concepts are the facts which force a reconsideration of underlying ideas and a search for a general theory.

2. This inquiry does not take the form of a survey of accounting practices nor of an appraisal of the lore of teachers and practitioners of accounting. There are eminent examples of such surveys and appraisals, and in the growth of a systematic body of knowledge their work has been invaluable. But confined as they were to accounting as it was taught or practised, these studies touched only tentatively or tangentially on fundamental ideas. What is now proposed is an examination of those ideas as such, without any attempt at the outset to relate them to any existing accounting system; the objective is to deduce from the nature of the environment of accounting the characteristics of a system which will serve the purposes for which it was or is designed.

3. The present exercise will have some defects and some limitations. It will be possible to consider at length only two classes of case—natural persons as producers and consumers; and simple trading enterprises. The generality of the argument may therefore be open to doubt in some respects; the doubt

---

* Prepared as a basis for the Annual Endowed Lecture of The Australian Society of Accountants in the University of Adelaide, 2 August, 1961. The invitation of Professor R. L. Mathews to give this lecture provided the spur to set down these ideas even though they are only a first approach to a complete and systematic presentation.

can only be resolved by extending the demonstration to other cases, which will be done on other occasions. There may be defects of another less obvious kind. The foundations of accounting are varied; it will be necessary to draw on a number of seemingly unrelated disciplines; it is hoped that none of these is misconstrued, though that possibility is open. The treatment given to those disciplines is necessarily simplified, and simplification and the selection it involves may be challenged.* One thing specifically excluded is the effect of governmental levies or taxes on the form of accounting. The basis of such levies is a matter of governmental policy and administrative convenience; it has no necessary connection with accounting concepts; it belongs to a different field of discourse.

4. The art of accounting is practised in a socio-economic setting. It concerns itself with representations to or for persons, singly, in groups or by classes, on the consequences of actions having financial characteristics. Its operations are designed, or expected, to add to the knowledge of persons for whom accounting statements are prepared. The study of it therefore requires and should be based on some knowledge of the ways in which people act, individually and collectively. Accounting represents transactions of persons in economic resources. Its study should therefore concern itself with that part of economics which deals with the characteristics of resources, their combination for the purposes of production and consumption, and the process of exchange. These processes are regulated by the laws and customs which prevail at the time, the legal and conventional framework cannot therefore be overlooked. Finally, accounting is a formal operation by which information is selected, processed and communicated; its study must therefore comprehend parts of the field of the communication sciences such as languages and epistemology.

5. Out of this mixture of psychological, economic, legal, conventional and formal considerations must be spun a coherent network of ideas which will represent the source of all specific prescriptions for accounting practices.

6. It may be useful before beginning the analysis to indicate what it is expected to demonstrate. It will be suggested that conventional accounting procedures are illogical; that they lead to results which are irrelevant and misleading; that they are internally inconsistent and inconsistent with the

---

* Throughout this paper no references are made to the work of other authors in the field of accounting or in any other field of inquiry on the findings of which argument depends. The list would be extensive, and as the system of ideas presented has been built up over many years it is unlikely that such a list as would now occur to me would be exhaustive. I can therefore acknowledge only generally my debt to others, hoping that in some future restatement more specific acnowledgement can be made.

realities they report on. It will be argued that a full historical record necessitates adjustments for shifts in value, that such a record is the closest approximation one can make to the representation of present reality for the purpose of future action. It will be argued that accounting to be useful will be oriented to future behaviour and that it will concern itself always with values—not with costs in the sense of money outlays. It will be argued that many of the practical imperfections of existing methods arise from makeshift devices adopted in the absence of a consistent theory of accounting. The theory represented in embryo in this paper is not designed specifically to overcome these deficiencies; but it results in a system which is free of most of them.

Individuals as Actors.

7. We begin by considering persons as actors. The human individual is a complex organism capable of perception, reflection and action. Perception, reflection and action have *time* dimensions; they are initiated at points of time and carried out over periods of time. But the total time available for these processes to any person is limited.

8. *Perception* is the observing or sensing in any way of characteristics of the environment or of the organism itself. At any time the environment and the organism itself offer for perception an extensive array of things and events. As the sensory devices are limited, the *span of attention* is limited; so that at any time only some of the perceivable things are in fact perceived, only some become the *focus of attention*.

9. *Reflection* includes all mental operations, such as relation, comparison, recollection and calculation. *Relation* is the apprehension of connections between things perceived including causal connections. *Comparison* is reflection on the similarities or differences between things. *Recollection* is bringing to immediate conscious attention things that have been perceived in the past. *Calculation* is the manipulation of qualities and quantities for the purpose of apprehending connections, of making comparisons or contrasts. The operations of relation and comparison give rise to *arrangement, classification* and *systematization*. The capacity for recollection of specific things and events varies inversely with the number of specific unrelated things perceived, and directly with the extent of reflection on and systematization of things perceived.

10. *Action* includes, besides bodily action, such mental actions as choice and appropriation. Perception and reflection are always directed towards action in the future. Through time actions need not necessarily be consistent; for any individual may assume different *roles* — either during successive

intervals or during a given interval. He may, for example, be at the same time father, breadwinner, worker, member or official of non-family groups; and some or all of these roles may be relinquished as time passes.

11. At any time an individual finds himself in a set of bodily and mental states. At the same time he has a set of preferred states. If the two sets are identical there is no incentive to change; but they are seldom identical. Perceived differences between existing and preferred states create *strains* or uneasiness. At any time there may be numerous strains; one may be hungry, thirsty, weary, elated and economically insecure simultaneously. Potentially the number of concurrent strains is equal to the number of states postulated above. And as there are mental states appropriate to each role (10)* filled by any individual, the *number and diversity of strains* vary with the number of concurrent roles.

12. The *intensity of a strain* varies with the extent of the perceived difference between an existing and a preferred state (11). Intensity is a product of comparison; it is a matter of more or less. It is possible to imagine a scale of intensities for each different kind of strain, but the mind does not find explicit scales necessary. Even though there are many contemporary strains, all different in character, the mind proceeds to rank them in order of intensity. The ranking of strains (arrangement or ordering) is not simple; the difficulty of ranking varies with the number and diversity of strains. Ranking implies an order of urgency. As ranking involves an expenditure of mental effort over time and time is scarce (7), explicit ranking may be limited to the strains felt with greatest intensity; to all others the mind may, for the time being, be indifferent.

13. Strains are accompanied by wants; *wants* are desires to be relieved of strains. Wants are correlates of strains. Thus, there are diverse concurrent wants; wants are felt with different intensities and wants are ranked according to intensity. The relief of strain or the satisfaction of wants is the incentive to and goal of action. *Goals* are correlates of wants. There are diverse concurrent goals; goals at any time have different values and are ranked according to those values. The *values* assigned to specific goals are the values placed on the satisfaction of their associated wants. The values placed on the satisfaction of wants are personal and therefore subjective and intensive. The values assigned to goals determine the order in which they become the focus of attention.

---

* The numbers appearing occasionally in the text are references to other paragraphs where the same ideas are dealt with.

14. The set of preferences of any person is variable. Attainment in whole or part of any goal will lead to a change in the ranking of goals. Or, of his own will a person may abandon one system of values for another, changing the whole structure of his wants and the values assigned to specific goals. Or he may recast his value system in response to characteristics of the environment. Any system of preferences may persist over a long time, but the possibility of change is ever present; its nature and extent are always unpredictable.

15. Because the span of attention is limited and the time for reflection may be short, the greater the extent of systematization the greater is the capacity to comprehend the variety of factors which are the environment of action, and the wants and values which direct action. The greater the number of sub-systems, the greater is the time and effort required to relate and co-ordinate them, and the greater is the possibility of lack of relation and co-ordination.

Means.

16. Goals are pursued by the appropriation of means. Means are all things other than free goods, *believed to be serviceable* in the attainment of goals or ends. Free goods are those which though useful involve no effort or sacrifice; they are part of the environment. Things with no perceived serviceability at any time are not then means; they are irrelevant. The *value* to a person of any means is derived from the values attached to the goals it serves. The expectation or belief that a means will be serviceable in satisfying a want is its *utility*.

17. Means are *scarce* relatively to wants; non-scarce means are excluded by the above definition. Means are varied in form; they include labour, natural things, artefacts and rights. With advances in knowledge and technology some things which were at one time considered as means cease to be so considered, and some things not previously considered to be means become means. Means vary in *specificity*, or in their appropriateness to the service of specific ends. Some means are said to be means of the first order; they are highly specific and have the capacity for directly satisfying wants, or *direct utility*. Other means are said to be goods of higher orders; they have the capacity for yielding means of the first order. Means vary in *durability;* some may continue indefinitely to serve wants, some may lose over more or less long periods their capacity to serve wants, and some are exhausted immediately in serving wants. Means vary in *divisibility;* in some cases the minimum unit is large, in other cases it is small.

The Environment.

18. The environment is the complex of things, persons, relationships and events which surround and impinge on an individual. The environment in part determines the state in which an actor finds himself at any time. It provides some of the things which gives rise to strain; it also provides some of the means of relieving strain. Those things which tend to create states divergent from a preferred state or to create new preferred states will be called *stimuli*. Environmental stimuli include natural events and circumstances and social events, circumstances and customs.

19. Environmental stimuli may be *fortuitous, recurrent* or *persistent;* and their impact may be more or less severe. Knowledge and experience may enable people to distinguish stimuli which are expected to be fortuitous, recurrent and persistent. This is not certain knowledge; it is probabilistic only. Against recurrent and persistent sources of strain persons may make provision; but against fortuitous stimuli and against the possibility of any stimulus being more or less severe no specific planned provision can be made. In at least some respects, therefore, the *environment is fluid and unpredictable*. This is one source of personal *uncertainty*.

20. The environment includes laws, customs and other devices relating things, persons and events. The predictability of the environment increases with the stability and effectiveness of such laws, customs and similar devices. But laws and customs themselves are responses to a given set of circumstances at a given level of knowledge and are therefore susceptible to change. The timing of such changes is not predictable. This is another source of uncertainty.

Categories of Action.

21. The characteristic activities of men are production and consumption. *Production* is the combination of means for the creation of things having greater utility than the sum of the utilities of the means used. The process may be as simple as the expenditure of effort in performing a service; or it may be quite complex, involving many stages and the use of many intermediate goods. The state of technology and the methods of production change from time to time, introducing additional uncertainties to the environment of action. The purpose of production of final goods or intermediate goods is the satisfaction of wants. The incentive to production is the increase in utility or value expected to result. The amount by which the value (16) of produced goods exceeds the value of goods used in production is the *income* from the process.

22. *Consumption* is the appropriation of means for the satisfaction of immediate wants. The difference between production and consumption is *saving*. Saving is the provision of means for the service of future wants; it involves the accumulation of a stock of means and depends therefore on there being some durable means. Individuals may save with the object of meeting unforeseen contingencies, or with the object of *investing* in productive operations. Prior saving is a condition of production by complex or roundabout processes. The incentive to invest is the expectation of increasing the income stream by improving the methods of production.

23. The accumulation of a stock of means, whether precautionary or for investment, is influenced by the predictability of the environment. Extreme uncertainty may dictate the immediate consumption of what one has. Short of extreme uncertainty, the greater the flexibility of one's goals and the less the predictability of the environment, the greater will be the tendency to accumulate non-specific means. Conversely, the greater the persistence or recurrence of wants and the more stable the environment, the greater will be the tendency to acquire specific and durable means. As, generally, the environment has some relatively stable elements (20) and personal goals have a measure of stability (14), persons will, if their means are above subsistence level, accumulate both specific and non-specific means. Some means are used alone, some are used in combinations dictated by technology and the planned scale of action, and some are substitutes for others. The proportions in which means of different kinds are accumulated depends on their *complementarity* and *substitutability* with respect to goals.

24. As there are concurrent competing wants, the greater the stock of a specific means the less is the desirability of adding to that stock; the utility of the n*th* unit is less han the utility of the (n-1)*th* unit. As action involves adding to or subtracting from stocks of means, interest focuses on the unit last added or sacrificed, the *marginal unit*. The *utility of the marginal unit* diminishes as the stock of a given means increases. In pursuit of maximum total satisfaction (40) the aggregate stock of means will tend to be so arranged that the marginal utilities of all stocks are equal.

Action in a Market Economy.

25. A society of individuals tends to arrange its productive processes so that the wants of its members may be satisfied in a greater measure than would be achieved by the efforts of each acting in isolation. All individuals have different innate and acquired capacities for action (*individual differences*). The greater the opportunities for *specialisation* (the exercise of specific individual skills) the greater the aggregate

product. But as individuals have diverse wants, the possibility of exchanging what one produces for what one wants is a condition of specialisation. *Exchange* is the process by which each individual arranges that the marginal utilities of different stocks are equal.

26. Both consumption and exchange entail that individuals shall have *control* over, or the right to dispose of, means. These rights are secured by the framework of laws and customs (20). Control may take the form of possession or ownership. *Possession* is a matter of fact; but the conditions under which one has possession are matters of law and custom. Freedom to use and dispose of goods in possession may be limited by the role in which one has possession — for example, one may have possession as agent, trustee, lessee or owner. *Ownership* of (or property in) means is a legally enforceable right against all other persons to have, use and dispose of means. One may have ownership with possession, in which case the subject goods are entirely under the control of one person. One may have ownership without possession, in which case one's rights as owner are limited by the contract under which possession was transferred. And one may have possession without ownership in which case one's rights as possessor are only those which have been ceded by the owner. Both goods themselves and limited rights in them are means in terms of the above definition. Laws and customs establish the conditions under which ownership and possession may be transferred between persons. Generally ownership and possession may be transferred gratuitously or for consideration.

27. Except in the case of gratuitous transfers, the owner of means will only part with possession if he is assured that the transferee will at a future date perform his part of the contract. Performance is assured by legal rights of recovery and damages. But owners will frequently transfer means in the expectation of performance by the transferee without recourse to legal remedies. All transfers in advance of settlement by the transferee are *credit* transactions. The extent to which means are exchanged is increased by the use of credit.

28. In the absence of exchange one would only acquire means specific to one's goals. But the possibility of exchange increases the range of goods one may acquire so that it includes goods to be held for exchange as well as for consumption. Goods may thus have a *value in exchange* as well as a value arising from the value attached to the ends they serve. Value in exchange is extensive and objective; it is independent of the private opinion of the owner or possessor for the time being of any good. Beyond the level of the stock of means necessary for planned consumption, no stock of goods may be considered irrevocably committed to any purpose. A change in the exchange

value of a good or a change in the composition of wants will induce a change in the composition of one's stock, and as noted above many such changes are unpredictable (14). For any contemplated action involving a change in the composition of one's stock the values in exchange of the components of that stock are the relevant values to consider.

29. The rate at which goods are exchanged is the *ratio of exchange*. An exchange occurs when both parties expect to gain from the sacrifice of what they offer for what they receive. The sacrifice of the satisfaction which would have been obtained from the use and possession of the goods given is the *cost* of the goods received. As both parties have different wants the ratio of exchange is a function of their current preferences and current stocks; and as these change, so will the ratio of exchange alter.

30. The ratio of exchange involves specific units of goods. Direct exchange depends on the willingness of the parties to exchange goods in the units in which they are produced or in multiples of those units. But some goods are large in size (17), or high in exchange value by comparison with others. The possibility of exchange is increased by the availability of a generally accepted *medium of exchange*. A medium of exchange must be generally acceptable, otherwise it would not be worth taking in exchange for things having direct utility. It must be divisible, otherwise it could not serve as a means of settling transactions diverse in size. It must be durable, otherwise it could not be accumulated for the purchase of goods of high exchange value or for the purchase of things of low exchange value at a point of time remote from its acquisition.

31. Media of exchange are means in terms of the definition of means given above (16). They differ from other means in that they are demanded not for themselves but for the ease with which they are *convertible* into other means required for consumption or production; the utility of a medium of exchange is a *derived utility*, not a direct utility. Money is a medium of exchange. It is the most easily convertible means, or the most liquid means, and serves as a base for describing the degree of liquidity of other means. But in terms of exchange, money is not essentially different from other means.

32. The exchange of goods for goods through the intermediate step of money is *indirect exchange*. The ratio of exchange of other goods for money is the *price*. It is customary to speak of the price of other goods being such and such a sum of money; it is equally proper to speak of the price of money being such and such a quantity of goods. The purpose of this latter contrast is to draw attention to the fact that money and other goods are both wanted; in different amounts

at different times, it is true, but because both provide means of relieving wants. The marginal utility of money diminishes at a slower rate than that of other goods, but simply because it is convertible with ease into any of a great range of other goods. But like other means money does not have a fixed ratio of exchange with respect to any other goods (29).

38. 33. Exchanges take place in *markets*. A market is simply a set of arrangements by which exchanges are facilitated. It need have neither specific location nor distinctive form. It is customary to consider markets as specialising in the exchange of a limited range of means, e.g., the wool market, the share market, the money market. But each such market is only a part of the wider market in which all goods and services are bought and sold. The function of the market is to establish prices. Prices may be established directly by the higgling and bargaining of buyers and sellers, or indirectly by sellers making offers at what they expect the market will stand. But whether directly or indirectly established, the price of any good depends on the conditions of supply and demand (29), both actual and anticipated, for the good itself and for substitutable and complementary goods (23).

34. The market is also a device by which stocks of scarce means are rationed among potential users. Where prices are flexible and goods are mobile, goods will flow to the highest bidders, to those who, for consumption or production, place the highest value on them. In this way goods are employed in directions in which the aggregate product or satisfaction from their use is expected to be at the maximum. In this way too users are able to indicate, by the prices they offer, which goods shall be produced in greater or smaller quantities and which shall no longer be produced. It is unnecessary for present purposes to consider at length the specific features of different markets; it is necessary only to observe that prices and the distribution of goods and services are not determined unilaterally, but by the simultaneous choices of buyers and sellers.

35. Many things may be used for money. A special form of money is *currency*. Currency is the legally established medium of exchange in any given community. A currency has a prescribed denomination per unit. The *monetary unit* is the unit in which all bargains or claims arising from bargains are expressed. It is also the unit in which all derived forms of money, such as bank deposits and other debts, are expressed. Its general use in these ways has established the monetary unit as the *unit of account*, the unit in which costs, prices and values are expressed, in which economic calculations are made and in terms of which records dealing with such transactions are kept.

36. It may be useful to summarize the consequences of the use of money and money units. *Monetary calculation* relieves men of the task of comparing satisfactions with sacrifices in diverse ordinal scales (12). Values of diverse means are reduced to a common cardinal scale in which actual or expected gains or losses from alternative courses of action may be expressed. The strain on the span of attention is eased, as also is the problem of choice. Because most of the means of satisfying wants are acquired at market prices in markets, it is possible to express goals in monetary terms, and to measure the rate, and extent at any time, of their attainment. As the effectiveness of action depends on the specificity of goals, the expression of goals in monetary terms increases the effectiveness of action. Again, reduction to a common scale enables values to be added, so that an aggregate value for a varied stock can be obtained. And if the scale is a monetary scale of present values, it is possible to set off money claims against the aggregate present value of a stock; both are brought into the framework of one system of calculation.

39

37. For all its convenience the monetary calculus has limitations. Reduction of the tangible and real characteristics of means to a monetary scale is an abstraction; a money value can represent only one characteristic—exchange value at some time. This is not the only characteristic which determines action; there are other relevant features of goods and services; but in its own field—actual or potential action in markets—monetary abstraction is a powerful aid. A second difficulty in using monetary calculations is that it may be assumed that all monetary representations are of equal significance. The very durability of units of currency and the fixed nature of money contracts nurture this idea; it is, nevertheless, false and misleading. Just as in the sale of merchandise different grades are distinguished, so also should the different qualities of money be distinguished. No five apples are thought to be equal to any other five apples; likewise monetary units may not without specific evidence be supposed to be identical in significance (32). Unless all monetary units in a given calculation are identical in significance—that is, in general purchasing power—the mere use of the conventional monetary unit does not provide a common denominator. A third difficulty is the ease with which people, seeing numbers, slip easily into the assumption that cardinal representation means precision. The monetary scale is not like a physical scale. It is always a scale with a significance for the moment, a significance depending on the actions of all buyers and sellers—and therefore quite lacking in stability through time. In spite of this its utility is enormous; but to disregard this limitation is to court confusion.

13

38. The extensive use of money and credit is one reason underlying the development of monetary accounting. *Accounting* is a systematic procedure by whch the monetary or financial aspects of transactions and events are recorded, classified and summarized so that informed choices may be made. Its link with the problems of acting man specifies its character. It is an aid. It has no justification of itself. It provides a *service* only; its methods are dictated by the modes of action of those it serves. A prime characteristic which its results will be expected to have is *relevance* to action; its components will be selected and its methods devised so that the results are relevant. Relevance does not however imply giving direction. Relevance means pertinence to the behaviour appropriate to the role for which an account is given. It is the function of actors to decide and to assess; to decide and to assess one requires information that is neutral. An actor sets his own goals; in pursuit of them he may err to his advantage or disadvantage; to decide whether in fact he did err is his prerogative. *Neutrality* with respect to any specific action is just as important as relevance with respect to a role in general. Accounting may influence choice; it has no criteria for determining choice. For, accounting is not to be understood as the sole source of information influencing choice. It presents a particular aspect of affairs only. For other aspects one must necessarily resort to other kinds of information. References to choice and action hereafter allude generally to financial criteria only; but the existence and importance of other criteria may never in practical situations be overlooked. Given the full range of financial and other criteria the mind can choose; lacking either, choice is in part blind.

Qualities of Action.

39. Human action is purposive, aggressively adaptive, oriented to the relief of strains (13). Action may be *spontaneous* (habitual, instinctive) or *deliberate*. The more urgent the need for action (the greater the intensity of strain), the greater is the tendency towards spontaneous action. The success of spontaneous action (in relieving strain) depends on ready perception (9) of the relationship between stimuli, strains and means. But the greater the variety of stimuli, strains and means, the greater is the difficulty of perceiving their relationship, the more complex is the goal system and the greater is the need for deliberate action. This study concerns itself with deliberate action.

40. As means are scarce relatively to wants, deliberate action will be directed towards securing the greatest possible advantage for a given sacrifice. It is not implied that "the greatest possible advantage" is of a specific kind; the phrase

does not mean the maximization of profit, for strains arise for other reasons than the mere scarcity of means; the phrase does not mean the maximization of money returns, for, firstly, money itself has no capacity for directly relieving strains and, secondly, money sums may have varying significance over time in terms of the power to purchase means having direct utility. "The greatest possible advantage" is to be understood with reference to the goal system as a whole (13). Nevertheless, the pursuit of the maximum profit or money return is part of the process of securing the greatest possible advantage. The goal system of an individual is beyond inquiry, but unless his overt actions are designed, in the framework of non-specific goals, to secure the maximization of economic goals, his capacity for achieving economic and other goals is needlessly sacrificed.

41. Further, in suggesting that action will be directed towards securing the greatest possible advantage, it is not implied that such an objective is attained. Nor is it a valid objection to this principle that people do not in fact maximize their gains. However carefully a course of action may be chosen, it is chosen at a point of time for a future period of time of which the actor has uncertain knowledge. As a point of reference it is useful to describe action which in fact achieves the goal to which it is directed as *optimal adaptation*. The more deliberate the action the greater is the probability of optimal adaptation.

42. Deliberate action always involves *choice* of a course of action from among a series of possible courses. The outcome of choosing depends on (a) the goal system (set and ranking) at the time of action, (b) knowledge of the possible courses of action available in the given environment, (c) knowledge of the means available and (d) expectations of the consequences of each possible course of action.

43. *Knowledge* of the available courses depends in turn on several factors. It depends on the breadth of *past experience* and on the *ability to recall* (9) past experience. It depends on the *propensity to search*, that is on the freedom from inertia and habit. And it depends of the *time available* for search, that is, on the urgency of action (12).

44. Knowledge of the means available likewise depends on other factors. It depends on the *ability to recall all means* available and to marshal them in terms of their characteristics; in particular in terms of their specificity for the purpose in mind and of their liquidity if no specific good is available. It also depends on the *ability to recall commitments* of means or restraints on their use or disposal.

45. *Expectations* depend on knowledge of the consequences of past actions; not simply on past experience, but on the

extent to which past experience has been the subject of reflection for the purpose of discerning cause and effect relationships (9). Expectations depend also on the predictability of the environment (20); expectations will be formed with greater precision and assurance if the environment is stable in significant respects. And the quality of expectations depends on the quality of *judgment* exercised in relating what has transpired in the past to the possible conditions of the future.

46. In the last three sections there have been persistent allusions to knowledge. All types of knowledge constitute information. But any actor may be informed—of his own affairs or of conditions about him—poorly or adequately. The better informed the actor the greater is the probability of optimal adaptation.

Qualities of Information.

47. Knowledge may be *formal* or *informal*. By informal is meant the accumulation of knowledge in the person, his memory and skill derived from his past experiences. But the greater the variety of past experiences the greater is the difficulty of recalling any particular experience in the detail necessary to establish its relevance to a present problem. By formal knowledge is meant the knowledge accumulated by a recording process and stored independently of the person. The greater the variety of stimuli, means, experiences and available actions, the greater is the need for formal knowledge.

48. Human adaptation is a continuous process; or more strictly a continuous cycle of processes. Man acts; he observes, reflects on, and appraises the consequences of his action; he refers his new state to his goal system (which may have changed from the original system), makes a new decision and acts again (7, 8, 9). The repetition of this cycle for every aspect of his behaviour is perhaps unnoticed; but it is constant, and by means of it he inches towards the satisfaction of his wants. As the process is continuous, the demand for knowledge is continuous. If his activities are limited in number and kind he may be able mentally to encompass the knowledge necessary for adapting his behaviour to his circumstances. But if his activities are varied so that it becomes necessary to augment his memory with a formal record (8), that record will necessarily be of a continuous kind.

49. A person may himself keep the record of his financial transactions and relationships. If he knows the technique and keeps the record he will know how relevant the result is to his purpose; and if it is not relevant the remedy lies in his own hands. On the other hand he may rely in the skill and knowledge of specialists in record keeping; the keeping of the record

and the making of decisions are divorced. In this situation the actor does not know the method used, the skill with which it is used or the relevance of the resulting figures or statements to his purposes. He depends on the technical skill and probity of the record-keeper. Two kinds of problem arise; one because the design of recording and information processing systems becomes the concern of others than actors themselves; the other because the result of the recording and processing systems must be communicated to persons who must act on the result but are uninformed as to the method.

50. Formal or processed information is conveyed by *signals* which differ from the original observable events and things. Signals are necessarily abstractions (37). The probability of optimal adaptation varies with the *correspondence* of the signals to the observable realities to which they relate. Signals may convey more or less completely the characteristics of observable real events and things; they may be so conventionalized that they represent in one dimension what may only be described adequately in more than one dimension. Correspondence is critical where the actor has no possibility of confirming or testing the quality of the signals.

43

51. The probability of optimal adaptation varies with the *processor's awareness* of what is relevant to the actor (38). The processor acts as an extension of the actor's sensory and manipulative apparatus; what he observes he observes for the actor; the calculations he makes he makes for the actor. He can have no independent viewpoint.

52. The probability of optimal adaptation varies with the *objectivity* of the record and process. By objectivity is meant freedom from the influence of personal judgment or bias. As the future actions of an actor are with respect to other persons through markets, personal opinion and evaluation are irrelevant. An observation is objective if other persons reasonably well informed would concur with it—exchange value or market value is in this sense objective (28). It is not a fancy of the actor's imagination only. Further the same objectivity is necessary in processing as in initial observation. No procedure or criterion of the processor may be inconsistent with the procedure or criterion which an actor would ideally adopt for himself. As to act deliberately requires that he shall know, without interposed distortion, states of affairs and rates of change, these are what the process should yield.

53. Distortion of information may take several forms. Distortion may be deliberate; deliberate distortion may be intentional (as, for example, to conceal fraud) or unintentional. The latter occurs when values or procedures continue to be used after they have ceased to be useful or to yield relevant information. Distortion may be due to the deficiencies of the

signals used. Typically signals abstract — morse code cannot convey an inflexion, a gesture, or a facial expression. Distortion may also be inadvertent; errors may be made, attitudes or beliefs may be adopted which are inconsistent with the needs of a situation. Formal checks may be incorporated in an information processing system to eliminate or reduce some of these possible causes of distortion, but there can be no routine safeguard against attitudes inconsistent with the service functions of recording and communicating.

54. The probability of optimal adaption varies with the *perceived significance* of signals on the part of the actor. Information processing is unlike many other forms of expert assistance; it accomplishes changes in mental equipment rather than in physical things. There are greater difficulties in conveying ideas than changing physical things; many persons can grasp the significance of a change in things, but the significance of ideas is not always self-evident. For this reason the terms of a communication, the words used, the measures involved, should be consistent where possible with general usage. The wider the range of recipients of a communication the greater is the necessity for consistency of its terms with general usage.

55. Processed information is accepted only subject to evaluation by the recipient. This evaluation is applied in part to the information yielded and in part to the processor. An actor will place greater confidence in processed information if it is found to be consistent with other knowledge, formal or informal, of the same matters. And, the greater the reliability of the process or the processor and the greater the prestige of the processor, the greater is the confidence with which processed information will be accepted. It follows that information prepared by experts (specialists) will tend to be accepted readily, even though it does not conform with the criteria of relevance, neutrality, correspondence and objectivity. Therefore, the greater the awareness among processors of these critical qualities of information, the greater is the probability of optimal adaptation.

The Entity.

56. It has been observed that an individual may simultaneously fill several roles (10). He must of necessity reconcile the demands of different roles, but in order to do this it is necessary first to consider each role separately. It may appear that a given individual assuming the roles of householder (consumer) and employee (producer) would be content to regard the consumer-role as dominant and to gear his behaviour to that role alone. But two entirely different modes of behaviour may readily be observed as his calculations shift from one role

to the other; he may be shrewd and crafty in his business relationships, but openhanded and generous to a fault as a consumer. The goals of consumption and production are different in kind; one counts the cost far less carefully in the case of consumption than in the case of production, because the satisfactions obtained from consumption are personal and incommensurable (13), whereas the gain from production, in terms of additions to means, is measurable in the same scale as the sacrifices or costs incurred.

57. An information system can deal only with one role at a time if it is to enable the actor to discern and to distinguish the issues governing his actions. Roles are filled not only by natural persons but by groups of natural persons and by artificial persons. These roles are so varied that it is possible that no single information system will serve all role playing entities equally well. This is a matter for further development. But the point made here is that information systems are concerned each with a specific role. The role may coincide with or cut across legally distinguishable categories of persons; its prime characteristic is that it represents a limited potential set of goals.

Financial Position of an Individual Person.

58. For any given role, the foundation of a plan of action involving a change in means is the existing state of one's affairs (24). As every such change takes place through bargains in which exchange values are expressed in monetary units, the state of one's affairs may be represented by a statement in monetary units.

59. Ability to engage in any exchange is represented by the means under the control of the entity expressed in terms of current exchange values. It is immaterial whether those means were acquired for a purpose other than exchange; a shift in relative prices may make it worthwhile to dispose of or replace any good in possession. Means in possession are desscribed as *assets* of the entity.

60. All means are the property of some entity (26). By virtue of loans and other forms of credit some of the means in possession are not the property of the entity under discussion; so that the freedom to use or dispose of specific assets or of assets generally is restrained by the claims or equities of others (*creditors*). The equities of creditors (*liabilities* of the entity) are determined as to their character and amount, by contract. The present value of such equities is the amount of the liabilities of the entity.

61. The difference between the aggregate of the exchange values of assets and the aggregate of the present values of liabilities represents the present *residual equity* of the entity in the assets. The amount of the residual equity is significant for two reasons. Firstly, it represents the exchange value of unrestricted assets, providing assurance to creditors that their claims are more than "covered" by the assets of the entity. Secondly, it represents a basis on which further advances from creditors may be obtained. For an individual person, residual equity represents net worth or wealth or capital.

62. *The financial position* of an entity at any time is defined by the relationship

    Assets = Equities
           = External equities + Residual equity
or A = L + R

each term being quantified in the manner described in the preceding paragraphs. This identity holds at successive instants of time; for whatever additions are made to assets a like addition must be made to equities (as all means are the property of some entity). It will in fact hold even if nonsensical values are given to assets and equities, provided only that the value assigned to a given asset corresponds to the value assigned to the equity by virtue of which it was acquired. However, whimsy is restrained by the requirement that the resulting information must be *relevant* to action (38).

63. In stating the financial position of an entity it is not sufficient to give the total amount of assets, liabilities and residual equity. The process of aggregation involves the loss of some information which may be important for any particular decision. On the other hand an indiscriminate listing of each asset and liability may present such an array that confusion results. The limited span of attention (8) dictates the *classification* of assets and liabilities into groups but the number of groups will be such that no serious *information losses* occur. It has been observed that stocks of means may be of varying durability, specificity and liquidity (17). Of these qualities the most significant in the adaptive process is liquidity. The utility of a statement of financial position is increased by *ranking* assets in order of liquidity. To some extent such a ranking will also be an inverse ranking according to specificity; for liquid assets are non-specific, and highly specific assets tend to be convertible only with difficulty ("specific" being related to goals, which may be shared by relatively few other entities). Similarly, the utility of a statement of financial position is increased by ranking equities in order of maturity, for in considering any change in the stock of assets, with or without any increase in external equities, one must first make provision for meeting existing commitments. These considerations relate

to form rather than substance but form is significant in the sense that it determines in a measure the order in which things become the focus of attention.

Changes in Financial Position.

64. The financial position of an entity will change over time. Consider a person who is a producer-consumer (say, a wage-earner) and suppose there are no lags between the initiation of any action and its consummation. In a given period he will earn a wage income, I, and receive cash, Mi, in the amount of it. He will incur expenditure, C, on consumption and pay out cash, Mc, in the amount of it. He will as a result have made savings, S, and there will be an increase in his cash holdings in the amount of it. In respect of each event there is an asset effect; resources are increased or decreased. But in each case, the increase or decrease is represented by a concept—income, expenditure, savings. These concepts are the same in kind as the concept residual equity; they represent effects on the residual equity equal in amount to changes in the assets.

65. Thus, if we write

$$A_1 = L_1 + R_1$$

to represent the financial position at time 1, and

$$Mi - Mc = I - C$$

to represent the events occurring between time 1 and time 2, the two equations may be added to obtain the financial position at time 2:

$$A_1 + Mi - Mc = L_1 + R_1 + I - C \qquad [1]$$

or

$$A_2 = L_1 + (R_1 + S)$$

66. The demonstration may be extended by removing the assumption that there are no lags between the initiation and the consummation of any action. If the cash received is less in amount than the amount of I, the wage-earner will have a contractual claim, D, against his employer; A_1 will be increased by the amount of it and cash receipts will be less than Mi in an equal amount, Md. But the effect on the aggregate assets of earning I will be the same. Similarly, if the cash spent on consumption is less in amount than the amount C, the wage-earner will have incurred a liability, Lc, to another party; L_1 will be increased by the amount of it and cash payments will be less than Mc in an equal amount Ml. By inspection it can be seen that the identity [1] of para. 65 will take the form

$$A_1 + D + (Mi-Md) - (Mc-Ml) = L_1 + Lc + R_1 + I - C,$$
$$\text{or, } A_2 = L_2 + R_1 + S,$$

if allowance is made for both lags mentioned in this paragraph.

Similarly again, if the wage-earner acquires assets by incurring liabilities—whether or not those assets are consumed or held—the identity will hold: A_2 and L_2 will simply be larger by equal amounts, but the residual equity will be as before.

67. The financial position at any time is the basis of action for the next ensuing period. But it offers no suggestion as to the mode of action. A person planning for a future period will find suggestive what happened in the last period. He will want to know his total income, its sources if there are more than one, and the regularity of the flow from each source. He will want to know his expenditure and the kinds of things for which it was incurred; in particular, he will find it useful to know which of his expenditures are periodically recurrent, which are occasional but predictable and which are unpredictable (19). He will want to know whether on balance he saved anything and how much, or whether he consumed part of his original wealth during the period. All of these have some bearing on expectations for the next period. Amounts representing income I, and consumption C, may be set down in a statement called an *income statement*, (I—C) being equal to savings, S, during the period. From para. 65, it will be clear that S also represents the change in the net assets (A—L) held; it could have been obtained by taking the difference between net assets at the beginning and end of the period. But in the absence of a continuous record linking two position statements, the systems of computing position from time to time are sub-systems. To avoid the limitations of sub-systems (15) accounting resorts to a system of continuous records yielding from time to time completely articulated statements of position and change in position.

68. It will be recalled that income is the value of the net addition to utilities through production and that direct utility attaches only to non-monetary goods. A money income and a money stock are useful only insofar as they enable one to acquire non-monetary goods. The calculation of income proceeds therefore from a basic reference level—the amount of or the capacity to command non-monetary goods at the beginning of a period, or the initial capital or wealth. The phrase "the maintenance of capital" is used to indicate this criterion for the measurement of income. It does not imply that individuals will wish to maintain their capital in the above sense; to add to or to draw from their capital is their choice; but choice is uninformed unless the effects of operations are related to an initial stock of direct utilities and/or monetary equivalents.

69. A regular or contractual income, such as the income of a wage-earner, may be described as predictable income; expenditure on consumption may be considered as predictable expenditure. But in any interval, a residual equity may be

increased and assets increased correspondingly by *windfall gains* such as the proceeds of a legacy or a gift; or it may be reduced with a corresponding reduction in assets by *windfall losses* such as the accidental loss or destruction of assets. These are unplanned incidents or events. One's reaction to windfall gains and losses will differ from one's attitude towards predictable income and expenditure. For this reason, it is necessary to distinguish between planned and windfall items. The assets arising from or dissipated by planned actions and by windfalls are, of course, the same in kind; the distinction is applied only to the conceptual designation of the source of the change.

70. As income and expediture are concepts, they can be made to denote whatever is found to be useful or necessary for action. For example, income could be used to embrace windfall gains, but to do so would result in the loss of a significant piece of information (63). Our wage-earner, on the other hand could adopt as a guide and limit to his actions the amount of cash he receives and spends during any income period, notwithstanding that the lags of para. 66 occur. It is sufficient for his purposes only because of the regularities in his receipts and payments patterns. A small business firm may find the same basis sufficient where there are substantial regularities in receipts and payments patterns. An accounting system in which transactions are recognized when cash is received or paid is said to be conducted on a *cash basis*. Where transactions are brought into account when they become effective, even though cash is received or paid at other dates, the accounting system is said to be conducted on an *accrual basis*.

71. If changes occur in the composition of assets and liabilities and if the composition of assets and liabilities is critical for action, the income statement of itself will be insufficient to describe the change. The differences in the statements of position will need to be set out in detail. This may be done by a summary statement showing the changes in the composition of assets and corresponding changes in the residual equity and in the composition of liabilities. The statement will be called a statement of the change in position, or a *funds statement*.

72. The formal framework outlined above may be restated as $$A + C = L + R + I$$
From this identity may be derived the rules for recording all transactions of an entity in such a way as to yield articulated income and position statements. The method of describing transactions in terms both of changes in a stock and the corresponding changes in equities is *double entry accounting*. It rests simply on the fact that all goods are the property of some entity (26). The demonstration of the preceding section has assumed that the monetary units, in terms of which the symbols

used are expressed, are homogeneous or of equal significance throughout. This does not necessarily conform with reality (32). The argument could be extended here by relaxing this assumption, because shifts in the purchasing power of money are as important to wage-earners as to anyone else using money as a medium of exchange; but the extension is deferred to the treatment of the next class of case. The relaxation of the assumption of the constant purchasing power of money does not in any way affect the validity of the identity given above.

Simple Trading Ventures.

73. Attention is now directed to trading ventures as such. Trading ventures include all ventures in which resources are converted, by combination or by holding against the future demands of consumers, into other means which are sold at a price per unit. A trading venture is a productive unit simply (21); its operations are not confused by the difficulties of evaluating satisfactions from consumption. It buys and sells. Its affairs may thus be regulated strictly according to economic sacrifices and gains. For the purposes of this paper, the trading venture contemplated has no investments or obligations unrelated to the production and sale of a line or lines of goods or services.

74. Trading ventures arise from decisions of persons to devote to or invest in (22) a productive activity part of their personal resources, in money or kind. The incentive to divest oneself of such resources is the expectation of gain—either in terms of a periodical division of the gains of the venture, or in terms of the proceeds from disposing of one's interest in it. No decision to invest is irrevocable (28); personal exigencies may at any time dictate the liquidation of an interest in a trading venture. Ease of withdrawal thus influences readiness to invest. The ease with which resources or the proceeds of their use may be withdrawn depends on the legal form and contractual capacity of the venture. Equities in a trading venture arise through loans or through capital contributions; the latter will be considered first.

75. A sole trader may contribute to his enterprise at will. He may withdraw resources in part or whole with ease as the matter is subject only to his discretion. He may, if he wish, disregard the equities of others in business assets. Legally, he and his business venture are indistinguishable, even though for the purpose of economic calculation it is useful to distinguish personal and business roles (57). However, he may shift the risks of his business by the sale of the whole of, or an interest in, it to others.

76. The limited liability business corporation differs in some significant respects. It is an independent creation of law arising in the first place from decisions of a group of people to devote part of their resources to a joint enterprise. That group, the members, acquire shares in the venture proportionate to their contributions; the corporation is thus a device for marshalling the savings of individuals for productive purposes (22). The corporation has an indeterminate life and an independent capacity to contract; its contracts may extend over long terms and some of the assets it acquires may not be reconverted to cash except over long periods. Individual members may, nevertheless, wish to convert their investments into cash for personal reasons in a much shorter time (63). To meet the unpredictable demand for cash on the part of members without disturbing long-term arrangements of the corporation, shares are transferable. A member, or shareholder, may thus shift the risks attaching to his interest by the sale of the whole or a part of his holding—in the same way as may a sole trader—but not by recourse to the corporation itself; he must sell in the securities market.

77. It will be clear that trading ventures are concerned with operations in three markets — the new money market, in which new securities are issued for new money contributions; the securities market, in which existing securities are exchanged; and the commodities market, in which goods and services are bought and sold. It will be useful to consider the nature of operations in each of these markets. But first a general view.

78. A trading enterprise is a co-operative system depending on the continued support of its participants. The participants may be grouped according to function—there are workers, suppliers, customers, financiers (lenders), and investors (risk bearers); and insofar as such ventures are restricted or authorised by law, it may be said that the public at large, through the instrumentality of government, is a participant. These groups participate in the expectation of receiving incomes or services appropriate to their functions. Workers, suppliers, customers and financiers may be described as freely contracting participants. Their rights are determined and secured by contract or the general law. Insofar as they may offer their services to a wide range of enterprises they are able to obtain prices consistent with those obtainable in other enterprises. They may bargain in such a way that the inducements offered by the subject enterprise tend to be sufficient to maintain their consumption levels in real terms.

Risk Information and Investment.

79. But all trading enterprises are subject to *risks*—from changes in tastes (14), from technological changes (21), from competition (34). The risks fall on investors. Investors par-

ticipate in the expectation of recovery of their contributions at some further time and of a periodical yield, appropriate to the risks assumed, in the interval between making and withdrawing their contributions. Although such expectations are held, the risks are acknowledged. No investor is of right entitled to the return of the whole of his contribution or to any determinate periodical yield. If the venture is successful he will obtain both; if it fails he may receive neither. But as investors are in another role consumers, it is reasonable to suppose that they envisage yield and contribution recovery in the same way as freely contracting participants, namely as providing the means for sustaining an expected level of consumption or a given amount of wealth in real terms.

80. In a manner analogous to the commodities markets, the *new money market* rations available new money among competing ventures (34). To those ventures money is a means of operating in the commodities markets; so that ventures compete in terms of the expectations they engender regarding the outcome of operations in the commodities markets. Funds flow most readily to the ventures in respect of which the expectation of gain is greatest—gain being understood to be the aggregate surplus above the investment, in real terms. Gain may take the form of periodical interest payments or dividends from the net proceeds of operations. In respect of residual equity holders it may take the additional form of increases in the market value of their securiites. These values will increase as the aggregate value of assets is increasd through the retention (re-investment) of part of the periodical surplus, for the increase in equity per share will be expected to lead to greater earnings—and dividends—per share.

81. To investors the new money market at any time offers a range of possible investments. In choosing between these investments, one consideration is the financial position of each venture—its solvency, the amounts and terms of its liabilities, the nature of its assets — for this represents its *readiness* to benefit from the opportunities the commodities markets offer. An equally important consideration is the rate of expected earnings on the residual equity of each, for residual equity earnings covers both the amounts available for distribution and the amounts available for reinvestment. The expected rate of residual equity earnings represents the *capacity* of a venture to benefit from the opportunities which the commodities markets offer. If an investor is to make valid comparisons between, and to form expectations relating to, investment opportunities, both capacity and readiness require expression in *consistent* terms; and because the choice is for immediately future operations in the commodities markets those terms will be current values (59), whether the venture is a new one or one with many years of operation behind it.

82. As investors invest at risk they are not indemnified against loss, however great may be their expectations. But if expectations change they may take their losses and shift their risks. The function of the *securities market* is to facilitate the realisation of securities or the conversion of risks of one kind into risks of another kind. It effects a redistribution of risks; but it does not raise the income or wealth of the community generally. If some gain, others lose. No less than new investors in existing ventures, existing investors are dependent, for periodical re-assessment of risks, on statements of income and position in current terms.

83. Lenders are equally interested in the same information even though their risks are limited. Lending is geared to the residual equity and the periodical increment to it. These provide margins of security; but security is only significant if at any time it is represented by current evaluations. It is of no consequence that at the time of granting a loan expectations were of a high order; the probability that the service charges will be met as they fall due and that the loan itself will be discharged on maturity is a function of present capacity to exploit opportunities. Further, inasmuch as borrowing is limited by the residual equity and borrowing at a lower yield than the customary yield on risk investments increases the yield of the latter, opportunities for further borrowing can only be fully exploited, with due regard to the rights of lenders, by reference to present capacity and readiness.

84. One final line of argument for the expression of capacity and readiness in present terms may be developed from the point that the public at large may be considered as a participant in trading enterprises (78). The laws under which private institutions engage in trade for profit are public grants of power. As trading enterprises employ a large proportion of the capital goods of a community, and as the stock of capital goods is the means of maintaining or improving the income stream or potential living standard, the policies of trading ventures as to the division and distribution of surpluses are of social importance. It should be expected that the surplus available in any period for distribution and potentially available for consumption will be calculated on the basis of the capital employed at the opening of the period converted to present values at the time of calculation. A system of calculation, which does not proceed from such a basis may not prevent *inadvertent consumption of capital* (68). Given the maintenance of the community's stock as a desirable minimal objective, the information systems in use will be such that they clearly indicate whether or not a proposed division of business resources would result in consumption of capital. Further, the complex of markets serves to determine, through the allocative mechanism of prices, what enterprises shall have the support

of the community, access to available savings and, through them, access to the resources of the community (34). For efficient allocation, the information systems in use will be such that the market is informed of the relative capacities of firms to add to the community's stock or supply of direct utilities. This capacity is represented by the relationship of the gain from trade to the capital employed, both being expressed in current terms.

85. It will be clear that new investors, existing security holders and lenders alike are dependent on information representing present capacity and readiness to exploit opportunities. It should also be clear that the objectives of the class of workers designated managers will include the preservation of the contractual equity of lenders and, at the minimum, the maintenance in real terms of the yield and capital contributions of investors. Managers direct the operations of firms in the commodities markets to which we now turn.

Trading Operations.

86. All goods acquired, held and used in the process of manufacture or trade are, in those uses, producers' goods. Producers' goods are themselves manufactured and acquired in anticipation of their final conversion into and sale as consumers' goods. The exchange value or price of producers' goods is thus a function of the exchange values or prices of the consumers' goods to which their use gives rise (16).

87. More specifically, the exchange value or price of producers' goods at the time they are acquired is a function of the expected future proceeds of their product. The purchase of any asset is evidence that the present value of the expected future return from its sale is not less than its price. Whether or not a particular asset is acquired depends on the prices at which the output is expected to be sold; if the margin between expected input prices and expected output prices is not sufficient to satisfy all participants, the venture will not be undertaken.

88. But once a course of action is undertaken expectations may change. After the date of acquisition it may be found that an alternative use of the present exchange value of existing assets may have a higher expected yield than the use to which those assets are presently being put. This may occur either because the original expectations are themselves found to have been inappropriate, or because changes in the environment have presented opportunities for more economical (better-yielding) investment. In either case the initial cost of the assets will have no bearing whatever on future income from their continued use. The value of an asset in a given employment is neither

more nor less than the present value of the future income expected to flow from its use. If there is an alternative employment expected to yield a greater income flow, it will be preferred (28); and however fixed the initial intention to use the asset for its initial purpose, it is economic wisdom to shift the investment from one asset to another. Adaptability, not constancy, is the characteristic of a going concern.

89. It should be pointed out that this does not entail constant revision of investments in specific durable assets. A plant built up of less specific items into an integrated and highly specific unit will tend to have a lower resale value— either as a whole or piecemeal — than the same items uncombined, because being highly specific there are few buyers whom it would serve equally well, or because of the dismantling costs of individual pieces. The investment, once made, can therefore be justified on a relatively lower income than may initially have been expected.

90. As was stated above, the value of an asset in any employment is the present value of the future income expected to flow from its use. How is this present value to be assessed? Its assessment is implied in present market prices for equivalent assets, replacement prices. *Replacement price* (or replacement cost) does not mean some hypothetical future price to be paid on some hypothetical future replacement date. It means the price currently ruling for equivalent service potential. The price currently ruling for producers' goods is the market's assessment of the present value of expected income flows from their use at the present level of prices, for all potential users of such goods. It is therefore an objective valuation, and is equally relevant to decisions involving the continued use or abandonment of the use of any asset. Barring imperfections in the market, replacement cost and realizable value will be equal. If at a given purchase (or replacement) price an asset is able to earn a higher return in one employment than another it is not required that it be stated at a higher value than current price in the record of the more profitable venture. The higher earnings rate will simply result in funds flowing more readily to the one than to the other. Similarly, if the rate of return on the investment calculated at replacement prices is lower than it would be in alternative employments, a clear indication is given of the desirability of switching the investment. It should perhaps be mentioned that reference to replacement price in the above argument means always current replacement price for equivalent service potential; thus if an asset has already yielded half of its original service potential, current replacement price is equal to half the replacement price as new.

91. It may be suggested that, if prices are expected to change, the formation of income expectations (and hence de-

cisions on investment in particular assets) must involve hypotheses or guesses about the degree and direction of such changes. But this is not so. One bases one's calculations (as distinct from one's speculations) on the present level of prices, that being the nearest one can get to the future. And such calculations are relevant. For if there is at the moment a certain functional relationship between present purchase prices of producers' goods and present selling prices of finished products, this relationship will be expected to continue. The prices of non-durable inventories and finished goods will go up or down the escalator together—both in fact and in the record; it is necessary to adjust the record to provide that the present value of the consumed services of durable inventories move in the same direction at the same rate. If changes in technology or in the relative prices of different producers' goods occur so that the functional relationship between purchase prices and selling prices is changed, the effect will show up in the rate of return, as suggested in para. 90, unless the consequential windfall loss or gain is taken into account immediately.

Continuity and Periodical Review.

92. Business ventures may be undertaken for various lengths of time; some for specific functions over short periods, others for a potentially wide range of functions over an indefinite period. We will consider the latter as including the former. An indefinite "expectation of life" does not imply persistence in an originally chosen course of action. Adaptation is as important as it is to individuals; the extent to which a business venture adapts itself determines the extent to which it meets the expectations of its participants (78). For adaptation it is necessary to know the present financial position and its rate of change.

93. Continuous adaptation necessitates a *continuous record* except in the most modest ventures (48). The investors and managers of an undertaking may at the outset lay down specific objectives and specific methods of achieving those objectives. But the environment is unpredictable in a measure so that no plan may be expected to be carried out without deviation. Every small action in some way promotes or hinders the attainment of the objective; but because actions are so numerous and their individual effects so slight, it is not possible to review them all piecemeal. Nevertheless, the aggregate effects of many such actions may cause a deviation from the plan which is material; and the same actions or the environment itself may give rise to a change in the relationship of the venture to its environment which is *material* — i.e., sufficient to induce a change in actions. For review and replanning, a statement of the results of actions and of the position arising from actions

is required at points of time no further apart than the interval in which material changes occur. This interval may be described as the *accounting period*.

94. The period contemplated is a function of the impact of actions and external events. If no actions having or expected to have material effects in themselves occur or are contemplated, the accounting period may be long; the greater the frequency of actions having, individually or collectively, material effects, the shorter will be the accounting period. The shorter the accounting period, the greater is the probability of optimal adaptation. Periodical summarization of results and position, however, adds to information processing costs; the accounting period is thus determined at the point where the marginal utility of information is equal to the marginal cost of producing it.

95. The assessment of the changes effected by action is made easier if the periods covered by summaries are equal in length. Planning for periods of equal length and reviewing operations over the same periods enables one to build up one's stock of comparable "period experiences", to improve one's judgment and capacity to plan (9). This advantage emerges for even greater reasons when the periods coincide with natural or social cycles—weeks, quarters, years.

96. These considerations have given rise to the customary procedure of summarizing the results and reporting on the position of business and other organizations yearly. Notwithstanding this custom, which, in terms of procedure and formality has its own justification, the predominant principle of periodical reporting lies in the materiality of actual or expected change. The same principles apply whether the summaries are for the use of management or investors; reporting for equal periods is useful to investors, but further reporting on the occasion of material changes in operations or prospects is no less necessary.

97. Periodic recurrence of certain summarizing processes does not, of course, mean that events and transactions fit neatly into periodical compartments. There is a continual flow of goods, services and money; periodic assessment of the rate of change and of the position is a device for ordering that flow but it does not interrupt it. The continuity of the flow poses problems in measurement.

98. In the first place, measurement cannot be exact or precise: for three reasons. The flow is continuous; there is no point of inaction or period of inaction long enough to refine methods of identifying changes with accounting periods. Further, the measurement of changes necessitates the selection of a base for forming expectations. Whether the base is the level of market prices or an indirect measure of present value these are inexact

in themselves. Further still, there can be no exact knowledge of the period over which existing commitments or investments will be continued. These reasons are operative whatever system of accounting is adopted. Accounting summaries are at best *approximations;* the periodical problem is how to make the best approximations. Where unique values are unobtainable, the best approximation may be an average, as an average is a more representative value than any of the values from which it is derived.

99. In the second place, to secure comparability as between statements for successive periods requires that all changes shall be identified with the periods in which they occur. Operations which are consummated (i.e. which complete the cycle "cash-goods-cash") in any period create no problem of identification. Operations which straddle two or more consecutive periods involve allocation. The greater the consistency of use of methods of allocation the greater will be the comparability of successive statements. No possibility of alternatives at the discretion of the record keeper can be admitted (51). Nor can any procedure be admitted which is consistently biassed in any direction (52). Nor can any external change which induces internal changes in a period or over successive periods be disregarded; for the impact of external changes will differ from period to period (the environment being fluid) destroying the comparability of successive statements. Comparability is not to be understood as similarity in size of results or effects; any device selected because this will be its effect operates to defeat the purpose of reporting and is inconsistent with the service function of the record (38). The very purpose of comparison is to discern the sizes of changes or deviations.

Recording Trading Operations.

100. The framework considered in para. 64 needs to be restated for trading ventures. For consumption must be substituted expense; for savings, net profit. In all other respects the original terms will serve, though they may be subdivided for some purposes. Assume that at the commencement of operations a trading venture has assets, liabilities and residual equity. Part of its assets and all its liabilities are fixed in money terms —they are either fixed amounts of money or claims to fixed amounts of money — monetary assets and liabilities. The remainder of its assets are real or non-monetary assets. Real assets embody services which are available for sale, or which by combination become available for sale, in different form. In the succeeding interval the venture will buy goods and services, combine them with the opening stock of real assets and purchases in the form of saleable products.

101. It is necessary to choose between the cash and accrual basis for recognising transactions. As in the case of individuals (70), firms which have a regular income and regular expense and little change in the periodical level of claims may find the cash basis a sufficient approximation. But generally the pattern of business transactions presents few such uniformities; a firm is subject to arrays of influences from the expectations of its officers, of influences from the actions and pressures of its participants, and of influences arising from market changes in which it takes no direct part. Comparability can only be approached in these circumstances by adopting the accrual basis.

102. Given that transactions have been recognized in the record, it is necessary to devise some test by which transactions may be attributed to periods. Now, the risks of holding monetary assets (cash and claims) and non-monetary assets are different in kind. The risks of holding monetary assets and liabilities are risks that their purchasing power or redemption costs may vary in real terms. All persons may be assumed to be equally well informed of these risks, but no person may, on the basis of any present knowledge, quantify their future extent or their incidence in time. One may speculate on the probability that prices will rise or fall, and arrange one's stocks accordingly; but the outcome is not predictable. The risks of holding non-monetary assets are risks that the incomes they yield may vary due to changes in the commodities markets. As these incomes arise from the sale of commodities having direct utility, expectations and plans may be formed with a degree of confidence. Further, these are the specific risks which investors undertook, risks on which they could not be assumed to have knowledge but in respect of which they would wish to have some basis for future assessment of their investments. It appears that it is useful to determine periodically the gain from trade and that to do so the income side of the calculation will be based on the change in the character of risks which occurs at the point of sale. This may be described as the *realization* principle.

103. If there is no change during an accounting period in market conditions, prices or technology—that is if the environment is completely stable—money outlays and money receipts are of equal real significance, unit for unit, and costs may be set off against income to obtain the net increment to the residual equity. It is relatively easy to fix the amount of income by the realization principle. The costs attributable to that income are of two kinds. Some costs of a period are not related directly to goods sold. They are general costs of being in business. They do not add to the value of inventories and are attributable directly to total income. Other costs are identifiable with inventories. The part of those costs attributable to the income of a period comprises—opening inventories plus purchases plus

wage costs plus other service costs plus plant costs less closing inventories. All items except plant costs may be measured directly; the indivisibility of plant makes indirect measurement necessary. Plant cost for a period is that part which bears to the total cost of plant the same relationship as the services consumed during the period bear to the total expected service; this is the *depreciation* of the plant during the period. Income less total costs gives the net increment to residual equity or *net profit*. Note that under the assumptions of the first sentence of this paragraph, costs are equal to present values throughout the period and throughout the calculation. Opening and closing financial positions are stated in sums representing equivalent real things and the amount of net profit may logically be related to residual equity.

Recording and Restatement under Instability.

104. If the assumption of complete stability is relaxed the problem increases in complexity. Prices are free to move and will move under the impact of charges in market conditions. Money receipts from sales of finished goods at the beginning of an accounting period will not be the same in amount as money receipts from sales of the same quantities at the end of the period; or to put it another way, equal amounts of money income at the beginning and end will have different significance in terms of goods. Initial outlays on commodity stocks and durables at the beginning of the period will not be the same in amount as outlays on similar stocks at the end of the period; nor will the values of stocks on hand at the end be the same as the money outlays per item at the time of acquisition. To match money outlays against money receipts in such a direct way that the money units paid out and received are of equal purchasing power is only possible if all goods acquired are completely disposed of before a change in purchasing power occurs; it is obviously impossible in the case of continuous trading ventures, for inventories must be carried, and no one can tell in advance when a change in purchasing power of the currency will occur or to what extent.

105. In these circumstances, money outlays are not equal to present values. The amounts paid for goods acquired represent values at the time of acquisition (28). The prices paid for goods by traders are derivatives of the expected values (prices expected to be charged) for final products, which are themselves a function of the then prevailing level of prices (87). If the level of prices shifts, purchase prices will shift but so also will the values of stocks on hand. Such shifts induced by price level movements are not productive of income. It is necessary to distinguish the gain from trade at current costs and prices from the induced shifts in value due to general price movements. The income from trade in terms of current values

is predictable insofar as demand is predictable. But changes in value due to general price movements are unpredictable in amount and incidence; and in any case they cannot be considered as increments to residual equity in any real sense. Unless the basic record is adjusted to take account of these shifts, income being represented by receipts of money or money claims at the contemporary price level would not be charged with the contemporary value of the services incorporated in goods sold, Such adjustment implies that the process of setting off costs against incomes is a process of assigning values rather than assigning parts of money outlays.

106. If the level of prices shifts, monetary assets and liabilities are affected as well as non-monetary items; if prices rise the value of monetary assets, in terms of goods, falls, and the cost, in terms of goods, of meeting liabilities falls, even though their monetary amounts remain the same. These changes, unlike changes in the valuation of non-monetary assets, do not enter into the costs of goods sold.

107. The consequences of a shift in price levels may be demonstrated as follows: Assume that a firm has monetary assets, M, non-monetary assets, N, liabilities, L, and residual equity, R, at the beginning of a period. Assume further that it engages in no transactions during a period in which the price level rises from 1 to $(1+p)$, p being the percentage rise in relation to a base 1. The position at the beginning then is

$$M + N = L + R \qquad [1]$$

Multiply throughout by $(1 + p)$:

$$M(1 + p) + N(1 + p) = L(1 + p) + R(1 + p) \qquad [2]$$

Now, by hypothesis, at the end of the period, the firm has the same monetary assets and liabilities as at the beginning. Restore the terms representing these to their original amount by transposing and taking the differences to residual equity:

$$M + N(1 + p) = L + [R(1 + p) + Lp - Mp] \qquad [3]$$

This represents the position at the end of the period restated in terms of the level of prices then ruling. Monetary assets and liabilities are in amount as at the beginning; non-monetary assets and initial residual equity are increased by the amount of the rise in the price level; and the residual equity is augmented by the "gain" on liabilities less monetary assets owing to the fall in the purchasing power of money.

108. The net adjustment to the residual equity may be obtained by a shorter process than by the adjustment of all items in the identity. For subtracting [1] from [3],

$$pN = pR + pL - pM \qquad [4]$$

The net adjustment to the residual equity, the right-hand side of [4], may thus be obtained by applying p to the initial value of N. Whether the adjustment is made by the process of the left-hand side of [4] or by the process of the right-hand side depends on the significance attached to the "gain" or "loss" on monetary items. In the first place, the decision to hold monetary assets and to have liabilities of given amounts is no different in kind from the decision to hold non-monetary assets of a given size; with given opportunities they are, in fact, mutually dependent decisions. The "loss" or "gain" from monetary items is the price of the advantage gained from or the sacrifice made by holding the consequential stock of non-monetary assets. This suggests that pN is an adequate adjustment. In the second place, one may consider whether the "gain" (if any) on holding monetary items is a divisible surplus. If the maintenance of the residual equity is adopted as the basis for measuring divisible surplus, no part of pR (=pN + pM—pL) is divisible. If, on the other hand, a policy is adopted of taking the maintenance of non-monetary assets as the basis for measuring divisible profits, on the ground that the maintenance of real assets is a condition of maintaining an income stream, then no part of pN (= pR + pL — pM) is divisible. In neither case is the separate calculation of pL and pM necessary. In the third place, one may look at the question from the viewpoint of the management of monetary balances. If the position given in [1] is an equilibrium position inasmuch as net monetary assets (M — L) are necessary to the employment of non-monetary assets N, then the position given in [2] would be the equilibrium position at the higher price level. It would be necessary therefore to have net monetary assets (M+Mp—L—Lp) or an increase of p(M—L). But net monetary balances are not independently determinable under fluid conditions, so that again the separate calculation of pM and pL seems to be unnecessary.

109. To take up the argument again from para. 105, it is now necessary to consider the combination of continuous basic recording and periodical restatement which will yield information relevant to action at the beginning of each successive accounting period. The difference between the positions at the beginning and the end of each period is to be accounted for completely. The conventional accounting procedures will serve as providing the basic record; it is necessary so to adjust the aggregates obtained that (a) only items relative to the period just ended are attributed to it and (b) that classification of aggregates is adequate to distinguish restatements of value from gains from trade. A simplification is introduced to overcome the difficulties referred to in para. 104. Matching transactions at specific value levels will be assumed to take place uniformly during the accounting period, in order to avoid restating the values of every single transaction in terms of prices at the close of the period. Periodical restatement avoids the accumulation

of errors of approximation in all but the residual equity balance. The error affects the distribution of the aggregate change in residual equity as between gain from trade and restatement. No further discussion of the possible error from such approximation is offered here.

110. Cash balances are readily determined. The present values of amounts owing under contractual interest obligations, discounted at the contract rate, are equal to their face value. For amounts owing and owed for short terms the present values may be taken as face values. For amounts owing and owed but not bearing interest the present values are obtained by discounting face values at current interest rates, adjustment being made at the same time to interest paid or received during the period.

111. In respect of commodity stocks at the end of a period, current replacement cost is the principle to be adopted in all cases; for basic materials this means current prices, for partly or wholly processed stocks it means the present prices of material, labour and expense components. The opening inventory appearing in the income account will be the inventory as shown in the balance sheet of the previous period restated in terms of closing prices. Where direct calculation from closing market prices is not possible, an approximattion may be made by applying a price index to the closing value of inventory of the last period. The amount of the restatement of inventory values would be credited to a residual equity adjustment account, the amount of which would not be available for dividend appropriation if the maintenance of capital were adopted as a policy (68). The value of commodity stocks to be charged against income from sales would then be the value of opening stocks at closing prices plus the value of goods and services purchased at actual prices plus the value of plant service calculated as below, less the value of closing stock at closing prices.

112. In the case of plant and other durables it is often not possible to obtain replacement cost quotations for the items in stock. An approximation may be made to replacement cost as new by applying a price index to initial money outlay. The differences between replacement costs as new at the ends of two consecutive periods would be entered in the record as adjustments to plant value and to the residual equity adjustment account mentioned in the previous paragraph. The value of plant service consumed in any period would then be approximated by applying to calculated replacement cost at the end of the period the ratio of service consumed to total expected service. Replacement cost at the end of the first period of use is replacement cost as new less the value of plant service consumed. At the end of the second period of use the replacement cost and the value of plant service consumed would fall short of the total value for plant service consumed if calculated as

for the two periods combined. The amount of the shortfall would be equal to the percentage increase in the price level in the second year applied to the value of plant service consumed as computed at the end of the first year. The rise of the second year could not have been foreseen in the first year. To make good the total charge against replacement cost new at any time therefore requires a retrospective adjustment. This would be made out of past surplus, not out of current income, for to charge current income would be to charge an amount in excess (in the above circumstances) of the current value of plant service consumed.

113. The question may now be raised as to the appropriate index for making the adjustments referred to in the two preceding paragraphs. In the first place at each point it was stated that an approximation was being made. This is important; it is impossible to do precision work in a fluid environment with crude tools; all estimates, however well attested, (including the estimates necessary in conventional accounting) lack precision. In the second place, as the prices of each item in a non-monetary stock may change at different rates it may appear that an index for each type of stock would be required. However, there is no certainty that any given item of a stock will be replaced; adaptation may involve quite different investments of the money proceeds of liquidating existing assets through the sale of their services. Furthermore, one of the purposes of the calculation is to determine the amount which can be divided and distributed without impairing the future potential income stream. This amount may be retained in part, and laid out in a variety of ways; and in part it may be distributed to residual equity holders, who likewise may lay it out in an even wider variety of ways. In these circumstances, a general index of the level of prices (or the reciprocal of an index of the purchasing power of money) seems to be indicated. But in so far as the prices of all producers' goods are based on the expected level of prices of consumers' goods — the ultimate product of and reason for production of all kinds (21)—a consumers' goods index is logically preferable.

114. The above adjustments will yield position statements and income statements which reflect financial position and its rate of change in comparable and relevant terms — as far as the imperfections of the methods of recording and restatement allow. If calculated adjustments are made, it may be necessary still from time to time to make *ad hoc* adjustments, for relative changes in demand and technology may cause the values of specific assets to diverge significantly from calculated values; but the magnitude of these adjustments will be of a much smaller order than those commonly occurring in quasi-reorganizations or asset revaluations within the conventional accounting framework.

Summary of Foundations, Assumptions or Postulates.

115. The sequence of the above argument has something of the appearance of a layer cake; it has been dictated by the desire to proceed piece by piece to build up the case from a simple example to a more complex one, and gradually to introduce principles relating to accounting method and to relax simplifying assumptions. It will be useful to draw together at this point the characteristics of the world of action which have been used as foundations for the derived statements relating to accounting. These characteristics represent the way in which the environment of accounting is visualized; it is believed that they are realistic and verifiable by observation or introspection.

		Para.	
1.*	*Individual differences.* Individual persons have different wants, different skills and different propensities for action	25*	65
2.	*Diversity of goals.* Persons have diverse concurrent and competing wants and corresponding goals	13	
3.	*Diversity of roles.* Persons may fill varied roles, concurrently or consecutively, and have sets of goals corresponding to each role	10	
4.	*Variability of goals.* Wants and goals vary from time to time	14	
5.	*Intensity of wants.* In any system of wants (2)* each will have a different ranking or intensity at any time; ranking will change from time to time (4)	13, 14	
6.	*Orientation.* Deliberate action is oriented to the satisfaction of wants, individually and as a set. An action may satisfy a want or wants in one or more respects	39	
7.	*Cerebration.* The choice of a course of action is the outcome of the processes of observation, recollection, calculation and comparison	8, 9	
8.	*Incapacity.* For all persons there are limits to the capacity for observation, to the capacity for recollection and to the span of attention	8, 9	

---

* The numbers in the left hand margin identify each concept for subsequent reference; such references are designated subsequently by numbers in parenthesis ( ). The numbers in the right hand margin refer to relevant paragraphs in the body of the paper.

		Para.
9.	*Choice.* For a given role choice depends on the intensity of wants (5), on present knowledge (7, 8) and on expectations of the outcomes of available courses of action (7)	16, 42
10.	*Revocability.* No choice is irrevocable	14
11.	*Abstraction.* Because there are various aspects of each actual or potential course of action (6), and because the span of attention is limited (8), each aspect of a series of possible actions is considered independently	37, 38
12.	*Means.* Wants are satisfied by the appropriation of means. Means are scarce resources which are believed to be serviceable in satisfying wants. The utility of a means subsists in the belief that it will be serviceable in satisfying a want	16
13.	*Diversity of means.* Means vary in specificity with respect to particular wants, in divisibilty, in durability, and in convertibility to other means .	17, 31
14.	*Valuation of means.* Means derive value from the value attached to the satisfaction of wants (5, 12). Any choice involving addition to, or sacrifice of part of, a homogenous stock is based on the utility (12) of the marginal unit, i.e. on marginal utility	16, 24
15.	*Possession.* Appropriation of means (12) depends on possession	26
16.	*Equities.* Possession (15) may be unrestricted, in which case the equity in means vests in the possessor; or restricted, in which case the use of means is subject to the equities of other parties	26
17.	*Legal framework.* The equity in and possession of means (16) are regulated by laws, rules and understanding relating to interpersonal relations, contracts and bargains: this framework lends predictability to the environment of action	26
18.	*Uncertainty.* The environment of action is fluid. Many aspects of the environment of action are fortuitous; their incidence and severity are unpredictable. Every aspect of choice may be affected by changes in the environment of action	19, 20
19.	*Accumulation.* The legal framework (17) makes possible and uncertainty (18) makes desirable the accumulation of means	23

		Para.
20.	*Optimization.* Because means are scarce (12) in relation to wants (2), deliberate actions are chosen according to their expected capacities for yielding the greatest aggregate satisfaction of a system of wants, e.g. the greatest gain for a given sacrifice (6, 9)	41
21.	*Diminishing marginal utility.* Because of the diversity of competing wants (2) and the scarcity of means (12), every increase in the stock of a given means reduces the utility of further additions to it	24
22.	*Combination.* A stock of heterogeneous means will tend to be so arranged that the marginal utilities of all types of means in the stock will be equal (14, 20, 21)	23, 24
23.	*Specialisation.* By making possible the exploitation of different individual capacities (1), specialisation increases the potential supply of means . ..	25
24.	*Exchange.* Specialisation of function (23) and the diversity of individual goals (2) require a mechanism for the exchange of means	25
25.	*Markets.* A market is a process by which the interplay of the wants and preferences of different persons (1, 20, 21, 22) establishes ratios of exchange or prices. Exchange values or prices are the resultant of the choices of more than one person: for any person they are objective valuations	28, 33
26.	*Money.* Money facilitates the exchange of goods which vary in divisibility (13). Money is a means of high convertibilty (13) and low specificity (13). Because of the convertibility of money, monetary units are accepted units for expressing ratios of exchange (25), or prices, of non-monetary means	31
27.	*Credit.* The existence of a legal framework (17) makes possible the exchange of goods and services (including money) at one point of time for goods and services to be made available at a subsequent time. Credit gives rise to specific equities (16). The capacity to obtain credit depends on the extent to which the control of means is restricted or unrestricted (16)	27

		Para.
28.	*Price.* In the case of an actual exchange, the ratio of exchange or price expresses the value attached to expected service yields from the good acquired at the time. Prices are derivatives of marginal utilities (14). Prices are the only values relevant to actions in markets (25)	28, 29
29.	*Variability of values.* Prices of goods and the purchasing power of money vary over time as the environment changes (18); the possibility of such changes subjects different parts of a stock of means to different risks	29, 102
30.	*Monetary expression.* Every good or service acquired or to be acquired by exchange and every sacrifice made or to be made to acquire such goods or services may be represented by an actual or estimated price. Monetary expression enables the economic characteristics (see 11) of diverse goals (2), diverse means (13), and diverse equities (16, 27) to be brought within one framework of calculation (7), increasing the effectiveness of attention (8) and making easier the problem of choice (9)	36
31.	*Monetary calculation.* Monetary calculation is concerned with market or exchange values, market values being measures of the sacrifices of means necessary to secure given ends (26, 28)	36
32.	*Continuous adaptation.* Optimization (20) in the face of the variability of goals (4) and the variability of values (29) makes necessary continuous adaptation. Continuous adaptation depends on successive assessments of financial capacity for action and of the probable effectiveness of possible courses of action (9)	48
33.	*Financial position.* Financial capacity for action is represented by the relationship between assets and equities at current valuations at a point of time	58, 62
34.	*Change of position.* The probable effectiveness of possible courses of action may be deduced by reference to the result of past courses of action ..	67
35.	*Complexity of organization.* Specialization (23) gives rise to complex organizations the existence of which depends on the actions of persons filling various roles (e.g. investors, financiers, managers, accountants, etc.). For each actor, action conforms with the propositions indicated above—see (9), (12), (20), (21), (22), for example	78

	Para.
36. *Conflict of goals.* Specialization tends to result in the adoption of sectional or personal goals or points of view which may be inconsistent with the goals of an entity as a whole, either by reason of extra-organizational influence on specialists themselves or by reason of the conflict of personal goals with organizational goals	53, 78
37. *Balancing of interests.* The viability of a complex organization depends on the continued provision of incentives for participants which (a) are adequate as rewards for service and (b) are deemed to be fair by comparison with the rewards of other participants. To form opinions on these matters participants require information	78
38. *Specialization in information processing.* One form of specialization in complex organizations is specialization in information processing and the consequential separation of decision-making from direct apprehension of information	49
39. *Information systems.* The processing of information so that the results are relevant to choice situations requires systemization. The function of an information processing system is to provide a substitute for and a supplement to direct observation (7, 8) and a supplement to the memory of actors (7, 8)	9, 52
40. *Objectivity.* As individuals have different propensities for judgment and action (1), as individuals may simultaneously occupy several roles with respect to any complex entity (3) and as the viability of the entity depends on the satisfaction of parties occupying different roles (37), information will be so processed that the rewards and interests of all participants are objectively represented—it will represent the entity as such, not the viewpoint of any class of participant	52

69

These postulates are selected for their relevance to the framework of behaviour in which accounting plays a part. For the derivation of specific propositions relating to accounting a definition is also necessary:

> *Definition.* Accounting is a method of monetary calculation designed to provide a continuous source of financial information as a guide to future action in markets 38

Summary of Derived Principles.

116. In this paragraph there are brought together and arranged the statements relating to the general nature of accounting which have emerged from the foundations just outlined. If a general description must be given to these statements they may be described as principles.

	Para.
(A) *Accounting entities.* Accounting systems relate to specific entities defined by roles of natural or artificial persons or groups (3, 9)*	56*, 57
(B) *Relevance.* The probability of optimal adaptation varies directly with the relevance of accounting information to action (9, 20, 39)	38
(C) *Neutrality.* The probability of optimal adaptation varies directly with the neutrality of accounting information (1, 4, 9, 20, 39)	38
(D) *Correspondence.* The relevance of accounting information varies directly with its correspondence with realities (i.e. market conditions, contractual relations, etc.) at the time of action (9)	50
(E) *Consistency.* Comparability and the legitimacy of inferences as to present position and expectations depend on consistency in the use of concepts and methods in accounting (7) 9, 52, 81, 99	
(F) *Communication.* The transferability of accounting information depends on the use of terms, concepts and measures having the same content and significance to all parties of interest (39, 40)	54
(G) *Objectivity.* The relevance of accounting information depends on its freedom from the bias, influence or opinion of persons connected with an entity, whether as actors on its behalf or as information processors (35, 36, 40)	52
(H) *Double entry.* Transactions of and events affecting an entity are fully described for accounting purposes by simultaneous recording of the manner in which they affect the values of the assets of an entity and the equities by virtue of which those assets were acquired (28, 33)	62
(I) *Accounting identity.* The aggregate values of the assets of, and the aggregate amount of the equities in, any entity are equal (16, 25)	62

---

* The numbers in parenthesis ( ) refer to points listed in paragraph 115. The numbers in the right hand margin refer to relevant paragraphs in the body of the paper. These references are rough indications of the grounds on which the statements depend and the places at which they are discussed.

	Para.
(J) *Basic record.* As a basis for any subsequent calculation or comparison, a continuous basic record is required which indicates the values attached to actions or events at designated points of time (7, 8, 9, 18)	93
(K) *Summarization.* Because the span of attention is limited, summarization of entries representing varied transactions improves comprehensibility of the record and thus increases the probability of optimal adaptation (8, 9, 20)	8, 9, 93
(L) *Classification.* Summarization in accordance with the characteristics of assets and equities which are pertinent to action — utility, durability, convertibility etc. — increases the probability of optimal adaptation (13, 16, 20)	63
(M) *Uniformity of valuation.* The operations of addition, subtraction and relation necessary in any form of summarization can only be performed validly if the separate items are valued on a uniform basis (7, 30, 31)	9, 81

71

(N) *Current valuation.* Insofar as the monetary values assigned to events, things and transactions are at the date of assignment, the current valuation, the principles of relevance, objectivity and uniformity of valuation are satisfied (9, 28, 31) 28, 59

Corollary 1. At the date of purchase or sale, i.e., at the point of making the initial record, the prices at which bargains are made are the values to be assigned.

Corollary 2. At any other date (e.g., for the purpose of any subsequent calculation) the values to be assigned are replacement prices in respect of assets, present values in respect of specific equities.

(O) *Periodical interval.* The frequency of summarization depends on the frequency with which material deviations from planned objectives or operations have occurred or may occur (9, 10, 18) 93

(P) *Periodic identification.* Transactions and other changes are attributed to the periods in which they become effective by changing the character of risks and by changing or inducing changes in the characteristics or values of assets or equities (9, 29) 99

(Q) *Periodic restatement.* If changes in the value of any asset or equity occur, restatement of the values entered in the basic record is required (a) to validate arithmetical and relational operations after such change in value and (b) to conform with the principle of correspondence (9, 29)   105

(R) *Status representation.* Financial position may be derived by summarization of the basic record subject to restatement of values if changes in values have occurred. Such summaries enable decisions to be made with respect to combinations of assets (21, 22) and the use of credit (27) 58, 85

(S) *Change representation.* Changes in financial position during a period may be represented by a statement or statements describing completely the nature, magnitude and sources of the differences between the financial positions at opening and terminal dates. Income and funds statements serve this purpose in different but complementary ways, assisting in the making of decisions having regard to the probable effectiveness of alternative courses of action (9, 34) 67, 71

(T) *Articulation.* The cause and effect relationship of transactions and events on financial position is reflected in an accounting system in which statements of financial position and changes in financial position are articulated by reason of their derivation from a basic record founded on market values (16, 24, 28)   67

(U) *Approximation.* Indivisibilities of assets, the fluidity of the environment, the flexibility of goals and the variability of values make statements of financial position and change approximations only (4, 13, 18)   98

117. The summaries given in the two preceding paragraphs seem to be sufficient as far as the demonstration has been taken. Until other cases than the two examined have been subjected to analysis, the "principles" derived may not be considered either sufficient or conclusive. It is believed, however, that they may be shown to be relevant over a wide field. It is repeated that a general theory or framework of concepts is sought by means of which accounting of varied kinds and for varied entities may be explained or described; it is believed that all the propositions of para. 116 are of this general kind. The method here adopted encompasses a range of ideas which conventional "theory" has taken for granted; for example, why account at all? why double entry? why classify? Conventional "theory" has concerned itself with the areas which have provoked controversy, and without a general

basic idea as a point of reference, the concepts adopted in those controversial areas have been special purpose concepts, often flying in the face of the brute facts of economic life.

Some Contrasts in Conclusion.

118. In conclusion, some contrasts with the existing framework of conventional accounting may demonstrate the superiority of the framework set out in this paper.

(a) One consistent principle is applied throughout—the relevance of information to human behaviour. Conventional accounting has no such explicit principle; it therefore disregards the need of men to know where they are in objective terms and the rate at which they are approaching real goals.

(b) As a corollary of relevance the proposed theory concerns itself with values—present market values. It avoids the melange which conventional accounting presents — with its different valuation bases for different things. It avoids the interminable arguments about the merits of H.I.F.O., L.I.F.O., F.I.F.O. and all the other F.O.'s. It avoids the contradictions of the conventional descriptions of the money valuation concept and the going concern concept; it has no special use for the notions of conservatism and disclosure and thus evades their inherent inconsistency. It substitutes for the false assumption that an investment is irrevocable the realistic assumption that adaptation is the essence of behaviour.

(c) By adhering to one set of values it permits of the logical application, over the whole array of entries in an accounting system, of the operations of addition, subtraction and relation. These operations cannot logically be applied to conventional accounts for, although all items are expressed in money units, those units lack similarity in substance.

(d) The proposed theory is disciplined by real circumstances. It does not resort to eclectic principles geared to the "uniformity" and "objectivity" conceived by protagonists of conventional accounting. It has its own uniformity and objectivity, based on the fact that all calculation in money is intended to guide action *vis-a-vis* the external world of men in markets.

(e) The proposed classification of assets into monetary and non-monetary groups is consistent with real differences. It cuts across the conventional current asset — non-current asset classification which has long stood in the way of clear understanding of the similarity of all commodity inventories and the application of consistent principles to both long-term and short-term commodity stocks.

(f) The proposed theory avoids the unrealistic assumption that money has a stable value. It treats the problem of shifts in purchasing power as an integral part of the problem of accounting, which indeed it is. Conventional accounting on the other hand persists in the delusion that only goods change in value, and treats the most obvious shifts in the purchasing power of money as occasional, pathological conditions from which the economy will soon recover.

(g) Adoption of the proposed model would do away with the many "grey" areas in which it is now considered that accountants may exercise discretion—areas which show up accounting as a vague and undisciplined product of circumstance and convention. Its adoption would sharpen the dim outlines of trends in results and position which rob investors of the means of review and criticism. Its adoption would provide accountants, businessmen and administrators with an unequivocal basis for determining the equity of the fiscal and regulatory policies of government. Its adoption would help remove the extensive opportunity for misallocation of resources which conventional accounting in inflationary periods provides. Its adoption would rationalize the merging of businesses which, under conventional accounting, makes every investor a speculator.

119. One final point. If conventional accounting has all the defects these contrasts suggest, how has it managed to survive so long? It has survived simply because of the enormous richness of the informal flows of information in and around business and other organisations. Cost accounts, budgets, *ad hoc* calculations, market prices, project successes and failures — countless pieces of information, all from unintegrated subsystems (para. 15), help men to manage in spite of the flaws in conventional accounting. Goethe had one of his characters describe double-entry book-keeping as one of the finest inventions of the human mind, because it enables one to see clearly the whole without becoming confused with details. Accounting, though it still has this original and basic function, today is frequently discounted, and relegated to the role of satisfying formal legal requirements. The hope of restoring it to consistency with reality and of restoring its internal consistency justifies the search for an accounting which is dynamic because it is related to the exigencies of human behaviour.

The Resolution of Some Paradoxes in Accounting

OCCASIONAL PAPER No. 2

FACULTY OF COMMERCE AND BUSINESS ADMINISTRATION
UNIVERSITY OF BRITISH COLUMBIA
VANCOUVER
1963

Introduction	paragraph 1 - 4
When is a service function not a service function?	5 - 10
When is information not information?	11 - 21
When is a going concern not a going concern?	22 - 27
When is a going concern value not a going concern value?	28 - 35
When is a cost not a cost?	36 - 44
When is a value not a value?	45 - 52
When is a principle not a principle?	53 - 61
A proposed set of Postulates and Principles	62 - 67

THE RESOLUTION OF SOME PARADOXES IN ACCOUNTING

"It may be said that in commercial or investment banking or any business extending credit, success depends on knowing what not to believe in accounting. Few concerns go into bankruptcy or reorganization whose books do not show them solvent, and often even profitable." Mr. Justice Jackson (quoted in Pinger, 1954; 652.)

Introduction

1. Consistency is not perhaps one of the outstanding characteristics of human behaviour. It is not difficult, if one wishes to be critical of another, to find examples of what may be alleged to be inconsistencies, and even to demonstrate that behaviour has been inconsistent. It is an entirely different matter to have the "accused" admit to inconsistency, or, if he does admit it, to think anything serious is involved. In some cases his indifference is quite legitimate. As a player, over any period, of several roles, he may be acting according to the requirements of each successively with due care but in a manner which appears to an observer, who does not appreciate the plurality of roles, to be inconsistent. On a more general level, few people want to think that living is such a perpetually serious business that inconsistency is inexcusable.

2. Those who assume the role of specialist or expert however can scarcely afford to indulge in such freedom from restraint when filling such a role. The "expert" is a phenomenon of social living; he is one deemed by others to be skilled and well informed in the field of his experience; and such a judgment on the part of others stems largely from the fact that he is of service to them. Few experts if any are expected by those who use their services to be expert opportunists; it is usually expected that they will show some evidence of consistency in their role as experts; that their knowledge will demonstrate such common understanding as will make their advice and skill reliable; and that where there is a body of such experts there will be evidence of mutual consistency in the actions and advice of individual members of that body. Mutual consistency depends in turn on there being a reasonably well-argued body of knowledge, consistent in itself. And insofar as the unskilled seek the advice of the expert, they usually expect that the advice and information they are given will be consistent with their purposes and with the real world with which they must contend. We shall be concerned with the extent to which these forms of consistency find expression in accounting. It should perhaps be pointed out that we are not concerned merely with uniformity. Uniformity may have quite different and less worthy justification than consistency. Uniformity may be adopted without serious thought, as a means of avoiding embarrassment. But consistency can only be achieved at the cost of deliberate and careful analysis of the circumstances with which the expert and his dependents are concerned.

3. In a lecture entitled <u>Towards a General Theory of Accounting</u>, given in the University of Adelaide in August, 1961, an attempt was made to set down the foundations of a general theory of accounting. The line there followed proceeded from the characteristics of human behaviour and the characteristics of the economic environment, to a set of ideas which are mutually consistent, yielding a system of accounting which gives information relevant to action in markets. The present purpose is to demonstrate that, insofar as there is a common body of ideas among accountants today it is self-contradictory or internally inconsistent, and quite inconsistent with the needs of those whom accounting purports to serve. It will be argued that the resolution of those inconsistencies is of importance, and that they may be resolved by adopting the same framework of ideas as was presented in the

---

* The Australian Society of Accountants Annual Endowed Lectures, University of Adelaide, 1961.

earlier lecture.

4. The procedure to be adopted will be as follows: At each of several points a paradoxical question will be set up. Each question relates to certain elements in the environment of accounting as they are understood among accountants. These questions will be explored by resorting to the literature of accounting. In each case a number of statements in the literature are referred to, in order to establish that the ideas under discussion are not isolated ideas of individuals or specific institutions, but are ideas which are widely and firmly held. The literature contains many statements which differ from and are more defensible than those examined here; but these statements do not form the basis of generally established practices whereas those to be discussed do. The quotations used may appear to be repetitious and for that reason tiresome: but it seems necessary adequately to authenticate the ideas under discussion to avoid the charge that they are minority views. It will transpire that some of these ideas are at odds with the facts of economic life, that some are inconsistent with other ideas on the same subject, and that some are so loosely expressed as to be useless. Care has been taken to avert the suspicion that any author or institution has been singled out for special mention. Such criticism as is offered is to be considered as general criticism of the present state of accounting theory; it is hoped that it will appear to be neither captious nor partisan. At the end of each section will be indicated the ideas which may be substituted for those generally held if the postulated defects are to be eliminated. In a final section these are drawn together and the set of accounting principles based on them is reproduced as it appears in the earlier paper.

When is a service function not a service function?

5. There is perhaps no better point to begin than with the picture of accounting as a function. How do accountants regard their art? One might expect to find the answer in definitions of accounting. Perhaps the most widely quoted definition is that offered by the A.I.C.P.A. Committee on Terminology (A.I.C.P.A., 1941; 67).* This takes the form of listing the types of operation which comprise accounting; no attempt is made in the definition to indicate the purpose of those operations. There is, no doubt, an implicit purpose, for the appendage "and interpreting the results thereof" involves a recipient of the interpretation. Sanders, Hatfield and Moore (1938; 113) assert that "accounting should make available all material information of a financial nature relating to (a) the financial condition or status of the business, (b) its progress in earning income." No statement of these kinds is in itself objectionable. But all such statements are sterile. They provide no explicit clue to the precise manner in which accounting serves or may serve human purposes. Implicit functions or purposes can be anything the reader chooses.

6. Some assert a purpose which is described as reporting on stewardship. "The primary purpose of the annual accounts of a business is to present information to the proprietors, showing how their funds have been utilized and the profits derived from such use" (I.C.A.E.W., 15; 1952). "Corporate financial statements are usually prepared as an accounting by the management for its stewardship of the stockholders' property..." (Broad, 1944; 190). "...financial stewardship is the paramount objective and rests at the base of accounting.... The whole process of accounting is geared to record funds entrusted and their subsequent disposal." (Irish, 1950; 216, 217.) An explicit statement of purpose is worth having, but any statement alluding to stewardship of this kind has several defects. Firstly, it seriously oversimplifies things. For unincorporated businesses it is quite proper to speak of the funds and property of the proprietor or proprietors. But it is an error of fact to speak of the funds or property of proprietors in the above context in the case of corporate business. An investor who divests himself of funds in

---

* A full description of all sources is given at the end of the paper.

exchange for a paper title to a share in a business can no longer speak of "his" funds. Further, the "funds" which he exchanged for his paper title may not have gone to the business in which he holds a share, but to a previous shareholder; there is no necessary connection between "his" funds and the funds available to the business. Secondly, the stewardship view of accounting implicitly represents managers as custodians rather than as businessmen. There is no particular point in knowing what has been done with the funds of the business unless one adopts the view that managers are fiduciaries - and this view is false. Investors may want to know how efficiently funds have been utilized - but not simply how they have been utilized; and they want to know this because they are buyers of managerial talent. It is in any case pretending too much to speak of the annual accounts as showing how funds have been utilized, for all sorts of things are quite legitimately eliminated in the process of drawing up the annual accounts. The accounts may show the net effect of utilizing funds - but this is a very different thing. And even if investors did have a comprehensive statement showing how funds have been utilized, would they be able to make any use of it? It is quite improbable, for seldom are they able as managers to assess the merits of a given deployment of funds or to know of alternative deployments and their prospects.

7. Statements such as those considered in the previous two paragraphs are still current; but there are more explicit and more useful statements. It is many years since Paton stated the setting of accounting in the following terms: "The conception of the manager must be exactly that of the business entity as an economic unit; and if, as is repeatedly said, the most important purpose which modern accounting can serve lies in the rationalization of business administration, the accountant must of necessity adopt the viewpoint of the manager in large measure." (Paton, 1922; 478.) If the managerial function is fully described it will embrace both the problems of investment in and use of a body of assets and the problems of maintaining the rights and interests of the various equity holders who make possible the use of that body of assets. Paton's view may legitimately be extended to include investors as "economic units"; but by the late 'thirties the investor was beginning to be specifically mentioned in descriptions of the accounting function. Sanders, Hatfield and Moore (1938; 4) wrote of "satisfying the need for information of all the parties of interest, especially of (a) the management of the business, (b) outside groups, such as investors and creditors, (c) government, in such matters as taxation and regulation." Paton and Littleton (1940; 1) commenced their monograph thus: "The purpose of accounting is to furnish financial data concerning a business enterprise, compiled and presented to meet the needs of management, investors and the public." Others have stated in general terms the governing idea, without alluding to any special class of users "...the fundamental principle of accounting is usefulness...this principle...provides a basis for accounting outside itself." (Wilcox and Hassler, 1941; 309.) "...fundamentally the objective (of accounting) is to make enterprise activities understandable." (Littleton, 1953; 77.) More recent statements make specific allusions to "communication" which is another way of indicating the needs of users; thus, "Effective measurement and communication of economic data on a business enterprise...represents the accounting function." (Bedford, Perry and Wyatt, 1961; 6), and, "Accounting's purposes are to serve as a language for communicating the financial facts about an enterprise to those who have an interest in interpreting and using those facts, and to provide a useful tool for analyzing, controlling and planning enterprise operations." (Black and Champion, 1961; v.)

8. There is sufficient evidence here to indicate that the notion of service to one or more groups of persons associated with business has long been a part of the general impression its exponents have had of the accounting function. But it is easy to use the appropriate words while having a confused and inadequate view of what the words mean in an operational context. Few objections can be taken to any of the above forms of words; but in so many cases they gloss over the implicit but

essential meanings of component phrases. For example, what do Sanders, Hatfield and Moore mean by "the need for information"? What do Paton and Littleton mean by "financial data" and "meeting the needs of management..."? What does Littleton mean by making enterprise activities "understandable"? What do Black and Champion mean by "financial facts"? It seems generally to be supposed that such words or phrases have an unequivocal and uniform meaning, or that they are self-explanatory. But this is far from the case as will be shown.

9. It is necessary, if the above types of description are to have any content which will be of use in formulating an accounting system, that the precise character of the service to be given be delineated. It is necessary to have a clear idea of the manner in which accounting fits into the framework of individual and business behaviour. Business men do not simply want to "understand" enterprise activities; they want to understand so that they can "control" and "plan"; but even these words do not say specifically what they want to do. Business-men, in fact all men, must act and every act involves a choice between available courses of action. What determines these choices and hence the actions which follow? Any group of persons will display individual differences; different wants, skills and propensities for action. At any time each will have a series of diverse goals which compete for attainment, because each will feel uneasiness or strain in a variety of directions simultaneously. These goals will depend on the diverse roles which an individual fills during the period in which each moment of action falls. But wants and goals will vary from time to time. To use time and other scarce resources with the greatest effect at any time goals will be ranked in order according to the intensity of wants, and because degrees of uneasiness will vary from time to time so will the order in which goals are ranked vary. At any time action will be directed towards the most urgent goal. But for thinking men, action will not be random; it will be deliberate, involving the mental processes of observation, recollection, calculation and comparison, and, in respect of each of these, every individual has limited capacity - both absolutely and with reference to the amount of time during which choices must be made. Choice is thus influenced by the intensity of wants, the amount of present knowledge and one's expectations of the consequences of various possible actions, the latter also being a consequence of present knowledge. But every course of action may have several aspects and bear on more than one goal; each of these aspects must be considered independently, the emergent action being finally the consequence of mentally synthesizing the various abstracted implications of each available course of action. Above all, the whole purpose of choice is that some person or persons may obtain satisfaction of wants, in terms of what can be consumed - sooner or later. The orientation of action is towards things or control over things, never towards money as such. It is believed that, unless such characteristics of behaviour as these are explicitly taken into account, it is impossible to stipulate the kind of service accounting can or should render. The portmanteau term "service function" may be good enough in everyday parlance; but it is far from enough for technical rigour, for it may equally connote things of incidental or questionable use as well as things of the utmost importance. If incidental, implicit or questionable functions steal the limelight, a service function may in fact give very little service.

10. When is a service function not a service function? When the modes of action of the entities it is supposed to serve are so poorly defined that no specific basis is provided for designing the service or for testing whether any task performed by a service unit is in fact a service; and when the service function itself is so poorly defined that no link is established with the entity served and its mode of action. In these circumstances its practitioners can quite blandly assert that they are giving service even though the service is trifling and inconsequential.

When is information not information?

11. It is an easy and comforting belief that all statements convey information. It is just as easy to show that this belief is mistaken. Logicians are partial to the invention of nonsense statements to demonstrate the error. Some lines from Lewis Carroll's Through the Looking Glass will serve:

> 'Twas brillig and the slithy toves
> Did gyre and gimble in the wabe;
> All mimsy were the borogoves,
> And the mome raths outgrabe.'

This is a useful example because it has sufficient recognisable words - 'twas... and...the...did...and...in the...etc. - to give it the form of a statement in the vernacular without conveying anything. Many political and ceremonial speeches are of the same kind. Carroll's lines may of course well convey some information, but only if the terms used are translated into terms which are generally understood by the reader. Likewise a code or cipher is a device for conveying nonsense to the unauthorised or misinformed, but conveying very much in the vernacular to the person who has the key. It is also easy to show that although some statements convey information, the information is not worth having, and the statement is not worth making. To fill up the silence, as a conversation piece, one may say "Ughrr. It's cold", when it is apparent to every shivering one of the audience that it is cold. Questions relating to the content and significance of statements will occupy this section.

12. Accounting records and reports consist of sets of statements. At early stages in the development of accounting, each entry in the record was in fact a detailed and sometimes lengthy statement of the facts behind it. (Peragallo, 1938; 4 ff.) The forms and formal conventions since adopted enable events and transactions to be recorded in abbreviated ways, but every entry is still a statement. "Cash, 1000 money units", "Plant, 10,000 money units", are statements. But they are statements in code. Plant and money units are not the same in kind. "Plant, 10,000 money units" is a statement relating "plant", "10,000" and "Money units". To understand the relationship one must have knowledge of the symbols used and the rules for putting symbols together in statement form. These are precisely the problems of language, and the similarity has not been overlooked by some accountants. Montgomery (1938) described accounting as "the language of finance". Goldberg (1957;.13) deals briefly with the "lingual" aspect of accounting. And a number of the extracts quoted in paragraph 7 imply that accounting serves as a form of language.

13. To be a little more precise, accounting is a form of language which concerns itself with quantities and magnitudes. The form of its statements is not the same as the form of some statements in economics: for example, it is not concerned simply with tendencies, with higher or lower, with more or less. A businessman does not simply want to know that his assets today are more than they were yesterday; he wants to know how much more. He does not simply want to know that last year's income was less than that of the year before: he wants to know how much less. He does not simply want to know that a new product will increase his profit; he wants to know by how much. Thus if accounting is to be the means by which he is informed, accounting will involve measurement and the propositions which appear in accounts will be expressive of measurements made.

14. This aspect of accounting is noticed far more frequently than reference is made to language. Paton says "accounting strives to measure economic forces in financial terms and to communicate the results of such measurement to interested parties" (1939-40; 87), and in another place speaks of accounting as "<u>measuring</u>

and arraying economic data" (Paton, 1955; 1; emphasis in original). Paton and Littleton say "The primary purpose of accounting...is the measurement of periodical income by means of a systematic process of matching costs and revenues" (1940; 123); and they use "measured consideration" of costs and revenues (1940: 11-12). Canning (1929) styles one of his chapters "The Measurement of Income"; he speaks more commonly of valuation when he refers to assets, but is impelled (p. 199) to offer some general rules which describe the characteristics which measures must possess if they are to be "merged". He does not however establish general principles of accounting which conform with the general rules relating to measurement. Kester (1946) repeatedly refers to measurement. His second chapter is styled "Measurement in Accounting" and he applies the term to specific items throughout the text. Of the significance of the measurement problem he writes "Regardless of what the items are which are given a place in the balance sheet...it is their measured amounts which give them their real significance when used to show financial position." (p. 29.)

15. But, in spite of the implied importance of measurement, the only type of measurement contemplated by Kester is measurement in terms of cash outlay or its equivalent, and the only justification offered is the "primary need of management" for "information as to the status of invested funds" (p. 30). He writes of the need for "remeasurement" of balance sheet items "at successive fiscal periods", but this turns out to be nothing more than an introduction to the usual conventional going concern methods of valuation: "going-concern measurement is not so much a distinct type of measurement as it is a term descriptive of the kinds of dollar measurements suitable for a going business" (p. 33). In these respects most accountants follow the same road. Canning, as an observer, is disillusioned about accountants' measurements. "What is set out as a measure of net income can never be supposed to be a fact in any sense at all except that it is the figure that results when the accountant has finished applying the procedure he adopts" (Canning, 1929; 98, 99). He notes six types of commonly accepted valuations for different classes of assets, and comments: "These diverse values of things are added ("merged"?) to find an asset total, that, dollar for dollar, cannot possibly have a common significance" (p. 319), ... "No competent student of the joint field of economics and accounting can doubt that the measurements in accountants' reports are of diverse statistical orders." (p. 320.) If this is the state of affairs, can the resulting information be informative?

16. All this is rather disappointing. One might be pardoned for supposing that measurement would entail a conscious, deliberate and skilled attempt to assign quantities to things by reference to a scale which applies equally to all the things to be measured. For such a scale to be applied equally, consistently, to all things measured, it must be applied to one and only one of the characteristics common to those things. Further one might be pardoned for supposing that any remeasurement would involve more than a simple mechanical adjustment to the original measurement. The reasons why these suppositions and expectations are disappointed may lie in the attitude accountants adopt towards the signs and symbols they use and towards their processes of assigning symbols.

17. Notwithstanding all references to communicating facts and information the accountant has reserved the right to dictate what information shall be communicated. What, for example, does Kester imply when he speaks of "the dollar amount of an item as measured for the accounting records" (1946; 29; emphasis added)? He seems to imply that there is a distinction between "for the accounting records" and "for business purposes". What does Gilman imply when he speaks of "the accounting viewpoint" which "has caused some difficulty to those who use accounting figures" (1939; 609)? He seems to imply a viewpoint which is different from that of users of accounting figures. What does Littleton imply when he refers to "objective reality in the accounting sense" (1953; 182; emphasis added)? He

seems to imply that there is an objective reality for accountants which is different from the objective reality for anyone else; but what can "objective" mean if this is so? Scores of such adjectival usages of "accounting" imply that there is a clear difference between the way accountants see things and the way businessmen and users of accounts see the same things. Montgomery (1938) speaks of this as a "tendency to expect business to conform to an accounting pattern rather than the reverse". This tendency is a bias which accountants perhaps do not find in themselves, but it is a bias which is well known to psychologists and logicians. It finds occasional mention in the literature relating to business problems; thus: "There is a widespread notion that an adult person can always discern facts that are exposed to observation.... This belief is illusory because a mental bias can operate to prevent a person from either ascertaining the relevant facts or from appropriately interrelating facts and drawing logical conclusions therefrom" (Campfield, 1959; 556). If accounting statements are to convey information, accountants must first see things as the users would see them if they were able; there is no room for a special accounting viewpoint interposed between the facts and those who must act upon them.

18. The recording of events, transactions and "facts" generally, can only be done in terms of symbols - words, numbers, positions and so on. Attention will be confined here to the numbers assigned to descriptive words. What do the numbers in accounts represent and what information do they communicate? The assignment of numbers is described by Gilman (1939; 26) as the valuation convention. "By this convention non-homogeneous assets and claims to assets are translated into financial equivalents or money values." At another point he says that valuation in the sense in which he uses it "is no more than a convenient method of symbolizing" (p. 56). And at another point still, "If it be conceded that dollar valuations are no more than symbols, then it follows, in theory at least, that consistency results from leaving the symbols unchanged. Thus, if the symbol $5 is used to represent one ton of fuel, as long as that ton of fuel remains intact, the symbol itself should theoretically remain unchanged.... Essentially all that the convention of valuation really accomplishes is substitution.... Instead of calling a ton of coal $5, it might be called X. Just so long as the ton of coal remained, it would be symbolized as X, but as soon as half of it was consumed, it would be symbolized as X/2" (p. 247). Though Gilman is the source of this particular demonstration, something of the same kind underlies all statements which sanction the assignment of numbers, other than numbers representing market values, to items in accounts. What is the character of Gilman's statement? If the numbers assigned are symbols, what are they symbols of? - for Gilman does not make this clear. If all that the assignment of numbers "accomplishes is substitution", what is substituted for what? Suppose a merchant has three trucks, one that is so old that it is held together with wire and Scotch tape, but is still usable, one that is three years old and rather battered, and one that is quite new. He can see the condition they are in, he knows what they can do and he can even estimate how long they will last. But, suppose his accountant gives him the following information - Trucks, 10,000 money units, less depreciation 6,000 money units, not 4,000 money units; now what does he know? According to Gilman, he knows that someone has substituted a money symbol for trucks and another for depreciation - no more than that. And that piece of information is not information worth having. Further, if Gilman offers his coal example seriously, the merchant can have no means of showing anything less than, say, Y, for a truck, for there is no such thing as half a truck - accounting is not concerned simply with quantities. Again, if a ton of coal were denoted by X presumably one would have to denote a truck by something not-X, say Y, so that a merchant having a truck and a ton of coal would have X + Y, and the "translation" of "non-homogeneous assets" into common terms would not have been accomplished.

19. It is not generally enough realized that every translation of facts and events into symbols involves a loss of some information. Whatever information his accountant gives the truck-owner mentioned above, it is less than all the facts about his trucks. But for specific purposes one may be prepared to forego much information in order to see clearly in its context some specific piece of information: the necessity of abstraction has been referred to in para. 9. It is the particular advantage of the use of money symbols in the formal framework of accounting that it can provide a specific class of information of which the parts may be related and from which inferences may be drawn with respect to the actual and potential flows of money - the only common means, in a monetary economy, which gives access to control over other means. Generally an information system may use symbols which simply denote items, for example, a catalogue, a chart of accounts. But if a system is to use symbols of such a kind that a common characteristic of all items is represented, and if the magnitudes of those characteristics are to be capable of summation or relation, any given symbol will necessarily have the same connotation wherever it appears in a list of items: thus "500" assigned to "plant" will mean the same thing as "500" assigned to "cash" or "500" assigned to "creditors". The intention to add, subtract and relate symbols will discipline the whole process of measurement and of determining what will be measured.

20. If we are to design an information system which conveys information it is necessary to start with the service notion dealt with in the preceding section. It is necessary to admit explicitly that where, as a consequence of specialization the processing of information and the choice of actions are divorced, processors and actors may see things differently; but it is necessary at the same time to demand, as a corollary of the service function, that accountants make every effort to convey relevant information in a manner free of their individual predilections. This is a critical aspect of the objectivity of information. Accountants have ostensibly feared that, without restraints, managers would report affairs in a manner favourable to themselves, but have disregarded the equally possible bias on their own part. If the symbols used are strictly relatable and contemporary it is possible to conceive that summary statements may be derived which are relevant to action - summaries representing financial position or the financial capacity for action, and changes in position, the results of past actions and a guide to future action. If symbolization is artificial and the results must be re-translated to be useful, then one of two undesirable things will follow: there will be unavoidable losses of information both at the point of symbolization and at the point of interpretation, and the resulting information will be less useful than it could be; or the re-translation will not be made and what appears to be information will in fact be useless.

21. When is information not information? When the information generating system has a low degree of selectivity due to inadequate definition of its purpose: when the transmitting system is subject to interference; and when the signals transmitted lack precise meaning to the receiver because the same symbols at any time have quite different significances. The conventional accounting model has all three defects. Though it has the appearance of an information system, the information units it produces and transmits are of mixed character, due in part to lack of definition of the function of the system and in part to bias in processing; and, as for the utility of its signals to receivers, the exponents and practitioners of conventional accounting alike freely admit that on many matters more precise and more relevant information is required than their system yields.

When is a Going Concern not a Going Concern?

22. The notion of the going concern has a well established place in the literature of accounting. But there is no consistency in the interpretation of its purpose or its implications. "(Following the convention of the going business) no attempt is made (at the end of each period) to value all the assets of a company on a realizable

basis. Rather the emphasis is shifted to the amortizing of initial costs...the resulting asset figures are not influenced by market price fluctuations ascribable to the law of supply and demand." (Gilman, 1939: 81.) "Business in general does not consist of an array of sporadic, short-term ventures and its accomplishments are not normally subject to the test of complete liquidation. Liquidation is not the normal expectation; continuity is." (Paton and Littleton, 1940; 9.) "The business is viewed as established and as expecting to operate continuously. Capital has become tied up in equipment essential to the undertaking, in the sense that to dispose of it in its entirety would mean a break-up of the business. It cannot therefore be freed or put to other uses without a reconstruction of the present enterprise" (Kester, 1946; 306). "The 'going concern' concept assumes the continuance of the general enterprise situation...the assets of the enterprise are expected to have continuing usefulness for the general purpose for which they were acquired, and its liabilities are expected to be paid at maturity." (A.A.A., 1957: 2.) "...it is assumed that the business entity has continuity of life... Properties used by the entity are deemed to have been irrevocably dedicated to the carrying on of its purposes and will remain in use as long as they serve those purposes" (Owen, 1958; 70).

23. Several threads run through every such series of statements. The first is most concisely expressed by Owen, the irrevocable dedication of properties to purposes. This concept of the character of a going concern is quite inconsistent with business behaviour. There are admittedly countless examples of firms which have acquired assets which they have held continuously over long periods for their original purposes. But there are probably no less numerous examples of assets which have been disposed of piece-meal before their full service potential was exhausted, of assets which have become technologically and economically valueless to one firm for its purposes but which are quite useful and valuable to other firms for their purposes. In a very real sense business does "consist of an array of short term ventures" for each of which the test is liquidation. Every purchase of an asset is potentially a short term purchase, and businessmen are quite concerned about the interval over which such investments may be liquidated. For the essence of the business enterprise is that it is surrounded by the ceaseless ebb and flow of technical and economic change. A vehicle, a machine, a security investment may for this reason be considered as a worth-while investment only so long as the present value of the expected services it will yield exceeds the present value of the yield from investing its present resale price in an alternative manner. If the alternative yield is greater it is sheer folly not to take it - liquidating the earlier investment in the process. The fact that certain assets are complementary in character is not overlooked; complementarity simply requires that in any re-examination of investment possibilities complementary assets must be considered together, as a unit. There is no more likely way of making a going concern defunct than to force it to dedicate its properties to one purpose as long as they will last.

24. Another thread running through such arguments as are quoted above seems to be the notion that the alternatives available to any business are continuation as it is or complete break-up. Kester makes the clearest statement of this view but it occurs also in the statement from Paton and Littleton, and in many similar statements by others. Quite apart from the possibility of alternative investment mentioned in the previous paragraph, liquidation at some time of the investment in any business asset is always and inevitably in contemplation; but not liquidation in the sense of forced sale as seems to be implied in most statements relating to the going concern which refer by antithesis to liquidation. Gradual liquidation is one of the most obvious characteristics of a going concern: if a business is not liquidating some of its assets, by sale of their services, it is not going. Every advocate of the importance of cash flows in business calculations attests the importance of liquidation as a feature of a going concern. And even those who deny the relevance

of liquidation have to fall back on it in the long run: e.g., "the complete picture (sic) of an enterprise is never discernible prior to final liquidation" (Paton and Littleton, 1940: 10). But, of what use is the "complete picture" then, when the business is gone? Surely it is important while the business is a going concern to consider each part of it as undergoing liquidation in a planned and orderly fashion!

25. The thing represented by the phrase "going concern" is not merely an abstraction. We may use abstract words to denote it, but any tendency to think of it as an abstraction will mislead. A going concern is a collection of live persons using tangible things and enforceable rights to change the form or the location of other tangible things and to create other enforceable rights. To keep going it is obliged to do these things in a manner consistent with its purposes and the environment at the time: its actions must be planned. It is misleading to assert that "the entity does not plan - it only acts" (Raby, 1959; 460); acting can only be dissociated from planning in the case of instinctive action, but a business entity can have no instincts. It is misleading to dissociate the accounting viewpoint from the trading viewpoint as does Gilman (1939; 247-8), when after stipulating that the accounting viewpoint requires unchanged symbols for assets he adds: "As soon as the trading viewpoint is adopted, it is inevitable that consideration will be given to changes in the market value (of an asset)". Going concerns are traders; the only viewpoint they can have is a trading viewpoint. It is also misleading to stipulate other "viewpoints" as if all were unrelated either to accounting or to trade. "Only when (the) question of valuation is approached from the ownership, credit or legal viewpoints does a non-cost basis become of serious import. It is only when the task of interpreting accounting figures is faced that the convention of dollar (cost) valuation causes trouble. Such interpretation is always from the ownership, legal or credit viewpoint, never from that of the entity", says Gilman (1939; 56). Ownership, credit and legality are not viewpoints separable from a trading entity; they describe some of its inseparable characteristics. If accounting statements must be translated from their conventional form into the form appropriate to actions affecting or affected by ownership, credit or legal considerations, then apparently they were pointlessly translated into the conventional form in the first place. A going concern is intimately involved in a network of ownership, credit and legal restraints, conditions or relationships. It cannot avoid them, nor can any accounting legitimately be devised which is so abstract that it ignores them.

26. There is little doubt about the utility of the idea of a going concern. It does set up a way of approaching the problems of recording, processing and restating the significances of events and transactions. But its implications need to be specified, otherwise an entirely amorphous entity will be imagined and there will be no definite characteristics which will point to the style of recording and reporting suited to it. These implications apply to a very large extent to individuals and business entities alike. A going concern, like an individual has a <u>goal system</u>; it and its goal system are both products of <u>specialization</u>, and the exploitation of <u>individual differences</u>. Its method of functioning is <u>complex,</u> for it operates in every market which provides means of attaining its goals, whether the market provides services in exchange for money or money in exchange or services. Its method of functioning involves giving satisfaction to every class of person associated with it. If any one class (customers, workers, financiers, etc.) ceases to be associated with it, because there is a <u>conflict of goals</u> it ceases to be a going concern. To give satisfaction to all classes entails a <u>balancing of interests,</u> a balancing of the rewards and incentives flowing to participants; in some cases to assure participants of the equity of their respective shares in the product, a statement of the results and their division is made available. The management group of participants is expected not only to balance conflicting claims but also to operate efficiently, so that the amount against which all claims can be made is the optimum. As the going concern operates through time in which the environment changes, <u>optimization</u> involves <u>continuous adaptation</u> of policies, physical

equipment and other arrangements to take advantage of the new circumstances. Continuous adaptation is possible only if no past action or choice is regarded as irrevocably binding; <u>revocability</u> of choice is a condition of survival. Changes in tastes and in the environment generally are in many respects unpredictable, so that there is an element of <u>uncertainty</u> as to the outcome of all actions or proposed actions. The legal framework makes possible, uncertainty makes desirable and indivisibility of means makes necessary the <u>accumulation</u> of means, but the accumulation of any class of means is necessarily related to the continuously changing nature of operations. A going concern is not an inert or passive thing; it takes an active part in changing or meeting changes in its environment - this is its dominant feature.

27. When is a going concern not a going concern? One cannot change the nature of a going concern by attributing to it characteristics which it does not have and by denying it characteristics which it does have. But if it is envisaged in terms which disregard the very nature of going - of constantly acting on and reacting to the environment - it is quite improbable that any worthwhile aid to its continuation will emerge. It may continue to go - but in spite of the actions of those who conceive it as a venture irrevocably committed to its past choices and unconcerned about the shifts of preferences and group pressures which surround it. The conventional going concern concept can only lead to its dissolution.

87

When is a going concern value not a going concern value?

28. The whole apparatus of accounting is concerned with the individual resources in which entities deal. The very reason for keeping separate accounts for different assets is so that each item may be considered on its merits from time to time, rather than that all assets shall be considered as an indivisible complex. There are of course occasions when an enterprise as a whole changes hands, lock, stock and barrel; but this may be assumed to occur only when the proceeds of selling the individual assets would fall short of the proceeds of the sale of the enterprise. In any case the frequency with which individual assets change hands is much greater than the frequency with which businesses change hands. All of which raises the question: When "going concern value" is used, is it used of the value of a business as a going concern, or is it used of the values of assets to a going concern?

29. There is some confusion on this point. Consider for example the following: "The fallacy of attempting to establish present values through the medium of the balance sheet is two-fold. In the first place it is frequently impossible to establish satisfactory present values for various items in the balance sheet. More important, a significant present value of an enterprise can be established only by dealing with all balance-sheet items as an entirety: 'enterprise value' is only rarely equal to the sum of the present values of its component parts" (Dohr, 1942; 44). This represents a positive answer to both parts of the question posed in the previous paragraph. Somewhat earlier George O. May asserted that present values of fixed assets "if ascertained would be irrelevant. What the investor is interested in is the value of the enterprise in which he is acquiring an interest as a whole.... If the enterprise is profitable its value will be determined mainly by consideration of its earning capacity" (May, 1940; 19, 20). This represents a positive answer to the first part of the question, as also the following appears to do: "Earning power - not cost price, not replacement price, not sale or liquidation price - is the significant basis of enterprise value. The income statement, therefore, is the most important accounting report." (Paton and Littleton, 1940; 10.)

30. These statements slip from one focus of attention to another without explanation; for example, the parenthetical section of the extract from Paton and Littleton appears clearly to refer to prices of individual assets, for in the context no reference is made to the price of a going concern, but the remainder of the

11

statement refers to the whole enterprise. Now it is quite true that enterprise value is significant to investors. But this gives no warrant for disregarding the individual assets and their individual earning powers. Every single investment in plant or other assets will, if efficient or rational management is assumed, be required to be justified in terms of its expected earnings. If the expected earnings of any asset fall it is proper to consider whether its use should continue. If the expected earnings of any asset become less than the expected earnings of an alternative asset, it is proper to consider whether the former should be replaced. If the expected earnings of any asset would be greater in the hands of another user than in those of its present user, it will pay the latter to sell if any alternative investment is expected to yield more than this asset to its present user. In all these cases the test is the present market price of the asset in question; for the present market price, on the one hand, is the amount which will be available for re-investment in the event of sale, and the amount which determines the scale of the expected yield from re-investment: and on the other hand, present market price is the market's assessment of the capitalised value of future yields from the asset in question itself.

31. The legitimacy of this argument may be challenged in respect of those assets which have no market. Why, for example, should a steel manufacturer be interested in the present value of a blast furnace or a rolling mill, for which break-up is the only alternative to continued use? He may not be an operator in the blast furnace market, but he is an operator in the market for his products. And if he wishes to remain in the business of making steel he will at any time expect his customers to pay the going rate for the output of a steel plant not only as a whole, but also piece by piece - the going rate for ore, coal, coke-ovens, blast furnaces, steel furnaces and rolling mills, individually. Insofar as the market permits, he will make sure that his prices allow him at least to maintain his physical capacity. His prices may remain steady while other prices rise if he can cut his costs; but once he reaches the limit of cost-cutting as he then sees it, he will raise his prices to ensure that they yield at least the present value of the plant service consumed.

32. It is sometimes suggested that an important attribute of a going concern is its attitude towards "the long run", and that short run (market) values are not therefore pertinent. Paton and Littleton (1940) aver that "accounting and business can follow a scientific pattern only by adapting themselves to the long run" (p. 20). But what is the long run? Does it fall short of liquidation, when a business has become an "unneeded industry" and capital cannot be used by it "effectively" (p. 3)? And if it falls short, how far short? It is quite unscientific to believe that business men only adapt themselves to the long run. They do not ignore the long run. But they want returns in the short run rather than the long run - the longer the run the less is the present value of their returns. And they want returns in the short run, for only by meeting the expectations of supporters in the short run will their businesses survive in the long run. They will not calculate their prices and formulate other policies on the basis of last year's outdated costs or conditions. They will not keep their prices down because they bought assets at a lower price than a more recent entrant to their industries. They will not gear their prices to initial money costs of plant for years and then on replacement raise prices by the whole of the difference between the appropriate parts of initial plant outlays and outlays on new plant. They will not assume that when an old piece of equipment comes to be sold its scrap value will make up the difference between the sum of all depreciation charges on the basis of initial outlay and the cost of a new piece of equipment of the same capacity. They will not adopt the equivocal position of expecting customers to pay the current price for labour service embodied in their products but not to pay the current value of plant service embodied in the same products.

33. Accounting is concerned with value in only one sense - the values of individual assets and claims. It is not concerned with the value of a going concern in

toto. The securities market is, on the other hand, concerned with the values of enterprises as units in toto. The price it puts on securities is an expression of this. The market value or price of securities is known to investors and prospective investors independently of the accounts; it may arise in part from what investors think of what appears in the income accounts of companies, but only in part; and, however it arises, knowledge of it is readily available. The other side of the picture however is the values - the present values - of individual assets. It is quite misleading to assert that "In a well-managed and profitable business, the current worth of assets is really only of academic importance." (Irish, 1950; 219) Dohr's statement is much more realistic: "the present value of property is generally speaking the factor of outstanding importance" (Dohr, 1944; 193). If the aggregate of the present values of assets exceeds by a significant amount the aggregate market value of the outstanding securities, investors are given an indication that they should consider whether to liquidate the assets, to change the management, or to cut their losses. If the aggregate of the present values of assets falls short, by a significant amount, of the aggregate market value of the outstanding securities, investors are warned that they should consider part of their incomes as a premium for the risk they run, either of inadequate cover for their investment or of the entry of new firms wishing to take advantage of apparently high returns. Similar types of argument may be adduced to cover the uses management may make of accounting which reports present values. No such series of tests can be made however if, by going concern valuation of assets, one means valuation on a cost basis. No such series of tests is even contemplated by those who, acknowledging the irrelevance of balance sheets prepared on a cost basis, assert the overriding importance of the income statement.

34. To summarize, "going concern value" in accounting has reference to the values of specific assets and claims of a going concern. Accountants in the ordinary course of accounting are not required to produce market assessments of the value of a going concern in toto or of particular shares in it. The market does this. But the right of investors and managers to have some comparable independent information on the values of assets and claims cannot be denied; comparison is essential to informed judgment, and comparison of security prices with balance sheet values is useless unless both are in current terms. As a going concern is constantly changing in every respect - financial supporters, customers, suppliers, workers, stocks, obligations, market conditions - the variability of values is an ever present reality. Financial position at any time can only have a useful meaning if it relates to the position a going concern occupies in the market situation then prevailing; and because of the severability of every asset, every claim and every specific relationship, the present value of every marketable thing or right is a necessary aspect of going concern value. It is pointless to consider the skill, acumen and foresight of management and the organized arrangement of its facilities as assets; they will both be reflected in earnings and hence in market evaluations of securities. It is unnecessary and incompetent for accounting to recognize them, for the skill of management may be lost or withdrawn and any given arrangement of facilities may be altered.

35. When is a going concern value not a going concern value? Investors are not simply concerned with the income which they receive as dividends - their probable receipts from dividends, from the sale of their securities and from the proceeds of liquidation are all significant to them. Accounting should aid them in making calculations in all these directions; and it can if present values are what it reports; the prices investors offer or demand will only then be informed indications of the going concern value of an enterprise as a whole. But accounting can only give the financial data behind investors' calculations. In its limited field, going concern values can only relate to the present values of items piece by piece, for a going concern treats them piece by piece for all investment or re-investment purposes. A going concern value which is rooted in the past is a contradiction; a going

concern value which incorporates imponderables is, for accounting, an impossibility.

When is a cost not a cost?

36. One of the most strongly entrenched ideas in accounting is that cost is the proper basis for entries in accounts. If cost is to be made the cornerstone of accounting one would expect to find the notion of cost defined. On recourse to the literature it will be found that cost has at least as many variants or expressions as value has (see for example, Greer, quoted in para. 56). But in spite of the alleged importance of cost it is difficult to find any reasonable discussion of its meaning in relation to human action. If one were inclined to accept operational definitions, that is, to assert that cost is only definable in terms of what can be measured, one may be content with some of the descriptions given. "...cost is measured by cash outlay or by the fair market value of property acquired in exchange for securities" (A.A.A., 1936). "Historical cost is cost measured by actual cash payments or their equivalent at the time of outlay" (A.A.A., 1952:176). "The price at the time of an exchange is 'cost'. Thus the cost of an item to a business is the cash outlay necessary to acquire the item. If property other than cash is given up in the exchange, then the cost of the item acquired is the cash equivalent of the property given up." (Wixon, 1956; 1.16.) "Cost, or the amount of cash or its equivalent paid to acquire an asset, is the dollar amount to be accounted for" (Smith and Ashburne, 1960; 49). But what has all this to do with human action?

37. It seems to be necessary to clarify the notion. Firstly, there is no such thing as cost unless it relates to <u>some thing</u>; only things or services cost. Secondly, the cost of things or services falls on <u>some person</u> or persons. And thirdly, the cost of any thing to any person is, regardless of the state of the market, potentially different at different times. The first two points may be obvious, but the third is apparently not so obvious for it is completely disregarded in accounting. At any time the cost of a thing to a person is what he must sacrifice or forego to acquire that thing. Thus, if a person has very little of a certain good but wants much of it, he will be prepared to pay much for an addition to his stock, provided he has the means of adding to it. On the other hand, if he has a large stock of a given good and wants little, if any, more than he has, he will only be prepared to pay little for an addition to it. One may test this by introspection. But a clear example can be obtained by trying to induce a retailer who believes he is adequately stocked to take in additional quantities; if the retailer is at all sensible he will only do so, if at all, at a reduced cost to himself. If, at another time, the retailer does not believe he is adequately stocked, he will be prepared to take additional quantities at the same cost as before. In other words the cost of acquiring a thing at any time to any person is a function of what he then has and what his other wants are at that time. The sacrifice he is prepared to make is an evaluation of the relative advantages of having more or less of some things and less or more of others.

38. The example may be extended. At any time a business firm has a certain combination of assets and obligations by reason of which it is able to exploit the demand for what it sells at that time. But as time passes, the combination of assets and obligations changes, not only in amount but also in quality and variety; and the demand for what it sells changes both by reason of changes in buyers' preferences and by reason of the actions of competitors through advertising or the provision of substitutes. At any time, therefore, the firm is in a different position than it was at a previous time or will be at a subsequent time. The sacrifices it will make or demand of others (its customers) will not at any of these times be the same unless every feature of the firm and its environment is the same, and this proviso is patently inconsistent with reality. As costs are sacrifices made

in the course of exchange, the cost of anything acquired or used for any purpose is always a dated cost.

39. It is a common practice to justify the initial cost basis of accounting on the ground that accounting records and statements give an historical record of activities. "...the balance-sheet is historical in character" (Sanders, Hatfield and Moore, 1938; 56). "Financial accounting is now generally recognized as being primarily historical in character" (May, 1943; vii). "...it is a fundamental convention that accounting is purely an historical record..." (Yorston, Smyth and Brown, 1957; 5). "...a balance sheet is...an historical record..."(I.C.A.E.W., 15, 1952). "From the viewpoint of the entity, accounting is historical only", (Raby, 1959; 460). "Accounting is a historical record...a balance sheet is an historical document..." (Ross, 1960; 386). Few writers link "history" directly with "action" and hence may overlook the connection. Not so Hill and Gordon (1959; 5): "...accounting may be viewed as a special type of history, a history of the capital committed to a business venture. ...it is of much interest only insofar as it provides bases for action, particularly as it increases our ability to predict and plan the future course of events." This implies that there are at any time open alternatives, and at that time various possible costs of those alternatives. The minimum cost of every alternative is the value attached to the pursuit of it, and the minimum cost of every alternative depends on the structure of financial and operating conditions at the time of action and at no other time. It is quite inconsistent therefore to add to the above statement: "the raw material of accounting is history, and hence unchanging regardless of end use" (Hill and Gordon, 1959; 12).

40. What is the "history" to which allusion is so commonly made? Or, to use the form of the paradoxical question, when is history not history? The amount paid for a good or service at a time in the past is an undeniable fact; it is history. It is also undeniable that the amount paid represents the buyer's evaluation of the good at that time; that too is history. It is also undeniable that after the date of acquisition the holding- or user-value of a good may vary; if such a variation takes place, and accountants admit that it may and does (see para. 48), that too is history. It is also undeniable that, if, for example, the user-value of a good has risen, the sacrifice made by using it then is greater than the sacrifice made by using it at the time of acquisition. It follows that unless one shows that the unit sacrifice made is greater at the later date than the unit sacrifice made at the earlier date, one does not write history. One in fact falsifies the history by disregarding critical determinants of the scale of revenues. History ceases to be history. Balance sheets become agglomerations of snippets of history - organically unrelated in spite of the appearance of relatedness which accounting processes give them.

41. Accountants who adhere to the cost doctrine as history and the service notion are caught on the horns of a dilemma. The cost doctrine has the consequence of showing assets at figures relevant at the time of acquisition (subject to subsequent adjustments formally based on the same figures). If the "raw material of accounting" is money cost at the time of acquisition and cost is "unchanging regardless of end use", how would one explain the facts that businessmen frequently discard assets before their "usefulness" is at an end, and as frequently go on using assets after they have been completely written out of the accounts? This behaviour is only explicable on the ground that the value of the subject assets is, in the first case, lower than the value of having the cash proceeds, and, in the second case, higher than the value of an equivalent new asset. But accounting systems and statements based on cost will give none of the relevant figures: in short they will be of no service in solving any such problem. And inasmuch as the whole of business is a matter of exchanging one thing for another, such accounting throws no direct light on business transactions at all.

42. It is possible to hold to "cost" and the "historical record" in a vital sense. But only if cost means value means price at the time of action, not only at the time of acquisition but for every subsequent use or disposal of a good - in other words, if cost always means current cost. And only if history is understood to include the history of changes in values as current costs represent them. Under conventional accounting, "cost" as used is irrelevant and "history" is a misnomer. If accounting is based on current market values, the costs it represents will be of service, the history it represents will be complete, and the two ideas will be quite compatible.

43. Cost only has significance in terms of the sacrifice of means, that is, of things which are believed by someone to be serviceable in satisfying wants of some kind. But means may only be sacrificed if one possesses them, whether one has the unrestricted right to dispose of them, or whether disposal is subject to the equities of others. These rights are governed by the <u>legal framework</u>. But neither an individual nor a business firm will consciously sacrifice more to achieve a given end than is necessary; each will strive to make the greatest gain for a given sacrifice, to <u>optimize</u> the result of acting. The more one has of a given means, the smaller will be the sacrifice one will make to add another unit to it; in other words, additions to the stock of any given means are subject to <u>diminishing</u> marginal utility. There are considerable <u>diversities</u> in means - differences in specificity to a given purpose, in diversibility, convertibility and so on; so that if one is able to accumulate a stock of means the optimum combination will be such that the marginal utilities of all types of means will be equal; that is to say, the total sacrifices or costs of having that combination will be at a minimum. Sacrifices may be made in the course of consumption and conversion of means, or in the course of exchanges with others in the market. Insofar as any means is bought and sold in a market place, the sacrifice one makes to acquire it or in consuming it or in converting it is measurable by the price at the time of acquiring, consuming or converting it. The price at the appropriate time is what one foregoes; that is its cost.

44. When is a cost not a cost? When accountants compute and set down, as cost, figures which have no relationship to present values presently sacrificed. The acquisition of anything in advance of the time of its use is an act of investment, not of use. One may speak of the cost of the investment, but every investment may increase or decrease in value, as time passes, without use. Cost is the loss in value of an investment through use; unless this loss in value, this sacrifice at the point of use, is measured, cost is not measured. Accounting of the conventional sort confuses loss in value with cost; its "costs" are not costs in any precise sense which is pertinent to action.

<u>When is a Value not a Value?</u>

45. Many attempts have been made to eradicate "value" from the accountant's vocabulary. Following Bonbright (1937), many have attempted to argue that value has no precise meaning and is therefore useless as a guide to the numbers or symbols to be assigned to things described in accounts. Many others have stated directly or implied that accounting is not concerned with values. An oft-quoted nutshell dictum runs "The purpose of accounting is to account - not to present opinions of value" (Healy, 1938; 6). George O. May (1940) averred, "We accountants...know, or can find out something about prices; we are less able to determine values. ...a price is the amount of money for which something can be bought or sold. It may be a buying price or a selling price; it may or may not coincide with value." The American Institute attempted to remove from the word every vestige of its everyday connotation: "Value as used in accounts signifies the amount at which an item is stated, in accordance with the accounting rules or principles relating to that item" (A.I.C.P.A., 1941; 76). Kohler (1957; 237) says that under

standard accounting procedures "going value...is synonymous with book value", which is the same in effect as the A.I.C.P.A. statement just quoted. Paton and Littleton (1940; 25) seek to avoid the cost-or-value dilemma by suggesting the use of the term "price-aggregate." Irish (1950; 228) asserts that "accounting...has no interest in value of any kind". Littleton (1953; 12) asserts that "accounting... deals with prices rather than values". Of the same genre are such statements as "accounting is essentially the allocation of historical costs and revenues to the current and succeeding fiscal periods" (Byrne, 1937; 372). The Institute of Chartered Accountants in England and Wales includes the following in its recommendations: "Assets are normally shown at cost less (amortization)... A balance sheet is mainly an historical document which does not purport to show the realizable value of assets such as goodwill, land, buildings, plant and machinery; nor does it normally purport to show the realisable value of assets such as stock in trade. Thus a balance sheet is not a statement of the net worth of the undertaking and this is normally so even where there has been a revaluation of assets and the balance sheet amounts are based on the revaluation instead of on cost" (I.C.A.E.W., 18, 1958). Cost and value are explicitly or implicitly set up as alternatives and the obvious weight of sentiment lies against value.

46. But all these attempts to eliminate "value" have failed. Try as they may, writers have been unable to avoid the use of "value" or "valuation". A bracket of examples from recent texts which otherwise adhere to the so-called "cost principle" will serve to show that the term is ineradicable. MacFarland, Avars and Stone (1957; 21) say that the statement of financial position "must show clearly the respective values of the assets, liabilities and owner's equity." Paton and Dixon (1958; 16) require the notion of value as a test for identifying assets: "...things and rights...which have...value to the enterprise." Husband (1960; 8) describing transactions, says "an item of value must have been received and another item given up", and speaks of "the value flow" on certain conversions of assets. Though Smith and Ashburne (1960) sedulously avoid the use of value and valuation in their table of contents and in their detailed index, they cannot avoid them in the text. They speak of current assets being reported "at realizable value" and of "accounting valuation" (p.77), and of the use of "appraised values as a substitute" for cost where a mixed parcel of assets changes hands for a single price (p.217). Even the more obviously theoretical work of Paton and Littleton (1940) has use for the term and the notion of valuation: "The price aggregate that emerges at the moment a bargaining exchange is consummated is a mutually acceptable 'valuation'"(p.26). They clearly visualize an act of valuation when they regard as a legitimate procedure the use of "the amount of money which would unquestionably be necessary to acquire the resource in its established commercial status" when "resources are discovered or developed which have an immediate economic significance far in excess of the actual outlay required for their acquisition" (p.28). The Institute of Chartered Accountants in England and Wales unashamedly uses valuation in respect of stock in trade (I.C.A.E.W., 10, 1945); the permissibility of a valuation of assets is implied in its statement on accountants' reports for prospectuses (I.C.A.E.W., 13, 1949). When dealing with appreciation in value of security investments held by trading companies, lengthy circumlocution is adopted to avoid any suggestion that revaluation is condoned: "Exceptional circumstances may arise in which an undertaking, wherein an important trade investment is held, has retained and accumulated profits on such a scale that the income which reaches the investor company and the amount at which the investment is carried in the accounts are a wholly inadequate reflection of the value of the investment, although this fact is not apparent from the trade investments item in the balance sheet or from the accounts as a whole. In such circumstances consideration should be given to the question whether the relative importance of the matter is such that without some explanation in the accounts they would fail to show a fair view" (I.C.A.E.W., 20, 1958). Not a word here about revaluation, but there can scarcely be any doubt that the statement implies a value other than cost.

47. Examples such as these can be multiplied. But the point emerges clearly enough that there must be something so crucial about "value" and "valuation" that no formula can be devised to eliminate them. What is this crucial thing? Looking back to the references cited in para. 45, it is noticeable that May, Paton and Littleton explicitly or implicitly are contrasting value and price to the disadvantage of value. But a price is a value! It is pointless to argue as May does, that a buying or a selling price may or may not coincide with value. A price is the only value of "economic significance", to use a test which Paton and Littleton have found useful (1940; 28, 123). Price is the only value contemplated in market economics. May's usage of "value" can only have legitimate reference to some form of non-market evaluation; and non-market evaluations, being a matter of private knowledge, can have no usefulness of themselves in determining the course of actions in markets. Value in this sense can have no relationship to accounting. Although he does not follow its implications, Kester (1946; 29) at one point states what, in a relevant sense, value is: "The value of anything is its worth in exchange or in use at a given time and is determined normally by the acts of buyers and sellers."

48. There is some evidence of the recognition of value in this sense even on the part of writers who would not be regarded as supporters of the value basis of accounting. Paton (1922; 489) says "The accountant...assumes that cost gives actual value for purposes of initial statement" (italics in original). The idea recurs in Paton and Littleton (1940; 122): "Under normal conditions cost incurred may be assumed to represent the market value of the factor involved at the date of acquisition; at the outset, in other words, cost and value are substantially identical in the typical case". Owen's review (1958; 72) includes it: "When acquisitions of properties or services) take place, ...value in the usual economic sense and cost in the accounting sense are one and the same." All these statements refer to value in connection either with initial acquisition or initial entry of the transaction by which goods or services are acquired. Now, if value is not the concern of accountants, why bother to make a point of the fact that at some time value and cost coincide? Why? - because it is necessary to establish that the first entry in the record is "objectively determined, inasmuch as it is, in most cases, the result of bargaining between two parties with opposing interests" (Owen, 1958; 72). The point made in para. 37 - that a bargain represents an evaluation - does not seem to be appreciated. But once it is admitted that market value is the figure which determined whether or not the two parties did business together, it is impossible to deny that for any and every acquisition or contemplated acquisition (or sale, too), the market value determines whether things will change hands, and it is impossible to deny that "values" meet the needs of interested parties. Logically, if one admits "values" into the accounting system one should proceed to show how, after initial acquisition, one continues to represent values. But the logical consequence of the fact that price equals value is disregarded. Paton and Littleton state the conditions quite clearly: "With the passing of time...the value of the particular productive factor...is subject to change in either direction, and when a change occurs it becomes clear that the actual cost...is not fully acceptable as a measure of immediate economic significance" (1940; 122-3). But, they ask, "would accounting meet...the...needs of the various parties concerned if...current values were regularly substituted for recorded costs incurred? There seem to be no convincing reasons for an affirmative answer." In short, the whole reference to value at the time of acquisition is pointless!

49. Some appear to appreciate the link between value and expected service potential but do not appear to appreciate the link between value and market price. "The value of an asset is the money equivalent of its service potentials. Conceptually, this is the sum of the future market prices of all streams of service to be derived, discounted by probability and interest factors to their present worths" (A.A.A., 1957; 4). This is precisely what the market price of any producers'

good represents, so that there is a clear indication of a method of measuring value, namely by using market price. But the A.A.A. statement continues: "However, this conception of value is an abstraction which yields but little practical basis for quantification. Consequently, the measurement of assets is commonly made by other more feasible methods". This is a rationalization for switching right away from the groundwork laid in the previous passage. The switch is evidenced by the use of "quantification" and "measurement" in the second part of the passage quoted, instead of continuing the use of "value", as in the first part. Far from offering "little practical basis" for valuation, insofar as the discounted value of all expected service flows from an asset is represented by its market price, the aggregate discounted flow concept offers the <u>only</u> practical basis for valuation. And what is offered as more feasible? For monetary assets, the discounted expected cash flow; for non-monetary assets, acquisition cost. In short two methods are offered; both represent quite different things; the second is in no way related to the notion of value as described at the outset, and therefore cannot be a "more feasible" method of measuring value.

50. But these are not the only inconsistencies. If it is contended that a balance sheet in which assets are represented by "unexpired costs" meets the needs of parties of interest, there can be no need for any other information than is yielded by the orthodox matching process. It would be quite unnecessary to use any other basis than cost for inventories; the cost-or-market rule would be abandoned; L.I.F.O., F.I.F.O. and other similar hypotheses would be superfluous. There would be no need to state market values of marketable securities. There would be no such thing as revaluing assets - up or down. And there could be no grounds for recommending the use of supplementary statements as a solution to the problem of accounting under conditions of price instability. But not one of the supporters of cost against value will go this far!! It follows that they do not really believe in the "unexpired cost" theory of the nature of the balance sheet or the "cost" theory of accounting; or, if they do believe, they have not analyzed the grounds for belief; or they have a double or multiple standard in which a wide range of mutually inconsistent behaviours is quite permissible - truly "Wonderland" material.

51. Value may be based on the importance a person attaches to an object or purpose. <u>This value is knowable only to the person.</u> One may manage to rank things as one values them, but there is no scale in which such private evaluations may be measured. Other persons can only know that one values something by his actions with respect to it; and others can only know how much one values something by what he will sacrifice to acquire it or what will induce him to part with it. The only values we can communicate to others and expect them to understand are the values which become explicit through <u>exchanges</u>. Values in exchange are significant to all actual and potential operators in <u>markets</u>; in an economy in which <u>money</u> and <u>credit</u> are used to facilitate exchanges, <u>price</u> is the measure of value in exchange. And because all means and equities are acquired or arise through exchanges the values of them all may be given <u>monetary expression</u>; and <u>monetary calculations</u> may be made in terms of these values at any time as guides to action. There can be no gainsaying the importance of value in exchange when contemplating actions which change the composition of the resources of persons or firms. No amount of evasion or circumlocution can destroy it. The only reasonable thing to do is face it and to design accounting systems which conform with it.

52. When is a value not a value? No money sum attributed to an asset is a value in an operative sense unless at some point its basis is an actual or possible evaluation by a person faced with a choice involving that asset. Such an evaluation is necessarily related to some market operations - so that it is not a personal evaluation only. If cost is taken as value after a shift in the level of prices, such a "value" is a non-market evaluation, specific to a person or an enterprise and is therefore subjective. It is not a value which is of any use or consequence once the

particular pattern of prices and markets shifts from the form it had at the time of acquisition. A value is not a value whenever the method of evaluation disregards the ineluctable fact that values change as the conditions of the values and of his environment change.

When is a principle not a principle?

53. A series of questions of this kind may be posed - about theories, postulates, conventions, doctrines and like terms. It will suffice to deal with a few only of such questions. In spite of the extensive literature on, and the enormous amount of time devoted to, accounting principles and theory, the whole area is confused. "Principles" has long been used of common ideas in accounting though many of the so-called principles were not stated with any precision. The term "standards" was adopted in American literature and practice during the 1930's, to avoid the implication, supposed to inhere in "principles", that universal rules could be laid down; but there is just as much haziness about "standards" as there was about "principles". The same ideas have been variously described - the going concern idea, for example, has been described as a concept (e.g. Kester, 1946; 306), a point of view (e.g. Paton and Paton, 1952; 504; Smith and Ashburne, 1960; 50), an assumption (e.g. Paton, 1922; 478), a convention (e.g. Sanders, Hatfield and Moore, 1938; 3) and a hypothesis (e.g. Blough, 1956; 13). Generally, in designating ideas, guidance has been sought from dictionary "definitions"; but this is not always helpful. A dictionary is a general purpose device designed to inform users of the customary usages and meanings of words. If we are to converse with lay people it is necessary to converse in terms that are generally understood; common sense or customary usages are highly desirable if not obligatory. Thus, in published financial statements, the users of which may be very sophisticated or quite unsophisticated, it might be expected that everyday usages would prevail; but it has been shown that precisely in this area, accountants tend to flee from every day usages and to invent highly specialised meanings for such everyday notions as cost and value. Yet, in the highly specialised and technical field of concept and theory formation the tendency to run to dictionary meanings is quite marked!

54. If we are concerned to discover the character of an art, a science, or an operation, it may well be found necessary to devise special notions for the purpose, notions specifically relevant to our inquiries. For example, "true" has in general usage a connotation of reliability, universality and even immutability; but in the usage of the logician and the philosopher it has no such meaning. When a logician says a statement is true he may mean that it is logically irrefutable. A philosopher may assign the label, "true", to certain statements which meet stated tests. It is not a matter of indifference what general designations are given to groups of ideas. Designations should convey some idea of the way in which concepts are regarded; they should indicate which ideas are primitive and which derived. The model adopted in conceptualizing is thus not necessarily that suggested by dictionary descriptions except insofar as those descriptions include scientific usages; for the process of discovering the character of a set of ideas or operations is essentially scientific and there are established scientific procedures for going about it. But this is no place for an extended discussion of methodology.

55. The prevailing attitude of accountants towards their principles, however designated, may be explored, as before, by reference to the literature. "In the opinion of accountants generally, accounting principles are not principles of nature but rules of human behavior. They are not inherent in nature to be discovered by man but are developed by man. They are, therefore, not immutable and they need to be changed to meet changing needs" (Blough, 1957). Again, "Action in accounting clearly does not rest on immutable laws" (Littleton, 1953; 170). Now statements of this kind are acceptable but not for the reasons usually given. No statement - and every principle, every law is a statement - is immutable. For a

statement expresses how some person at a given time and place visualizes the thing or the relationship which is the subject of the statement. Many persons may agree with any such statement at a given time, but this does not prevent other persons at other times from formulating quite different statements about the same thing. The thing itself may not have changed one whit; but people may picture it quite differently, and the statements - principles or laws - which express the picture will therefore be different from the statements made in a different environment of knowledge. There are thus not even any immutable laws of nature that man can describe. The contrast made or implied in the above quotations is pointless, and no distinction can be drawn between the natural sciences and accounting to the latter's disadvantage, so far as the formulation of principles is concerned.

56. Just as the formulation of statements in the natural sciences will vary with changes in the state of knowledge so also will the statements in the field of accounting. One can agree with Blough that "principles...need to be changed to meet changing needs" and with the statement "Accounting rules or principles must be flexible and in continuous process of evolution" (A.I.C.P.A., 1938). But this does not mean that *at any time* any given principle, as then understood and stated, may have a variety of mutually exclusive meanings. The cost-or-market rule for inventory valuation is a well-established "principle" - using principle in a loose sense. But it is not one principle; it is a combination of two conflicting, mutually exclusive principles which, taken separately, can yield results which diverge by material amounts. Or, to take a more extensive recommendation on the same problem, consider the following: "The portion of the original cost of each class of product, materials, and supplies inventories to be carried forward as applicable to future operations, should be not more than the least of the following: (a) actual cost, determined on a first-in first-out basis, with substitution of standard for actual cost components where appropriate, (b) current replacement cost, similarly computed, (c) current net realizable value. Alternative valuation bases, permissible as a measure of conservatism, include (a) original cost, determined on a last-in first-out basis, (b) initial cost of a normal base stock plus actual cost of subsequent additions, (c) prospective realization value less expenses remaining to be incurred, including a normal profit margin, (d) other procedures appropriate to the conditions of individual industries and enterprises, when consistently and reasonably applied". (Greer, 1956; 12.) According to my calculations there are seven specific "principles" and one completely open-ended "principle" in this statement; (d) in the last sentence virtually permits any basis of valuation! It is no defence to point out that "the least of the following" unifies the statement. It does not. In any given series of situations any one of these bases may become the "appropriate" basis; so that the statement as a whole sanctions them all individually. The above statement could in effect be condensed into a three-word principle: "Anything will do."

57. Let it be noted that the Greer quotation is not an isolated example. It expresses the sense of many other statements of the same kind by individual writers and professional organizations. The general attitude towards principles is evident in many statements relating to uniformity and the exercise of judgment. "To the extent that personal judgment is involved, standards are subjective; to the extent that standards are formulated by authoritative bodies, standards are objective. It follows that objective standards narrow the spheres of individual judgment and personal opinion as to what the standards are; but it does not follow that they restrict the reasonably free play of judgment and individual opinion as to the propriety of applications of generally accepted principles." (Stempf, 1941; 106.) "An accounting principle is not a principle in the sense that it admits of no variation, nor in the sense that it cannot conflict with other principles." (A.I.C.P.A., 1940; 60.) "There...remains ample scope for the exercise of professional judgment; in determining, for example, what principle or standard applies in particular circumstances where a choice is possible; or in deciding the manner or extent to which it

is to be applied." (Broad, 1944; 186.) "Uniformity of accounting method is neither expected nor necessarily desirable" (A.A.A., 1957; 9). The trouble about the latitude which these views allow is that they serve as a licence for disregarding any discipline or stricture such as one usually means by "a matter of principle" - to turn a phrase, accounting as a result is "unprincipled". It should be no cause for wonder that "today it is difficult to decide just what significance may be attached to the annual accounts of a corporation." (May, 1955; 43.) Nor should one be surprised that "there remains a widespread belief that published financial statements still leave too much to imagination and guess-work, and that the variety and inconsistency of corporate accounting practice bring needless confusion and uncertainty into the study of business affairs." (Greer, 1956; 9.)

58. In what sense, if any, may it be said a principle may be varied? that uniformity is not necessarily desirable? that choice of principles is possible? Only in one sense; namely, that as knowledge increases, as new points of view are put forward, the whole of the previously accepted body of ideas is seen in a new light and an entirely new set, or a set related in new ways, emerges. Or, to put it another way, when one set of principles, accepted as a working hypothesis, is found to be invalid a superior hypothesis is set up in its place. This, of course, is counsel of perfection. It is not pretended that in other sciences mutually inconsistent theories are unheard of. They do occur; but their appearance is not considered to be an occasion for accepting both. It is a spur to efforts to resolve the inconsistency, by seeking out the flaws in one or the other or both. One may not according to one or the other, while the problem is unresolved; but one may act legitimately take bits and pieces of both and hope to act consistently. All talk of flexibility and expedience is simply an excuse for evading the discipline of vigorous analysis. One may be permitted a fictional allusion, to a passage in Ayn Rand's "Atlas Shrugged" (The New American Library, New York, 1959; 343):

> "You know, Mr. Rearden, there are no absolute standards. We can't go by rigid principles, we've got to be flexible, we've got to adjust to the reality of the day and act on the expediency of the moment".
>
> "Run along, punk. Go and try to pour a ton of steel without rigid principles on the expediency of the moment."

59. If accounting were concerned with physical things the futility of attempting to hold simultaneously two or more inconsistent principles would become apparent. It is equally possible to drive a car on either side of a road; but let a driver attempt to drive on both sides, or on the left hand side in North America, or on the right hand side in Britain; he will soon discover that there is no middle ground, and that there are no subtle verbal devices he can adopt to escape disaster. Why should such behaviour be permissible in accounting? Gilman (1938; e.g., 235) long ago pointed out the inconsistency of certain generally held ideas; but their existence has bothered little his successors. Some scarcely seem to notice them. Dohr (1944; 193), for example, states categorically that "the present value of property is generally speaking the factor of outstanding importance", but later in the same article reaches the conclusion "that accounting is generally on a cost basis and that there is and should be a strong presumption in favour of statement in terms of cost" (p. 195) - a conclusion which appears in italics as if cost were of greater importance than "the factor of outstanding importance". Others attempt to argue inconsistencies out of existence (e.g. Blough, 1956; 14), but they have to resort to the use of ideas which are inconsistent with reality or with the service function of accounting. Others admit them without a blush. None of these reactions is likely to clear the air.

60. One might expect of a rule or a principle that it should state an ideal procedure or notion in unequivocal terms. If there is a key concept or set of concepts to which it is geared this should not be difficult. There may well be ways of interpreting a specific rule or principle so that some discretion is allowed, but the statement of the key concept should circumscribe this discretion. Further if a key concept were formulated and incorporated in the definition of accounting, all elaborations of rules and principles which would follow it would be freed of loose expressions and readers would have some clear guidance. But statements of or on accounting principles are noticeably deficient in this direction. For example, the Recommendations of the Institute of Chartered Accountants in England and Wales include no such statement. It is believed to be a consequence of this that the recommendations give clear and unequivocal direction on very few things; categorical statements are almost invariably qualified, suggesting that two or more principles are involved; "normally" appears frequently, carrying the implication that the principle will not stand up in all circumstances other than undefined "normal" circumstances; "preferably", "where practicable" and similar qualifications are employed, so that one is apparently allowed a discretion in respect of what is stated to be "preferable", and one is given a clear sanction for ignoring the rules if one deems that in a given case the recommended procedure is impracticable.

61. It is not for one moment suggested that the authorities have been in error in prescribing the characteristics which a theory or statement of principles should possess. Thus "...a corporation's periodic financial statements should be continuously in accord with a single coordinated body of accounting theory." (A. A. A., 1936; 61.) "...accounting standards should be orderly, systematic, coherent; they should be in harmony with observable, objective conditions; they should be impersonal and impartial" (Paton and Littleton, 1940; 6). "Theory (should have) clarity...orderliness...pattern; (it) should be in harmony with observable, objective factors and conditions... (and have) impartiality...consistency." (Paton, 1939-40). "A fairly broad set of coordinated accounting principles should be formulated on the basis of the postulates." (A.I.C.P.A., 1958; 63.) All these descriptive words and phrases one would have no hesitation in endorsing. But the whole purpose of this paper is to demonstrate that the requirements of these statements are not in fact met. Nor can they be met while practitioners and writers adopt multiple standards, conflicting principles and inconsistent rules. No "principle" which has these consequences is worth designating by the term principle.

A proposed set of Postulates and Principles

62. This paper may appear to be a wordy wrangle about words. It is not. It is concerned with meanings. Its purpose has been to show that many words have a chameleon-like character which poorly serves the demand for precision which rigorous discourse requires. Terms such as service function, information, going concern, cost, value, very often do not mean what they appear to mean. Consequently their users, and more so their readers, frequently jump to conclusions for which no foundation is laid and which are at variance with realities and with one another. A rich and varied language is the principal feature which differentiates man from other creatures. Users of the language assume the obligations of being precise, of defining their terms and of submitting to the discipline of their definitions. This is not a plea for definitions for their own sake: nothing is so sterile as arguments over terminology as such. But no proponent of a concept, a principle or a theory is thereby absolved from defining his terms adequately for his purposes if he wishes his propositions to be understood by others. If he fails to do so, both he and his readers may unwittingly fall into the trap of assuming more than is intended; every such interpretation is then privy to the interpreter and is not a matter of public knowledge nor of ascertainable reliability. This possibility falls with multiplied severity on accounting, for it affects both knowledge

about accounting and the knowledge which accounting processes and statements yield. Inconsistency in both directions is tolerated because none of the ideas put forward is considered to be part of a systematic set of ideas, each of which is as necessarily related to the others as are the pieces of a mosaic or a jig-saw puzzle. It might be argued that accounting has its system builders. Does not Gilman (1939) provide a system? A categorization of ideas, maybe, but certainly not a set of interlinked ideas. Does not Stead (1948; 355) provide a system? Certainly a categorization of over twenty ideas, but none of them is described in sufficient detail to demonstrate that the system is coherent in substance. Can such a set of ideas be devised? It is believed to be possible.

63. At the conclusion of each of the preceding sections of this paper there is a paragraph which states what are believed to be pertinent concepts denoting conditions which govern the type of accounting which will be of use to adaptive entities in a changing environment. They apply in fact to all organizations and persons, for all seek to adapt themselves aggressively or passively to their environments. These paragraphs are numbered 9, 20, 26, 34, 43 and 51. Some forty specific ideas are emphasized. In the following paragraph they are described and rearranged in the same manner as they were presented in the earlier paper, Towards a General Theory of Accounting. It is believed that every one of these ideas is directly or indirectly apposite to accounting and that their separate identification is necessary to provide an adequate and realistic foundation for accounting. They represent the way in which the environment of accounting is visualized. It is believed that they are all verifiable by observation or introspection.

64. Proposed Foundations, Assumptions or Postulates   Para.

1.* Individual differences. Individual persons have different wants, different skills and different propensities for action.   9, 26*

2. Diversity of goals. Persons have diverse concurrent and competing wants and corresponding goals.   9, 26

3. Diversity of roles. Persons may fill varied roles, concurrently or consecutively, and have sets of goals corresponding to each role.   9

4. Variability of goals. Wants and goals vary from time to time.   9

5. Intensity of wants. In any system of wants (2)* each will have a different ranking or intensity at any time; ranking will change from time to time (4).   9

6. Orientation. Deliberate action is oriented to the satisfaction of wants, individually and as a set. An action may satisfy a want or wants in one or more respects.   9

7. Cerebration. The choice of a course of action is the outcome of the processes of observation, recollection, calculation and comparison.   9

8. Incapacity. For all persons there are limits to the capacity for observation, to the capacity for recollection and to the span of attention.   9

---

* The numbers in the left hand margin identity each concept for subsequent reference; such references are designated subsequently by numbers in parenthesis ( ). The numbers in the right hand margin refer to relevant paragraphs in the body of the paper where these ideas are mentioned.

			Para.
9.	Choice.	For a given role choice depends on the intensity of wants (5), on present knowledge (7, 8) and on expectations of the outcomes of available courses of action (7).	9
10.	Revocability.	No choice is irrevocable.	26
11.	Abstraction.	Because there are various aspects of each actual or potential course of action (6), and because the span of attention is limited (8), each aspect of a series of possible actions is considered independently.	9
12.	Means.	Wants are satisfied by the appropriation of means. Means are scarce resources which are believed to be serviceable in satisfying wants. The utility of a means subsists in the belief that it will be serviceable in satisfying a want.	43
13.	Diversity of means.	Means vary in specificity with respect to particular wants, in divisibility, in durability, and in convertibility to other means.	43
14.	Valuation of means.	Means derive value from the value attached to the satisfaction of wants (5, 12). Any choice involving addition to, or sacrifice of part of, a homogeneous stock is based on the utility (12) of the marginal unit, i.e. on marginal utility.	43
15.	Possession.	Appropriation of means (12) depends on possession.	43
16.	Equities.	Possession (15) may be unrestricted, in which case the equity in means vests in the possessor; or restricted, in which case the use of means is subject to the equities of other parties.	43
17.	Legal framework.	The equity in and possession of means (16) are regulated by laws, rules and understandings relating to interpersonal relations, contracts and bargains: this framework leads predictability to the environment of action.	43
18.	Uncertainty.	The environment of action is fluid. Many aspects of the environment of action are fortuitous; their incidence and severity are unpredictable. Every aspect of choice may be affected by changes in the environment of action.	26
19.	Accumulation.	The legal framework (17) makes possible and uncertainty (18) makes desirable the accumulation of means.	26, 43
20.	Optimization.	Because means are scarce (12) in relation to wants (2), deliberate actions are chosen according to their expected capacities for yielding the greatest aggregate satisfactions of a system of wants, e.g. the greatest gain for a given sacrifice. (6, 9)	26, 43
21.	Diminishing Marginal Utility.	Because of the diversity of competing wants (2) and the scarcity of means (12), every increase in the stock of a given means reduces the utility of further additions to it.	43
22.	Combination.	A stock of heterogeneous means will tend to be so arranged that the marginal utilities of all types of means in the stock will be equal. (14, 20, 21)	43

101

Para.

23. Specialisation. By making possible the exploitation of different individual capacities (1), specialisation increases the potential supply of means.
20, 26

24. Exchange. Specialisation of function (23) and the diversity of individual goals (2) requires a mechanism for the exchange of means.
26, 43

25. Markets. A market is a process by which the interplay of the wants and preferences of different persons (1, 20, 21, 22) establishes ratios of exchange or prices. Exchange values or prices are the resultant of the choices of more than one person: for any person they are objective valuations.
26, 43

26. Money. Money facilitates the exchange of goods which vary in divisibility (13). Money is a means of high convertibility (13) and low specificity (13). Because of the convertibility of money monetary units are accepted units for expressing ratios of exchange of non-monetary means.
43

27. Credit. The existence of a legal framework (17) makes possible the exchange of goods and services (including money) at one point of time for goods and services to be made available at a subsequent time. Credit gives rise to specific equities (16). The capacity to obtain credit depends on the extent to which the control of means is restricted or unrestricted (16).
43

28. Price. In the case of an actual exchange, the ratio of exchange or price expresses the value attached to expected service yields from the good acquired at the time. Prices are derivatives of marginal utilities (14). Prices are the only values relevant to actions in markets (25).
43

29. Variability of Values. Prices of goods and the purchasing power of money vary over time as the environment changes (18); the possibility of such changes subjects different parts of a stock of means to different risks.
34

30. Monetary Expression. Every good or service acquired or to be acquired by exchange and every sacrifice made or to be made to acquire such goods or services may be represented by an actual or estimated price. Monetary expression enables the economic characteristics (see 11) of diverse goals (2), diverse means (13), and diverse equities (16, 27) to be brought within one framework of calculation (7), increasing the effectiveness of attention (8) and making easier the problem of choice (9).
43

31. Monetary calculation. Monetary calculation is concerned with market or exchange values, market values being measures of the sacrifices of means necessary to secure given ends. (26, 28).
43

32. Continuous adaptation. Optimization (20) in the face of the variability of goals (4) and the variability of values (29) makes necessary continuous adaptation. Continous adaptation depends on successive

		Para.
	assessments of financial capacity for action and of the probable effectiveness of possible courses of action (9).	26
33.	Financial position. Financial capacity for action is represented by the relationship between assets and equities at current valuations at a point of time.	20, 34
34.	Change of position. The probable effectiveness of possible courses of action may be deduced by reference to the result of past courses of action.	20
35.	Complexity of organization. Specialization (23) gives rise to complex organizations the existence of which depends on the actions of persons filling various roles (e.g. investors, financiers, managers, accountants etc.). For each actor, action conforms with the propositions indicated above - see (9), (12), (20), (21), (22), for example.	26
36.	Conflict of goals. Specialization tends to result in the adoption of sectional or personal goals or points of view which may be inconsistent with the goals of an entity as a whole, either by reason of extra-organizational influence on specialists themselves or by reason of the conflict of personal goals with organizational goals.	26
37.	Balancing of interests. The viability of a complex organization depends on the continued provision of incentives for participants which (a) are adequate as rewards for service and (b) are deemed to be fair by comparison with the rewards of other participants. To form opinions on these matters participants require information.	26
38.	Specialization in Information Processing. One form of specialization in complex organizations is specialization in information processing and the consequential separation of decision-making from direct apprehension of information.	20
39.	Information Systems. The processing of information so that the results are relevant to choice situations requires systemization. The function of an information processing system is to provide a substitute for and a supplement to direct observation (7, 8) and a supplement to the memory of actors.	20
40.	Objectivity. As individuals have different propensities for judgment and action (1), as individuals may simultaneously occupy several roles with respect to any complex entity (3) and as the viability of the entity depends on the satisfaction of parties occupying different roles (37), information will be so processed that the rewards and interests of all participants are objectively represented - it will represent the entity as such, not the viewpoint of any class of participant.	20

103

These postulates are selected for their relevance to the framework of behaviour in which accounting plays a part. For the derivation of specific propositions relating to accounting a definition is also necessary:

Definition. Accounting is a method of monetary calculation designed to provide a continuous source of financial information as a guide to future action in markets.

65. Derived Principles. This paragraph sets out a series of statements which follow from the foundations given above. It is possible to present an argument in detail, based on various combinations of the postulates, supporting each of the principles to be enumerated. This is not attempted here, but the numbers in parenthesis designate the main postulates (as numbered in para. 64) on which the stated principles depend.

(A) Accounting entities. Accounting systems relate to specific entities defined by roles of natural or artificial persons or groups. (3, 9)

(B) Relevance. The probability of optimal adaptation varies directly with the relevance of accounting information to action. (9, 20, 39)

(C) Neutrality. The probability of optimal adaptation varies directly with the neutrality of accounting information. (1, 4, 9, 20, 39)

(D) Correspondence. The relevance of accounting information varies directly with its correspondence with realities (i.e. market conditions, contractual relations, etc.) at the time of action. (9)

(E) Consistency. Comparability and the legitimacy of inference as to present position and expectations depend on consistency in the use of concepts and methods in accounting. (7)

(F) Communication. The transferability of accounting information depends on the use of terms, concepts and measures having the same content and significance to all parties of interest. (39, 40)

(G) Objectivity. The relevance of accounting information depends on its freedom from the bias, influence or opinion of persons connected with an activity, whether as actors on its behalf or as information processors. (35, 36, 40)

(H) Double entry. Transactions of and events affecting an entity are fully described for accounting purposes by simultaneous recording of the manner in which they affect the values of the assets of an entity and the equities by virtue of which those assets were acquired. (28, 33)

(I) Accounting Identity. The aggregate values of the assets of, and the aggregate amount of the equities in, any entity are equal. (16, 25)

(J) Basic Record. As a basis for any subsequent calculation or comparison, a continuous basic record is required which indicates the values attached to actions or events at designated points of time. (7, 8, 9, 18)

(K) Summarization. Because the span of attention is limited, summarization of entries representing varied transactions improves comprehensibility of the record, and thus increases the probability of optimal adaptation. (8, 9, 20)

(L) Classification. Summarization in accordance with the characteristics of assets and equities which are pertinent to action - utility, durability, convertibility etc. - increases the probability of optimal adaptation. (13, 16, 20)

(M) Uniformity of Valuation. The operations of addition, subtraction and relation necessary in any form of summarization can only be performed validly if the separate items are valued on a uniform basis. (7, 30, 31)

(N) <u>Current Valuation</u>. Insofar as the monetary values assigned to events things and transactions are, at the date of assignment, the current valuation, the principles of relevance, objectivity and uniformity of valuation are satisfied. (9, 28, 31)

<u>Corollary 1.</u> At the date of purchase or sale, i.e. at the point of making the initial record, the prices at which bargains are made are the values to be assigned.

<u>Corollary 2.</u> At any other date, (e.g. for the purpose of any subsequent calculation) the values to be assigned are replacement prices in respect of assets, present values in respect of specific equities.

(O) <u>Periodic Interval</u>. The frequency of summarization depends on the frequency with which material deviations from planned objectives or operations have occurred or may occur. (9, 10, 18)

(P) <u>Periodic Identification</u>. Transactions and other changes are attributed to the periods in which they become effective by changing the character of risks and by changing or inducing changes in the characteristics or values of assets or equities. (9, 29)

(Q) <u>Periodic Restatement.</u> If changes in the value of any asset or equity occur, restatement of the values entered in the basic record is required (a) to validate arithmetical and relational operations after such change in value and (b) to conform with the principle of correspondence. (9, 29)

(R) <u>Status Representation.</u> Financial position may be derived by summarization of the basic record subject to restatement of values if changes in values have occurred. Such summaries enable decisions to be made with respect to combinations of assets (21, 22) and the use of credit (27).

(S) <u>Change Representation.</u> Changes in financial position during a period may be represented by a statement or statements describing completely the nature, magnitude and sources of the differences between the financial positions at opening and terminal dates. Income and funds statements serve this purpose in different but complementary ways, assisting in the making of decisions having regard to the probable effectiveness of alternative courses of action. (9, 34)

(T) <u>Articulation.</u> The cause and effect relationship of transactions and events on financial position is reflected in an accounting system in which statements of financial position and changes in financial position are articulated by reason of their derivation from a basic record founded on market values. (16, 24, 28)

(U) <u>Approximation.</u> Indivisibilities of assets, the fluidity of the environment, the flexibility of goals and the variability of values make statements of financial position and change approximations only. (4, 13, 18)

105

66. The two sets of statements in the preceding paragraphs constitute a body of ideas which are believed to be self-consistent and consistent with the environment of accounting, the world of economic action. The cross references in para. 65 to the numbered postulates indicate the coherence of the system; it will be apparent that the whole system is closely interwoven. Every postulate is necessary directly or indirectly to provide a basis for one or more of the derived principles, and no principle is stated which is independent of one or more of the postulates. The number of postulates and principles identified may appear to be large but it is no

larger than is necessary to eliminate ambiguity and to avoid the paradoxes which a paucity of concepts forces on exponents of accounting. The complex interrelationships of thinking, acting, recording and reporting in a market economy cannot be described in terms of a smaller number. This system leaves no ground for doubt about the kind of information required for intelligent action; it states clearly the character of a going concern and the meaning of value to a going concern; it links cost and value to current price, for current price is the only objective evidence of value and the only measure of cost which is relevant to action. The whole system is based on one general idea, namely that the function of accounting is to provide a continuous objective representation of the transactions of and events financially affecting an entity so that its participants are assisted to act in a rational and informed manner.

67. It will soon be 1984. The persistence of anomalies and contradictions in accounting over the last twenty-two years makes one wonder whether they will survive the next twenty-two years. No doubt they will if accountants continue to follow the philosophy of double-think so well described in George Orwell's Nineteen Eighty-Four: "Doublethink means the power of holding two contradictory beliefs in one's mind simultaneously, and accepting both of them.... The process has to be conscious, or it would not be carried out with sufficient precision, but it also has to be unconscious, or it would bring with it a feeling of falsity and hence of guilt.... To forget any fact that has become inconvenient, and then, when it becomes necessary again, to draw it back from oblivion for just so long as it is needed, to deny the existence of objective reality and all the while to take account of the reality which one denies - all this is indispensably necessary". Doublethink and doubletalk will not resolve the paradoxes of accounting. If it were not for doublethink and doubletalk there would be no paradoxes.

REFERENCES

A. A. A., American Accounting Association
- (1936) A Tentative Statement of Accounting Principles, The Accounting Review, June 1936 (Reprinted in pamphlet with A.A.A. (1957) etc.)
- (1952) Report of the Committee on Cost Concepts and Standards, The Accounting Review, April 1952.
- (1957) Accounting and Reporting Standards for Corporate Financial Statements, 1957 Revision (Pamphlet).

A. I. C. P. A., American Institute of (Certified Public) Accountants
- (1938) Editorial The Journal of Accountancy, Feb. 1938.
- (1940) Accounting Research Bulletin, No. 7, Report of the Committee on Terminology.
- (1941) Accounting Research Bulletin, No. 9, Report of the Committee on Terminology.
- (1958) Report to Council of the Special Committee on Research Program, The Journal of Accountancy, December 1958.

Bedford, Perry and Wyatt, (1961), Advanced Accounting, John Wiley & Sons, Inc., New York.

Black & Champion, (1961), Accounting in Business Decisions, Prentice-Hall, Inc., Englewood Cliffs.

Blough, (1957), Carman G. Accounting Principles and their Application, C. P. A. Handbook, Vol. 2, Ch. 17. American Institute of Certified Public Accountants, New York.

Bonbright, (1937), J. C., The Valuation of Property. McGraw-Hill Book Company, Inc., New York.

Broad, (1944), Samuel J., Recent Developments in Accounting and Auditing. The Journal of Accountancy, September 1944.

Byrne, (1937), Gilbert R., To What Extent can the Practice of Accounting be reduced to Rules and Standards? The Journal of Accountancy, November 1937.

Campfield, (1959), William L., Re-examination of Bases and Opportunities for Applying Accounting Judgment, The Accounting Review, October 1959

Canning, (1929), John B., The Economics of Accountancy, The Ronald Press Company, New York.

Dohr, (1942), James L., Reflections on the Development of Accounting Procedures, The Journal of Accountancy, July 1942.

Dohr, (1944), Cost and Value, The Journal of Accountancy, March 1944.

Gilman, (1939), Stephen, Accounting Concepts of Profit. The Ronald Press Company, New York.

Goldberg, (1957), L., An Outline of Accounting, The Law Book Co. of Australasia, Pty., Ltd., Sydney.

Greer, (1956), Howard C., Benchmarks and Beacons, <u>The Accounting Review</u>, January, 1956.

Healy, (1938), R.E., The Next Step in Accounting, <u>The Accounting Review</u>, March, 1938.

Hill and Gordon, (1959), <u>Accounting: A Management Approach,</u> Richard D. Irwin, Inc., Homewood, Ill.

Husband, (1960), George R., <u>Accounting: Administrative and Financial</u>, Chilton Company, Philadelphia.

I.C.A.E.W., The Institute of Chartered Accountants in England and Wales.
    (1945) <u>Recommendation 10</u>, The valuation of stock-in-trade.
    (1949) <u>Recommendation 13</u>, Accountants' reports for prospectuses: fixed assets and depreciation.
    (1952) <u>Recommendation 15,</u> Accounting in relation to changes in the purchasing power of money.
    (1958) <u>Recommendation 18,</u> Presentation of balance sheet and profit and loss account.
    (1958) <u>Recommendation 20,</u> Treatment of investments in the balance sheets of trading companies.

Irish, (1950), R.A., Fundamental Concepts of Corporate Accounting, <u>The Australian Accountant,</u> June, 1950.

Kester, (1946), Roy B., <u>Advanced Accounting</u>, The Ronald Press Company, New York.

Kohler, (1957), Eric L., <u>A Dictionary for Accountants</u>, Prentice-Hall, Inc., Englewood Cliffs.

Littleton, (1953), A.C., <u>Structure of Accounting Theory</u>, American Accounting Association, Urbana.

Macfarland, Ayars and Stone, (1957), <u>Accounting Fundamentals</u>, McGraw-Hill Book Company, Inc., New York.

May, George O.,
    (1940) Valuation or Historical Cost: Some Recent Developments, <u>The Journal of Accountancy,</u> January, 1940.
    (1943) <u>Financial Accounting,</u> The Macmillan Company, New York.
    (1955) Talk with George O. May on His 80th Birthday, <u>The Journal of Accountancy</u>, June, 1955.

Montgomery, (1938), Foreword to Feragallo's <u>Origin and Evolution of Double Entry Bookkeeping</u>, American Institute Publishing Company, New York.

Owen, (1958), James N., A Review of the Basic Concepts of Financial Accounting, <u>N.A.A. Bulletin,</u> June, 1958.

Paton, William A.,
    (1922) <u>Accounting Theory</u>, The Ronald Press Company, New York.
    (1939-40) Recent and Prospective Developments in Accounting Theory. <u>Dickinson Lectures, 1939-40</u>, Harvard University Press, Cambridge, Mass., 1943.
    (1955) <u>Essentials of Accounting</u>, The Macmillan Company, New York.

Paton and Dixon, (1959), Essentials of Accounting, The Macmillan Company, New York.

Paton and Paton, (1952), Asset Accounting, The Macmillan Company, New York.

Paton and Littleton, (1940), An Introduction to Corporate Accounting Standards, American Accounting Association, Urbana.

Peragallo, (1938), Edward., Origin and Evolution of Double Entry Bookkeeping, American Institute Publishing Company, New York.

Pinger, (1954), R.W., The Semantics of Accounting, The Accounting Review, October, 1954.

Raby, (1959), Wm. L., The Two Faces of Accounting, The Accounting Review, July, 1959.

Ross, (1960), E.B., Notes on Accounting Theory, The Accountants' Journal (New Zealand), June, 1960.

Sanders, Hatfield and Moore, (1938), A Statement of Accounting Principles (Reprint, 1959, by American Accounting Association).

Stead, (1948), Gordon W., Toward a Synthesis of Accounting Doctrine, The Accounting Review, October, 1948.

Smith and Ashburne, (1960), Financial and Administrative Accounting, McGraw-Hill Book Company Inc., New York.

Stempf, (1941), Victor H., Critique of "Accounting Principles Underlying Corporate Financial Statements", The Journal of Accountancy, August, 1941.

Wilcox and Hassler, (1941), A Foundation for Accounting Principles, The Journal of Accountancy, October, 1941.

Wixon, (1956), Rufus, (Editor), Accountants' Handbook, The Ronald Press Company, New York.

Yorston, Smyth and Brown, (1957), Advanced Accounting, Vol. 1, The Law Book Co. of Australasia Pty. Ltd., Sydney.

THE FOUNDATIONS OF FINANCIAL ACCOUNTING

The widespread contemporary concern with the quality of the products of financial accounting prompts me to take the view that we should be, and are, engaged in a discussion of an aspect of practical affairs which is a matter of some urgency. I take it that this is not the occasion for a mere academic excursion, and I do not propose to consider, except by way of illustration, the merits of antecedent academic excursions. There in ample evidence of belief in the inadequacies of the present mode of financial reporting. There is also ample evidence to the effect that the existence of these beliefs is not taken lightly by the appropriate professional and regulatory authorities. These are concerned with practical matters. And, as it seems to me, the foundations of financial accounting are to be found by contemplation of the practical contexts in which its products are used, not by contemplation of the justifications and rationalizations by which any existing body of accounting rules is sustained.

I shall take the position that we are concerned with accounting in the economic and commercial context of the present. There is a widespread phobia about being positive or definite or unequivocal about statements of principle and rules. It purports to be founded on the idea that accounting should evolve as the economic context changes, and that to be positive or definite or unequivocal now will foreclose the possibility of further development. But this is mere temporizing, procrastination. There will be no better financial accounting or reporting in the future, in a different context the style of which we cannot possibly envisage, unless, by resolute inquiry and willingness to act upon its reasoned outcome, we are prepared to learn from the circumstances and context of the present. Some say that accounting should be allowed to "evolve". But, just as there was no such thing as the evolution of power-driven vehicles from horse-drawn vehicles, there is no evolution in accounting. There have been and should be changes. But to use the metaphor of evolution in respect of a matter which properly is the outcome of deliberation and choice is to confuse. Likewise, to suppose that the alternative to evolution is revolution is to confuse. To label necessary or conceivable changes is not to bring them about. The invention of the phrase "generally accepted accounting principles" has not brought about the *general* acceptance of any principle, not even of any rule, as a glance at *Accounting Trends and Techniques* will show.

For strong practical reasons we are concerned with general acceptance, with the general acceptance of some principles and the concomitant or consequential rejection of others. The basic matters with which we deal are interrelated elements of the concrete world in respect of which some persons expect to be informed. Toleration of conflicting principles and vacillation between principles can only lead to confusion on the part of those who expect enlightenment, to mistrust between issuers and users of financial information or mistrust of the specialism which provokes misunderstanding. On the other hand, as long as conflicts of principle and vacillation persist they rob the practicing expert of the sense of direction which is the foundation of a professional ethic. The only sense in which general acceptance can have a valid and useful meaning among experts, however, is with reference to acceptance by conviction and on the incontestable evidence of the observable world. Experts naturally, as experts, tend to expect their views to be respected by others, even by other brother-experts. But comprehension of the foundations of an expertise is not so much a matter of having "views" as of grappling with the events and things to which it is related. It is a matter of being impressed by what one observes, not of pressing what one observes into an already fixed mold. The sooner and the further we fly from the world of events and things to the ethereal world of third, fourth and fifth level abstractions, the sooner we reach the point where nothing we say can be tested and much we say is mere gobbledegook. There is abundant evidence in the literature of the tendency to run in the direction of the higher abstractions and to shun the attempt to seek the order which pertains among the observable events and things.

In the following outline I have attempted to keep to the commonly observable events and things—to goods and money and transactions; to people having and people wanting money; to what they want and what they can know and what they can only expect. The propositions to be presented commend themselves to me as yielding a financial accounting which is superior in demonstrable usefulness to the financial accounting now in use, and as foundations they seem to be demonstrably superior to the foundations of many present practices.

Following a common custom, reference will be made primarily to corporations, but the argument is quite general in application. Where it is used, "firm" will generally mean corporation.

1. *Financial accounting*

Financial accounting is concerned with the representation of the monetary consequences of the transactions of single entities (firms) and the monetary consequences of non-transaction events which effect the economic or commercial characteristics of those entities.

Every such entity is conceived to be a going concern engaged in continuous adaptation to the markets in which it operates, adaptation stimulated by the prices of goods and services as these are disclosed in those markets. The decisions of its managers may, and generally will, be based in part on expectations of future prices, but the capacity of the firm to give effect to those decisions depends on the relationship between the firm's holdings of cash (and the equivalent of cash) and the prices of required goods and services at the time.

By transaction we mean any wholly completed or partially completed engagement between the firm and other entities, already settled by the giving or receiving of money, or giving rise to a right to such a settlement in money at a future time. Transactions thus include purchases, sales, loans, subscriptions to security issues.

By non-transaction event we mean any event which bears on the monetary measures (or cash equivalents) of goods or rights held or obligations owed by the firm during the holding or owing. Non-transaction events include gifts, losses by theft or other such causes, changes in prices and changes in price levels.

By monetary consequences we mean actual effects on the cash holdings and monetary equivalents of goods held and obligations owed. The purport of the definition of financial accounting, or rather, of its scope, is to require the representation of all such actual effects in the accounts. The monetary measures of the consequences of all transactions are given by prices expressed in monetary units at the time of such transactions. The monetary consequences of all non-transaction events are given by prices if those events occur at identifiable points of time, and by differences in prices if those events occur through an interval of time during which goods or money are held or obligations are owed.

The definition of the scope of financial accounting and the other necessary definitions are framed in contemplation of the usual understanding of finance, namely, money and money's worth and the provision of money and money's worth. Financial accounting is concerned with these matters alone. Other characteristics of goods, transactions and so on may not be disregarded by managers and other officers of firms, but the monetary calculus has a capacity for representing only monetary aspects of rights, goods, transactions and events. Its significance is not to be disparaged on the ground that its scope is limited, for

THE FOUNDATIONS OF FINANCIAL ACCOUNTING   29

all specialized devices are limited in scope. Its significance lies in the fact that in a monetary economy the provision and the continual renewal of the provision of money is a condition of survival.

2. *Money, cash equivalents and financial position*

The possession of money (currency or bank deposits) confers the right to demand any and all goods having prices equal in the aggregate to the amount of money held. The usefulness of money and of calculations in terms of the monetary unit depends on this freedom to demand any goods up to the limit of the money held. As it is said, money and money holdings are valued by reason of their general command over goods and services.

If a holder of money has also holdings of other goods and rights, he may be deemed to hold a number of money units equal to the sum of the actual money units held and the number of money units which represent the several resale prices of those other goods and rights. As in the simpler case, this sum represents the holder's command over goods and services in general at any given point of time, and the extent to which the holder is able to liquidate any debt or make any other payment in money at that time.

The quantity of money necessary to buy a given quantity of goods-and-services-in-general changes from time to time; the purchasing power of money changes. If the purchasing power of money falls (rises), a firm will be able to buy less (more) in general than previously. A change in the purchasing power of money is clearly a non-transaction event having a monetary consequence; as allowance must be made for the depreciation of durable goods (one type of non-transaction event), so also must allowance be made for the depreciation of the purchasing power of money—but each in its own way.

Although a firm may hold specific goods and trade in specific lines of goods, the prices of those goods are all and always expressed in units of the same general currency at any given time. It might appear that a firm in a particular class of business or industry is concerned only with the purchasing power of money in that industry. But any such idea does violence to the idea of money as a *common* medium of exchange, and to the idea of the monetary unit being a *common* denominator at a point of time. A businessman in a specific industry cannot pay his workers, his creditors, his suppliers and his taxes in units of purchasing power, peculiar to his industry. What he is concerned with is the relationship between units of general purchasing power and the *specific* prices of particular goods. His wisdom expresses itself in the use to which he puts common monetary units in his industry, as, for example, when he purchases goods whose prices move upwards at no less a rate than any rise in the general level of prices. It seems entirely proper that the consequence of such exercises should be made known to managers and to investors; not separately, but as part of the net result of the period or periods in which the advantage becomes apparent. The treatment of asset holdings which we propose would secure this.

The relationship between the monetary measures of the holdings of money, claims to money and goods (collectively the assets) of a firm and the monetary measures of the obligations (equities) of the firm is its financial position. A statement of financial position at a point of time is significant only insofar as it represents the monetary measures of assets and equities in terms of the monetary unit of prevailing purchasing power at that time, and only insofar as the monetary measures of assets are, or are approximations to, resale prices ruling at that time.

114 The evidence for this view is extensive. The granting of credit by or to a firm may be determined in part by its current ratio; the use of this ratio is misleading unless the numerator approximates the current monetary equivalent of the current assets. The granting of loans for medium and long terms may be determined in part by the borrower's debt to equity ratio; the use of this ratio is misleading unless its denominator represents (through the representation of assets at contemporary cash equivalents) the then current measure of the stockholders' equity. The magnitude of loans against specific collateral is always a function of the contemporary prices of the assets charged, and it may be increased or decreased by the lender as the prices of those assets change. Prior consideration by management of the possibility of obtaining finance in any of these ways would involve resort to the same criteria. In any of these cases, as in all choices, other factors, such as the reputation of the borrower or its managers, may enter into the lender's considerations; but insofar as the lender is guided by the *financial facts* of the borrower, only the contemporary financial facts are relevant. Furthermore, any calculation of future cash inflows or outflows will be closer approximations if based on contemporary prices than if based on any other prices.

It follows that every transaction shall be recorded at the amount of the price paid, for this is the amount of the actual cash outflow or inflow consequent upon each transaction. It follows also that changes in prices of goods held shall be brought into the accounts for such goods, so that those accounts will always approximate the contemporary cash equivalents of holdings at any time and the financial position of the firm at that time. The different treatments of accounts for cash balances and goods account balances are due to the fact that the representation of money (and other monetary asset) holdings in terms of money involves a one-to-one relationship, whereas the monetary measurements of goods, their prices, are variable relationships.

The traditional objections to the modification of the account balances of non-monetary assets are without logical or practical foundation. It is said, for example, that increases in the prices of goods held should not be brought into the accounts because they are not objectively determined. But every market price is an objectively determinable price; a firm may or may not buy or sell at that price, but this in no way bears on the objectivity of the price. It is said that increases should not be brought in because they may only be temporary; but the same reason is not invoked against bringing into the accounts *decreases* in prices. It is said that increases in the monetary measures of goods held should not be brought into account until the point of sale, when the amount of the increase in assets is unequivocally determined; by the same reasoning no allowance for depreciation should be brought into the accounts until the amount is unequivocally determined when the asset is finally put out of use; the one event, final sale, determines the magnitude in both cases, yet the accrual principle is applied to one and not to the other. None of the objections is sustained or sustainable on grounds consistent with principles accepted in traditional accounting even now. They can only be sustained by invoking principles which contradict the accrual principle, and which defeat the practically significant object of providing presently relevant and useful information.

3. *Expectations of investors and financiers*

The time-preferences of different persons and firms for the immediate use of money for transaction purposes differ. Those having preferences for the immediate use of money are able to bid for the use of the limited supply available from those who have immediate possession but have preferences for the direct use of money themselves at a later date. The suppliers of money are investors and financiers (creditors); bids are made by virtue of the types of securities offered and the issue prices and other terms at which they are offered.

The outcome expected of an investment in securities is subjective for each investor or financier. But the several kinds of expected outcome may be specified. (1) In general, investors and financiers expect to be able to convert their securities into money when their time preferences for having money become immediate; hence the transferability of securities, and the differing maturities of some classes of security. (2) They expect to be able to convert when alternative opportunities occur for which the prospective gain (loss) appears to them to be greater (less). (3) They expect to be better off by making the investments they in fact make than by making no investment at all. By "being better off" is meant having a greater capacity to command goods and services in general; whether they are or become better off in any other sense depends on how they use this capacity. This greater capacity may arise through periodical dividend or interest payments and through differences between purchase prices and resale prices of securities. (4) They may be presumed to expect to be better off by a greater margin, as a result of their choice of securities, than they would be by the choice of any alternative investment; this because the greater the margin the greater the capacity to satisfy their wants by the direct use of money, and because in general wants exceed means.

The expectations may be described briefly as the time preference for money, the safety of the investment in terms of purchasing power, and the yield in terms of purchasing power. Safety and yield are in no case absolutes; relative safety and relative yield, by comparison with other opportunities, are the criteria. No issuer of securities can know what combination of these three criteria any buyer will prefer. Nor can any buyer be supposed always to give the same weight to each of them, for buyers may make up their portfolios from securities of which they expect quite different outcomes in terms of the three factors. But issuers may be presumed, for their part, to issue securities having features which they expect will be sufficiently attractive, again in terms of these criteria, to ensure that their issues will be taken up in the conditions of the securities market at the time. The reference to safety of investment and yield "in terms of purchasing power" is justified not only on the logical ground that purchasing power rather than numbers of monetary units determines the recipients' capacity for satisfying wants. There is also the evidence of preference for common stocks on the practical ground that appreciation in market prices, rights issues, and rises in dividends are believed to offset diminutions in the purchasing power of money. It may not be argued that holders of preferred stocks and bonds do not conform with the set of expectations we have suggested. Their preferences must be supposed to give less weight to yield and more to safety than the preferences of investors in common stocks.

The characteristics of securities and the nature of the institutions for dealing in securities are predicated on the idea that all holders of securities may at any time want to dispose of them. All holders are potentially short-term holders, either by virtue of the uncertainty of personal exigencies or by virtue of the emergence of opportunities for which superior expectations are entertained. This does not preclude the possibility of some holders turning out to be long-term holders; but even long-term holders may sell and there is no way of foretelling when any holder will want to sell. In order that there shall always be a fair and informed market in securities, a periodical supply of information on financial position and results is necessary. There can be no justification for taking the view, in accounting, that "in the long run total profits will equal the sum of periodical profits however much the profits of particular periods may be influenced by conservatism or other elements of judgement". Conservative representation robs the holder of securities who is obliged to sell during the period in which conservatism is applied of the advantage of knowledge of the actual rights then attaching to his securities, and confers an equivalent advantage of an unrequited and windfall nature on holders during periods in which conservative representation is relaxed. Insofar as accounting is expected to provide certain kinds of knowledge it is no part of its function to withhold knowledge of those kinds, whether the withholding is described as conservatism, prudence or by any other name.

4. *Financial information and financial supporters*

All choices, including all choices of investors and financiers, depend upon both information and expectations. In particular, information on security prices influences choices, for security prices constitute the amounts of money to be invested in securities to obtain the gains expected; expected dividend yields vary as prices vary, inducing some to buy and others to sell as yields move into or out of the preferred range of yields of buyers and sellers as these stand from time to time. Further, information on earnings yields and earnings per share influences the expectations of dividend yields. Further still, information on the present composition of a firm's investment in business assets and the composition of its liabilities influences the expectation of safety of investment and the expectation of gains by way of dividends, interest and shifts in security prices. For example, other things being equal, a firm with a high debt to equity ratio and a low current ratio will be considered to be a more risky investment, requiring a higher dividend yield, than a firm with a low debt to equity ratio; it will be considered to be more risky both because the fixed interest charges take up a large proportion of gross earnings, making net income volatile under shifts in the amount of gross earnings, and because the firm's capacity to adapt its operations to shifts in business is restricted by the extent of its borrowings and the poverty of its net working capital. These considerations apply equally to investors in common stocks and to lenders, for the priorities of lenders are affected as firms shift towards the limits at which the safety of investment and the regularity of interest receipts by lenders become questionable.

117

At the lower limit, choice depends on the relative advantage of an investment in company securities by comparison with a pure monetary contract with minimal risk, such as an investment in governmental or semi-governmental bonds backed by taxing powers. Much less doubt attends the assessment of the probable monetary outcome of a pure monetary contract than the outcome of a business investment. As the investment of business firms is an investment at varying risks as business conditions change and firms attempt to meet those changes, it is necessary that investors and financiers shall be able to choose whether any given firm shall remain in business or shall be liquidated or sold as a going concern. As long as a firm remains a going business, the several amounts of the present resale prices of its assets determines its capacity to adapt itself, and the total amount of net assets (measured severally at resale prices) is the basis for determining the rate of return—current earnings as a percentage per annum of the current measure of the capital employed. If the liquidation or sale of the business *in toto* is contemplated, it may be possible by inquiry and bargaining to obtain a higher price for the business *in toto* than the aggregate amount of its net assets. But, in the first place, it is the drift in the rate of return which triggers this type of inquiry, and in the second place it is necessary to know the amount of the net assets in order to know whether it is preferable to liquidate than to sell the business *in toto* at any price obtainable from a prospective buyer.

Above this lower limit investors' choices depend on the relative advantage of investments in the securities of different companies. But the calculation of rates of return on the same footing is the only valid way to obtain comparable foundations for expectations.

It will be clear that even though investors and financiers may inform themselves of the general state and trend of business conditions and the general state and trend of particular industries, this itself is insufficient to inform the choice of particular firms as investment opportunities. It should also be clear that to invest merely on the basis of security price movements—for example, by buying when security prices begin to rise, in expectation of further rises—is to commit oneself at least in part to the judgments and expectations of other investors, rather than to the substantive capacities of firms. The securities market in such circumstances is merely a device for shifting wealth from one person to another (through outguessing others) rather than an auxiliary device in the augmentation of general wealth through the selection of the more efficient and the rejection of the less efficient firms.

5. *Alternate bases of accounting*

A number of bases of accounting are in use or have been proposed, the implications of which are that present resale prices of assets are irrelevant to going concerns and irrelevant as information to investors in them. In keeping with the proposition that choice is based on comparison, some brief comparative observations on these are made.

First, there is the position that the prices relevant to going concerns are the original purchase prices of assets, modified by such things as depreciation allowances. This position disregards the perennial flux of prices and the bearing which contemporary prices have on business behavior. If the prices of goods held by a firm rise the firm has a broader equity base for additional borrowing. The firm also has expectations of a greater cash flow than would be indicated by original purchase prices. Present prices are, on both scores, more pertinent to managers', investors' and financiers' judgments and expectations than original purchase prices. Again, original purchase prices represent the consequences of expectations held at the time of purchase; but expectations, like prices, are continually changing, and investors need to have some indication of expectations at a more recent date than the dates at which assets were bought. The resale price at the latest balancing date gives an indication of more recent expectations; for, insofar as a firm still holds an asset, at the prevailing market resale price, the expectation entertained by the management is that the proceeds of continuing to hold and use the asset exceed the expected proceeds of any alternative investment of the amount of the resale price.

119

It is also said that the original purchase prices provide a foundation for judgments of stewardship, of fiduciary responsibility, insofar as they represent what has been done with the funds subscribed to the firm. If this means only that investors need assurance from time to time that no unwarranted loss or misappropriation of assets has occurred at the hands of or through the negligence of managers, then elementary periodical audit processes should provide that assurance, even without the publication of financial statements. In any case, once the assurance has been given in respect of any year, it is not necessary to give the same assurance about *that* year in the following year, and the next, and the next . . . as reporting in successive years on the basis of initial cost implies. Further, insofar as financial statements are summaries of the net consequences of past transactions and events, they do not give an account of *all* the resources which may have come under the control of managers and *all* the dispositions made of those resources. Nor is it necessary that they should do so. The responsibility of managers is to use the resources under their control from time to time in the most efficient manner they can devise. Whether they have succeeded in this as well as others have succeeded can only be judged by reference to the express consequences of their actions as these are represented by the prices prevailing through the periods reported upon and at the dates of reporting. Indeed, perpetuation of the use of original purchase prices enables better rates of return to be shown the older a firm is (granted a secular tendency for prices to rise), interfering with the possibility of comparing performances of older and more recently established firms on the same footing of contemporary prices.

Second, there is the position that what investors and others need to know is what the future earnings of firms are likely to be; and that the relevant magnitudes are not the purchase prices nor the present market prices but the future yields of assets. However much investors and managers would like to know this, it is of course impossible to know. Like the initial price basis, this basis entails that the future course of events is already given and definite and unalterable, for one can only calculate the probable flows in the future from one single hypothesis of the complex of future operations if one statement of present value is to be presented. Adaptation is brushed aside. Further, there is abundant evidence in the failures of firms, in the failures of managers and in the failures of particular projects to the effect that all such future calculations are hazardous. Further, inasmuch as they represent present position in terms which are the product of calculations upon hypothetical outcomes, they do not represent the magnitude of the resources by which the firm may attempt to secure those outcomes; a hoped for end, but no knowledge of the means of reaching it. These calculations may be made, indeed must be made, to discover whether the commitment of present resources to a given course of action is likely to be worthwhile; but they do not tell us what the magnitudes of the present resources are. The making of these calculations may enable managers to avoid gross errors, but, being entirely subjective and hypothetical, they may also lead into error. The information they yield is complementary to the information yielded by financial accounting; but, being expressions of expectations only, they do not constitute any part of financial accounting which, as we see it, is concerned with expressions of fact.

There can be no legitimate ground, in our opinion, for supposing that investors should be as well-informed as to the detailed operations of firms as managers, nor as understanding of the various specific alternatives open to firms, nor as capable of judging for themselves the expectations of managers. The phenomenon which has become widely and popularly known as the separation of ownership and control is, in fact, nothing more than an example of the specialization of functions, the object of which has always been to make possible the doing of things more efficiently than before. In effect, investors choose those firms and managers which shall have the use of money; managers choose those projects which seem to promise the better returns; both operate in different markets, but they are linked by the fact that operations in the goods and services market provide the prices (i.e., profits, hence dividends and rises in share prices) at which money is made available in the securities markets. Thus, while *general* knowledge of particular trades is pertinent to investors, no particular knowledge can be expected of them (the alternative is to expect them to be encyclopedists, having particular knowledge of all industries), and no technical explanations of business or accounting methods are likely to be comprehensible to them. They may, however, be presumed to be able to understand the monetary outcomes of business, for safety and yield are matters of common experience to all who have ever had the most elementary form of savings account or bond investment. Managers, on the other hand, are expected to have or to have access to *detailed* technical knowledge of their own trades, and general knowledge of the effects on firms of evaluations made in the securities market. The focal points of interest of the two classes are different but complementary.

121 The belief that great detail should be given to investors, including, as some have suggested, statements of divisional profits, and even budgets of future operations, has arisen from too great a preoccupation with the minutiae of particular firms, and too little regard for the fact that investors and financiers must choose *between firms*. It is well known that too great a supply of signals can lead to vacillation and complete breakdown of the processes of thought as one signal jams another; overelaboration of detail is likely to produce just this effect, for in matters of detail all firms differ and publication of such details increases exponentially the difficulties of comparing firms. Perhaps the suggestions and demands for the publication of greater amounts of detail arise from perceived shortcomings of financial accounting, but they are no substitute for uniformity and contemporaneity in financial accounting; for monetary measurement and representation constitute the one respect in which diversity of business activities is reducible to common denominators and the one respect which bears on the common interest of all investors and financiers, managers and others, namely monetary returns.

A *third* position, intermediate to the original purchase price and the present value positions, holds that the monetary measures which are relevant in accounting are replacement prices. This certainly comes closer to a representation in contemporary terms, and one conceivably based on ascertainable prices. But it suffers from the defect that the replacement price of a good does not give an indication of the firm's capacity to meet future conditions, its capacity for adaptation; and from the defect that it presumes replacement of specific assets with identical assets to be among the regular *modi operandi* of firms; by implication it disregards the continuous changes in tastes and technique which modify the operations of firms, making replacement sometimes impossible and sometimes uneconomic.

6. *Individual and aggregate measures*

The preceding argument has been limited to the establishment of the importance of obtaining aggregates in terms of contemporary prices at each balancing date. We wish to stress that the obtaining of aggregates or aggregate measures is the necessary end of financial accounting. It has been objected that to take the several assets of a firm and to add their present resale prices does not give the expected proceeds of any possible grouping of those assets. This we freely admit, as we admit that the present resale price may well be more or less than the firm does subsequently obtain by use or sale. Resale prices, and indeed current purchase prices in some cases, are, however, surrogates for the general property, current monetary equivalent. The object of accounting seems to be, from our examination of the uses to which its products may be put, to discover positions and changes in position, expressed in monetary equivalents from time to time. It is not to assert that any precise given sum *will* be realized on the sale of any asset or combination of assets; it is rather to give the best possible indication of position and results, so that actions thereafter may be taken in the light of this knowledge. Only when investors and others obtain a representation of the financial position and results is it possible to decide whether past policies have been as effective as the policies of other firms or as effective as they were expected to be; and only then does it become apparent to managers whether they should aim for greater liquidity of assets, whether greater investments in assets of different liquidities is possible, whether efforts to make profits should be intensified, and so on. In short, it is the discovered aggregate result which influences behavior in the following period, not some possible future action which influences discovery of the results of the past period.

The mechanism by which these responses to a financial position and result are put into effect is the series of directives given by management, directives which, of course, may be changed from time to time during any accounting period as the firm interacts with the commodities and securities markets. Buying and selling operations and the concomitant bargaining are not done with reference to balance sheet or other account balances; they are done within the framework of managerial directives and the present potentialities of the market. But because at the year's end, or more frequently, the results come under review by investors and creditors, managers themselves must try to ensure that the rate of return, solvency and other aspects of the firm will continue to justify the support of stockholders and creditors.

It is not expected, nor can it be expected, that managers will not make mistakes of judgment. Inasmuch as decisions and choices are made for an unknown future, expectations are always likely to be at variance with subsequent attainments. What *is* expected, however, is that on balance there will be a favorable aggregate outcome in any period. It is the business of managers to change their directives when the outcomes are or are expected to be unfavorable. And if, in their judgment, it is impossible to change from one directive or policy to another, or possible only at an uneconomic cost, it is their business to find additional ways of offsetting unfavorable outcomes. These steps are all part of the adaptive process.

It follows that to break down operations and results may do injustice to managers and may misrepresent the adaptability and performance of them and of the firm. It seems reasonable to treat the whole complex of activities and effects of decisions as integrally related to one another, for they are so related. It cannot be known, independently of the subjective assertions of managers, whether a course of action was taken entirely on its own merits or for its side-effects, or to what extent for both reasons. Gains in command of purchasing power from traders' margins, from borrowing in anticipation of a fall in the purchasing power of money, from buying in anticipation of rises in particular prices of inventories or durable assets, from so-called non-operating activities, are all gains to be sought; none is intrinsically more desirable than another, and a gain of one kind may necessarily entail a loss of some other kind. Gain in the aggregate is what matters; the only kind of gain (or loss) which it seems to be legitimate to isolate is a pure windfall, the consequence of an event which was in principle unforeseeable.

Now, although all buying and selling is done in the context of the day-to-day state of markets, of buying and selling prices, the periodical determination of aggregate gains must take account of the drift in the purchasing power of money. There is no simple way of doing this except on an aggregate basis. The monetary measures of all bargains during a period are in units of the purchasing power prevailing from time to time during the period; the sum of the measures of all transactions will be a sum expressed in units of various purchasing powers. This applies alike to sales, purchases, common costs of production and administration and to specific price adjustments made during the holding of goods. It is necessary to set off against the resultant of these transactions the effect of the drift in purchasing power, indicators of which only become available periodically. The double entry process gives a ready method of periodical reduction or augmentation as the case may be. If the opening (closing) stock of assets is represented at then current prices, the amount of the stockholders' equity will be in monetary units of the then current purchasing power. But if the purchasing powers of the monetary unit at the two dates differ, the opening measure of stockholders' equity must be augmented (reduced) by a sufficient number of monetary units, if purchasing power of the unit has fallen (risen), to secure the maintenance of capital in purchasing power terms. This number is obtained by applying to the opening measure of the opening stockholders' equity the proportionate change in the index of the purchasing power of money. The amount does not represent an increase in command over resources in general (when prices have risen), and the amount of the total surpluses of the year must be reduced by it to obtain net income (before tax). Thus, even though the component items of an income account may be expressed in monetary units of mixed purchasing power, this method of adjustment gives the net income of the year in monetary units of the purchasing power prevailing at the end of the year. It is logically permissible, then, to relate this amount to the adjusted opening amount or to the closing amount of stockholders' equity to obtain a rate of return, for both numerator and denominator will be in units of the same purchasing power.

In further defense of this procedure we make a comparison with a *fourth* proposed method of accounting, a method of adjusting original purchase prices of assets by the use of indexes of changes in the price level, price-level accounting. This process results in the representation of assets in monetary amounts which may differ materially from the contemporary prices of specific goods held by a firm; the emergent representation of financial position may diverge from the actual position of the firm in relation to the rest of the environment, and the net income will be affected correspondingly. Suppose, for example, that a firm is running down, its products are suffering a decline in demand and its plant and machinery are therefore falling in value; and suppose that the general level of prices is rising. These are all eminently possible; firms fail even in boom years. Price-level accounting would in these circumstances show rising amounts for specific assets the values of which were falling, a rising stockholders' equity when in fact it was falling, a falling debt to equity ratio when in fact the effective ratio is rising. It would also show lower net profits than in fact were being made, because of the higher depreciation charges on fictitiously higher asset values. These divergences between the substantive facts and the representations work at cross purposes to some extent; but, insofar as decisions are made on the basis of the rate of return, they both conspire to interfere with the rehabilitation of the firm and to hasten its demise. In conditions of the reverse kind, in which the rate of growth of a firm exceeds that of firms in general, financial position would be understated relatively to the prevailing prices of the firm's assets, and income would be overstated to the extent of the difference between depreciation charges based on price-level adjusted values and charges based on prevailing prices.

Furthermore, price-level accounting appears to involve the implication that, say, a rise in the general level of prices automatically leads to a rise in well-offness, inasmuch as assets come to be represented by greater monetary amounts and the stockholders' equity is equally augmented. But, in fact, the effect of a rise in the general level of prices *of itself* is to *diminish* well-offness; only if the actual prices of specific goods rise at the same rate is well-offness maintained. The disregard of the counteracting effects of changes in specific prices and changes in the purchasing power of the monetary unit constitutes what may be described as a logical solecism of price-level accounting. The procedure we proposed earlier in this section gives explicit recognition to these separate and counteracting effects.

7. *Accounting as feedback and foundation* 125

The conclusion to which we are led is that, to serve managers, investors and financiers, accounting on a continuously contemporary basis is required; and that such an accounting will serve them all equally well in the only way accounting can serve, namely by aggregate representation of the financial consequences of what has transpired.

As informational feedback, financial accounting serves a function which is not otherwise served. The consequences of small, localized, specific acts can be observed by those on the spot; they can modify their actions (decisions, policies) in the light of what they observe, from observational feedback. But at the level of general administration and of the financial supporters of the firm, organizational and spatial distance, and the complexity of internal relationships and effects, prevent direct observation of consequences. The pertinent consequences are, of course, the changes in the firm's financial position in relation to the rest of the community in which it operates; changes in other than financial respects must be observed in other ways. If we assume the necessity of adaptive behavior, neither the management nor the financial supporters of firms can wait for the long-run consummation of the stream of events which constitute the life of the firm; they require periodical reports of what has transpired in the recent past from time to time, of *all* that has transpired in the immediately past period, whether by action or inaction on the part of the management. Informational feedback, descriptive of the change in the firm's position in relation to its economic environment is the only way they have of knowing whether, in general, the firm's operations and the policies of its managers are as effective, in terms of financial outcome, as the operations and policies of other firms in the same economic environment. There are no absolute tests of effectiveness; these tests are all relative. And this entails that all firms shall do their accounting on uniform principles, regardless of diversity in specific business operations.

As informational foundation for expectations of the future, again accounting serves a function which is not otherwise served. Businessmen and investors must formulate their own expectations of firms; but expectations which have no basis in the financial facts of a firm's operations and position from time to time are nothing more than vague guessing; the frustration and the satisfaction of such expectations are equiprobable. It is, however, a function of accounting to increase the probability of favorable choices; it will only do so if the financial position represented from time to time coincides with the position as prevailing prices establish it.

On these grounds we hold that continuously contemporary accounting is logically and practically imperative, and that the following principles constitute the foundations of financial accounting:

(a) The users of financial statements have varied points of view and entertain varied expectations. These require to be informed from time to time by statements of fact, as well and reliably as the facts of the time can be ascertained and stated.

(b) Buyers, sellers and holders of securities may variously interpret the facts, giving different weight to the facts in the light of information from other sources and their general expectations; but no worthwhile expectation may be formed of any specific investment at any specific time without knowledge of the facts.

(c) Present facts are ascertainable; the facts of a company's financial position at a point of time are ascertainable by reference to the market prices of assets and the amounts of its equities or by deliberately selected approximations to prices, but independently of wishes or expectations.

(d) Only if financial position is ascertained, independently of expectations, at successive dates is it possible to deduce the incomes of the periods denoted by those dates.

(e) Only if all measures appearing in financial statements are measures as of the point of time or the period to which the statements relate can valid inferences be drawn from ratios of different aggregates.

(f) As investors choose between alternative security investments on the basis of expected financial outcomes (capital safety, dividends and other gains), and as choice involves comparison of the factual basis of expectations, uniformity of principles and practices (yielding information of uniform quality) for all firms is indicated.

APPENDIX.

At the beginning of the paper it was suggested that a choice must be made between alternative systems of accounting if vacillation and recurrent exposure to recrimination are to be avoided, and indeed if accounting is to perform a specialized function well. An attempt is made here to present an evaluation of the main types of system used or suggested.

The main differences between the systems relate to methods of asset valuation and the five systems compared differ primarily in this respect; the names used reflect the general principles of asset valuation employed; variants are disregarded in all cases. The systems are:

Original cost accounting (O.C.A.): the general basis of asset valuation is the initial purchase price of each asset in possession at balance date.

Price level accounting (P.L.A.): the general basis is the original cost modified by application of a general index of changes in prices. Because of its link with original cost, this system has many of the characteristics of O.C.A.

Discounted value accounting (D.V.A.): the general basis is the discounted expected net product of each asset. In essence all such values are based on sets of hypotheses about the future, including the primary hypothesis that the firm's operations will remain substantially the same.

Replacement cost accounting (R.C.A.): the general basis is the replacement cost of assets. This entails that replacement is intended and feasible, and is thus akin to D.V.A. in the assumption that the firm's operations will remain substantially the same.

Continuously contemporary accounting (C.C.A.): the general basis is the measure given by prices of assets held as they are evidenced, at balance dates, in the resale markets of those assets. The system is the system alluded to in the paper, and developed at length in the writer's *Accounting, Evaluation and Economic Behavior*.

In the following table the criteria are of two classes: A, technical accounting questions, and B, questions on the practical utility of the products of the systems. The questions in each group and in the set as a whole are not mutually exclusive, so that the mere number of "yes" and "no" entries is not to be taken as giving the weight of evidence conclusively. These numbers do, however, indicate the relative positions of the systems in such an evaluation scheme. There may be other criteria, and the reader may not agree with the scores given in every case. But, if a choice is to be made, some such scheme must be employed, and must include at least these questions.

Comparison of Five Accounting Systems

		O.C.A.	P.L.A.	D.V.A.	R.C.A.	C.C.A.
A1	Is it, in principle, a double entry system?	Yes	Yes	Yes	Yes	Yes
A2	Are its transaction inputs, in principle, facts?	Yes	Yes	Yes	Yes	Yes

44   THE FOUNDATIONS OF FINANCIAL ACCOUNTING

		O.C.A.	P.L.A.	D.V.A.	R.C.A.	C.C.A.
A3	Are its transformations (depreciation, inventory valuations, etc.), in principle, facts?	No	No	No	Yes	Yes
A4	Are its transformed magnitudes measures?	No	No	No	Yes	Yes
A5	Are its transformed magnitudes contemporary?	No	No	Yes	Yes	Yes
A6	Do its transformations give prompt effect to relative price changes?	No	No	No	Yes	Yes
A7	Does it give a comprehensive history of the relationships and transactions of the firm? (Is it isomorphic?)	No	No	No	No	Yes
A8	Is aggregation of measures of items logically possible?	No	Yes	Yes	Yes	Yes
A9	Is it a representation of facts, or, alternatively, does its theory provide for other ways of getting contemporary facts?	No	No	No	No	Yes
B1	Are the results neutral as to specific future actions?	Yes	Yes	No	No	Yes
B2	Are individual measures relevant at stated dates to choice or adaptation?	No	No	No	No	Yes
B3	Is income a measure of general command of goods and services?	No	No	No	No	Yes
B4	Do magnitudes provide a basis for comparison of present operations with future potential variants?	No	No	No	No	Yes
B5	Is a valid current ratio given?	No	No	No	No	Yes
B6	Is a valid debt to equity ratio given?	No	No	No	No	Yes
B7	Is a valid rate of return given? (Is rate of return comparable with rates of return on pure money contracts and other opportunities?)	No	No	No	No	Yes
B8	Are interfirm comparisons of ratios valid?	No	No	No	Yes	Yes
B9	Do balance sheets and income accounts fairly present positions at stated dates and changes between those dates?	No	No	No	No	Yes

Continuously Contemporary Accounting—Additivity and Action

This note is prompted by criticisms of some elements of the theory of accounting presented in *Accounting Evaluation and Economic Behavior*.[1] The differences of Professors Larson and Schattke appear to lie in their concept of "financial action." The alleged refutation of the additivity of current cash equivalents, it will be found, turns on argument relating to *mercantile action*, rather than to financial action or even metrological action. Such mixtures of considerations have provided the justification for many rules and practices in accounting that are inconsistent with other rules. Thus, for example, although it is said to be one of the functions of accounting to disclose what has taken place, it is also held to be legitimate that accounting statements should not overstate (but, by implication, may understate) what has taken place. And in case it may be contended that conservatism is not now an avowed principle, the fact remains that the lower of cost and market rule and the last in first out rule for inventories (both tending to the understatement of the monetary measures of inventories) are still endorsed and used. This inconsistency between disclosure and conservatism only rises if we regard the accounting function as appropriating part of the managerial function. It may well be a safe rule of business behavior to be conservative in some respects; but I find it impossible to accept any justification for an accounting procedure which, by being "conservative," fails to disclose or discloses in a distorted manner the consequences of what has happened. "Distorted" is used quite deliberately, for it is known, even by those who practice it, that the effect of the rules mentioned is to represent inventory measures by smaller monetary amounts than more recent and therefore more relevant purchase prices would justify.

It has been one of my aims to avoid the confusion to which the mixing of ascribed functions gives rise. The emphasis on the specialization of functions and on the consequent differentiation of orientations of specialists within firms is an important element of my position. Larson and

---

[1] Kermit Larson and R. W. Schattke, "Current Cash Equivalent, Additivity and Financial Action", THE ACCOUNTING REVIEW, October 1966, pp. 634–641.

No short name was given to the theory in that place. At other times subsequently the phrase "continuously contemporary accounting" has been used as the theory is directed towards the provision of continuously contemporary financial information. I will continue to use it, hoping to avoid the possibility that the theory may be dubbed a CCE theory, alluding to the use of current cash equivalents, whereas the implications of the theory are much broader than the particular concepts it employs.

Schattke's criticism shows that my explication has been less than convincing, at least to some, and I welcome the opportunity of attempting to clarify the issues.

Macroscopic and Microscopic Considerations

It is beyond dispute that financial statements have reference, in some sense, to the financial outcomes of past actions: to the net change in the residual equity and to the change in the composition of assets and equities. They relate only to financial consequences and characteristics. They say nothing about purely technical or purely mercantile outcomes of possibilities or positions. They do not indicate the age, the technical capacity, the spatial distribution or any similar characteristic of assets; they say nothing about the numbers and types of customers, suppliers, or workers of firms. For information on all such matters as these, business managers turn to other sources. The capacity of accounting to represent the aggregative consequences of actions taken, in terms of the current monetary unit and the value of aggregative statements of results and positions from time to time as indicators of possibilities and constraints (for the present command of resources constitutes the constraints of future actions), are the reasons for the widespread use of financial statements and the sources of the usefulness of accounting. Accounting may serve other functions. But because aggregate consequences are the financial measure of success, and because aggregate positions from time are determinants of future actions, the importance of the function of providing aggregative statements cannot be gainsaid. No process other than accounting serves this function.

It is both convenient and consistent with the way in which business is done to distinguish two types of action and two types of consideration antecedent to action. To these two types different contrasting designations may be given; we will use the terms "macroscopic" and "microscopic" as having some allusion to the scope or breadth of view required for the two types. A macroscopic action (or consideration) is one which has or contemplates effects of a substantial kind on the position of the firm, one which entails a series of consequences ramifying through several or many divisions or functions of the firm. A microscopic action (or consideration) is one which has or contemplates effects of a localized kind.

Thus, by way of contrast, a liquidity crisis is a macroscopic consideration; an excessive investment or overstocking of any given line of inventory is generally a microscopic consideration. The effects of many microscopic actions are in the aggregate a macroscopic consequence; a macroscopic consequence of a series of past actions may become a macroscopic consideration leading to a change in the criteria for subsequent microscopic actions. For example, a liquidity crisis may lead to reductions of individual purchases, to sales at reduced prices, to limitations of the credit given to particular customers. But no single microscopic action can influence future macroscopic considerations or actions. The distinction is consistent with the fact that all minor decisions are expected to be taken within the framework of, and subject to, the constraints of major decisions.

Financial statements relate only to macroscopic effects and considerations. Accounting embraces the recording of the financial effects of all specific transactions and events, it is true, and with an object —the protection of an entity's specific resources—that has merit of its own. There are strong grounds on which it can be argued that the protective function is served only by accounts dealing with minutiae, and never by aggregative statements. Yet aggregative statements are prepared periodically, for an additional purpose, namely, to give the aggregative effects of some sub-classes of transactions or events. Business income, business capital are macroscopic concepts; rates of return and measures of solvency are macroscopic concepts. All are necessary in the process of appraising the performances, positions, and prospects of firms. The requirement of additivity is not only "vitally important" in the system I described; it is an unavoidable requirement under any circumstances in which the magnitudes of the variables just mentioned and others like them are informational premises of choice.

Larson and Schattke observe that "additivity of course occupies an important place in traditional accounting" (p. 637). But this is patently false. *Addition*, not additivity, occupies an important place; but whether the magnitudes added are in fact addable is a question which is not explicitly raised, and is implicitly disregarded, in traditional accounting. Magnitudes measured in different scales and under different environmental conditions are added as if the differences were of no consequence whatever. Such a form of accounting cannot represent the macroscopic outcome of past events and transactions, nor, therefore, the macroscopic considerations pertinent to future actions.

The ex post relationship between the macroscopic and the microscopic is merely a matter of faithful recording and of careful transformation of recorded measures to units of common dimension and common temporal significance for the purpose of aggregation. The ex ante relationship between macroscopic facts, macroscopic financial objectives, and microscopic future actions is a matter of managerial choice. Given the position of a firm at a point of time (its solvency, the composition of its assets and equities) and the expectations and aspirations of its managers, there will be established such things as gross-profit rates and mark-up rates, the volume of credit business permissible, the expected collection period, all for the guidance of the buyers and sales personnel of the firm. These are all macroscopic constraints, not microscopic constraints.

The discretion given to the firm's officers is usually a discretion to sell particular goods above, at, or below, the target rates, but so that the aggregate consequence is the result and position which the macroscopic constraints entail. Some goods may be sold at losses, some at high profit rates, and so on; but the maintenance of solvency and the earning of an income consistent with continued financial support condition the particular (microscopic) bargains which the sales and purchasing officers strike. The target rates may be changed by senior management from time to time, even during any accounting period, as the cumulative effects of a period's transactions and conditions become known through the accounting system. But the targets that stand at any time are what buyers and salesmen must take into account in making bargains. They are engaged in *mercantile* operations subject to specified financial constraints.

The Larson and Schattke Example

The Larson and Schattke interpretation has no place for such constraints, no way of ascertaining the macroscopic conditions that influence particular *mercantile* transactions. They cite as an example a firm having goods x and y whose separate resale prices are $10 and $15 at a given balance sheet date. The resale price of x and y together may be greater than, equal to, or less than $25. We consider the case before indicating its inconsistency with the system we proposed. If the resale price of x and y together is less than $25, the firm would not sell the combination at such a smaller price at the time. If the resale price of x and y together exceeds $25, the excess is a potential profit which buyers may, in the event, not pay and which the firm, in any case, may not anticipate. Whether or not a buyer will take x and y will be determined by many things; whether or not he wants both at the time of any offer; whether the vendor wants to part with both rather than one only at any time; and so on. We do not know the answers to these questions. The object of finding resale prices is not to discover what is expected of any future transaction; it is simply to assign a contemporary measure to an asset. If therefore there are any reasons why $25 is a less satisfactory measure of the current cash equivalent than any other measure, I do not as yet apprehend them; and Larson and Schattke do not provide any circumstance in which it is obviously appropriate to take some other measure.

But further, the Larson and Schattke criticism disregards at least three principles (specialization, ignorance of the future, and the temporal sequence of information and choice) which are part of the theory of continuously contemporary accounting—and this in spite of their repeated insistence (pp. 634, 636, 640) that they are taking all elements of the theory, other than the additivity of current cash equivalents, for granted. Their example presumes that the accountant knows what goods will be sold and in what combinations and at what prices before the point of sale is reached. The theory of continuously contemporary accounting depends on no such presumption. It recognizes the impossibility of knowing future events and their outcomes in the present. By virtue of the principle of the specialization of functions it grants the superior knowledge of sales personnel as to what goods can be sold and in what combinations; and it grants the possibility that buying and selling personnel may influence the price of every bargain struck on behalf of the firm. And it recognizes knowledge of past events and present position as temporally antecedent to the determination of profit objectives and hence of prices for the period in which goods on hand are expected to be sold. The theory has a defined logical and temporal structure for the steps which different officers of a firm take in the course of setting financial constraints, buying and selling; the Larson and Schattke example appears instead to assume, simply, an all-knowing accountant which to say the least is quite unrealistic.

The theory of continuously contemporary accounting does not represent a system giving certain knowledge of present position and past events, much less certain knowledge of the future. In specifying CCE as the property to be measured and resale prices as the ideal measures of CCE, it is concerned with obtaining the *most probable* monetary measures of assets and equities at a point of time; it says nothing of what the future may bring, of what package deals marketing divisions may find possible. It is concerned only with providing financial information.

Additivity

In dealing with additivity I made frequent use of the words "combine" and "combination." The context of the discussion indicates that these terms have reference to monetary measures; to the combining of monetary measures, not to the combining of goods or rights, nor to the monetary measures of any specific combination of goods and/or rights as such. The discussion is directed to the resolution of the problem of aggregating differing measures through time, measures taken in a scale which itself varies through time. In contemplating a future action which appears to require a sum of money larger than the proceeds of any particular asset, managers will wish to consider the various combinations of assets whose sale will yield the necessary sum, so that they may choose the combination which is expected to have the optimum effect on future earnings. Only if they may make alternative hypothetical combinations of the present measures of assets can they discover which combinations to examine further for their effects on future earnings. And only if the measures themselves are in the same contemporary scale may they make alternative hypothetical combinations of the measures of assets at a given time.[2] Larson and Schattke say nothing whatever about the problem of reducing diverse measures to units of homogeneous dimension; clearly they miss the whole point of this part of the argument.

But we consider their views. They say "we may argue ... that CCE and numerosity are separate and distinct properties, and that, while measurements of each may be attempted, it is not appropriate to attribute characteristics of the latter to measurements of the former" (p. 638). I am at a loss to understand this. Consider an analogous example. A rod has a given length; to obtain the measure of its length we apply to it a scale calibrated in inches. The function of such a scale is to give the number of inches (the numerosity of the units of length) in the length of the rod (and all other such objects). It cannot be said that the measure of the length of the rod and the numerosity of inches corresponding to that length are "separate and distinct properties." Rather, the choice of a certain unit is necessary in order to enable us to quantify the property, length, of the rod. So also with current cash equivalent and the numerosity of monetary units by which it is denoted.

Larson and Schattke appeal to Hempel on additivity, but they make no attempt to apply Hempel's terms to the theory they criticize. We make good the omission. Hempel's definition is as follows: A quantity s is additive relatively to a combining operation o is $s\ (x\ o\ y) = s(x) + s(y)$ whenever x, y and $x\ o\ y$ belong to the domain in which s is defined.

Let x and y be two parcels of money of a given currency, and let o be the operation of putting the two parcels together. Let s be the scale of units of money of the given currency. There is an "operational interpretation for the numerical addition of the s values of the two different objects" x and y, as Hempel requires (see the reference on p. 638). And x, y and $x\ o\ y$ belong to the same domain in which s is defined; they are all sums of money. There is nothing "artificial" (pp. 638, 639) about the operation o; an operational interpretation can be given for the numerical addition of the s values of the two objects x and y even if x consists entirely of metallic tokens and y entirely of currency bills. Likewise there is an operational interpretation for the numerical addition of the s values of x and y if x is entirely in currency and y is entirely in things for which the monetary equivalent is discoverable, for monetary equivalent is simply the s value of such things as such value is given by market prices. The theory of continuously contemporary accounting meets the Hempel test exactly.

A Fruitful Theory

Larson and Schattke are equally reticent about the grounds for their assertion that the theory of continuously contemporary accounting does not lead to a "simple and fruitful theory" (p. 639). Again we will make good the deficiency; we give only some of the considerations.

The summation of current cash equivalents of assets gives the firm's present

[2] See *Accounting, Evaluation and Economic Behavior*, pp. 92-3.

command of purchasing power, for any and every possible action for which it may need purchasing power, and without any special presumptions about the firm's possibilities of taking a long time to dispose of any assets in order to obtain the best possible prices, or about the strains it may be under to dispose of assets in minimal time. If we assume informed choice, special presumptions about future behavior must be avoided in the course of finding the facts on which future behavior will be decided. The total or some sub-total of the current cash equivalents of assets is relevant:

(i) To any consideration of the solvency of the firm;

(ii) To any consideration of the settlement of any obligations of the firm;

(iii) To any consideration of the capacity of the firm to buy any good or goods it does not at the time possess, the possession of which is expected to be more advantageous than the least advantageous of the goods presently in possession and whose aggregate current cash equivalent would furnish the price of the more advantageous goods;

(iv) To any consideration of the capacity of the firm to borrow on the collateral security of goods in possession, for current cash equivalents are the only objectively determinable basis for the security of creditors' advances;

(v) To any consideration of ways and means of increasing profitability (by seeking out markets which will pay higher prices, a time-consuming process not available to firms under liquidity strains) or of increasing liquidity if this appears to be necessary for survival (survival being the preferable alternative to allowing creditors to interfere with the firm's independence);

(vi) To any consideration of the merits of the whole undertaking relative to alternative investment of the proceeds of liquidation. (If switching to an alternative investment comes to be preferred, the net assets or the firm sold as a going concern may realize more or less (not necessarily either) than the current cash equivalents, but this cannot be discovered until bargains are actually driven.)

These examples will suffice. Note that (i), (ii) and (iv) relate to the money or securities market; (iii), (iv) and (vi) relate to the firm's factor markets; and (iv) and (v) relate to the firm's product markets. In short, then, we have one concept which is relevant to considerations in all classes of market in which firms operate. In each of the examples, of course, current cash equivalents of assets are not the only considerations, for every choice involves contrasting one set of considerations with another or others. But current cash equivalents are the only considerations common to all. A concept the quantification of which enters into so many problem situations surely has the merit of simplifying the theory of choice in response to financial information. As for the fruitfulness of the theory, let it be demonstrated that any other theory yields a homogeneous magnitude or set of magnitudes which can enter so freely into combination or comparison with other magnitudes in the contemplation of financial aspects of business problems. The theory surely is fruitful insofar as it entails a form of accounting in which individual measures are additive because they are, in principle, taken in the same context in units of the same dimension. If it is to be deposed, let it be shown that some other theory is equally fruitful.

Some Other Matters

Larson and Schattke's attempt to introduce intangibles into the counterargument is, of course, a departure from the "other aspects of the theory" which they proposed to accept. But it puts them in a position of asserting some things which appear to lack support. "... individually nonseverable, intangible factors ... are of great importance ... in setting the limits of financial action in markets," they say (p. 640). If this is so, why, then, do companies eliminate intangibles from their balance sheets? And why do analysts disregard the magnitudes shown for intangibles in balance sheets? And why do accountants protest that non-purchased goodwill should never be written into balance sheets?

Again: "As assets are combined into various collections, the CCE of the collection, due to positive or negative goodwill, may be greater or less than the summation of the CCE's of all constituent assets. These intangible factors become 'embodied' only in asset collections..." (p. 639). Now if intangible factors become "embodied" we should first be told how, but we are not told. And if the measure of their embodiment may be positive or negative we must know in advance what the measure of goodwill is. But of course we cannot say a firm has a goodwill (or its opposite) until by its actions it proves to have earned superior profits (that is, if we follow the traditional ideas on goodwill), which means that in order to measure the monetary property of the assets at the end of a year, and hence to discover its profits, we have to know a magnitude which we cannot discover until we have calculated its profits. It should be obvious that this is an untenable position, a position which the theory under criticism escapes altogether.

Larson and Schattke have whetted my anxiety to clarify. Perhaps they will reveal the "many points" it is possible to criticize –their disagreement with the "basic assumptions about human behavior," the faults they pick with basic definitions adopted for economic terms, the "certain factors" which are left out, the technical faults in the deductive approach (p. 634). Perhaps they will say in what sense I excluded discounted cash flows from "the accounting discipline" (p. 636) when I did no such thing; nowhere did I discuss "the accounting discipline" to the best of my recollection. Perhaps they will explain how the importance of CCE is asserted and the role of discounted net cash proceeds is de-emphasized (p. 636), when in fact the roles of *both* in the process of choice is a fundamental point in the theory of continuously contemporary accounting. Perhaps they will answer the "interesting question—should accounting be a valuation system, rather than a measurement system?" (p. 636), a question which I thought I had taken pains to answer.

As for their conclusions, they do not, as they assert, demonstrate that CCE is a non-additive property, because they do not discuss the criteria for addition. They only disagree with the manner in which the singular measures are taken and that is a very different matter. But then, of course, they did not take cognizance of the fact that exactly the same problem must arise in the case of any inventory valuation method in traditional accounting which has reference to "market," and indeed to "cost"; and presumably there is some evidence to the effect that it is solved in some manner. If two theories have some point in common there seems little point in attacking only one of them, for what we need from criticism is a demonstration of relative superiority or inferiority. The "apparent forcefulness" of their criticism is not "apparent" to me.

The Canons of Criticism*

On first reading Richard Leftwich's "Critical Analysis of Some Behavioural Assumptions Underlying R.J. Chambers' **Accounting, Evaluation and Economic Behavior**" (University of Queensland Press, 1969) I wondered whether it was to be taken seriously – or whether it was some kind of spoof. I am quite serious about that, for reasons which will presently be given. There are classic examples of spoofing the experts, and there can be nothing more funny than a first class hoax. But on reflection I found the absence of authorities such as Mother Shipton and Nostrodamus, the presence of authorities such as Arrow and Barnard and Simon, and the presence of the imprint of a University Press, sufficient to quell my doubts.

Criticism in my view is a respectable exercise. I am not one to condemn what some call destructive criticism, and to plead only for constructive criticism. Any legitimate criticism is constructive, for one must clear away rubbish before one can start to build. But there are certain canons of criticism. First, criticism of any evidential or descriptive statement requires that contrary evidence of sufficient weight be adduced. Second, criticism of any line of argument requires that the alleged logical fallacy be exposed. Third, criticism of any premise or argument of any person requires that what is alleged to have been said shall in fact have been said. Fourth, criticism of any substantial exercise requires care, insofar as conclusions may depend on the convergence of evidence introduced at various stages in the development of a demonstration.

The third of these is a matter of courtesy – to all. If a critic distorts or misrepresents what he purports to criticise, his criticism ceases to be legitimate. He seduces his audience. Instead of criticism he offers the spectacle of the demolition of a collection of straw men of his own making. This may be entertaining. But entertainment and scholarship are rather different kinds of endeavour. Both those who share and those who oppose the views of the subject of such excursions may be gleeful – on the one hand, because the critic has exposed his own

---

* Written as for publication, but communicated in 1969 only to Richard Leftwich.

flanks, on the other hand because the subject of criticism is not being allowed "to get away with it". But on neither count is the enjoyment contributory to cleaning up confusion; the distortion only compounds confusion.

Let me say, as I have said elsewhere, distortion is not necessarily intentional or malicious. I do not know Mr Leftwich. I will take it for granted that he has written without malice, even though he has a goodly stock of the invective words. I trust he, in turn, will take it for granted that I write with no malice, notwithstanding a little invective of my own. The reader of p.220 of Leftwich's paper will find there generous remarks on his part which it would be churlish of me to treat with ingratitude. With these preliminaries, let's get down to business.

Leftwich purports to demolish my conclusions by demolishing my "behavioral" premises. Those premises are, as in other fields of empirical study, generalizations from recurrent or plentiful instances. As I have said empirical premises may be rebutted by the weight of evidence of contrary instances. And this, it may be expected, is the line along which Leftwich's choice of "grounds" would lead him. As we shall see he offers no contrary evidence whatever.

The substance of Leftwich's analysis begins with a section headed "The Process of Homeostasis". I did not use the phrase. I did use "homeostatic system", a purely descriptive term for a system having the means of restoring itself to a condition appropriate to survival and functioning if disturbances in its internal economy or its environment threaten its survival. Like all descriptive terms, "homeostatic system" is a short-hand way of saying a number of things which have already been identified in an exposition. If human organisms as wholes do not have such features as I identified, it should be possible to show in what respects they do not. As to human physiology, Leftwich defers to Cannon; and as to psychology, his authorities provide no clear examples. The very citations from Stagner, Weber and Herzberg, of the strain which arises from the striving for ideals and from the contrast of achievements with aspirations, illustrate the spur to action which produces relief from strain.

It is not even entertaining to read of the disputes of the

psychologists over words. I do not pretend to be a psychologist. I am not therefore able to say whether Fletcher or Stagner or Maze or Davis or any of the others is the more reliable. But Leftwich offers no credentials of his own in the field either. One is left wondering therefore whether the "biting criticism" of Maze, or the "adamant" rejection by Davis [of the use of "homeostasis" in psychology] are justified at all. Much of the debate seems to be on whether survival is what the adaptive mechanisms may be supposed to secure. But Cannon, for obvious reasons, dealt with the breakdown of these mechanisms, a possibility which was necessary to my analysis and which I gave notice of, on pp.21, 161, for example. If the psychologists must quibble because some have disregarded the possibility of breakdown, there is no reason why their quibbles should be regarded as proof that the ideas for which the word "homeostasis" stands are of dubious value.

But quibbling apart, it is undeniable that men feel strains - from bodily unease to states of doubt and insecurity. It is undeniable that when they feel strains they seek relief. It is undeniable that bodily strains they do not even feel are eased, or their ease by deliberate action is prompted, by bodily mechanisms of which they are generally unconscious. It is undeniable that relief from doubt and insecurity of all kinds is sought in ways varying from the hard, calculating processes of disciplined thought to the invention of fantasies - and even to use of the dicta of authorities. Leftwich makes no attempt to deny these things. After some six pages on the psychologists, his scanty reference to my exposition suggests he would rather not "analyze" what was so plainly stated. And his occasional allusions to "equilibrium", after citing Cannon's reason for preferring "homeostasis", suggest that he would rather talk about something else than the matter supposedly at issue. And that is just an illustration of one mode of seeking relief from strain.

On to rational behaviour. Leftwich heads the section "Rational Human Behaviour". In using this phrase he disregards von Mises' judgement that "the term 'rational action' is pleonastic and must be regarded as such". Leftwich is of course at liberty to be pleonastic; or even to deny that the phrase he uses is pleonastic. However he introduces these words of von Mises to show that they and other following sentences throw a "different light on the assumption" [of rationality] than the brief sentence from von Mises which I quoted, namely, "Human action is necessarily always rational". Leftwich continues: "Thus von Mises says that such an assumption of rationality serves no purpose because it is tautologous" [i.e., pleonastic]. von Mises says no such thing. He says only that the **term** "rational action" is tautologous; that is, it uses "rational" unnecessarily. How Leftwich can reject the judgement of von Mises which he quotes, then misrepresent it, and then offer the misrepresentation as criticism of the statement which von Mises made, and which I adopted as a premise, is not easy to follow. I am forbidden, by adoption of the view that human action is rational, from asserting that Leftwich is irrational; but there must be curious reasons for so curious a line of non-argument.

Skip over the next three pleonastic pages; pleonastic, for, as Leftwich admits, I used the notion of rationality in a purely descriptive sense. Leftwich seems to agree with the position I took. On p.231 he writes: "it should be obvious that the criteria of the observer cannot validly be used as standards . . . it is not relevant, when evaluating the **actor's** rationality for the observer to judge those [the actor's] standards in terms of **his** [the observer's] set of values". Note that he affirms that an observer's standards provide no criteria for judging the rationality of the decisions of another. But having said that, it is surely impossible then to speak of an observer "evaluating" an actor's rationality. An observer can only "evaluate" anything by reference to standards of his own choosing. The only way out of this dilemma is to admit that no one can evaluate the rationality of another's decisions; to admit, as I do, that everyone acts **for what seem to him** to be good reasons. Rational can mean nothing more than this. Of course, if Leftwich thinks rational means more than this he could say so. He doesn't.

I hesitate to deduce from Leftwich any conclusion which he does not clearly assert. But he seems surprised that I do not require "expectations to be realized as a necessary condition for judging an action to be rational". I take it, then, that if, in spite of great exercises in discovery and calculation, I choose to do something which turns out otherwise than I expected, my decision was irrational! If that is how we "judge" rationality, we must mean by it either chance or omniscience; or we must have supposed such a loose set of expectations that a very wide range of consequences will constitute realization of expectations. We have to make up our minds whether we are to use rationality of a human attribute or of the outcome of a human action. I choose the former. Given that choice, I may not say anything about the rationality of another; but I may say that I like or do not like the **outcome** of the other's actions. Observers can pass such judgements; they can evaluate outcomes. They cannot evaluate what goes on inside a man's skin.

Striving to clinch the point Leftwich takes issue with my introduction of the costs of search preparatory to choice and the consequent delay in action. He says "what is then substituted for the original decision is another decision regarding the anticipated cost-benefit relationship of further search" (p.232). He repeats the "substitution" allegation on pp.233, 246. To describe a treatment of two aspects of a problem as "substitution" of one problem for another is the same kind of verbal legerdemain as has already been noticed. Further, to assert that I did "not propose any criteria whereby the decision maker is able to solve the substituted problem" may be literally correct. But as it is a problem of relating expected costs and benefits, the solution lies in exactly the same direction as any other economic problem. Did it need saying?

Leftwich continues: "It is difficult to reconcile the characteristics of rational behaviour as defined by Chambers with the limitations of man which he recognizes" (p.233). His difficulty arises, however, from his importation of a different notion of rationality altogether. A man may know less than another, and yet be no less rational, in my terms. Knowledge is one thing; forethought, insight, skill and judgement are something else. Says Leftwich: ". . . the picture . . . of an optimizing man acting to select the best alternative . . . is invalidated by the limitations which, as Chambers admits, are common to all men" (p.233). Not at all. My optimizer can, by virtue of his limited knowledge, choose only the best alternative **from the alternatives he knows**. No one can ask any more of him than that. Beg pardon; Simon can. He postulates an idea, "objective rationality", which is that kind of choice which **in fact** results in the maximization of ends. Having thus posed a quality which only omniscients can have, he is then forced to say that men cannot reach such a "high degree of rationality". Of course they can't. Why then should Simon set up a non-observable omniscient as a hypothesis, so that he can knock it down? I was content to follow Occam's maxim, and to stick with observable man. And, curiously, my observable man has all the characteristics which Simon's "knocked-down" man has (see Leftwich at p.234).

After quoting at length (pp.232-3) my explicit description of the limitations of man, it seems strange to find my "man" caricatured as being able to consider "all possible alternatives" (p.234). A passage of mine which is purely descriptive of the variety of opportunities available to any person is taken as evidence that any given person is supposed by me to consider them all. Leftwich then asserts that because man rarely ventures beyond his customary range of markets, "his behaviour is not characteristically flexible" (p.234). Why not? Flexible does not mean infinitely flexible. Leftwich avers: "the model must contain factors to explain man's consideration of only a limited number of alternatives and his criteria for selecting a particular alternative". Of course; but Leftwich simply fails to see that limited knowledge, the desire for relief from strain, the recourse to habit, the strain and cost of search, the desire to optimize and the diminishing marginal utility principle - all of which I made use of - are all factors which explain the limited number of alternatives considered by man.

And of course it might have been expected that Simon's "satisficing" would be thrown in, for good measure (p.235). It is Simon's postulation of "objective rationality" which obliges him to have recourse to "satisficing". If one frankly admits that man is limited, and that he seeks to maximize his ends as well as he is able even though he is limited, one has the same result as Simon but without two superfluous notions - objective rationality and satisficing. On this matter I have been quite explicit. In an organization, the ends of participants are in partial conflict. Whatever each may seek, he can expect no more than the wants of others will allow. The wants of others and their bargaining power are among what Simon calls "givens". Given these constraints each will seek the maximum he can get for whatever costs he is prepared to meet. This is a far more definite description, in my prejudiced view, than some vague notion of satisficing, because it explains the failure to get what an individual in isolation may want in terms of the very compromises which non-isolation entails.

The next section "Behaviour of an Entity", as may be expected by now, proceeds by the use of similar tactics. Contrary to my own view (which he quotes) that "adaptation . . . is the dominant mode of economic behaviour", Leftwich contends that rigidity is predominant (p.238). This leaves him in a predicament, though he does not seem to realize it. If so much behaviour is rigid behaviour, why have so many people spent so many acres of printed matter on the discussion of decision-making? Why are there so many managers and sub-managers in any firm of even modest size, if all persons respond rigidly to their directives? What does competition in business mean if it doesn't mean trying out newly-decided tactics in the market place? And that is a daily occurrence, as any reader of the newspapers, any housewife, will know. Leftwich confuses the issue repeatedly by such phrases as "deviates **significantly**" (p.239), "diverges **greatly**" (p.239), "**high degree** of rigidity" and "**high degree** of flexibility" (p.240); I have emphasized the quantifiers because, although they are meaningless, they are the only distinctions Leftwich seems able to make to sustain his case. Nowhere have I denied that behaviour is in many respects persistent, habitual, non-deliberate (p.241). I have held only that when strain occurs men do give thought to its removal; that no one knows when strain will occur; that there are many users of information, each susceptible to different strains at different times and that therefore the information available at any time should be such as will enable its users to give **informed** thought to strain when strain arises for any one of them.

Leftwich has some unusual ideas about the relation of investors to companies and managers. At pp.237 and 242 one suspects that he thinks investors can or do own the assets of companies, or can and should interfere in managerial policy making. Of course the law expressly excludes these possibilities. It is useless to complain that investors do not do something which the legal structure prevents them from doing, or to suggest that indifference is the reason why they do not do what the law prevents (p.243). How they can be expected "to operate the entity and to switch entity assets" (p.245) is beyond comprehension.

It seems an odd thing to say that my bald description of the powers and perquisites of management entails "mistrust of management" (p.243). I do not mistrust anyone without cause. I only like to have information which assures me that my trust is well placed. I do not want soothing syrup or "advice" (p.243). The history of commerce is bespattered with cases of "advisers" who were frauds, of persons trusted in all kinds of circles who were found to be fakers. If Leftwich wishes to dispute the evidence, at least he could try; but, in spite of numerous references to empirical evidence, he does not try.

I am not a little intrigued by what Leftwich calls "the docile role of the accountant in Chambers' model" (p.244). The disciplines of science are by no means easy. The characteristic objectivity and neutrality of scientific knowledge are hardly won. They are won against the common wish to believe in what we believed in yesterday, against habits of thought which are comforting and comfortable. There is nothing docile about this. The task of finding out the contemporary facts, as I described it, is a task demanding a much less docile attitude than the mere acceptance and transmission of opinions obtained from management, as Leftwich suggests (p.243). Indeed, Leftwich unwittingly shows how docile some of today's accountants are. Although, he says, "the writings of leading academics and publications of the professional bodies . . . show little evidence of widespread agreement, they do at least represent the judgements of men of experience of accounting and experience of what users of accounting expect from it". If the experts disagree, why should anyone, Leftwich and I included, accept their judgements as guidance or authority? To do so is docile in the extreme, supine even. It is especially piquant to find Leftwich chiding me for ignoring the experts when already in his introductory pages he indicated at length the messy state in which accounting theory and practice now stand.

I return to the canons of criticism. First, to what extent does Leftwich supply empirical evidence in rebuttal of my premises? None at all. There is only one empirical illustration in the paper (at p.233), and even that is explicable in terms of my set of ideas, notwithstanding Leftwich's denial. Second, to what extent does Leftwich expose logical fallacies? None that I have discovered. On the other hand he seems to have perpetrated quite a few. Third, to what extent is the object of the criticism clearly presented and free of distortion? In a goodly number of cases there is manifest distortion. Fourth, to what extent is the whole of the object of criticism taken into account? It might seem that this is improper in this case, as Leftwich expressed the intention to confine himself to certain behavioural assumptions. But the rejection (p.245) of my conclusion on the utility of the kind of accounting I proposed goes beyond his stated brief, and thus exposes him to the charge that he did not take the whole of the argument into account.

Accounting, Evaluation and Economic Behavior may be open to many kinds of criticism. I do not myself now agree with the details of some of the suggestions I made. The premises are a different matter. A little inspection of the behaviour of others and a little introspection on our own part will, I think, confirm the propriety of them all. Unless we have been entirely unobservant and uninstructed we will have found examples of them every day in every kind of context. I think it requires more than juggling with the dicta of authorities to upset them. A little ingenuity will enable anyone to unearth "authorities" for anything, sense or nonsense, relevant or irrelevant. But the elementary features of behaviour are so open to observation that a little ingenuity in that direction is all that is required to upset my premises - if they can be upset. But this is a discipline to which no critics of those premises have yet seen fit to submit themselves.

September 1969

Second Thoughts on Continuously Contemporary Accounting[1]

First thoughts

I do have second thoughts on some elements of the argument in *Accounting, Evaluation and Economic Behavior*. But I would like to begin with some of my 'first' thoughts — the ideas and circumstances which prompted the development of the theory in the first place.

Some twenty-five years ago I was engaged in a government regulatory agency which, for its purposes, required the analysis and comparison of the financial positions, results and costs of business firms in all kinds of industries. For a time this work was my sole preoccupation. The conventional accounting processes on which the financial statements were based made comparisons between firms, even in the same trade, most difficult. The pressing tasks of administration prevented us from seeking a solution which would treat firms of different ages and sizes equitably. But the experience left a great sense of uneasiness, a sense of dealing with something quite undisciplined, subject to no firm principles. When I left that position I was quite disenchanted about accounting, although it had been the major subject of my studies and work for the previous ten years.

For the following nine years I was engaged in the teaching of aspects of management. My main interest was in financial aspects of business; but as these aspects of business touch every participant in the activities of a firm in some way, their study I considered to provide, in microcosm, examples of the whole of the relations between a business entity and its owners, managers, creditors, customers, competitors, and so on. Changes in the attitudes and actions of any of these parties would require changes in the actions, tactics and strategies of the firm. The immediate post-war years provided numerous frequent and varied examples of the shuffling and bargaining and haggling which go by the general description of adaptation.

The idea of a firm which went on doing the same things year by year, or which set up plans and stuck to them — an idea which many describe as the going concern concept — did not match the observable behaviour of the business

[1]. This paper owes its origin to a suggestion of Dr Horace Brock, North Texas State University. It was prepared as the basis of a discussion in that University in February 1970. The present text has benefited from comments, objections and doubts expressed on presentation of the paper in several U.S. universities. To my hosts and interlocutors I am grateful.

community. Changes in the environment and in the expectations of businessmen constantly obliged business firms to respond, sometimes aggressively, sometimes defensively. According to my undergraduate economics, all this was 'old hat'. But in learning it anew, by observation, it became clear that the form which adaptation took depended in part, often a crucial part, on the means at the disposal of a firm. Knowledge of the present facts, in particular the present financial facts, of a business was a necessary condition of informed adaptation. And as adaptation is continuous, knowledge of the financial facts must be continuously brought up to date.

Accounting as it was then expounded and practised did not provide this information. Perhaps it could. In any case I had by this time (1950) become disenchanted with the literature, the 'theory', of management. Apart from the works of Barnard and Simon, it was too full of unargued prescriptions, which may well serve as rules of thumb but which one could see 'violated' in almost every firm, and which lacked any coherent, reasoned foundation. I turned back to accounting, as a university teacher, in 1953.

Fortunately for me, there was evidence in Australia to the point that the long-established doctrine of conventional accounting — the initial cost doctrine — was not in fact endorsed and followed in practice. Poring over company reports, prospectuses, loan indentures and press reports, I found that this evidence was substantial. Hundreds of companies had revalued their assets upwards in spite of the cost doctrine. And the terms of issue of preference shares and loan securities made it clear that there were good commercial reasons for doing so. For if one did not know the contemporary worth of the assets of a company from time to time one could not know whether the terms of contracts and indentures were in fact violated.

The observed revaluations were, of course, made on various kinds of evidence; more frequently than not their bases were not disclosed. But they did confirm the view that more up-to-date information than original costs was needed in practice. And as general commercial practice is substantially the same around the world, there seemed good grounds for supposing that up-to-date information was necessary everywhere, notwithstanding extant doctrines and accounting practices. That there were and are good grounds for this belief has since been confirmed by many more observations than I had then made. Even in the United States, where upward revaluation was virtually outlawed in the 'thirties, up-to-date information was regarded by accountants as significant when market prices of assets fell; and by some security analysts as significant in a wider range of circumstances. Why then didn't the textbooks take notice of these things?

They were worth closer analysis. I began to find that they contained vague and inconsistent propositions, that those propositions did not constitute coherent systems of ideas from which rules could be deduced, that particular terms had widely variant meanings as between texts, that firmly stated propositions were virtually cancelled by appended provisos, and that there were numerous other difficulties.

For some years I had no clear idea of what should be regarded as contemporary information. That it should be contemporary was the main thing. I wrote of replacement prices sometimes, of price-level adjustments at other times and of the present value of expected proceeds at other times.[2] It was not until I began (in 1963) to put the product of my past thinking into comprehensive and systematic form that the solution of the problem occurred to me. Neither replacement prices nor price-level adjusted costs nor present values provided the *generally* usable premises of financial calculations. The argument I developed in *Accounting, Evaluation and Economic Behavior* led to the conclusion that resale prices were the kind of contemporary information which was useful in making *all* judgements about the past and *all* plans for the future of business firms.

I have given this brief account of some twenty years' thinking — about practical experiences, about observed financial events and about the state of accounting doctrine — simply to show that the outcome was not just a novelty. It was a conclusion to which everything pointed — provided one could only free oneself from the 'sanctity' of established doctrine long enough to allow the evidence to accumulate. I had in fact taken some steps to free myself from existing dogma. About fifteen years ago I tried diligently for some years to find some common core in the principal expositions of accounting, the expositions of the conventional mode and of modes of accounting which would reduce the alleged flaws in conventional accounting. I had little success. I had also, meanwhile, read the accounts of the histories of a number of business firms, and of mergers, disputes, frauds and failures; accounts written by lawyers, journalists, and businessmen themselves, and thus free of the overtones or verbal uses of accountants. I concluded that only by the persistent attempt to construct a theory independently of the existing dogma, but with an open eye to commercial and financial events, could one circumvent the contradictions and inconsistencies of existing expositions and recommendations on accounting practices.

Old habits die hard, however. I will indicate presently some respects in which I failed to shake off old ideas. And I will give examples of points where attempts to add force to my argument led me into improper extensions of my chosen set of ideas.

But first may I say that my second thoughts on continuously contemporary accounting have only served to confirm my belief in the validity of the main ideas. Critics have attacked my exposition. I invited this. In the Preface I foreshadowed that others would judge whether the development of my ideas had been in the direction of 'maturity or senility'; and in the Epilogue I said: 'We have not come to the end of the road. In a very real sense, much of the journey lies ahead'. But none of the critics has attacked the main features of the argument. These are (a) that informed choice of future actions and informed appraisals of past actions depend on present knowledge of a present state; (b) that in respect of financial information there is no business function other than accounting which

2. Examples will be found in the articles brought together in *Accounting, Finance and Management*, Butterworth, Sydney 1969.

accumulates such knowledge; and (c) that such knowledge is only part of the premises of choice or judgement, the other parts being presently available external information and the (subjective) expectations of managers, investors and others who exercise choice and judgement. If these points remain unchallenged, and as they are the main grounds for the details of the whole system, I can only feel that my critics have left the main part of the structure unscarred.

Perhaps the most pointed way of proceeding will be to consider some of the criticisms to which my work has been exposed. I hope I can convey the burden of the criticisms fairly. I will acknowledge their propriety in some cases. But, in respect of other criticisms I will offer some defences, the better to show that, in the more significant particulars, my original position is unaffected. I acknowledge the generous remarks of reviewers and others on the general character of my exercise. What I may say in rebuttal of particular objections I hope will be taken as an attempt to clarify what I must have left in doubt, and without any suspicion of animosity on my part.

Alleged inconsistency

The most widely noticed element of my exposition is its treatment of inventories and durable assets. After developing the case for the use of resale prices, I introduced the possibility of using replacement prices and indexed calculations. This move was interpreted variously. After the establishment of 'a consistent theoretical rationale for using realizable price', McDonald found the 'switch . . . less than compelling'.[3] Wright suggested that I was obliged to use replacement prices because the use of current resale prices 'fails to deal satisfactorily with the problem of inventory measurement', and that I was led to 'present two quite different methods of accounting for durable goods, without being able to provide any useful criterion for choosing among them'.[4] Baxter alleged that when my argument comes 'to deal with each type of asset in detail, it abandons the sale price principle and substitutes replacement cost'.[5] Benston implies a charge of inconsistency. 'It would seem that . . . Chambers would favor accounting statements in which assets are valued on several bases. But he rejects this notion emphatically, on the grounds that only one method can be correct'.[6] Hendriksen points to inconsistency in my firm adherence to resale price for durables while demanding the application of the 'rigid realization rule' for inventories: '. . . current output prices are more consistent with Chambers' postulates than are current input prices'.[7] Iselin pointed out that to use any other price than net realizable value

3. Daniel L. McDonald, review in *The Canadian Chartered Accountant*, August 1966, pp. 78-9.

4. F. K. Wright, 'Capacity for Adaptation and the Asset Measurement Problem', *Abacus*, August 1967, pp. 74-9, at p. 77.

5. W. T. Baxter, 'Accounting Values: Sale Price versus Replacement Cost', *Journal of Accounting Research*, Autumn 1967, pp. 208-14, at p. 213.

6. George J. Benston, review in *The American Economic Review*, March 1967, pp. 297-9, at p. 299.

7. Eldon S. Hendriksen, review in *Journal of Business*, April 1967, pp. 211-13, at p. 213.

would be inconsistent with my own definition of financial position.[8]

To some of these 'charges' I plead 'not guilty'; to others 'guilty — but under extenuating circumstances'!

Had I been content to develop a theory without regard for the availability of the information which the theory presumed to be available, I could have avoided the possibility of charges of inconsistency. But I believe that theory is closely related to practice, and I did not wish to evade the practical difficulties which might stand in the way of endorsement. That is why I undertook the discussion of different kinds of inventories and durables in some detail. And it is on just those parts of the analysis that critical attention has focused, relatively few pages in Chapter 10.

But I did make one serious mistake; it is hinted at most directly by Hendriksen, and it had, before that, been pointed out to me by my own colleague, W. P. Birkett, in Sydney. The mistake was to make use of the idea of realization, in the conventional sense, in discussing the relation between inventory values and income. The conventional idea is that profit should not be anticipated. The balances which turn up in the balance sheet are what they are because this dictum is applied. My own system strictly has no use for this notion. Asset balances are indicative of the present prices of assets on hand; income is the difference between residual equities at two dates based on assets at prices ruling at those dates.

How did I come to make this mistake, especially as I regarded 'realization' as a term relating to revenues only and made this point even after perpetrating the inconsistency under examination? Looking back, it seems due, in part, to inadvertent adherence to an old verbal habit, an old and familiar formula. The difficulties of shaking off old habits are notorious. But I suspect also that I was intimidated by the novelty of the resale price idea which, to my knowledge, has no respectable antecedent in the literature. Perhaps, too, I was cowed by the possibility that a strict use of the resale price rule would entail the elimination of monetary representations of many assets. Whatever the cause or causes, I was inconsistent in this respect. I can scarcely blame my critics for the appellations they gave — 'switch', 'defection', 'abandons . . . and . . . substitutes' — to what I did. And I can scarcely blame them for alleging that I countenanced the use of two kinds of contemporary price. Certainly I said repeatedly that I was seeking resale prices and that any other device was merely an attempt to approximate resale prices, and that their use did not mean I was departing from the principle of resale price. But the deliberate use of the old test of realization properly confused the matter. I will presently indicate what I now see as the way through the dilemma which then confronted me.

Resale price

A number of critics have challenged the propriety of using resale prices. Baxter, even after listing five of my arguments without any hint of real objection, still

---
8. Errol R. Iselin, 'Chambers on Accounting Theory', *The Accounting Review*, April 1968, pp. 231-8, at p. 233.

found 'the case for selling price quite unconvincing' (p. 211). He was in favour of 'qualified' replacement price. Benston said that the measurement of assets and the derivation of income by reference to contemporary prices 'differs from the present value approach favored by most economists' (p. 298). Staubus put up an extensive defence of the use of discounted values as a counter to my proposals.[9] Solomons said that in his view 'it is "value to the owner" that is relevant'.[10] I am not sure what this phrase 'value to the owner' means exactly. Baxter (p. 212) attributes it to Bonbright; both Baxter and Solomons, following Bonbright, suggest that value to the owner has the limiting values, replacement price and selling price. This does not give us a clear warrant for supposing that value to the owner is the discounted value of expected net proceeds, favoured by 'most economists' (Benston) and Staubus. But Baxter said 'the present value of the asset's future net contribution should be used when it is lower than replacement price (p. 212); so we will presume that value to the owner is the net present value for purpose of our later analysis. Wright contended that 'resale price measures capacity for adaptation if existing activities are to be contracted, whereas replacement cost measures capacity for adaptation if existing activities are to be expanded' (p. 78); otherwise his views on the 'relation' between resale price, replacement price and value to the owner are substantially the same as those of Baxter and Solomons. Dein contended: 'The proposed statement of financial position seems to emphasize for the continuing entity approximately the dimension which the statement of affairs emphasizes for the financially embarrassed entity'. As for contemporary financial information, he said, 'a cash projection schedule extending several years into the future' would be more informative than the proposed balance sheet. He himself is content with accounting as it now is.[11]

How does one come to grips with the criticisms of so many who among themselves are champions of quite different proposals? I will try — by indicating the general drift of *Accounting, Evaluation and Economic Behavior* and by treating generically the objections.

In the book I tried to set out all the kinds of figures which would be usable in any judgement, on financial grounds, of past actions or future possibilities. I indicated the necessity of calculating net present values for *prospective* projects.[12] I indicated that the purchase price of a new asset (whether or not it was a 'replacement' of an old asset) was necessary information in the calculation of net present values. I indicated that resale prices of assets were necessary information in the calculation of the net present values of prospective projects. I indicated that resale prices were necessary to the determination of any present position and hence to the assessment of past performance and to the estimation of the better-

---

9. George J. Staubus, 'Current Cash Equivalent for Assets: A Dissent', *The Accounting Review*, October 1967, pp. 650-61.
10. David Solomons, review in *Abacus*, December 1966, pp. 205-9, at p. 208.
11. Raymond C. Dein, review in *The Journal of Accountancy*, October 1966, pp. 89-90.
12. For a subsequent and different statement of the case, see my reply to Staubus: 'Measures and Values', *The Accounting Review*, April 1968, pp. 239-47.

ment to be expected from any future action. It should be noticed that my analysis of the range of specific calculations and assessments included specific uses of all the kinds of information (present values, replacement prices, and resale prices) the need for which has been the justification of systems other than my own. I rejected present values and replacement prices as bases for the preparation of factual financial statements, on the grounds (a) that they are both transient or ephemeral in character and are ascertainable directly at any time, and (b) that they do not in any case yield an indication of the present state of the financial affairs of a firm at any time — information which is necessary to every retrospective and prospective judgement.

As for the criticisms, consider first the idea of the value of an asset to a firm. We must consider Solomons' reference to 'value to the owner', cited above, as meaning value to the firm, since we are dealing with representations of assets in the accounts of firms. If the value of an asset to a firm means the net present value or discounted value of the expected proceeds *of an asset*, the term can only be used of assets which yield identifiable incomes without the aid of other assets or inputs. There are some assets of this kind; but they can be few only, for even the occasional attention which must be given to such things as leased property or security holdings entails that the *net* proceeds is not a figure independent of the net proceeds of other activities. In the typical case revenues arise from the use of assets in combination. In this case it is not possible to assign a significant net present value to each of the assets used in combination.

Usually, of course, net present values are calculated for *projects* which require the use in combination of plant, inventories and labour-service. But even in this case the net present value of a project must be considered in an incremental sense; it is the present value of a project to be undertaken given the existing state of the firm. It is contingent on that state. It follows that the present value of any project cannot be related to anything else than the present value of an alternative project given the same state of the firm. It also follows that to obtain the values of all the projects of the firm, each would have to be considered as if the firm were a different firm. Thus, to obtain the present value of project J of a firm whose projects are J, K, L, M, N, PV_J would have to be obtained by recourse to assumptions about the firm in the absence of J: similarly for each of the other projects. The interdependences of the variables stand in the way of making any unequivocal statement about any asset.

Yet it is demonstrable that some firm indication of the present financial characteristics of particular assets or classes of asset is of interest and use to firms, their managers and their creditors. Specific assets can be, and are, mortgaged or pledged. A charge may be given over a class of assets or a collection of assets, never over a project (unless it corresponds with an identified collection of assets). Some asset values enter directly into calculations made to indicate drifts in efficiency. It is difficult to imagine what meaning could be assigned to a receivables turnover, inventory turnover or working capital turnover rate, in which the numerators were present values of the relevant assets. No proponent of the use of present values has suggested what tests may be applied, when attempting to assess drifts in efficiency, if present value figures alone were available for analysis. The long-established practice of accounting for assets in terms other than their values to the firm is not lacking in claims to legitimacy.

But suppose we could calculate the net present values of assets. What of the assertions of Baxter, Bonbright, Solomons, and Wright to the effect that this value has as its limiting magnitudes resale price and replacement price, assuming rational behaviour. We may consider four possible combinations of the magnitudes.

Let A be the asset now held. Let B be the best alternative use of the proceeds of A; B may be a replacement of A, or an entirely different asset, or either of the former plus the investment of the surplus cash (if any) at interest or in an additional asset. Let PV_A be the present value of holding A; and PV_B the present value of the course of action B, i.e., the present value of investing $800 in B.

	Resale price A	Replacement price A	PV_A	Indicated action
(a)	$800	$1,000	$1,200	Invest in B if $PV_B > \$1,200$
(b)	$800	$1,000	$ 900	Invest in B if $PV_B > \$ 900$.
(c)	$800	$ 600	$1,000	Course B should already have been taken.
(d)	$800	$ 600	$ 750	

Note first, that it may be said that cases (c) and (d) are not feasible, assuming rational behaviour. There is, however, a difference between rational behaviour and rational *and informed* behaviour. If resale prices are not somehow kept under observation, it is quite possible for cases (c) and (d) to occur.

In cases (a) and (c) the present value of A exceeds both the resale price and the replacement price of A. These are quite feasible situations. But they are certainly not covered by the view that these two prices are outside limits to the value of A to the firm. In cases (b) and (d), the present value of A falls between the resale price and the replacement price of A. But in case (b), if the asset A were shown as $900 (i.e., PV_A), or as $1,000 (replacement price of A) these figures would be of no use in deciding whether B was a possible alternative (i.e., whether $800 would be available to invest in B) and hence, also, no use in discovering what PV_B is; for both depend on knowledge of the resale price of A. And in case (d), if the asset A were shown as $750 (i.e., PV_A) or as $600 (replacement price of A), neither of these figures would be of use in deciding the feasibility of alternatives.

In respect of cases (c) and (d) where resale price exceeds replacement price, it should be remembered that the replacement of A is only one of the forms course B can take. To discover which form B should take, it is necessary to know how much is available (i.e., $800), not only the replacement price of A; for some other course than the replacement of A could have a greater present value.

Now consider Wright's contention that the use of resale prices represents 'capacity for adaptation if existing activities are to be contracted' (p. 78). It will be noticed that we made no reference whatever, in the cases used above, to contraction or expansion. The criterion of choice between holding an asset and doing other things (including replacing the asset) is simply which has the greatest present value (other considerations being equal). If a firm knows its position on a resale price basis it knows approximately what cash it can lay its hands on; and that is one of the facts which determine whether a firm can expand or must contract.

The constancy with which the resale price of A occurs in the discussion of the example indicates its necessity and the variety of its uses. Replacement prices and new goods prices and present values are used in all such choice-making deliberations; but the one thing to which all are tied is the resale price of the present asset. This is a different and more extensive role than Solomons' description of it — 'an occasional surrogate' for replacement cost (p. 208) — suggests.

We take up, next, an objection raised by Baxter, Solomons, and Benston. Suppose an asset is bought which immediately has a low or zero resale price to the firm. Said Solomons: 'The use of resale prices in this situation leads to what I can only regard as an absurdity and a flagrant failure to measure up to the criterion of correspondence with the economic events which are being recorded' (p. 208).

Suppose a firm buys a specialized asset A for $10,000, the present value of its expected net proceeds being $20,000. The purchase for $10,000, an economic event, will be recorded. If the resale price to the firm becomes zero immediately, that too is an economic event. The loss of the firm's adaptive capacity is an economic event for the firm. To record it is to measure up fully to the criterion of correspondence with events which occurred. But we need to follow through the example to see whether it produces absurdities.

Suppose the firm's net trading income for the first year is $5,000. Its balance sheet at the end of the year would appear thus:

Asset A (cost $10,000)	0	Owners' equity 1 January	10,000
Cash	5,000	Less investment in non-vendible asset	10,000
			0
		Plus net trading income	5,000
	$5,000		$5,000

The mere fact that the resale price of A is zero has no necessary effect on the firm's income expectations. For the firm could have anticipated that the asset would have no resale price. Or, if its sale was estimated to be at some distance, the expected proceeds would have only a slight effect on the present value calculation; for the discount rate on such a specialized asset would tend to be high. We may suppose that the only factor affecting income expectations at the end of the first year is that $5,000 of the originally expected income has already been yielded.

The way in which the firm's affairs are reported puts investors on notice of several things. First, it indicates that the firm has a high rate of return on the sum of money it can invest in any alternative; an infinite rate of return even if the net income is only $1, for the sum it could invest (apart from retained income) is zero. Second, it indicates that the firm has no means of securing a continuing income, if the asset becomes exhausted or obsolete, other than by retaining and reinvesting some of the cash generated each year. If the asset were shown at cost less amortization, investors would be entitled to suppose that the asset (by association in the balance sheet with other money-like assets) is salable and that continuity of the firm's income may be secured otherwise than by retaining profits. Third, it indicates that the firm has no property-base for borrowing, though it might be able to borrow on the strength of its expected earnings. If the asset were shown at cost less amortization, there would seem to be a property-base for borrowing when in fact there is not. Fourth, it indicates that the firm's original cash is now locked in. Investors will be prepared to pay less for a share in this firm than in other firms having salable assets and the same income expectations, because of this lack of asset-coverage. Whatever they pay they will know they are paying for *their* share in the firm's income prospects only.

I have used an extreme example, stripped of complexity. It may be worth pointing out that, by appropriate arrangement, all the background information given in the balance sheet for the first year could be carried into the balance sheet of a subsequent year. It may be objected that the immediate depreciation charge of $10,000 should be shown as a charge in the income account, resulting in a net loss of $5,000. But the manner in which it has been represented is logically identical and informationally superior in the extreme circumstance I have chosen. There can surely be no grounds for refusing to show an unusual event in an explicit if unusual manner.

In short, the mode of reporting is not unrealistic, though it may seem odd when we have long been accustomed to something else. It is certainly not 'absurd'. It discloses some things which conventional balance sheets do not disclose, things which are pertinent to investors. It enables investors to distinguish between this firm and other firms having the same income prospects but salable assets also. It does represent the firm's financial position, and it does represent its capacity for adaptation.

It is difficult to forbear quoting observations which are intended to be critical but which merely strengthen my case. Solomons observed: 'The failure to recognize that the owner of an asset which is not for sale does not directly suffer if its resale price drops, unless this change is associated with some change in his expectations (as indeed it may be, indirectly, or in the long run) must be regarded as a serious flaw in Chambers' theory' (p. 208). If we recognize what Solomons said I failed to recognize, there is no reason to be squeamish about accounting for the drop. That I proposed to account for it indicates that I did recognize the point, and on Solomons' own grounds my treatment has strength rather than a serious flaw. My treatment also covers the proviso which begins with 'unless . . .' in the sentence cited. The firm owning the asset does suffer indirectly (as does every firm whose assets fall in resale price), in the sense that its adaptability and its property-base for borrowing are reduced. (No automobile buyer is thought to be foolish when he pays $3,000 for a car which, immediately on leaving the showroom, has a cash value of, say, $2,700. But it would be foolish to assert that nothing had happened to the buyer's financial position in the same circumstances.) What is more to the point, however, is that unless *investors* in the firm know of the drop in resale price they do not know of these indirect effects on the firm, and can take no account of them in forming or revising *their* expectations. To hold back information which does no direct harm to the firm, but which would have an effect on the expectations of rational investors, is to fail to represent material facts, to fail in disclosure. No mention of the investor's calculations, reflections and choices is made by Solomons, Baxter or Benston, except perhaps in an oblique or vague way.

Current cash equivalent

I introduced this phrase as a generalization which would cover all assets. It would be curious to speak of the resale price of cash; and also, as I contemplated ways of approximating resale price, some general term seemed to be necessary. I do not believe that my exposition made it perfectly clear what I intended; and I know there are several points at which I would now like to make amendments. But what I intended was, I hope, reasonably clear from much of the detail of my argument.

We speak quite generally of *financial* statements and *financial* position. I suspect we often use the adjective loosely. Finance means money, cash or its substitutes. 'Financial' has therefore to do with money. It seems reasonable that a financial statement should deal with money and the equivalents in terms of money of claims and other assets and of obligations. The money equivalent of anything is its price. Things which have no money equivalent, no price, have no present financial characteristic.

When speaking of the money or cash equivalent of assets I did not mean what I or you *expect* or a firm *expects* or hopes to get. What we expect or hope an asset will yield, by use or by sale, is not a characteristic of the asset. What we expect or hope is a characteristic of ourselves. We are entitled to expect or hope what we please. But in any form of calculating which we hope will inform us of our present capacity for action, we would be naïve to suppose that others will concur with the prices we put on things unless there is some evidence to the effect that they do concur. This evidence is the fact that, at any given date, transactions occur or have recently occurred at stated prices. In setting down assets at these selling prices, it is not assumed that the goods on hand will in fact be sold at those prices.[13] Selling those goods is something which will be done after the balancing date. We make no assumptions about what will be done after that date, because

---

13. The point is made more fully in 'Continuously Contemporary Accounting — Additivity and Action', *The Accounting Review*, October 1967, pp. 751-7.

one of the premises of what we then decide to do is the state of affairs as we find it at balancing date. We are simply using the prices quoted in the market as the indicators of present cash equivalents.

The phrase has been interpreted by some as indicating what is expected to be received in cash. And I think there are some points at which vagueness or a poor choice of words on my part contributed to this interpretation. But as early as Chapter 4 of the book it is made clear that the quoted market price is what is intended. One may of course entertain expectations of receiving a market price; but the crucial point for our purpose is not the expectations we entertain but the existence of a market price. If the resale price of a good I hold is $100, that is the cash equivalent of the good, regardless of its price in the future and regardless of whether I sell in the near or distant future.

I may have confused the matter somewhat by reference to the discounting of payables on p. 107 and by the implication of my recourse to the authority of Sprouse and Moonitz on p. 196 for abandoning discounting for 'roughly' matched short-term receivables and payables. These are mistakes, due, I imagine, to my difficulties in weaving my way among so many conflicting ideas. Discounting has a place in present value calculations. But it has no place in my notion of a dated financial position. The matter may also have been confused by my treatment of bonds as obligations. For bonds held as assets I suggested market prices; but for bonds as liabilities I suggested their face value. Hendriksen questioned the differential treatment (p. 213). My defence is simply that, at a given time, the issuer owes the bondholders the contractual amount of the bonds, whatever the price at which the bonds are traded.

The contractual amount of a bond at any time may be more or less than the face value, by virtue of redemption provisions in the bond indenture. It can readily be calculated from those provisions. But even if the market price is materially different from this contractual amount, the latter is the relevant figure for assessment of a present financial position. In recent years, in some countries, certain outstanding bond issues have sold at discounts as high as fifty per cent of face value. Suppose that a company has $10,000 in assets, and an outstanding bond the contractual amount of which is $5,000: and suppose that the bond is selling at 60. Certainly no creditor would accept the notion that he was holding a $60 bond if its contractual amount were $100. As long as the company's affairs are reasonably secure, the bond price is a function of the coupon rate and the current market rate of interest. It has nothing to do directly with the equity of bondholders and others in the assets of the company. It is the quite separate function of the balance sheet to show just this.

The position is perhaps analogous to that of stockholders. The equity of stockholders in the assets of a firm is not given by the prices at which the stock is traded. I suppose that in any calculation of the leverage of a firm, the face value of liabilities would be used rather than their market value; and that in any calculation for re-funding or liquidating the loan, the face value would be used in ignorance of the bondholders' reaction to the proposal. In short, equities are not just negative assets, and there is no reason that I can yet see why the same general rule should apply to both assets and equities. The current cash equivalent of the assets or any set of assets can be meaningfully set off against an amount now owing, no matter when the amount now owing has to be paid; this possibility is a significant feature of the utility of figures available for use in financial calculations.

The additivity of current cash equivalents has been called in question by Benston (p. 299) and by Larson and Schattke.[14] Both, however, confuse the notion of additivity of numbers of monetary units assigned to assets with the question of the way in which a seller may combine or group assets in any given sale. The additivity of such numbers subsists in the similarity of what they designate, not in their magnitudes. Numbers of monetary units designating the same kinds of prices in monetary units of the same kind are additive. In what groupings assets will, in fact, be sold, is dependent on the proceeds expected at the time and in the circumstances in which they are offered. As I hold that knowledge of financial position is one of these circumstances, it would be circular reasoning to assume any particular grouping for the purpose of finding out the position which will, in part, influence the grouping at the time of sale.[15] I would be satisfied to consider the prices of assets in the quantities, parcels or combinations in which the firm customarily sells or offers them for sale. If we are concerned with the production of figures which may be embodied in a variety of distinctive calculations, what we seek is their most probable values; or perhaps the values which depend on the fewest *ad hoc* stipulations. It seems to be incontestable that the quantities, parcels and combinations within the usual and ordinary experience of the firm best meet this test.

Refer now to Dein's remark on the utility of a cash projection schedule. Whatever uses a cash projection schedule may have, its preparation entails the use of resale prices — for inventories; for such other assets as may be intended to be sold in the period covered; and, in the event that borrowing is necessary, for such assets as may be pledged as security, and that means potentially any and all assets. Instead of being an argument against the continuous availability of information based on resale prices, the cash budgeting suggestion of Dein and others is a strong argument in favour. Further, it would be useless to offer a cash projection schedule which was inconsistent with the figures appearing in a balance sheet which purports to represent the position at the date from which the cash projection schedule proceeds. No reader of the two could form a legitimate view of the consequences of the projected cash movements from two statements prepared on inconsistent bases.

One final comment on the relation between the present and the future. Wright alleged that my difficulties arose from my assertion that 'accounting is not con-

---

14. Kermit Larson and R. W. Schattke, 'Current Cash Equivalent, Additivity and Financial Action', *The Accounting Review*, October 1966, pp. 634-41.
15. This objection was answered more fully in the article referred to in footnote 13.

cerned with the future'. In pointing out at the same time that I *do* make some assumptions about the future (the firm has at least some future; adaptation itself is future) he implies inconsistency in my premises (p. 77). The juxtaposition of such statements is a caricature. What I held was that *in the derivation of figures* descriptive of a present position no account can be taken of the future. It should be obvious that we always estimate the future from the present, never the other way round. Even in present value calculations we must estimate the future from a known present if the result is to be informative. It is only in that sense that accounting is not concerned with the future. If assumptions are made about the future in deriving a representation of the present, the result will be the same vicious circularity we mentioned when dealing with the grouping of assets for sale. The same objection may be taken to Baxter's observation: 'so long as all is going well, sale price has little relevance' (p. 212). We are required to suppose that all is going well, when we are preparing statements to show whether or not all is going well!

Second thoughts

What then are my second thoughts? In a number of respects the criticisms have, in fact, provided occasion for additional arguments in favour of my main argument. And a number of other things have made me more confident than I was six or seven years ago of the feasibility of adhering to the resale price principle in practice.

The accessibility of resale prices At the time of writing I was aware that newspapers and trade periodicals carried classified advertisements from which some idea of contemporary prices could be obtained for a wide range of industrial goods. I knew that in the second-hand motor vehicle business and in the wholesale grocery business there were, in Australia, trade publications giving extensive lists of prices. I have since been informed by my colleague, R. P. Brooker (now deceased), that there are extensive catalogues of used machinery prices available to the trade in the United Kingdom. A recent Sydney graduate[16] has shown that in the mining industry resale prices of minerals, in partly processed and fully processed states, are available for a wide range of basic mineral products. A graduate student of Michigan State University[17] has drawn attention to the existence of extensive catalogues of used equipment prices in the earthmoving and road-building industry and of used motor vehicles in the United States. And of course any reader of the newspapers and business and trade journals will find prices of other primary products and equipment than those mentioned above. Even if one thinks about it ever so little, one cannot help believing that knowledge of prices of all kinds of things, new and second-hand, must be available to people

---

16. George J. Foster, 'Mining Inventories in a Current Price Accounting System', *Abacus*, December 1969.

17. James C. McKeown, 'An Application of a Current Market Value Accounting Model'. (Unpublished thesis, 1969). McKeown also compares the system, to its advantage, with conventional accounting.

who use particular kinds of assets for particular kinds of operations. Yet we are prone to overlook the extensive service industries (specialists, exchanges, second-hand merchants, trade periodicals) which grow up on the fringe of the main manufacturing and distributive trades.

The necessity of judgement None of these sources will necessarily give *unequivocal* resale prices. But their existence certainly gives assurance that there is extensive evidence on which informed judgement could be exercised with the object of approximating resale prices. There may be some who have supposed that my proposals were so tightly phrased that I excluded the exercise of judgement. The tightness of my specification, however, relates to the principles to be used, not to the identity of the magnitudes derived. I wrote explicitly of approximation, and 'the best possible approximation to cash equivalents'. These very words imply the use of judgement.

The exercise of judgement has long been the trump card of those who favour freedom of choice among the vast array of 'invented' accounting rules. We are asked to suppose that, from this array of rules, all having different effects on the computed profit residual and on the statement of position, the accountant can choose just that set of particular rules which, in a given firm for a given year, will yield a fair representation of results and position. But so great is the range of possibilities that this desired end could only be attained by chance, certainly not by judgement. Indeed all the usual talk of judgement seems rather hollow in the light of the common dependence on *managerial* judgement for many of the figures incorporated in annual statements. How often are we told that the statements are the statements of management!

But when we set up an ideal type of information, and ask that accountants use their best skill and judgement in approximating it, then there is a real opportunity for using judgement. Skill and judgement are demonstrated only when one has to work within limits, or to an ideal. One does not need judgement of a high order to drive a car over an open field. One does when driving under the rules of the road, on a three-lane highway, in the midst of unpredictable traffic.

The inventory problem Now, for the inventory problem which has caused me the greatest consequential trouble. My attempts to suggest a practicable 'second best' when resale prices are not available show that I wished all 'assets' presently represented in balance sheets to have some monetary magnitude (as the main figure in the list of assets, not merely a memorandum figure) under my system. I do not now hold this view, as an earlier illustration in this paper shows.

It is not difficult, I think, to find resale prices for undifferentiated raw materials, (i.e., unprocessed by the present owner). The owner could generally dispose of these materials without substantial loss; but because he occupies a different position from his supplier in the chain of physical distribution, his resale price will generally be lower than his purchase price. Nor is it difficult to assign a selling price to his finished goods in the manner in which they are usually sold, in gross lots, as made up goods, as spare parts, as the case may be. There is, however, a difficulty in dealing with goods in the course of production. For some partly processed goods there are markets from which indications of resale prices in their then condition can be obtained. But for the rest, let them be shown at zero value.

This may seem drastic, but only by reason of our long-standing habits. However, notwithstanding those habits, there must be thousands of machines in daily use across the country which have been written off, or down to a purely nominal value, under existing methods of accounting. No fuss is made about that. Again there are thousands of instances of assets being shown at less than they are expected to produce in cash, now or in the future. No fuss is made about that. But there is the positive argument from my own theory. If, as we claim, the cash equivalents of assets provide the kinds of magnitude which we can presently relate to other financial magnitudes when reflecting on immediate possibilities, then any 'asset' which has no present cash equivalent can properly be shown to have none.

Two other kinds of comfort may be offered. First, there is no reason why the direct cost of work in process which has no resale price should not be shown in parenthesis, without extension.[18] Second, we are prone to think of the effect of any such change in methods on the closing values of assets and on the profits of a single year. But as the closing figures of one year become the opening figures of the next it is unlikely that the aggregate of the profit figures over a number of years would differ materially, from this cause, from the aggregate obtained under many other ways of accounting. We would, however, have the advantage of knowing exactly what those figures represented at any time, and the advantage of a consistent general rule.

Method and product Technical features of my argument and theory aside, there are two general observations with which I might close.

Much of the discussion of alternative accounting methods, and most of the reviews and criticisms of my theory, make scanty use of illustrative examples of the substantive choices of managers and investors. I am convinced that unless we ask 'how could this or that piece of information, or this or that calculated magnitude, be used by an investor or manager in judging or choosing?', we will not find out what is worth producing. That is the way in which I have proceeded in deriving my own conclusions and in the above analysis of some contrary assertions. Unless by this means we can be sure that a specific piece of information has a quite specific place in some thought process in a class of imaginable situations, it is vain to attempt to argue its merits.

Finally, as I have said, the critics have left the main structure of my theory unscarred. None saw fit to comment on the way in which my theory provides a synthesis in which there is a fit and proper place for all the kinds of information which have been said to be needed for informed judgements and choices on financial grounds. There is a place for original prices — at the original point of

---

18. More generally, there is no reason why 'cost' figures could not be shown in parentheses for all assets, with current cash equivalents in the main balance sheet columns — at least until it is generally realized how useless the cost figures are.

purchase. There is a place for replacement prices — not in periodical reporting, but in the course of reflections on future alternatives. There is a place for present values of expected proceeds — again, not in periodical reporting, but in the course of reflections on future alternatives. There is a place for corrections for general price level movements — in the calculation of the capital maintenance adjustment and net income. And there is a place for resale prices — in *every one* of the contexts just mentioned. To fit these various pieces of information together into a coherent system does not require me to deny the utility of any one of them as pieces of information. But any theory which neglects the utility of knowledge of resale prices in all problem contexts leaves out of account the one kind of information which is a necessary premise of all judgements and choices. I should like to know of any other systematic way in which these different kinds of information can be reconciled. Until I hear of any such alternative I have no second thoughts on this, the distinctive characteristic of my theory.

The Commercial Foundations of Accounting Theory

THE LAST DECADE has seen the adequacy of existing methods of accounting, and their products, brought sharply into question. Around the world, commercial events, business failures, and the merger movement have obliged regulatory bodies to give more attention to the financial publicity provisions of the company codes than in any other decade. In the same decade there have been many symposia on accounting theory. Ten years ago we might have hoped that there would have emerged by now some clear and positive line of thought, some conclusions which would warrant the advancement with confidence of improvements in technique. There has been no such result.

Had it been a matter of only ten years, we could perhaps excuse ourselves. But the criticisms of Canning, Sweeney, and Macneal of some thirty to forty years ago have not been met, either in the general body of theory or in practice. I believe this failure to be explicable in terms of the modes of inquiry and exposition which have prevailed and seem to still prevail in accounting. For, first, there is a noticeable reluctance to assign quite definite and limited functions to accounting. Attempts to limit the field of discourse and the function of accounting proper are treated almost with scorn by teachers as well as practitioners. Yet, it was only when naturalists gave up mixing metaphysics with physics, and concentrated on a limited range of phenomena and ideas, that they laid the foundation of modern scientific knowledge. When one has mastered one's own speciality, it is profitable to consider what greater power, knowledge, or service it may in future put within one's grasp. But it is futile to adopt the role of visionary unless one knows how first to get rid of the follies of present doctrine and practice.

Second, almost everyone seems to think he is entitled to an opinion on the subject matter and the nature of accounting theory—an opinion, what is more, which others will respect. This belief may have been fostered by the prominence given to opinion and judgment in statements on practices. However, there can be no more mischievous idea than that the choice of the magnitudes recorded and reported and the choice of rules of processing are matters of opinion. There can be no greater source of disruption and confusion. For if these things are matters of opinion, there can be no solid core of principles, no ascertainable function, no systematic knowledge. It should be well known that it is profitless to debate matters of opinion. But to a considerable extent the literature consists of free-wheeling debate rather than the systematic, intensive, and consciously controlled analysis of present and proposed schemes of accounting.

Reluctance to assign precise and limited functions to accounting and an easy attitude toward the merit of mere opinion have doubtless contributed to the present methodological chaos. There has been relatively little accumulation of factual evidence, or recourse to available factual evidence, in the derivation of basic ideas. There has been much talk of the use of deduction,[1] but there is little evidence of its use. Some have attempted to align thinking about accounting with thinking about "economic matters" in the wider sense of the term. The phenomena under consideration have been described in such general terms that no clear accounting rules can be deduced.[2] Some have felt it impossible to proceed to clear conclusions, protesting ignorance of how people behave in commercial situations.[3] Some, while restricting at-

---

1. E.g., Carl Thomas Devine, "Research Methodology and Accounting Theory Formation," *The Accounting Review* (July 1960); Maurice Moonitz, *The Basic Postulates of Accounting* (New York, 1961), p. 6; Eldon S. Hendriksen, *Accounting Theory* (Homewood, Ill., 1965), chap. 1.

2. The use of such portmanteau terms as communication, measurement, resource, entity, information, environment, *without* any description or analysis of what is meant, is so common that it needs no documentation.

3. E.g., AAA, *A Statement of Basic Accounting Theory* (Evanston, Ill., 1966), p. 69. Perhaps the statement reflects the views of only some of its authors; see

tention to the actions of individuals and firms, have found it impossible to avoid mixing commercial, political, and psychic elements of choice and behavior.[4] And hardly anywhere is there presented evidence, from commercial and financial affairs, of the necessity of the information it is proposed that accounting should produce. In all, the linkage of theory with practical affairs, both at the initial postulational stage and at the final testing stage, is at best tenuous, and at worst missing altogether.

I have chosen to use the words "commercial foundations" in the title of this paper, first, because in my view accounting is concerned strictly with commercial experiences, events, and considerations; second, because to concentrate on specific particulars enables us to follow exactly the same course as others have followed in the pursuit of certain, or highly probable, generalized knowledge. I could as well have used the words "economic foundations" or "empirical foundations." I rejected them, because I wished to leave in no doubt my concern with specific particulars, the consideration of which, alone, can yield grounds for belief and tests of belief in one kind of accounting or another.

Events and Records

Much of the discussion of accounting deals in a general way with commercial affairs, buying, selling, borrowing, lending, and so on. But by far the greater part of it deals with the *records* of commercial affairs. Commercial affairs and the records of commercial affairs are not the same thing. A record is a construction, an artefact. The way it is constructed depends on how we see or understand the matters recorded and on how the matters recorded are subsequently to be seen or understood. A purchase, a sale, simply occurs. It can be recorded in many ways, from the long descriptive paragraphs of the early bookkeepers to the abbreviated symbols of mechanical devices. If it is an isolated event, it is sufficient to describe it as it occurred. But if it is part of an on-going mixed sequence of events, the consequences of which affect later choices and commercial dealing, it must be so em-

---

Norton M. Bedford, "The Nature of Future Accounting Theory," *The Accounting Review* (Jan. 1967); and George H. Sorter, "An 'Events' Approach to Basic Accounting Theory," *The Accounting Review* (Jan. 1969).

4. As witness, the rising occurrence in the literature of references to organizational and individual goals and social ends and values, in wider senses than the commercial or financial sense.

bedded in the record of those events that subsequently the effects of the mixture and the sequence can be seen and understood.

That a record is a construction is emphasized. If I keep a cash book, the balance it shows of cash on hand at any time is not necessarily the amount of cash I have. I and everyone else can make errors and lose money accidentally. The amount of money I have, not the amount in the cash book (unless the amounts are the same), determines what I can buy, and the usefulness to me of any reckoning I make before buying. If I keep a more complex record of cash movements and other movements in the things I buy, use, and sell for my own purposes, I am at liberty to do as I please—on the record. But, as in the case of the cash book, that record will only be indicative of what has happened and what I can now do if it is constructed with that object, and if in fact I have taken care to see that it records *all* the events which have affected my present capacity, and knowledge of which may affect my present judgment in respect of my commercial affairs.

I hope everyone would assent to the propriety of the two conditions mentioned. Whatever my likes and dislikes may be about the manner of keeping records, they cannot be allowed to affect the substance of the record if the product of the record is to help me in the two ways specified. If I choose to disregard any event or class of events which has had a bearing on my present capacity for buying, selling, borrowing, lending, paying debts, and so on, the statement of capacity which I deduce from the record will be inconsistent with my actual capacity. Similarly, if I choose to incorporate in the record any *expected* event or class of events which *may* in the future affect my capacity for commercial action, the deduced statement of capacity at any time will not be consistent with my actual capacity at that time. In both cases, my present judgments about the past and the possibilities of the present and the future will be mistaken if I base them on the statement deduced from the record.

I hope everyone would assent to these two propositions. I mention them because both the exclusion of things that have happened and the inclusion of things that are expected to happen seem to be countenanced by many extant and proposed practices. It is not denied that men may wish to classify past events the better to make judgments about the future. But classifying past events does not mean disregarding the effects of some of them. Nor is it denied that men may wish to speculate about future events, the better to choose which will serve them best. But speculation about the future does not warrant the introduction, into any statement of present capacity, of the substance of those speculations or of any one of them.

It seems highly probable that the confusion of past, present, and future in present and proposed practices has arisen because, in personal affairs, we very seldom have to think very closely about the distinction. We are familiar with our past experiences—at least we think we are. We are familiar with our present state; as individuals we have a rough idea at any time of the commercial worth of what we own. The thing that looms largest in our minds is thinking about what we might do next; how much will it cost us to have that vacation, furnish that room, run that additional car, and so on.

In business affairs, however, the things done are so numerous that only a small proportion of them comes under the notice of managers, and the experience of only that proportion is known to them. And none of them is known to investors and other outsiders. The effects of those and all other things must be brought together in some way which represents the whole experience of the firm. Similarly, the assets and obligations are generally so numerous that an account of them all must be prepared deliberately, if managers and investors are to be familiar with the present state of the firm. Certainly what the firm might do in the future is of consequence, as in the case of individuals thinking of their own affairs. But the discovery of what has occurred and of the resulting present position provides the major factual premises, of a financial kind, for speculation about the future. It cannot be brushed aside as readily as we might brush it aside in our personal affairs because of our own familiarity with those personal affairs. We hold this process of discovery to be the prime function of accounting. If it is not done as well as is possible, judgments about past and future lack that contact with the factual present which alone provides a trustworthy foundation for choice and action.

Commercially Necessary Information

There can be little doubt that the present states of business firms from time to time are of immediate concern to managers, at least in some obvious respects. Knowledge of cash flows, for example, is widely said to be of consequence. Anyone familiar with the care and attention given to cash positions, arrangements with bankers, short-term borrowing and lending, and such matters, by company treasurers and boards of directors, will know that in this respect what the literature says is matched by what is done in commercial practice.

Balances of receivables and payables are closely linked to cash balances. It would be futile to attempt to project cash movements from any point of time without firm knowledge of the cash balances and receivables and payables balances at that point of time. It would be equally futile to attempt to explain the past drift in net monetary balances without firm knowledge of those balances at the moment of the attempt.

For cash resources, firms are not limited to the amounts they can generate by way of revenues. They may pledge assets, singly or in total, as security for cash advances. The immediate security for lenders is the market selling price of the assets pledged. It is often said that the significant value of an asset to a firm is its calculated net present value in its present use. But no lender on the security of the firm's assets is concerned with the value of those assets to the firm in this sense. He is concerned with the value of those assets as generators of cash for himself in the event that he must enforce his claim against the borrower by sale of the charged asset. Furthermore, a borrower in this position will want to know the market prices of his assets in order to be free to make his own choice of arrangements to meet his creditors, so that he is not entirely at their mercy if he is unable to meet his obligations from ready cash.

For confirmation of this view, one may have recourse to bond indentures and similar instruments. Wherever a charge over particular assets or groups of assets is given as security for borrowings, there will be found some provision restricting other borrowing by reference to the amount of the assets of the borrower. Now the term "the amount of the assets" in such an indenture can have only one kind of meaning. The object of the provision is to cover the amount borrowed. This cover is given, not by the book values of assets, however determined, but by the market values of assets. It would be unwarranted to regard "the amount of the assets" as a term of art, having a meaning derived solely from accounting rules, whatever they might be. As we have said, a record is a construction. Unless what it yields is consistent with the real state of affairs, creditors' interests, in financial information for their protection, cannot be served. Nor indeed can the interests of borrowers be served.

There is ample evidence in the history of commerce of the correctness of the point we are making. A very simple and almost everyday instance is the buying of stock on margin. It must be widely known that if the market price of a stock bought on margin falls, the buyer must pay up, put up further security, or be sold out. On a more extensive level, there are many cases in which book values, which seemed to provide adequate cover for secured loans, have been found to be entirely misleading, to the very great cost of creditors.

It may be contended that lenders are accustomed to lend only a certain proportion of the amount of any pledged assets. But the safety margin can only be known to be safe if at any time the market value of pledged assets is known. Further, few firms have only one creditor. If a firm has only one creditor, and that creditor is sufficiently important to the firm to oblige it to disclose the market value of its assets, perhaps it would not matter (at least for the creditor's protection) that its balance sheet did not disclose the market values of its assets. But the typical situation is that a firm has many creditors, some secured, some unsecured. And all are entitled to know whether they may reasonably expect their claims to be met. Private disclosure of market values of assets to a few privileged creditors would not cover this case. Nor would it be possible for stockholders to judge whether or not a firm is approaching the limits of its borrowing power if they are in ignorance of the market prices of assets; yet, for any informed opinion on the prospects of changes in leverage and asset backing, this information is necessary.

Consider now the stockholders of a company. It would be generally agreed that the relative worths of two ventures determine which is to be preferred. Every classroom exercise and every real-life exercise in choosing between alternative investments has somewhere in it a present amount of cash or cash substitutes or cash equivalents. In addition, every such exercise contains particulars of two or more alternative courses of action and their expected financial outcomes. Whatever method of appraisal is used, it is expected that a conclusion will be reached of the kind "Course X is preferable (or preferred) to Course Y" or, in other words, "Course X is worth more than Course Y."

Now suppose that a firm has $10,000 in cash and has two courses of action open to it, X of which the net present value is $12,000, and Y of which the net present value is $11,000. We would not, at the date in question, say that the firm had a greater cash balance than $10,000. Suppose next that the firm has not $10,000 in cash but an asset A which has a resale price of $10,000. And suppose that course X is to sell the asset A and use the proceeds otherwise, and course Y is to continue to use the asset. And suppose the net present values of X and Y are as before. As in the previous case, course X is worth more than course Y.

But it would be just as useless in this case to show the asset A in an amount different from $10,000 as it would be to show the cash in the previous case in an amount different from $10,000.

But suppose the *book value* of the present asset A is $8000 and that is the only information known. If this were taken to be the limit of the financial capacity of the venture, course X could not even be considered. But if it were possible to borrow another $2000 and the borrowing of this was taken into account in assessing course X, the net present value of course X would be loaded with an additional $2000 initial outlay plus the interest charges—all quite improperly, since the (undisclosed) resale price is sufficient to make course X possible.

The example shows several things. First, we need to know the cash we have, or the cash equivalent of the cash and other things we have, if we are to do any calculating in respect of future alternatives. If we do not know this, our choices between alternatives will be mistaken; indeed, some feasible alternatives we may not even consider. And, as every judgment of relative worth is based on present facts and *expected* financial outcomes given the present facts, the only presently verifiable element in the calculations and the only uniformly used component of the calculations is the cash equivalent (or sum of the resale prices) of the assets.

The stockholders and the managers of companies are both faced with problems of the above kind: managers with choices between projects, stockholders with choices between companies (or, more generally still, between companies and other forms of investment). Now stockholders can discover day by day the cash equivalents of their present holdings and alternative stocks. What they need is something to inform their expectations of the financial outcomes of alternative investments on their part. As in the earlier example, it is impossible to form expectations of the performance of companies unless one knows how they are presently placed financially, that is to say, what they own and in what proportions the equities in those assets run to different classes of equity holder. But stockholders cannot be expected to form any idea of the inflows and outflows from the specific operations of the many firms in which they may invest. They can, however, be informed of the effectiveness of the *whole* of the past operations of companies and their managements; they are so informed by the rates at which the equities of residual equity holders have been increased. These, the achieved rates of return of companies, may be modified by actual or prospective investors when forming their expectations, in the light of their views on the expected impact of general or specific trade conditions. The process is exactly analogous to the formation of managerial expectations, even though the calculations are of a less specific kind. But none of these calculations or expectations can be serviceable unless it is based on financial statements expressing positions and results in contemporary, and therefore comparable, terms.[5]

There are, of course, some who hold that, when a set of assets and equities is put together, we have something greater than the sum of the parts. It is implied that the aggregation of the cash equivalents of assets represents, if anything, less than the whole firm. Of course this is true. The whole firm in its concrete manifestation, however, is not what balance sheets represent. They represent in some sense the amount of the investment in assets and the apportionment of that amount among the classes of equity holders. It is true that any given collection of assets may be put together in different ways by different managers of them. But the effect of putting them together and to work in a given way is the net income yielded, year by year. When we know the amounts and composition of the assets and equities of any firm and what it produces (in financial terms) from time to time, we have all that is necessary to describe it and with what effect it has been managed. We can compare these characteristics with like characteristics of any other company, and with any more general form of investment; on the basis of knowledge of the past and present and of *general* expectations of the future, we may formulate specific expectations in respect of future possibilities for as many alternatives as we choose to consider.

In much of the literature the kinds of comparison we have been mentioning seem to be regarded as occasional or unusual. For example, the arguments against uniformity in accounting and the arguments for diversity with specification of the methods used give scant regard to the conditions under which comparison is possible. They are, in this respect, quite at odds with the reflective exercises which are part of judging and choosing. We cannot judge anything without some other past or present thing in mind. We do not choose unless we have at least two possible things in mind. Far from being unusual, comparison is of the essence in judging and choosing. And judging and choosing are potentially everyday exercises. But we cannot judge, choose, or compare commercial propositions in terms of all their specific differences by reference only to financial statements. We use financial statements

---

5. The argument is presented in more elaborate form in "Measures and Values," *The Accounting Review* (Apr. 1968).

to inform us only of financial elements of judgments and choices. However, in respect to their commercial outcomes, whatever specific nonfinancial elements we may want to consider, we cannot judge or choose unless we can reduce all the financial facts to common order—equally up-to-date and equally inclusive of the effects of past decisions and of the impact of past events of the nondecided kind.

It is vain to pretend that the prices of things have not risen when in fact they have. It is vain to contend that these changes are immaterial and that their consequences should be omitted from accounts. It is vain to pretend that the purchasing power of money has not risen or fallen when in fact it has. It is vain to expect managers or outsiders to be able to take cognizance, in their reflections, of the specific effects of these changes on particular firms and their results. For it is quite possible that, for any common class of assets, the prices of the holdings of one company may move at a different rate from, and even in opposite direction to, the prices of the holdings of another company. And it is quite possible that the different asset compositions of two companies will expose them quite differently to the effects of changes in the purchasing power of money.

It is also vain to attempt to exclude or separately to identify the effects of these different kinds of change. It is widely said that some of these effects are controllable, or at least are subject to managerial choice, while others are not. In simple thought experiments it is possible to isolate all kinds of possible variation. But in the complex of commercial operations of any firm, any kind of variation is intimately associated with other kinds. And few are strictly controllable. If the C company sold $1 million worth of goods in one year and planned to sell the same in the next year, and yet only half of its customers placed orders in the next year, it cannot be said that sales were, in any worthwhile sense, controllable by its managers. The risks of business are that fashions will change, wants will change, techniques will change, personnel will change, prices will change, the purchasing power of money will change. It is unrealistic to suppose that managers can cope with, make provision against, or respond to some of these changes and not others. And there are so many ways in which they can respond that the only safe way to treat the effects of these changes is to capture them all as well as is possible.[6]

6. Arguments against the separate identification of elements of the increment in residual equity are given at several points in *Accounting, Evaluation, and Economic Behavior*, pp. 118–19, 226–27, 236–37.

It seems unnecessary to illustrate further the particular ways in which present knowledge bears on judgments of the past and expectations of the future. The present is the link between past and future. Present financial position is the link between past events and future events. If it is not known, we cannot knowledgeably review the past or plan for the future. The past and present are in principle knowable and unalterable; the future is not knowable, but we can guess, calculate, and plan its shape if we know what the past has yielded and how we stand presently. These distinctions between past, present, and future have been the basis of much of my own work. I can readily admit the necessity of future calculations; but I cannot see how those calculations can be made or, if made, can be worthwhile without the fullest possible knowledge of the present financial state of a firm and the fullest possible account of its past.

175

Some Contrasts

The method of analysis we have illustrated proceeds from particular kinds of problem situations to which any person or firm may be exposed. It may well be asked in what way this method differs from the methods of others who have advanced proposals different from our own. The difference lies in the particularity with which we examined the situations we described and with which we could have examined other such problem situations. Lest it be supposed that this is not a material difference in method, it will be instructive to look at the methods used in developing some other proposed bodies of principles. It will be found that, in general, the authors of these proposals do not go back to the specific commercial settings in which financial information is used; their method is to expound or to reformulate ideas which are held or debated *among accountants*. It is as if the proof of the pudding were in the mixing, not in the eating.

Moonitz' study *The Basic Postulates of Accounting*, as indeed other studies to be mentioned, has a specific professional and temporal setting. It will be recalled that the work of the reconstituted Research Division of the AICPA was viewed as a potential corrective of the piecemeal examination of professional problems over the previous two decades. The antecedent research bulletins addressed themselves to accounting technicalities, however, not to the utility of the resulting information. The connections between information and its use were never established. Had they been established, it would perhaps have been sufficient, in the postulates study, to deal with the users and uses of accounting information in summary fashion and to pass on to the terms of art, which are at least one stage removed from commercial calculation and dealing. The Moonitz study concerns itself principally with these terms of art—the particular constructs and language forms common in debates among accountants. There will not be found in the study any illustration of the precise way in which accounting information enters into the processes of choice or judgment, although examples of certain kinds of decision are named (e.g., pp. 28–29) and decision-making is elsewhere referred to in less specific terms (e.g., p. 27).

We are not here concerned with the merits of the discussion in the study of such terms of art as "assets," "entities," "accounting periods," "going concerns," and so on. We are simply pointing out that, in the absence of proven connections between choices and certain antecedent financial information, the discussion of higher-level abstractions is premature. We choose only one example of the effect of the absence of explicit and admitted connection. We are told that, "without statements of position we have no starting point, no end, no check points to verify our measures of change" (p. 16). Then later: "For the most part, accounting data rely on *past* prices, but not entirely. Pressures have been building up in recent years for more use of future, and hence estimated, events and prices in order to make accounting reports 'more useful' "; it is suggested that nothing "stands in the way of such a development" (p. 29). The two stated views are, of course, inconsistent. Analysis of the particular elements of any financial or quasi-financial problem would have suggested that complete *information* on past events and present position and future *estimates* based on present position are *both* essential in choosing and that the mixing of past and future, of events and expectations, in reports of one kind (as the second quoted passage suggests), cannot serve to inform choices.

The Illinois study, *A Statement of Basic Accounting Postulates and Principles*, makes no direct reference to specific uses or users of accounting information. There are, of course, references to stewardship (pp. 2, 3), to "maximization of the benefits of resource utilization" (pp. 2, 3), to "decisions to be made by the various interests in an enterprise" (p. 3), and to serving "the needs of a variety of interests . . . whose needs vary" (p. 15). Notice that the components of all these phrases are abstractions, or constructs. None refers to such specific details as concern any person or persons engaged in trade or persons having to consider the merits of alternative courses of action. The whole discourse is lifted away from the context of the marketplace. We do not claim that discourse in general terms or by recourse to constructs is improper. We do claim, however, that in the absence of examples of the particular uses of the information generated by any process we are given no ground for supposing that one kind of accounting is any better than any other; what is more to the point, we have no ground for supposing that any particular kind of accounting is of any use at all.

True, the statement has a section on transactions. But nowhere are we given the anatomy or mechanics of the reflective process which precedes transactions, nor of the parts played by various kinds of financial magnitude and calculation in that process. True, we are told that "accounting fulfils a social need by reporting data which provide a basis for evaluating the success with which enterprise management has utilized the scarce resources entrusted to it" (p. 32). But nowhere are we given a single illustration of an evaluative device used by society or by individuals.

The AAA statement, ASOBAT, is much more specific in dealing with the actual or potential users of accounting information than the Moonitz study and the Illinois statement. There are statements of the kinds of decision which are made by named classes of parties—investors, suppliers, creditors, employees, and others (p. 21). But nowhere is there a suggestion of the ways in which particular pieces of financial information enter into those decisions and choices. We are told specifically that information on earnings, financial position, and liquidity is necessary (pp. 23–25). But we are treated to no discussion of the variant meanings of these terms and no particular definition or analysis of any one of them. Indeed, most of the discussion is devoted to the prediction of future earnings, positions, and cash-flows without any ostensible connection between specific present knowledge and specific estimations or predictions.

There are occasional pieces of evidence or occasional dicta which may be taken as indicating the futility of some kinds of accounting. Thus historical cost accounting is said to lead to undervaluation of assets and overstatement of earnings following inflation (p. 28). It is alleged that accounting on the basis of "current values (however defined) fails to satisfy a number of [unspecified] uses" (p. 30). But there is no illustration of the ways in which the alleged defects would distort judgments or estimates in any specified commercial circumstance.

Perhaps our request for definition and specific illustration will be considered pedantic. But we may very well believe that to define and illustrate would be much too uncomfortable a task when the authors were committed to the parallel reporting of positions and results on *two* bases. Their conclusion inevitably means that earnings, working capital, net assets, owners' equity, rate of return, leverage ratio, and other such aggregates and relations can have two different magnitudes at the same time. But analysis of the particular uses which can be made of these magnitudes in commercial reckoning would show that their components could ideally be of one kind only.

As in other cases, the discussion is removed entirely from contact with the commercial choices which, because there is no other source of information of the same kind, accounting might be expected to inform. The greater part of the statement employs terms and phrases which relate to debates among accountants and notions peculiar to accountants. It does not come down to the level of the city's haggling, choosing, and economizing. Its propositions are not, therefore, based on explicit inferences from observables, and its conclusions are not submitted to the test of usefulness in identified problem-contexts.

Time and space prevent us from dealing here with other recent theoretical works and the textbooks which purport to deal with accounting as an aid to decision-making. Generally, their style is the same as the examples noticed above. Allusions to particular situations in which factual and hypothetical financial magnitudes and relationships are used are missing. There is no discussion of the commercial significance of asset-backing, achieved ratio of return, debt to equity ratios, indicators of liquidity—which among them embrace all the figures which appear in periodical financial statements. The reader is left to suppose that these things are of no account (a conclusion flatly contradicted by the literature and practice of security analysis); that, if they are of importance, the necessary figures must be obtained otherwise than from accounting statements (yet no indication is given in the literature of any systematic alternative source); or that the specific magnitudes of these indicators may be used without regard for the effects of the different accounting rules used by any firm, or as between firms, on the component elements of the indicators (which is patently false).

In the absence of this analysis, there is no foundation for conclusions by way of deductive inference. The occasional allusions to deduction, as a method of reaching conclusions, are generally pointless, for seldom are they followed by explicit application of the deductive process to any set of premises for the reaching of any stated conclusion; where a line of deductive argument *is* begun, it is dropped in mid-course, and attention is switched to more palatable assertions.[7]

Finally, there is no attempt to indicate how the magnitudes derivable by any proposed accounting process would eliminate specified defects of alternative processes or would positively advance the capacity for informed judgment of users of accounting statements. Seldom are there references to reported failures, misdemeanors, or disputes as evidence of the propriety or impropriety of any process or conception. The world of commerce is just disregarded, instead of being regarded as the laboratory in which proposals and theories are refined and put under test. It seems unlikely that progress will be made as long as accountants are content to find shelter under the idea that magnitudes and methods are matters of opinion and are content to disregard the confusion which stems from the coexistence of materially different conceptions of what matters in daily commercial experience.

An Analogy

The kinds of exercise we have described in the previous section arise from the belief that what accountants do provides the empirical foundation of principles and theories.[8] Given this belief, it is easy to understand the consequential belief that to proceed from observable practices to principles is to follow the same steps as other sciences follow. We hold that this is a mistaken view.

We may use an analogy from, say, chemistry. If we watch closely the things which a chemist does in a laboratory, we can report every step he takes. We can collect descriptions of what many chemists do—put measured quantities of solids and fluids of certain kinds into test tubes and retorts; observe their interaction in atmospheric air or under exposure to heat, and so on; and weigh or otherwise measure the products. None of these observations, however, would provide any knowledge at all of the laws, principles, or theories of chemistry. We could say it is generally accepted practice among chemists always to use clean instruments or containers, always to weigh or measure inputs

---

7. Examples are the switch in treatment between the first half and the second half of Canning's *The Economics of Accountancy*; the switch from exit prices, after making a strong case for their use, by Edwards and Bell (*The Theory and Measurement of Business Income*); and the switch from dual values to a single value in Ijiri's *The Foundations of Accounting Measurement*.

8. This belief is at least implicit in all attempts to provide a rationalization for existing practices.

and outputs in particular ways, and always to write down or otherwise record what they have done. But all this describes only the overt and superficial elements of what chemists do. Chemical knowledge subsists in statements of the ways in which chemical substances can be related to one another or mixed with one another, and with what effects. The routines of chemists are intended to insure that they do not draw false inferences from the reactions and other events they bring about and observe. But they are not the empirical foundations of chemical knowledge.

It is exactly the same in accounting. Knowledge of financial calculation subsists in statements of the ways in which specific kinds of financial magnitudes can be related to one another or mixed with one another, and with what effects. If we know the effects we wish to bring about—magnitudes which will inform others of what has happened, of how firms stand in financial relation to the rest of the community, of the present capacity for varied but unspecified actions at any time—we can devise routines which will bring about just those effects. The empirical foundations of accounting knowledge lie in the kinds of financial magnitudes which men find it necessary and reasonable to relate, add, subtract, and compare if certain kinds of judgments are to be made or certain kinds of conclusions are to be drawn in respect of commercial or financial matters. They do not lie in the kinds of practices accountants have become accustomed to following.

There seem to be grounds for supposing that the widely held dictum, that different kinds of information are necessary for different kinds of decision, also has its roots in the variant practices of accountants rather than in close examination of reflective processes. We may use another analogy. The properties of common salt are numerous. Its components are sodium and chlorine in a fixed proportion; its specific gravity is given by a fixed number; its molecular weight is a fixed number; its solubility is known; and the ways in which it combines with other chemicals are known. Any given user of sodium chloride in a chemical process may make use of knowledge of these properties in any combination, depending on what process he is concerned with and what he intends to produce. But it would be futile to expect to produce what he intends if specific gravity, molecular weight, solubility, and so on did not have unequivocal values.

It is exactly the same in the case of the financial properties of firms. If we know (1) the financial position of a firm at a given time, (2) the composition of its assets and equities, (3) the net income it has recently earned, we can put these pieces of information together in any way which is relevant to the kind of choice or judgment we may wish to make. If we happen to be investors, we can relate these magnitudes or any pertinent combination of them to their counterparts for other firms and other forms of investment and to the prices of other securities and investments, which we can discover independently of financial statements. But only if they are unequivocal magnitudes. If we happen to be managers, we can relate these magnitudes or any pertinent combination of them to the counterparts mentioned and to the prices of any other potential assets which we can discover, at any time, independently of the accounting process.

What is necessary for different kinds of decision is not, therefore, different kinds of information, but different combinations of the components of a body of information of the same kind. Investors as a class are not solely concerned with the magnitude of a year's income; some are concerned with the magnitude of net assets, some with the relationship between assets and equities. As the composition of some will change in the light of the firm's performance and external commercial events, it is necessary to provide the kind of information which is usable by all. Similarly creditors and financiers as a class are not concerned solely with asset coverage; some, at times, are concerned with net income and its components—but not a *different* net income or one calculated on different principles from the net income which is of interest to stockholders. Managers as a class are not solely concerned with any particular financial property of a firm, but with them all—and with such quantified expressions of those properties as will serve them in as many possible problem contexts as possible.

As we have said, we will not find the empirical foundations of accounting in the variant practices and conceptions of accountants. They will be found only from the widest survey of the potential uses of financial information in commercial reckoning and from the attempt to find just that kind of information which is commonly usable by all parties to commercial and financial dealings.

Conclusion

To devise and subsequently to test theories by reference to the phenomena they deal with is the normal and accepted course of all empirical science. We have aimed to illustrate the same processes in this paper. The phenomena in question are statements about the effects of particular transactions and other events which bear on the financial positions and results of firms. The questions at issue are: "What kinds of particular and aggregate statements are usable and necessary in the specific contexts of specific problem situations?" and "Of those kinds, which are worthwhile continuously recording and periodically reporting because they are parts of the ongoing history of the financial affairs of firms?"

We considered a number of typical problem situations which indicate that contemporary resale prices are pertinent to judgments of past results and choices based on present potentials at any time. We found no use or need for book-values which are inconsistent with market prices. We concluded that representations of the effects on a given firm of all its transactions, and of all changes in the prices of its assets, and of changes in the purchasing power of money, are necessary if those without immediate knowledge of acquaintance are not to be misinformed.

The types of transaction and event we discussed are factual in character, and the modes of reckoning and dealing considered we hold to be typical and verifiable. These constitute the core of factual premises for our conclusions. They are the real stuff of commerce. They must somehow be embraced by any theory of the generation of pertinent financial information.

Every theory makes use of some generalized terms, idealizations, or constructs. These are inventions. But if they are to be serviceable they must have demonstrable empirical correlates. It may be said that any theorist is entitled, is free, to choose his own constructs. But with that freedom runs the obligation to show how the constructs are related to observed and experienced events and to show how the products his theory entails engage with the reflections and actions of men in active commerce. There can be no useful construct in a theory of accounting which is not firmly tied, directly or indirectly, to some choice or action of a commercial kind. We noticed however that the literature generally fails to deal with observable events in their temporal and circumstantial settings and fails to consider the specific connections of the products of the theories propounded with the known criteria of choice in commercial matters.

I have not in this paper attempted to illustrate all the commercial situations in which statements of financial position based on resale prices, and statements of results embracing the effects of changes in prices and the purchasing power of money, are relevant. The general ideas of continuously contemporary accounting,[9] as I have expounded them elsewhere, have arisen from consideration of such situations. They have been supported by observation of commercial events, disputes, frauds, and failures, as well as by analysis of the notorious conflicts in the present body of doctrine.

The theory of continuously contemporary accounting takes cognizance of all the factors which have given rise to suggestions for different forms of accounting. It is more fully historical than historical cost accounting. It embraces the effects which price-level-adjusted accounting attempts to cope with. It embraces the effects which replacement-price accounting attempts to cope with. It is geared to the calculation of expected outcomes of future possibilities. Its products are capable of being related to any other financial magnitudes at a given time. Each of the types of accounting just mentioned has the recognition of some element of commercial reality as its justification. But each ignores some other aspects of that reality, and in that sense each falls short of the ideal system which would cope with all of the elements of commercial experience.

My object has been to suggest that the methods of empirical science have scarcely been tried in accounting. The common observables and experiences of commercial reckoning and dealing are generally disregarded; yet they are the only legitimate foundation for a viable theory and serviceable practices. In place of their analysis, we have discussions of higher-level abstractions, discussions which drift away from or point only vaguely in the direction of the very points of choice and judgment at which accounting information is used.

Whatever confidence I have in my own inference from these experiences and observables may be shaken by demonstration of their falsity. But I do not believe that any worthwhile theory of accounting or any worthwhile practice can emerge otherwise than from examination of the exigencies of men engaged in the calculating, choosing, and dealing characteristic of the marketplace.

9. I allude here to the main ideas mentioned in the previous sentence. Some of the suggestions made in *Accounting, Evaluation, and Economic Behavior* I would now modify, but only through stronger belief in the propriety of the main ideas. A paper on these modifications is forthcoming.

Evidence for a Market—Selling Price—Accounting System

I. Schema

A SYSTEM is a contraption for doing one or more things. A well-designed system is a contraption for doing that or those things well. We cannot pretend we are designing a system, or repairing a system or modifying a system unless we have clearly in mind the things we intend it to do, and unless we are concerned with fashioning its parts or elements so that it does just those things. The design of the system is, thus, primarily dependent on what it is expected to produce.

A complex system is a contraption for doing complex things. Commonly, it consists of subsystems, each doing or designed to do its own thing, but each designed to fit into and be part of the complex system. No subsystem in a well-designed system is inconsistent with the whole system, and no subsystem is designed to do just the same thing as any other subsystem. If they were, we would not call such a system well-designed, for inconsistencies will require additional subsystems to offset them, and superfluous subsystems are just in the way, uneconomical.

For analytical purposes we may take for examination a system as large or as small as we please. But, if it is locked in with other systems or is part of a larger system, we will know little of it and, hence, have

Evidence for a Market—Selling Price—Accounting System 75

little chance of designing it well, unless we take account of the larger system of which it is a part.

The economic organization of a community is a system. We shall consider just some parts of it. To avoid cumbersome expression, we shall speak of two systems which are really subsystems of the whole economic organization: the F-system, a single firm; and the W-system, the rest of the world or community. And we shall speak only of the financial features of these two systems.

There is a subsystem of F which engages in trading relations (having financial characteristics) with W. Call it the transactions subsystem F(T). There is a subsystem of F which sets the framework of these transactions. Call it the managerial subsystem F(M). If transactions are many and the relations between F and W persist over time, there is a subsystem of F which keeps track of the transactions and relations between F and W. Call it the accounting subsystem F(A). If F is a well-designed system, each of its subsystems will engage smoothly with one another, without gaps, inconsistencies or irrelevancies, as the parts of any well-designed machine. F(T) concerns itself with market prices, buying and selling prices. F(M) sets the framework or policy within which F(T) operates. F(A) provides the information on what has occurred and the consequences of what has occurred in F(T), so that F(M) may vary the framework of F(T) from time to time. As F(T) engages with the system W in terms of buying and selling prices, the function of F(A) in the system F will be to accumulate, arrange and digest buying and selling price information. If F(A) produces any information which is not in the nature of a price, F(M) will have to convert it to price information or seek price information from other sources or guess what framework it should set for F(T) from time to time. The system F will not be a well-designed system.

The system W has subsystems which correspond with the subsystems of F, namely W(T), W(M) and W(A). As the two systems W and F engage through their transactions subsystems, both F(T) and W(T) will engage on the same terms; namely prices—and at any given time, the prices at that time. And F(A) and W(A) will produce information in terms of those prices if F(M) and W(M) are to set the subsequent framework or policy for F(T) and W(T).

Now in the system which is (W + F), no single F is indispensable.

W is larger than F; there may be other firms in W which can produce what F produces, consume what F consumes, employ the labor which F employs, use the money funds which F uses. F(M) must, therefore, set the framework for F(T) from time to time in the light of what is occurring in W and the expectations of the components of W(T) with which it presently engages and may find it useful to engage. And, because the system F is at any time in a specific financial state or relation to W, that state or relation is one of the premises on which F(M) must proceed in setting the framework for F(T); for, certainly W(M) will proceed on that basis.

Now, there are effects on F due to W which do not arise merely from transactions. When the prices of particular inputs to F change through events in the system (W + F), F(M) may vary the framework of F(T) in one or more ways—direct it to seek less expensive inputs, to raise output prices, to change the composition of what it buys and sells (i.e., the production mix)—according to the expectations of W entertained by F(M). Those changes in prices have immediate effects, notwithstanding that F may not replenish its "inventory" at any given price. Furthermore, when prices of all things rise or fall, the unit in which transactions (and hence, relations) are expressed acquires a different meaning than it had before with reference to goods and services.

If F(M) is to set the framework of F(T) on the basis, *inter alia*, of the present state of F, the present state of F must be defined so that it has reference to the ability of F(T) to procure the effects proposed by F(M). F(T) can procure those effects only by having cash or getting cash from W by the sale of what F has at the time. So that we can say that the present state of F is defined by reference to the selling prices of what it has at any time.

We will call F(A) a well-designed subsystem if it meets the requirements of the last two paragraphs.

We have said that one of the premises of F(M) in proceeding to choose a course to be followed by F(T) is the state of F at the time. There are many such possible courses—"sell this and buy that," "borrow this and buy that," "discharge this debt and incur that one." The state of F is a common premise for all. Which of these courses is deemed to be feasible depends on the expectations of F(M) regarding W; for

F(T) can only operate by engagements with W. Which of the feasible courses is deemed to be preferable to other feasible courses depends on what state of F at some future time is preferred by F(M) to other possible states at that time. Notice that these last two elements in the process of choice are non-factual; one relates to expectations of F(M) at a point of time, the other to a preference of F(M) based on expectations at a point of time.

Two features of the products of F(A) are distinctively different from these features of F(M). The recorded history of F, as developed by F(A) is, in a sense, continuous. Given one state, say at t_0, and the transactions and events between t_0 and t_1, the state at t_1 can be deduced. Thus, F(M) can discover states at any time by reference to F(A). If, although F(A) is a well designed system, it does not operate perfectly, its output can be readily checked externally from time to time by reference to the prices ruling in W. There is no such continuity or possibility of independent corroboration (and correction, if necessary) of the expectations and calculations which are contributory to choice. For, if F(M) expects F to be in a certain state at t_1 in the light of the actual state at t_0 and some expected events, there is no apparent way (in a varying world) of deducing either the actual state of F at t_1 or the expectation F(M) will entertain at t_1 or the state F will be in at t_2. The contingent nature of future events, and the reasonable requirement that F(M) will always proceed to calculate from the actual state at a point of time, entail that all calculations about the future will be temporally isolated events, making use of the knowledge of the present state and of such other market prices as are relevant. These calculations are necessary events, certainly, but unique and evanescent. It should scarcely be necessary to argue that there is no way of verifying the content of any statement or calculation about the future at the time the statement is made.

There is a further point, generally disregarded. All problems of project evaluation emphasize in some way the expected cash flows and the net present values. It is not universally correct to say that that project which has the greater net present value is to be preferred. It would always be the case if the horizon of calculation were the terminus of the whole venture and if no other condition required by W were violated up to that time. But, if F is to be a continuing system, then its state at any time must be such that W will continue to engage with it. Solvency, contractual or conventional leverage conditions and the capacity to make dividend payments are all part of the requirements of W, so that any preferred state must meet these requirements. There is, thus, a link between F(A) and W(T), which a well designed F(A) will serve.

The preceding style of analysis, of a line of argument given elsewhere in different terms, has been designed to bring under notice one major point. The products of any F(A) enter as premises into the processes of analysis and calculation of *other* parts of the systems F and W, many other parts. They will be related to many other prices. There is no way in which, if they are not cash amounts or prices themselves, they can be related to other prices. There is no way in which, if they are not contemporary prices themselves, they, or any combination of them, can be related to other prices which are contemporary. If any of them has any relation to the payment of any existing debt or the securing of any new debt, they must be in the nature of cash or have a cash equivalent.

The use of the impersonal idea of systems is intended to lift the argument away from the vague term "usefulness" which, though it is seldom defined, is running riot in the literature. I think it might be preferable to speak of functional information rather than of useful information. If we ask what is useful, we tend to suggest useful to someone; we are then confronted with the possibility that any piece of "information" may be said by someone to be useful. There is no way of tying practices down to a tight description of "useful." I am not sure the term "functional" is vastly superior. But, in the context of the description of the firm and its relations which I have just given, what it signifies is not hard to see. A piece of information is functional if it is a necessary premise of any other party in the systems F or W for any kind of calculation which that party wishes to make. And information relating to a financial state is functional if it can be confidently taken by any party as a basis for calculating backward, presently, or forward. Of course, if all F(A) subsystems are well-designed, their products can be used generally and with confidence throughout a community, for they will be uniform in substance and significance and equally relatable to one another and to all conceivable transactions at a given time.

II. Inconsistencies Between Accounting Practice and Commercial Behavior

I came to my own conclusions on the inconsistencies between accounting practice and commercial behavior by a devious route. The kind of accounting commonly done is not consistent with the kind of data one ordinarily employs in one's own calculations. Nor with the kinds of analysis one finds in elementary economics. Yet, it is claimed, almost universally and by large groups of professional and academic people, that it yields useful information. One may satisfy oneself on the one hand by analysis or model-building. One may construct a theoretical system, necessarily on the basis of one's own presuppositions (original or learned; mostly learned). But, as accounting is a real-world phenomenon, there should be evidence, beyond oneself and one's convictions, of the inconsistency between accounting practice and commercial behavior, if indeed there is inconsistency.

The kind of evidence which would be acceptable, I decided, would be occurrences which arose more or less spontaneously. It would be better to avoid manufacturing evidence. Most forms of opinion inquiry, questionnaire or contrived experiment could be challenged on the ground that the way they were structured would "create" a situation biased in some way, or would "force" into play whatever sympathies and antipathies may surround customary or habitual practices. It would be better just to look, to see what was happening *independently of prompting in the particular direction of my own ideas*. There are many kinds of such evidence: What companies do in their accounting; what their chairmen or presidents say by way of augmenting or qualifying what their financial statements say; what businessmen say about accounting; what legal documents designed to protect the rights of contracting parties contain; what accountants and professional bodies say (since none of what they have said has been consciously directed towards or against my own ideas); what analysts do; what the information services provide; what economists say about accounting and the context in which accounting information is used; and so on.

It should be obvious that if one is looking at what goes on, the sayers and doers are acting free of the suspicion that what they say or do will be used in the particular way I choose to use it. On my part, therefore, the evidence is independent of me. Such a form of observation is similar, in this respect, to any form of strictly scientific inquiry.

It should also be obvious that some of the evidence will be indicative only. For example, if the practice in accounting is to use for one kind of asset a contemporary price, and for all other kinds of asset some other number or price, the use of a contemporary price in one instance is some evidence. But if, from many directions, there are such fragments of evidence, and if there are no such fragments of evidence in equal quantities for any alternative practice, we may consider the *convergence* of such evidence to be in the nature of empirical confirmation.

The remainder of this paper will present some of the indications. As there are so many possible sources of evidence, I cannot pretend to have examined all or any of them exhaustively. But I hold that the scraps I shall offer are mere samples or specimens of kinds of observation which could be made in great abundance by anyone who cares to look in similar directions. These scraps have come under my notice at different times over the past twenty years.[1] They have affected the views I have held from time to time, yielding at last what confidence I have in my present conclusions. They are drawn indiscriminately from the literature and practices of people in different countries who have been concerned with business and accounting in the kind of developed industrial economy with which we are familiar. As the conduct of *business* is substantially the same in such economies, the kind of accounting appropriate to that kind of business is the same kind. Drawing on illustrations from different economies enables one, therefore, to skirt the purely local habits and practices which have arisen from the idiosyncratic experiences of particular communities.

III. Functional Information—Comprehensible Signals

As we said in the introduction, when two or more parties are engaged in an operation in any sense interdependently, the communications between them are unlikely to produce responses appropriate to their positions unless those communications are understandable alike to all. Business managers, investors, financiers, analysts and advisers,

---

[1] Some of them have been used in earlier publications. The collection of some of these in *Accounting, Finance and Management* (Sydney, Australia: Butterworth & Co., 1969) makes it easier to cite one source. I shall refer to these articles by the abbreviated reference A.F.M.

Evidence for a Market—Selling Price—Accounting System

suppliers and customers and others are engaged in interdependent operations, giving and receiving money and other financial instruments of or relating to a given firm. All communications embodying amounts of money are understood in the normal course of affairs as having reference to the capacity to pay a price (e.g., a statement about cash holdings) or a reference to some price or prices expressed in money. As the structure of prices and the general level of prices change from time to time, any communication expressed in money is commonly interpretable only in the light of prices ruling at or about the time of the communication. And any money sum which is an aggregate of other sums will be interpretable only if the component sums and the aggregate are themselves prices or are relatable to prices at or about the same time. Among these communications are the financial statements which accountants prepare.

We might, therefore, expect to find some evidence of the use of contemporary prices or of amounts which can be directly related to contemporary prices. And we might expect to find signs of dissatisfaction with the use of other kinds of numbers, vacillation in the prescription and use of other kinds of numbers, and suggestions that the other kinds be supplemented or replaced by more or less contemporary numbers, if not contemporary prices.

The Evidence

1. We do, in fact, find in the practice of accounting some contemporary monetary magnitudes. Universally, we find the actual present amounts of cash: and generally, we find the present amounts of receivables and payables, even though in some cases we may doubt the ways in which the amounts of receivables are determined. And we do find the use of market prices in respect to inventories at least some of the time. The lower of cost or market, and the use of net realizable value, and the outright use of market prices in some trades, all signify that market prices are indeed used at least some of the time.

2. We do, in fact, find vacillation in the general prescriptions relating to the valuation of assets on other bases. In the recommendations and prescriptions of professional bodies, we find numerous alternative valuation bases mentioned. No firm grounds for any of the

alternatives are given. Many alternatives are not even in the nature of contemporary prices. And the choice is left open to accountants or managers, without any guidance in the prescriptions. Analysis of the accounts of almost every company will show that the same components have been valued on different bases through time. Reference to the consecutive issues of *Accounting Trends and Techniques* will show the extent of this vacillation. *Trends* of 1967 shows that in 1960, 1965, 1966 there were 54, 43, 29 cases, respectively, of "changes in consistent application of generally accepted principles of accounting."[2] It can confidently be said, from the tabulations throughout *Trends*, that changes in particulars are much more numerous. Recent shifts in depreciation accounting and merger accounting are conspicuous examples of idiosyncratic accounting. All such changes are unaccountable, except on the hypothesis that there is no confident belief in the functional quality of any one of the methods used, the newly adopted or the method rejected—for while some companies are adopting one method, others are rejecting it.

3. Bearing on the same point, we do find strong suggestions that steps should be taken to reduce "unnecessary diversity" in accounting methods. The suggestions have come from leaders of the accounting profession and from officials of the SEC. The argument for "narrowing the differences" is sometimes couched in terms of improving the comparability of the resulting figures, which is just one facet of interpreting the figures or producing comprehensible figures.

4. We do, in fact, find critical comments on the use in accounting of figures other than contemporary prices in the reports of presidents and chairmen of companies. References to a number of examples from the United Kingdom, the United States and Australia are given in "The Formal Basis of Business Decisions"[3] and in *The Function and Design of Company Annual Reports*.[4]

---

[2] *Accounting Trends & Techniques*, Twenty-First Edition (New York: American Institute of Certified Public Accountants, 1967), Table 4, p. 273.

[3] Chambers, A.F.M., p. 70.

[4] R. J. Chambers, *The Function and Design of Company Annual Reports* (Sydney, Australia: The Law Book Co., 1955).

5. Every argument for replacement price accounting and price level adjusted accounting is, at bottom, an argument for approximating figures which are currently interpretable. (We are not concerned at this point with other elements of these proposals.) There have been and are many supporters of both among professional accountants and academics. The Institute of Chartered Accountants in England and Wales in 1952 produced Recommendation XV "Accounting in Relation to Changes in the Purchasing Power of Money." The Institute of Cost and Works Accounts (England) produced in 1952 *The Accountancy of Changing Price Levels*. The Association of Certified and Corporate Accountants produced in 1952 *Accounting for Inflation*. The American Accounting Association supported the works on the effects of price level changes of Mason and Jones in the mid-fifties.[5] In 1963 we had ARS 6,[6] which incidentally reports a number of companies, in different countries, whose accounting is in the direction we are discussing. More recently we have the APB Statement No. 3.[7] The number of individual supporters of one or the other of these proposals and the number of articles supporting them have never been estimated. Both must be large. There have been eminent individual contributors, from commerce, the profession and the universities in Germany, the Netherlands, Japan, Britain, the United States and Australia, and no doubt in many other countries, too.

6. The common statutory requirement that certain kinds of companies shall publish periodically a statement of financial position and results which shall contain no untrue statements or omissions likely to mislead (or other equivalent words) is a pointless requirement, unless the statements so published are commonly interpretable. The broad foundation of such a law is, that if men pursue their

---

[5] Perry Mason, *Price Level Changes and Financial Statements: Basic Concepts and Methods* (Columbus, Ohio: American Accounting Association, 1956). Ralph Coughenour Jones, *Price Level Changes and Financial Statements: Case Studies of Four Companies* (Evanston, Illinois: American Accounting Association, 1955).

[6] Staff of the Accounting Research Division, American Institute of Certified Public Accountants, *Reporting the Financial Effects of Price-Level Changes*, Accounting Research Study No. 6 (New York: American Institute of Certified Public Accountants, Inc., 1963).

[7] Accounting Principles Board, *APB Statement No. 3*, "Financial Statements Restated for General Price-Level Changes" (New York: American Institute of Certified Public Accountants, Inc., 1969).

own interests knowledgeably, the welfare of a community as a whole is advanced. The narrower foundation is, that if each investor or lender is periodically informed of the affairs of companies in which he invests or may invest, he can protect his interest. As the quantities *and* the prices of company assets rise and fall, no investor can be informed by statements which embody the effects of changes in quantities but not of changes in prices. To so report would be to make an "omission likely to mislead." The law clearly seems to contemplate financial statements which are presently interpretable and presently indicative, because they are in terms of present prices. Writing close to the date of the Securities Act of 1933, Professor Sanders was of the opinion that Congress "doubtless was thinking of the balance sheet mainly as . . . a statement of *present* conditions."[8] As creditors are quitted by cash payments, and as investors may divest themselves of their interests by sale of their "share" or by liquidation of a company or by swapping securities, protection is, in fact, assured only by using present resale market prices of assets in statements of present condition.

7. Such general publicity laws have been very loosely interpreted, or misinterpreted, in practice. Following notable instances of the divergence of published "information" from factual information and consequential losses by investors, more explicit stipulations of the modes of valuing some assets have been made in the publicity laws of some jurisdictions. In 1948, the English legislation required that the market values of listed securities be given in the financial statements, by note if not otherwise. The same requirement has been adopted since in some other jurisdictions. An amendment of the English Act in 1967 required that, where assets were revalued, subsequent reports should show the dates, amounts and sources of the newer valuations. This does not secure that contemporary prices would be used, either for all assets or in any given year. But the dating, at least, provides some basis on which users can judge how out-of-date the figures are. It seems reasonable to suppose that the requirement contemplates that up-to-date prices yield functional information. Amendments to some Australian statutes in 1964

[8] Thomas H. Sanders, "Accounting Aspects of the Securities Act," *Law and Contemporary Problems*, IV (April 1937), p. 195.

Evidence for a Market—Selling Price—Accounting System 85

required up-to-date valuations to be given for any real property to be charged as collateral security for any issue of senior securities.

IV. Functional Information—Particulars

Men frame their actions or choices on the basis of their general goals, their expectations and their present states. Of the three, the last is dominant. Knowledge of a present state may influence the goals that will be sought and the expectations that will be entertained. But neither goals nor expectations can influence a present state.

Though we have spoken of a present financial state in a general way with reference to market prices, it is made up of particulars, and it is analyzed by managers and others who combine those particulars in various ways. Let us say that there are at least three such combinations which are of interest—a measure of solvency such as the current ratio, a measure of debt to equity, and a measure of the rate of return or net income to residual equity. The numerators and denominators of these three ratios constitute six combinations of the particular components of a set of financial statements, and between them embrace all the usual components. The former two ratios may be of special interest to creditors, the latter two of interest to stockholders; and because F is smaller than W and more dependent on W than W is on F, F(M) will be concerned with all three. Knowing these ratios at a given date, F(M) may specify the state of F which is preferred at some future date; knowing what means are available at a given date, F(M) may specify, in general, by what steps the preferred future state may be reached; and knowing the change of state from some past date to the present date, F(M) may form some idea of what future change can be expected or should be expected. Of course, none of these particular bits of knowledge is functional unless in terms of contemporary resale prices.

We might, therefore, expect to find that accounting is done on a contemporary price basis. As we do not find this, we would expect to find that if the kinds of relationship we mention are used or discussed, there will be critical observations on the products of the kind of accounting in present use. Or, we would expect to find knowledgeable discussions of the affairs of firms which clearly entail or require the use of contemporary resale prices, even though they make no reference to accounting.

86   Asset Valuation and Income Determination

The Evidence

1. First, there are some accountants who doubt that the users of financial statements take any notice of the contents of balance sheets; perhaps this is rationalization of the inadequacy (known to accountants) of balance sheets to give the kinds of contemporary figures we stipulate. But, if analysts make reference to the use of balance sheet figures, we will have settled the question of what users use. Dun and Bradstreet and Robert Morris Associates have for some years published tabulations of some fourteen ratios for an extensive range of companies and industries.[9] The three types of ratios we mentioned appear in these series.

2. As the "source material" of analysis is not of the ideal kind, we expect to find suggestions of the manner in which the source material may be adjusted. We do.

   (a) "At the end of 1960 Bishop Oil Company owned 88,000 shares of Flintkote Corporation . . . carried at cost of $164,000 but worth $2,550,000 at market. For analytical purposes these shares should be considered as current assets at their market value less capital-gain tax on the indicated profit."[10]

   (b) "In December 1960 Kaiser Industries showed investments in Affiliated Companies of $182 million with a footnote indicating that their market value was $388 million. This market appreciation of $206 million is relevant to an analysis of Kaiser Industries shares."[11]

   (c) Commenting on two companies which reported the insured values of buildings and machinery at figures vastly greater than reported book values: "If figures such as these were required to be supplied by all companies as a footnote to the balance sheet a much more informative picture of the plant account would be available to [stockholders]."[12] The practice

---

[9] See *Annual Statement Studies*, The Staff of Robert Morris Associates; and of a different kind, R. A. Foulke, *Practical Financial Statement Analysis*, Third Edition (New York: McGraw-Hill Book Co., 1961).

[10] Benjamin Graham, David L. Dodd and Sidney Cottle, *Security Analysis: Principles and Technique*, Fourth Edition (New York: McGraw-Hill Book Company, Inc., 1962), p. 206.

[11] *Ibid.*, p. 207.

[12] *Ibid.*, p. 208.

here mentioned is also followed in some European countries. It has also been used and recommended for use in estimating national wealth and income.[13]

(d) In "The Missing Link in Supervision of the Securities Market,"[14] I cited a sample of comments of English financial statement analysts in the professional periodicals on the inadequacy of reported book values as bases for investors' judgments and the need for information more closely related to present market values.

3. Related to this kind of evidence is the view long held among some accountants that, if investors wish to have more up-to-date information they may go back over past reports, find when the assets were purchased and make their own estimations of what the present prices of assets might be. In an English case, *Re Press Caps Ltd* (1949), it seems likely that such a view was expressed in expert evidence or, if not, was expressed from the bench. The suggestion does not deny, implicitly it admits, the functional character of up-to-date information. But, the impossibility of an investor doing what is suggested is glossed over.

4. In jurisdictions in which the practice is not legally barred, occasional upward revaluation of assets is quite common. In view of the doctrine that cost is the proper basis for fixed asset accounting (a doctrine taught and said to be held by practitioners in those countries), this practice is anomalous. It is explicable only in terms of the inadequacy of the products of traditional accounting, and the resulting distortions of the ratios named at the beginning of this section. In a study of Australian listed companies for the ten years 1948–57, some 288 cases were found of stock dividends made from the "proceeds" of asset revaluations.[15] A subsequent study of Australian and New Zealand companies by McKee and Clarke, for the ten years ended June 1960, showed that 60 percent of the companies which continued through the decade had revalued

---

[13] See *Measuring the Nation's Wealth* (New York: Columbia University Press, 1964), p. 334. Papers from the Wealth Inventory Planning Study, George Washington University, National Bureau of Economic Research.

[14] R. J. Chambers, "The Missing Link in Supervision of the Securities Market," *Abacus*, V (September 1969), p. 16.

[15] Chambers, A.F.M., pp. 107 ff.

assets at least once.[16] The practice has continued. It has been extensively followed also in England, and, I believe, in a number of other countries.

5. In jurisdictions in which the practice of revaluing assets upwards is barred, it might be expected that there would be other evidence of the inconsistency between actual asset prices and book values, if the pressure of commercial circumstance can be relied upon to flush out such inconsistencies. The only evidence I know of at present is indirect. Undervaluation is permissible, gross undervaluation is permissible. Where commercial circumstance makes it desirable, the amount of undervaluation can be reduced (e.g., by varying the depreciation or inventory valuation method). But, being corseted by a law believed to limit valuations to cost, the system cannot directly disclose the extent of the discrepancy between book values and the current prices of assets. The only counter to this is to use supplementary statements, which have been suggested and have occasionally been used. This is an obviously weak line of evidence; but it is some evidence.

6. A stronger line is given by the nature of mutual funds and unit trusts. These operate on the principle that contributors may generally withdraw at a price determined by the market prices of the assets. There seems to be no difference in principle between this kind and any other kind of investment *qua* investment. But, if it is not possible to allow stockholders of industrial corporations to withdraw from the corporation in exactly the same way, there seems to be every reason why they should be able to withdraw (by sale of their securities on the market) with the same kind of knowledge of what the underlying assets are currently worth at market resale prices.

7. This last observation comes close to one of the possibilities available to creditors of and stockholders of companies. They have the nominal right to resolve to liquidate a company, creditors subject to constraints, stockholders without constraints. It is of no consequence that this is a nominal right, nor that stockholders seldom exercise it. If there is such a right, it entails that information shall be available which will enable stockholders to decide whether

---

[16] Chambers, A.F.M., p. 194.

to liquidate a company if ever they should want so to decide. If assets are stated in amounts higher than resale prices, they would be misled as to the possible scale of alternative investments if they ever consider the liquidation possibility. If assets are stated in amounts lower than resale prices, they would also be misled, but in the opposite direction. In the first case, they would suppose a larger scale alternative than is possible, in the second, a smaller scale than is possible. The evidential point is simply the existence in law of the right to consider the alternative of liquidation. As for the managerial side of the matter, it is desired to avoid liquidation (in deference to the wishes or rights of any party whatsoever), the only way to avoid it is to keep constantly under observation the facts which are indicative of solvency—the relationships of debts to assets at market prices. A recent and apposite example of the relevance of market prices will be found in the report of the judgment in the Court of Appeals in the Continental Vending case.[17]

8. We have noticed the independently stated views of some analysts. We may notice the independently stated views of some economists. Analysis of the opportunities available to firms (in microeconomic theory) begins with the supposition that the firm is financially able to operate through the whole range of outputs contemplated in the examples used; in short, it has the money (or money and goods whose resale prices will make good the deficiency in money). The comparison of alternative courses thus proceeds from a known present state. Point one. Point two. Those writers who make reference to that state specify it by reference to resale prices. The discussion is sometimes related to income, that is, the difference between two states.

(a) "Personal income may be defined as the algebraic sum of (1) the market value of rights exercised in consumption and (2) the change in the store of property of rights between the beginning and end of the period in question ... measured ... by appeal to market prices ... [or] according to objective market standards."[18]

---

[17] See "Continental Vending Decision Affirmed," *The Journal of Accountancy*, CXXIX (February 1970), p. 61.

[18] H. C. Simons, *Personal Income Taxation* (Chicago: University of Chicago Press, 1938), p. 50.

90　　　　　　　　*Asset Valuation and Income Determination*

(b) The definition of income *ex post* "which is the most important" of three possible definitions is that it "equals the value of the individual's consumption plus the increment in the money value of his prospect which has accrued during the week; it equals consumption plus capital accumulation . . . it is an objective magnitude . . . [involving] a comparison between present values and values which belong wholly to the past."[19]

(c) Edwards and Bell make a stronger case for opportunity cost valuation (resale prices) than any other of the alternatives they considered.[20] The reason why they did not adopt it seems to be in the position taken that opportunity cost valuation relates to complete liquidation as an alternative, whereas the liquidation of any asset at any time is just as feasible an alternative, and indeed a more common one.

(d) Perhaps plainer than any form of verbal description is the example given in Lipsey and Steiner's *Economics*.[21] With the object of distinguishing the conventional accounting procedure from the procedure entailed in the mode of economic analysis, they set up the accounts of an imaginary firm on both bases. The "economist's balance sheet" is there shown quite clearly to be based on market prices at opening and closing dates, the depreciation is shown as the difference between two market prices, and the income of the period as the difference between the opening and closing values of the net equity calculated in that way.

V. *Functional Information—Comparison*

Choosing between two or more possibilities is the easier if one or more properties common to the possibilities can be measured in a common scale. Assessing the relative performances and other features of two or more entities engaged in different activities is made easier

---

[19] J. R. Hicks, *Value and Capital: An Inquiry into Some Fundamental Principles of Economic Theory*, Second Edition (London: Oxford University Press, 1939), pp. 178–9.

[20] Edgar O. Edwards and Philip W. Bell, *The Theory and Measurement of Business Income* (Berkeley, California: University of California Press, 1961), pp. 80 ff.

[21] Richard G. Lipsey and Peter O. Steiner, *Economics* (New York: Harper & Row Publishers, 1966), p. 207.

Evidence for a Market—Selling Price—Accounting System

if one or more of the characteristics of those entities can be measured in a common scale. It is commonly claimed that the publication of accounts provides the basis on which comparisons may be made of the financial properties of companies. Some do not readily admit this, but these simply fly in the face of the necessities and practices of men.

The object of any measurement scheme is to supply measured magnitudes which may be used in a wide variety of contexts—by one user in many kinds of calculations, or by many users each in his own calculations. Any balance sheet or income figure which is derived by a combination of rules unique to its issuer is, at best, limited in use to those who "derived" it. For they alone know how it was derived. But, typically, those who derive the figures do not use them. In the terms we employed earlier, the products of $F(A)$ are used by $F(M)$. If $F(M)$ wishes to compare F with any other firm in W, $F(M)$ can perhaps ask $F(A)$ to what extent the products of $F(A)$ should be adjusted to make them comparable. But this is not fruitful, for any other firm G in W may also have unique products of its $G(A)$, the effects of which cannot be discovered by $F(A)$.

Comparisons of the states and the rates of change of state of two or more firms are impossible unless the component items are expressed in the same (contemporary) terms, both as to the units used and as to the prices expressed in those units (and, in particular, as to the use of resale prices, since they alone express elements of the claims of firms as against the rest of the community).

We would expect either that such a form of accounting is used; or that there would be expressions of objection and attempts at correction on the part of those who must use the products of the system of accounting that is used; or that there would be evidence of losses falling unexpectedly on those who rely on published figures which are not comparable.

The Evidence

1. First, the point that comparisons *are* necessary to some parties of interest. Information services associated with the securities markets publish extensive tabulations of figures drawn from and based on financial statements. *Standard NYSE Stock Reports*, for example, gives up to ten years statistics of income, balance sheet figures and security prices, including such deduced figures as the current ratio

and the book value of common stock. We have already mentioned the Dun and Bradstreet and Robert Morris Associates compilations. The latter give the median and upper and lower quartile values of the ratios they compute for each industry in their systems. This type of calculation is technically meaningless if the component figures are not of the same kind (i.e., if they are derived by rules unique to each company). All of these services would be meaningless unless it were expected (and confirmed by the sale of the services) that comparisons would be and are made in forming judgments on securities.

2. Those parts of the literatures of accounting and security analysis which deal with financial statement analysis commonly contain warnings about making direct comparisons of different companies, because of the different rules available generally to each and all companies. If comparison were not a natural or legitimate response to the appearance of financial statements, there would be no occasion for the warnings and the elaborate descriptions of the differences which different ways of accounting yield.

3. The use of common words and the whole case for standardizing terminology rests on the supposition that the amounts corresponding with the verbal notations are similar in kind and, therefore, comparable. If it were not so, we should find an elaborate description of the particulars represented. Instead of just "net income," we should find "net income—FIFO—SYD—GA—TA—variety," for example (meaning FIFO inventory; sum of year's digits depreciation; goodwill amortization; tax allocation), and many similar or fancier varieties. In the absence of this kind of full disclosure, it can only be supposed that accountants intend that the figures should be compared. (This may seem at odds with the point of the previous paragraph, but such oddities are to be expected when the product does not meet all of its tests simultaneously.)

4. Arguments for common dollar accounting are all partially in contemplation of the comparison of the resulting figures, whether or not the common dollars are "contemporary" dollars (a condition of interpretability, already mentioned) or dollars of any other specified date. All such arguments are, in effect, criticisms of the adequacy of the prevailing mode of accounting.

Evidence for a Market—Selling Price—Accounting System 93

5. The problem of comparison is particularly of concern to regulatory and concession-granting agencies which administer particular trades or classes of trade or terms of trade, where comparisons of particular firms or aggregations of characteristics of classes of firms must be made. As two recent examples:

   (a) In June 1969, *The Journal of Accountancy* noted a revision of the regulations of the Small Business Administration, requiring that Small Business Investment Companies shall report "unrealized appreciation of assets" of each concern which the Small Business Investment Company has helped to finance. The amount would be the difference between "total assets as recorded in the small business concern's books" and "total assets based on their estimated market value or fair value as of the close of the fiscal year."[22]

   (b) In December 1969, *The Journal of Accountancy* reported on a Federal Trade Commission study which said that existing accounting practices "have granted merger-minded companies almost limitless opportunity to understate the market value of investments in acquired enterprises." Calling for the elimination of pooling of interests accounting, the study said: "Insofar as possible, every merger transaction should be accounted for in a way that will most accurately represent the true value of the individual assets acquired."[23]

6. Comparison of the financial characteristics of companies is one element in the decision to merge or not, to sell one's shareholding to a takeover bidder at one price or another, and all similar decisions. Many bids are clearly in contemplation of acquiring the the assets of a company at a lower price than they could otherwise be acquired. There may, in some cases, be other expectations also, but these will simply be "causes" of the extent to which the bidder is prepared to bid *above* the prices at which the assets could be acquired. Where a bid is by way of an exchange of shares, the *ostensible* comparison is of the market prices of the shares. The

---

[22] "SBA Revises Reporting Requirements for SBICs," *The Journal of Accountancy*, CXXVII (June 1969), p. 20.

[23] "FTC Study Urges Elimination of Pooling of Interests," *The Journal of Accountancy*, CXXVIII (December 1969), p. 12.

underlying comparison of the bidder is of what he has to pay (the market price of the shares offered) with what he expects to get. If the assets of an offeree company are understated by comparison with their contemporary market prices, the extent of the past gains of the company will also have been understated. On one ground or the other, the shares will tend to be priced in the market at less than the price could be if the actual extent of the gains and the net assets had been disclosed, hence, the opportunity of the bidder, through the ignorance of the shareholder of the offeree company.

(a) Loss cites an action brought successfully against Transamerica Corporation which turned on an undervaluation of the tobacco inventory of Axton-Fisher Tobacco Company, which Transamerica had acquired. The action was based on Rule 10b-5 under the Securities Exchange Act of 1934, relating to insider trading to the detriment of uninformed public security holders. Commenting on the case and the judgment, Loss observes: "It is no answer that accounting practice normally favors the carrying of assets at cost or market, whichever is *lower*, so as to present a conservative rather than a roseate view of the company's affairs. The cost-or-market-whichever-is-lower formula operates in quite the reverse manner, of course, when the company is *buying* rather than *selling* its securities. Nor is it an answer that the Commission's accounting rules do not specifically require inventory to be priced at market value. For Regulation S-X does provide that the specified information shall be furnished 'as a minimum requirement to which shall be added such further material information as is necessary to make the required statements . . . not misleading.' "[24]

(b) Elsewhere I have shown that from a selection of Australian takeovers, share prices can rise by over 100 percent on the announcement of a bid. I interpret this as the reaction of the market to new information (the offer), indicative, at least to some extent, of asset values in excess of reported values.[25] There are also cases in which asset revaluation has been

---

[24] Louis Loss, *Securities Regulation*, Second Edition, Vol. III (Boston: Little, Brown and Co., 1961), pp. 1058–62. Footnotes omitted.
[25] Chambers, A.F.M., pp. 191–3.

Evidence for a Market—Selling Price—Accounting System

explicitly described as a defense against takeovers.[26] Shareholders who bought or sold prior to the announcements of bids clearly did not know what they were buying or selling. The unexpected "losses" of some (through unsuspected ignorance) yielded unexpected gains to others.

(c) There are numerous cases where bidders have been able to acquire substantial properties, without or nearly without cost, through purchasing securities and meeting the purchase price out of disposal of only part of the assets which came under their control. One Australian company thus acquired an airline, liquidating the airline company's investment portfolio for the cost of the airline securities purchased. Examples of English cases are given in Bull and Vice, *Bid for Power*,[27] and Marriott, *The Property Boom*.[28] No doubt there are many such cases in the U.S. Their success depends on knowledge of asset values which bidders are able to acquire by search, but of which stockholders are kept in ignorance.

7. There are, on the other hand, examples of companies whose shareholders and creditors have sustained substantial losses through belief in financial statements which represented at cost assets which had or came to have much lower market prices than their costs. Some Australian examples are given in A.F.M.[29]

8. On numerous occasions, members and officials of the SEC have stressed the importance of the comparability of the information yielded by accounting and made available to the public. There would be no occasion for the stress were it not that comparison is necessary to choice and that the present forms of accounting do not permit proper comparisons.

Conclusion

The bits of evidence cited are only examples of larger masses of evidence in the same direction under each of the heads mentioned. It

---

[26] Chambers, A.F.M., p. 111.
[27] George Bull and Anthony Vice, *Bid for Power*, Third Edition (London: Elek Books, Ltd., 1961).
[28] Oliver Marriott, *The Property Boom* (London: Hamish, Hamilton, Ltd., 1967).
[29] Chambers, A.F.M., pp. 204 ff.

is emphasized that all of this evidence is observational; it relates to events which do or did occur; none of it is manufactured or hypothetical. It all points to the functional property of contemporary information and, in particular, to the functional significance of market resale prices. It tends to the confirmation of the conclusions which may be reached, on empirico-logical grounds, in respect of the functional character of the products of a system of accounting on the basis of market selling prices.

The variety and weight of this evidence may be set against the variety and weight of similar evidence for any other system of accounting. Let it be remembered that the argument given in the introduction recognizes the necessity of present value *calculations*, as and when necessary, but such calculations depend on knowledge of present market prices of assets and present states. Let it be remembered that initial prices are necessary inputs of a market price system, but the latter does not arbitrarily exclude the effects of subsequent changes in prices; the system we here support is more completely historical than historical cost accounting. Let it be remembered that continuously contemporary accounting takes account of the differential effects of changes in prices and changes in price levels, whereas this differential is disregarded in price level adjusted historical cost accounting. Let it be remembered that an entry (or replacement) price system does not yield information indicative of the present state of a firm in its relations with the rest of the world. On all these grounds, it seems extremely unlikely that the quantity of independent evidence for any other system can approach the evidence for a market-selling price system. The supporters of other systems are invited to attempt to match it.

At least until contrary evidence is tendered, we conclude that a market-selling price accounting system is a functional part of a well-designed business system.

R. J. CHAMBERS, JOHN W. KENNELLY, THOMAS W. McRAE,
FRANK K. REILLY and W. KEITH WELTMER

Historical Cost Accounting[1]

Continuously contemporary accounting is the only complete and legitimate form of historical cost accounting.

---

[1]. The authors wish to acknowledge their debt to Professor Robert R. Sterling, organizer of the 1970 Touche Ross Symposium in the University of Kansas on 'Asset Valuation and Income Determination', and The Touche Ross Foundation, without whose assistance the collaboration of the authors could not have been possible.

R. J. CHAMBERS is Professor of Accounting, University of Sydney; JOHN W. KENNELLY is Assistant Professor of Accounting, University of Iowa; THOMAS W. McRAE is on the staff of the Research Division, American Institute of Certified Public Accountants; FRANK K. REILLY is Associate Professor of Business Administration, University of Kansas; W. KEITH WELTMER is Professor of Business Administration, University of Kansas.

Accounting in an International Economic Community

> *In this article, Professor Chambers describes the concept of continuously contemporary accounting and suggests that adoption of this idea would overcome present difficulties of international differences in accounting practice, and increase the reliability of inter-firm and international comparisons.*

In some significant respects accounting has, in the past, developed along localised, national lines. There is much that is similar in the basic processes of bookkeeping. But the rules which determine the significant aggregates yielded by financial statements are much less uniform.

There are several reasons for the differences as between countries. Differences in the economic endowment and development of countries may be expected to produce differences in the style and quality of accounting; in a country which is largely agricultural or in which commerce and industry is largely in the hands of small firms run by owner-managers, much less, and much less sophisticated, accounting may be expected than in a country the commerce and industry of which is dominated by large corporations. Differences in the legal forms of business organization available may yield differences in the accounting required, primarily because in designing the legal forms (partnerships, public and private companies) legislators may prescribe different devices for securing the rights of contributors of capital. Differences in the general financial institutions and in the prevailing modes of financing may give rise to differences in accounting; where investment in business enterprises is done largely through financial intermediaries a different mode of accounting and reporting may serve than is required in a country in which individual security investment is common.

Perhaps the greatest single source of differences, however, is the taxation codes of different countries. Although taxation laws are primarily revenue-raising laws, they are widely regarded as means of giving discriminating aid to particular firms, or industries, through the concessions which are commonly embodied in them. Thus, aid may be given to primary producers in some countries, and in different degrees to different kinds of primary producers. In other cases, aid may be given for the rehabilitation of specific industries, for the encouragement of investment in advanced technology, for the encouragement of foreign investment, for the encouragement of exporters, and so on. The rules by which these concessions are granted may or may not become embodied in the corpus of commercial accounting rules. If they are so embodied they may appear as new rules entirely or they may supplant established commercial accounting rules. But it is almost certain that this secondary effect of taxation laws is not foreseen when relief provisions are introduced piece-meal into the tax codes. Furthermore, it has been found that some modes of calculating taxable income are themselves onerous or inequitable, particularly in periods of inflation when the replacement of inventories and plant requires larger outlays than the original outlays on the items already consumed in production. *Ad hoc* forms of tax relief are then superimposed on the existing fiscal rules and these, too, may become embodied in the corpus of commercial accounting rules. The use of the L.I.F.O. rule for inventories in the United States had such an origin.

The consequence of these and similar influences is the diversity in quality of the financial statements prepared in different countries mentioned at the outset. There could, perhaps, be little ground for concern about the diversity as long as countries are substantially self-contained, economically. The concern would be largely internal. There may well be controversy over the extent to which one industry is favoured by comparison with others, due to the accounting rules available to it, under the tax laws for example. But where two or more countries become linked through substantial investment of one in another or by substantial and competing commerce between them, diversity in accounting may well lead to misallocation of resources, mistaken domestic fiscal policies, and poorly-founded agreements and understandings among them. (Diversity of accounting rules within any country may also lead to misallocation of resources, to erroneous expectations, and to conflict of interests through misunderstanding. This is a particular case of the general effects of the accounting rules which are common to most countries. The proposal to be outlined covers both the intra-national and the international aspects of financial information).

The necessity of factual financial information

There can be no question about the necessity of factual information about the financial positions and results of business firms from time to time. In all forms of activity which involve progression from some condition or position to another the ascertainment of a present position and of the change in position since the last reading is a prerequisite of making any decision to proceed as before or to change the previous course. The navigation of ships, airplanes, spacecraft; the diagnosis of physical health; the conduct of industrial operations; the scoring of competitive games — all illustrate the principle.

Emphasis is laid on factual information on the present position from time to time. In the examples just mentioned great care is taken to secure that factual information is provided. Improvements are continually being sought in the counting and measuring devices by which present positions or states are ascertained. The possibility of human errors of observation is reduced by the use of automatic devices which give continuous records of the state of objects or processes. Indeed in many cases it is impossible to give effect to ideas requiring the use of sophisticated operating devices unless adequate instrumentation is first developed — high-speed and high-altitude aircraft, high temperature furnaces, the use of radioactive substances, illustrate the point.

Although the modern business corporation is a complex device, and many corporations are highly sophisticated devices, much less care has been given to the design of the financial instrumentation that it requires. There has been no lack of willingness to debate the superficial elements of competing ideas for reform. That is not the issue. The lack has been in arranging the many elements which must be accomodated in a reformed system in such a way that all are interdependent and logically consistent, and that the needs of all users of accounting information are satisfied.

The common users of accounting information are managers, investors and creditors. These classes may, on occasion, have conflicting interests. But none is able to manage its interest in the affairs of a company without factual financial information. Those who are interested in solvency need up-to-date factual information; otherwise they can form no valid judgement of the security for creditors' advances. Those who are interested in income cannot be properly informed without recourse to the factual state of a company from time to time, for the amount of income is the difference between certain features of the states of a company at successive dates. To make assessments of the past, to know the present state, and to form expectations about the future, all require that factual information about the present be available from time to time.

We propose to outline a system which provides this kind of information. But first we deal in some detail with the information which users require for their purposes.

The ideal functions of financial statements

Balance sheets and income accounts are prepared periodically in order to give investors and others information of an aggregative kind. Ideally they should enable readers to gain some idea of the liquidity of assets, the solvency of the firm, the relationship between equity and debt and the rate of return on net assets employed. These are key indicators of general position and performance for any and all firms. To be useful indicators, the figures on which they are based must be contemporary. Eeach of the indicators is a sum or a difference or a ratio. Summation, subtraction and comparison by ratio are illegitimate unless the components are represented in terms of the same general market situation (that is, prevailing prices) and in terms of monetary units of the same purchasing power. These two conditions are satisfied by the use of contemporary market prices at any year's end for the values of assets.

As investors and others are confronted with choosing between particular forms of investment, indicators of rates of return and safety of capital should be similar to those available for investments in say, governmental securities, or in assets other than corporation securities. As these are always determinable in contemporary terms, so therefore should indicators for corporations be in contemporary terms. But as one of the forms of choice open to investors is as between any two or more corporations, the accounting for all corporations should be in the same terms; there should be uniform rules, without significantly different optional treatments for assets of any given class.

Outline of a proposal

Using contemporary prices it is possible to draw up a balance sheet indicative of the financial position of a firm; that is, showing how it stands in relation to the rest of the community at a given time. The difference between two such discovered positions at different points of time will be due in part to changes in assets, liabilities and shareholders' equity. The difference between two such measures of the latter will be the income of the period, provided new shareholders' contributions and dividend payments are eliminated and provided there has been no change in the purchasing power of the monetary unit.

The measure of income just mentioned will include the effects of all rises or falls in the prices of goods used by a company during the period. But if the price of any such good rises in the period and the purchasing power of money falls, the company does not become better off by the whole amount of the rise in the price of the good. Account must be taken of the change in the purchasing power of money, as well as of changes in the prices of particular assets, if a measure of income in contemporary terms is to be obtained.

It is not possible to trace these two effects for all assets individually; for some assets held at the beginning of a year are not held at the end, and new assets will have been acquired during any year. It is legitimate to make a general adjustment for the effect of changes in the purchasing power of money during a period. If the shareholders' equity in the assets of a firm at 1 January 1970 is $ 100.000, and if all assets are then represented by contemporary prices and if the purchasing power of money changes so that $ 100.000 at 1 January 1970 is equal in purchasing power to $ 110.000 at 31 December 1970, the additional $ 10.000 is not income. If the shareholders' equity at 31 December 1970 is $ 120.000 (assets being represented at prices prevailing at 31 December 1970), the income of the year will be $ 10.000 only, of dollars representing purchasing power at 31 December 1970.

This suggests that, if during the year we take account regularly of changes in the prices of goods held, we can take account of any change in the purchasing power of money by a single adjustment at the years' end. We multiply the opening measure of shareholders' equity (or of net assets) by the proportionate change in an index of the general level of prices (the reciprocal of the purchasing power of money). Call the number so obtained a capital maintenance adjustment, as it is the number of additional monetary units which must be held at the end of the year to make up for the effect of the fall in the purchasing power of money on the shareholders' equity. If we add this to the number of dollars which is the measure of the opening shareholders' equity, we obtain a measure of the opening shareholders' equity in terms of the purchasing power of the dollar at the end of the year. The difference between the opening and closing measures of shareholders' equity (both expressed in units of purchasing power at the close of the period) will be the net income of the year.

The system may be represented symbolically as follows.

Let S_1 and S_2 represent dollars of the purchasing power prevailing at dates t_1 and t_2, the opening and closing dates of a period.

Let $S_1 M_1$ and $S_2 M_2$ be the measures of net monetary assets at the two dates. Net monetary assets are cash and receivables less payables.

Let $S_1 N_1$ and $S_2 N_2$ be the measures of non-monetary assets at the two dates, that is to say, the sums of the resale prices of assets other than monetary assets.

Let $S_1 R_1$ and $S_2 R_2$ be the measures of the shareholders' equity at the two dates.

Now at t_1, $S_1 M_1 + S_1 N_1 = S_1 R_1$
And at t_2, $S_2 M_2 + S_2 N_2 = S_2 R_2$

The left-hand sides of these equations are true representations; they are discovered and verifiable by observation of the assets in possession and discovery of the resale prices of the non-monetary assets at the two dates. The right-hand sides of the equations are thus also true representations.

Let the proportionate change in the general level of prices be p (expressed as a decimal fraction), so that $S_1 1 = S_2 (1 + p)$. The shareholders' equity at t_1 may therefore be represented by $S_2 (1 + p) R_1$; and the capital maintenance adjustment will be $S p R_1$. (We use S without a subscript to indicate it is an adjusting number of dollars only). We may therefore obtain the profit of the period thus:

Closing shareholders' equity $\quad S_2 R_2$
Less opening shareholders' equity $\quad S_1 R_1$
Less capital maintenance adjustement $\quad S p R_1$
Profit of period $\quad \overline{S_2(R_2 - R_1 - p R_1)}$

In case there is any doubt about the mathematical legitimacy of this operation, a rearrangement will demonstrate its propriety:

Opening shareholders' equity $S_1 R_1$
Capital maintenance adjustment $\quad S p R_1$ $\quad \} = S_2(1+p)R_1$
Profit of period $\quad S_2 R_2 - S_2(1+p)R_1$
Closing shareholders' equity $\quad \overline{S_2 R_2}$

It is possible to accumulate revenues and charges against revenues in a manner similar to that of conventional accounting. The amounts shown as revenues will be the selling prices of all goods sold, whether they are inventories, plant or other assets. The amounts shown as charges against revenues will be (i) all outlays during the period (or opening balances) for which no asset having a resale price remains at the end of the period, (ii) all charges (less credits, if any) due to changes in the resale prices of assets during the periods over which they are held, and (iii) the amount of the capital maintenance adjustment already mentioned.

This mode of accounting may seem strange, based as it is on resale prices instead of the traditional method of using initial purchase prices. But it is more rigorous and more realistic than the traditional method.

It is clearly dynamic. It takes account of changes in prices and in the purchasing power of money in the periods in which they occur. Traditional accounting takes account of changes in asset prices often long after they have occurred; and it takes no account at all of changes in the purchasing power of money.

The balance sheet yielded by the proposed system contains balances in terms of up to date prices; it therefore represents the financial position of the company in its relationships with the rest of the community at the time. Traditional accounting yields balance sheets which are not up to date, which contain prices of various ages, and which cannot therefore represent financial position at a stated date.

Balance sheets under the proposed system will give proper indications of solvency and of the relationship of debt to equity. Only the use of resale prices will yield proper indications of these matters. Traditional accounting does not give such indications; cost prices may have no bearing whatever on solvency and relations with creditors, especially if they are prices long since out of date and of mixed date.

Balance sheet contents and the amount of net income, being always in up to date terms, are readily understandable and interpretable against the prevailing state of the markets in goods, services and investment opportunities*.

Technical features of the proposal

It will be noticed that the proposal is not backward-looking. For any period its emphasis is on closing prices. It does not carry in the accounts residues which are merely end-products of original prices and "book-work" calculations. The residues are always verifiable amounts based on closing prices. The proposal thus gives effect to all of the changes, upwards and downwards, in the particular prices of the goods which the firm uses or buys and sells. It takes account of specific price changes.

When, for the calculation of income, it is necessary to subtract the amount of the shareholders' equity at the opening date from that at the closing date, it makes use of an index of changes in the general purchasing power of money to bring the two amounts to units of similar meaning. This one calculation (the capital maintenance adjustment) gives effect to the changes in the purchasing power of the amounts in which all assets and external liabilities were denominated at the beginning of the year. If we add this amount to the opening actual amount of shareholders' equity we obtain the opening amount of the latter in terms of units of closing purchasing power. By deducting the same adjustment from the increment obtained by setting off cash expenses and the effects of price falls against revenues and the effects of price rises, we obtain net income, also in terms of units of closing purchasing power. The consequence is that income is calculated by reference to the maintenance of capital in purchasing power terms. In brief, the proposal takes account of changes in price levels as well as changes in specific prices.

The rate of net income on net assets (or on shareholders' equity) can be calculated on a legitimate basis, as both numerator and denominator are in units of the same purchasing power. This rate may be compared directly with the rate for the previous year (if accounts were then kept on the same basis), even though the purchasing power of money has changed, for the rate is a pure number having no purchasing power or other dimension. The same applies to other ratios used in analysis.

Viewed as an exercise in measurement, the proposal contains all the elements of correction which may be found in metrological work in other fields. There is, however, one difference. Whereas in work in the physical sciences and technologies there are basic standards of reference for determining the unit dimension, there is in commerce a continually shifting standard, the *contemporary* purchasing power of money. All calculations are made and expectations are formed on the basis of present prices and the present purchasing power of money. If financial statements are to serve as bases for calculations backwards or forwards, or as bases for forming or constraining expectations, they must take account, from time to time, of the changes in the effective dimension (purchasing power) of the monetary unit as well as of changes in the prices of assets.

Again, as an exercise in measurement, the proposal carries no policy overtones. It does not imply that firms must maintain their capitals in purchasing power. It does entail that income shall be deemed to have emerged only insofar as provision is made for maintaining the purchasing power of an original investment; but in the context of an exercise in the measurement of an increment, this requirement is merely a requirement of the rules of measurement *per se*. The proposal does not imply that taxation authorities may or should tax only the income which emerges from the calculations. But insofar as any tax does, or any proposed tax is likeley to, encroach on capital, the proposal will reveal it.

---

* Only a brief outline is given here. The argument for the proposed style of accounting is given at length in the author's *Accounting, Evaluation and Economic Behavior*, Englewood Cliffs, Prentice Hall Inc., 1966. See also "Second Thoughts on Continuously Contemporary Accounting", *Abacus* Vol. 6 No. 1, 1970. Much of the preliminary work which led to the conclusions presented in these places will be found in the *Accounting, Finance and Management*, Butterworth, 1969.

In some countries the rules for calculating taxable income have been adopted for general commercial accounting; this may be true of many countries. This side effect of fiscal policies is undesirable. Economic efficiency cannot satisfactorily be assessed if its measurement is confused by rules adopted for purely fiscal reasons. It is possible that a government may wish to encourage development of an industry at one time, but to constrain its development at another; and to do this it may vary allowable deductions for taxation purposes (in respect of depreciation or for new investment, for example) accordingly. These variations have no necessary bearing on the economic realities of firms, on the actual depreciation and the present values of assets. Insofar as they affect the commercial accounting process they distort the representation of periodical income and financial position. And if the vestiges of the varied modes of calculation remain in use after the removal of the discriminatory tax relief or burden, the distortion will continue. It seems eminently preferable to maintain the distinction between the determination of a liability to taxation and the determination of net income and financial position for commercial purposes, as long as the first is not based directly on the same principles as the latter.

Consider the case of a country in which, say, investment allowances are made as a lump sum in the year of new investment (by grant or by credit against tax otherwise assessed). If the amount of the allowance is immediately set off against the balance of the asset account, the amount of the net assets will imperfectly represent the extent of the firm's investment in assets; and rates of return will subsequently be overstated. Our proposal, by virtue of its recourse to selling prices, avoids this kind of distortion, and any other kinds which may arise from fiscal policies made effective through depreciation and similar charges.

If we consider the case where comparison must be made between firms in different countries the need for realistic and contemporary financial information on a uniform basis is even greater. It would be bold to expect that any two or more countries would adopt substantially the same rules for taxation or for other methods of supporting or constraining particular industries. If such rules are, or were to become, embodied in the general corpus of commercial accounting rules, the possibility of legitimate comparison is, or would be, seriously endangered. The occasions for making comparisons between firms in different countries, for comparing the opportunities for profitable investment at home and abroad, for assessing the relative efficiencies of firms or industries at home and abroad, increase as international commerce and financing increase. But unless the accounting systems employed uniformly represent the results and positions of firms, and unless they are as free as possible of distorting conventions, the credence which can properly be given to financial information will be limited.

But we are not concerned solely with international differences in fiscal policy. For many reasons the specific prices of identical goods may rise or fall in different degrees in different countries through any given year. And the general levels of prices (or the purchasing powers of money) in different countries may change at different rates. These various changes or the expectations of them will have induced some of the decisions and actions of companies. If a company has in fact gained from its responses, or lost through failure to respond, to such changes, its statement of results and position should embody the consequences. It would, for example, be misleading to show the positive effect of a policy directed to avoiding the worst consequences of an anticipated change without setting off against it the negative effects of the actual change.

Suppose two companies A and B do business in imaginary countries X and Y which have as their domestic currencies francs (F) and marks (M). Suppose the companies make no physical change in their non-monetary assets during a year to which the following particulars relate. (We use symbols and subscripts similar to those used in the earlier formal example).

	A(X)		B(Y)	
	Open	Close	Open	Close
	F_1	F_2	M_1	M_2
Net monetary assets (M)	100	300	100	350
Non-monetary assets (N) at resale prices	500	600	500	550
Shareholders' equity (R)	600	900	600	900
Rise in general level of prices (p)		.08		.10
Capital maintenance adjustment		48		60
Net income		252		240

If we were to disregard changes in the market prices of non-monetary assets and changes in the general level of prices, we would rank B ahead of A. B's net income and the increase in its net assets would be M250 (the amount of the increase in net monetary assets above); the corresponding figure for A would be F200; the rates of return on opening net assets would be B — — 42%, A — — 33%. This is the result under traditional accounting. If we were to take account of changes in the specific prices of non-monetary assets and disregard the changes in the general level of prices, we would rank both equally; the rates of return would be 33%. If we take account of both kinds of change we would rank A ahead of B. We would calculate the rate of return by relating net income to the price-level adjusted opening capital F₂648 for A, M₂660 for B; the rates of return would then be 39% and 36% respectively.

In this simple exercise we have not been concerned with the rate of exchange of francs for marks. But the interpretation of the absolute magnitudes is rendered easier by the proposal; for as the figures are in terms of contemporary prices the current rate of exchange provides a means of direct translation or transformation of all the reported figures.

The buying and selling prices of goods and the general levels of prices in different countries do not always move in step or in the same direction. The variations we have illustrated are modest by comparison with those which may be found in the numbers of countries in which some firms operate or in the countries which make up an economic community. The greater the number of local variations which are "caught" in a given mode of accounting, the smaller is the need for *ad hoc* speculation about the meaning of the figures or *ad hoc* adjustment of the reported figures. It follows that decisions, whoever makes them, will be based on facts which are more reliable than the approximations which must otherwise be used.

Value of the proposal

If a company operating in many countries wishes to compare the rates of return of its branches or subsidiaries, it can do so directly given the figures produced in the manner proposed. If it wishes to compare the inclusive effects of its policies and those of other companies to assess the comparative total economic efficiencies of different companies, it can readily do so.

If the fiscal authority of any country wishes to impose taxes or to raise or lower tariffs or otherwise to influence particular kinds of industry, it can consider the effects of its proposals on the results of firms in any such industry in the knowledge that the reported results are inclusive of all gains and losses, in current terms, falling on firms in that industry. To some extent this may be a domestic matter. But insofar as taxes, tariffs and bounties may influence the capacity of domestic firms to compete with foreign firms, at home or abroad, it is not simply a domestic matter.

A community of countries may seek to promote trade and commerce between its members by reducing fiscal and other barriers. As a basis for rationalization, its secretariat may wish to be informed of the present (or recently past) effects of existing economic and fiscal policies on firms in its member countries. Where companies may choose their own sets of accounting rules (as is presently common), the information yielded by financial statements is a hazardous guide. Where the rules are uniform in each country, but different as between countries, the information is still of dubious value, since no transformation is possible from the result of using one set of rules to the result of using another set without recourse to the original data in respect of each firm; the interdependence of the components of financial statements hinders external transformations of this kind. Where the rules are uniform for all countries and where the rules cover the impact of variations in domestic prices and price levels, comparisons and assessments of the differential effects of old and proposed fiscal policies are far more likely to give rise to appropriate measures than if the information is varied or fragmentary.

Further, we may suppose that any company operating under any such new fiscal policy may still wish to rearrange its international business, or to make representations for domestic relief from the effects of international agreements, or at the very least to discover the effects of the new fiscal policy on its affairs. Only a comprehensive form of accounting will enable it to deduce the overall effects of any such change.

Counterargument and its rebuttal

It has long been held that to disclose a firm's results and position fully would expose it unfairly to its competitors. This has been one of the grounds for the use of secret reserves and other income-smoothing devices. The proposition is however baseless. Mere financial figures will only indicate whether one firm is more profitable, or successful, than another. They will not indicate whether its superiority lies in its financing, its buying, its product development, its marketing or its management, or in what combination of these. If competitors seek information on these matters they must seek elsewhere.

On the other hand the costs of distortion or misrepresentation of financial facts by the use of inappropriate conventions and rules are potentially enormous. There are the costs of guessing the meaning of information which purports to be factual but which known to be highly conventionalized. There are the potential costs of error and rehabilitation, if decisions made are found to have been inappropriate because the information available at the time was inaccurate. There are the costs of negotiations when for any purpose factual information is demanded instead of conventionalized information. There are the costs of inefficiency where conventionalized accounting enables the inefficient to escape scrutiny and prevents the efficient from being distinguished. And there are the costs of compiling information which is just not contemporarily relevant as it is expected to be.

Neither domestic nor international commerce can be as productive as technology warrants if the principal indicator of the aggregate efficiency of firms fails to represent relative efficiencies and positions in continuously contemporary terms. Neither the competition between firms nor the cooperation between countries can be expected to be as fruitful as technology warrants if the bases of contracts, negotiations and governmental policies lie in financial representations which diverge from the realities of commercial and industrial relationships and performance. It is believed that the system proposed would eliminate many of the grounds for doubt or mistrust of accounting information, and provide a more reliable foundation for private negotiation and public policy than the divergent modes of accounting now in use.

Trial—and Error: A Reply

Trial—and Error: A Reply

The object of a book review or review article is to put the subject of it under scrutiny. It is a trial, of a sort. But it can be a wayward or a disciplined trial. A book may be judged for what it claims to be. Or it may be judged for what a reviewer believes it should have claimed to be. Or it may be judged for what a reviewer thinks was claimed, but what was in fact disclaimed. Indeed, a review may be a summary execution, without much in the way of trial. Which of these possibilities resembles the critique of Anderson and Leftwich (A & L) the reader may presently judge.

Securities and Obscurities is "substantially a book of evidence" (p. 7). Of what? As the subtitle suggests, evidence of the necessity of reform of "the law of company accounts." The book could be attacked, therefore, on the ground that it makes no case for reform of the law. It is odd that A & L make no reference to this, the primary (and obvious) function of the book. They pass no judgment on whether the book is what it claims to be.

There is, in the title, an implied indication that practice under the law, as it stands, is far from satisfactory. And the book presents a great deal of evidence to the point. But does it establish the point? The closest A & L seem prepared to go on this is a vague allusion embedded in other comment—"if we are prepared to assume that the evidence may support the hypothesis." It is a neat way of damning the evidence without appraising it.

Criticism without some suggestion for reform has seemed to me to be only "half the job." So the book cites a substantial amount of evidence in favor of accounting for assets on a market price basis. But A & L "are not prepared to evaluate" the suggested reform or the evidence for it solely on the ground that contemporary information "impounds more information" than the products of traditional accounting. Thus, on the three central features of the book mentioned in the preceding paragraphs, A & L are unprepared to pass any judgment or opinion. The exercise begins to look like a nontrial.

Although its principal object was to collate a great variety of evidence, the book is not short on argument. Each of its chapters represents a particular line of argument, and for each line of argument there is quite specific evidence. A & L favor the reader with nine examples—and they lift them right out of the contexts of the arguments to which they relate. That is an excellent way of confusing the drift of the argument and evidence and of escaping the task of appraising the aptness of the evidence to the argument in any particular section. At a later point (to which I shall presently return), A & L charge me with failure to examine the relative frequency with which certain things occur. However, they exempt themselves from the obligation to say what proportion of the total evidence their nine examples represent—a task which, by the way, is far easier than the burden they would force on me.

In fact, the book alludes to events, accounting practices, and other features of over 280 named companies, drawn almost equally from Australia, the United States, and the United Kingdom. They were so chosen to show that the faults and defects under examination are widespread—territorially, industrially, and temporally. Besides these companies, at least 2,000 companies are represented in the summary tables and digests used—again, American, Australian, Canadian, and English. There are over 300 particular quotations and abstracts in respect of particular companies, or in respect of the law and practice of accounting, or in respect of the case for and the direction of reform. They include numerous citations of or references to opinions and judgments and dicta of the courts, of legal scholars, of economists, of accountants, of professional and official bodies, and of top business executives. It is all there, within the compass of 240 pages, certainly accessible enough for A & L to see that their nine examples represent about one-half of one percent of the material used. And the book points out that "the examples cited are only a fraction of what could have been tendered." A & L's "case" (their footnote 3; presumably a case for the prosecution, in the light of their later criticisms) looks flimsy indeed—no indication of the size of the population from which they selected, no suggestion that their selection amounts to a tiny fraction of the evidential material, no indication of the variety of material, and no indication of the matrix in which their examples were embedded.

A & L proceed to review the book by reference to a "framework" of their choice. What the framework is they do not say—but it seems, at this point, that the book is not to be judged on what it claims to be, but on what A & L think it should have been. Using their framework, they "express three major reservations concerning the evidence."

First, they say they are unable to determine whether the evidence is offered as the source of a hypothesis or as independent verification of the hypothesis. Granting for the moment that the distinction is of consequence, the inability of A & L to distinguish the two roles of the evidence is their fault, not the fault of the book. They noted my claim that the conclusions reached in *Accounting, Evaluation and Economic Behavior* (1966) stemmed from evidence presented in *Securities and Obscurities*. It is a simple matter to discover how much of the evidence could have been available before 1966 and how much of it was not available until later. All the material in the book is dated, and what I used in articles before 1966 is readily discoverable. But A & L are careless of such details. They simply treat the evidence *en bloc*.

In any case, the distinction they draw is a quibble. Anything which, by way of argument or evidence, "leads to" a conclusion (or hypothesis) surely "supports" the conclusion; otherwise, it could not be said to "lead to" the conclusion. If, on the basis of evidence available at a certain date, a conclusion is reached, the value of *that* evidence in no way diminishes as time passes. If at a later date more evidence for the same conclusion becomes available, the conclusion becomes better established. But the function of the earlier evidence is no different from that of the later. And it is all "independent"; nothing that I have done gave rise to it.

The temporal sequence is, of course, of some consequence where predictions are made on the basis of a hypothesis. Prediction in respect of socially influenced affairs is notoriously hazardous, and I am not inclined to play the role of seer in public. But the evidence available in 1964 (when *A.E.E.B.* was finished) would have supported the prediction that the disclosure of up-to-date information would be increasingly required by law. There have in fact been changes since then in the English and Australian statutes in this direction—not sweeping changes, admittedly, but certainly changes in the direction I have expected. They are mentioned simply as part of the present state of the legislation on pages 11–13. The evidence would also have supported the prediction that in the future, not distant from 1964, the professional bodies would become increasingly concerned with the inadequacies of traditional accounting. This too has happened.

Second, A & L contest the pertinence of the evidence to the hypothesis that valuation of assets on a market price basis is the best way of improving the utility of financial statements. Now, if we know how a particular kind of information is used, we can deduce what kind of information must be produced. As evidence of the uses made of accounting information, the book cites four financial information services, three textbooks on investment analysis, and fourteen examples of press comment and analysis. As examples of direct or implicit endorsement of the propriety of using market price information, it cites six accounting authors, six economists, two writers on investment analysis, three determinations by regulatory bodies, and two kinds of legally required disclosure of market values (with seventeen examples). As less direct evidence of the belief in, or of the necessity of, disclosing up-to-date asset values, the book refers summarily to over 900 companies, with specific illustrations of over 70 named companies. Of the amount and diversity of this evidence and its convergence on a common conclusion A & L say nothing. Their gratuitous assertion that "the evidence does not exist" flies in the face of all problem-solving experience. None of the particular things we choose or decide to do *exists* at the moment of choice. Always we act on the basis of some evidence of the appropriateness of means (the courses of action open to us) to ends. That is the function of the evidence I cited—to indicate the appropriateness of information of a certain kind to the exploratory calculations and deliberations of users of financial statements.

A & L assert that evidence of the superiority of the system I propose will only be available when firms produce financial statements "incorporating the various suggested alternative asset valuation bases." This means either that different firms shall use different bases, or that some or all firms shall use some or all of the alternative bases simultaneously. Whichever it means, I cannot conceive a method by which the superiority of any of the alternatives could be established. I invite A & L to share with us their blueprint for such a test, in such circumstantial detail that a clear identification of cause and effect (accounting method and consequence) can be made. The world of commerce is not so kind that it serves up the evidence which is a researcher's dream of heaven. In the present case, I suspect that the lifetimes of A & L will not yield the kind of evidence they want. Practical people, dealing with a capricious world, however, must use what is available—and that is what I did.

Third, A & L take issue with the link I posited between investors' losses and frauds, on the one hand, and the products of traditional accounting, on the other. As before, they fail to indicate the extent to which I drew on material of this kind. Only about fifteen out of the hundreds of examples used fall into this category. I played these cases in low key; quite deliberately, since I was much more concerned with flaws in the reporting of going concerns. But they are supplementary evidence to the more substantial evidence of other kinds. They deserved notice in the context of the book. As it seems, they are the kind of molehills out of which reviewers may make mountains.

As for the evidence of losses, A & L again suggest an impossible test. They would like to know how frequently investors fail to get the returns they expected; they want some indication of the proportion of such failures to the "totality of investment decisions." I frankly admit I do not know how to do it. Perhaps, given the whole lifetimes of A & L, they will be able to establish whether or not investors' failures are a significant proportion of the totality of investment decisions. But the information will throw no special light on the problem to which the book is directed. For myself, all I wanted was to show that misrepresentation of the financial positions and results of firms was associated with heavier losses than investors and creditors may otherwise have faced. The concluding sections of chapter 13 make this quite plain—as do the cases cited in that chapter and elsewhere. The investors and creditors who lost in these cases number tens of thousands. To A & L that number may not be statistically significant. But I am simpleminded enough to believe that even ten thousand people are too many losers to ignore, if something could have been done to make good their ignorance and prevent their misdirection.

As for the frauds, A & L are not convinced that my proposal would reduce their incidence. The very point of the examples cited, however, is that the frauds could not have been perpetrated, or if perpetrated not concealed, if published information had been required to conform with the market price rule. Here, as repeatedly, the bland and generalized statements of A & L about the book's material fail to come to grips with the particular inferences from that material. They point out that closing one avenue for fraud or concealment will not make other forms inaccessible. In effect, they imply that if we cannot solve all problems, it is pointless to solve one. This seems a trifle absurd. In any case, in the preface, I pointed out that the proposals "are not a panacea for all commercial ills." Their objection amounts to judging the book on what they think I claimed, when in fact I explicitly entered a disclaimer.

Fourth, A & L allege that the case for reform is based on the "implicit assumption" that to produce contemporary information is costless. They challenge this on the basis of "casual observations." Now, on the one hand, there is no such implicit assumption. The book is concerned with the *quality* of information, not with its cost. And, on the other hand, it takes something better than unspecified casual observation to assert anything about the costs of getting information. The objection is something of a red herring. But as they raise it, let us consider it.

It is pointless to talk about costs without at the same time dealing with benefits. And it is pointless to talk about the costs and benefits of one style of action (or accounting) in isolation. To make a judgment between two styles of accounting there are required (a) the costs of getting the information and (b) the consequences, good or bad, of using the information, for each style.

The costs of getting up traditional accounts may seem small. But things are not always what they seem. I do not know, and A & L could never know by casual observation, the costs associated with choosing from the alternatives available under traditional accounting, the costs of discussions with auditors and regulatory bodies where the methods chosen are in dispute, and the costs of the interminable debates about alternative methods among practitioners, academics, and others. I have been a noncasual participant or observer in all of these settings, and I know many others who have been. I say I do not know these costs. But I am prepared to wager, on the evidence available, that to particular firms they are considerable, and to the community at large enormous.

The costs of getting up accounts of the style I propose may seem substantial. But, again, things are not what they seem. In respect of cash, receivables, inventories, and marketable securities, there is obviously no greater cost than for traditional accounts. As for all other assets, if managements of firms are alert, opportunity-seeking, cost-avoiding, and under pressure of competition, they will of necessity know the approximate market values of many, if not all, of these assets from time to time. I say "of necessity," since market prices enter into proper calculations relating to changes in operations, projections in the nature of budgets, insurance coverage, takeover bids and offers, and so on. The information required for the accounts is a by-product of other inquiries. And given one principle of valuation, the costs of deliberation, dispute, and debate associated with the alternatives of traditional accounting would be saved. I guess now, but I suspect that there could be a "saving" under my proposal by comparison with traditional accounting. Of course, if managements are not of the kind supposed above, there seems to be good reason, in the public interest, to force them to take notice of the market prices of assets, the wealth they control—just as it is necessary to force on those who are careless of the interests of others the strictures of the safety laws, the food and drug laws, the labor laws, and the fair trade laws.

Turn to the benefits. Who will assess the benefits of traditional accounts? The book shows in numerous ways the confusion, misdirection, manipulation, and concealment which are possible—and, by implication, the inefficiency of some firms and the difficulty of judging the financial efficiency of all. "No one can guess the cost [in its widest sense] of generating and publishing *irrelevant* information. Much of it is concealed, since the inefficiency that flows from its use is not traceable and the personal misfortunes of the many who suffer its consequences are not reported" (p. 228). And what of the benefits of the proposed system? At least, they would entail the avoidance of confusion, misdirection, and inefficiency which arise from the products of traditional accounting. The net benefit, by comparison, lies entirely with the proposed system. If A & L wish to contest any element of this assessment, let them do so. But, please, with something better than unspecified casual observation.

So much for the reservations and objections. But was there nothing good about the book? Has it no saving graces—nothing that would abate the severity of A & L's "conclusions"? It was constructed from many pieces, so arranged that they interlock—argument with evidence, the particular with the general, section by section, and one section with another. The direct evidence *against* the "status quo" stands as indirect evidence *for* what the book proposes; and the direct evidence for those proposals stands as indirect evidence against the status quo. Opinions of diverse experts in diverse places and at diverse times, the sense and content of the relevant statutes, judgments of the courts, determinations of regulatory bodies, analyses by the financial press—all are interwoven, adding their combined strength to the book's conclusions. Every separate piece of evidence could be countered by a contradictory piece, I freely admit. But taken as a whole and in conjunction with the argument, the drift of it is, I believe, incontestable. A & L make nothing of the mutually supporting foundations on which the themes of the book and its conclusions are constructed.

It has happened before. *Accounting, Evaluation and Economic Behavior* was designed on similar lines, drawing on the support of many disciplines related in one way or another. Few of its critics have noticed this. Some have challenged, piecemeal, the way in which I associated ideas of one field with those of another. Leftwich, in fact, did this in "A Critical Analysis of Some Behavioural Assumptions [of *A.E.E.B.*]" (1969). On the basis of a handful of "alleged" flaws, he purported to demolish the foundations and conclusions of that book. But the allegations are all contestable (and, for the record, they are contested in a response to "Analysis" which I communicated to Leftwich but have not published). And even if the flaws were incontestable, they were not crucial to the conclusions of that book. A structure with many interlaced foundations does not crumple under a few stresses. As in that case, so also in the present case—there is much shadowboxing, but the substance is bypassed.

For credits, A & L have probably scored a notable "first." I have never hitherto seen a review or review article of which 40 percent consisted of straight extracts from the book and another 10 percent of simple connectives between those extracts. Nor have I ever been able to "lift" so much from one book without paying for the privilege. Perhaps my notions of the conventions of reviewing are old-fashioned.

Was the review a trial? or a summary execution? or what?

Third Thoughts[1]

It is of some importance in dealing with the theoretical basis of any technical operation, that the theory be judged on its merits as a theory, quite apart from the necessarily variant and contingent circumstances in which the practices it entails are applied. A theory is essentially an idealization. It strips away the idiosyncratic elements of a class of situations or phenomena the better to grasp the common elements and their relations.

The theory of continuously contemporary accounting is essentially a theory about the qualities of (a certain class of) information as an input to the deliberative processes of users of that information. The qualities of a class of information can be judged with reference to a posited set of circumstances, a posited set of mental operations in a posited set of contexts. The posits—the assumed circumstances, operations and contexts—will, ideally, correspond with some observed or observable circumstances, operations and contexts. A theory in respect of a limited class of situations or phenomena does not *necessarily* concern itself with other such classes, but its conclusions will, ideally, be consistent (or not inconsistent) with theories in respect of those other classes. A theory of exchanges under perfect competition, for example, does not concern itself with the means by which the conditions of perfect competition may be brought about. Similarly, the theory of continuously contemporary accounting does not concern itself with the means by which current cash equivalents are discovered, in any particular case, provided what is meant, *in general,* by current cash equivalents (or money equivalents) is clear.

The point of these remarks is that I know of no criticism of the theory which purports to demonstrate that its arguments or conclusions are invalid. Such criticism as there is has turned on the derivation of money equivalents in specific cases (particular assets or firms). Perhaps this criticism was 'invited' by the attempt, in *Accounting, Evaluation and Economic Behavior,* to provide some clues for deriving the data in what seemed to be 'difficult' cases. This was done with the object of suggesting that the mode of accounting which the theory entailed was feasible, practically. The use of replacement costs and specific indexes was proposed for no other reason than the derivation of an *approximation* to cash equivalents. The propriety of current resale prices for non-monetary assets 'is maintained as a matter of principle' (p. 248). This position is still held. It will

---

1. Prompted by Ronald Ma, 'On Chambers' Second Thoughts', *Abacus,* December 1974. Page references in the text relate to *Accounting, Evaluation and Economic Behavior.*

be understood therefore that any comments hereafter on methods of deriving approximations to a money equivalent have nothing to do with the validity of the theory. They relate to attempts to do what, in principle, the theory entails.

Accounts receivable

The term 'current cash equivalent' was introduced to the argument in the context of a discussion of *nonmonetary* goods (p. 92). It was adopted as a perfectly general term descriptive of a characteristic of all classes of asset. It would have seemed curious to speak, for example, of the 'resale price' of a cash balance; a general term avoids this curiosity. There are references to current cash equivalent elsewhere (pp. 104, 218) which allude to market resale prices without specific reference to nonmonetary assets. These may lend colour to the idea that resale price is to be taken for receivables. Against, as far as I can recall, there is no reference anywhere to factoring receivables. It might well have been expected to be mentioned if I had had any such notion in mind. Iselin's allegation of 'inconsistency', which Ma endorses, holds up if current cash equivalent is interpreted as resale price in all circumstances. But it was never intended that current cash equivalent and resale price should be considered as identical in all respects.

There are other indications. It was said that 'the current cash equivalents of the assets of a going concern are the sums obtainable in the short run in the ordinary course of business; that is market resale prices in the short run' (p. 218). I was trying, by this formulation, to insist that no value which was asserted to be a value to the business in the long run could properly be included in a dated balance sheet. That is why the passage refers to 'sums obtainable in the short run'. I was also trying to avoid the charge (made by some) that accounting on the basis described was 'liquidation' accounting. That is why the passage refers to 'the ordinary course of business'. The whole of the accounting was intended to be accounting for going concerns. If, therefore, a given firm in the ordinary course of business factors its receivables, the resale price of receivables would be a proper figure. But if a firm does not factor its receivables, the resale price of the receivables inventory is not the appropriate figure. Ma makes no reference to the phrase 'in the ordinary course of business'. But this limitation on the prescription is of its very nature; I do not want to force round firms into square pigeon holes.

Ma objects to a suggestion of Iselin, to the effect that to represent receivables by face value less a provision for doubtful debts is inconsistent with my system, 'since management expectations are taken into account'. Two points deserve attention, the taking account of expectations and the making of the valuation provision.

If there is a process by which a magnitude is discoverable at a given date, and if the process is recognized as an apt process, there would be no need to make a point of proscribing reference to expectations. There are such processes in the sciences. Hence there is no suggestion, in the literature of measurement in the sciences, that a physicist, for example, should report what his instruments say now rather than what he expects they might say at some future date. But in accounting there was, and is, a strong line of belief that the contents of a dated balance sheet should be influenced by what is expected to happen. There was, and continues to be, ample evidence of the capacity for misdirection of financial statements produced in this belief. Furthermore, as a general rule, the possible courses of future action, in non-financial and financial settings alike, cannot be considered without knowledge of one's present state, for that state is the point of departure into the future. Knowing these things, it seemed necessary to state categorically that expectations should not influence what purport to be dated statements of fact. In principle, the point seems unchallengeable. It is supported by a second line of argument; namely, that, as feedback on the consequences of operating under past expectations, financial statements cannot properly include the expected consequences of future events and actions.

Now, it may seem that, if the reported amount of receivables is less than the face value of debtors' balances, account is being taken of management's expectations. However, it is no less possible or reasonable to put a different construction on the exercise. What is required is an indication of the amount of money which, for practical purposes, claims agaitns debtors represent. Consider some cases. If the firm is an unsecured creditor of a bankrupt, and it is discovered that there are insufficient assets of the debtor to meet preferred creditors, the amount of the debt would be written off. If the firm is a secured creditor of a bankrupt, and it has been reported that secured creditors might receive 25 cents in the dollar, the remainder of the debt would be written off. If the firm is a creditor of a debtor whose account is overdue, an amount could be written off so that the balance represents what is deemed at the balance date to be recoverable. In all three cases there is available some evidence on which a judgment may be based. And the judgment is a judgment about the money equivalent of claims against debtors. In all three cases the judgment may turn out to have been in error, in the same way as the money equivalent of any other asset at a given date may turn out in due course to be different from the money amount realized. But that is a matter to be determined and reported upon in a subsequent period. In short, there is no better reason for regarding the write-off or write-down as an expression of a judgment about the future than there is for regarding it as a judgment about the magnitude of receivables at a stated date.

Finally, in dealing with the examples of the previous paragraph, reference was made in all cases to writing off an amount. The creation of a general provision for doubtful debts is not intended. Most provisions are near enough to being pointless in practice. It is common in practice to write off debts deemed to be bad. It is also common (or if not common, it is quite reasonable) to keep a memorandum record of bad debts written off until it is certain that they are not recoverable. If a provision for doubtful debts is made as well, the income of some past or present period will have been charged both with actual losses and with expected losses—there must have been a kind of double-charging somewhere if there remains a credit in the provision, a charge for the past (amounts written off) and a charge for the future (amounts provided). This double-charging is a proper enough ground for the rejection by taxation authorities of deductions by way of provisions for doubtful debts. It seems also a proper enough ground, whatever applies to taxation, for rejecting the creation of general provisions for doubtful debts.

Bonds payable

Ma contends that for publicly traded bonds 'the appropriate measure of their current cash equivalent is the market price'. Although I introduced current cash equivalent when dealing with assets, I applied the term also to equities (p. 107). If assets are worth in the aggregate $1,000 and debts amount to $500, the residual equity in the assets is $500. Because the first is a money sum (the money equivalent of what is owned) and the second is a money sum, the difference is a genuine money sum. The use of 'current cash equivalent' in respect of all three amounts suggests a unifying idea—it's all money.

But assets are not equities, and there is no ground for supposing that the same rules apply to both. The amount of the assets represents the claims of the firm, as against the rest of the community, to the use of resources. The amount of the liabilities represents the claims of creditors against the assets of the firm. The claims of creditors against the assets of the firm do not become the less (or the greater) as a consequence of transactions between bondholders. Ma asserts that to report a '5-year bond liability at its contractual amount imparts no useful information on the net resources available for adaptation'. But indeed it does. In the simple case of my previous paragraph it indicates that the debt to equity ratio is one-to-one; and that, to the extent of $500, the company has made use of its borrowing power; for these reasons its future freedom to borrow (and in some cases, its freedom to deal in its assets) is constrained.

Suppose the company issued at par $500 in 10 per cent bonds for a term of four years, redeemable at par, on condition that the ratio of debt to equity should not exceed one-to-one. Bond indentures or trust deeds contain such stipulations; any specified ratio would serve our purpose. Suppose now that the market price of the bonds fell to 50. If the market price of the bonds were used in the balance sheet, the bondholders' equity would be shown to be $250 and the owners' equity $750. The *debt to equity* ratio would then appear to be one-to-three, and the bondholders should therefore be quite satisfied if the company borrows another $500 (which would restore the ratio to one-to-one). This is inconceivable. For the object of the restriction clause was to provide an *asset-cover* of two-to-one for the debt, whereas the new borrowing would reduce the cover to three-to-two. If it were conceivable we will have learned how to circumvent an indenture condition without really trying.

Turn to the viewpoint of the company. Ma suggests that, where an indenture restricts the company's dealing in its own assets, the restriction may be removed by buying in its bonds. But first it must get the money. Now the market price of the bonds will have fallen to 50 because the market rate of interest has risen—very substantially for a bond with a short term to maturity, less so for a bond with a long term—or because the company has become a risky debtor. In the latter case, its prospect of raising new money is dubious, at least; so we set that case aside.

A $100 bond that has, say, four years to run at 10 per cent, will yield in cash $140. If the market rate is 10 per cent, the present value of the bond to maturity is $100. If the market rate rose to 35 per cent, that bond would sell at 50, the price alluded to in the previous paragraph. (The figures may seem unrealistic; but they will serve as well as any others to illustrate the point). Now in order to buy in the outstanding bond, the company could issue a $50 bond at 35 per cent redeemable at par in four years time. The company is confronted with the two possible payouts:

Original bond	10	10	10	110
Replacement bond	17.5	17.5	17.5	67.5

the present values of both of which, discounted at 35 per cent, are approximately $50. Certainly, to replace the original bond would reduce the debt to equity ratio. But for a given income (before charging interest) it would also reduce the interest cover, and an even higher rate of interest might have to be paid. Why then, at any balance date, will the company not have bought in its bonds? Either because no lender is willing to lend at the higher risk of interest income, or because the alternatives are not judged by the company to be as 'comfortable' or as 'satisfactory' as allowing the original issue to run. The companys' capacity for adaptation has in fact been constrained by the commitment, not only to pay 10 per cent per annum but also to pay $500 at maturity. The posited 'advantage' is not as great as it may see, superficially, to be. If the company has not taken the 'advantage', it is simply because it can't.

Some may suppose that the same can be said of assets: if a company has not sold an asset it has not taken advantage of the difference between book value and resale price. But a company does not in this case have to sell to get the advantage. It already has it; as resale price is a money equivalent it already has the greater money's worth, the greater command of goods and services generally. It can, if it wishes, turn the asset into cash, which is only changing the form without changing the magnitude of assets. It can borrow on the strength of the (greater) market value. In a nutshell, the possession of assets represents freedom to act; obligations to pay creditors are restraints on that freedom. Greater freedom to act accrues (without deliberate action) if the market prices of assets rise; it does not accrue (without deliberate action) if the market prices of outstanding bonds falls.

Now consider two series of outstanding bonds, at 10 per cent and at 5 per cent, as in Ma's example, having, say, four years to run. The future outlay on the servicing and redemption of the 10 per cent issue will be $140 per $100, and for the 5 per cent issue $120. Ma suggests that to report both at the contractual amount of $100 is not meaningful. But indeed it is. For in both cases the amount of $100 is the present (discounted) value of the outlays, discounting each at its rate of interest. Ma avers that 'it is conceptually wrong to employ the internal rate of return for valuation purposes'; the allusion seems to be to the use of the two rates, 5 and 10 per cent, in the calculation just mentioned. But the calculation is not a calculation made 'for valuation purposes'; its object is simply to show that, in reporting both issues at $100, the present face values and the discounted values of the *commitments* are simultaneously reported.

Work in process
Under this caption Ma deals with a passage occurring in the wider context of 'inventories' in the 'Second Thoughts' paper. If indeed I was 'skating over the very real difficulties in interpreting the reported periodical profit figure', it seems to me that Ma has skated over specification of the difficulties. A new and expanding firm which increases its inventories of the work-in-process, zero-value, variety, may well report a smaller profit than if it were operating at a stable level. But there seems no occasion for calling this a 'downward bias'. Surely we do not expect growth for nothing; and surely we do not expect instantaneous profits from a process of expansion the outcome of which is time consuming. Investment in the building up of a higher quantum of work in process is no different in principle from investment in other appurtenances of growth. If it reduces the immediate net outcome that seems understandable—it does not seem difficult at all to interpret.

That firm application of the resale price rule to work in process opens more widely the possibility of manipulation needs more support than mere assertion. The sloppiness of conventional accounting does not subsist in the variety of optional rules for valuing any one asset, but in the variety of options available for all assets. However, if, by the use of resale prices, the possibility of varying one's options in respect of other assets is reduced, there is also less possibility of forcing all the latitude which might otherwise be gained on to one asset class such as work in process. A greater degree of consistency in respect of that asset seems to be a highly probable consequence.

Rules and judgements
Many of the questions raised by Ma in the final section of his paper have to do with what some would consider as 'refinements' in reporting or in discovering the magnitudes to be reported. I am, frankly, sceptical of the value of being painstakingly exact in a world which is gross and volatile. In the domain of reason, of theory, one can be tightly discriminating. In the laboratory one can test and test, and measure and measure, till one knows in great detail the characteristics of what is under observation. But the whole apparatus of statistical description and analysis seems to have little meaning when the facts under observation are in essence unique 'point facts' which, by the time they have been ascertained, are already out of date.[2] That is the inevitable characteristic of dated financial statements.

2. See also R. J. Chambers, *The Mathematics of Accounting and Estimating, Abacus,* December 1967, p. 163, esp. pp. 168-72.

Ma is of the opinion that 'there has not been adequate recognition of the fact that the current cash equivalent . . . is an average or expected value (employing the term in the statistical sense)'. But I have never considered it as a value about which one could or should put statistical hedges. When an inventory is counted, the result can be considered as a discovered fact, or as one of a series of possible results or values which are distributed in some statistically describable fashion. I do not deny that the discovered value is a possible value and that a statement in which it occurs should be regarded as a statement of a probabilistic kind. But it is not a statement to which one can assign a statistical probability for the unique observation or set of observations will not have occurred before and will not recur.

In suggesting that the average of a number of observations may be taken (where there are different values of the observable), I sought merely to avoid the possibility of 'biassed' selection of a particular value. I did not suggest that a 'scientific sample' be taken. I can imagine so many reasons why individual observations may be unique in style and setting, that I find it hard to imagine what a scientific sample would be. I suspect, therefore, that any attempt to refine by statistical manipulation the process of discovering a reliable value will merely give a pseudo-scientific result, based at least as much on the assumptions of the refiners as on the raw data. Whatever doubt the user may have of the reliability of a reported value may be stilled; but he may nevertheless be the unwitting victim of the refiner's imagination and technique.

I value any attempt to improve 'the superstructure' of the system I have proposed. But Ma forgoes attempting a 'definitive solution' of the problems he raises; indeed he forgoes an exploratory attempt. It may be very instructive to see the form of a set of financial statements which meet Ma's minimum disclosure requirements, and a pro forma statement of the steps which yield the information he requires (see his third last paragraph). Perhaps he will undertake the exercise. Until there is some such demonstration, it is impossible to avoid the suspicion that the result will be 'sophisticated' beyond the bounds of practical necessity, and even that the result will be refined beyond what the substantive (as distinct from the speculative or normalizing) inputs will justify.[3]

There seems to be a widespread tendency to discuss the use of financial information in a general way, as if *every* kind of information must meet all the stipulated requirements of any *one* kind of information.[4] This is unwarranted, and confusing. A particular officer of a particular company may wish to know in great

---

3. None of this is to be taken to apply to intensive *ad hoc* inquiries, either by researchers or by functional specialists in business firms. When dealing with a limited range of phenomena (say, the management of a securities portfolio) with some specified object or series of possible objects in mind, it would be sheer folly to disregard elaborate tools appropriate to the task.

4. The evidence is extensive. The most general indication of it is the widespread neglect of the requirement that figures in financial statements shall be of the same generic kind, and therefore 'additive'. There is no reference to it in Grady's *Inventory* (1965), or in *A Statement of Basic Accounting Theory* (1966), or in the Report of the Study Group, *Objectives of Financial Statements* (1973).

detail the financial magnitude, and the characteristics of that magnitude, of a particular event or asset. For example, he may wish to know the price of a particular share at the close of business on a given day, the range of prices during that day, the range of prices during the preceding week, the total turnover on that day or in that week, the average price at which it is traded, and so on. All of these bits of information may tell him more 'about' the closing share price than a simple statement of the price. But other officers do not want and cannot use all that information. To insist that they shall have it is to insist on overloading them with information which is useless in their setting. Not only are they inexpert in the analysis of the securities market, their interest in the closing price is a different kind of interest, and, being concerned with many things other than the prices of shares, they have not the time to grapple with particulars of one share price. The very first formal propositions of *Accounting, Evaluation and Economic Behavior* (p. 35) take this into account.

Overload is, of course, one of the causes of breakdown. In the present case, if a receiver is overloaded with information, either he may neglect it in order to get on with things other than the task of digesting it, or he may attempt to digest the information and neglect some of the other things he is required as a functionary to do. In the first case, he preserves his capacity for functioning, but the overload entails a cost without benefit. In the second case his capacity for functioning is diminished as he strives to cope with the putative benefit for which the cost was incurred. By matching the degree of particularity (or generality) of information with the tasks of classes of users of the information, both the above causes of 'waste' may be avoided. The whole drift of my work on accounting and financial statements is based on this.

The object of accounting and the financial statements which are its end products is to present the aggregative positions and results of firms as wholes, for the benefit of classes of person who deal with firms as wholes. These classes, of course, include all classes of managerial person whose acts must be related to the position and results of a firm as a whole, and all external classes of person whose acts are the better informed by knowledge of the firm as a whole—and, in both cases, even though any particular act of any of those classes affects only some part of the whole. The reason why I have repeatedly drawn attention to the uses of indicators of solvency, debt-cover and rate of return is that they represent features of firms as wholes. (Incidentally, they also embrace between them all the figures which might be expected to be found in financial statements.) Trends of aggregates, sub-aggregates and the indicators just mentioned also represent aspects of firms as wholes. In all these respects the use-values of the aggregates are greater than the use-values of any of the particulars which enter into the aggregates. But of necessity the particulars should not be inconsistent with the amplified particulars which any specialist within the firm will use for specialist purposes.

Given, then, that financial statements deal summarily with a wide range of particulars (from petty cash to real estate), and that even within classes of particulars there is great diversity (consider receivables or inventories), it does not seem feasible that their utility for the purposes specified would be greatly improved by statistical hedges and qualifications. There is in the system already, a rule (the money equivalent rule) which sharply constricts the options. There is already a means (the independent audit) of giving assurance that what is reported under the proposal is not systematically biassed. Given these checks there seems no reason to believe that the analytical measures derived from financial statements would be sensitive to the net effects of random observational errors. If, of course, there are reasons or examples which lead to a contrary view, I for one would like to know of them.

ACCOUNTING FOR INFLATION

Exposure Draft

Conventional (historical cost based) accounting is almost universally recognized to be defective under inflationary conditions. Experience under these conditions has prompted the search for a dependable alternative.

There are at present in circulation in Australia "preliminary exposure drafts", prepared by the Australian Accounting Standards Committee, entitled

"A Method of 'Accounting for Changes in the Purchasing Power of Money'" (issued December 1974), and
"A Method of 'Current Value Accounting'" (issued June 1975).

Notwithstanding the express need of a method of accounting for inflation, neither of these statements is, or claims to be, a method of accounting for inflation. The first deals with ways of taking account of some of the effects of changes in the purchasing power of money, but disregards the effects of changes in the prices of particular assets. The second proposes the use of the replacement prices of assets in financial statements, but disregards the general effects of changes in the purchasing power of money. As both types of change occur concurrently during inflationary periods, both of the above methods are partial or incomplete, and therefore potentially misleading.

The object of the publication of the preliminary exposure drafts was to encourage discussion and comment, preparatory to the publication of an "accounting standard". But discussion of two quite different and incomplete methods can scarcely be well-informed, if there is also a method which does not suffer from their defects.

This Exposure Draft deals with a method of accounting -continuously contemporary accounting - which takes into account both changes in particular prices and changes in the general level of prices. It is thus more comprehensive than the two methods previously mentioned. And the financial statements it yields are up-to-date, more realistic and more readily comprehensible.

September 1975.

ACCOUNTING FOR INFLATION

CONTENTS

		Paragraphs
I	Accounting Generally	1 - 8
II	The Effects of Inflation	9 - 14
III	General Principles of Continuously Contemporary Accounting	15 - 21
IV	The Determination of Money Equivalents	22 - 30
V	Owners' Equity Accounts	31 - 36
VI	Some Features of the System	37 - 43
VII	Summary of Rules	44

APPENDIXES

A	Illustration of Method of Continuously Contemporary Accounting.
B	Comparative Evaluation of Price Level Adjusted Historical Cost Accounting (C.P.P.), Replacement Price Accounting (R.P.A.) and Continuously Contemporary Accounting CoCoA .

PART I — ACCOUNTING GENERALLY

1. **The discussion and conclusions to be presented will have reference to business firms generally.**

   Any method of business accounting should be expected to be serviceable in substantially the same ways, no matter what the form of ownership of the business to which accounts relate. However, the most extensive array of uses of accounting information is exemplified by the relationships between companies and their shareholders, creditors and others. For this reason much of the discussion will relate to companies and company accounting. But, because the principles or rules which emerge are equally pertinent to companies and other types of business ownership, the general term "business firm" or simply "firm" will be commonly used. Also the terms "net profit" and "net income" will be used interchangeably, as synonyms.

2. **Financial statements are expected to represent fairly and in up-to-date terms the financial characteristics of firms.**

   The products of the accounting process are dated balance sheets and income (profit and loss) statements. These are expected, by the laws relating to companies, to give a true and fair view of the financial positions and of the results of companies as at the dates and for the periods to which they relate. They are put to use by a variety of parties; by actual and potential investors and creditors; by investment advisers and underwriters and trustees for creditors; by tribunals concerned with wages and prices; and by governmental authorities for fiscal and other regulatory purposes. The decisions and actions of all of these parties are taken in the light of what they know, at the time, of the past results and present financial positions of companies (or of firms generally). Unless the financial statements of companies correspond fairly well with their actual positions and results, actions based upon them may affect adversely, and quite unexpectedly, the interests of companies or of other parties related to them.

3. **The survival and growth of firms depends on their command of money and money's worth.**

   The actions of all the above mentioned parties are directly related to money receipts and payments of a company - receipts by way of sales income, loans or credits, subsidies or bounties, and the proceeds of new share issues; payments by way of purchases, wages, taxes, interest, and loan repayments. The capacity of a company to grow or to change its operations, on a small or large scale, as new opportunities arise and present operations become less attractive, depends on its command of money or money's worth. In the ordinary course of events, companies are expected to pay their debts to others when they fall due. In some circumstances they may find it worth while, or be forced, to repay debts before they fall due. Generally, then, the ability to meet debts owed is a condition of survival. For all these reasons, it is a matter of importance that the managers of companies, and that other parties having financial interests in companies, shall know from time to time the money and money's worth at the command of companies and their outstanding financial obligations.

4. Financial position is a dated relationship between assets and equities.

The money and money's worth at the command of a company at a point of time is given by the sum of its holdings of cash and receivables and the market (resale) prices of its other (non-monetary) assets. The resale price of an asset at a given date is its money equivalent at that date. Possession of the asset is financially equal to possession of the sum of money representing its resale price. It is therefore possible to add amounts of cash and receivables and the money equivalents of other assets to obtain a financially significant aggregate. The total amount of liabilities to short and long term creditors represents money claims against the aggregate money's worth of assets. The difference between total assets and total liabilities is a genuine money amount, since the amounts of total assets and total liabilities are genuine money amounts. This difference represents the residual interest of shareholders or owners in the total assets, or the total investment at risk in the business of the company. It also represents the amount of net assets, or assets financed otherwise than by credit.

5. The amount of income is deduced from changes in dated financial positions.

A balance sheet in which assets are represented at their money equivalents gives to all users of it an up-to-date indication of the total wealth of a company at a point of time and total claims against or interests in that wealth. Given two such balance sheets, in the absence of inflation, the increment in the amount of net assets represents the retained profit of the intervening period (provided there has been no new share issue). The sum of retained profit and the dividends paid in the period is the net profit or net income of the period. Net income may be calculated by setting out the several classes of gain or loss of a company in a period. But the amount so obtained is necessarily equal to the difference between the opening and closing money amounts of net assets. It is a genuine increment in money's worth, since the net assets figures are genuine money amounts (para. 4)

6. Financial positions and results are aggregative; their elements must satisfy the rules of addition and relation.

Total wealth, total liabilities, the amount of net assets, the calculation of net profits, all entail addition and subtraction. Other calculations made by investors and creditors, such as rates of return and debt to equity ratios, are relations between aggregates. All particular elements of financial statements must therefore be capable of proper addition and relation. The money amounts and money equivalents referred to in the two previous paragraphs satisfy this condition. By contrast, no logical or financial significance can be assigned to the sum of an amount of money and the purchase price, past, present or future (including replacement price) of any good. No such sum can properly be related to any debt outstanding, or to any plan to purchase goods or services, or to pay taxes and dividends.

7. Financial positions and results are both the consequences of past actions and the bases of future actions.

The financial position of a firm is a consequence of past (historical) events up to the date for which it is ascertained. No future event or expectation of a future event has any bearing on it. But given an ascertained financial position (and other information and expectations), choices may be made among the courses of action available to the firm. If at a given date the liquidity of a firm is strained, action to restore its liquidity is necessary. If at a given date a firm is heavily in debt, liquidity cannot readily be restored by further borrowing. If the results of the immediately past period are unsatisfactory in any sense, action must be taken to improve the result in the following period. All deliberate actions having financial consequences must be considered in the light of the aggregative financial characteristics of the firm at the time of choice. And all estimations of the probable financial consequences of future actions must be based on the position of the firm at the time of choice of future courses of action. Financial position as described is the one common element in all calculations relating to choices of future actions.

8. **The money equivalents of assets, the purchase prices (replacement prices) of assets and the user-values of assets are used in conjunction; none is a substitute for the other.**

    If a prospective course of action entails the "replacement" of an asset, it is necessary to know the money equivalent of the present asset and the purchase price of the new asset. If a prospective action entails the purchase of additional assets, their purchase prices must be known. Whether or not any such course is financially "feasible" can only be ascertained by comparison of those purchase prices with the money equivalents of present assets, or some selection of present assets. Which is to be preferred of the feasible courses of action is indicated, inter alia, by comparisons of the expected net proceeds of the alternative projects or investments in assets. Expected net proceeds, or present (discounted) values, are user-values. They are personal estimates based on expectations of the future; they are therefore subjective. They represent the expected outcomes of specific possible future actions. They cannot therefore be used in balance sheets as indicative of the financial feasibility of *any* course of action, even of those courses to which they relate. In short, the money equivalents of assets, the purchase prices of goods not presently held, and user-values of assets or projects are used when considering specific possible courses of action. But each is used for its own purpose and in its own way. None is a substitute for the other. None of them may properly be added together. Only the money equivalents of assets are properly useable for the representation of financial position at a given date.

PART II — THE EFFECTS OF INFLATION

9. **Changes in the structure and in the general level of prices occur concurrently but not equally.**

    In an inflationary period two things occur which affect the positions and results of companies. The prices of particular goods change relatively to one another. There is a change in the *structure* of prices. Such changes may occur at any time as the wants of consumers change, technology changes or the policies and outputs of companies change (collectively, supply and demand conditions). There is also a change in the general *level* of prices. "Inflation" is descriptive of a rise in the general level of prices, or of its counterpart, a fall in the general purchasing power of money. When inflation occurs all prices do not rise to the same extent or at the same time. Some may fall as rises in others force business firms and consumers to change their spending habits. Inflation may thus cause changes in the structure of prices, to the benefit of some firms and to the detriment of others. The beneficial or detrimental effects may arise from changes in the money equivalents of assets held, or from changes in the profit margins obtainable for goods and services sold.

10. The effects on a firm of changes in the structure and level of prices can only be ascertained in the aggregate.

When changes in the structure of prices and changes in the general level of prices occur in the same period, it is not possible to say that any particular price change is caused by inflation, or by the shift in the relation between the supply and demand conditions, or partly by the one and partly by the other. All that is known is that prices and the level of prices are different from those of an earlier date. Nevertheless, it is possible to calculate the aggregate effects of changes in prices and the general level of prices on the positions and results of firms. Because changes in particular prices and changes in the general level of prices influence one another, the effects of both should be brought into account. One cannot be considered as isolated from the other. Whatever the outcome, it cannot be said whether any part of the result is due solely to managerial judgements or solely to accidental or unforeseeable factors. Managers may be expected to use their best judgements at all times. Only the results in aggregate will indicate with what effect firms have been able to meet the conditions through which they have passed.

11. The conventional money unit, in terms of which financial positions are represented, is equally serviceable for that purpose in inflation.

Financial position has been described as the dated relationship between amounts of assets and equities (para 4). The dating of a financial statement represents both (a) that the money unit used in it has reference to that date and (b) that the number of money units appearing beside any item is the appropriate money equivalent of that item at that date. To suppose otherwise would be anachronistic, and confusing. The money unit is by its nature the unit of general purchasing power and debt-paying power at any specified date whatever, and the unit in which the money equivalents (resale prices) of assets are expressed. That the same nominal money unit may have a different general purchasing power at some other date is of no consequence when determining a dated financial position.

12. The increment in the nominal amount of net assets during a year is not serviceable as indicating net income in an inflationary period.

Calculation of net income in the manner described in para 5 brings into account the effects of all changes in the money equivalents of assets, in the absence of inflation. If particular assets have risen or fallen in price during a year, for whatever reason, these changes in the structure of prices will be captured by taking the resale prices of assets at the opening and closing dates of the year. Since, in the absence of inflation, there is no change in the general purchasing power of money, the net income so calculated will represent a genuine increment in the general purchasing power or debt-paying power of the net assets of a firm. Part of it will be the resultant of trading costs and revenues, and part the resultant of rises and falls in the money equivalents of assets since the beginning of the period or since (the subsequent) date of purchase. The rises and falls during the year in the money equivalents of assets held at the end of a year may be described as *price variation adjustments*. But if the purchasing power of the money unit has changed during the year, the difference between the opening and closing amounts of net assets will not represent a genuine increment in general purchasing or debt-paying power.

13. Provision must be made for the loss of purchasing power in an inflationary period of the amount of net assets (or capital employed) at the beginning of the accounting period.

Money holdings and claims to fixed amounts of money may be described as monetary assets. Their money equivalents at any date may be discovered directly. All other assets are non-monetary assets. Their money equivalents at any date must be discovered by reference to market resale prices at or near that date. Monetary assets held during an inflationary period lose general purchasing power. Likewise every dollar representing the money equivalent of non-monetary assets at the beginning of a period loses general purchasing power. And likewise every dollar owed during an inflationary period loses general purchasing power; borrowings thus constitute a "hedge" against losses in

243

the purchasing power of money. By subtraction, the amount at risk of loss in general purchasing power during inflation is the amount of net assets (total assets less liabilities) at the beginning of the accounting period. The amount of the loss thus sustained must be made good out of other surpluses before it can be said that a surplus in the nature of net income has arisen. This amount may be described as a *capital maintenance adjustment,* since its object is to secure that, in calculating net income, provision is made for the maintenance of the general purchasing power of the opening amount of net assets (or capital employed).

It may be noted that, across a whole community, the aggregate amount of price variation adjustments might be expected to correspond with the aggregate amount of capital maintenance adjustments, since the general price index is indicative of the average of changes in specific prices. But particular firms are affected differentially by changes in prices and in the price level. Rises in the prices of particular goods do not correspond with or offset falls in the general purchasing power of money. That is why the aggregates of both should be taken separately in the accounts of firms.

14. Net income is the algebraic sum of trading surpluses, price variation adjustments and the capital maintenance adjustment.

The amount of the capital maintenance adjustment is the opening amount of net assets multiplied by the proportionate change in the general level of prices. Thus, if a firm begins a period with net assets of $1,000 and an index of changes in the general level of prices rises from 130 to 143 in the period, the amount of the capital maintenance adjustment is $1,000 x 13/130, or $100. A general price index is used because the amount of net assets is a genuine dated money sum, irrespective of the composition of assets, and because the firm is considered to be free to lay out any part of its assets or the increment in its assets in any way it pleases. The index to be used would be chosen on the basis of competent statistical advice. From the two preceding paragraphs, net income will be the algebraic sum of trading surpluses, price variation adjustments and the capital maintenance adjustment. The amount charged as capital maintenance adjustment will be credited to a capital maintenance reserve. If any part of this reserve were appropriated as a dividend, it would impair the general purchasing power of the opening amount of net assets. (See also para 34).

PART III — GENERAL PRINCIPLES OF CONTINUOUSLY CONTEMPORARY ACCOUNTING

15. The method of accounting described is called continuously contemporary accounting CoCoA.

Asset valuations are brought up-to-date, at least at the end of each accounting period, by reference to independent sources of information. Those valuations are in terms of the purchasing power unit at the time. That the balance sheet is a dated statement implies that the amounts stated in it relate to that date and that the dollars in which those amounts are expressed are dollars of dated purchasing power (see para 11). CoCoA satisfies this requirement. Shareholders' equity amounts are augmented by the capital maintenance adjustment periodically and the balance of net income is a sum also expressed in dollars of the same dated purchasing power as other items in the balance sheet. All reported balances of a given date are therefore contemporary with that date. There are no prices of different dates nor purchasing power units of different dates in the balance sheet of any date. Hence the description "continuously contemporary accounting".

16. Accounts may be brought up to date periodically or more frequently.

The price changes affecting a firm may be occasional or frequent, and individually large or small. As up-to-date information on a firm's assets and liabilities is the only dependable basis for managerial action, the accounts may be continually adjusted for changes in the prices of assets. In principle this is the most desirable mode of accounting. But for external reporting it is sufficient to bring the account balances to their money equivalents at the end of each reporting period. Accounts could be kept just as they are presently kept during the accounting period. But at the end of the period all account balances are adjusted to their current money equivalents. The variations of money equivalents from book balances are summarized and charged or credited, as price variation adjustments, in the income account. And of course the capital maintenance adjustment is computed and charged. The method may be called "continuously contemporary" because, in principle, accounts can be kept continuously up-to-date, even though in practice adjustments may be made less frequently than price changes occur. Under either process the results will be exactly the same.

17. **CoCoA. conforms with the established principle of periodical, independent verification of account balances (the objectivity principle).**

   To verify the physical existence of, and legal title to, assets at balance date is a well established principle. Independent checking of cash balances and receivables balances has long been regarded as a necessary safeguard against misrepresentation. But the same process of verification is not applied, under traditional historical cost accounting, to the money amounts assigned to other assets. The mere checking of physical existence and legal title is inconsistent with the fact that financial statements relate to the *financial* characteristics of firms, not to physical or purely legal characteristics. The financial characteristics of assets should be independently verified, no less than other characteristics. CoCoA applies this principle uniformly to all assets.

18. **CoCoA conforms with the well-established accrual principle.**

   The accrual principle entails accounting for changes in the financial characteristics of a firm independently of the conversion of assets and obligations to cash. Revenue is brought into account when customers are billed; earlier, that is, than cash is received from customers. Depreciation is brought into account periodically; that is, long before the diminution in value of an asset is discovered on its resale. Applications of the principle pervade current practice. Yet there are also numerous cases in traditional practice where the principle is not applied. Changes in the prices of assets are not accrued usually, unless they are downward changes. And quite generally the effects of advantageous changes are not accrued but the effects of disadvantageous changes are accrued; thus depreciation is charged, but appreciation is not brought into account. These inconsistencies cannot yield realistic and up-to-date statements of financial position and results. CoCoA avoids inconsistency by applying the accrual principle uniformly to all assets and liabilities, and hence also to shareholders' equity.

19. **CoCoA conforms with the well-established going concern principle.**

   The going concern principle entails that the financial position as represented in a balance sheet shall be indicative of the position of a firm as a going concern. The significant financial characteristics of a going concern are its ability to pay its debts

12

when due, to pay for its supplies of goods and labour service, to change the composition of its assets, liabilities and operations if the present composition hinders its survival or growth, and the ability to earn a rate of profit consistent with the risks of the business. The ability of a firm to pay its debts, to pay for its necessary inputs, to borrow on the security of its assets, and to change the composition of its assets and operations, is indicated only if assets are shown at their money equivalents, since all the matters mentioned entail receipts and payments of money. The ability of a firm to earn an adequate rate of profit may be judged only if the profit earned is a genuine increment in purchasing power and the amount of net assets (or shareholders' equity) to which it is related is a genuine money sum. The use of market (resale) prices in CoCoA has nothing to do with liquidation of a business; it is simply the only way to find the present money equivalents of non-monetary assets from time to time.

247

20. CoCoA satisfies the requirements of stewardship accounts.

As financial statements indicate in general terms the disposition of assets and increments in assets from time to time they are regarded as the basis upon which the performance of a company and its management may be judged. Such judgements must be supposed to be made periodically in respect of the year recently past; their formal expression lies in the resolutions of annual general meetings. It is necessary, therefore, to know the amount of the assets available for use and disposition by the management at the beginning of each year, if a satisfactory account is to be given of the use, disposition and increase of assets in that year. If the amounts of assets from time to time were stated on any basis other than their money equivalents, there would be no firm and satisfactory basis for determining the use and disposition of assets. Since all uses and dispositions in a period entail movements of money or money equivalents, financial statements based on the money equivalents of assets provide information on which periodical performance may fairly be judged.

21. CoCoA adheres closely to the principle of periodical accounting.

Financial statements generally purport to represent dated positions and the results of defined periods. But the effects of events in one period are frequently allowed to influence what is reported of another. This occurs whenever some future event or outcome is anticipated (as in the usual calculation of depreciation charges), or whenever some actual effect on results or position is

13

"deferred' for recognition in a later period. CoCoA makes no such concessions, on the ground that reports which do not represent the effects of events in a defined period cannot properly be interpreted, singly or in series, by reference to the dated context of business events and circumstances. It may be objected that to base accounts on a dated selling price could be misleading if the price were anomalous. But exactly the same can be said of dated purchase prices which are used in other forms of accounting. In any such case the anomaly might be expected to be explained rather than concealed.

PART IV — THE DETERMINATION OF MONEY EQUIVALENTS

22. Any asset for which there is not a present resale price cannot be considered to have a present financial significance.

A company may have assets for which there is no present resale price. They may have a high user-value (see para 8), but they cannot be considered to have financial significance in the sense of purchasing or debt-paying power or as security for loans. Investors, creditors, suppliers and others would be misinformed of the financial capacity for action by balance sheets in which money amounts were assigned to assets having no current money equivalents. The assets to which this rule applies include some work in progress, and specialized plant and equipment for which there is no market in the ordinary course of business. The same rule applies to expenditures on exploratory or developmental work which has yielded no vendible product or asset. The notion of conservatism in traditional accounting would tend to have the same effect as the treatment suggested. But that notion is vague and loosely applied, whereas the principle here stated is definite and it yields information which is relevant to the judgements and decisions of parties financially interested in companies. If it is desired, on any ground, to indicate that a company has assets, or has incurred costs and outlays, having no present money equivalent, parenthetical or footnote information may be given.

23. The determination of the money equivalents of assets at a stated date is necessarily approximate.

Prices may vary from place to place for the same goods on any given day. What is required is a fair approximation to the current money equivalent of each asset. This may require the exercise of judgement, but abuse of judgement is constrained by the necessity of approximating a definite characteristic of the asset and by the prices discovered at or about the balance date. In any case, no form of accounting escapes the use of dated prices; even historical cost accounting uses dated prices which may or may not have been the only prices, or representative prices, at dates of purchase. Any attempt to distort results and positions by the choice of prices which are not fair approximations to money equivalents is constrained by the independent inspection and judgement of auditors. It is also constrained by the fact that the whole of the asset balances of one year determine the amounts of the price variation adjustments, and hence the income, of the following year. There are no alternative permissible rules by resort to which this constraint may be avoided.

24. Resale prices are accessible to most firms for most assets.

249

All proposals considered in anticipation of purchases and the settlement of debts include at some point sums of money which are presently available, or which could shortly become available by the sale of assets (inventory or other assets), or which could be borrowed on the security of assets. In the latter two cases some approximation to the money equivalent or resale price of non-monetary assets is required. Changes in the prices of goods and services used and in the markets for a firm's products may at any time force its management to reconsider the costs of its present mode of operations. And if it is assumed that one of the functions of management is the pursuit of efficiency or economies, the possibility of changes in its operations and assets will be under examination from time to time. It follows that some person or persons will be acquainted with the approximate market prices of the assets the firm presently holds, and with changes in those prices from time to time. It is possible for any firm to draw on its purchasing officers, salesmen, engineers and project evaluation officers for information on the prices of assets; and to have recourse to prices published in trade journals and the general press as well as direct inquiry. A greal deal of information of this kind is readily available without recourse to specialist valuers. But valuations by specialists on an asset resale basis may also be obtained, where necessary of themselves, or as a check on the information available otherwise.

25. Receivables: The amount to be reported will be the amount deemed, on the evidence available, to be recoverable from debtors in the ordinary course of business.

15

Generally this will be the face value or book value of debtors' accounts, for that is the amount of the claims against debtors at balance date. There is no need to speculate about the possibility that some debtors may take advantage of discounts offered for prompt settlement. Whether they do so or not, the consequence will lie in the following period and will be then reported. Where there is evidence that the full amount of a debt will not be recovered, the amount of the debt may be reduced or written off according to the evidence then available. The amount of receivables yielded by these rules will be the best approximation to the money equivalent of receivables in the light of the information then available, without speculative allowances for what may subsequently occur.

26. Inventories will be valued consistently on the basis of their present market selling prices in the parcels or quantities in which they are customarily sold by the firm.

In the ordinary course of events, raw materials will have a somewhat lower money equivalent than their recent purchase prices, since the user is not a trader in those materials. Work in progress inventories may have a substantially lower money equivalent than their costs, for such work in progress may not be salable in its then state and condition. Finished goods inventories will generally have higher money equivalents (current selling prices) than their costs.

To report inventories at market resale prices is not novel. Nor is it novel that work in progress may appear at a low or zero value; for the traditional rule, "lower of cost and market", should produce the same result. By comparison with the recorded costs, the higher money equivalents of finished goods will to some extent "offset" the lower money equivalents of raw materials and work in progress. But whether the resulting aggregate differs much or little from a cost-based aggregate is less important than the fact that a uniform rule - market price - is used throughout, and that the aggregate has a definite, dated money significance which "cost" and the "lower of cost and market" do not have.

27. Plant and equipment will be valued at market resale prices, in the units or combinations in which, in the ordinary course of business, they are bought, sold, or put out of use.

The object of the traditional method of accounting for plant is to record its cost and to provide out of periodical revenues sufficient to reduce that cost to its market resale price, or scrap value, by the time it is put out of service. The method of CoCoA has exactly the same object; but it is attained by direct reference to market prices year by year, rather than by relying on an arithmetical formula and disregarding the actual changes, up or down, in market prices from time to time. Market resale prices may be estimated from information obtained by the methods mentioned in para 24. The prices sought are not prices obtainable on liquidation or under duress. They are to be the best approximations to the money equivalents of assets in the ordinary course of business. To determine the best approximation entails skill and judgement; but judgement is to be applied to the information obtainable on prices, not to construct imaginative valuations. Checks on the possibility of manipulation are (i) that auditors must be satisfied that the assigned market values are based on current price information, (ii) that excessive understatement reduces the profit of the year and the asset backing of shares and debt at the end of the year, and (iii) that excessive overstatement reduces the profit of a subsequent year and improperly boosts the asset backing of shares and debt. The use of market resale prices may entail heavy charges, due to the sharp drop from cost to money equivalent of some plant, in the early years of use. Some assets may have virtually no resale price, but high user-value. Such occurrences necessarily reduce the adaptive capacity of firms, their command of money and money's worth. The reduction is made explicit in the amounts by charges against revenues, or against other shareholders' equity accounts if the amounts are extraordinary. (See also para 22 above).

28. Land and buildings will be valued at market resale prices, or approximations based on official valuations, prices of similar property and expert valuations.

The same considerations apply to land and buildings as to plant and equipment. Local government valuations (for taxing or rating purposes) provide evidence additional to that from other sources. No single valuation or price need necessarily be taken as a proper approximation to money equivalent; but the chosen valuation must be justifiable in the circumstances. The checks mentioned in para 27 tend to limit arbitrary or unusual valuations.

29. **Investments in the shares of other companies will be valued at net market prices where the shares are publicly traded; otherwise at the proportionate interest in the net assets of the investee company.**

Holdings of listed shares are readily priced by reference to stock exchange quotations (i.e. "buyer"). Allowance may be made for commissions payable on sale, to obtain the net money equivalent of the investment. There is no readily available and dependable price for non-listed shares. An alternative is required which yields the best approximation to the money equivalent of the investment. If CoCoA is used uniformly, the proportionate interest in the net assets of the investee will provide an approximation; for the accounts of the investee will represent assets at money equivalents. Strictly the amount so calculated will not be the same as a share price; but it is a better approximation than the original cost, or a valuation related to user-value (e.g. based on capitalized prospective earnings).

30. **Liabilities will be represented by the amounts owed and payable to creditors in the ordinary course of business.**

No amount shall be shown as a liability unless it represents an amount owed to and legally recoverable by a creditor. Whether the due date is near or distant is immaterial. Long-dated obligations may become due and payable if any circumstance threatens the security of creditors.

PART V — OWNERS' EQUITY ACCOUNTS

31. **All transactions of a period will be recorded at their actual effective prices, and so charged in the income (profit and loss) account.**

All transactions have determinate effects on balances of cash or receivables and payables. The general purchasing power of the cash receipts and payments during an inflationary period will change from time to time. But the aggregate effect of changes in the purchasing power of the money unit is brought into account by way of the capital maintenance adjustment at the end of the accounting period. By showing the actual amounts of receipts and payments, all such amounts are traceable, and identical with their counterparts elsewhere in the accounts.

32. **Price variation accounts will be credited with all increases in the book values of assets, and debited with all decreases, during the period.**

   The book balances of accounts, other than monetary item accounts, may be adjusted for changes in asset prices during the year. The valuation of all assets at the end of the year at their resale prices gives effect to all variations in prices which have not previously been brought into account. The amounts by which the book values of assets are increased (decreased) during the year to correspond with market resale prices will be debited (credited) to the asset accounts and credited (debited) to the price variation accounts. There may be price variation accounts for as many separate asset classes as is deemed necessary. Under CoCoA, the depreciation account, representing a fall in the market resale price of an asset or class of assets, is a price variation account. The price variation accounts are closed by transfer of their balances to the income account.

33. **The capital maintenance adjustment will be calculated by applying to the opening amount of net assets the proportionate change in the index of changes in the general level of prices.**

   The net amount of price variations will tend to be (but will not necessarily be) positive during inflation. But these are gross increments, and the resulting asset balances are in units of year-end purchasing power. The full effect of the change in the purchasing power of money on the results of the year is given by the calculation of the capital maintenance adjustment. The calculation is a mathematically proper calculation, since under CoCoA the opening amount of net assets is a genuine, dated money sum to which a change in the index may legitimately be applied. The capital maintenance adjustment is debited in the income account (in inflationary years).

34. **The amount of the capital maintenance adjustment will be credited proportionately to the opening balance of undistributed profits and to other opening balances of owners' equity accounts.**

   The amount of net assets at the beginning of a year is equal to the sum of the balances of the owners' equity accounts. The object of crediting the amount of the capital maintenance adjustment to owners' equity accounts is to restate the aggregate of the opening balances in units of purchasing power at the end of the year. Part of the capital maintenance adjustment may therefore be credited directly to the retained profits account, a part equal to the opening balance of retained profits multiplied by the proportionate change in the index of changes in the general level of prices. The remainder of the adjustment will be the appropriate amount to credit to a capital maintenance reserve. Where the amount subscribed by shareholders is required to be shown in balance sheets, this money amount may be carried indefinitely in the accounts. Following the above rules, the sum of the amount subscribed and the balance of the capital maintenance reserve at the end of any year will be the purchasing power equivalent at that time of all sums deemed to have been subscribed by shareholders.

35. Where there are outstanding issues of preference shares, these shall be treated as equivalent to outstanding debt, for the purpose of calculating the capital maintenance adjustment.

Preference shares are, like debts, redeemable at fixed, contractual money amounts. Therefore, like debts, they provide a hedge against the effects of changes in the general purchasing power of money. The amount of outstanding preference shares will therefore be deducted (together with all other liabilities) from total assets to obtain the amount of net assets to be used in the calculation of the capital maintenance adjustment.

36. Net income of a year will be the algebraic sum of transaction surpluses (para 31), price variation adjustments (para 32), and the capital maintenance adjustment (para 33).

The balance of the income account after incorporating the consequences of transactions and the price variation and capital maintenance adjustments will be the net income in units of year-end purchasing power. The whole of it may be paid out without impairing the purchasing power of the opening amount of net assets. Or if it or any part of it is transferred to a retained profits account, the whole of the balance of that account could be paid out (as dividends) without impairing the purchasing power of the amounts subscribed or deemed to have been subscribed by ordinary shareholders.

PART VI — SOME FEATURES OF THE SYSTEM

37. All original entries relate to the amounts of transactions; all adjustments are based on information from sources external to the firm.

These features ensure that all amounts represent actually experienced or accrued effects on a firm's position and results. Doubts about the magnitudes of accrued effects are resolved by recourse to external information, not to internal formulae. There are no arbitrary apportionments, no questionable assumptions about future events or uniformities, and no arbitrary demarcations between outcomes which are and which are not controllable, in some sense, by firms and their managements. The accounts and financial statements may be audited, therefore, with reference to independent sources of information; and the representations they make will be pertinent to the financial relations of the firm with the rest of the world.

38. CoCoA applies a single valuation rule throughout, avoiding the addition of different kinds of magnitudes in balance sheets.

There are no optional rules for asset valuation, as there are in all other systems. There is no possibility, therefore, that the significance of aggregates will be distorted by the addition of magnitudes of different kinds. Although the transactions figures and price variation adjustments are magnitudes expressed in money units of different purchasing powers, the combined effect of them and the capital maintenance adjustment is a net income in units of the same purchasing power as other items in a closing balance sheet.

39. CoCoA entails uniform valuation rules for all companies, making possible comparison of the financial features of companies.

Under accounting systems which allow optional valuation rules, the financial significance of the resulting figures is always open to doubt, and strictly no direct comparison of financial magnitudes, rates and ratios is possible. Financial statements based on market resale prices, on the other hand, yield technically proper and practically significant indications of the composition of assets, of current ratios, debt to equity ratios, and rates of return - all of which may be directly compared with

255

21

corresponding features of other companies and with corresponding features of the same company in prior years.

40. Some of the figures yielded by CoCoA may seem unusual by contrast with traditional accounting; they should be considered, not separately, but as parts of the whole system.

To value finished goods inventory at market price, when higher than cost, may seem unusual; and to value raw materials and work in progress at current market price, when lower than cost, may also seem unusual. It may appear that to calculate net income on such a footing is to "anticipate profits". But in the first place, the use of one valuation rule yields a comprehensible aggregate. Second, the "unusual" effects are to some extent offsetting. And third, the overriding charge for the capital maintenance adjustment is built-in protection against the overstatement of periodical net income. The same reasoning applies to the bringing to account of changes in the market prices of other non-monetary assets.

41. No right or advantage which arises only on disposal of the company as a whole is brought into the accounts.

CoCoA is strictly concerned with a company as a going concern. No value is assigned to such things as developmental costs, goodwill and specialized plant having no resale value, which are realizable only on liquidation or disposal of part or whole of the company. Insofar as any amount has been paid out in respect of these items, it constitutes a sunk cost, and is not available as such for any financial purpose in the ordinary course of business. Such amounts may be charged against shareholders' equity directly, or treated in the manner of the "double account" system, above the balance sheet proper. This treatment is in accordance with the practice of financial analysis, and avoids the impression that the company has assets which are convertible to cash in the ordinary course of business. The mixing of subjective user-values with objective financial values has led, in many cases, to serious misdirection of investors and other financial supporters (see also para 8).

42. The information given by CoCoA is consistent with that demanded by lenders and analysts of business affairs, and with the sense of the legislation relating to financial disclosure.

Lenders on the security of property are concerned with the up-to-date market values of assets; they alone constitute effective cover for debt. Press discussion of company affairs has drawn attention repeatedly to the differences between "accounting values" and market values - both when specific prices have been rising and when they have been falling. The statutory requirements relating to financial disclosure have increasingly stipulated the publication (by footnote or otherwise) of market values, or have indicated that realisable value is important information to users of financial statements. Examples are the disclosure of the market values of listed securities, general provisions relating to the valuation of current assets, provisions relation to the valuation of property charged as security by borrowing companies, and the U.K. provision requiring directors to comment on differences between market values and book values of interests in property. CoCoA does systematically what all these practices, in piecemeal fashion, imply.

257

43. The financial statements yielded by CoCoA constitute, in series, a continuous history of the financial affairs of a company.

Because the method of CoCoA embraces the consequences of actual transactions and of external changes which affect the wealth and results of companies, the statements for any period and at any date are all-inclusive. Taken in series, they represent a continuous record of shifts in wealth, solvency, gearing or leverage and achieved results. They are historical, avoiding the defects of dated speculation about the future; they are fully historical, avoiding the defects of partial representation of what has occurred up to any date or between any two dates.

PART VII — SUMMARY

44. The rules of continuously contemporary accounting are:

   (a) All assets should be stated at the best approximation to their money equivalents, in their then state and condition, at the date of the balance sheet.

23

(b) All transactions shall be accounted for in the amounts at which they occurred.
(c) All variations from the costs or book values of assets, which are not already brought into account by the sale of assets in the period, shall be brought into the income account at the end of the period as price variation adjustments.
(d) There shall be charged against total revenues, in calculating net income, the amount of a capital maintenance adjustment, so that the amount of net income is a surplus by reference to the maintenance of the general purchasing power of the opening amount of net assets.
(e) Net income is the algebraic sum of the outcomes of transactions, price variation adjustments and the capital maintenance adjustment.

APPENDIX A

ILLUSTRATION OF METHOD OF CONTINUOUSLY CONTEMPORARY ACCOUNTING

The simplified example which follows traces the recording of transactions, the making of closing adjustments and the derivation of the final statements. All transactions are recorded at their cost throughout the year. The closing price adjustments convert closing book balances to their ascertained money equivalents, represented in the final two columns of the Work Sheet. The workings are shown fully in the Work Sheet. The transactions and adjustments are alphabetically keyed, in the following description and in the Work Sheet, so that the counterparts of all entries may be traced. The figures in the columns headed "Balances" are the money equivalents at the respective dates.

The paragraph numbers in the right hand column of the table of data are the paragraphs in the text of this Draft where the accounting treatment is described.

		$	Para.
Transactions of the year			
A	Credit sales	410	31
B	Receivables collected	390	31
C	Raw materials purchased (on credit)	160	31
D	Suppliers on credit paid	140	31
E	Wages and other costs (to Work in progress)	90	31
F	Raw materials to Work in Progress	145	
G	Work in progress to Finished Goods	225	
H	Cost of finished goods to Income Account	270	
J	Administrative and other cash costs	60	31
K	Interest paid	4	31
L	Taxes paid	20	31
M	Dividends paid	14	31
N	Dividends received	2	31
P	Plant purchased	25	31

	Year-end adjustments	$	Para.
	Price variation adjustments (differences between book values and ascertained money equivalents at year-end)		
Q	- raw materials	10	32
R	- work in progress	15	32
S	- finished goods	-55	32
T	- plant and buildings	20	32
U	- land	-6	32
V	- shares	3	32
W	Provision for taxes	30	30
X	Provision for dividends	26	30
	Capital maintenance adjustment (assuming the general price index rose by 10 per cent in the year). Apply this to the opening balance.		
Y	- undistributed profits (71 x 10/100)	7	34
Z	- capital maintenance reserve (150 x 10/100)	15	34
AA	Net profit transferred to Undistributed profits	39	36

WORK SHEET FOR YEAR ENDED 31 DECEMBER 19x4

	Balances 31 Dec. 19x3		Transactions and Adjustments		Balances 31 Dec. 19x4	
	Dr	Cr	Dr	Cr	Dr	Cr
Assets						
Cash	20		390 (B)	140 (D)	59	
			2 (N)	90 (E)		
				60 (J)		
				4 (K)		
				20 (L)		
				14 (M)		
				25 (P)		
Trade debtors (receivables)	40		410 (A)	390 (B)	60	
Inventories — raw materials	25		160 (C)	145 (F)	30	
				10 (Q)		
— work in progress	30		145 (F)	225 (G)	25	
			90 (E)	15 (R)		
— finished goods	80		225 (G)	270 (H)	90	
			55 (S)			
Investments in listed shares	15			3 (V)	12	
Plant and buildings	80		25 (P)	20 (T)	85	
Land	40		6 (U)		46	
Equities						
Trade creditors (payables)		30	140 (D)	160 (C)		50
Provision for taxes		20	20 (L)	30 (W)		30
Provision for dividends		14	14 (M)	26 (X)		26
Long-term creditors (10% p.a.)		25				25
Preferred shareholders (10% p.a.)		20				20
Ordinary shareholders						
— paid in		120				120
— capital maintenance reserve		30		15 (Z)		45
— undistributed profits		71	26 (X)	7 (Y)		91
				39 (AA)		
Income (profit and loss) items						
Sales				410 (A)		
Finished goods sold — book value			270 (H)			
Price variation adjustments						
— raw materials			10 (Q)			
— work in progress			15 (R)			
— finished goods				55 (S)		
— plant and buildings			20 (T)			
— land				6 (U)		
— shares			3 (V)			
Administrative and other cash costs			60 (J)			
Interest paid			4 (K)			
Dividends received				2 (N)		
Provision for taxes			30 (W)			
Capital maintenance adjustment						
— undistributed profits			7 (Y)			
— capital maintenance reserve			15 (Z)			
Net profit			39 (AA)			
Totals	330	330	2,181	2,181	407	407

261

p.30 follows

INCOME [PROFIT AND LOSS] ACCOUNT FOR THE YEAR ENDED 31 DECEMBER 19x4

Sales		410
Dividends received		2
		412
Finished goods sold (book value)	270	
Inventory price variation adjustments (net)	(30)	
Depreciation, plant and buildings	20	
Price variation adjustment, land	(6)	
Price variation adjustment, shares	3	
Administrative costs	60	
Interest paid	4	
Capital maintenance adjustment		
-undistributed profits	7	
- capital maintenance reserve	15	343
Profit before tax		69
Provision for taxes		30
Net income		39

BALANCE SHEETS AT 31 DECEMBER

	19x3	19x4
Assets		
Cash	20	59
Trade debtors	40	60
Inventories	135	145
Investments in listed shares	15	12
Plant and buildings	80	85
Land	40	46
	330	407
Equities		
Trade creditors	30	50
Provision for taxes	20	30
Provision for dividends	14	26
Long term creditors (10%)	25	25
Preferred shareholders (10%p.a.)	20	20
Ordinary shareholders		
- paid in	120	120
- capital maintenance reserve	30	45
- undistributed profits	71	91
	330	407

Note: All assets are shown at the best available approximations to their money equivalents at the respective balance dates.

APPENDIX B

COMPARATIVE EVALUATION OF PRICE LEVEL ADJUSTED HISTORICAL COST ACCOUNTING [C.P.P.] REPLACEMENT PRICE ACCOUNTING [R.P.A.] AND CONTINUOUSLY CONTEMPORARY ACCOUNTING [CoCoA]

If a choice is to be made from the above alternatives to historical cost accounting, it must be based on the respective capacities of the systems to provide information which is unambiguous and significant for the purposes of investors, creditors, managers and others. There are many particular calculations and comparisons which these parties, and others concerned with the regulation and assistance of business, may make. The three systems may therefore be ranked according to their capacities to give reliable, significant and readily understandable figures. That system should be considered as the best which satisfies these tests.

The following assessment indicates whether or not each system satisfies the listed "test" points. For its preparation the three systems have been analyzed in detail, on the basis of the Australian Exposure Drafts, "A Method of 'Accounting for Changes in the Purchasing Power of Money'" and "A Method of 'Current Value Accounting'" and the present Draft. The analyses are lengthy and cannot be reproduced here. They are given in the related publication, *Accounting for Inflation - Methods and Problems*. But each of the assessments can be substantiated by reference to the source materials. The three systems are described briefly in terms of their salient features.

Price level adjusted historical cost accounting has been given its popular description "current purchasing power accounting". "Replacement price accounting" is used here of the method of current value accounting expounded in the second exposure draft above. The "current cost accounting" proposal of the U.K. Sandilands Committee is of the same family. With few exceptions, it would score similarly to R.P.A. in the following evaluation.

Current purchasing power accounting (C.P.P.) The general basis of asset valuation is, for monetary assets their face values, for non-monetary assets, original cost "indexed" by changes in an index of the general level of prices. Discretionary variations from the rule for non-monetary assets are permissible. Periodical charges against gross revenues in respect of non-monetary assets are based on the "indexed" cost figures. Gains or losses of purchasing power in respect of monetary items are brought into account in income calculation.

Replacement price accounting (R.P.A.). This is the variety of "current value accounting" dealt with in the abovementioned exposure draft. The general basis of asset valuation is, for monetary items their face values, for non-monetary assets the current replacement prices of assets expected or intended to be replaced; for non-monetary assets not intended to be replaced, their net market selling prices. Periodical charges against gross revenues in respect of non-monetary assets are based on replacement prices.

Continuously contemporary accounting (CoCoA). The general basis of asset valuation is the money's worth, or money equivalents, of assets, which in the case of non-monetary assets means the best approximation to their resale prices at balance date. Charges against (or credits to) gross revenues are based on changes in the money equivalents of assets. Gains or losses of purchasing power are brought into account in respect of the whole of the opening amount for the year of net assets (or net owners' equity) by use of a readily calculated capital maintenance adjustment.

There are possible tests beside those listed below. There is, for example, the cost of doing the accounting. As C.P.P. and R.P.A. require numerous calculations to be made additional to the processing of original entries, and CoCoA requires only one additional calculation, the last is the least costly. There is the cost of getting the closing balance sheet valuations. Under C.P.P. (taking the historical cost accounts and supplementary C.P.P. accounts together), there are costs of getting several valuations and choosing between alternative valuation rules. Under R.P.A., there are the costs of getting replacement prices and choosing between alternative valuation rules. Under CoCoA, there are the costs of getting values according to only one valuation rule; and, as para 24 of the main text indicates, most of the valuations required are generally accessible. It could also be shown that CoCoA is superior in respect of most of the general "principles" of accounting; consistency of method, application of the accrual principle, representation of the facts of a company as a going concern, periodical matching of revenues and costs, and so on.

However, as financial statements are expected to be serviceable to their users, all the tests which follow relate to the usefulness of the products of the three systems.

EVALUATION

	CPP	RPA	CoCoA
1. Are assets shown at their money (or purchasing power) equivalents at each balance date?	No	No	Yes
2. Does net income, as calculated, represent a genuine increment in purchasing power up to balance date?	No	No	Yes
3. Can particular figures in balance sheets properly be added and related?	No	No	Yes

Monetary items are, in all systems, represented by money equivalents. It is logically improper and practically misleading to add to these figures any others which are not money equivalents. Hence the answer to (3). From (1), (2) and (3) flow the following consequences:

	CPP	RPA	CoCoA
4. Does the balance sheet yield a proper current ratio?	No	No	Yes
5. Does the balance sheet yield a proper debt to equity ratio?	No	No	Yes
6. Do the statements yield a proper rate of return?	No	No	Yes
7. Does the aggregate of asset values fairly represent gross wealth?	No	No	Yes

To make certain judgements or decisions it is necessary to compare the positions and results of different companies as at a given time and of the same company in successive years. Comparisons of the first kind are invalid unless all companies use the same valuation rules; comparisons of the second kind are invalid unless a given company uses the same rules from year to year and those rules embrace all types of change in financial position and results. Therefore:

		CPP	RPA	CoCoA
8.	Is the rate of return technically comparable with the rates of return on other types of investment?	No	No	Yes
9.	Are the aggregates and ratios yielded comparable from year to year and fair indicators of trends?	No	No	Yes
10.	Are the main ratios comparable as between firms?	No	No	Yes

The information in financial statements is used by managers and by outsiders in a variety of settings. The particulars and aggregates must be understandable by and useful to those parties.

		CPP	RPA	CoCoA
11.	Are the figures free of ambiguity and equally interpretable by and useful to managers and others?	No	No	Yes
12.	Do particular asset figures represent amounts of money accessible for alternative use?	No	No	Yes
13.	Are the figures a firm basis from which to calculate prospective results and positions?	No	No	Yes
14.	Does the net asset figure suggest a minimum acceptable takeover bid?	No	No	Yes
15.	Are the statements fair and serviceable for negotiations and other relations with public and other bodies?	No	No	Yes
16.	Are the statements complete as statements of results and position, needing no supplementary information or statements?	No	No	Yes
17.	Are the statements a fair basis for periodical "stewardship" evaluation?	No	No	Yes
18.	Do the statements give a true and fair view of financial results and position?	No	No	Yes
19.	Are the amounts representing assets and liabilities verifiable independently of the company's internal calculations?	No	No	Yes

No specific reference has been made above to inflation or its effects, except by references to purchasing power (1), (2), and to supplementary statements (16). There are several specific tests, however, which should be satisfied.

	CPP	RPA	CoCoA
20. Are retrospective corrections or adjustments to previously reported figures avoided?	No	No	Yes
21. Are any adjustments made in respect of changes in the prices of particular assets?	No	Yes	Yes
22. Are any adjustments made in respect of changes in the purchasing power of money?	Yes	Yes	Yes
23. Are adjustments made for the gain or loss of purchasing power during each period in respect of all assets and liabilities?	No	No	Yes
24. Is the method of accounting a method of accounting for inflation?	No	No	Yes

Two further points might be made. Although C.P.P. accounting makes reference to current purchasing power, a C.P.P. balance sheet does *not* represent assets by amounts which are in fact their current purchasing power (or money) equivalents. The point is covered in (1) above; but it may escape notice because of the description of the system.

Secondly, although replacement price accounting purports to provide for the replacement of assets by charges against gross revenues, the figures it yields do *not* indicate whether or not a firm could in fact replace those assets; a replacement price valuation does not represent purchasing power at the command of the firm, yet purchasing power is the only means of buying a "replacement" asset.

These inconsistencies with their apparent or avowed aims score against the two systems mentioned.

The practical superiority of CoCoA is demonstrated.

Accounting for Changing Prices*

1. I have tendered a critical note on the CVA Exposure Draft on the standard form. I have supplied to the Standards Committee copies of an Exposure Draft, "Accounting for Inflation", descriptive of continuously contemporary accounting - which I shall call CoCoA. I have supplied a booklet "Accounting for Inflation - Methods and Problems" which deals singularly and comparatively with current purchasing power (CPP) accounting, current value accounting (CVA as expounded in the Second Preliminary Exposure Draft) and with CoCoA. The Standards Committee will have seen an article "Accounting for Inflation - The Case for Continuously Contemporary Accounting" in **The Australian Accountant** of December 1975. I have supplied copies to the Standards Committee of a mimeographed paper entitled "Continuously Contemporary Accounting - Misunderstandings and Misrepresentations". The Standards Committee will be aware of a book **Securities and Obscurities** which presents evidence of great variety from Australian, American and English companies, of the demand for information of the kind generated by CoCoA.

2. CoCoA is based on observations of accounting practices, debates and proposals over some 25 years. In the course of that interval I have endorsed successively historical cost, CPP and CVA until it became clear that each (in turn) had practical and technical defects. It is the continual search for ways of eliminating those defects that led to the present form of the proposal. In that search, I have retained, as significant, most of the well-established **principles** of accounting:

(a) that accounting is properly a continuous historical record (CoCoA does not take account of any imagined event of the future in deriving dated financial statements),

(b) that increments or decrements may be accrued at the end of any period,

(c) that the processes of accounting must be consistent from time to time notwithstanding their conversion to cash at earlier or later dates,

---

* Presentation to Hearings of a Review Committee set up by the Australian Accounting Standards Committee of the Australian Accounting Research Foundation, Melbourne, 2 March 1976.

- d) that the balances of accounts from time to time must be independently verifiable (i.e. without necessary recourse to the personal judgements or preferences of the managers or accountants of firms),
- e) that accounts must relate to the assets and equities of going concerns (not the values of firms as wholes, which are only ascertainable from the share market),
- f) that accounts relate to set periods, and should fully represent the financial consequences of events period by period, regardless of what did or may occur in other periods.

3. In brief CoCoA has several **premises**:
- (a) Financial statements are intended to inform managers, investors, creditors and other decision-makers on the financial positions and results of firms from time to time.
- (b) If financial positions and results are not represented fully, realistically, and in up to date terms, judgements about the past and choices from future possibilities cannot be made with confidence.
- (c) Since all financial statements are aggregative, all of the components of dated statements must be capable of proper addition, subtraction and relation.
- (d) Since all decisions relate to prospective cash inflows and outflows and dated increments in the money equivalents of assets and equities, the components of financial statements must be in terms of their dated money equivalents.
- (e) Since the purchasing power of the dollar differs from time to time, dated dollar amounts may not be added or subtracted or related without correction for the shift in general purchasing power (the general financial significance) of the dollar.
- (f) The characteristic influences of inflation on the affairs of companies are shifts in the prices of the assets held from time to time and shifts in the general purchasing power of money. These are interlocked and generally work in opposite directions. A method of accounting for the effects of inflation must take account of both.
- (g) Accounts taken in series over a period of years should constitute a continuous historical record of the financial affairs of firms.

4. The **technical processes** have been fully described in the material

available to the Standards Committee. They are indicated concisely in para. 44 of the Exposure Draft. Most of the technical difficulties have been considered in the booklet "Methods and Problems".

5. The **advantages** of CoCoA lie in

(a) its simplicity. It requires no change whatever in the day to day accounting of firms; its adjustments may all be made at the end of the period, like the year end adjustments now made.

(b) its continuity. There are no "unbooked" changes in the balances of accounts. All the "historical" figures of any period appear in the financial statements without indexing or other manipulation. There are no retrospective adjustments. Its results can be readily reconciled with historical cost accounts in any changeover period.

(c) its feasibility. The money equivalent rule is already implied in the rule for giving market values of listed securities (even though in parenthesis); in the net realizable or market value rule for certain kinds of inventories; and in the negotiations surrounding mergers, takeovers, restorations of liquidity and so on. The text of **Securities and Obscurities** gives numerous and varied illustrations. I tender, as giving an actual example, a note on the 1974 accounts of Challenge Corporation, a New Zealand company with group assets of $200 million and net income of $9 million.

(d) the reality of its output. The net income figure it yields is a genuine increment in general purchasing power in the period. The balance sheet is a proper basis for realistic calculations of current ratios, gearing ratios, rates of return, asset backing and other critical indicators.

(e) the comparability of its outputs. As its rules are uniform and take full account of the effects on each firm of its own trading and its own composition of assets and equities, the results and positions of firms (expressed as dated ratios) are fully comparable.

6. By **contrast** with other methods, CoCoA is superior in that

(a) it is complete in dealing with the specific effects on firms of changes in the prices of **its** assets and of changes in the general purchasing power of money. No other proposal is complete in these respects.

(b) its arithmetic, additions, subtractions and relations are correct

and technically proper throughout. No other system has this feature.
(c) its rules are applied consistently. All other systems specify multiple and conflicting rules; they therefore violate the requirement that only like things may be added and related.
(d) it yields financial statements which give realistic indicators, and therefore a true and fair view, of dated financial positions and results, as required by statute. No partial system can be said to give such a true and fair view.
(e) because its component items are indicative of events which have occurred and the magnitudes of their effects, they can be independently checked. The component items of no other system can be so checked.
(f) because the figures it yields are up to date money amounts they may be compared with other such amounts or rates of return and so on. They are freely and generally interpretable by all who engage in financial dealings. No other system yields figures which are thus readily comparable and interpretable.

7. General

There are numerous other practical and technical arguments for CoCoA, which I have presented in other published work. I summarise some of them:

(a) CoCoA as a tax base is more equitable and more general than any other. It would result in taxing only genuine increments in general purchasing power. It is more inclusive than the Mathews Report proposals [a variety of current cost accounting] and requires no restrictions or retrospective adjustments as do those proposals.
(b) CoCoA is amply supported by the basic doctrines of economics. It embraces what Hicks (one of the most widely quoted writers on income calculation) describes as the most dependable of all notions of income.
(c) CoCoA is consistent with all calculations of past results and future effects which taxing and regulatory bodies and prices and wages tribunals might wish to make.
(d) CoCoA is consistent with the efficient administration of business and the efficient conduct of the trade in shares, since its indications of liquidity, income, rate of return and so on are

continuously up to date and relevant to present judgements.
(e) CoCoA is consistent with management in the interest of survival, since its indicators of liquidity strains, prospects of varying the style of business and the composition of assets, and similar matters, are realistic.
(f) CoCoA is consistent with all reasoning relative to cash flows, since, by its nature it is concerned with flows of money and the money equivalents of non-monetary assets.
(g) Unlike systems based on current replacement costs of present assets, CoCoA requires no hypothetical assumptions about the future style of business of any firm.
(h) CoCoA is consistent with the professional ideal of giving the fullest possible service to all users of the products of accounting. I believe the profession can accept no less an objective than this.

Applications of Continuously Contemporary Accounting
A Note

The 1974 report of Challenge Corporation contains an innovation which is among world "firsts". Challenge is a New Zealand company with group assets in excess of $200 million. The report includes a supplementary set of financial statements which shows in full the effects of changes in asset prices and the effects of inflation for the year. This method of accounting, described as continuously contemporary accounting, is the only method which takes account of both kinds of change.

As the Challenge report says: "The Statement of Financial Position shows all assets at their full net realisable values and reflects the group's ability to engage in any future operations and to readily adapt to changing circumstances. It also reflects more realistically the scope for borrowing and the present value of resources and shareholders' funds on which a reasonable rate of return should be obtained".

Coming at a time when business firms and professional bodies are vexed with the problem of dealing with inflation in accounts, the Challenge exercise deserves attention. The method is very simple. The group income figure includes the rises in prices during the year of inventories ($0.9 million) and of land and buildings ($8.5 million). To obtain the group income figure, there is deducted a "capital maintenance charge" which is the loss in purchasing power during the year of the net investment (assets less liabilities) at the beginning of the year. The effect in the case of Challenge is a group income $1.8 million greater than the conventionally calculated group income of $9.3 million.

Due to the up-to-date valuation of assets, the shareholders' funds are $97.2 million compared with $63.3 million under the traditional mode of accounting. And although the "inflation and price adjusted" profit is higher than traditional profit, the rate of return is lower.

The following comparisons illustrate the differences in the figures yielded by traditional accounting and continuously contemporary accounting (CoCoA):

	Traditional	CoCoA
Return on Shareholders' Funds	15.3%	12.4%
Debt to Equity (times)	2.2	1.4
Assets per share	$2.14	$3.37

As the CoCoA figures are all based on up-to-date asset valuations they are obviously of greater use in analysis than the mixed valuations of traditional accounts.

Some particular features of the method are worth noting.

Critics of the CoCoA method have made much of the difficulty of getting approximate up-to-date prices of assets. The Challenge Corporation had a total revenue of $668 million in 1974 from over 20 subsidiaries in general merchandising, vehicle distribution, domestic and farm machinery manufacturing and distribution, wool scouring, finance and other operations. Yet it has made or obtained up-to-date valuations for the range of assets it held.

The difficulties are overrated in any case. Any firm actively engaged in dealing in or with its assets, borrowing on their security, or switching their composition as opportunities open and close, will have reasonably reliable knowledge of its asset values from time to time.

The capital maintenance adjustment is a simple calculation based on the change in the price index and the opening shareholders' funds. It is the net effect of inflation, as such, on the opening net investment. The opening amount of total assets in any year is hedged against inflation by the total amount of liabilities. Only the amount of shareholders' funds (net investment) is therefore at the risks of inflation, and the effect of inflation is thus easily calculable.

The prices of the particular assets of a firm cannot be expected to move at the same rate (or even in the same direction) as a general price index. The method used indicates whether or not they have done so. In the case of the Challenge group the increment through price movements upwards was $9.4 million; the loss of purchasing power through inflation was $8.2 million. By virtue of the assets it held and its mode of financing them, the group more than offset the effect of inflation during the year - a "plus" for any investor.

The CoCoA method may be compared, to its advantage, with current purchasing power (CPP) accounting which has been widely discussed. CPP accounting brings into the income calculation only the inflationary gain or loss on monetary items (cash, receivables and payables). It disregards the inflationary loss on investments in other assets and the gain or loss on price movements of other assets. CPP accounting is therefore only a partial treatment of the effects of price movements during a year.

Partial treatments of changes in prices and price levels will necessarily lead to odd consequences. If companies only account for inflationary losses and not for price gains (or losses), the disadvantageous effects of inflation will be overstated; and the accounts will not show up those companies which, through asset price gains or losses, did better or worse than just offset the effects of the fall in the purchasing power of money. And, by contrast, if companies only account for asset price gains or losses (as when revaluations are made under traditional accounting), disregarding the effects of inflation on the purchasing power of money, reported profits will not distinguish those companies which have and those which have not hedged successfully against inflation. Investors need clues such as these to make informed judgements as between companies.

The CoCoA method relies on actual or estimated prices from year to year. As they are approximate current prices they represent the "real wealth" of a company in terms of current purchasing power. The CPP method claims to do this, but fails. Asset values under CPP accounting are found by applying a general price index to the original costs of assets. It is therefore possible that assets whose prices have actually fallen, while the general price index has risen, will be shown at higher prices than their costs and much higher prices than their market prices at the end of any financial year. And technically, the CPP method is far more complex than the method used by the Challenge group.

The method may be compared to its advantage also with the replacement price method, or what has widely been called current value accounting (CVA). Replacement price accounting makes no attempt to deal with the effects of inflation as such. It deals with inventory and depreciation charges on a replacement price basis (the proposals of the Mathews Report are an example of it). But only by chance will this secure that working capital is sufficient to service out-of-pocket costs at the higher prices of an inflationary period. By making provision for the maintenance of the purchasing power of the whole of the net investment at the beginning of a year, the CoCoA method sustains the working capital either directly or through the increase in borrowing power which flows from increases in the market values of assets.

Some of the calculations made by brokers and others of the effects of using CPP accounting and CVA accounting have yielded vastly different figures for net profit (some higher, some lower) than the traditional accounts. This is due to the fact that each of those systems deals with only one side of the effects of inflation - CPP with the change in the purchasing power of money, CVA with changes in the prices of specific goods. Yet, on a common sense view, any company with large and varied assets might find that one of these effects is almost (but never quite) equal and opposite to the other. Two other N.Z. companies which have used the CoCOA method are Haywrights (an associate of Challenge) and Skellerup Industries. The 1974 figures of the three companies were as follows:

	Conventional		CoCoA	
	Profit	Rate of Return	Profit	Rate of Return
Challenge Corporation	$9.3m	15.3%	$11.1m	12.4%
Haywrights	$0.9m	11.7%	$ 9.7m	6.8%
Skellerup Industries	$2.4m	20.0%	$ 2.3m	13.0%

The differences between conventional and CoCoA profits are significant, but not enormous. The CoCoA rates of return are in each case lower, of course, because the asset values which affect the denominator are up to date, by contrast with the out of date values of historical cost (conventional) accounts.

The CoCoA method is complete, taking account of both particular asset price movements and movements in the general level of prices. The figures in the accounts are up to date and realistic; they are not merely indexed figures or hypothetical figures. The system merits the attention of the professional and other bodies now considering ways of accounting for inflation - and of the Treasury in respect of tax proposals, and of the Attorney General in respect of the proposed securities and companies legislation.

***

The following pages give sections from the annual reports of
   Skellerup Industries Limited, to 31 March 1974
   Challenge Corporation Limited, to 30 June 1974
   Haywrights Limited, to 31 July 1974
   Midland Coachlines Limited, to 30 June 1975
   Firth Industries Limited, to 27 March 1976
all New Zealand companies which gave supplementary statements on a CoCoA basis. The auditors of the Companies were four different professional firms. Supplementary statements on a CoCoA basis were abandoned after professional sentiment hardened in favour of current value or replacement cost accounting in the latter part of the 1970s.

Skellerup Industries Limited and Subsidiaries

Statement by the Chairman

INFLATION

Inflation, as mentioned earlier, has become the most disruptive influence of commercial activity and is rushing along at such a rate that one is deluding oneself if one ignores it. For the year ended 31st March, 1974 the rate of inflation was modest compared to that which we have experienced since that date, but even so this "modest" rate was greater than any we have experienced in recent times. It is perhaps prudent to look again at our profitability

in the light of these conditions and we find there are many advocates of various systems to show the effect of inflation on accounting. A restated financial statement appears on Page 24 of this report and it is gratifying to see that the method we elected to use does not greatly diminish the Group's overall profitability. The return on shareholders' funds however is markedly reduced. During the year under review the cost of living index rose 6.2% and we have used this in determining the sum of money necessary to maintain the purchasing power of Shareholders' Funds in March, 1973. This would be totally inadequate under today's prevailing conditions but is relevant to the period covered. To carry out the exercise in the 1974-75 financial year a very much larger amount than $1.1 million, as shown in the restated financial statement, will be required to maintain the purchasing power of Shareholders' Funds.

Skellerup Industries Limited and Subsidiaries

ACCOUNTING FOR INFLATION

Restated Financial Accounts for the Year Ended 31st March, 1974

INCOME STATEMENT

	Notes	Realisable Values $M	Conventional Basis $M
Total Group Income		39.7	39.7
Less Purchases of goods, services and taxation		36.5	36.7
	1	3.2	3.0
Depreciation: Buildings		—	0.1
Other Fixed Assets		0.5	0.5
		0.5	0.6
NET GROUP INCOME FROM TRADING		2.7	2.4
Other Income: Increase in value of property and investments	2	0.7	—
Surplus before Capital Maintenance Charge		3.4	2.4
Capital Maintenance Charge to maintain intact the purchasing power of Shareholders' Funds	3	1.1	—
GROUP INCOME FOR THE YEAR		$2.3	$2.4

BALANCE SHEET as at 31st March, 1974

	Notes	Realisable Values $M	Conventional Basis $M
Assets			
Land and Buildings		7.4	3.3
Investments		1.2	0.7
Stock		10.5	8.3
All Other Assets	4	7.4	7.4
		$26.5	$19.7
Liabilities			
Liabilities and Pension Fund Reserve		6.7	6.7
Preference Capital		0.4	0.4
Interests of Ordinary Shareholders		19.4	12.6
		$26.5	$19.7
Return on Average Shareholders' Funds		13%	20%

Note 1. The increase of $.2millions represents the gain in unrealised profit on stocks held at balance date.
Note 2. All properties have been valued at indemnity value which in the opinion of the directors fairly represents the net realisable value of these assets. Investments are in associated companies and are not traded. However, a recent professional valuation was used for shares in Dominion Salt Ltd., others are at par plus a proportion of undistributed profits.
Note 3. Based on Cost of Living Index for year ended March, 1974.
Note 4. Other assets are stated at their book value as this is regarded to be a fair and reasonable realisable value.

ACCOUNTING FOR INFLATION

Challenge Corporation Limited and Subsidiary Companies

The following financial statements have been prepared using a method of price level accounting which is based on the current market value of assets. This is considered relevant for the circumstances of the company and the users of the resulting information. The method is based on the theory of continuous contemporary accounting, described by Professor R. J. Chambers in his book entitled "Accounting Evaluation and Economic Behaviour".

The income statement measures the change in the real wealth of the company for the year and is therefore adjusted from the conventional basis by adding the unrealised gain from holding assets, and deducting an amount equal to the fall in purchasing power of actual shareholders' funds at the beginning of the year.

The Statement of Financial Position shows all assets at their full net realisable values and reflects the group's ability to engage in any future operations and to readily adapt to changing circumstances. It also reflects more realistically the scope for borrowing and the present value of resources and shareholders' funds on which a reasonable rate of return should be obtained.

FINANCIAL STATEMENTS FOR YEAR ENDED 30 JUNE 1974
REFLECTING CURRENT VALUES AND THE IMPACT OF INFLATION

	Notes	Current Values $M	As shown in the Consolidated Accounts $M
INCOME FOR YEAR TO JUNE 30 1974			
GROUP INCOME from commissions and trading	1	64.7	63.8
DEPRECIATION – Land and Buildings		—	0.6
Plant, Vehicles and Equipment		1.9	1.9
OTHER EXPENSES including taxation and after deducting other income and exceptional items		52.0	52.0
		53.9	54.5
NET GROUP INCOME from operations		10.8	9.3
deduct CAPITAL MAINTENANCE CHARGE required to maintain intact the purchasing power of Shareholders' Funds	2	8.2	
SURPLUS before gain in fixed assets		2.6	—
add GAIN IN VALUE of Land and Buildings held during the year		8.5	—
TOTAL GROUP INCOME FOR THE YEAR	3	11.1	9.3
FINANCIAL POSITION AT 30 JUNE 1974			
ASSETS	4		
Stock in Trade		49.0	43.1
Land and Buildings		65.0	37.0
All other assets		120.8	120.8
TOTAL ASSETS		234.8	200.9
LIABILITIES and minority interest		137.6	137.6
SHAREHOLDERS' FUNDS		97.2	63.3
TOTAL LIABILITIES		234.8	200.9
Return on Average Shareholders' Funds		12.4%	15.3%

NOTE 1. **Group Income**
The increase of $.9M represents the unrealised gain for the year in holding stocks.

NOTE 2. **Capital Maintenance Charge**
This amount of $8.2 million reflects the loss of purchasing power of shareholders' funds during the year, due to inflation. It has been calculated by applying the rate of increase in the consumers' price index for the year to 30 June 1974, of 10%, to the current value of shareholders' funds at the beginning of the year.

Notes continued on page 34.

Notes continued

NOTE 3. **Total Group Income for the Year**
The Group shows a final surplus for the year of $11.1M after taking account of an increase of $8.5M in the market value of land and buildings. A similar substantial gain in property values has been enjoyed for several years in the recent past. However, because of changing conditions in the property market, it is not expected that there will be any material gain in the market value of land and buildings during the next year to 30 June 1975.

NOTE 4. **Assets**
Assets have been shown at their current cash equivalent, calculated on the following bases.
Land and Buildings: Valued separately at 30 June 1974 by qualified staff of our property division. The increment in value for the year was calculated by the application of a factor of 15% which, in the opinion of the valuers concerned, was a fair reflection of the average movement of prices during the period.
Stock on Hand: Valued at estimated net sales value at 30 June 1974 and 30 June 1973. Net sales value was calculated by increasing the stock as shown in the conventional accounts by the average gross profit earned on these stocks, less the normal direct selling expenses necessary to realise them.
Plant Vehicles & Equipment: Valued at net depreciated value, as recorded in the conventional accounts. In the opinion of the company, these values fairly represent the net realisable value of these assets.
Other Assets and Liabilities: Stated at the amount recorded in the accounts, which represents their realisable values.

AUDITORS' REPORT
We have examined the consolidated financial statements expressed in current values, set out on pages 33 and 34. In our opinion, these financial statements have been correctly prepared in accordance with the bases disclosed in notes 2 and 4.

17 September, 1974

BARR, BURGESS & STEWART
Chartered Accountants

281

Chairman's Letter to Shareholders

Effects of Inflation

Inflation is the single greatest economic problem facing the world today. In reviewing our own performance, we are most conscious of its impact.

Because of the potentially harmful and certainly misleading effects of inflation upon profits, assets and shareholders' funds, we have devoted a section in this year's Report to indicating its effects. This has been done by adjusting our figures on the principles of "continuous contemporary accounting" which is being quite widely advocated in academic accounting circles in New Zealand.

In essence, our profits are re-calculated to include the unrealised profits arising from the holding of assets and are charged with the cost of maintaining the purchasing power of our shareholders' funds at current values. The surplus, or "profit", therefore reflects the real increase in our wealth for the period.

On this basis, our overall surplus this year is good, but is due almost entirely to the increase in value of our relatively high investment in property assets. The results illustrate the misleading nature of conventional accounting statements and the dangers in using them as a basis for taxation, price control, wage negotiation, and securities market comparisons.

HAYWRIGHTS LIMITED

ACCOUNTING FOR INFLATION

The following financial statements have been prepared using a method of price level accounting which is based on the current market value of assets. The income statement measures the change in the real wealth of the company for the year and is therefore adjusted from the historical cost basis by adding the unrealised gain from holding assets, and deducting an amount equal to the fall in purchasing power of actual shareholders' funds at the beginning of the year.

The Statement of Financial Position shows all assets at their full net realisable values and reflects more realistically the shareholders' funds on which a reasonable rate of return should be obtained.

FINANCIAL STATEMENTS FOR YEAR ENDED 31st JULY, 1974
REFLECTING CURRENT VALUES AND THE IMPACT OF INFLATION.

	Notes	Current Values $000	As shown in the Consolidated Accounts $000
INCOME FOR YEAR TO 31st JULY 1974			
Total Income	1	10,775	10,486
Depreciation —			
Land and Buildings			33
Fixtures, Plant, Motor Vehicles		382	382
Other expenses including taxation		9,187	9,187
		9,569	9,602
Net Income from Trading		1,206	884
Deduct Capital Maintenance Charge required to maintain intact the purchasing power of Shareholders' Funds	2	957	—
Surplus before gain in fixed assets		249	884
Add Gain in value of Land and Buildings held during the year		484	—
CONSOLIDATED NET PROFIT FOR YEAR		$733	$884

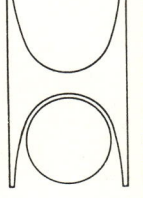

	Notes	Current Values $000	As shown in the Consolidated Accounts $000
FINANCIAL POSITION AT 31 JULY 1974			
Assets	3		
Stock on Hand		9,766	8,335
Land and Buildings		3,790	1,917
All other Assets		6,191	6,191
Total Assets		$19,747	$16,443
Liabilities and Minority interest		8,940	8,940
Shareholders' Funds		10,807	7,503
		$19,747	$16,443
Return on Shareholders' Funds		6.8%	11.7%

Note 1 **TOTAL INCOME**
The increase of $289,000 represents the unrealised gain for the year in holding stocks.

Note 2 **CAPITAL MAINTENANCE CHARGE.**
This amount of $957,000 represents the loss of purchasing power of Shareholders' funds during the year, due to inflation. It has been calculated by applying the rate of increase in the Consumers' Price Index for the year to 30th June 1974, of 10% to the current value of Shareholders' funds at the beginning of the year.

Note 3 **ASSETS**
Assets have been shown at their current cash equivalent, calculated on the following basis.
Land and Buildings: Included at estimated market value as at 31st July 1974. The increment in value for the year was calculated by the application of a factor of 15% which is considered a fair reflection of the average increment of prices during the period.
Stock on Hand: Valued at estimated net sales value at 31st July 1974 and 31st July 1973. Net Sales Value was calculated by increasing the stock as shown in the conventional accounts by the average gross profit earned on these stocks, less the normal direct selling expenses necessary to realise them.
Fixtures, Plant and Motor Vehicles: Valued at net depreciated value, as recorded in the conventional accounts. In the opinion of the company, these values fairly represent the net realisable value of these assets.
Other Assets and Liabilities: Stated at the amount recorded in the accounts, which represents their realisable values.

Midland Coachlines Limited and Subsidiary Companies for the year ended 30th June 1975

Accounting for Inflation

The following financial statements have been prepared using a method of price level accounting which is based on the current market value of assets. This is considered relevant for the circumstances of the company and the users of the resulting information. The method is based on the theory of continuous contemporary accounting, described by Professor R. J. Chambers in his book entitled "Accounting Evaluation and Economic Behaviour".

The income statement measures the change in the real wealth of the company for the year and is therefore adjusted from the conventional basis by adding the unrealised gain from holding non-monetary assets, such as vehicles, investments and fixed assets and deducting an amount equal to the fall in purchasing power of actual shareholders funds at the beginning of the year.

The Statement of Financial Position shows all assets at their full net realisable values and reflects the ability of the group to engage in any future operations and to readily adapt to changing circumstances. It also reflects more realistically the scope for borrowing and the present value of resources and shareholders funds on which a reasonable rate of return should be obtained.

FINANCIAL STATEMENTS FOR YEAR ENDED 30TH JUNE 1975
REFLECTING CURRENT VALUES AND THE EFFECT OF INFLATION

	Notes	Current Values $ 000's	As shown in the Consolidated Accounts $ 000's
Group income for year ended 30th June 1975			
Revenue		5,323	5,323
Expenses			
Loss in value of assets (depreciation)			
— Coach fleet and rental vehicles	1	840	746
— Building		—	23
— Plant and business vehicles		42	42
Other Expenses — including transfer to deferred taxation account		4,038	4,038
		4,920	4,849
Net Profit from Operations		403	474
Deduct Capital Maintenance Charge required to maintain the purchasing power of shareholders' funds	2	489	—
		(86)	
Add Net Gain in value of land and buildings and investments		101	—
Total Group income for the year		$ 15	$ 474

(Continued overleaf)

19

Financial position at 30th June 1975

Assets	3		
Current assets		1,098	1,098
Coach fleet and rental vehicles		3,825	3,562
Investments and advances		107	87
Land and buildings		1,991	1,975
Other assets		134	134
Total Assets		7,155	6,856
Deduct Liabilities		3,348	3,348
Shareholders' Funds		$3,807	$3,508
Return on average shareholders' funds		.4%	16.6%

Note 1 Loss in value of assets (depreciation)
Under continuous contemporary accounting, depreciation is the loss between the opening value of the asset plus purchases at cost less proceeds from sales compared with the closing net realisable value.

Note 2 Capital maintenance charge
This amount of $489,000 reflects the loss of purchasing power of shareholders' funds during the year due to inflation. It has been calculated by applying the rate of increase in the consumers price index for the year to 30th June 1975 of 14.9% to the current value of shareholders' funds at the beginning of the year.

Note 3 Assets
Assets have been shown at their current cash equivalent calculated on the following bases:
Coach Fleet and Rental Vehicles: Valued separately at 30th June 1975 by experienced employees of the company whose values in the past have fairly represented the net realisable value of the assets concerned.

Investments: Valued at cost which is also their net realisable value.

Land and Buildings: These are valued at the latest Government valuation except for those properties where cost exceeds that valuation. A major revaluation was undertaken as at 1st July 1974 and it is the opinion of the directors that these values represent the net realisable value of land and buildings.

Other Assets and Liabilities: Stated at the amount recorded in the accounts, which represents their realisable value.

REPORT OF THE AUDITORS
We have examined the consolidated financial statements expressed in current values set out on pages 19 and 20. In our opinion these financial statements have been correctly prepared in accordance with the bases in Notes 1 to 3 above.

Christchurch
26 August 1975

WILKINSON NANKERVIS & STEWART
Chartered Accountants

Firth Industries Ltd
Accounting for Inflation

In line with the recommendations of the New Zealand Society of Accountants, and with the assistance of the University of Waikato, the Company has adjusted its Annual Accounts to show the effects of inflation on its assets and operations over the last year. The three recognised methods used and the subsequent adjustments are explained in the accompanying notes on the following page.

CONSOLIDATED REVENUE STATEMENT
FOR THE YEAR ENDED 27TH MARCH 1976.

	As Shown in Consolidated Accounts.	CPP	CRC	COCOA
Group Income	12,279,000	13,340,000	12,279,000	12,279,000
Expenses – including taxation				
– excluding depreciation	10,581,000	11,720,000	10,707,000	11,116,000
Depreciation	732,000	1,073,000	994,000	—
Net Profit from Operations	966,000	547,000	578,000	1,163,000
Gain on holding net Monetary Liabilities		317,000	10,000	
Capital Maintenance Charge				(1,328,000)
Holding Gain on Assets				472,000
Net Profit for Year	$966,000	864,000	588,000	$307,000

CONSOLIDATED FINANCIAL POSITION
AS AT 27TH MARCH 1976

Properties, Plant, Equipment and Investments (Less accumulated depreciation)				
Land	853,000	1,667,000	3,157,000)	
Buildings	1,155,000	2,027,000	2,446,000)	5,603,000
Plant and Machinery	1,789,000	2,504,000	4,247,000	1,143,000
Motor Vehicles	2,236,000	2,838,000	5,091,000	2,676,000
Other Assets & Investments	168,000	187,000	148,000	141,000
Total Properties, Plant Equipment & Investments	6,201,000	9,223,000	15,089,000	9,563,000
Working Capital	1,450,000	1,481,000	1,616,000	1,955,000
	7,651,000	10,704,000	16,705,000	11,518,000
Less Long Term Payable	2,200,000	2,200,000	2,200,000	2,200,000
Total Shareholders Investment	$5,451,000	8,504,000	14,505,000	9,318,000
Return on Average Shareholders Investment	19.1%	10.7%	4.5%	3.6%

1. **CURRENT PURCHASING POWER (CPP)**
   1.1 Under this method of accounting for changing price levels, the Consolidated Accounts are adjusted to allow for changes in the General Purchasing Power of Money as measured by the Consumer Price Index (CPI). The basis of the application of this method was the New Zealand Society of Accountants Exposure Draft No. 10 of Statement of Standard Accounting Practice "Accounting for Changes in the Purchasing Power of Money".
   1.2 The purchase dates of all Fixed Assets were determined and their historical costs were adjusted to restate their purchase price in terms of 1975 and 1976 dollars. The adjustments were made in accordance with changes in the CPI. Opening and closing inventories were restated upwards on the basis of changes in the CPI since their average date of purchase. Monetary assets and liabilities are already stated in current 1976 dollars.
   1.3 Expenses (other than Depreciation) are assumed to have been incurred evenly throughout the year and therefore these have been adjusted by the average increase in the Consumer Price Index over the year.
   1.4 Depreciation expense has been calculated on the basis of the assets cost adjusted to current purchasing power terms.
   1.5 The gain from holding net monetary liabilities of $317,000 represents the increase in purchasing power calculated on the average holding of monetary liabilites in excess of monetary assets during the period.

2. **CURRENT REPLACEMENT COST (CRC)**
   2.1 This method involves the restatement of assets on the basis of their current replacement cost. The objective of this method is to maintain the operating capacity of the firm. Consequently the profit resulting is that amount which may be distributed without effecting the operating capacity of the firm.
   2.2 Profit is determined at average for the period prices. The difference in expenses between the Consolidated Accounts and the CRC accounts of $126,000 is due to adjustments to opening and closing inventories, to eliminate any profit arising from changing prices.
   2.3 The increase in depreciation expense of $262,000 is the result of depreciation for the period being assessed on the average replacement cost of the assets held.
   2.4 The holding gain of $10,000 represents the gain from holding net short term monetary liabilities.
   2.5 The statement of financial position shows assets at their replacement cost less accumulated depreciation. Valuations were obtained where possible from outside suppliers. Land and buildings were valued in some cases by registered valuers and in other cases by using land agents' estimates and current building costs.
   2.6 Inventories were valued at replacement cost. An adjustment of $166,000 was made as a result of this revaluation.
   2.7 Last year a similar application of the current replacement cost method produced a net profit after maintaining operating capacity of $410,000. This represented a 3.9% return on average shareholders funds compared with 4.5% in 1976.

3. **CONTINUOUSLY CONTEMPORARY ACCOUNTING (COCOA)**
   3.1 This method adopts a realisable value concept of asset measurement. Professor R. J. Chambers' book "Accounting for Inflation – Methods and Problems" was used as the basis of applying COCOA.
   3.2 The increase in expenses, other than depreciation of $535,000 is the result of increasing cost of sales by valuing inventories at net selling price. The depreciation charge is included as part of the price variation adjustment. (see 3.4. below).
   3.3 For the year ended 31st March 1976 the rate of increase of the Consumer Price Index was 17.2 per cent. A charge of $1,328,000 has therefore been necessary to maintain the purchasing power of shareholders funds during the year. This charge was calculated by applying 17.2 per cent to the opening shareholders funds of $7,710,000.
   3.4 Assets held by the company increased in resale value by $472,000 during the period. This is reported as a gain in the Profit & Loss Account.
   3.5 For the valuation of land and buildings depreciated replacement cost was used as an approximation of net realisable value. These two groups of assets were valued as one as they would usually be sold together.
   3.6 Plant and Machinery was valued at 15% – 25% of current replacement cost depending on the age and type of asset. In the opinion of the company this valuation fairly represented the average resale value of its plant and machinery.
   3.7 Motor vehicles were valued at current selling prices which were obtained from motor vehicle dealers.
   3.8 Inventories were valued at estimated net selling value. This was calculated by applying the various markups to the stocks as shown in the Consolidated Accounts, then deducting 10% of finished manufactured goods selling price, representing trade discounts. The subsequent adjustment increased working capital by $505,000.

287

Whatever Happened to CCE?

I think I can fairly claim to have introduced the term "current cash equivalent" into the literature, but I disavow any responsibility for the confusion with which some have surrounded it. Larson and Schattke [1966] claimed to have demolished my contention that current cash equivalents were additive. Professor Vickrey [1975] now contends that their arguments fail "if CCE is defined as the numerosity of a set of homogeneous monetary units which can be obtained for a severable mean (*sic*) in the market." But he still contends that CCEs are not additive. Larson and Schattke [1975] apparently are satisfied that Vickrey's argument is "convincing," that it is "more cogent" than their original exposition.

It is a little curious, to say the least, that neither Vickrey nor Larson and Schattke now make any reference to my response [Chambers, 1967] to the original criticism of Larson and Schattke. The latter purported to show, by relying on an argument of Hempel, that additivity could not be asserted of CCEs. In my response, I showed that my claim satisfied exactly the conditions which Hempel stipulated. Larson and Schattke have not taken up that challenge to this day, to my knowledge, and Vickrey seems to ignore it. I have noticed that others of my critics also have cited Larson and Schattke without any reference to my rebuttal. I shall try first to explain the idea from scratch and will turn, presently, to the fallacies of others.

Suppose you have a $10 bill. You can buy with it anything you like up to an aggregate of things the prices of which add to $10. Suppose you have another $10 bill as well. You now have two separate pieces of paper with which you can buy what you like up to $20 worth of goods. Suppose you have two $10 bills and a check of mine payable to you for $20; also suppose that my check account is in funds. You now have three pieces of paper which will enable you to buy anything you like up to $40 worth of goods. Suppose that besides those three pieces of paper you have another piece of paper which says you own 100 shares of A.T.&T. stock, and suppose you find that buyers are offering $50 per share. You will have the capacity to buy up to $5,040 worth of goods, or to pay debts up to that amount (less in each case, of course, the brokerage charges on the sale of the stock).

In every case but the first, you will have added two or more "amounts of money" in accordance with the usual rules of arithmetic. Perhaps, you may even assert that it is "logical" to do so; but if you say

289

this, it usually will mean nothing more than that you cannot imagine anyone doing otherwise. You will be confident that the sums of the several amounts of money are the aggregate amounts you could spend if you wished to spend or to liquidate debts.

The cash equivalent of a "$10 bill" is $10; the cash equivalent of the "$20 check" is $20; the cash equivalent of the A.T.&T. stock is $5,000. The cash equivalent of any combination of these things is the number of dollars to which the cash equivalents of each item in the combination aggregates. The term cash equivalent is readily comprehensible in ordinary speech, but a few words are in order to explain why I chose to use it.

Accounting is essentially aggregative. As like can only be added to like, it is necessary to specify a characteristic or property which all things represented in an aggregative statement have in common. All things other than money have resale prices (even though some of those prices may be zero). But it is a trifle odd to speak of the price of a sum of money; and sums of money in possession occur in the aggregative statement which is a balance sheet. "Cash equivalent" was chosen as a general term to describe the common property of sums of money and resale prices of non-monetary assets. But the cash held at any point of time and the prices of goods at any point of time have particular significance at that point of time only. If aggregative statements are to be serviceable, for retrospective analysis up to a point of time or for the analysis of prospects from that point of time forward, their components always should be up-to-date, contemporary or "current." Hence, *current* cash equivalent. I also have used the term "current money equivalent" or "current monetary equivalent" to express the same notion.

There is nothing complex about the idea.

People make use of it all the time. Its critics, however, seem to think it too naive a notion. We turn to Vickrey's discussion and show its critical elements to be based on verbal twists, logical fallacies or misapprehensions.

First, he says that *A.E.E.B.* [Chambers, 1966, pp. 93-94] indicates "that any monetary unit is a unit of measure which can be used to obtain measures of CCE" (p. 142). Then: "This contention implies that current cash equivalents are measures of some property other than numerosity . . . " These two extracts confuse a property with a measurement of it. The confusion will be apparent by substituting one term in the second extract for an identical term in the first. The first would then read "any monetary unit is a unit of measure which can be used to obtain measures of (measures of some property other than numerosity)"!

As for numerosity, the cash equivalent of any asset at any time, being its realizable price (or its nominal amount, in the case of cash), is expressed in a number of dollars. Numbers of things are exactly what "numerosity" refers to; "things" in the present context are dollars. The sum of the cash equivalents of any collection of assets is such a number. It expresses, in a number of dollars, the extent to which the possessor of the assets could buy any other assets or services or pay any debt at the time. Of course it is a form of counting. I cannot see how Vickrey can be "confident" that I am not referring to the process of discovering the numerosity of the dollars equivalent to the assets of a firm (see his footnote 4), when the passages he cites [*A.E.E.B.*, pp. 91-92, 101] make it quite plain that I am referring to that process.

"Second," says Vickrey, "Chambers contends contradictorily that severable means and equities are the phenomena that are subjected to measurement when CCE is measured and that current cash equivalents are meant to be measures of the amounts of CCE that are possessed by these phenomena." Here there is confusion of an object with a particular property of it. I did not assert that severable means and equities are the phenomena that are subjected to measurement when CCE is measured. Vickrey makes it appear that way by omitting my acknowledgment of a quotation from Margenau in the footnote to page 104 of *A.E.E.B.* I pointed out in Chapter 4 that monetary calculation is concerned with a particular *property* or *properties* of assets and equities, not with the measurement of assets and equities. The distinction is important. The literature persistently has referred to the representation or quantification or measurement of assets and equities, and I am disposed to believe that that is the reason why the fallacious practice of using so many different kinds of valuation in a single balance sheet has been perpetuated. I determined to avoid that error by stipulating (as is customary in all exercises in measurement), the particular characteristic or property being measured. Hence, in the footnote just mentioned, I said "the subject is an individual asset or equity; the observable [i.e., the property to be quantified or measured] is its cash equivalent." The alleged contradiction arises only from inaccurate paraphrasing of the text on Vickrey's part. (Incidentally, it almost seems as though Vickrey means two different things by "current cash equivalent" and "CCE"; otherwise, it is simply tautologous to say "current cash equivalents are meant to be measures of the amounts of CCE"!)

"Third," writes Vickrey, "Chambers says that the dimension of the monetary unit (i.e., the alleged unit of measure for CCE) is its general purchasing power . . . this statement means, in effect, that a current cash equivalent is a measure of the purchasing power of some phenomenon."

Of course, and why not? If I find I have a 10-dollar bill the cash or monetary equivalent of which is $10, surely I have general purchasing power to the extent of $10. The numerosity of monetary units is 10, the units are dollars; therefore, $10 expresses the numerosity of the dollars I command. As the dollar gives me the power to command any goods up to one dollars' worth, $10 represents my command of general purchasing power. The point that Vickrey glosses over is that the context of the passages he cites is a discussion of the change in the purchasing power of money through time. At two points of time I may have 10 dollars, but "dollar" may not have the same significance, or "dimension." It takes the addition of a date to any such statement as "I have $10" in order to indicate my command of general purchasing power at that date, as distinct from the number of dollars in my possession. A statement about a number of dollars can be interpreted, at any time, both by reference to other numbers of dollars and by reference to the prices of goods and services at that time. But, the change represented by an increment in the number of dollars between two dates at which the general purchasing powers of the dollar differed cannot be specified, let alone interpreted, without converting the two numbers of dollars to a common base or dimension.[1]

This is taken up in Vickrey's fourth and fifth points. His allegation there is that the

---

[1] Since 1966, I have improved the original notation to distinguish dollars of different dates having different general purchasing powers; thus $\$_0$, $\$_1$ represent general purchasing powers of dollars at t_0 and t_1. See, *inter alia*, "Price Variation Accounting—A General Notation" in Chambers (1969). In a paper presently awaiting publication, I show that it is possible to avoid using the phrase "general purchasing power of money" by recourse to the notion of a "coefficient of variation in the general level of prices" which is analogous to the coefficient of expansion of, say, a metal. This does not alter the form of accounting which my theory entails, but it eliminates a bone of contention and makes it even clearer that continuously contemporary accounting is of the same family as measurement in other fields.

transformation of a quantity of dollars at one date into a quantity having equivalent purchasing power at another date entails a similarity transformation, whereas, the only admissible transformation of representations of numerosity is an identity transformation. In the first place, it seems as though Vickrey has overlooked his earlier decision (p. 141) to use numerosity as shorthand for "number of dollars." A number (or numeral, see Vickrey's footnote 7) is quite different from a number of dollars. The numbers which appear in accounts are not numerals; they are numbers of dollars, and dated dollars at that. If n is any numeral, n plus one equals $(n+1)$, always. But n dollars of 1974 plus one dollar of 1975 does not equal $(n+1)$ dollars of any specific purchasing power. In the second place, nowhere in the pages cited by Vickrey did I say that measures of CCE can be transformed into other measures of CCE. I did say that a number of dollars of specified general purchasing power may be transformed into another number of dollars of different specified general purchasing power (*A.E.E.B.*, p. 95). This may seem to be the same as Vickrey's paraphrase, but it is not. I did not intend that the CCE of any asset at a point of time should be transformed into an equivalent CCE at another time by the use of a price index. In my system, the only transformation used is a transformation of the opening residual equity which, by reason of its derivation, is a number of dollars of specified (dated) general purchasing power.

In the third place, Vickrey alleges a misconception of the characteristics of the scale to which I referred, a misconception which "may be attributable to some of the relatively early works on measurement theory" such as Stevens (footnote 8, p. 143). There is no misconception on my part that I can see. The scale of natural numbers ("the scale we use when we count"—Stevens) is a ratio scale, in Stevens' terminology. Suppes and Zinnes (p. 9) say:

"Counting is an example of an absolute scale. The number of members in a given collection of objects is determined uniquely. There is no arbitrary choice of unit or zero available. In contrast, the usual measurement of mass or weight is an example of a ratio scale . . . the choice of a unit [being] an empirically arbitrary decision . . . Of course, once a unit of measurement has been chosen, such as the gram or pound, the numerical mass of every other object in the universe is uniquely determined."

There is, it seems, a distinction here without a difference. With reference to counting, "the number of members in a given collection of objects is determined uniquely only when the unit, "member," has been chosen. The number of eggs in a given collection of eggs will be a different number if the unit is a single egg than if the unit were a dozen eggs; both are cases of counting. On the other hand, with reference to mass (or distance), given the unit of mass, the measurement of the mass of a specific object is simply a matter of counting. Therefore, in substance, Suppes and Zinnes are not at odds with Stevens, except by reason of an elision on their part. (There are examples of another type of elision in the same passage. Strictly counting is an example of *the use of* a particular scale. The scale is the scale of numbers.)

Sixth, Vickrey points out that I have asserted that measures of CCE are measures of purchasing power and concludes that CCEs cannot "logically" be construed as "measures of the numerosities of sets of homogeneous monetary units" (p. 144). Here, as elsewhere, Vickrey fails to grasp the significance of the first C in CCE. *Current* cash equivalent means the cash equivalent at any specified date. The whole tenor of my argument bears this out. The number of dollars by which a CCE is denoted at a given date is, thus, the number of homogeneous monetary units of dated general purchasing power which the possessor of the asset commands at that date.

Finally, Vickrey explores the "additivity of purchasing power." It should not be necessary to labor the points that dollars at a given date represent general purchasing power at that date, and that the addition of dollars at that date gives aggregate command of general purchasing power. But Vickrey turns to a line of argument used by Larson and Schattke. As I have mentioned, in responding to Larson and Schattke I demonstrated that Hempel's conditions of additivity are satisfied completely by the ideas I have advanced. By contrast, Vickrey's proposal (p. 144) for testing the additivity of purchasing powers rests on two logical fallacies. We will take the argument in two steps, since Vickrey proposes that the "denominator" of purchasing power may be either monetary units or amounts of other types of goods.

First, take the monetary unit as a denominator. In effect, Vickrey says, let the selling price of x (i.e., the power of x to purchase dollars) be $\$X$ and the selling price of y be $\$Y$. Find also the selling price of $(x+y)$; let this be $\$Z$. Compare ($\$X + \$Y$) with $\$Z$. If they are equivalent, that will be one piece of evidence for the additivity of purchasing powers. Here is the first fallacy; the comparison cannot be made unless $\$X$ and $\$Y$ can be added. Thus, we assume that they can be added in order to proceed to the final point where it is demonstrated whether they can be added. This is the fallacy, *petitio principii*, begging the question, or assuming what is to be proved. And, of course, the exercise of comparison shows, not whether $\$X$ and $\$Y$ can be added, but only whether the selling price of the combination is equal or unequal to the sum of the selling prices of the components. This shows that the argument also involves an example of *ignoratio elenchi*, the fallacy of arguing beside the point.

Second, Vickrey allows the use of amounts of other goods as denominators of purchasing power. This also must fail for the above reason; namely, that it assumes that the purchasing powers of x and y in terms of say, potatoes, are additive. Again, there is a second fallacy. To find the "barter" equivalents of x and y in potatoes is to find a *specific* purchasing power, and one, indeed, which is subject to much greater variation than a money price, since the marginal utility of potatoes diminishes at a faster rate than the marginal utility of wealth in general. The virtue of money is that it represents wealth or command of resources or purchasing power in general. The whole of my discussions of money and selling prices, with reference to CCEs, have reference to the *general* purchasing power of money. A barter equivalent of the kind proposed by Vickrey is not an amount of general purchasing power at all. Since accounts are representations in monetary units, and since monetary units are units of general (nonspecific) purchasing power, Vickrey's proposal involves another case of *ignoratio elenchi*.

In sum, it seems to me that Vickrey's comments are confused throughout by third- or fourth- or higher-level abstractions [Hayakawa, Ch. 10]. There is nothing wrong with abstraction, as long as one keeps one's feet on the ground. But it is fatally easy to slip to "Cloud 9." A CCE is simply a selling price in the case of nonmonetary assets, a price denominated in dollars. The additivity question is simply: what kinds of dollar amounts legitimately can be added, subtracted and related. Certainly, the amounts of money I now can get for anything I possess can be added to the amount of money I possess; and the sum can be related to what I owe; and the difference is my net command of money's worth, now.

Whatever happened to CCE? It hasn't really suffered from the assaults of fallacious logic; and its consistency with the views of classical writers on measurement has not been demolished. In fact, it is alive and doing well in the company of all who buy and sell, and who borrow and lend on the security of assets—a very numerous company.

REFERENCES

Chambers, Raymond, J., *Accounting, Evaluation and Economic Behavior* (1966).
———, "Continuously Contemporary Accounting—Additivity and Action," THE ACCOUNTING REVIEW (October 1967), pp. 751–757.
———, "Price Variation Accounting—A General Notation" in Chambers, *Accounting, Finance and Management* (Arthur Andersen & Co. and Butterworths, Sydney, 1969), pp. 636–642.
Hayakawa, S. I., *Language in Thought and Action* (Allen and Unwin, 1965).
Hempel, Carl G., *Fundamentals of Concept Formation in Empirical Science* (The University of Chicago Press, 1952).
Larson, Kermit and R. W. Schattke "Current Cash Equivalent, Additivity and Financial Action," THE ACCOUNTING REVIEW (October 1966), pp. 634–641.
———, "A Note on Vickrey's Comment," THE ACCOUNTING REVIEW (January 1975), p. 147.
Stevens, S. S., "On the Theory of Scales of Measurement," *Science* (7 June 1946), pp. 677–680.
Suppes, Patrick and Joseph L. Zinnes, "Basic Measurement Theory," in Duncan Luce, Robert R. Bush and Eugene Galanter, eds., *Handbook of Mathematical Psychology*, Vol. 1 (Wiley, 1963), pp. 1–76.
Vickrey, Don, "A Comment on the Larson-Schattke and Chambers Debate over the Additivity of CCE," THE ACCOUNTING REVIEW (January 1975), pp. 140–146.

Continuously Contemporary Accounting: Misunderstandings and Misrepresentations

In the context of the current debate about the future style of accounting, the partiality of the critics of continuously contemporary accounting deserves attention. Some widely distributed publications positively misrepresent the system and take no notice whatever of practically significant features which other systems lack. Recourse to such devices suggests that continuously contemporary accounting is beyond more legitimate forms of criticism, and that the claims of other systems are less substantial than they appear.

It is just about ten years since *Accounting, Evaluation and Economic Behavior* was published.[1] As far as I recall, the method of accounting it proposed was first called 'continuously contemporary accounting' in a paper presented in the University of California at Berkeley in January 1967.[2] The method has been amplified and refined in some respects in papers since then, but its key features remain. Those features are the use of resale prices (or dated money equivalents) for nonmonetary assets, and the use of price variation and capital maintenance adjustments in the calculation of periodical incomes, to take account of the effects of changes in asset prices and changes in the general purchasing power of money.

The Berkeley paper mentioned above was, to the best of my knowledge, the first paper in the literature to compare, on a uniform set of tests, the salient features of the main systems of accounting which then, and now, 'compete' for adoption as the most comprehensive, consistent and serviceable system. There have since been other such comparisons.[3] Most of them have been partial, some fragmentary. Most of them have occurred in the course of expositions of systems other than continuously contemporary accounting, particularly in the debates over methods of taking account of the effects of inflation.

It might be supposed, by those who have not followed closely the literature of the last ten years, that the descriptions and appraisals of critics of continuously

---

[1] Prentice-Hall, Englewood Cliffs, N.J. 1966. Reprinted, Scholars Book Co., Houston 1974.
[2] 'The Foundations of Financial Accounting', *Berkeley Symposium on the Foundations of Financial Accounting,* University of California, Berkeley 1967, pp. 26-44.
[3] E.g., Reg S. Gynther, 'Capital Maintenance, Price Changes and Profit Determination', *Accounting Review,* October 1970, pp. 712-30; Daniel L. McDonald, *Comparative Accounting Theory,* Addison-Wesley, Reading, Mass. 1972; John R. Hanna, *Accounting Income Models,* The Society of Industrial Accountants of Canada, Hamilton 1973.

contemporary accounting and proponents of other systems would have fairly represented that system. But that supposition is at odds with the evidence. The system (which I have since called COCOA, for short) has been widely misunderstood or misrepresented, notwithstanding the numerous articles on it over the period.[4] This may not matter if the misrepresentations had occurred in relatively insignificant places. But the very wide publicity given to documents which unfairly represent COCOA prompts me to attempt to put the record straight.

The appraisals and criticisms to be considered occur in the following publications (in order of dates of publication):

A. *Report of the Committee of Inquiry into Inflation and Taxation* (Mathews Committee Report), Australian Government publication, May 1975 (official publication, circulation unknown, but significant).

B. Preliminary Exposure Draft, *A Method of 'Current Value Accounting'*, published by the Australian Accounting Research Foundation, June 1975 (circulation in excess of 40,000).

C. *A Comparison of Accounting Measurement Systems*, an Evaluative Paper, published by the Australian Accounting Research Foundation, August 1975 (circulation in excess of 40,000).

D. *Report of the Inflation Accounting Committee* (Sandilands Committee Report), U.K. Government, H.M.S.O., September 1975 (official publication, circulation unknown, but significant).

The discussion which follows relates only to the comments on COCOA embodied in these publications. It is *not* an appraisal of the substance of the methods proposed by the committees responsible for the publications. A brief appraisal of the three main systems (other than historical cost accounting) is given in an appendix to the present author's Exposure Draft, *Accounting for Inflation*, and an extended critique is given in *Accounting for Inflation—Methods and Problems*.[5] A later section of this paper deals with significant claims which the abovementioned publications (and many other such comparisons) disregard completely. In effect, the accounts widely given of the features of COCOA are so bowdlerized as to be completely misleading.

A. *The Mathews Report*

A.1 In the course of its inquiry, the Committee considered a number of methods of accounting. When dealing with COCOA, the Report disregards completely the prime feature of the system, namely its recourse to the money equivalents

---

[4] E.g., 'Continuously Contemporary Accounting—Additivity and Action', *Accounting Review*, October 1967, pp. 751-7; 'Measures and Values . . .', *Accounting Review*, April 1968, pp. 239-47; 'Continuously Contemporary Accounting', *Accountant*, 30 April 1970, pp. 643-7; 'Second Thoughts on Continuously Contemporary Accounting', *Abacus*, September 1970, pp. 39-55; 'Evidence for a Market Selling Price Accounting System' in Robert R. Sterling (ed.), *Asset Valuation and Income Determination*, Scholars Book Co., 1971, pp. 74-96; *Securities and Obscurities*, Gower Press, Melbourne 1973.

[5] Both published 1975, and available from the Department of Accounting, University of Sydney, N.S.W. 2006, Australia.

of assets at balance dates for the purpose of calculating financial positions and results. The Report describes COCOA as 'Relative Price Level Accounting'. It says 'this approach effectively combines a current value system with a CPP system' (para. 10.38). When dealing with current value accounting ('CVA' hereafter), current values are said to be current replacement costs or market selling values, according to the intention of the firm to replace or not to replace an asset (para. 10.22). COCOA does not make use of current replacement cost for any purpose.[6] When dealing with CPP accounting, the Report says that 'financial statements prepared on the basis of historical cost accounting are adjusted for changes in the general price level . . .' (para. 10.32). Clearly the adjusted (CPP) figures for assets are based on costs. COCOA does not make any use of the costs of assets or index-adjusted costs for the purpose of deriving dated asset values. In describing COCOA as 'relative price level accounting' the Report appears to be characterizing it by reference to its asset-valuation method. But in failing to point out that, by contrast with CPP and CVA, it uses dated money equivalents or resale prices, it disregards a crucial difference.

A.2 The Report correctly points out that COCOA income has three components. The first, it says, is 'the difference between revenues and expenses expressed in current prices, and is thus equivalent to the current value concept of income' (para. 10.38). This is not the case. The first component is net revenues, that is, all receipts less all payments made in the course of business. (For the sake of simplicity, we exclude new financing, dividends, and purchases and sales of assets other than inventories, as does the Report.) The current value concept of income entails charging revenues with updated inventory and depreciation costs; the first component of income under COCOA does not. Further, the reference to 'revenues and expenses expressed in current prices' may imply that revenues and expenses (or even cash payments) are index-adjusted or averaged; the Australian draft on CVA entails such adjustments. This is not done under COCOA; revenues and payments are actual amounts. The first component of income under COCOA is thus *not* equivalent to the current value concept of income.

A.3 The Report says that 'the second component of income [under COCOA] is represented by the changes in current value . . . on nonmonetary assets; by contrast with current value accounting, these are regarded not as valuation adjustments but as income available for distribution' (para. 10.38). Neither of these statements is the case. The second component of income under COCOA is the 'price variation adjustment'. This is the net amount of all changes in money equivalents (or resale prices) of assets, other than those which have already been taken up in net revenues. Where price variation adjustments are made only at the end of a year, this component is simply the difference between book values and the independently determined money equivalents of nonmonetary assets. The amount of this component is *not* regarded as income available for distribution;

---

[6] Replacement price was suggested as an approximation in 1966, but it has since been completely abandoned; see 'Second Thoughts on Continuously Contemporary Accounting' (note 4 above).

against the first and second components must be set off the third; the net income which results is the income available for distribution.

A.4 The third component of income calculation under COCOA, the capital maintenance adjustment, is described in the Report as the 'purchasing power loss (or gain) on proprietorship capital or net assets' (para. 10.38). This is correct if 'or' is understood as an alternative description of equal amounts of money. It seems preferable, however, to speak of the 'proprietors' equity' to avoid confusion with 'paid up capital', or to speak of the 'capital of the firm' using capital in a sense common among economists. But to say that the effect of this adjustment 'is to adopt a capital maintenance requirement that is the same as that used under CPP accounting' (para. 10.39) is to misrepresent both. CPP accounting is justified in the official statements on it by reference to the maintenance of the general purchasing power of the amount invested in it by its owners.[7] That is not the same thing, however, as calculating periodical income by reference to maintenance of the general purchasing power of the amount of net assets with which a period begins, the method of COCOA. Further, notwithstanding its claims, CPP accounting does not in fact ascertain whether the general purchasing power of a dated amount is maintained at a later date. It *assumes* that there is *no* change in the general purchasing power equivalent of nonmonetary assets from year to year. COCOA makes no such assumption. It proceeds by the only way in which general purchasing power may be ascertained at any date—namely by using the market selling prices (general purchasing power equivalents) of nonmonetary assets.

A.5 The notation used in paras 10.40-10.42 of the Report is far from satisfactory. It has no symbol for the change in the financial significance of the money unit and the other symbols used are open to misunderstanding on that account if on no other. But there are others. The alleged similarities or equivalences referred to in earlier paragraphs of this discussion of the Report lead to the use of symbols which are the same as those used in the Report's discussion of other systems. It should be apparent (from A.2, A.3 and A.4 above) that this does violence to COCOA.

A.6 Paragraphs 10.41 and 10.42 purport to show that, if the 'income from trading activities is ignored', and if the net income under COCOA is distributed, the purchasing power of the opening net assets is maintained but the composition of the assets is altered. The amount of the net assets 'does not command the same quantity of the kinds of assets' which were held at the beginning of the income period (para. 10.42). The analysis of the Report stops at this point, as if the quoted observation settled the case against COCOA. Of course it does not settle the case. Business firms of every class and kind are continually changing the compositions of their assets. There is no ground whatever for supposing that to maintain a given quantity of given kinds of assets is a legitimate or

---

[7] See Australian Preliminary Exposure Draft, *A Method of 'Accounting for Changes in the Purchasing Power of Money'*, December 1974, Appendix 1, para. 3.

reasonable object of business. In any case, if the assumption of no trading income were relaxed, it is quite possible in principle that both the composition of assets and the general purchasing power of the opening amount of net assets could be maintained.

I think I can fairly claim to have been the first to propose the form of notation used in the Report, and the notion of a 'transactionless interval' (no trading income) as a means of simplifying the problem and sorting out the issues. But having sorted out the issues, the notation and the inferences from its use have been generalized to the point where the transactionless interval is no longer necessary as an expository device. As well, the newer notation has symbols for the different financial significances of the money unit at different dates, avoiding any confusion about what it represents.[8] Of these forms of improvement and their consequences, the Report takes no notice.

A.7 Clearly the Report misrepresents COCOA to a material extent. It is difficult to grant that this is due to faulty exposition of the system, since its main thrust—the use of market selling prices and the calculation of the capital maintenance adjustment—has been well understood by others. But the extent of the misrepresentations casts serious doubt on the propriety of the conclusions which emerge from the Report's survey of alternatives, and hence on the merits of the Report's chosen proposal.

B. *The CVA Exposure Draft*

B.1 The Preliminary Exposure Draft, *A Method of Current Value Accounting* was published by the Australian professional bodies in June 1975. It offers a 'classification' of proposals for remedying the shortcomings of traditional accounting (para. 4). The classes are (a) 'General price level accounting', (b) 'Specific price change accounting' and (c) 'Methods combining specific price change accounting with some features of general price level accounting'. Class (a) is generally described as CPP accounting and was the subject of the first Preliminary Exposure Draft of December 1974.[9] Its balance sheets are based on *costs* adjusted by reference to changes in an index of the general level of prices. Its profit includes gains or losses on monetary items. Class (b) takes account of changes in the prices of specific assets. Its balance sheets are based generally on the up-to-date *costs* of assets; revaluation amounts are taken directly to revaluation reserves; and inventory and depreciation charges against revenues are based on average or up-to-date costs. It does not take account of gains or losses on

---

[8] The development of the notation may be traced through Chambers, 'Price Variation Accounting—An Improved Representation', *Journal of Accounting Research*, Autumn 1967, pp. 215-20; 'New Pathways in Accounting Thought and Action', *Accountants' Journal* (N.Z.), July 1968, pp. 434-41; and 'Price Variation Accounting—A General Notation' in Chambers, *Accounting, Finance and Management*, Butterworth, 1969, pp. 636-42. The general solution, abandoning the transactionless interval, was first published in 'Continuously Contemporary Accounting', *Accountant*, 30 April 1970.

[9] Preliminary Exposure Draft, *A Method of 'Accounting for Changes in the Purchasing Power of Money'*, Australian Accounting Research Foundation, December 1974.

monetary items. Class (c) includes a method similar to (b), but which brings into account gains or losses on monetary items. Class (c) also includes a method called 'Relative Price Change Accounting' (call it (C, 2)) which is said to proceed as in (b) except that it splits the revaluation surplus into a part which represents the change which would correspond with the movement in the general price index, and a part which is the balance of the change in asset prices. Under (C, 2), gains or losses on monetary items are brought into account. 'Some supporters' of (C, 2) hold that 'movements in the specific prices of nonmonetary assets also represent real gains or losses which should be included in the profit and loss statement as part of the profit for the period'.

B.2 Now, curiously, COCOA seems to be completely excluded from this classification. The balance sheets of (a) and (b) are based on cost prices; the balance sheets of (c) must therefore be based on cost prices, according to its description quoted above. It seems as though the description of method (C, 2) is intended to cover a system such as COCOA. But COCOA does *not* use cost prices (past, present or future) in deriving asset values; it uses dated money equivalents. COCOA does *not* split the amounts of price changes in the manner indicated. And COCOA does *not* carry the movements in asset prices into profit without offset; it offsets the amount of a capital maintenance adjustment, which appears nowhere in the description given in the CVA Exposure Draft. It follows that either the compilers of the Draft misunderstand the nature of COCOA; or they misrepresent it; or they disregard it—for the purposes of the classification at least.

B.3 The CVA Draft expounds the methods of class (b). To be exact, para. 4 (b) when speaking of changes in asset prices, does not refer to the 'costs' of assets. However, the method expounded employs replacement cost for all assets 'essential to the continuance of operations'; by way of 'refinement' it employs net realizable value for assets not essential for continuance of operations (paras 16, 17). These rules are said to be justified on the assumption of 'continuity of the entity'. The Draft then says: 'In recent years the going concern assumption has been attacked by those who have advocated that current value accounting should be based entirely on net realizable value or, as it is also described, current cash equivalent. They argue that to assume continuity of an entity is a questionable procedure, when in fact an important objective of accounting is to provide evidence as to whether the continuity of the entity is justified' (para. 19). Here again is either a misrepresentation or a misunderstanding of COCOA (COCOA being the only system in which the term 'current cash equivalent' has been used). The going concern assumption is as much an element of COCOA as it is claimed to be of other systems. More so, indeed; for it envisages a much wider range of possible operations, to keep a firm 'going', than the replacement of particular assets. It regards the entity as typically adaptive to its circumstances and opportunities in the interest of continuity of the entity (see, e.g., *Accounting, Evaluation and Economic Behavior*, pp. 202-5). What the exponents of COCOA attack is not the assumption of continuity of the entity, but the assumption of continuity of use of particular assets or classes of assets. This means, of course, that they attack the relevance of replacement costs, since replacement costs or figures based on them do not represent capacity, if needed, to pay wages, debts, taxes or dividends, to buy inventories, plant or shares in other companies, to replace any asset, or to borrow on the security of present assets. The allegation that COCOA attacks the assumption of continuity of the entity is thus false. Whether the allegation is deliberately 'self-serving' or inadvertent cannot be judged. But clearly it is intended as defence of the Draft's proposal, by improper denigration of an alternative.

B.4 It may appear that the CVA Draft is not altogether unfair to COCOA. It suggests that if, by the use of the method it proposes, the results 'put in doubt the viability of the entity', it may become necessary to use accounting information based entirely on net realizable values. In the first place, this is an odd conclusion. If replacement price accounting is not able of itself to indicate the capacities referred to in the previous paragraph, it is not indicative of the 'viability' of the entity. It will not necessarily, therefore, prompt a redraft of the financial statements using net realizable values! In the second place, if the viability of the entity were 'put in doubt', it would have to go to the expense of redrafting the statements on entirely different principles. Two inconsistent sets of accounts, in respect of the same transactions and the same period, would not only be curious, but would be a positive nuisance.[10] COCOA was never intended to be contributory to the confusion which would result. And, in any case, COCOA is not simply a 'net realizable value system'.

C. *The A.A.R.F. Evaluative Paper*

C.1 Subsequent to the publication of the Australian Exposure Drafts of December 1974 and June 1975, the Australian Accounting Research Foundation published an 'evaluative paper', styled *A Comparison of Accounting Measurement Systems* (CAMS hereafter). It was expected to assist accountants 'to obtain a better appreciation of the problems involved in accounting for inflation'. Each of a number of proposals is described, and 'evaluated'. The section on COCOA (pp. 17-19) is headed 'Current Exit Values'.

At the outset CAMS suggests that the unit of account may be 'money' *or* 'current purchasing power'. Both are to be 'expressed in dollars' (p. 4). If both are to be expressed in dollars (money units, or units of account), what is there that distinguishes them? It can only be their dates. Is it conceivable that there can be a 'current purchasing power unit', that is not 'money' but is 'expressed in dollars'? No; a dated dollar is a dated general purchasing power unit. CAMS describes COCOA as using 'purchasing power as the unit of account' (p. 17). What this means is not at all clear; but certainly it is not correct. COCOA uses dollars as the unit of account. When goods are bought and sold COCOA uses dollars spent and received. Only when income is to be computed does COCOA

[10] For some indication of the confusion, though in a different setting, see Chambers, *Accounting for Inflation—Methods and Problems*, pp. 68-70.

take account of the fact that opening and closing dollars have unequal general purchasing powers; and it makes one adjustment to take account of that fact. COCOA does use dated dollars to represent dated financial positions; and dated dollars are dated purchasing power units. But that does not introduce some other kind of unit as CAMS implies.

C.2 CAMS says 'there can be little argument about the theoretical relevance of exit values for managerial decisions about assets currently held' (p. 17). It notes the claim that resale price is the only asset value 'which is relevant in every business decision about an asset once it has been acquired' (p. 18). But then it says 'it is important to recognize that this point has limited applicability in practice' (p. 18). These passages appear to set up what is 'theoretically' pertinent against what is 'practically' pertinent. CAMS offers no evidence of what is practically pertinent; but by implication or omission it disregards the substantial amount of evidence to the point that resale prices are practically pertinent. The most convenient collection of such evidence occurs in the present author's *Securities and Obscurities*.[11] CAMS cites this work at one point, so that ignorance of its contents cannot be pleaded. The allegation of 'limited applicability in practice' is belied by the variety of practical circumstances and cases in which knowledge of the resale prices of assets is shown, by exponents of COCOA, to be practically important.

C.3 On the determination of market resale prices, CAMS notes that in one exposition of COCOA (*Securities and Obscurities,* p. 219) it was said that the prices reported are to be 'the best possible approximations to the net selling prices of those assets in the ordinary course of business in their then condition as at the date of the balance sheet'. CAMS omits to note that, in other expositions, the quantities or combinations of assets to be used in ascertaining market resale prices are said to be the quantities or combinations in which the asset or assets in question are customarily sold or would be sold or put out of use in the ordinary course of business. (It also apparently disregards the fact that in all budgeting in the ordinary course of business, some notion of quantities and combinations of goods sold, of any class or kind, must be used.) It also omits to note that, elsewhere than in the passage cited, liquidation prices or prices under duress are not the class of prices intended to be used.[12] For want of fair examination of expositions of COCOA, CAMS implies that the method is quite inadequately specified. It asks (p. 19) 'sale under what conditions?'—when 'the ordinary course of business' indicates the conditions. It asks 'what is being sold?' —when, as indicated above, there are quite specific indications. It points out that liquidation prices may be well below prices obtainable by a continuing enterprise —when, in expositions of COCOA, it is clearly stated that liquidation prices are not intended. It asks 'in what combinations should assets be priced?'—when the answer is clearly suggested in expositions of the system. By innuendo (i.e. by

[11] Gower Press, Melbourne 1973.
[12] E.g., *Accounting, Evaluation and Economic Behavior,* p. 204.

asking these questions as if they were just not answered), CAMS quite misrepresents the expositions of COCOA and the extent to which its rules are specified.

C.4 In its evaluation, CAMS alludes briefly to the problem of non-vendibles—highly specific assets, premiums paid 'for goodwill', research and development costs and like items. Under COCOA, the reported money equivalent of any such item may be as little as zero at the end of the year of acquisition. CAMS points out that the 'adaptability' of a firm is indicated by the use of 'exit values'. It does not point out that 'adaptability' embraces every action related to survival—capacity to pay short-run debts, cover for long-term debts, capacity to pay wages, trade accounts, dividends and taxes and so on. Insofar as any firm has sunk a large part of its funds in non-vendibles, it has reduced its capacity for short-run adjustments to its circumstances. Unless this is made clear in the accounts, investors and creditors can have no idea of the risks to which they are subject. Only COCOA, of all the main proposals, makes it clear, for only COCOA takes the position that asset costs, past, present or future, are irrelevant to the representation and assessment of financial position.

C.5 In addition to the brief statement and evaluation of each a number of proposals, CAMS gives a comparative presentation of accounts for two years of a given hypothetical firm under five systems (pp. 31-7). The impression yielded by any such example depends, of course, on the figures chosen. It happens that at the end of the second year, the 'accumulated losses' range from zero under historical cost accounting, between $8,200 and $31,000 for three other systems, to $283,000 under 'exit values' (the CAMS description nearest to COCOA). The greater part ($240,000) of the last amount is due to a fall in the money equivalent of plant immediately following installation. The potential reality of this fall is not questioned, even though it is not a common occurrence. But there is no necessary reason for describing the fall as accumulated losses.

The notion of sunk costs, descriptive of outlays yielding no asset having value in exchange, is not novel. In the double-account system once generally used by utilities, sunk costs were represented separately from financial operations on current account. There are good reasons for recourse to the same device in respect of purchased goodwill, mine development costs, highly specialized plant and other 'costly' items. The reasons are that (i) the accounts would show what had been done with contributed funds, (ii) the *financial* position would not be confused with financially insignificant residual balances, (iii) the 'riskiness' due to reduced 'disposable-asset-backing' would be made evident, and the higher rate of return on net assets would correspond with that risk. The balance sheet of the CAMS example would appear then as follows:

ABACUS

COCOA Balance Sheet at 30 June 19x2

Plant (specialized or non-vendible)	$240,000	Contributed funds employed	$240,000

Financial Position

Assets	$607,000	Contributed funds	$660,000
		Less Sunk Costs (above)	240,000
			420,000
		Accumulated losses	(43,000)
			377,000
		Liabilities	230,000
	607,000		607,000

The impression this gives is very different from that given in CAMS.

Much of the apparent 'uneasiness' about writing off large sums of the above kind appears to stem from a belief in the periodical regularity of incomes and the stability of prices. The belief is a myth. It may well be true that some firms enjoy regular incomes and that some do not experience marked swings in asset values. It may also be true that companies prefer the *appearance* of regularity of incomes and stability of asset values, even when they are experiencing neither. But any reasonable examination of results and asset values even under traditional accounting will show that many companies have had to face marked shifts in reported incomes and reported asset values—even in single years. There is nothing unusual about COCOA in this respect. What is more pertinent, though, is that COCOA recognizes the swings when they occur; it does not allow long-run expectations (which may or may not eventuate) to influence what is reported from time to time about dated financial positions and results. The present point is that, by the choice of specific assumptions, the illustrations of CAMS suggest that COCOA is anomalous in some sense; whereas more elaborate argument and the choice of other specific assumptions would yield quite different and defensible conclusions.

C.6 Dealing with liabilities, CAMS impugns the logic of COCOA. The amount of any liability under COCOA is the amount for which a debtor stands in debt at balance date. 'However', says CAMS, 'where the enterprise has the opportunity to redeem a liability before maturity at a price other than the contractual amount owed, it would seem logical to conclude that this value would constitute the liability's current cash equivalent or exit value' (p. 19). Now, for a going concern in the ordinary course of business, as long as a debt is outstanding its amount is the amount payable out of its assets. Its amount is the money equivalent or cash equivalent of the debt at the date of the statement in which it appears. No creditor would tolerate it being written down to some lower figure; and any potential creditor who was told, when about to lend, that the firm owed less than in fact it owed would be entitled, on discovery, to claim misrepresentation. If there is any lack of logic in all this, CAMS is not prepared to demonstrate it.[13] Allegation and innuendo are made to serve as 'evaluation'.

D. *The Sandilands Report*

D.1 The Report devotes something over two pages to continuously contemporary accounting. It points out first that the method 'so far as we know' is not practised by any company (para. 503). Perhaps the Sandilands Committee was not to know that it has been used (as supplementary information) by several companies in New Zealand. But the Committee should have known that the valuation of assets at market prices has a great deal to do with the capacities of companies to meet their debts and to modify their operations, as they are prone to do.[14] The Report, indeed, goes so far as to admit the value of information based on the market value of assets to creditors and lenders (paras 505, 506). But it makes no suggestion about the way in which creditors and lenders will be able to get this information under the method it proposes.

D.2 The Report quotes some words of mine: 'as, for any particular purpose, a company may wish to redeploy its wealth, or any part of it, or to borrow on any scale up to the limit which creditors will stand (on the basis of its present wealth and past earnings), its balance sheet or financial statement should carry all assets severally at such market prices'. The Committee 'doubts, however, whether the majority of companies regard their assets either as "means of buying other things" or as a means of "paying off debts"' (para. 505). Now the question at issue is not 'how the majority of [or any] companies regard their assets'; it is: 'how may the financial positions of companies be fairly represented'. The Committee could have satisfied its doubts, in any case, by reference to what companies do. They sell some assets to buy others continuously. And not only inventories. They buy and sell land, buildings, equipment, shares in other companies. Certainly some companies don't do each of these things continuously. But there would be few companies which do not in any year sell some non-inventory assets or buy some or both sell and buy. And there are many companies in any year which sell assets they did not previously 'regard' as assets for sale—either to abandon worthless projects, or to take advantage of new opportunities or to pay back debts or to pay dividends or taxes. One need have recourse to no better source of information than the financial press to verify this.

D.3 The Report continues: 'In normal circumstances, most companies would expect to pay off their debts and purchase the materials and supplies for their continued operation out of the earnings generated by the assets, not from the

---

[13] No attempt is made in CAMS to rebut the argument on this matter presented in 'Second Thoughts on Continuously Contemporary Accounting', p. 50.
[14] The Committee had access to *Securities and Obscurities* which presents a substantial amount of evidence to the point.

assets themselves' (para. 505). True: but what are earnings if they do not turn up as increments in assets (i.e. as assets themselves)? And, even in the context of the quoted sentence, of what use are earnings if they are not means of payment, money or things convertible into money? The attempt to dodge the money equivalent of assets (and increments in assets) fails on the very grounds which the Report holds out as critical of COCOA.

D.4 The Report avers that income calculation under COCOA is 'based on the preservation of the "purchasing power" of the shareholders' interest as the concept of capital maintenance, rather than on the maintenance of the value of the assets (including stock) consumed during the year' (para. 507). In the absence of borrowing (which is not mentioned at this point) there is no necessary difference between these two concepts. The purchasing power of the shareholders' interest at the beginning of a year is equal to the value of the assets at the beginning of the year, if 'value' is defined as purchasing power or, as economists say, 'value in exchange'. The criticism implied by 'rather than' fails for lack of specification of what 'value' was intended to mean.

D.5 Under COCOA, the Report continues, 'large elements of unrealized holding gain may find their way into profit for the year' if the money equivalents of assets rise faster 'than the index used to measure the change in the "purchasing power" of shareholders' equity' (para. 507). So what is wrong with that? If a company has become especially better off by virtue of the assets it has held and what has happened to their prices, should not shareholders and others be told of it? Yes, they should, is the inference to be drawn from the Committee's own proposal— unrealized holding gains are to be shown in revaluation reserves in the balance sheet (para. 621). But the method of COCOA sets off against the so-called holding gains the capital maintenance adjustment, whereas the Committee's proposal does not. Thus, although the quoted words from para. 507 suggest that COCOA is far too liberal, in fact it is less liberal than the Sandilands proposal! Further, there has for some time been a movement towards showing all kinds of gain or loss in the profit and loss account, rather than taking some of them directly to reserve accounts; gain or loss is surely what a profit and loss account is all about. But Sandilands turns back the clock. Movements in stock adjustment reserves and revaluation reserves are to by-pass the profit and loss account, but are to be picked up in a separate summary statement of total gains or losses (para. 624). On the other hand, because all sources of gains and losses are necessarily interlocked in the conduct of a business, COCOA puts them all through the profit and loss account. The implied criticism of COCOA has not been established.

D.6 The Report notes the treatment under COCOA of 'non-vendible durables', and the heavy charge this may entail in the year of purchase. (The matter is dealt with more fully in C.5 above.) The Committee says 'this leads to a legitimate and consistent concept of profit but, if applied universally, it would not meet the criteria we put forward in Chapter 5' (para. 508). A concept of profit that is both legitimate and consistent seems to have a lot 'going for' it; yet it is rejected. Are the criteria of Chapter 5, then, 'more legitimate' or 'more consistent'?

Tracing the Committee's preferred concept of profit through Chapter 5 (para. 199) to Chapter 4 (paras. 143, 128), there is no firm claim that it is either legitimate or consistent. 'Profit is regarded as any gains arising during the year which may be distributed after charging for the "value" of the company's assets consumed during the year' (para. 128). The 'values' of a company's assets are to be their 'values to the business'. The closest the Report comes to claiming 'legitimacy' for its proposal is to say (e.g.) that, in respect of assets, 'the dominant requirement is *probably* for information on the "value to the business" of net assets'; and in respect of profit, the Committee's method *'appears to be more useful* to many users than other concepts of profit' (para. 199, emphasis added). This is a far cry from *proof* of utility or legitimacy. As for 'consistency', there are three possible values for 'value to the owner', replacement cost, realizable value and net present value. It is possible, then, that any balance sheet may contain an instance of each, making their addition illegitimate. And it is possible that the same assets may be valued on different bases in successive years making the accounting inconsistent from year to year. Neither of these possibilities occurs under COCOA. In the light of all this, it is impossible to see how COCOA fails to meet the criteria of usefulness given in Chapter 5 of the Report.

D.7 The Report offers the Committee's view that COCOA 'is an interesting example of a hybrid system using a "purchasing power of shareholders' equity" concept of capital maintenance and a basis for the valuation of assets other than historic cost' (para. 510). There is really nothing 'hybrid' about the system. If we wish to find whether the purchasing power of the opening amount of shareholders' equity in any year is maintained, we must find what its closing amount is. The only way of finding what the general purchasing power of shareholders' equity (or net assets) is at any date is to find the purchasing power—or money equivalent—of the assets and to deduct from it the amount of liabilities. This COCOA does. It is 'pure bred'. The 'hybrid' notion may well stem from the Committee's ideas of the significances of 'the monetary unit' and 'the current purchasing power unit'. The Report seems to imply that the two are necessarily different (para. 504, for example). But as is noted in C.1 above, any *dated* monetary unit *is* a *dated* general purchasing power unit. To suppose otherwise is to fly in the face of economic theory and ordinary commercial and financial practice. COCOA is quite fastidious in respect of the dating of money amounts. In this respect it is the only 'pure-bred' system. The Report's suggestion that COCOA is a hybrid system certainly does not seem to have been meant unkindly. But it is false nevertheless.[15]

---

[15] For a more extensive treatment of the points mentioned and other facets of the Report, see Chambers, *Current Cost Accounting—A Critique of the Sandilands Report*, International Centre for Research in Accounting, Lancaster 1976.

Summary

Taking the four publications together, it appears that:

(a) the following features of COCOA are misrepresented
- —the use of dated money equivalents of nonmonetary assets as balance sheet values (A.1, B.1)
- —the 'unit of account' used (C.1)
- —the method of income calculation or the amount of income available for distribution (A.3, D.5)
- —similarities and differences between COCOA and other systems (A.2, A.4, A.5, B.2, D.4, D.7)

(b) the following are disregarded
- —evidence of the practical serviceability of knowledge of the resale prices of assets (C.2, D.1, D.2)
- —refinements in the exposition of COCOA since it was proposed (A.6)

(c) the following improper judgements or allegations are made explicitly or implicitly
- —that COCOA does not in principle tend to the maintenance of a given combination of given kinds of assets (A.6)
- —that COCOA rejects the 'continuity of the entity' assumption (B.3)
- —that the specification of the manner of obtaining resale prices is inadequate or non-existent (C.3)
- —that the treatment, under COCOA, of non-vendible assets and payments for intangibles is objectionable (C.5, D.6)
- —that the representation, under COCOA, of the amounts of debts (liabilities) actually outstanding is objectionable (C.6)
- —that the notion of 'net profit' under COCOA is objectional even though it is 'legitimate' and 'consistent' (D.6).

General Omissions

Apart from these instances of misrepresentation, disregard and questionable judgement, there are several characteristics of COCOA on which the critics are noticeably silent.

(a) The arithmetic of COCOA is technically legitimate throughout. All the amounts of money which appear in any one of its balance sheets are capable of proper addition, subtraction and relation.

(b) The method of COCOA yields a balance sheet which is a practically significant statement of a dated financial position, a position which is both a full acccunt of the consequences of events and transactions up to its date and a proper basis for all exploratory and budgeting exercises from that date forward.

(c) The asset valuation rule of COCOA is a single unequivocal rule, and the products of its application are generally comprehensible, being dated amounts of available wealth expressed in dated money units.

150

(d) The statements yield a representation of dated positions and results which conforms with the statutory requirement that a true and fair view of positions and results shall be given.

(e) The particulars which make up the balance sheet under COCOA are independently verifiable or testable without recourse to the judgements, intentions, expectations or internal calculations of the officers of a firm.

None of the other systems described or proposed in the publications considered lays claim to any of these five features, each of which is of importance if financial statements are to be reliable grounds of judgement. Is that the reason why the exponents of other systems do not mention these features, and hence escape the need to give credit to COCOA in respect of them?

What's in a name?

Finally, as I noted at the outset, 'continuously contemporary accounting', as the name of a method or system, has been in use since 1967. Yet the Mathews Committee Report avoids it, choosing to refer to the system as 'Relative Price Level Accounting'; the CVA Exposure Draft avoids naming it; the A.A.R.F. Evaluative Paper describes it as a current exit value system; only the Sandilands Report uses its name boldly. The names assigned to COCOA are in all cases descriptions; but those assigned by its critics are inadequate—and therefore partial or improper—descriptions. Evasive references and exercises in 're-christening' do nothing but confuse readers.

More recently the confusion threatens to be compounded. Since 1967 I have used CCA as an abbreviation for the system. The Sandilands Committee, in 1975, proposed a system which it described as Current Cost Accounting—and a Statement of the Consultative Committee of Accountancy Bodies in the U.K. published in November 1975 referred to the Sandilands proposal as 'CCA'! The abbreviation has since gained general currency. It is not possible to go back and rewrite all my references to CCA to avoid confusion with the Sandilands system. But since late in 1975, as in this paper, I have been obliged to refer to continuously contemporary accounting as COCOA.

Conclusion

To legitimate criticism based on fair representation of COCOA, no objection could be taken. But when so many questionable representations and allegations are made against COCOA, and when the points at which it is clearly superior to other systems are so carefully avoided (as it seems), must there not be something *incontrovertibly right* about COCOA?

9 "THE TAXI COMPANY" UNDER COCOA

THIS IS AN EXERCISE in accounting for a simple company having one kind of nonmonetary asset and dealing for cash. Continuously contemporary accounting (CoCoA) accounts for the financial consequences of operations on an all-inclusive basis, period by period. Nonmonetary assets are represented by dated money equivalents from time to time. Income is the increase in a period in the general purchasing power represented by the net assets.

The exercise proceeds through a series of years from the simplest setting to an example of project evaluations and budgeting and then to settings in which there are changes in specific prices without general inflation and changes in specific prices with general inflation. It demonstrates that, in the face of shifts in circumstances, to which the company adapts itself, the accounting represents continuously and cumulatively the financial effects of what has occurred.

The concluding section offers some general observations on CoCoA; for more extensive treatment, see other work of the author.

I shall deal with the problem in the first person and in the capacity as manager-accountant of The Taxi Company. I do this so that, as accountant, I need make no assumptions about the manager's plans or intentions, for, as manager, I know what they are and how they vary from time to time. I do all this work "for the fun of it," since, under the specification of the problem, "there are no other employees" than taxi drivers.

I shall suppose the company to start from scratch in order to avoid any assumptions about where the company stands (e.g., in accordance

184   Chapter 9 (Exit Values)

with any other accounting process) at the beginning of any later period. It is specified that "the company knows what it has done in the past in regard to how long it kept the taxis operating and the proceeds of sales when the taxis were put out of use." To accommodate or get around this, I shall suppose that I have been the manager of another similar taxi company in the recent past. (Of course, all the figures are hypothetical; I do not know anything specific about taxi charges, costs, commissions, and so on.)

Further Specifications

Suppose The Taxi Company issues stock for $25,000 with a stated expectation (based on the figures of Table 9-1) of paying a dividend to stockholders of 15–20 per cent per annum. The stock is listed on a stock exhange.

The company purchases, at the end of 19x0, four taxis, all of the same model, for $4,500 each. There are no lump sum payments by way of "franchise" or otherwise. The remainder of the proceeds of the stock issue are to finance running costs and to meet contingencies. Funds retained (as undivided profits or by reason of depreciation charges) are kept in liquid form, e.g., as noninterest-bearing bank deposits.

Suppose there is no change in the new price of the model over the period of the life of the taxis; no change in the prices of gas, oil, service, and so forth; and no change in the general level of prices. Suppose each taxi is expected to run 80,000 miles per year for four years and that only part of the total mileage is income-earning (i.e., the metered mileage). Suppose that taxi service, being heavier usage of a car than personal usage, is ranked as "rough usage" by car dealers and that the ("Blue Book") buying and selling prices of resellers for rough usage are:

Age of model (years)	1	2	3	4	5
Buy	3,000	2,000	1,000	500	400
Sell	3,500	2,500	1,300	700	500

Operations—The Simplest Case

The expected annual operations are given in Table 9-1. The budget per taxi and the actual operations of all taxis are given in Table 9-2. All items (except depreciation) are variable. Four plausible tests of performance (in different respects) are given at the foot of the operating data.

Table 9-1
Expected Operations of The Taxi Company

	1 Taxi	4 Taxis
Purchase cost	4,500	18,000
Expected resale price, end 19x4	500	2,000
Depreciation	4,000	16,000
Annual Operations (over 4 years)		
Expected mileage per annum	80,000	320,000
Expected metered mileage p.a.	50,000	200,000
Revenue—40¢ per metered mile	20,000	80,000
Drivers' commission—20¢ per m.m.	10,000	40,000
Gas, tires, etc.—8¢ per mile (total mileage)	6,400	25,600
Total variable costs	16,400	65,600
Depreciation (average over life)	1,000	4,000
Total Costs	17,400	69,600
Expected net income before tax	2,600	10,400
Tax (50%)	1,300	5,200
Net income after tax	1,300	5,200
Dividend (20% on $25,000)		5,000
Retained profit		200

On these assumptions, stockholders will have received, by the end of 19x4, $5,000 per annum in dividends, and The Taxi Company will have as assets:

Cash	23,800
Taxis	2,000
	$25,800

By definition under CoCoA, depreciation is the change in a period in the resale price of an asset. Operating usage affects this change only by virtue of the classification of cars (e.g., as between "above average," "average," and "rough") in the car dealers' "Blue Book." The depreciation charge thus varies independently of mileage. The "average depreciation per annum" is shown in Table 9-1, as this is intended as an indication of general feasibility and prospects. The depreciation charge in Table 9-2 is the difference between the purchase price and the reseller's buying price (the taxi company's selling price) for a model one-year-old.

Table 9-2
Operations—19x1

	Budget	Actual				
Taxis	Each Taxi	A	B	C	D	Total
Total miles	80,000	82,000	70,000	85,000	88,000	325,000
Metered miles	50,000	50,000	45,000	56,000	55,000	206,000
Revenue—						
40¢/m.m.	$20,000	20,500	18,500	22,000	21,500	82,500
Commission—						
20¢/m.m.	10,000	10,000	9,000	11,200	11,000	41,200
Gas, tires, etc. (service)	6,400	6,600	6,000	7,000	7,200	26,800
Net revenue	3,600	3,900	3,500	3,800	3,300	14,500
Depreciation	1,500	1,500	1,500	1,500	1,500	6,000
Income	2,100	2,400	2,000	2,300	1,800	8,500
Taxation 50%						4,250
Net income						4,250
Dividend (16%)						4,000
Retained profit						250
Metered/total miles	.63	.61	.64	.66	.63	.63
Revenue/m.m. (cents)	40.0	41.0	41.1	39.3	39.1	40.0
Service costs/mile (cents)	8.0	8.0	8.6	8.2	8.2	8.2
Variable costs/revenue %	82	81	81	83	85	82

Balance sheet at end of 19x1

Cash on hand	13,250
Taxis, at market resale price	12,000
	25,250
Owners' equity	
Paid in	25,000
Retained profits	250
	25,250

The final column of Table 9-2 represents the income account of the company. Its balance sheet at the end of 19x1 is given at the foot of the table. The balance of cash on hand is the sum of initially unspent cash ($7,000), depreciation charges ($6,000), and retained profit ($250). It is unnecessary to work out the accounts for the following three years on similar assumptions. They would take the same form. Only three features of the system deserve comment.

The figures are independently testable. Total mileage, metered mileage, and initial hire charges are mechanically recorded and, together with out-of-pocket running costs, would be part of the drivers' logs. The only other item is the depreciation charge which is verifiable by reference to information independent of the drivers and the management.

Secondly, the depreciation charges over the period, being based on resale prices, match the actual decline in the company's command of money and money's worth. If straight-line depreciation charges had been made ($1,000 per annum per taxi, as in Table 9-1), the income before tax would have been $10,500 in year 1; the tax payable, if levied on the income so computed, would be $5,250; and a dividend of 20 per cent would appear to be feasible from the net income of $5,250. But this would be inconsistent with the maintenance of the opening capital in genuine purchasing power terms. The cash on hand would be $11,250; the taxis, though shown at $14,000, would have a money equivalent of only $12,000. In genuine purchasing power terms, the assets would be worth $23,250 against an initial $25,000 input. If the company survived and operated according to its expectations, the short-fall would be made good subsequently. But the accounts in series would not represent the actual accretion in accessible wealth year by year.

Thirdly, (a) there is no good reason why taxes should be paid in advance of genuine increments in accessible wealth (as would occur under straight-line depreciation); (b) it makes more sense to pay a lower dividend in an initial year than the expected average than to pay a high dividend and create expectations of its continuation when the future is uncertain; and (c) in the event of merger or similar negotiations, which may occur at any time, it is better to know the financial state of the company as it is than to know its conventionalized state (as under the straight-line method).

Variation 1—Choice between Projects (19x3)

Suppose that the operations of 19x2 and the position of the Company at its end were as shown in Table 9-3. For the whole firm, the metered

Table 9-3
Operations—19x2

	Budget	Actual		
	Each taxi	A+B+C	D	Total
Total miles	80,000	220,000	78,000	298,000
Metered miles	50,000	140,000	51,000	191,000
Revenue—40¢/m.m.	$20,000	55,000	20,200	75,200
Commission—20¢/m.m.	10,000	28,000	10,200	38,200
Service costs	6,400	18,500	7,200	25,700
Net revenue	3,600	8,500	2,800	11,300
Depreciation	1,000	3,000	1,000	4,000
Income	2,600	5,500	1,800	7,300
Taxation 50%				3,650
Net income				3,650
Dividend (14%)				3,500
Retained profit				150
Metered/total miles	.63	.64	.65	.64
Revenue/m.m. (cents)	40.0	39.3	39.6	39.4
Service costs/mile	8.0	8.4	9.2	8.6
Variable costs/rev. %	82	85	86	85

Balance Sheet at end of 19x2

Cash on hand	17,400
Taxis, at market resale price	8,000
	25,400
Owners' Equity	
Paid in	25,000
Retained profits	400
	25,400

mileage rate has improved; the revenue per metered mile has declined; the service costs per mile have risen. The income before tax was substantially less than the budgeted figure. (The depreciation charges, budgeted and actual, are based on the "Blue Book" figures.) The lower profits necessitated a cut in the dividend rate to 14 per cent. Some re-thinking by the manager was necessary. Taxi D appeared to have unusually high service costs and recurrent though minor mechanical trouble. The previously budgeted figures for the taxis seemed still to be feasible except for service costs. The budget figure would need to be raised to 8.5 cents per mile (for total mileage). Two possible courses of action occurred to the manager.

Alternative (a): Invest any cash in excess of $2,400 that is available at the beginning of each year at 10 per cent per annum (subject to an institutional restriction that such investments be made in $1,000 units, the cash not invested being a reserve for contingencies). Operate the four taxis as previously, replacing them all at the end of 19x4 with similar cars at the same price. The budget for 19x3 and the projected results under these arrangements through 19x6 are given in Table 9-4(a).

Alternative (b): Sell taxi D immediately at the "Blue Book" price ($2,000); buy a superior limousine for $7,000, offering a superior service (at different tariffs and costs); operate the other three taxis as before, replacing them as in (a) at the end of 19x4; invest all cash in excess of $3,400, available at the beginning of each year, at 10 per cent per annum under the same "even thousands" restriction as before. The "Blue Book" lists the following prices for the limousine for "average use," which is assumed to be appropriate for the business it is to undertake:

Age of model (years)	1	2	3	4	5
Buy	5,000	3,500	2,800	2,200	1,500
Sell	6,000	4,500	3,500	2,800	2,000

The budget for 19x3 and the projected results under these arrangements through 19x6 are given in Table 9-4(b).

Under both alternatives a dividend of $5,000 is expected to be paid each year.

Present value analysis. By simple inspection, Alternative (b) is clearly superior. In other cases, the style of problem considered may require treatment in the manner of present value analysis. The standard procedure involves the discounting of net cash proceeds. Although all assets and operations may be expected to yield a net cash flow at *some* time, at any intermediate time conversion to cash may not be complete. And in any case, the object of trading is to secure increments in total wealth, not simply in cash. As it seems to me, increments and decrements in total wealth, whether they are by way of cash or not, should enter into present value calculations.

In particular, if depreciation charges represent actual diminutions

Chapter 9 (Exit Values)

Table 9-4(a)

Alternative (a): Run 4 taxis; invest surplus funds at 10 per cent p.a.

Budget 19x3	Each Taxi	Total
Total miles	80,000	320,000
Metered miles	50,000	200,000
Revenue—40¢/m.m.	20,000	80,000
Drivers' commissions— 20¢/m.m.	10,000	40,000
Service costs—8.5¢/m	6,800	27,200
Net taxi revenue	3,200	12,800
Depreciation	1,000	4,000
Net taxi income	2,200	8,800
Interest income		1,500
Net company income		10,300
Tax, 50 per cent		5,150
Net income after tax		5,150
Dividend, 20 per cent		5,000
Retained profit		150

Projected Summary 19x3–x6

Year	19x3	19x4	19x5	19x6
Net taxi revenue	12,800	12,800	12,800	12,800
Depreciation	4,000	2,000	6,000	4,000
Net taxi income	8,800	10,800	6,800	8,800
Interest income	1,500	1,900	600	1,100
Total income	10,300	12,700	7,400	9,900
Tax	5,150	6,350	3,700	4,950
Income after tax	5,150	6,350	3,700	4,950
Balance Sheet				
Cash on hand	6,550	5,900	7,600	6,550
Cash on loan	15,000	19,000	6,000	11,000
Taxis (resale price)	4,000	2,000	12,000	8,000
Total	25,550	26,900	25,600	25,550
Owners' equity:				
Paid in	25,000	25,000	25,000	25,000
Retained profits	550	1,900	600	550
Total	25,550	26,900	25,600	25,550

in the cash equivalents of assets, the amount initially paid does not fall wholly in the period of purchase as long as the asset has a cash value at the ends of the periods immediately following. Or, to put it another way, if the purchase price is shown as a cash outflow in the period of purchase, there should be offset against it at the end of that period the remaining cash equivalent of the asset; and a like amount should be shown as a cash outflow of the next succeeding period, and so on.

The matter may be illustrated by an example in less detail than that of the taxi company. Suppose there are two possible projects available to a company, each requiring investment in a durable asset, A for Project A, B for Project B, and that:

1. A and B require the same initial outlay, $3,000;
2. A and B are expected to have the same "service lives," three years, and to have zero resale values at the end of that time;
3. the projects are expected to yield the same net cash inflows yearly; and
4. whereas A has no money equivalent after its purchase, B has a diminishing money equivalent.

These highly simplified assumptions are selected to illustrate only one point. The figures of Table 9-4(c) give the assumed data.

Under conventional expositions of present value calculations, both projects would have the same net present value—that shown under project A. The outlays on A and B are treated as "spot" and irrevocable outlays at the date of purchase. But, under B, there is a spot outlay and a spot loss of $500 (the immediate resale price of B being lower to the user company than the price which the vendor of B could command), and the company thereafter has access to the money equivalent of B. The operation is not irrevocable; that fact should be built into the mode of calculation, for although the advantage of Project B is apparent from the simplicity of the example, it would not be apparent in more complex examples.

Project B is treated as though cash outlays were made by installments at the four dates. It may be intended that the balances carried forward of the cash equivalents of B (2,500, 1,500, 500 in periods 1, 2, 3, respectively) should be treated as outlays at the beginning of each period, in which case the present value of Project B would be the same as that of Project A. But it is usual to assume that receipts and outlays occur at the ends of periods to avoid further assumptions about their distributions through any year. And the process illustrated does indicate a difference in the worth of the two projects which accords with the advantage of having an asset which is convertible to cash in the event

Table 9-4(b)

Alternative (b): Replace 1 taxi with 1 limousine; invest surplus funds at 10 per cent.

Budget 19x3	3 Taxis	Limo.	Total
Total miles	240,000	75,000	
Metered miles	150,000	50,000	
Revenue—40¢/m.m.	60,000		
50¢/m.m.		25,000	85,000
Drivers' commissions—20¢/m.m.	30,000		
22¢/m.m.		11,000	41,000
Service costs—8.5¢/mile	20,400		
9.0¢/mile		6,550	26,950
Net taxi revenue	9,600	7,450	17,050
Depreciation	3,000	2,000	5,000
Net taxi income	6,600	5,450	12,050
Interest income			900
Net company income			12,950
Tax, 50 per cent			6,475
Net income after tax			6,475
Dividend, 20 per cent			5,000
Retained profit			1,475

Projected Summary 19x3–x6

Year	19x3	19x4	19x5	19x6
Net taxi revenue	17,050	17,050	17,050	17,050
Depreciation	5,000	3,000	5,200	3,600
Net taxi income	12,050	14,050	11,850	13,450
Interest income	900	1,500	900	1,500
Total income	12,950	15,550	12,750	14,950
Tax	6,475	7,775	6,375	7,475
Income after tax	6,475	7,775	6,375	7,475
Balance Sheet				
Cash on hand	9,875	9,650	10,225	10,300
Cash on loan	9,000	15,000	9,000	15,000
Taxis (resale price)	3,000	1,500	9,000	6,000
Limousine (resale price)	5,000	3,500	2,800	2,200
Total	26,875	29,650	31,025	33,500

Table 9-4(b) Continued

Owners' equity:				
Paid in	25,000	25,000	25,000	25,000
Retained profits	1,875	4,650	6,025	8,500
Total	26,875	29,650	31,025	33,500

Table 9-4(c)
Alternative Projects of a Non-Taxi Company
(DCEF = Discounted Cash Equivalent Flows)

Year-end	0	1	2	3
Project A				
Purchase of asset A	(3,000)			
Net cash inflow (revenue)		1,000	1,500	1,500
Total	(3,000)	1,000	1,500	1,500
DCEF at 10 per cent	(3,000)	909	1,239	1,127
Net DCEF (present value)	275			
Project B				
Asset B				
—opening cash equivalent	(3,000)	(2,500)	(1,500)	(500)
—closing cash equivalent	2,500	1,500	500	0
Net cash equivalent outflow	(500)	(1,000)	(1,000)	(500)
Net cash inflow (revenue)		1,000	1,500	1,500
Total cash equivalent inflow	(500)	0	500	1,000
DCEF at 10 per cent	(500)	0	413	751
Net DCEF (present value)	664			

that Project B ceases to be viable before its expected terminal date.

All present value calculations are, of course, hypothetical only. They are made for the purpose of quantifying approximately the stipulated features of different projects, not of quantifying the absolute amount at any date of the money equivalent of an asset or any other valuation of an asset for balance sheet purposes. A balance sheet under CoCoA represents means accessible and claims against those means at a stated date. Clearly a discounted value of expected net receipts does not represent means available to meet claims at any stated date. But as CoCoA balance sheets represent assets at their money equivalents, the progress of any chosen project and the expected values from time

194   Chapter 9   (Exit Values)

to time on which the choice depends may readily come under review. Further, the components of any DCEF calculation would also be components of budgets indicative of the progressive consequences of any chosen course of action. These linkages ensure that the choice of projects and the appraisal of choices are based on consistent data.

Some general features of CoCoA. Variation 1 illustrates several features of CoCoA:

1. CoCoA represents dated money equivalents. It makes no use of physical capacity, operating capacity, or service potential, none of which can be shown to have a linear or other regular relationship to money equivalents or prices. It, therefore, avoids the problem of relating or aggregating different "capacities," which arises under any system which purports to deal with the maintenance of aggregate service potential or capability or capacity. (Notice that in Table 9-4(b) the mileages of taxi service and limousine service are not aggregated; they are not the same thing nor are they convertible into a common denominator.)

2. The balance sheet figures under CoCoA are all of equal significance, dollar for dollar, and all of immediate (dated) significance. It is equally possible to consider the spending of the amount representing any noncash asset as to consider spending any amount of cash. The figures provide a direct basis for any future budgeting and for any present value calculation for any feasible project or variation in present projects. (Incidentally, except in the most obvious cases, both present value calculations and budgetary calculations are necessary for choice between projects; it is of no use to choose the project having the highest net present value if it entails a liquidity emergency before the expected inflows occur.) And, of course, the balance sheet represents the outcome of past operations in the only terms significant to all who have interests in or claims against a firm—their current cash or financial significance. The past and the future are thus linked by common reference to the present (balance date).

Variation 2—Changes in Specific prices (19x4)

Suppose that The Taxi Company adopted Alternative (b) and that in 19x3 it actually achieved the results and position shown in Table 9-4(b) as "projected." The projected figures were computed for the purpose of choosing between the two alternatives. They have no necessary value thereafter except in respect of the chosen project (the figures of Table 9-4(a), for example, are of no further use). And even in respect of the chosen project they are of no use if some of the parameters change.

Suppose that the service costs were expected to rise in unit prices by the equivalent of 0.5 cents per mile from the beginning of 19x4. (The assumption is so expressed for convenience; the individual prices of gas, tires, and so on, would in fact change at different rates.) Suppose also that the price of the taxi model rose from $4,500 to $5,500 and of the limousine model from $7,000 to $8,000. Suppose that consequentially the "Blue Book" figures became as follows:

Age of model (years)	1	2	3	4	5
Taxi—buy	3,800	2,700	1,900	1,300	900
sell	4,400	3,300	2,500	1,800	1,300
Limousine—buy	6,200	4,800	3,700	2,800	2,200
sell	7,000	6,000	4,500	3,500	2,800

And suppose that no change was expected in the general level of prices.

Over a four-year life, on this basis, each taxi would cost $(5,500 − 1,300), or $4,200, against the previous $4,000; and the limousine would cost $(8,000 − 2,800), or $5,200, against the previous $4,800. The total additional cost is $600 over four years. The additional service costs, 0.5 cents per mile, over four years would cost $1,575. These costs spread over 200,000 metered miles amount to just over 1 cent per metered mile. Suppose the company raises its tariffs by 1 cent per metered mile for taxis and 2 cents per metered mile for the limousine. The net effect of these changes would be to increase net taxi revenue by $925, or $462 after tax, on average over four years, and on the basic budgeted figures of Table 9-4(b).

What of the asset accounts? The figures are as follows:

End of year	19x3	19x4
Resale price—3 taxis	$3,000	3,900
—limousine	5,000	4,800
	8,000	8,700

There will thus have been an appreciation of $700 in total, which, as part of the consequences of being in the taxi business, is a legitimate and genuine gain. Whether or not there is an appreciation or a depreciation in any other case depends on the goods held and the shifts in their prices. Under CoCoA the amount of this appreciation or depreciation is described generally as a price variation adjustment. On all the above assumptions, the projected results and balance sheet

196 Chapter 9 (Exit Values)

of The Taxi Company for 19x4 would be as represented in Table 9-5. The actual financial statements of 19x4, though differing in numerical detail from these budgeted figures, would be the same in form. For the purpose of the next section, these budgeted figures are assumed to be actual for 19x4.

Table 9-5

Budgeted Operations 19x4

Net taxi revenue	17,975
Price variation adjustment (appreciation)	700
Net taxi income	18,675
Interest income	1,500
Income before tax	20,175
Tax	10,087
Net income after tax	10,088
Dividend	5,000
Retained profit	5,088

Balance Sheet, end 19x4

Cash on hand	8,263
Cash on loan	15,000
Taxis (resale price)	3,900
Limousine (resale price)	4,800
Total	31,963
Owners' equity:	
Paid in	25,000
Retained profit	6,963
Total	31,963

Variation 3—Changes in Specific Prices and in the General Level of Prices (19x5)

Suppose that the shift in the prices of services and cars in 19x4 was the precursor of a change in prices generally. The Taxi Companies Association considered that wages would rise 10 per cent, service costs 12 per cent, and new car prices about 7–15 per cent above 19x4 levels. To cope with these changes, even though they cannot be quantified in advance with any precision, the price of taxi service was raised to 45 cents and of limousine service to 55 cents per metered mile.

The company replaced the three taxis at the beginning of 19x5. Though the "Blue Book" price was $3,900 (see Variation 2), the company was allowed $4,200 against the purchase of three taxis at a newly announced price of $6,000 each. By the end of the year the price (new) had risen to $6,300 and the new price of limousines to $8,400. Consequentially the "Blue Book" figures at the end of 19x5 were:

Age of model (years)	1	2	3	4	5
Taxi—buy	4,100	2,900	2,000	1,400	900
Limousine—buy	6,500	5,000	3,800	3,000	2,300

Suppose also that, in view of the rise in prices and the uncertainty of their extent, the company revised its investment rule to invest all even thousands of dollars above $4,000 at the beginning of the year and that there was no change in the interest rate. The sale of three taxis for $4,200, the purchase of three for $18,000, and the cash balance of $8,263 (all at the beginning of the year) entail an investment of $5,000 (down from $15,000 at the close of 19x4) and a free cash balance of $4,463.

Finally, suppose the net revenues of 19x5 were $19,500 and that the change in the general level of prices during 19x5 was 8 per cent. The accounts (actual, on the above assumptions) under CoCoA would be as in Table 9-6.

Some brief explanations of items in Table 9-6:

1. Although the "Blue Book" and other sources of resale prices provide approximations to resale prices, actual prices may be expected to vary from these approximations but by less than the difference between actual selling prices and "book values" derived in any other way. The difference is shown separately here simply on account of the sale at the beginning of 19x5. In the case of the new taxis and the limousine, the effects of the rises in the resale prices during the year are captured in the new "Blue Book" prices, and the depreciation charge is simply the difference between the book value at the beginning of the year and the "Blue Book" buying price for models one year older than at the beginning of the year. Under CoCoA, "depreciation" is given its strict financial meaning, a fall in price. To break the discovered amount into one part due to the shift in the new price and one part due to so-called "technical depreciation or obsolescence" is arbitrary and unnecessary.

2. The use of "increment" rather than "income" is in recognition of the fact that up to this point a dollar increment is calculated regardless of the differences in "dollars." The definition of income under CoCoA, the increase in the general purchasing power represented by the opening

198   Chapter 9   (Exit Values)

Table 9-6
Operations 19x5 (Capital stock only)

	Net revenues		19,500	
(a)	Price variation adjustment, old taxis		300	
	Price variation adj. (depreciation) new taxis		(5,700)	(3 × 1,900)
	Price variation adj. (depreciation) limousine		(1,000)	
(b)	Net taxi increment		13,100	
	Interest income		500	
(c)	Total increment		13,600	
(d)	Capital maintenance adjustment		2,557	(.08 × 31,963)
	Income before tax		11,043	
(e)	Tax 50%		5,521	
(f)	Net income after tax		5,522	
	Dividend		5,000	
	Retained profit		522	

Balance Sheet, end 19x5

Cash on hand		13,942	
Cash on loan		5,000	
Taxis (resale price)		12,300	(3 × 4.100)
Limousine (resale price)		3,800	
Total		35,042	
Owners' equity:			
Paid in	25,000		
Capital maintenance adj.	2,000	27,000	
Retained profit, end 19x4	6,963		
Capital maintenance adj.	557		
Retained 19x5	522	8,042	
Total		35,042	

(For notes, see pp. 197–99)

net assets, necessitates a correction of the dollar increment by the amount of the capital maintenance adjustment.

3. The total increment is the increment in dollars (or dollar equivalents of all assets) by "operations" and by other events which affect the money equivalents of assets because of the operations it conducts and the assets it holds for the purpose. Abnormal items in either category may

deserve separate reporting or footnotes. But the financial effects of all are the same in kind, and no purpose is served by an arbitrary distinction between "operating" and "nonoperating" items.

4. Under the assumptions of this case, the dollars at the beginning and at the end of the year are different "common denominators" of debts and prices and net wealth. Every dollar of net assets at the beginning of 19x5 is subject to this depreciation of the dollar. Since all figures in the 19x4 balance sheet are in 19x4 dollars and 19x5 figures are in 19x5 dollars (all assets are at cash or discovered money equivalent figures), the shift in the "common denominator" is provided for by applying the proportionate change (8 per cent) in the index of the general level of prices to the opening amount of net assets ($31,963, as in the 19x4 balance sheet), charging the result against the nominal dollar increment and crediting the owners' equity. All 19x5 balance sheet figures are then in 19x5 common denominators.

The company took steps, by changing its tariffs, to cope with those price increases which would fall on it. Those price increases may or may not (in any specific case) be elements of the calculation of the shift in the common denominator; certainly the two are not necessarily related since some dollar prices may fall while the general level of prices rises. The object of the calculation of results after the event is to indicate the net consequence of decisions followed and of nonoptional events which occurred in the period.

In the balance sheet the amount of the capital maintenance reserve is split proportionately between paid-in capital and retained profits, a simple case again of stating opening balances in their equivalents in closing "common denominators."

5. Tax is calculated at 50 per cent on the assumption that such a tax rate is applied to the income as calculated. As net income before tax is a genuine increment in general purchasing power, it is a proper and equitable tax base as between all taxpayers.

6. It will have been observed that the net income fluctuates through the years covered, even though the taxi operations are substantially similar. But the net income does represent the net increase in general purchasing power year by year. If the fluctuations were "normalized" (by a flat rate assumption for depreciation, the principal cause of the variations in the present case), the reported position and the results from year to year would not be consistent with the facts; and any attempt to "project" the future, by budgetary or other exercises, would be based on nonfactual premises. The managers or any outsiders could average the results of any series of periods they wished or for any purpose they entertained, given the raw data as in the examples used.

Variation 4—Equity and Debt

In the preceding section, the possession of vehicles represents a partial hedge against the decline in the value of the dollar as a common denominator of prices and net wealth. The "Blue Book" price of a three-year old limousine, for example, rose from $3,700 to $3,800. To hold money, of course, is to suffer the decline in the purchasing power of the dollar. But so, also, is to hold any asset, the price of which does not rise at the same rate as the general level of prices. As no one and no firm can deliberately purchase assets which rise in aggregate price at the same rate as the general level of prices (at least the odds against it are astronomical), CoCoA takes into account the price variations in aggregate and the capital maintenance adjustment in the aggregate and offsets the two, as in Table 9-6.

One dependable hedge against the decline in the value of the dollar is to borrow. Because of the size of its cash holdings, The Taxi Company is not a plausible case (in a realistic sense) to illustrate the consequence of borrowing. But it will suffice in an illustrative sense. Suppose that (for whatever reason, e.g., by undertaking to raise the dividend rate to 30 per cent) The Taxi Company converted $10,000 (nominal) of its stock to 9 per cent loan stock at the beginning of 19×5, repayable some years later at par. To this extent it hedges against the effect on the company of inflation, the fall in the purchasing power of the dollar, for this effect is made to fall on holders of loan stock. Suppose that interest on debt is tax-allowable and that otherwise the operations of the company were as in Table 9-6. The statements for 19x5 would be as shown in Table 9-7.

The main differences between Table 9-7 and Table 9-6 are the interest paid on loan stock, the capital maintenance adjustment (with the issue of loan stock the opening amount of net assets, or assets less liabilities, is reduced by $10,000), the consequential effect on tax, the dividend amount, and the retained profit. The net income after tax is slightly lower in Table 9-7 than in Table 9-6 but on a substantially lower opening net assets (or owners' equity) base. After converting the opening net assets to 19x5 dollars in both tables, the rate of return is 16 per cent under Table 9-6 and 23 per cent under Table 9-7.

General Observations

The simplified example does not permit illustration of all the details of the use of CoCoA or all the features of accounting for other types

Table 9-7
Operations 19x5 (Capital and Loan Stock)

Net revenue	19,500	
Price variation adjustments (net)	(6,400)	as in Table 9-6
Net taxi increment	13,100	
Interest income	500	
Interest paid	(900)	
Total increment	12,700	
Capital maintenance adjustment	1,757	(.08 × 21,963)
Income before tax	10,943	
Tax 50%	5,471	
Net income after tax	5,472	
Dividend 30% of $15,000	4,500	
Retained profit	972	

Balance Sheet, end 19x5

Cash on hand		13,592
Cash on loan		5,000
Taxis (resale price)		12,300
Limousine (resale price)		3,800
Total		34,692
Loan Stock, 9 per cent		10,000
Owners' equity:		
Paid in	15,000	
Capital maintenance adjustment	1,200	16,200
Retained profit, end 19x4	6,963	
Capital maintenance adjustment	557	
Retained 19x5	972	8,492
Total		34,692

of enterprise. Some additional points might be made.

Price variation adjustment. The amount of this is the difference between book value and the discovered resale price at balance date for assets in possession at balance date. If there were rises (or falls) in the resale prices of assets which were realized during the year, the effects of these will have flowed through as part of net revenues. The price variation adjustment at the end of the year then represents unrealized (but not unreal) increments or decrements in dollar amounts. Any person who is interested in the realized increment can see for himself what it is by ignoring the price variation adjustment. Where a variety of assets is held and if it is of consequence to know the price variation adjustments in respect of each class, the class figures can be tallied and reported separately.

Sunk costs. Where a company pays for goodwill, development costs, or highly specialized assets, which are not salable otherwise than by sale of the business as a going concern or on liquidation, the amounts of such payments are treated as sunk costs. The amount paid is set off against owners' equity in the balance sheet separately from the statement of financial position. Being sunk and gone, it does not represent accessible purchasing or debt paying power and, therefore, is not subject to any rise or fall in the general purchasing power of the dollar.

If, for example, The Taxi Company had begun with $30,000, from which $5,000 was paid for some transferable but not separately vendible right or advantage (e.g., goodwill), the condensed balance sheet corresponding to Table 9-7 would read:

Balance Sheet, end 19x5		
Goodwill		5,000
Financed out of issue of capital stock		5,000
Financial Position		
Cash on hand and on loan		18,592
Taxis and limousine (at resale price)		16,100
		34,692
Loan Stock		10,000
Owners' equity		
Paid in	20,000	
Less paid for goodwill (above)	5,000	
	15,000	
Capital maintenance adjustment	1,200	16,200
Retained profit, end 19x4	6,963	
Capital maintenance adjustment	557	
Retained 19x5	972	8,492
		34,692

The facts are fully disclosed, and the nonseverable or nonrealizable item is isolated from the statement of financial position.

Group operations. Transfers of assets between companies in a group at nominal prices would not persist in the accounts of the recipient or the group at artificially inflated or deflated prices. Recourse to market prices at the end of the year would wipe out the artificial element. Aggregate or group figures would be interpretable since all figures of all firms at any date would be expressed in money equivalents as at that date.

Independent testability. The components and results are all testable or verifiable independently of the opinions, guidance, or direction of managers or other officers of a company.

Statement analysis. All ratios based on balance sheet figures would be mathematically legitimate because all components are dated money equivalents. They should be practically realistic because they are used to indicate financial relationships, and they would do so since they are based on money equivalents. Interperiod comparisons of ratios are valid because the ratios are mathematically legitimate, and ratios are unaffected by equal changes in the unit in which numerators and denominators are expressed. Interfirm comparisons are valid because the same valuation rules are used by all firms.

Systematic consistency. As indicated earlier, the resulting financial statements are indicative of dated positions and results and are directly relatable to exploratory and budgetary calculations. The notions of wealth, net wealth, and income are consistent with economic doctrine on micro-economic matters and with practical usage and understanding.

The Use and Abuse of a Notation: A History of an Idea

Introduction

In 1961 I devised a notation for dealing in general symbolic terms with the features of the financial position and changes in the financial position of a firm from time to time. The object of the notation was to give rigour to the demonstration of the consequences of changes in the prices of assets and changes in the general purchasing power of money. Much of the 'argument' occurring in the expositions of accounting was characterized by *ad hoc* supplements to stated (often vaguely stated) general rules. One way of cutting through the labyrinth is to reduce the elements of the matter to their simplest form, and to derive results from stipulated premises by explicit reasoning. That is the method of explication used in other fields, from formal logic and mathematics to natural science and economics. I believed it was possible, and potentially fruitful, to follow the same course, and had already developed one theorem by way of illustration of the possibility [4]. A general notation would help.

In the following ten years I developed the notation. Over those years and since, others have made use of or reference to it. But, in most cases, those uses have diverged from the original intention and setting of the notation; and the arguments purporting to be based on it have often been at variance with the canons of rigorous formal demonstration. What is more, many of the users of the notation have disregarded the developments or refinements introduced from time to time. A survey of those developments and uses may be illustrative of what may happen to an idea, which appears to have the virtue of rigour, when it is used without exact stipulation of the elements of the problem contemplated by the user.

This paper is in two main parts. The first part outlines my development of the notation and the argument based on it through designated stages — Stages I to IV. The second part deals with uses made by others of the notation. Both parts are chronological. The development of the notation was at some points prompted by ambiguities which became apparent through other uses and the debates which those uses engendered. Delays in responding and delays in publication resulted in some of the developments being 'out of phase' with the discussions, comments and applications of others. And some of the symbols used by others have varied from the symbols I have used. For that reason it seemed desirable to deal first with Stages I to IV, to use the final form as a basis for analysis, and to convert variant symbols to those used in that final form. This introduces some anachronisms. But it seems to be the only way of dealing comprehensively with the uses made and the inferences drawn from time to time. Where, in the second main part of the paper, reference is made to numbered formal expressions of other writers, the identifying number as used by the author is given with a prefix identifying the article or book under notice. Where, in the first main part, reference is made to work of my own, the numbered expressions are prefixed by roman numerals indicative of the 'stage' of the development. All works cited are listed at the end of the paper.

Some Potential Fallacies

A short-cut identification of fallacies or solecisms will make it possible to designate the kinds of problems which have arisen in the literature. They are based on certain logical or practical considerations or imperatives. It is presumed that we are seeking a rigorously specified system of which the operations of addition, subtraction and relation are necessary elements. We shall refer to 'addition', as subsuming subtraction and relation.

If the amounts (or quantities) of the properties (or characteristics) of two or more elements of such a system are to be validly aggregated, those amounts must be amounts of the same property of each of the elements. In particular, if M represents an amount of money and N represents the money equivalent (or resale price) of a non-monetary asset, the two amounts may be validly added; for the amount of the money equivalent of an asset is equivalent to the possession of a corresponding amount of money. If, however, N represents the quantity of any other property of non-monetary assets, M and N may not validly be added. Such an addition may be described as an example of the *fallacy of heterogeneous aggregation*.

If the amounts of a common property of two or more elements are to be validly aggregated, those amounts must be denominated in units of the same kind in all respects. In particular, if the money unit $\$_1$ at t_1 is the same in all respects as the money unit $\$_2$ at t_2, then $\$_1 M_1$ and $\$_2 M_2$ may be validly aggregated. If the units are unequal in any respect, the two amounts may not be validly aggregated. If they are aggregated, the aggregate may be described as a product of the *fallacy of heterogeneous calibration*.

If any term or terms in an argument have an assigned meaning or significance, no other meaning may be assigned to the same term within the argument. If there are similar or analogous terms in a similar or analogous argument, they must be recognized as logically different terms, and assigned a distinctively different meaning (and a different symbol, if the terms are symbolized). To attribute the same meaning to terms or symbols which have different significance is an example of the *fallacy of mistaken identity*.

If any terms have the same significance in a sense material to any argument, none of those terms may be assigned a different significance within the argument. Thus, it is not logically possible to assign different significances to a term which is a member of a class of terms to which a single common significance has been assigned. If any such different assignments are made, the consequence is an example of the *fallacy of improper subdivision*.

DEVELOPMENT OF THE NOTATION

Stage I

My explorations of accounting ideas had, until 1960, been concerned principally with ideas other than those relating to rigorous quantification or measurement. I was critical of a number of the notions current in the literature, and sought to clarify some of them by examination of the context of economic action and of the characteristics of actors in that context. The result was an attempt in 1961 to put a modified set of ideas into a coherent exposition, linking the context, the actor and the accounting information (provided by an income account and a balance sheet) which would be serviceable to him. The first 103 paragraphs of *Towards a General Theory of Accounting* [5] set out those ideas.

It was said 'a money value can represent only one characteristic [of any means] — exchange value at some time'; and that 'unless all monetary units in a given calculation are identical in significance — that is, in general purchasing power — the mere use of the conventional monetary unit does not provide a common denominator' (para. 37). As for the balance sheet, 'the difference between the aggregate of the exchange values of assets and the aggregate of the present values of liabilities represents the present residual equity of the entity in the assets' (para. 61). As for income, 'the calculation of income proceeds from a basic reference level — the amount of or the capacity to command non-monetary goods at the beginning of a period, or the initial capital or wealth' (para. 68), where capital or wealth is synonymous with residual equity (para. 61).

These specifications are reasonably clear cut. If, at a given date, M is an amount of money (a value in exchange), N is the aggregate of the exchange values of non-monetary assets, L is the amount of the liabilities, and R is the amount of the residual equity, R will be an amount of money or general purchasing power (or 'capacity to command non-monetary goods') at that date. My long-standing interest in proposals to give effect in accounts to the consequences of changes in prices of assets and changes in the purchasing power of the monetary unit, prompted me to try to give a formal illustration in general terms. The argument proceeded thus:

Assume (1) that a firm had monetary assets M, non-monetary assets N, liabilities L, and residual equity R at the beginning of a period; (2) that there were no transactions during the period; (3) that the 'price level' rose during the period by the proportion p. The position of the firm at the beginning of the period was represented by

$$M + N = L + R \qquad \text{I[1]}$$

Multiply throughout by $(1 + p)$:

$$M(1+p) + N(1+p) = L(1+p) + R(1+p) \qquad \text{I[2]}$$

Since the nominal amounts of monetary assets and liabilities remain the same through the period, restate I[2] by transferring the terms pM and pL to the residual equity:

$$M + N(1+p) = L + [R(1+p) - Mp + Lp] \qquad \text{I[3]}$$

This was represented as the position of the firm at the end of the period, 'in terms of the level of prices then ruling'.

Subtracting I[1] from I[3],

$$pN = pR + pL - pM \qquad\qquad \text{I[4]}$$

From this it is clear that the net adjustment to the residual equity R is equal to pN; it could be calculated directly without calculating the amounts on the right-hand side of I[4]; and 'if a policy is adopted of taking the maintenance of non-monetary assets as the basis for measuring divisible profits, on the ground that the maintenance of real assets is a condition of maintaining an income stream, then no part of pN is divisible' (para. 108).

I well recall the difficulties I had in setting up the argument. I had previously supported the use of replacement costs, and I had some lingering allegiance to the idea. Uncertain of a way of dealing with a change in the prices of specific assets as well as with the change p, I was disinclined to push the argument any further. But I was anxious to expose the symbolic notation as a promising means of tackling the problem, and in that anxiety I had been less than cautious. It is permissible when exploring the 'shape' of an argument to proceed from assumptions to conclusions. It is also permissible to seek to shape the argument by working backwards from intuitive conclusions, for in doing so one may find flaws in the assumptions. But one's intuitions may be based on subconscious allegiance to ideas foreign to the object of the argument, or on vague associations of ideas, or on oversimplifications. In retrospect, it seems that the argument of 1961 suffered from a number of defects.

(a) Although the foundation was laid (in the extracts from paras 37, 61, 68 mentioned above) for assigning values in exchange (or dated amounts of general purchasing power) to M, N, L and P, the formal argument simply referred to the firm having 'monetary assets M . . . etc'. In adjacent paragraphs there were clear references to the use of replacement costs for non-monetary items. Reference was made to the setting off, in the calculation of income, of 'the contemporary value of the services incorporated in goods sold' against the revenues of a period (para. 105); and to the use in the balance sheet of current replacement costs for all commodity stocks (para. 110). This inconsistency between the earlier and later paragraphs of the paper has never been pointed out elsewhere, to the best of my recollection. It could have been said to be an example of the *fallacy of heterogeneous aggregation*. As will be shown, my subsequent development of the demonstration proceeded by refinements reinstating the use of values in exchange, whereas others who have used the demonstration of 1961 may well have taken it at its face value, as supporting replacement cost, or current cost, accounting.

(b) In the formal argument, p was used of the proportionate rise in the 'price level'. It was intended that p would represent the rise in the 'general price level'; for, of course, no multiplication by p of amounts such as M and L would have any meaning unless p were an adjustment for the shift in the general purchasing power of money (the obverse or reciprocal of the change in the general price level). So, in the first place, the specification of p was insufficiently exact. In the second place, if the formal multiplication yielding expression I[2] is to be valid, the amount of N would have to be the money equivalent of non-monetary assets at the beginning of the period. This could only be the case (in the immediate context of the argument) where the replacement cost was equal to the resale price — an altogether unrealistic case. But the inadequate specification of p left it open for p to be interpreted as the proportionate change in a specific price level.

(c) The formal multiplication yielding expression I[2] was, in the argument, a convenient way of obtaining an expression of equality. But as there is no amount $M(1+p)$ in any real sense, the justification for the multiplication was intuitive; even though the consequence seemed reasonable, there was no demonstrated reason for the multiplication.

(d) The money units of I[1] are different from those of I[3], due to the postulated change in the price level. This is not made explicit in the symbolic notation. The legitimacy of the subtraction at I[4] and the empirical significance of the result may therefore be dubious. The problems here indicated by (c) and (d) were not removed until Stage III of the development of the notation. But at Stage I it looked suspiciously like an example of the *fallacy of heterogeneous calibration*.

(e) Although it was said that no part of pN was divisible, no definition of profit was offered. The conclusion that pN was not divisible was made to rest on the 'policy' of 'maintaining real assets'. This simply evaded the definition of profit. It would give rise to problems where the prices of non-monetary assets rose at a different rate from p; but the Stage I argument did not extend to that case.

(f) The transactionless interval was a legitimate simplifying device. But it left in limbo the problems of dealing with transactions — until Stage IV.

Thus, the Stage I exposition was in some senses ambiguous; the symbols were inadequate; and the argument was far from sufficient to deal with all of the possibilities with which an accounting system must cope.

Stage II — *Accounting, Evaluation and Economic Behavior*

As accounting is, in principle, a process of continuous aggregation, and as its results have been described as measurements, some light might be expected to be thrown on the propriety of its method and rules by the literature of scientific measurement. I studied some of that literature relating to physics and economics in 1962. The upshot was a paper 'Measurement in Accounting', mimeographed in 1963 and published later after some revision [6].

Aggregative measurement entails measurement of a common property of the components. The common property of assets that is relevant to the representation of financial position, described in 1961 as value in exchange, was now described as 'current cash equivalent'. The use of replacement costs was rejected in principle; but it was retained as an expedient for assets for which a resale price could not be found, in the belief that *some* value must be shown for all items usually appearing in balance sheets. It persisted also in the description of income calculation as the deduction from revenue of 'the direct cost of all goods sold at the contemporary cost at time of sale'.

Again, following the scientific literature, and practice in technologies to which it relates, measurements made under different conditions or in different scales must be converted to equivalent measurements under similar conditions or in the same scale if they are to be added, subtracted or compared. The conversion to equivalent conditions or scales is based on empirical laws. (The coefficients of expansion of solids, liquids and gases are expressions of such laws.) No problems arise in respect of balance sheet amounts at a stated date; for all amounts discovered to be indicative of the current cash equivalents of assets and the amounts of liabilities are expressed in the money unit of general purchasing power at that date. But where a difference, such as income, is to be found by reference to measurements at successive dates at which the money unit is not in all respects the same unit, an adjustment must be made to one or other of the initial and terminal measures. That is the adjustment for which p was used in Stage I.

At the time of the measurement paper, and in the light of the use, as expedient, of the replacement costs of some assets, no alternative was seen to the calculation of depreciation charges by reference to the remaining expected service life of an asset. As representing the cash equivalent of a depreciating asset, the result of using such a calculation was less than ideal, but it was made to suffice.

The 1961 and 1963 papers provided much of the groundwork for *Accounting, Evaluation and Economic Behavior* [8] the manuscript of which was written in 1963-4. There, the two problems of changes in prices and changes in the general purchasing power of the money unit were dealt with separately at first, then merged. The notation of Stage I was used but since changes in the general purchasing power of money affect equally, unit for unit, the amounts of monetary assets and liabilities, the net effect could be captured by eliminating L and using M for net monetary assets. As before, a transactionless period was assumed.

For the change in the general level of prices between dates t_1 and t_2, the position at t_2 became

$$M + N(1+p) = R(1+p) - pM \qquad \text{II[3]}$$

if the prices of non-monetary assets rose at the rate p. This corresponds with expression I[3] above. In the assumed circumstances, $(-pM)$ represents a gain or loss of general purchasing power, depending on the sign of M.

For a change in the prices of non-monetary assets *only*, by the proportion q, the position at t_2 would become

$$M + N(1+q) = R + qN \qquad \text{II[4]}$$

In the assumed circumstances, qN represents a gain or loss in general purchasing power. (Whereas p must be obtained by reference to a general price index series, it was specifically stated that q is obtained by reference to actual prices, at the opening and closing dates, of the assets. Two non-monetary assets were used in the demonstration to emphasize that the prices of assets may vary at different rates; but this is dispensed with for present purposes.)

Effect may be given to *both* of the changes by adding $N(q-p)$ to both sides of expression II[3] above, resulting after simplification in:

$$M + N(1+q) = R(1+p) + qN - p(M+N) \qquad \text{II[8]}$$

In terms of 'depreciated' units, the terms of the left-hand side represent the command of general purchasing power at t_2; $R(1+p)$ represents the same general purchasing power at t_2 as R did at t_1; and the increment in general purchasing power $[qN - p(M+N)]$ represents income. In particular, qN represents the 'price variation adjustments' and $[-p(M + N)]$ which is equal to $-pR$, represents the 'capital maintenance adjustment' of the system.

As noted above, although the 'current cash equivalents of assets' was a clearer specification of the quantification or measurement rule, the use of replacement prices was still tolerated. This drew critical notice from reviewers of the book in 1966-7 which, in turn, caused me to abandon explicitly that position [12]. On the positive side, the Stage II exposition had introduced explicitly the effect of changes in the prices of non-monetary assets at a rate different from p; and the *pro forma* representation of the resulting accounts (pp. 254-6) embodied all the elements, including transactions, of a full accounting system.

Stage III — A Dollar Symbol

In 1965, before the publication of *Accounting, Evaluation and Economic Behavior*, Mathews made use of the notation in an article [22] critical of AICPA Study *ARS6* [1]. Both the AICPA Study and Mathews' critique dealt with two-period or three-date material. Without subscripts to indicate the date of any stated amount and without distinctive signs indicating the units in which those amounts are denominated, it is difficult to follow the threads of a three-date argument.

An interchange with Mathews led me to attribute the possibility of misunderstandings to the lack of explicit symbols for 'dated dollars' or dollars of dated general purchasing power. Such symbols would avoid the necessity of using, in the text surrounding any symbolic demonstration, such phrases as 'in terms of dollars of t_1'; and avert the possibility of oversight of such phrases. Further, if there were different symbols, it would be possible to give effect in the symbolic representation to the empirical law by which units in one scale are converted into units in another scale. That 'law' is given by $\$_1 = \$_2(1+p)$, where $\$_1$, $\$_2$ represent dollars of the general purchasing power of the dollar at t_1 and t_2; '=' represents 'equal in general purchasing power' and p is the proportionate rise in the general level of prices. Different dollar signs were introduced in [9] and [10].

This 'improved representation' was personally satisfying. It removed the necessity of saying 'multiply throughout by $(1+p)$' without saying why, as in expression I[2] above. And it confirmed that the amount of income derived by the process previously developed was a valid amount expressed in $\$_2$. Thus, supposing a transactionless period, at t_1,

$$\$_1 M + \$_1 N = \$_1 R \qquad \text{III[1]}$$

and at t_2, if the general level of prices rose by p, and the prices of non-monetary assets rose by q,

$$\$_2 M + \$_2 N(1+q) = \$_2 R_2 \qquad \text{III[2]}$$

Now, the difference between the residual equities at the two dates is the amount of income, Y, for the period; and this is equal to the difference between the left-hand sides of III[2] and III[1];

$$Y = (\$_2 M - \$_1 M) + (\$_2 N(1+q) - \$_1 N)$$

And since $\$_1 = \$_2(1+p)$, on simplification,

$$Y = \$_2 qN - \$_2 p(M+N) \qquad \text{III[3]}$$

It will be noted that this is the same as the increment in command of general purchasing power given in expression II[8] above.

Stage IV — The Inclusion of Transactions

By early 1969 it occurred to me that the assumption of a 'transactionless period' could be abandoned. Under the cash equivalent or money equivalent rule, we have a set of measured amounts at t_1 expressed in a common denominator, and a set of measured amounts at t_2 expressed in a different common denominator. Whatever may have occurred in the interval is captured by the difference. The changes in the nominal amounts of specific non-monetary assets are brought into account by adding or subtracting 'price variation adjustments' based on discovered prices at t_2. This is legitimate since, although the book balance before adjustment may have been expressed in say $\$_1$ (or in dollars of specifiable general purchasing power at different dates between t_1 and t_2), by t_2 all dollars will automatically have become $\$_2$. The same, of course, applies to the balances at t_2 of all monetary account items. We say 'automatically', since all amounts in $\$_1$ are gradually becoming expressed in $\$_2$ as the general level of prices rises. The fact validates the accumulation of amounts in accounts; for, all discovered or real balances of accounts *at any date at all* are in dollars of that date, and the effects of any transaction at that date are represented in dollars of that date. The only term of an expression of the position at t_1 (of the form of, say, III[1] above) which has not automatically become an amount in $\$_2$ is the term in $\$_1 R$. The equivalent of $\$_1 R$ in $\$_2$ is obtained by the conversion rule $\$_1 = \$_2(1+p)$.

It matters not how many changes have occurred during the period in monetary and non-monetary items, the independent discovery and recording of their cash equivalents at t_1 and t_2 will have brought into account those changes. Since the amounts of assets are variable when the effects of transactions are brought into account, it is necessary to assign subscripts to M and N, so that those terms represent numbers of dollars at specified dates and to use dated dollar signs as denominators of those numbers of dollars. Thus:

Let $\$_1$ and $\$_2$ represent dollars of the general purchasing power of the dollar at dates t_1 and t_2, the opening and closing dates of a period;

Let $\$_1 M_1$ and $\$_2 M_2$ be the amounts of net monetary assets at the two dates;

Let $\$_1 N_1$ and $\$_2 N_2$ be the sums of the money equivalents or net resale prices of non-monetary assets at the two dates.

Now, at t_1,

$$\$_1 M_1 + \$_1 N_1 = \$_1 R_1 \qquad \text{IV[1]}$$

and at t_2,

$$\$_2M_2 + \$_2N_2 = \$_2R_2 \qquad \text{IV[2]}$$

Let $\$_2Y_2$ be the net income (or profit) of the year ended t_2, that is to say, the increment in general purchasing power during the year in the amount of R.
Then,

$$\$_2Y_2 = \$_2R_2 - \$_1R_1$$

and, since $\$_1 = \$_2(1+p)$, in general purchasing power,

$$\$_2Y_2 = \$_2R_2 - \$_2(1+p)R_1 \qquad \text{IV[3]}$$

Substituting (M_1+N_1) for R_1 and (M_2+N_2) for R_2 in this expression

$$\$_2Y_2 = \$_2(M_2+N_2) - \$_2(1+p)(M_1+N_1) \qquad \text{IV[4]}$$
$$= \$_2(M_2-M_1) + \$_2(N_2-N_1) - \$_2p(M_1+N_1) \qquad \text{IV[5]}$$

This demonstrates how the amount $\$_2Y_2$ is related to the observed or ascertained values of monetary items and non-monetary assets and the change in the general level of prices. Since those values are ascertained independently of the accounts, and are so ascertained in order to prevent the accumulation of errors in the accounts, the amount of income is capable of independent authentication (as in auditing) by authentication of the components.

Formal demonstrations up to this point were given in [11], [12] and [14]. The effects of transactions are implicit in the process described. But an extension of the demonstration, making explicit provision for transactions, may be made to show the form of day-to-day accounting which is entailed, and the nature of the components of $\$_2Y_2$.

In respect of all non-monetary assets (inventories and other assets) *sold* during the period, let I represent the sum of the nominal differences between their selling prices and their actual purchase prices (or their recorded money equivalents at t_1 for non-monetary assets in possession at that date).

Let T represent the nominal amount of the aggregate net cash proceeds of all transactions (buying and selling) in non-monetary assets during the period.

Let E represent the aggregate nominal amount of all payments in the nature of expenses during the period (i.e., all payments which do not give rise to possession of non-monetary assets).

Let V represent the sum of the differences between the book-values (before terminal date adjustments) of non-monetary assets at t_2 and their discovered money equivalents at that date. V is thus inclusive of the fall in the money equivalents of depreciating assets and of all other rises and falls in the money equivalents of non-monetary assets.

Then, in nominal amounts,

$$M_2 = M_1 + T - E$$
$$\text{and } N_2 = N_1 + I + V - T$$

Substitute these values of M_2 and N_2 in IV[4]:

$$\$_2Y_2 = \$_2[(M_1 + T - E) + (N_1 + I + V - T) - \$_2(1+p)(M_1+N_1)]$$
$$= \$_2[(I-E) + V - p(M_1+N_1)] \qquad\qquad \text{IV[6]}$$

The result is interpreted as follows, from the definitions of the terms. The amount $(I-E)$ is the *realized* net cash proceeds (or *net revenues*) of the period from all transactions. It is obtained by the usual process of accumulating the amounts of transactions upon the opening balances of the accounts. It may be subdivided into any categories deemed necessary (e.g., as between transactions in inventories and transactions in other assets). Where revenue is derived by rendering services, to that extent there would be no component $(-T)$ in the above expression for N_2. The amount V is equal to the amount qN in expression III[3] above. It is the *price variation adjustment*, the sum of the *unrealized* increments and decrements in the money equivalents of non-monetary assets in possession at t_2 as ascertained at that date. This amount also may be subdivided in any way deemed necessary (e.g., as between inventories, plant, security investments, and so on). The component amounts, for which there would be corresponding adjustments to the asset account balances, are the same in principle as the terminal date adjustments made under accrual accounting generally. The third term in IV[6] is the *capital maintenance adjustment* appearing in II[8] and III[3] above. It is calculated from the independently determined values of its elements.

It will be noted that the individual components of the right-hand side of IV[6] are nominal amounts; only their aggregate is denominated in $\$_2$. It may seem that the accumulation in accounts of the effects of transactions at different dates and in differently dated dollars constitutes an example of the *fallacy of heterogeneous calibration*. But, on a day-to-day basis, it is not fallacious to add the money effect of a transaction to the balance of an account on the previous day; for, overnight, so to speak, the dollars of yesterday have *in fact* become the dollars of today. On the other hand, the shift in the general purchasing power of the dollar is not taken into account day-by-day. For it would be foolish to account for the minuscule day-to-day variations; and, in any case the value of p is not ascertainable daily. But if, notionally, all such variations were taken into account day-by-day over a succession of days, the cumulative amount of such adjustments can be shown to be equal to $p(M_1+N_1)$ for the period to which p refers. That this is the case should be apparent from the facts that the positions at t_1 and t_2 are expressed in $\$_1$ and $\$_2$, that the relationship between $\$_1$ and $\$_2$ is given by p and that the income amount in $\$_2$ is a difference between $\$_2R_2$ and the equivalent in $\$_2$ of $\$_1R_1$. The effects of all shifts in the general purchasing power of the dollar are encapsulated in the capital maintenance adjustment, the effect of which is substantially the same as adding to the nominal amount 'one' an 'adjustment' of 1.54 to obtain a length in centimetres equivalent to one inch. The adjustment to the nominal amount $(I-E+V)$ compensates for the heterogeneity of denominators; and the process yields a stated position and result at t_2 in homogeneous terms.

The transfer of the amount of the capital maintenance adjustment to a 'residual equity account' was refined in [14]. Since all amounts in $\$_1$ at t_1 become other amounts in $\$_2$ at t_2, it is appropriate that the amount of undivided profits at t_1 be adjusted. It was therefore proposed that credits corresponding to the amount of the capital maintenance adjustment of any year be made proportionately to the opening balances at t_1 of undivided profits and 'other residual equity'.

The Stage IV demonstration appears to be free of logical fallacies. It embraces the three (the only three) possible causes of changes in financial position — transactions, unrealized changes in the money equivalents of assets, and the change in the general purchasing power of the dollar. It is thus complete. And since the balance sheets and the amounts of income it yields are in dollars of the balance date, they are more readily interpretable than statements embodying amounts in mixed or temporally distant denominators.

OTHER USERS OF THE NOTATION

General Price Level Adjusted Accounting (1963)

The first use by others of the symbolic notation of Stage I occurred in *Reporting the Financial Effects of Price Level Changes* [1]. That Study proposed the application of changes in an index of the general level of prices to the original costs of non-monetary assets and the calculation of gains or losses in general purchasing power in respect of monetary items. Expression I[2] above appears to be a 'model' for general price-level adjusted accounting (since described as 'CPP' in the United Kingdom and 'GPL' or 'GPP' in the United States). But that expression, in the context of the 1961 paper, could have been interpreted as suggesting a form of effective current purchasing power (value in exchange) accounting, or a form of replacement cost accounting. In no way did the paper suggest the use of general price indices for the adjustment of all historical cost figures. It may have appeared to do so, since the Stage I demonstration *assumed* that all prices changed in the proportion p, and did not deal with the observable fact that the prices of particular assets do not move in unison with the general level of prices.

The proposal of the Study entailed restatement from time to time of the costs of non-monetary assets in current general purchasing power equivalents. But that does not yield a balance sheet in current general purchasing power terms, for an indexed original cost disregards the shifts in the relative prices of goods since the dates of purchase of the assets. On the other hand, monetary items are stated in the balance sheet at their nominal amounts (current general purchasing power) from time to time; and a gain or loss in general purchasing power in respect of those items is calculated, in the nature of the adjustment (pL−pM) of I[3]. It thus appeared that general purchasing power gains or losses arose only in respect of monetary items, instead of in respect of all initial wealth, in an inflationary period.

The method of calculating that gain or loss was complex and its 'averaging' assumptions make the result questionable. That aside, the aggregate income is based, in part, on changes in index-adjusted costs (which are not representative of the effects of changes in the general purchasing power accessible to the firm) and, in part, on changes in the general purchasing power (represented by monetary items) accessible to the firm. The significance of such a mixed aggregate cannot be described otherwise than as the amount which results from performing the prescribed calculations. The proposal is a clear case of the *fallacy of heterogeneous aggregation*.

The Study pointed out that it was not concerned with replacement costs. It mentioned a number of difficulties to which replacement cost accounting is subject. But it did not refer to the association of the Stage I exposition with replacement costs; nor to the earlier paragraphs of the 1961 paper which contemplated financial statements in homogeneous units of dated and effective general purchasing power.

Current Value or Current Cost Accounting (1965-7)

Mathews [22] made use of the notation in the course of an exposition of a method of current value accounting that he had long advanced. The 'current valuation approach only revalues non-monetary items, adding the amount of the revaluation as a separate item to the funds or equities side of the balance sheet'. More exactly, the current valuation method restates the *costs* of non-monetary items.

Mathews observed that the use in [1] of the simple terms of Stage I above yielded an increment in the year ended t_2 of pN. The current valuation approach, in which r represents the proportionate rise in the cost of non-monetary assets, yields an increment of rN. Thus, one step, the use of r, was taken to distinguish his demonstration from the case in which p represents the change in the general level of prices and the prices of non-monetary assets rise in the same proportion. But a second step is necessary if the consequence is to be distinguished from other cases. If NC had been used to represent the current cost of non-monetary assets, ambiguity would have been avoided.

But, if the position at t_1 is represented by

$$M + NC = R,$$

we have an instance of the *fallacy of heterogeneous aggregation*. The amount M is an amount of accessible general purchasing power; the amount NC is not. The aggregation of the left-hand side is, thus, invalid; and the amount of R is not interpretable. Historically it may have been true that an initial owner's contribution had been deployed partly in monetary and partly in non-monetary assets; and the two parts are necessarily equal to the whole. But this mere deployment of an original cash sum is not what the balance sheet at t_1 represents. The above expression should yield some describable aggregate representing a position; but it does not do so.

At the time (1965), the fact that the general purchasing power of the money unit had changed between t_1 and t_2 was embodied in the text adjacent to symbolic expressions. But given that there is such a change, it is logically improper to add the amount of the revaluation up to current cost (i.e., $\$_2 NC_1(1+r)$) to the 'funds or equities' side of the t_1 balance sheet (i.e., $\$_1 R_1$). Observing the different dollar denominators, this is a case of the *fallacy of heterogeneous calibration*.

In a later article [23] Mathews said that the 'income' of a transactionless period is represented by $[Nr - p(M+N)]$ in the terms of my system. But I had contended that income was equal to $[Nq - p(M+N)]$, where N and Nq relate to the money equivalents of non-monetary items. Now, since r is related to NC (current cost) and q is related to N (money equivalent), it is clearly improper to associate N and r as Mathews did. It is a case of the *fallacy of mistaken identity*.

Mathews proceeded to argue that, by treating rNC as a capital maintenance adjustment, the firm would be able to 'command the same quantity of operating assets [as at t_1] at their new prices $N(1+r)$' at t_2. '... thus capital is always maintained.' It seems from this that command of a given quantity of operating assets is equated with capital, and that operating assets (and, therefore, capital) is exclusive of monetary items. To restrict the meaning of 'capital' in this way creates difficulties. If, for example, a company commences business with assets $\$_1 M_1$, presumably it has no capital at that date. If it carries on the business of lending money (which it may well do without having non-monetary assets), presumably it has no capital. If it spends some part of $\$_1 M_1$ on non-monetary assets (say, $\$_2 NC_2$), presumably it has acquired a capital which it did not have before; when all that has happened is a change in the composition of its assets. All of these 'anomalies' are avoided if capital is defined as the dated amount of the net assets expressed in dollars of the same date.

Setting aside the fallacy of heterogeneous aggregation, implicit in the addition of an amount of money and the price paid for non-monetary assets, the consequence of Mathews' proposal is as follows, in the case where there are transactions during the period, and the costs of non-monetary assets rise by the proportion r.

At t_1,

$$\$_1 M_1 + \$_1 NC_1 = \$_1 R_1$$

At t_2,

$$\$_2 M_2 + \$_2 NC_1 (1+r) = \$_2 R_2$$

Since $\$_1 = \$_2(1+p)$, the first expression may be stated

$$\$_2(1+p)M_1 + \$_2(1+p)NC_1 = \$_2(1+p)R_1$$

Subtracting this from the second expression,

$$\$_2(M_2 - M_1) + \$_2 rNC_1 - \$_2 p(M_1 + NC_1) = \$_2[R_2 - (1+p)R_1]$$

Now, under Mathews' proposal p is, in effect, assigned a zero value and the second term on the left-hand side is treated as a capital maintenance adjustment and is not divisible. Suppose, then, that a dividend is paid out of $\$_2 M_2$ equal to $\$_2[M_2 - M_1]$ which is the only amount divisible under Mathews' proposal. The balance of the assets after paying the dividend is then

$$\$_2 M_1 + \$_2 NC_1 (1+r)$$

Clearly the command of the same quantity of operating assets at their higher prices has been secured. However, the command over other goods and services and the capacity to support net receivables at higher prices has suffered; for the amount of net monetary assets M_1 is nominally the same as at t_1, but it is an amount in the depreciated dollars of t_2. If p had been assigned a positive value, an additional amount would have been retained out of the total increment during the period, towards sustaining the firm's capacity to buy goods and services generally, at their higher prices at the end of the period.

In a response to Mathews' suggestion that 'capital' in his sense would not be maintained under my definition of income, I attempted [9] to show that it would be. But, as it now seems, that attempt was vitiated by confusion of N with NC, an instance on my part of the *fallacy of mistaken identity*. It should be clear that if N and NC are defined differentially, and are subject to proportionate price variations q and r respectively, it is impossible to establish whether one system will yield the 'same result' as another; for 'result' does not mean the same thing in two different systems, one of which rests on the *fallacy of heterogeneous aggregation* while the other does not.

The formulation of Stage I(1961) was adapted by Gynther [15] in the setting of advocacy of a form of current cost accounting. As did Mathews, Gynther used N as representing the *costs* of non-monetary assets. For reasons already given, the initial and terminal expressions representing balance sheets are examples of the *fallacy of heterogeneous aggregation*.

Gynther was concerned to show that, to 'protect' a 'capital' in a period in which the 'price level' rises by the proportion p, 'it is necessary to supplement the automatic increase in non-monetary assets', (pN), by p(M−L), where M represents monetary assets and L represents *current* liabilities. '... the profit-determining process must include profits and losses on monetary assets and non-permanent monetary liabilities in times of changing prices.' Presumably 'include' means 'take account of', since the amount of pN was to be transferred to an asset revaluation account and the amount p(M−L) was to be transferred to a 'capital reserve'.

The symbolic demonstration was not extended to the case where the current costs of non-monetary assets rose by a proportion different from p; nor to the case where there are long-term liabilities. But following the demonstration, Gynther argued that gains in respect of long-term liabilities should not be taken into account in calculating the profit of a period. Now, why gains on short-term liabilities should be taken into account, and not gains on long-term liabilities, is difficult to understand in the context of an exercise in measurement. For, first, short-term liabilities may, by renewal, have the same effect as long-term liabilities; and second, lenders for short and long terms both suffer losses in general purchasing power, which must correspond with the gains of borrowers, since there are no other parties to the transaction. The separate and distinctive treatment of different classes of liability is an example of the *fallacy of improper subdivision*.

Gynther sought to justify the distinction on the ground that long-term debt forms 'part of the permanent capital of the firm' as are amounts contributed by shareholders. Of course, long-term debt is not the same as shareholders' contributions, in law or in financial effect. To assert that it is, is an example of the *fallacy of mistaken identity*.

The argument, furthermore, ignores the fact that all amounts that are at any date relevant to choice or action, or constitute part of the representation of a financial position, are necessarily denominated in dollars of that date; and the fact that S_1 at t_1 gradually and inevitably becomes S_2 at t_2. Account must be taken of the change in the denominators between the two dates. Failure to do so represents an example of the *fallacy of heterogeneous calibration*.

Like Mathews, Gynther adopted a physical capital maintenance basis for the calculation of income, a procedure which is subject to some observations to be made on that matter at the end of this paper.

Income Measurement (1969)
Parker and Harcourt [27] made use of the notation in the introductory essay to their 'readings'. They were concerned primarily with income measurement; but, in the context of business operations, that entails consideration of accounting methods generally. They began with the *ex post* concept of income which, of the various concepts considered by Hicks, he considered to be 'almost completely objective', namely, 'the value of the individual's consumption *plus* the money value of his prospect which has accrued during the week'. Hicks' comment on the objectivity of this 'income' was related to income from property, that is to say, the kind of income which is generated by business firms ([17], pp. 178-9).

Now the 'money value of a prospect' may reasonably be described as the quantum of general purchasing power accessible by virtue of the possession of a stock of assets (net of debts); for that is the amount one has the prospect of spending. Parker and Harcourt quoted a definition from Meade and Stone, which, though in slightly different terms, appears to have the same connotation as Hicks' definition: 'a man's money income in any period is equal to the money value of his consumption plus the increase in the money value of his capital assets. For the sum of these two is the amount which he could have spent on consumption *while maintaining the money value of his capital stock intact*' ([26], p. 219, emphasis in original). Hicks had called this briefly 'consumption plus capital accumulation'. Similarly, Simons had defined income as 'the value of the rights which he might have exercised in consumption without altering the value of his store of rights' ([28], pp. 49-50). Kaldor's formulation, $(K_2 - K_1)$, in which the terms are the actual market values of assets at successive dates, may be interpreted similarly ([20], p. 63).

Parker and Harcourt went on to suggest that the Kaldor and Hicks definitions 'are not too far away from contemporary accounting practice'. But there is no clear evidence that any of the economists cited envisaged the calculation of income by reference to a statement of capital which consisted of the sum of an amount of dated general purchasing power (the amount of net monetary items) and the costs or unamortized costs of non-monetary assets, which is the method of contemporary accounting practice. That practice entails the *fallacy of heterogeneous aggregation*. There is no ground for presuming that such a notion of capital was intended in the sources cited.

None of the authors referred to 'money amounts' of assets or capital. They referred to 'money values'. Since all would have been aware of the fallacy of adding or subtracting amounts expressed in different denominators, it seems reasonable to interpret dated initial and terminal 'money values' as expressions in terms of dated general purchasing power, and to interpret the increment described as income as the difference between two amounts expressed in units of the same general purchasing power. This plausible inference was not drawn.

Proceeding, Parker and Harcourt acknowledged their debt to Edwards and Bell and set up a relationship between money income, current operating profit, holding gains, accounting profit and real income. For a business firm, they said, money income may be divided into current operating profit and holding gains. The *money income* of a period ended at t_2, in which there were no transactions and the prices of non-monetary assets rose by the proportion q, is

$$M_1 + N_1(1+q) - (M_1+N_1) = qN_1 \qquad \text{PH[3]}$$

The terms M_1 and N_1 related to 'quantities'. This confuses the meaning of the expression. In the context of contemporary accounting practice and the exposition of Edwards and Bell, non-monetary assets are represented by costs (original or current) and, as was pointed out above, the expression is consequently an example of the *fallacy of heterogeneous aggregation*.

However, Parker and Harcourt proceeded to derive the *real income* '*after* allowing for the change in the general price level', p, and making a corresponding adjustment to the residual equity; real income is

$$M_1 + N_1(1+q) - (M_1+N_1)(1+p) = qN_1 - p(M_1+N_1) \qquad \text{PH[4]}$$

Since there were no operations, there is no *current operating profit*; the amount of real income is therefore described as *real holding gains* accruing during the period.

If there were transactions during the period, so that the amount of the net assets at t_2 became (M_2+N_2), *real income* would be

$$(M_2+N_2) - (M_1+N_1)(1+p) \qquad \text{PH[5]}$$

Subtracting the holding gains element of PH[4], current operating profit would be

$$(M_2+N_2) - [M_1+N_1(1+q)] \qquad \text{PH[6]}$$

In words: 'current operating profit is equal to the difference between the current values of the net assets at the end of the period and the end-of-year values of the opening net assets'.

It has already been pointed out, with reference to Mathews [23], that the symbols in N should be in NC or some other differential symbol. Parker and Harcourt noted that 'many assets have market values which differ according to whether one is a buyer or a seller'. This should have posed a dilemma in respect of their demonstration, for one would suppose that if N were to be a buying price in some cases and a selling price in others, the meaning of the symbolic expressions would be indeterminate. The dilemma could be resolved by noticing that, in respect of assets one has, one can only be a seller. The consequential step, the use of N to denote selling prices, was not taken.

Instead, Parker and Harcourt turned to a line of argument purporting to be based on the work of Bonbright. They proposed a 'general rule of asset valuation'; the value to the firm of an asset is its current replacement cost (a market buying price), except in certain stated circumstances in which the present value of the expected net receipts from the asset (a hypothetical calculation) and the net realizable value (a market selling price) may be used. Now a market price (buying or selling) is an ascertainable price at a given date in dollars of that date. But a present value is not. Though its components are discounted to a present date, they are amounts of differently dated dollars, e.g., $\$_1C_1, \$_2C_2, \$_3C_3 \ldots$, where C represents the net cash receipts of a given year and the subscripts represent successive dates. To take the present value as a dated measurement is an example of the *fallacy of heterogeneous calibration*.

The 'general rule' thus entails that a dated statement of position may take the following form where there are several non-monetary assets some of which are subject to the 'exceptions' of the rule:

$$M_2 + N_2 + NC_2 + NPV_2 = R_2$$

where N_2 is a net realizable value at t_2, (M_2+N_2) is an amount of accessible general purchasing power; NC_2 is a purchase price which has not been paid at t_2; and NPV_2 is a hypothetical amount. This is an exacerbated example of the *fallacy of heterogeneous aggregation*. And the splitting of one class of assets into three classes is an example of the *fallacy of improper subdivision*; since, for the purpose of discovering a financial state or position, three different properties of the components of a class of assets cannot simultaneously be material.

If Parker and Harcourt had attempted to incorporate the effects of the 'general rule' in the symbolic notation, and especially if dated dollar signs had been used, it may have become apparent that the meaning of 'income' would be extraordinarily complex, and variant from time to time as the 'exceptions' of the rule became operative or inoperative. The task was not attempted.

Comparative Analysis (1970-7)

Hendriksen [16] introduced the notation in a comparative analysis of different income determination proposals. A transactionless interval was assumed; no distinguishing signs for differently dated dollars were used. For the case where there are changes in the prices of non-monetary assets and in the general purchasing power of the money unit, Hendriksen derived a position at t_2 in terms equivalent to

$$M_1 + N_1(1+q) = R_1(1+p) + [qN_1 - p(M_1+N_1)] \qquad H[17]$$

This, he said, is significant, since 'it points out the major difference between those who propose adjustments for only specific price changes and those who propose adjustments for general and relative price changes'. The former cancel pR_1 against $[-p(M_1+N_1)]$, since their amounts are equal. And they interpret qN_1 as an adjustment of capital, whereas those who propose both adjustments, as in the above expression, treat that amount as part of the calculation of income.

Hendriksen did not, however, notice that those who have proposed adjustments only for specific price changes have invariably used N as representing costs, whereas in H[17], which he says follows my suggestion, N represents resale prices. This is the same oversight as has been described as the *fallacy of mistaken identity*.

The third (1971) edition of Mathews' *The Accounting Framework* [25] made use of some elements of the notation. It was introduced first when dealing with 'general price level accounting'. There, M, N and R are valued 'in accordance with the assumptions underlying the historical record approach'. Of course, one is free to assign whatever meaning he wishes to a set of terms. But in a formal demonstration, at least '+' and '=' are expected to have common meanings; and if an expression in which they occur is intended to have some empirical content, those common terms condition the meanings which may be assigned to the variables. As I have pointed out, if M and N are assigned meanings of the kind found in historical cost accounting, their aggregation is heterogeneous; and multiplication throughout by $(1+p)$, the next step in the demonstration, is invalid.

In the mid-'fifties one of the suggestions made for dealing with inflation in accounts was to deduct from historical cost income the product of a change in a general index of prices and the opening amount of shareholders' funds. (The same proposal has recently been made in the Hofstra recommendation in The Netherlands [19].) I considered that suggestion unacceptable on the ground that the opening amount of shareholders' funds is derived by a set of variant and variable rules. The original (1961) use of the notation, though ambiguous in some respects, certainly required that M and N should be empirically determinate amounts at a specified date. To use the same symbols in respect of historical cost accounting disregards the constraints implicit in their original use.

Proceeding to deal with the 'relative price change approach', Mathews described income under that system as the surplus arising after providing for the preservation of the opening amount of the 'generalized purchasing power of the firm's residual equity'. This would entail that the symbol N represents the resale price of non-monetary assets, and qN the rise in the price of those assets during the period. These terms appeared in the demonstration. But no reference to resale prices was made in the text; the terms 'initial value' and 'current value' which were used suffer from the ambiguity of 'value'. Nevertheless, it is presumed that the system under discussion was a resale price system.

Mathews derived the increment in residual equity, $[qN-p(M+N)]$ for the conditions stipulated. He repeated some of the objections he had taken in 1967 and 1968 to the treatment of that increment as divisible income. He contended that the system was defective, in that it measured income 'by reference to the difference between two *hypothetical* measures of wealth, namely the generalized purchasing power of measures of proprietorship funds at the beginning and end of the income period' (emphasis added). But at any date, the money unit is the factual unit of general purchasing power; and the amounts of monetary items and of the resale prices of non-monetary assets are discovered, and therefore factual, amounts of accessible general purchasing power. Further, the change in the general purchasing power of the money unit is a factual change, even though the means of discovering it may be subject to errors of estimation. There is nothing hypothetical about the process; it simply seeks to follow through, in the accounts, the impact of occurrences that have actually affected the firm.

Turning to current value accounting, Mathews used the same symbols, but assigned to N and N(1+q) the meaning 'current purchase price' or 'current cost' of non-monetary assets. It is almost inevitable, when in one work the same symbols are assigned three different meanings, that confusion will arise; especially as Mathews used q for the proportionate rise in the current cost of non-monetary assets, which in 1965 had been represented by the distinctive symbol r. The argument proceeded without reference to a change in the general purchasing power of the money unit. As in his previous expositions of the system, the amount qN is not treated as a profit (in the absence of transactions) but as a holding gain transferred directly to an asset revaluation adjustment (part of the residual equity balances). The argument and the conclusion are similar to those referred to when dealing above with Mathews [23] and the result is subject to the drawback there mentioned.

The effect of a shift in the general purchasing power of the money denominator was then introduced in a section on the 'relationship between current value adjustments and general price level adjustments'. That shift was used as a means of converting successive sets of accounts at differently dated prices to sets of accounts 'in terms of a common price level'. (The argument is similar to that of [23].) The conversion was represented as a 'statistical procedure'; the fact that the significance of the amounts in accounts changes when the denominator changes was not regarded as a matter to be taken into the accounts. Statistical deflation and inflation are, of course, common practices in the treatment of economic aggregates when the level of prices changes. But they rest on the presumption that the aggregates are homogeneous and properly dated aggregates, a presumption which is not tenable where N represents the costs or current costs of certain assets.

Mathews proceeded to demonstrate that following such a process of statistical deflation, the change in the residual equity under current value accounting is the same as that 'which results from relative price change accounting'. As I have said above, no such equality can be established where the terms used in two systems under comparison are significantly different. The proof of equality is a consequence of the *fallacy of mistaken identity*, induced by the use of common symbols for magnitudes of materially different kinds.

Lee [21] made use of the notation with particular reference to the 'restatement of accounting income' and the 'restatement of current value income' when dealing with 'the price-level problem'. A transactionless interval was assumed; distinctive symbols were not used to distinguish money units of different general purchasing powers. The expressions derived were similar to those given above as II[3] and II[8].

Like others, Lee used the same symbols in differently structured settings. Perhaps this was due to his view of the symbolic statement of position, of the form M+N = R; he described this as a 'basic identity'. Now, of course, under any system of double-entry accounting M+N = R numerically. But if any such statement is to have empirical referents, 'identity' must mean more than numerical equality. The symbolic expression is an identity of an empirically significant kind only when the symbols are given interpretations which establish 'identity'. That is only the case where N represents the money equivalents or resale prices of non-monetary assets.

The use of terms such as 'restatement of accounting income', a usage not limited to Lee, carries the connotation that there is such an empirical thing as 'accounting income' (or other sorts of income) which can be 'restated' under certain conditions or for certain purposes. But varieties of income, such as 'accounting income', arise from certain specifiable assumptions, or expressed intentions to include 'this' or exclude 'that' from the accounting process. If, for example, there were no accrual accounting, many real consequences of the experiences of firms would be omitted from the accounts of a period. If there were no accounting for changes in the prices of assets and changes in the general purchasing power of the money denominator, other quite real consequences of the experiences of firms would be omitted. If the effect of any such real experience is omitted we do not obtain a particular 'income type' but a distortion of income, a distortion which cannot readily be corrected unless the 'formula' for the design of the system is a well-designed and complete formula at the outset. If the formula is well-designed, differences in circumstances, such as the non-occurrence or negative occurrence of any variable provided for in the formula, will be accommodated by zero or negative values, not by a complete or partial shift in the meanings attributed to the variables. It is the attempt to build adjustments and restatements on to a basically inadequate cost-based formulation of the income notion that leads to the *fallacies of heterogeneous aggregation, heterogeneous calibration and mistaken identity.*

Barton [3] made use of the symbolic notation as part of discussions of 'constant dollar value' accounting, 'real value (current cost)' accounting and 'real value (selling price)' accounting. Having envisaged two varieties of 'real value' accounting, Barton might have proceeded to signify the difference by some such terms as NC and NS for the amounts of non-monetary assets under the systems; he might then have proceeded to distinguish the change in current cost (say, rNC) from the change in market resale price (say, qNS), and to note that r is not necessarily equal to q. But definitional and empirical differences are passed over when similar symbols are used without adequate discriminatory specification or qualification. And that leads almost inevitably to the *fallacies of heterogeneous aggregation, heterogeneous calibration and mistaken identity.*

It may be noted that similar demonstrations to those of Mathews (1971) and Barton occurred in the *Report* of the Committee of Inquiry into Inflation and Taxation [2]. Mathews was Chairman of the Committee and the relevant sections of the Report were based on a paper by Barton.

CONCLUSION

A Matter of Logic

The notation was introduced as a means of giving formal rigour to discussions encompassing a variety of variables, and in the context of a specified set of ideas. Its initial form has been augmented as inadequacies and the possibility of confusion became apparent. Based originally on a transactionless period, it became clear that the consequences of transactions could be accommodated, since the whole of the change in position through a period must be explicable in terms of transactions and non-transaction events. *The Stage IV formulation does not rest on any argument of the kind — 'in order to be as well off at the end of the period, this or that must be maintained'. It rests entirely on (1) the empirical observations that* $N_1 \neq N_2$ *and* $\$_1 \neq \$_2$, *(2) the empirical law that* $\$_1 = \$_2(1+p)$ *in general purchasing power, and (3) the mathematical rule that only terms with the same denominators may be added, subtracted or related.* Of course this entails the calculation of income by reference to an initial stock of general purchasing power; but if the matters under discussion are financial positions and shifts in financial position expressed in money units, which are units of general purchasing power, that calculation is entirely proper.

Users of the notation have almost invariably assigned to the same symbols different connotations. Most of the users have 'favoured' a different style of accounting, for the exposition of which different symbols would have been appropriate. For lack of specification, the demonstrations have embodied one or more of the fallacies identified.

It may seem to be of no great moment to point out that a line of argument is fallacious. But the upshot of a line of argument is a proposal for action. Most of the authors cited, for example, would have fairly significant leanings towards the courses of action entailed in the Sandilands Report, the Australian Provisional Standard on current cost accounting, the Richardson Report (New Zealand) and like proposals. That those proposals are based on logical fallacies may be observed by the appeals made by their proponents to auxiliary or irrelevant considerations. But logical fallacies have a habit of producing dilemmas, confusion and downright damage — consequences which, in the interest of all, should be averted.

'Materialist' or 'Fundist'?

Being concerned largely with the logic of a formal demonstration, little has been said about the empirical validity of the use of a 'physical capital' as an object of managerial concern or the maintenance of a physical capital as a desideratum for the calculation of income. Hicks [18] has characterized the differences between two kinds of viewpoint by the terms 'fundist' and 'materialist'.

There are some economists whose expositions run in terms of stocks and changes in stocks of material wealth, physical goods. But such stocks are treated in general terms, seldom if ever in terms of specific quantities of specific goods. It may be said, for example, that if a community's stock of constructed 'capital' goods is allowed to run down, its capacity for generating income will suffer. In the setting of discussions of the welfare of a community as a whole, no account need be taken of the money balances and debts of its members, for money balances and debts cancel out as between all members (individual and corporate).

On the other hand, there are some who conceive capital as a 'fund', expressed as a money-quantified stock of means. Hicks considered accountants as falling usually within this category. Now, whereas it may be proper to disregard debts and money balances as irrelevant in the context of a community as a whole, it is not proper when account must be taken of individual rights in the means of exchange, as in treatments of the wealth of individuals and firms. And that is the function of accounting for individuals and firms.

The 'fundist' and 'materialist' notions, on these grounds, are neither compatible nor incompatible *per se*. They simply relate to quite different contexts of discourse. If we suppose that they are alternative permissible means of dealing with the *same* context we fall under the *fallacy of mistaken identity*. That seems to be the case of those 'materialist' accountants whose notions of wealth and income have reference to physical capital or physical capacity. They rely on a materialist notion in a context in which it is irrelevant and with which it is incompatible.

It is notable that no 'materialist' economist has attempted to quantify material wealth in terms other than those used by fundists. Material wealth or physical capital is not quantifiable in terms of a common denominator. Indeed, it is notorious that none of the materialist accountants has attempted to specify what is meant by physical capacity, operating capacity or operating capability. In the absence of a specification, no firm meaning can be assigned to the maintenance of physical capacity, and no dependable calculation of the 'financial' variety can be based on notions of the 'physical' variety. That is why the makeshift substitution of replacement and replacement cost has been made to serve.

But there is no rule of business administration or economic behaviour which entails that a physical capacity or a stock of material goods should be maintained. The adaptive behaviour characterized by the description 'economically rational behaviour' entails that firms will seek the most promising deployment of the money (general purchasing power) that comes under their control day by day. In the face of shifts in demand and technology, it would be folly to insist routinely on replacing physical goods.

The matter is not overlooked in the proposals of the materialist accountants. But to accommodate it they are obliged to introduce *ad hoc* or auxiliary propositions of the kind, 'where replacement is not contemplated, value assets at net realizable value'. That Parker and Harcourt, following others, introduced such *ad hoc* considerations has been noted. The same line was followed in the Sandilands Report and in the Australian and other current cost accounting proposals. But since the 'contemplation of replacement' may come and go as shifts in demand and shifts in asset usage vary, such *ad hoc* rules may never yield a firm and consistent mode of accounting for and reporting the factual consequences of past transactions and events.

Of course, the replacement in kind of non-monetary assets is *one* of the courses of action available to any firm in the short-run. But the provision of financial information of the most general utility cannot be made to rest on a replacement assumption that is consistent with the general pattern of economic action only in a limited class of cases. Since accounting is concerned with finances or funds, a 'fundist' rather than a 'materialist' view is pertinent. It alone provides a means of dealing with monetary and non-monetary items on equal terms and without the necessity of *ad hoc* auxiliaries. Continuously contemporary accounting, as represented by the Stage IV development above, is an expression of that view.

REFERENCES

1. American Institute of Certified Public Accountants, Accounting Research Study No. 6, *Reporting the Financial Effects of Price Level Changes*, 1963.
2. Australian Government, *Report of the Committee of Inquiry into Inflation and Taxation* (Mathews Committee), 1975.
3. Barton, A. D. *The Anatomy of Accounting*, 2nd edn., University of Queensland Press, 1977.
4. Chambers, R. J., 'Detail for a Blueprint', *Accounting Review*, April 1957.
5. ———, *Towards a General Theory of Accounting*, 1961.
6. ———, 'Measurement in Accounting', *Journal of Accounting Research*, Spring 1965.
7. ———, 'The Price Level Problem and Some Intellectual Grooves', *Journal of Accounting Research*, Autumn 1965.
8. ———, *Accounting, Evaluation and Economic Behavior*, Prentice-Hall, Englewood Cliffs, N. J. 1966.
9. ———, 'Price Variation Accounting — An Improved Representation', *Journal of Accounting Research*, Autumn 1967.
10. ———, 'Price Variation Accounting — A General Notation' in Chambers, *Accounting, Finance and Management*, Butterworth, Sydney 1969.
11. ———, 'Continuously Contemporary Accounting', *The Accountant*, 30 April 1970.
12. ———, 'Second Thoughts on Continuously Contemporary Accounting', *Abacus*, September 1970.
13. ———, 'Towards a Theory of Business Accounting' in Roy Sidebotham, *Introduction to the Theory and Context of Accounting*, 2nd edn, 1970.
14. ———, *Accounting for Inflation — Methods and Problems*, Department of Accounting, University of Sydney, 1975.
15. Gynther, R. S., *Accounting for Price Level Changes*, Pergamon Press, 1966.
16. Hendriksen, Eldcn S., *Accounting Theory*, rev. edn, Irwin, 1970.
17. Hicks, J. R., *Value and Capital*, 2nd edn, Oxford University Press, 1946.
18. ———, 'Capital Controversies: Ancient and Modern', *American Economic Association Papers and Proceedings*, May 1974.
19. Hofstra, H. J., *An Inflation-Adjusted Tax System*, Staatsdrukkerij & Uitgeverij, The Hague 1978.
20. Kaldor, N., *An Expenditure Tax*, Allen & Unwin, London 1955.
21. Lee, T. A., *Income and Value Measurement*, Nelson, London 1974.
22. Mathews, R. L., 'Price-Level Changes and Useless Information', *Journal of Accounting Research*, Spring 1965.
23. ———, 'The Price Level Controversy: A Reply', *Journal of Accounting Research*, Spring 1967.
24. ———, 'Price Variation Accounting — A Rejoinder', *Journal of Accounting Research*, Autumn 1968.
25. ———, *The Accounting Framework*, 3rd edn, Cheshire, 1971.
26. Meade, J. E. and J. R. N. Stone, 'The Construction of Tables of National Income, Expenditure, Savings and Investment', *Economic Journal*, 1941.
27. Parker, R. H. and G. C., Harcourt, *Readings in the Concept and Measurement of Income*, Cambridge University Press, 1961.
28. Simons, H. C., *Personal Income Taxation*, University of Chicago Press, 1938.

Inflation Accounting in the Mining Industry*

The mining industry is a riskier industry generally, than most other industries. Its products are bought and sold on world markets and their prices are influenced by economic conditions in diverse places. Discoveries of new deposits or ore bodies may make existing operations less economical. New extractive or refining processes may make feasible operations that were formerly uneconomical. Discovery itself may be very costly, and development may add enormous amounts to the outlays necessary before returns begin to flow in. Beside all these sources of risk, the risks of inflation may seem a modest additional burden. But the investments and incomes are so large that inflation at even low rates may significantly affect the assessment of returns from the industry.

My subject is inflation accounting in the industry. Inflation accounting has come to have a rather mixed and confused meaning. The flurry of interest in it over the last decade sprung from the very high rates of inflation experienced in some countries at the beginning of the seventies, and the prevailing mode of accounting which disregarded its effects. The effect of inflation is that every dollar or every dollar's worth, owned or owed, depreciates in general purchasing power between the beginning and the end of a year. The early inflation accounting proposals sought to take account of this by indexing historical accounting balances at the beginning of a year to their general (current) purchasing power equivalents at the end of the year. Those proposals were swept aside in the mid-seventies in favour of proposals of the current or replacement cost variety. These proposals explicitly disregarded the effects of inflation as such and concentrated on the replacement or current purchase costs of assets, or the costs of purchasing equivalent operating capacity or service potential. In some expositions of CCA it was pointed out explicitly that it was not a method of inflation accounting; and indeed it is not. But the names of the committees which fathered it referred to inflation accounting, and I suspect that it is still widely regarded as a method of inflation accounting.

---

* Presented at Silver City Accountants Silver Anniversary Convention, Broken Hill, September 1979.

Sketch of a Proposal

That confusion requires that I explain what I understand by inflation accounting. I take it that the function of a statement of financial position (a balance sheet) is to represent the gross wealth of a company (its assets), the claims of others against that wealth (its liabilities) and the residual interest of the company in that wealth (its net wealth), at a stated date. The residual interest is often described as owners' equity or shareholders' equity or shareholders' funds. But it does not represent shareholders' interests in a company's assets except on liquidation. For a going concern it represents only the wealth of the company that is free of commitment to pay debts.

The gross wealth of a company is the aggregate of the funds accessible to it by virtue of its possession of assets - and that is given by the aggregate of its monetary assets and the money equivalents (market values or net resale prices) of its other assets. That is a common sense notion that is put to use by all who consider spending more than the cash immediately at their disposal. Since it is the money equivalent of a company's possessions, it can be related to the company's liabilities and to its necessary or expected outlays in the near future. The importance of market resale prices is made evident in every case in which, through the use of other values, the capacity of a company to continue as a going concern is misrepresented.

The net wealth or net assets of a company at any date is represented in dollars of the common general purchasing power at that date. The net income of a company between two dates is the increment in the general purchasing power of the amount of net assets between those dates. The nominal difference between the amounts of net assets is meaningless, since the two amounts are expressed in dollars of different general purchasing power. It must be ascertained as a first step; but it must then be reduced by an inflation adjustment. The inflation adjustment is the product of the opening amount of net assets and the proportionate change in an index of changes in the general level of prices between the two dates. In bookkeeping terms, the amount of the inflation adjustment is charged against the total nominal increment and credited to the opening balance of the company's equity in its assets. The resulting income, the difference between the nominal increment and the inflation adjustment, is then a genuine increase in the period in the general adjustment, is then a genuine increase in the period in the general purchasing power accessible to the company.

I have skipped quickly through this process to keep attention on the effects of inflation. But some details should be filled in. The market values of assets must be ascertained at balance dates, for only then is their aggregate a valid aggregate, and only to a valid dated aggregate (the amount of net wealth) may the change in a price index be applied. Where the market values of assets differ from their balance date book values, those book values must be increased or decreased so that they represent market values. The aggregate of those differences is described as a price variation adjustment. It includes all upwards variations (appreciation) and all downwards variations (depreciation).

Besides those price variations there will have been increments in the net assets due to the difference between the proceeds of sales and the sum of the pre-sale book values of assets and the cash outlays for wages and other expenses. The amount of those increments may be described as net revenues. The net income of a period is then the algebraic sum of net revenues, price variation adjustments and the inflation (or capital maintenance) adjustment.

Mining Limited – First Year

With those ideas in mind, turn now to consideration of a mining company, any mining company. Suppose Mining Limited is floated to exploit a mineral deposit which, on the basis of expert evidence of geologists, is sufficiently promising to justify the expenditure of a considerable sum on surface works, shafts, ventilation, vertical and horizontal transport, earthmoving equipment, crushers and concentrators, and so on. Suppose that by the issue of shares the company raised $100m at t_1, the beginning of a year. At t_1 its balance sheet would read:

Cash $\$_1 100m$ Equity $\$_1 100m$

The sign $\$_1$ signifies dollars of the general purchasing power of the dollar at t_1. The dollar signs with subscripts indicating "dated dollars" will not be used in subsequent balance sheets since their dates indicate the kinds of dollars in which they are expressed.

Suppose that during the year the company spent on **development** of the mining area and the shafts and other outlays preparatory to actual mining, $60m. Suppose that all this work is specific to the site, so quarters, and other surface assets that could be sold (if necessary or desirable) separately from the mine and site. Suppose $5m was spent on a city building to be used as a head office, and partly as lettable space. And suppose that idle funds were invested in the money market during the year, yielding revenue of $4m; that rental income was $0.5m; and that management and related expenses amounted to $2m. The transactions are summarized in the cash account up to t_2, the end of the year, in Table 1.

Suppose that at the end of the year the plant is found to have a net resale value of $10.0m, and the H.O. building a value of $6.0m. Those assets would be revalued accordingly and they would represent a total price variation adjustment (downwards) of $4.0m. We have described the development costs as sunk costs, as they represent preparatory work which cannot be converted back into money for any purpose the company may choose. We shall not take them into account in calculating the income of the year for reasons I shall presently explain.

Suppose that during the year, the index of changes in the general level of prices rose from 100 to 108, i.e. by 8 per cent. To be as well off as at the beginning of the year, the company would have to have $108m in assets at the end of the year. But the money sunk in development costs is no longer available to the company, and it is not therefore subject to the loss in purchasing power through inflation. The initial funds that were subject to depreciation in general purchasing power were therefore $40m; and to have command of the same general purchasing power at the end of the year, the company would have to have $$_2$43.2m. The amount of the inflation or capital maintenance adjustment referred to earlier is then $3.2m (i.e. $40m x 0.08 for the 8 per cent rise in the general level of prices).

Several things should be noted about these results.
(a) Mine development costs are shown, but not as part of the financial position of Mining Limited. The amount "sunk" is not available for any other purpose of the company; it does not represent funds accessible to the company as a going concern, and should be removed forthwith from the body of information representing funds accessible for the payment of debts and the continuation of operations. Any practice or standard which entails that the amount should be included in a statement of financial position will lead to misrepresentation of financial position. Any practice or standard which requires that the amount be amortized over

some period will also misrepresent financial position; for it entails that only part of the total outlay has become "inaccessible" in the period, or "lost" as far as future financial operations are concerned.

(b) The isolation of development costs from other assets and the income account is consistent with the case law relating to divisible profits. In **Lee v. The Neuchatel Asphalte Company Ltd** (1889), it was held that the law does not require that the paid in capital shall be maintained before any amount in the nature of revenues may be divisible. Said Lindley L.J., "If a company is formed to acquire a property of a wasting nature – for example, a mine, a quarry, or a patent – the capital expended in acquiring the property may be regarded as sunk and gone; and if the company retains assets to pay its creditors, it appears to me there is nothing in the Act of Parliament to prevent any excess of money obtained, by working the property over the cost of working it, from being divided amongst the shareholders". The development costs in the present example are in the nature of amounts paid to acquire a mine. It is quite legitimate therefore to treat them as sunk, once and for all time, in the venture.

(c) For the same reason the adjustment for inflation is not applied to them. If we wished, we could have indexed the funds invested in development costs; but the amount of development costs would then have been indexed correspondingly. No difference would arise in the amounts shown for the capital maintenance reserve and the net loss. But we have chosen not to do this indexing; first, because, once sunk, the amount is no longer subject to depreciation of the dollar; second, because we are concerned with ascertaining the change in the equity of the company in its assets, not with the change in the equity of shareholders in their shares (which is a matter of what happens in the share market); and third, because the original amount expended represents exactly what was expended and the record therefore corresponds with the facts.

(d) By t_2, all dollars of record at t_1 will have become $\$_2$. By discovering the money equivalents of assets at t_2, the assets are all represented in $\$_2$; and so is the amount of equity, and in particular the amount of the net profit or loss. The net loss and the financial position is therefore interpretable in terms of the general purchasing power of the dollar at t_2; as it should be, for no one at t_2 can interpret dollar amounts except by reference to what a dollar stands for

Table 1

Mining Limited – First Year

Cash Account to t_2

	$m		$m
Share issue	100.0	Development costs	60.0
Interest revenue	4.0	Plant purchased	15.0
Rental income	0.5	H.O. building	5.0
		Administrative costs	2.0
		Balance – on hand	2.5
		– on deposit	20.0
	104.5		104.5

Income Account for year ended t_2

Administrative costs	2.0	Interest received	4.0
Price variation adjustments		Rentals received	0.5
– plant	5.0	Net loss	4.7
– H.O. building	(1.0)		
Capital maintenance adjustment	3.2		
	9.2		9.2

Balance Sheet as at t_2

Mine development	60.0	Funds invested	60.0

Financial Position

Cash on hand	2.5	Equity	
– on deposit	20.0	– paid in	100.0
Plant	10.0	– less Mine development	(60.0)
H.O. building	6.0	– capital maintenance reserve	3.2
		– net loss	(4.7)
	38.5		38.5

Notes: (i) Non-monetary assets are valued at the best approximations to their money equivalents at balance date.
(ii) The capital maintenance adjustment is based on the rate of inflation during the year, 8 percent.

(its general purchasing power) at t_2.

(e) The fall in the money equivalent of plant assets from $15 to $_2$10 is due in part to whatever appreciation there may have been concurrently with the fall in the general purchasing power of the dollar and in part to the depreciation of the assets through use or simply through being second-hand. But there is no way of identifying these "parts"; and there is no point in trying, if we are concerned to find the aggregate consequence of what has occurred. Discovery of the money equivalent of the assets at t_2 does it all. Further, to calculate depreciation on some expected service-life basis will only by chance give the money equivalents of the assets. It is guesswork, and the result is fictional. A calculated **cash** balance would not be accepted if it disagreed with the actual discovered balance. There is no reason to adopt any other principle in respect of other assets.

(f) The rise in the money equivalent of the H.O. building is one of the many rises and falls in prices that occur concurrently with a fall in the general purchasing power of the dollar. It is a matter of common knowledge that many companies (including mining companies) occasionally revalue assets by tens and hundreds of millions, when book values are vastly different from current values. To bring these revaluations into account as they occur (instead of infrequently) is to apply the accrual principle consistently and systematically. And in the context of inflation accounting, it is necessary to bring them in, in order to make a proper calculation of the inflation (or capital maintenance) adjustment year by year.

Mining Limited – Second Year

Suppose, now, that during its second year, the company continued to establish its operational apparatus; that it installed processing equipment and proceeded to mine and process ore. Suppose that it found its present funds inadequate and was able to negotiate a loan of $20m on the security of its assets and its prospects. Suppose that the whole of its operations, financial and mining, were as represented in the cash account, income account and balance sheet given in Table 2, up to t_3, the end of the second year.

For convenience, it is assumed that there were no receivables or payables at the end of the year. The plant assets are assumed to have a money equivalent of $27m, entailing a price variation adjustment of $8m to reconcile this with the book value at t_2 (opening balance $10m. plus purchases $25m.) The H.O. building is assumed to have a money equivalent of $6.5m. And it is assumed that the money equivalent of the closing inventory (of ore or concentrates) was $1.7m. The rate of inflation during the year was 9 per cent.

Table 2

Mining Limited – Second Year

Cash Account to t_3

	$m		$m
Opening balance – on hand	2.5	Development costs	15.0
– on deposit	20.0	Plant purchased	25.0
Loan (5 years, 10%)	20.0	Operating outlays	65.0
Mining revenues	80.0	Administration outlays	4.0
Interest revenue	1.0	Interest paid	1.5
Rental income	0.6	Closing balance – on hand	3.6
		– on deposit	10.0
	124.1		124.1

Income Account for year ended t_3

Operating outlays	65.0	Mining revenues	80.0
Administration outlays	4.0	Interest revenue	1.0
Interest paid	1.5	Rental income	0.6
Price variation adjustments		Closing inventory	
– plant	8.0	(at money equivalent)	1.7
– H.O. building	(0.5)		
Capital maintenance adjustment			
– opening equity excl. loss	3.9		
– opening loss	(0.4)		
Net income	1.8		
	83.3		83.3

Balance Sheet as at t_3

Mine development	75.0	Funds invested	75.0

Financial Position

Cash – on hand	3.6	Loan (5 years, 10%)	20.0
– on deposit	10.0	Equity	
Inventory	1.7	– Paid in 100.0	
Plant	27.0	– Less Mine development 75.0	25.0
H.O. building	6.5	– Capital maintenance reserve	7.1
		– Net loss	(3.3)
	48.8		48.8

Notes: (i) Non-monetary assets are valued at the best approximations to their money equivalents at balance date.
(ii) The capital maintenance adjustment for the year is based on the rate of inflation during the year, 9 per cent.

Several points of Table 2 deserve notice.

(a) No inflation adjustment is calculated in respect of the amount of liabilities, no matter when the debt was incurred. On borrowing, the company assumed a liability to repay $20m, neither more nor less. The effect of inflation (the depreciation of the general purchasing power of the dollar) thus falls on the creditors, not on the company, and there is no reason to bring it into the company's accounts. The company still owes $20m, but in depreciated dollars; and, of course, everything else in the t_3 balance sheet is in depreciated dollars. The same principle applies where there is an opening balance of current liabilities. All opening liabilities are a hedge against inflation. That is why the inflation adjustment is calculated by reference to the opening amount of equity (including accumulated profits or losses).

(b) The amount of additional development costs is added directly (without indexation) to the previous balance. And for the same reason as in the first year. The dollars spent are depreciated dollars (by contrast with the dollars initially invested in the company), but so are all the other dollars in the accounts of the second year. Further, the amount spent is the amount "sunk", the amount that is no longer subject to the influence of inflation.

(c) The closing inventory is valued at its money equivalent or net resale price. The use of selling prices is not a novelty in the mining industry. It is said, by those who have other industries in mind, that the use of selling prices entails "anticipation of profits". But if income is considered as the increment in the general purchasing power of net assets - the difference between two measurements - the process of discovering its amount cannot be described as "anticipating" anything. Mining Limited might have calculated its "costs of production" by the customary process of accumulating classes of cost and allocations of costs. In that case the closing inventory would have had a "book value" which would have to be converted to a money equivalent in the same way as the plant and building balances, by a price variation adjustment.

(d) The total amount of the inflation (capital maintenance) adjustment is calculated on the total amount of opening equity (9 per cent of $38.5m = $3465m, rounded to $3.5m). But where the amount of opening equity includes a balance of profit or loss and "other" balances, both parts must be adjusted out of the inflation adjustment. In the present case, the adjustment entails adding $0.4m to the opening loss and $3.9m to other balances (both "rounded figures"), as shown in the income account and the resultant balance sheet.

Mining Limited – Subsequent Years

The example could be extended to illustrate what may occur in a full year's operation. But most of the technicalities have been covered, and others can be covered without elaborate example.

Those who set score by the customary process of cost-amortization by the use of depreciation formulae may find the large initial depreciation (price variation adjustment) of plant unpalatable; and they may object to the recording of appreciation (rather than depreciation) on the head office building. But no such formula follows the financial consequences of events; the result of its use is fictional, not realistic, whereas the discovered resale prices or money equivalents, even if only approximations, do capture the consequences of what has occurred. Those who support the customary process may contend that the loss of the first two years is only a loss because of the heavy depreciation on plant. But that overlooks the fact that the customary process also entails amortization of the development costs. In the hypothetical example this could result in an even greater loss. But the argument for the method depends on the necessity of tracing the effects of what has occurred, not on the magnitudes of the resulting figures or on a comparison of the different magnitudes arising under different methods.

On the face of it, Mining Limited had not earned sufficient in the second year to wipe out the loss of the first year. Following the **Neuchatel** case, this would not have prevented it from paying a dividend out of the $1.8m profit of the second year. There is nothing unusual about failing to declare early dividends, however. Investors in mining companies do not expect instant dividends (though many may expect to make speculative profits on stock market transactions). But when dividends are declared and paid, is the amount paid to be adjusted in any way on account of inflation?

Suppose that, in the third year, the company earned sufficient profits to declare an interim dividend of $5m and that the dividend was paid during the year. Does this require any inflation adjustment? No. The stock of assets with which the year began was in dollars which forthwith began to depreciate. Whenever the dividend was paid it was paid in dollars depreciated to that date and the amount of equity was correspondingly reduced, by an equal number of depreciated dollars. Up to the payment date the loss in purchasing power was borne by the recipients of the dividend, and after that date the amount is not in the hands of the company. The increment in net assets as a consequence of operations (i.e. income of the year) will therefore tally with the change in net equity **plus** the nominal amount of the dividend.

If, on the other hand, new capital contributions from shareholders were received, their amount would be subject to a capital maintenance adjustment proportionate to the rise in the general level of prices between the date of receipt and the end of the year.

The use of money equivalents is relevant to the surveillance of solvency and borrowing powers. The current ratio is serviceable as an indicator of short run solvency only if its numerator represents funds accessible to meet its denominator, current liabilities. This is only the case if all current assets (including inventories) are represented by their money equivalents or selling prices in the ordinary course of business. Borrowing powers under trust deeds are usually constrained by provisions limiting total borrowings to some proportion of equity. The ratio of debt to equity is only a safeguard if the amount of equity represents a genuine money sum, and that depends on the total amount of assets also being a genuine money sum.

The planning of future operations and the assessment by outsiders of future prospects depend on knowledge of the funds accessible to a company. Only the use of money equivalents yields information on funds accessible from time to time. The calculation of an achieved rate of return, as an indicator of performance and as a guide to prospects, is only valid if its numerator and denominator are in dollars of the same kind. The calculation can readily be made under the method illustrated. For suppose the opening equity was $_4$50m, the net income was $_5$8m, and the rate of inflation in the year was 10 per cent. Then $_4$50m = $_5$55m and the rate of return was 8 x 100/55 = 14.5%.

Suppose a mining operation is conducted in one country by a company domiciled in another. The use of money equivalents enables the company readily to convert the results of its foreign operations (balance sheet and net profit) to domestic currency terms. Since all the figures are in dated money amounts, the current rate of exchange may be applied to them all. No other system makes possible such a ready conversion from statements in one currency to statements in another.

Or suppose a mining company has operations in several countries and wishes to appraise their relative financial performances. The method illustrated enables the differential inflation factors in the different countries to be isolated from other factors, a feature which no other system possesses.

Some General Matters

The example covers most of the technicalities. But there are several matters of general significance that are related to the results derived by the process illustrated.

Pricing. It is often supposed that companies should adopt a pricing policy which will secure their ability to replace necessary assets. No doubt those who can do so will do so. Companies the demand for whose products is insensitive to price changes will be able to do so. But companies producing mineral products sold on wide markets or in competition with substitute minerals are not able to do this. To a considerable extent they are price-takers. They must, for the sake of cash flow (and subject to the limits of stock-piling, itself a matter of cash flow) take the prices the market offers. Further, it makes no sense in the case of a mining company to speak of replacing a mine. A company may seek to stay in the mining business to exploit its expertise; but there is no commercial principle by reason of which its shareholders or its present customers can be obliged to finance such additional ventures. Incidentally, since replacement is irrelevant, the CCA proposals, as a style of inflation accounting, are irrelevant.

Maintenance of capital. As the **Neuchatel** case showed, there is no law which requires a contributed capital to be maintained before a dividend can be paid. There is no commercial reason either. But a capital maintenance idea is entailed in the process described. Capital is the money amount or equivalent of a stock of assets less the debt payable out of that stock. The amount invested in mine development in the example is not severable from the company as long as the company continues to exploit the mine. The mine is removed from the market by the intention to exploit it. It has no money equivalent. It is not itself a source of cash flow. That can easily be seen by reference to notorious experiences in the industry. If the market price of the product specific to a mine falls to a level that is insufficient to cover the direct cost of getting and processing it, production will cease. Neither the hole in the ground nor the body of ore can be sold to keep the company exploiting it afloat. The history of mining is full of abandoned holes, sunk capital. That is why mine development costs are set aside in the balance sheet proposed, and excluded from all further calculations.

The capital to be used as the base point for reckoning periodical income is the general purchasing power represented by the opening equity or net assets of any period. The capital maintenance or inflation adjustment is designed to secure that the net income is calculated by reference to that opening stock of accessible general purchasing power. That is why the adjustment of the second year of the example is calculated on the gross amount of equity at the end of the first year ($38.5m) and not on the $40m (after development costs) at some point during the first year. The adjustment does not imply that that capital **must** be maintained; obviously some part of it was lost during the first year. It is only a means of ensuring systematic calculation of periodical income in such a way that its amount is a genuine increment in accessible general purchasing power expressed in depreciated (and factual) year-end dollars.

Security and Rate of Return. Investors generally acquire share interests which entail a proportionate interest in dividends declared (or ultimately in all profits) and a proportionate interest in assets on liquidation. Their security turns on the stock of net assets from time to time (for their convenience, often expressed as net tangible assets per share) and their income prospects turn on the net income of the venture from time to time. Of course, assets per share is not an indicator of security (capacity to withstand or adapt to changes in circumstances) unless the amount represents money accessible for the continued conduct of the business; and net income or income per share is not an indicator of performance or prospects unless its amount represents a genuine surplus arising in a year. For a secure investment investors will tend to expect a lower rate of return than for a risky investment. Mining being a risky business, the security of an investment in it is the less to the extent of the sunk costs, for their amount cannot reasonably be expected to be available to shareholders if the venture fails. A high rate of return should therefore be expected on the funds accessible to the company. If calculations are based on the statement of financial position in the kind of balance sheet proposed, both of these effects will be apparent. Assets per share will be low on account of the elimination of sunk costs from the calculation, and the rate of return will be the higher if calculated on opening (index-adjusted) equity than if sunk costs were included in the denominator.

Alternative Investment. The appraisal of a mining (or any other) investment is a matter of comparing alternatives. If the prospect of continued operation at a rate of return commensurate with the risk is in doubt, the management (or the shareholders) will compare the present (or expected) rate of return with the prospective rate of return from investing the accessible funds elsewhere. Clearly the sum available for alternative investment is limited to the money equivalent of the assets (i.e. the amount of the equity based on asset resale prices). That figure will be available under the proposed form of accounting. The task, then, is to find whether that sum invested elsewhere is likely to yield a greater income than the present income. But no valid exploration of alternative prospects is possible without knowledge of the amount available to be invested in alternatives. Of course, it may turn out that, on actual disposal (piecemeal or as a going concern), the mining assets will fetch more or less than the money equivalents of assets on a going concern (or orderly re-adjustment) basis. But the "figure-work" must be done before one goes into the market to negotiate, so that the negotiator has some realistic idea of the order of magnitude of the proceeds. For that purpose the money equivalents are a far better approximation than any figure based on total costs or unamortized costs of development or any other assets; they are the only relevant figures.

Sale: Lock, Stock and Hole. The kind of accounting illustrated relates to a mining venture as a going concern. It does not entail, however, that on the sale of such a venture as a going concern, no account would be taken of developnment and other sunk costs. Sellers are not so soft that they would forgo the opportunity of trying to squeeze all they can from buyers; and buyers are equally hard-headed. In that case the whole venture will go for what it will fetch, without regard for the original outlays. They are simply irrelevant. But the disclosure of the sunk costs in the balance sheet, in the manner suggested, serves to indicate, to shareholders what has happened to the funds contributed, and to prospective buyers the amount sunk in development, but without any necessary implication that the sunk costs have anything to do with the financing of a going business or the price at which it may sell. It is not infrequent that businesses or parts of businesses change hands for much less than it cost to establish them; at a lower capitalization they may be feasible, when they do not appear to yield adequate returns on establishment cost. Whether continuation of a given mining operation or its abandonment is in contemplation, the style of accounting suggested provides relevant information.

Standards and Taxes

Two matters, one already mentioned briefly and one not mentioned at all, deserve notice.

The Australian accounting standard relating to the extractive industries perpetuates a notion of "matching" based on cost allocation or amortization related to physical outputs. In the first place, a balance sheet based on costs does not give an indication of dated financial position in any sense pertinent to judgements of solvency, asset composition, gearing and rate of return. In the second place, progressive amortization by any formula entails failure to match increases and decreases in the amounts of accessible funds with the periods in which they occur. In particular, a sunk cost removes the sunk funds from any possibility of further use by the company; it is unrealistic to imply that the "removal" occurs partially over a period of years. Physical outputs and fund outlays are not temporally related, even in industries other than mining; and physical capacities have no fixed or determinate relationship to income yields, as the abandonment from time to time of mining operations testifies.

The second matter is taxation. The example has deliberately excluded reference to taxation, because I wish to make a suggestion at variance with present tax rules. There has been much talk of providing incentives to mining and exploration (and other things) by way of tax concession. And in many arguments the effects of inflation play a part. In some countries, companies have the option for tax purposes, of charging off outlays, especially those in the nature of sunk costs, in the years in which they ocur or over some shorter period than is provided by the amortization rules of other countries. The virtue of this is that a mining company is able to recoup its development costs and sustain its operations by reason of the early allowances. And in an inflationary interval, the allowances are allowances expressed in substantially the same dollars as those spent on mining works and plant. By contrast, the periodical amortization practice results in charges in units of depreciated general purchasing power from year to year; they are not therefore equivalent to, they represent less than, the general purchasing power of the initial outlays.

Apart from the sunk costs, the suggested mode of calculating periodical net income allows for the effect of inflation. Unless that effect is removed from the sum described as net income, the net income figure will include a nominal increment that is not a genuine surplus but merely the effect of the depreciation of the dollar. Wage and salary earners are protected to some extent from the effects of inflation by wage adjustment mechanisms. And the government revenue is protected by percentage tax rates. Only the business sector has, as yet, no mechanism which makes specific allowance for inflation; for the market in commodities is not a market in which business firms may expect automatically to be covered by proportionate shifts in prices when inflation occurs.

Of course my suggestion entails bringing into account price variation adjustments in respect of some items not usually included in income calculation - the appreciation or depreciation of buildings, security investments, and so on. But if the object of accounting is to give realistic indications of what has occurred, and if a valid calculation of the effect of inflation is to be made, there is no ground for excluding these variations from the income calculation. Their effects may be more or less than the capital maintenance adjustment. If more, there will be a taxable surplus; if less, there will be a charge against other revenues. But the result in either case is a more equitable tax base than one which excludes, arbitrarily, some gains or losses of some taxpayers.

Conclusion

The whole of these suggestions may **seem** at odds with well-established practices. But in many respects they are not. The resulting record is entirely **historical**, and the years in which increases or reductions occur in real equity are the years in which the accounts will show them. The method is **systematic** and applies the accrual rule **consistently**. The resulting figures are **realistic**, in every sense related to the financial calculations made in the course of appraising financial positions and results. The possibility of systematic **error is removed** by the periodical discovery of the money equivalents of assets; and the fictional elements which arise from allocations and apportionments are eliminated. The financial statements themselves are internally consistent; all assets being expressed in dated money equivalents, their amounts may validly be added, and validly be related to liabilities; and being expressed uniformly in up-to-date dollars they may be readily interpreted; no other style of accounting has these features. If there are any defects in the suggestions that are more serious than the defects of present practice, I would be pleased to hear of them.

Groundwork for Accounting Standards

or

30 Reasons for CoCoA*

The setting of accounting standards dates from over 100 years ago. That periodical financial statements of companies should give "a true and correct view" of their states of affairs and their results from time to time was held in the U.K. in the 1840s. A similar verbal formula survives today in countries that have followed the pattern of English law on commercial corporations. It has its counterpart in the "fair presentation" doctrine in the U.S. The Securities Act of 1933 was intended to provide for the "full and fair disclosure of the character of securities" in registration documents and prospectuses, and to make untrue statements and the omission of material facts culpable and actionable. The Securities Exchange Act of 1934 extended the disclosure principle to secure that the information initially filed would be kept up to date by the filing of periodical financial statements. "True", "true and correct", "true and fair", "full and fair" - these are reporting standards, standards for published financial statements.

These words, embodied in the public statutes, cannot lightly be set aside. Companies were not to be permitted to make any statements they chose about their positions and results. That company officers should make optimistic claims about future operations and yields was to be expected. But those (creditors and investors) who responded to those claims were to be entitled to know the outcome, so that they could protect their interests in the future. The report on results and position was to be a true report, not a fabrication of imaginative or cosmetic art. Unhappily things have not turned out that way; for, if they had, there would not have been the persistent search for better accounting that has engaged the attention of the accounting profession

---

* This paper was prepared and presented for discussion in a number of Universities and by the staff of the Financial Accounting Standards Board in the United States in 1980. Many of the lines of argument and bits of evidence alluded to have appeared in more elaborate form elsewhere.

and related professions for fifty years.

There is a substantial body of opinion to the effect that present doctrine and practice need improvement in three general directions. First, the diverse array of permissible rules for dealing with specific types of events, transactions or objects, should be reduced. Second, a systematic way of dealing with shifts in asset prices should be devised. And, third, a systematic way of dealing with the effects of shifts in the general purchasing power of the money unit (the unit of account) should be devised. All three have engaged the attention of professionals and researchers for about 50 years - but without notable progress. For many years the first problem seemed dominant, but there seemed to be no progress in reducing multiplicity and diversity. More recently the second and third problems have moved to center-stage, and the diversity problem has been pushed into the wings. The lack of progress is exemplified by the facts that (a) in many countries we have, concurrently, officially endorsed standards some of which are actual cost-based (in principle) and some of which depart radically from that base - wholesale inconsistency, in fact; and (b) there is a greater supply of differently based bits or arrays of information to plague the users of accounts than ever before. In the very decade in which the term "accounting standards" has come to common use, there is less standardization or prospect of standardization than ever before!

That situation has arisen, it seems to me, from the tendency to treat the three problems mentioned above as separate and separately soluble. But the origin of diverse rules was in fact the tendency of prices (or costs) and levels of prices (or costs) to vary. All three problems are interlocked; therefore the solving of all three problems simultaneously may be the only way of solving any one of them.

That was the conclusion I reached about 20 years ago. It has a simple mathematical analogue. Many values of x and y will satisfy the expression $x = 3y$ (e.g., $x = 3$, $y = 1$; $x = 6$, $y = 2$; etc.). There is no "true" value of x and y given only that relationship. But if x and y must satisfy an additional condition, there is a single set of values of x and y that uniquely satisfies the two conditions. Thus: What values of x and y satisfy the conditions: $x = 3y$ and $x + y = 2$? Only $x = 1.5$ and $y = 0.5$ satisfy. Thus, the truth, the propriety, the uniqueness of a solution to any problem may be approached the more closely, the greater the number of tests (or conditions) it must satisfy. Thus, if a rule seemed reasonable or logical **and** people were found to abide by it, the ground for relying on it would be the stronger than if only one of the two conditions was satisfied. Similarly if a rule yielded what seemed to be a "truer" income statement but simultaneously a "less true" financial position statement, the propriety of the rule could not be maintained. That, in fact, is one of the reasons why so much dispute has surrounded so many of the rules of traditional accounting.

The possibility of increasing the determinacy of a solution to any problem of accounting principle by increasing the tests to be satisfied led me to think of the simultaneous solution of the three problems mentioned above. If a given rule was to be adopted in the absence of price changes and changes in the general purchasing power of the money unit, it would have to be serviceable both in the absence and the presence of those changes. If any two rules on a given matter seemed to be equally serviceable under several stated conditions, an additional (but not unusual) set of conditions must be found which will test their serviceability under more exacting (more numerous) conditions. That procedural principle in due course led me to continuously contemporary accounting (CoCoA, for short). Its single valuation rule eliminates a principal cause of diversity in accounting. Its price variation and capital maintenance adjustments take explicit and systematic account of shifts in prices and the effects of inflation. It solves the three problems simultaneously.

It might seem that a scheme that has such sought-for consequences should commend itself to standard setting bodies. Yet such bodies in the five countries with whose accounting I am most familiar currently endorse and proclaim schemes which are contrary in effect. Thus current cost accounting provides more scope for varietal accounting than has been available hitherto; and all proposals so far endorsed for dealing with price changes and inflation are frankly admitted by their endorsers to be partial - and for that reason of questionable merit.

It might seem, too, that a proposal having the three sought-for consequences would commend itself to the academic community, for that community has long been believed to cherish the logical, the consistent, the systematic and the economical and to disparage the merely pragmatic, the ad hoc, the chaotic and the unnecessarily complex. But, with few individual exceptions, the academic communities in the five countries seem to be quite complacent about the prospect of increasingly diverse accounting which present accounting standards entail.

It would be odd if I had not asked myself at some time why so many - all reasonable and honorable men - should be so reluctant, indifferent or antipathetic to a style of accounting that disposes of so many difficulties, dilemmas and solecisms. I have asked; and I have not been able to answer myself. So I ask you. But to substantiate an earlier intimation, that CoCoA emerged from the simultaneous consideration of a number of the criteria that any worthwhile proposal must meet - and to focus your attention on the question I asked - the following pages lay out a number of the heads of argument and the evidence and reasoning on which the superiority of continuously contemporary accounting is claimed to rest.

----oOo----

30 Reasons for CoCoA

#1. Debtor Protection. In most countries there are punitive rules or laws against continuing to conduct business operations while knowing oneself (or one's business venture, firm or corporation) to be insolvent. The low yields of liquid assets, the higher yields of non-liquid assets, and the advantages of borrowing predispose persons and firms to take the risks of illiquidity and debt. Since the bankruptcy or insolvency laws may be invoked by any creditor **at any time** (given due cause), the debtor will require information indicative of his capacity to meet his debts **at any time** if he is to manage his affairs so as to avoid the penalties of insolvency and of continuing to trade while insolvent. That information necessarily includes the money amounts owed to creditors and the money in possession, or accessible by virtue of other goods in possession, of the debtor from time to time. Given that information, the debtor may consider the rate at which he should incur or reduce debt; and the goods he might sell and those he might pledge to improve his short-run liquidity. A systematic and continuous record of changes in debts and changes in the money equivalents of assets is a means of averting the legal penalties and the practical penalties and constraints of asset sales or compositions with creditors under duress.

By contrast, valuations of assets on any other basis than their money amounts or money equivalents will not assist debtors to keep solvency under attention nor provide "first indications" of the options open to them.

#2. **Creditor Protection under Limited Liability.** Creditors of a natural person have the right to sue for recovery on default of the debtor up to the whole amount of the actionable estate of the debtor. Corporate business would have been impossible if the members of debtor companies had been made liable to the same extent for corporate debts. Hence the limited liability principle. The right to incorporate with limited liability is a grant of the state. In lieu of the right to sue members of a corporation to the extent of their personal estates, corporate creditors were to be informed of the assets and liabilities of corporations from time to time. If fairly informed, creditors could judge for themselves the debt-dependence of debtor corporations; and, in the light of their debts and assets, extend or restrict the credit given to debtors accordingly. The only effective indicator of a debtor-corporation's capacity to meet its debts is a statement of those debts and the money amounts or money equivalents of its assets from time to time.

#3. **Creditor Protection: Long and Short Run.** A debtor is insolvent if unable to meet his debts as they fall due. Debts falling due in the near future are of more immediate concern to a debtor than those of distant maturity. The usual test of short-run solvency is the current ratio (current assets to current liabilities). It has long been recognized, in accounting textbooks and in the publications of the stock exchange information services, as such a test. But it is useless as a test unless **all** current asset amounts are amounts indicative of debt-paying capacity, i.e., are money amounts or money equivalents. It may not seem that the money amounts and money equivalents of assets at any date have a bearing on the capacity to meet debts of distant maturity. But the date of maturity is indicative of the term of a debt only when a debtor meets and continues to meet all the terms of the loan agreement. In default of any one of them, the creditor may sue to enforce the terms, and long-term debts may become due forthwith. Current ratios and debt to equity ratios, when based on the current money equivalents of assets, are signals of current debt-cover (degree of creditor protection) and of still available borrowing power (financial flexibility). No other asset valuation basis provides signals related to the maintenance of solvency.

#4 **Creditor Protection: Secured Debt.** Bonds, notes and debentures are commonly issued on the security of charges over specific assets or of floating charges over all the assets of the borrower. The borrower may have substantial freedom to deal with his assets; but because assets may vary and because their values (as security) may vary, borrowers undertake to limit their aggregate borrowings to some stipulated fraction or multiple of shareholders' equity. This debt to equity ratio expresses the creditor's risk-limit. But it is serviceable as a constraint on borrowers only if assets are valued at their money amounts or money equivalents.

Some hold that the debt to equity ratio is inadequate for the planning of debt repayment and as assurance to creditors. A cash budget is the appropriate device, they say. But, first, a cash budget is a statement of expectations; it does not serve as feedback in the manner of a statement of recently dated debt-paying capacity. Second, the calculated ability to meet debts (expressed in a budget) depends not only on expected inflows and outflows, but also on what is accessible at the beginning of the period - and that is given only by the money equivalents of net assets at the beginning. Third, repayment schedules and the related cash budgets by which borrowers assure lenders are available only to **few** creditors, usually large and secured creditors. Yet the disclosure laws were written for the protection of **all** creditors. It follows that only the generally accessible financial statements of firms can serve all creditors equally, fairly, without prejudice or privilege; and that those are the statements in which, for serviceable indicators of solvency, debt-dependence, and borrowing potential, assets should be represented by money amounts or money equivalents.

#5. **Fair Disclosure.** The statutes and regulations governing the publication of financial statements by companies make reference to the giving of "a true and fair view" (in some jurisdictions) and to "full and fair disclosure" (in other jurisdictions) of the states of affairs (or financial positions) and profits or losses from time to time. The publication or disclosure in question is publication to parties external to the firm. External parties may include investors, creditors, prospective investors and creditors and all parties whose interests may lie in the profits and financial viability of companies. The interests of all these parties are different and potentially in conflict. It follows that whatever one class of party gives to or receives from a company influences what others must contribute to or can expect to receive from it. Those parties cannot knowledgeably pursue their several interests (through negotiations with the company or by market actions affecting the company) unless the information on those interests is **fair to each** of them; "fair" in the sense that each is informed in such a way that its disposition to act in its own interest is not prejudiced. If that condition is satisfied in respect to each of the parties related to the company, the resulting information will be **fair to all**. Now, insofar as each class of party has an interest in the money inflows and outflows of a company, only an accounting based on dated money inflows and outflows and up-to-date balances of money amounts and money equivalents will satisfy the sense of the statutes: will enable each party to know and appraise his payoffs from association with the company, and to appraise the company's capacity to meet any pressure for varied payoffs by his own or any other class of party.

#6. **Financial Position or State of Affairs.** Though freely used of what a balance sheet is held to represent, these terms are not defined in statutes or in the general technical literature. By inference from common experience and common practice, a financial position is the financial relationship between an entity (company, person, etc.) and the rest of the world at a specified date. The relationship arises from the entity's rights of possession of specific assets as against the rest of the world and the rights of the entity and others in the general wealth represented by those specific assets. It is a dated relationship, the consequence up to a dated **present** of **past** actions and events, and the capacity at that dated **present** to proceed to a **future**. If it were not possible to change the course of events from time to time there would be no point in discovering a present position. Since financial position **is** required to be discovered from time to time, its discovery must be presumed to be intended for information on (or analysis of) the past with the object of choosing a future. Since the choice of a future depends on present assets and present debts (or their difference, wealth) and since future actions depend on available spending or debt-paying power, amounts representing the present assets in any statement of financial position must be money amounts or money equivalents.

#7. **Financial Position in Early Corporate Practice.** What was intended by the terms of contracts and statutes may become obscure with the passage of time, through misuse, misinterpretation, misunderstanding or deliberate evasion. There has been little evidence of what was intended by "a true and correct view of the state of affairs" of a company when those words were finding their way into the U.K. companies law. But we have some. Before "incorporation by registration" became generally available, companies were formed by charter or under deed. The deed of settlement of the Carlisle City and District Banking Company (1838) required its directors twice yearly to

> "make out and declare a full, true and explicit statement and balance sheet, exhibiting the debts and credits . . . the profits . . . and the losses . . . and the amount and nature of the Capital and Property . . . which shall be estimated, not at the cost, but at the then selling price thereof . . . and all other matters and things requisite for fully truly and explicitly manifesting the state of affairs of the said Company . . ." (Ma and Morris, 1980/1982, 52).

Similar terms and associations of terms occurred in the deeds and articles of other banking companies of the mid-nineteenth century. Since legal specifications, in statutes or contracts, are often based on prior experience in similar or related settings, it seems likely that the same words will be found in the charter documents of non-banking companies. The explicit proscription of cost and prescription of selling price seem to suggest that, although cost prices may have been used in balance sheets by some firms (such as those not having significant financial relationships with other persons), the state of affairs of a company could only properly be represented if assets were shown at selling prices.

#8 **Financial Position as Generally Understood.** As the previous section suggested, words and phrases may acquire different meanings as time passes. It is of interest, therefore, to inquire whether the present notion of a financial position is similar to or different from that of the early years of corporate legislation. A recent Australian survey (Chambers, 1980) was made of persons having some association with business and financial affairs - a sample of 1,126 persons, about 65 per cent of whom were qualified accountants. They were asked, in effect, which method of valuing non-money assets would give the best indication of their "financial positions" - what the assets would fetch if sold, what the assets cost, or what it would cost to replace the assets. Of the total sample 83 per cent said "what the assets would fetch if sold"; and 82 per cent of the accounting class of the sample gave that response. In response to a quantified question on "wealth" (in the absence of debt), 93 per cent of the whole sample chose an asset resale price quantification; and 92 per cent of the accounting class gave that response. The professional training and experience of the accounting respondents may have predisposed them to give a cost-related answer. The fact that a large majority gave resale price answers suggests a strong undercurrent of dissociation of cost-based figures from the common understanding of financial position and wealth among people associated with business and professional affairs.

#9. **Financial Affairs and the Interpretation of Statutes.** The terms "state of affairs", "financial position", "results", "profits or losses", "a true and fair view", "full and fair disclosure", are terms used in, or associated with the purport of, statutes. Interpretations given to any of those terms should therefore be consistent with the rules governing and guiding the interpretation of statutes. The general rules are: (a) the plain and natural meanings of words used are to be adopted unless such a meaning is contrary to the interpretation of the statute, is contrary to other parts of the statute, or leads to patent absurdity; and (b) where words or phrases may have both an ordinary and popular meaning and a technical meaning, they are to be interpreted in their ordinary sense, unless from the context it is clear that they should be interpreted according to the usage of a special trade or profession. Now, there has never been an explicit technical interpretation of any of the terms mentioned above in the statutes or by any of the professional accounting bodies. It cannot therefore be held, under (b), that those terms have a technical meaning that is specific to accountants or to any class of persons associated with the financial affairs of business. And it follows from (a) that the cited terms must be given their plain and natural meanings. It is legitimate therefore to interpret financial position as a capacity to buy goods and pay debts; to uphold the valuation of assets at resale prices because of the relationship of those prices to that capacity; and to regard the commonsense argument of #6 and the discovered understandings of #8 as consistent with the relevant statutes.

#10. **Financial Statements as Aggregative Statements.** The notions "state of affairs", "financial position", "results", "profits and losses" are aggregative notions. The officers of companies may be expected to manage corporate affairs with attention to all details, to all particular components of those aggregates. But the top managements of companies and all external parties (a) are unlikely to be knowledgeable about and able to appraise details, and (b) are concerned principally with the performance, progress and status of a company **as a whole.** That is why the disclosure laws and regulations refer to aggregative notions. If aggregative notions are to be represented by sub-classes of particulars, it follows that all particulars shall be significantly similar in kind or quality at the time for which the aggregative representation is made. For otherwise the aggregation of particulars would be mathematically improper and practically misleading. This entails (i) that only amounts representing what is the case on or about a given date may be included in dated representations of position (historical cost figures are thus invalid; current resale prices are figures that may be valid); (ii) that only amounts representing what occurred within a period may be included in an account of the results of a period (figures that depend on strings of prior events or subsequent events - as in depreciation accounting, and price-level adjusted accounting - are invalid; the differences between discovered prices during a period or between the beginning and the end of a period are figures that may be valid); and (iii) that amounts which represent the accessible wealth of a company at any date cannot include both the money amounts or money equivalents of assets at that date and the purchase prices (past, present or future) of any goods in the company's possession. All balance sheets in which asset values are shown at cost or amounts based on cost are invalid for these reasons, since no financial or commercial significance may be assigned to the sum of an amount of cash in hand and the amount paid in the past for a present asset. Current resale prices on the other hand may be added to current cash balances, and their sum may properly be related, as in a statement of financial position, to debts outstanding.

#11. **Wealth in Economics.** The general literature and practice of accounting refer only seldom to the wealth of a person, a company or any other entity. "Assets" and "resources" are terms commonly used for goods and money and claims; the residual interest of the entity in its stock of those things - what would be called the wealth of the entity - is commonly described as "owners' equity". Yet a number of accountants have alluded to wealth and changes in wealth in descriptions of the functions of balance sheets and income statements (e.g., Sanders, Hatfield & Moore, 1938, 11; MacNeal, 1939, 271-2; Sands, 1963, 4; Arthur Andersen & Co., 1972, 13). What "wealth" signifies may reasonably be sought in the works of those who have analyzed the production and distribution of wealth. The definitions and descriptions of economists have remained substantially similar over at least two centuries. Wealth has been held to subsist in exchangeable goods; the amount of a man's wealth is the amount of purchasing power commanded at a given time by virtue of the money and other goods in his possession; the amount of a man's wealth is the value in exchange of the objects he possesses, the product of the number of articles possessed and the price each article "would or should fetch" (Smith, 1776/1937, 26-7; Cournot, 1838/1960, 6; Mill, 1848/1926, 3,7,9; Fawcett, 1863/1883, 7; Sidgwick, 1883/1887, 68; Keynes, 1890/1930, 95; Marshall, 1890/1910, 56; Fisher, 1906/1965, 12-13; Hobson, 1911/1919, 9). The capital of a firm has been described as "the sum of the money equivalent of all assets minus the sum of the money equivalent of all liabilities, as dedicated at a definite date to the conduct of a definite business unit" (von Mises, 1949, 262). And "the firm's fortune" as the money it has **plus** the market value of material objects and legal rights it possesses, **plus** the debts owed to it **less** those it owes to others (Shackle, 1970, 28). Discussing the valuation of a series of assets for balance sheet purposes, Morgenstern (1950/1965, 76) referred exclusively to realizable values. Clearly, expert opinion in a related discipline strongly supports the use of resale prices - values in exchange - in representations of wealth and of changes in wealth.

#12. **Asset Valuation - Value in Exchange Endorsed.** Though "cost" is held to be the generally accepted basis of valuation, asset selling prices have been advanced by accountants as a general valuation rule at least as far back as the early eighteenth century. Stephens (1735, 2,17) wrote of the "worth" of a thing to its possessor, meaning that "people will give so much for it"; and of being "the richer" (i.e. of having made a profit) when goods in a man's possession become able to "purchase more money" than was laid out on their purchase at an earlier date. Hayes (1741) wrote of merchants valuing their goods "at the market price they then go at" when they wish to make a general balance of their books. Dicksee (1909, 192) spoke of the selling prices of assets as going concern values. And more recently: "The value of an asset to an enterprise must be regarded as an estimate of its present exchange power . . . Financial status as expressed by the balance sheet must be regarded as the present value of the exchange capacity of the various items" (Rorem, 1928, 282). "To value any asset whatever means to indicate the amount of money current in the particular country, which, at that moment, and under those existent conditions, it is possible to obtain in exchange for the thing valued". (Bottini, 1929, 645).

#13. **Asset Valuation - Market Selling Price Permitted.** Much greater than the supporters of the use of market selling price as a general valuation base is the number who prescribe or permit the use of selling prices for some classes of assets, or in certain specified circumstances. The prescription and use of market selling prices for primary products (precious metals, livestock, and other produce) are widespread (e.g., Montgomery, 1949, 191). In respect of these things it is said that they have reached the point at which the profit or loss in respect of them can be ascertained and can be realized, for there are ready markets in them. But any supporter of the use of cost prices "in principle" would, it seems, have to adduce a stronger argument than "ease of discovery" of resale prices to warrant the rejection of the cost principle. Others would permit the use of selling prices for such things as packing-house products, on the ground that it is impossible to find the costs of the inputs to the variety of such products which a head of livestock may yield (A.I.A. Committee, 1932, 81). But that would justify the use of selling prices for all products yielded jointly by any set of material, labor and machine service inputs - all manufactured goods! The most general case of permissible departure from the cost basis is the "lower of cost and market" rule for inventory. It is permitted almost universally. Now, if there were firm practical and logical reasons for the use of cost prices for assets in balance sheets, we would expect "cost" to be displaced only if stronger reasons for the use of market could be adduced. But since no such strong reasons are given, the reasons for the use of cost must themselves be slight. It seems that, since cash, receivables and payables are generally shown at amounts which are values in exchange, and since the use of values in exchange **may** be extended to other assets, the cost dictum should long ago have been regarded as the exception rather than the rule!

#14. **Asset Revaluation.** Notwithstanding "avowed allegiance" to the cost dictum, the practice of revaluing assets, upwards and downwards is not uncommon. Revaluations of assets other than current assets are occasional for any specific firm or company; but their number, across the total of companies is substantial. Revaluations upwards and downwards were permitted in the U.S. prior to the era of the S.E.C. Companies may revalue assets, up or down, in most countries that have followed the pattern of U.K. Company law and practice, and in many jurisdictions that have followed the practices of other European countries (Price Waterhouse International, 1973, 225). Revaluation has been permitted or encouraged by government in a number of countries where the money costs of assets had ceased to have any relation to their then prices; in European, Asian and American countries that have experienced marked inflation. All price variation and inflation accounting proposals are in effect proposals for revaluation and departures from the cost dictum. As mentioned elsewhere, recourse to revaluation entails rejection of the cost dictum; and, given the allegiance to that dictum, powerful pressure may be necessary to force its rejection. That pressure is in the force of circumstance; the practical necessity of providing up-to-date information on asset values to justify higher borrowing; the urge to provide up-to-date information on asset values to counter raiders and takeover bidders; and the necessity of providing higher dividends (in inflationary conditions) to sustain real income. Companies which revalued assets and made bonus share issues (stock dividends) from the proceeds had, in effect, a practical method of coping with price changes and inflation long before the "new deal" in accounting. And although revaluations have not always been to market resale prices at revaluation dates, their rationale (in the borrowing and takeover situations mentioned above) is the same as the rationale of resale price valuation. Some details on Australian and U.K. revaluations are given in Chambers, 1973.

#15. **Independent Comment, Criticism and Litigation.** The professional, financial and general news media have provided numerous examples of comment and criticism when what has been represented in published and audited balance sheets and income statements turns out to have been grossly astray. The evidence may not emerge until it is revealed by bankruptcy or litigation, but there have been many cases in which financial journalists and analysts have been able to unearth pertinent information that was not generally accessible to shareholders and creditors. In almost all cases criticism has turned on the gap between reported values and "market values" where market value appears usually to mean resale or realizable value. And, of course bankruptcy and other litigation have frequently been associated with the reporting of asset values significantly in excess of market values. Many examples are given in Chambers, 1973. In the study of accounting practices, comments on them, and related financial events over some 30 years, I can recall no spontaneous demand by financial journalists, commercial historians, or bankers, analysts and similar persons, for replacement prices or price-indexed original costs of assets to be reported. This is consistent with the findings of the survey mentioned in #8 above; however, the kinds and sources of the evidence are different and they support independent lines of argument.

#16. **Asset Composition.** Different kinds of assets are subject to different kinds of risk, and engender different kinds of expectations. The deployment of the total funds of a company will be conditioned by these risks and expectations and variations in them from time to time. But no satisfactory assessment of the riskiness of a given deployment or of alternative deployments is possible unless the assessor (internal or external) is informed of the amounts presently deployed in assets of different kinds, and unless those amounts are in fact amounts that may be redeployed (i.e., money equivalents). No such assessment can be made if the amounts of assets are derived by cost-based calculations; and internal and external users in any such case would be misled if assessment were attempted, for the potential deviation of recorded amounts from discoverable amounts is not the same for all classes of asset.

#17. **Income Determination.** Business income is in the nature of income from property or from the investment of capital. Its derivation is described by some as a matching of costs with revenues. The definition of income is, under that view, dependent on the definitions of cost and revenue. An alternative view is that income is an increment in equity, or the fruit of the employment of a capital; definition then turns on the definition of "equity" (or capital) and "increment". As noted in #11, some treat income explicitly as an increment; but even in the ordinary course of double-entry accounting the amount shown as income is an increment in the amount shown as net wealth or owners' equity. An important question is whether income is a genuine increment of some kind or a difference by definition. Established practices include the recording of all inflows and outflows of cash and changes in receivables and payables, and the adjustment of the net effects of these to take account of differences between recorded balances and discovered balances. The same process, of adjustment on independent discovery, is not applied to the money amounts or dated prices of other assets - an inconsistency in traditional practice. Under continuously contemporary accounting the "adjustment on discovery" rule is applied uniformly to all assets and liabilities. A rule followed inconsistently in traditional practice is followed consistently under CoCoA; and because the amounts of assets and liabilities at opening and closing dates of a period are discovered amounts, income is a genuine increment, not a fictitious or "book" increment.

#18. **Income in Cognate Disciplines.** If income is regarded as an increment in wealth, all of the economists cited in #11 as defining wealth with reference to values in exchange may be held to support the use of values in exchange (market selling prices) for the calculation of income. There are other more explicit examples. Haig (1921/1959, 59) gave as the economist's definition of income "the money value of the net accretion in one's economic power between two points of time". Simons (1938, 49-51) defined personal income of a period as the algebraic sum of the market value of rights exercised in consumption and the change in the market value of the store of property rights during the period. Similarly Hicks (1939/1953, 178-9) defined income as comsumption plus capital accumulation in a period, both determined by reference to market prices. Such definitions as these are consistent with the notion of income as a realistic increment mentioned in #17. Substantially similar ideas recur in one of the few judicial dicta that relate to income as such, a judgement in the English 1911 case of The Spanish Prospecting Co. Ltd.:

"Profits implies a comparison between the state of a business at two specific dates . . . The fundamental meaning is the amount of gain made by the business during the year . . . by a comparison of the assets . . . at the two dates . . . For practical purposes these assets . . . must be valued and not merely enumerated . . . [for] the values in exchange of these assets may have altered greatly . . . To render the ascertainment of the profits of a business of practical use it is evident that the assets, of whatever nature they may be, must be represented by their money value".

The judge described this as the "well-defined legal meaning" of profits and said that it coincided "with the fundamental conception of profits in general parlance". The opinions here cited are all consistent with the use of money equivalents of assets to determine changes in wealth (amounts of income) from time to time. Of course, where a firm has assets **and** debt the change in wealth would be the change in the amount of net assets (total assets less debt) - see the references to von Mises and Shackle in #11.

#19. **The Realization/Accrual Dilemma.** The difference between cash laid out and cash received on the completion (the realization of the whole of the assets) of a venture is accepted as the income from a short-run venture. (It may be called a realized income, though strictly it is the income arising on realization of the assets). But realization is not a workable basis of itself, for income calculation where ventures, assets and debts may have long lives, and where short-run adaptation of investments, tactics and arrangements to meet the circumstances of a firm depend on knowledge of its performance and position from time to time. In those circumstances, the realization rule is applied to transactions having consequences wholly **within** the period of account, and the accrual principle is applied to transactions and events having consequences which straddle balancing dates. If the accrual and realization principles are to be similar in effect, or consistent, the rule for determining the closing values of assets must be analogous to the rule for determining the financial outcome of consummated transactions - e.g., for unsold goods the price they would fetch if sold; for sold goods the price at which they were sold. On this construction (the construction of continuously contemporary accounting) there is no dilemma.

The dilemma arises under cost-based accounting. Cost-based accounting entails the **non-accrual** of price changes, but the **accrual** of depreciation charges, and of closing inventory balances, both "unrealized". The result of the calculation is described as "realized" income, which it is not; and the method of calculation is held to be the preferred method, and realization the preferred "test" of the emergence of income, contentions which cannot be sustained. Forms of cost-based accounting are thus confronted with seemingly conflicting principles, from which dilemma they escape only by ad hoc and inconsistent application of both principles. The use under CoCoA of the same principle for consummated and unconsummated transactions and events gives it a consistency not characteristic of other styles of accounting.

#20. **Capital Maintenance.** The reference in #17 to income as an increment in wealth entails that income is considered to run only beyond the point where the opening capital has been maintained. There must therefore be some quantitative element in common in opening capital, closing capital and income. Only if they represent dated amounts of general purchasing power will they have such an element in common. The use of "capital maintenance" as a measurement rule (the increment in an original stock) is to be distinguished from "capital maintenance" as a rule or policy of prudent consumption. Only the former is pertinent in accounting for the past up to a dated present. In that setting it is clear that capital maintenance can have reference only to an opening stock of general purchasing power in any period. For, all capital paid in, or dedicated to the conduct of a business, is in the first place money or dated general purchasing power; all profits "ploughed back" are in the first place money or dated general purchasing power; and all capital subsequently raised from stockholders is in the first place money or dated general purchasing power. A company may deploy its capital in varied ways at any time and in different ways from time to time. The calculation of income by reference to the maintenance of capital can have no reference to the necessarily varying composition of assets of a firm; it can have reference only to the aggregate quantum, represented from time to time by the market selling prices of assets (#6 ff. above). Only continuously contemporary accounting makes use of such a notion of capital maintenance. Proposals which make use of a notion of "physical capital maintenance" are either mistaken or misrepresented; for there is no financial measure by which the maintenance of a physical capital may be represented, and any scheme by which it is sought to calculate income with reference to physical capital maintenance disregards the deployment of capital in other ways than in physical goods.

#21. **The Real Income Problem.** The difference between discovered amounts of net assets at successive dates is the income of the intervening period when there has been no shift in the general level of prices and the general purchasing power of the money unit. It will include all increments from trading (net revenues) and all accruals or price variation adjustments (#19). But the difference is a nominal difference only (the subtraction is mathematically improper) when the opening and closing amounts of net assets of any period are expressed in dollars of different general purchasing power. The difficulty is readily overcome under continuously contemporary accounting. A capital maintenance adjustment is derived by the multiplication of the opening amount of net assets and the proportionate rise in the interval in a general price index; for every dollar of the amount of net assets will have suffered from the depreciation of the dollar. This adjustment is charged against the sum of net revenues and price variation adjustments (the result is net income) and credited to opening equity (the result is opening equity in terms of closing dollars). Income is thus calculated by reference to the maintenance of opening capital, and it represents a genuine increment in purchasing power expressed in closing dollars. The use of an index representing or indicating shifts in the general purchasing power of the money unit is legitimate, of course, only when the sum to which the index is applied is itself a genuine dated amount of general purchasing power; and that condition is not satisfied where asset values are cost-based. The simple and inclusive adjustment under CoCoA is not available under other modes of accounting. Even Edwards and Bell (1961, 48) acknowledge that real income is calculable under exit price accounting but make no similar claim for the current entry price accounting that they endorse.

#22. **Rate of Return as Performance Indicator.** The achieved rate of return (net income or profit on opening capital) is widely regarded as an index of economic performance of firms. As an indicator of the performance of a firm **as a whole**, the net income figure will necessarily include the effects or consequences of trading, of shifts in asset prices, and of shifts in the general purchasing power of the money unit;

for if the effects of any one of these are omitted, performance may **appear** to be more or less satisfactory than was the case, and reactions to the performance reported may be out of step with what the factual performance demands or permits. The inclusive income amount is to be related to the inclusive amount of opening capital; but the rate will be an invalid rate unless the opening capital is expressed in the equivalent number of dollars of closing general purchasing power, for those are the dollars in which net income is expressed. The amount is derivable by the process described in #21. No other mode of accounting ensures that the numerator and the denominator of the rate of return calculation are dated real amounts expressed in money units of the same significance.

#23. **Alternative Opportunity Comparisons.** There is no absolute test of the adequacy of a rate of return; there are only comparative tests - "this has a better yield (pay off, rate of return) than that". An achieved rate of return should therefore be computed in the same fashion for an investment in a company as for an investment in public bonds, for the rate of return on bonds approximates the yield of a riskless investment, and is the bedrock standard for the appraisal of other rates of return. The market yield of a bond is inclusive of realized (interest) payments and accrued changes in market selling prices (e.g., Dopuch, Birnberg and Demski, 1969/1974, 192): the same rule applies to the yield of a firm as a whole under continuously contemporary accounting. The achieved rate of return should also be computable in the same manner for all firms. Different firms may choose differing profit-seeking tactics, different combinations of trading, speculating and hedging operations. Unless net incomes and capitals employed are calculated by substantially the same rules, and are inclusive of all gains and actual funds employed, rates of return may induce differential reactions to the debts and securities of different firms that are not justified by the facts taken whole. The single valuation rule of CoCoA and the use under that rule of objective (discovered) market prices rather than internal judgements or stipulations makes the rate of return a more discriminating indicator under CoCoA than under alternative systems. And, on the principle that the more efficient opportunity is discovered by comparison of what alternative opportunities yield, the rate of return maybe a more sensitive indicator of opportunities under CoCoA than under other systems. Certainly, under other systems the availability of optional rules, having divergent effects on reported positions and results, interferes with intelligent cross-comparison of the significant financial features of different firms.

#24. **Intertemporal Comparisons.** Internal and external parties have interests in the shifts through time in the financial characteristics of single firms as well as in the comparison of different firms at a specific time. The optimal combination of trading, speculative and hedging operations of a firm may vary from year to year; and its managers may seek periodical profits which from year to year are different combinations of net revenues, price variation adjustments and capital maintenance adjustments. Unless all three are properly accounted for, reactions to intertemporal shifts may be inapt. Of course, intertemporal comparisons may encounter the occurrence of shifts in the general purchasing power of the money unit. But almost all such comparisons are made by way of ratios. If all balance sheet amounts and the net income are expressed in year-end dollars (as they are under CoCoA) all ratios will be mathematically valid and serviceable in the general administration of the financial affairs of a firm. Mixed valuations of assets make the corresponding ratios under other systems invalid and unserviceable.

#25. **Stewardship.** The contention that a function of accounts is to provide an accounting for stewardship has long been held to justify accounting on a cost basis. But that contention could have survived, if at all, only as long as "cost" meant the actual outlay for legitimate purposes of money funds entrusted to the steward (the managers of a firm). When "cost" has come to mean "price-level adjusted historical cost" or "current cost", the connection between stewardship and entrusted funds has been broken. But it was already a pointless connection before that. If the managers of a firm were entrusted with a money sum they were entrusted with general purchasing power. If the outcome of their management was a cost-based financial result and position, the managers would not have been given the approval they deserved when prices were falling. They would have had the use of general purchasing power, while prices were rising, without the knowledge of those to whom they were accountable. And if, with the passage of time, the managers were replaced, credit or blame may have been assigned to successors which should have been assigned to their precursors. No such inequitable assignments of praise or blame would be made under continuously contemporary accounting; for increments and decrements in the general purchasing power accessible to managers from time to time would be clearly represented in the financial statements. Further the amounts of those increments and decrements would be determined by market prices, independently of the judgements of those whose stewardship is supposed to be under scrutiny, an independence which (it might be said) is necessary to a fair judgement of performance or stewardship.

#26. **Integral Policy Selection.** Internal and external parties alike are concerned with the solvency, leverage, rate of return and asset composition of companies. It would seem therefore that any system of accounting that is to be serviceable in exploring ways of maintaining or improving any of these facets of financial affairs must enable managers to explore systematically the available possibilities. This is only possible if all magnitudes are relatable to one another in any temporally specific situation. The major concerns in management are solvency and the rate of return. Consider only the latter. The equation -

$$\text{Return on capital} = \frac{\text{Net income}}{\text{Sales}} \times \frac{\text{Sales}}{\text{Total assets}} \times \frac{\text{Total assets}}{\text{Net assets}} = \frac{\text{Net income}}{\text{Net assets}}$$

links rate of return to profit on sales and total asset turnover and leverage. But if the rate of return is to say anything about the increment in real wealth, all the components of the three contributory ratios must represent money prices or money equivalents. This is one example of a class of devices by which the prospective consequences of sets of specific actions (volumes, turnovers, prices etc.) may be explored. Since definite increments in money or money quantified wealth are sought, all calculations and all budgets which describe the operations that are expected to yield those increments should be consistent with all accounts after the event. They are consistent only under CoCoA.

#27. **Intelligibility.** The disclosure laws clearly entail that what is disclosed shall be intelligible - otherwise it would be "unfair". To be intelligible, a statement must convey to a reader something that corresponds with his experience or his training and that is not contrary to his commonsense. On one or more of these grounds a number of accounting rules or principles fail. There is no such thing as "lower of cost and market" in commercial experience; there is no such thing as "sum of the years digits depreciation" in commercial experience; there is no such thing as a "deferred debit" or "deferred credit" in ordinary commercial experience. There is no circumstance for which a merchant would want to know the sum of an amount of cash presently on hand and the sum paid in the past for any other asset on hand. There is no situation in which a merchant could or would think of adding the net present value of an asset or project to a present amount of cash to discover whether he could pay his debts or to discover his present wealth. There is no situation in which any person or corporation manager would want to know the profit he made up to December 31, 1980, expressed in "average-1980 dollars". By contrast with the ordinary conduct of commercial affairs, most of the things mentioned are absurdities - occurring nowhere else in human experience than in accounts. And in the light of the rule against absurdities in the interpretation of statutes (#9), it seems unlikely that any of these practices could withstand challenge in the courts. The principles and rules of continuously contemporary accounting have recourse to or entail no such oddities. The fact that a large majority of the respondents to the survey mentioned in #8 associated financial position with resale prices of goods in possession suggests that those are the amounts they expect to find in balance sheets; and that balance sheets in which those amounts occur would be intelligible.

28. **Unique Functions of Temporally Distinctive Statements.**
Traditionally the financial statements of companies have been historical. Periodical accounting makes the statements histories of temporal segments, and the sum of the histories of temporal segments is the history of a firm. But there is no ground for holding that what was part of the history of one segment continues to be the history or part of the history of succeeding segments. In the theories of personal action, economic action, administrative action and biological action, action is treated as goal-directed or protective response to a present, in the light of the past from time to time. There are thus statements about the past that serve as feedback for the appraisal of past performance and as guidance in the choice of future actions. There are statements about the present, representing the consequences of the past and the basis on which performance in the succeeding segment will be judged. There are statements about the future - expectations and preferences and volitions.

There are three temporally distinct kinds of statement, **all** inputs to choosing or decision-making, and **all** having distinctive functions - respectively as account of past performance, as indication of what may presently be necessary and what is presently feasible, and as statement of what is possible or desirable or desired. It follows that no one of these kinds of statement can be a stand-in, substitute or surrogate for another; and that no statement purporting to be of one kind can properly include elements of another kind. With reference to financial statements - no statement of the past may properly be influenced by or contain elements that are related to expected futures; no statement of the present may properly contain elements that are strictly of the past or strictly of the future. These inferences from the analysis of the choosing process are violated by traditional and newer styles of cost-based accounting - historical, current or replacement cost systems; and the uneasy mixture of temporal settings seems to be the cause of the multiplicity and diversity of rules in practice under those systems. The burden of proof that financial statements containing mixtures of past, present and future amounts are serviceable, or that an account of the past is unnecessary for those who must make present decisions about the future, or that an account of the past may be made into a guide to the future, rests on those who so contend. By contrast, it is claimed for continuously contemporary accounting only that, in principle, it provides a full account of the past, and a full and authentic statement about the present. If any statement about the future is to be prepared for internal or external use, it is necessarily a statement additional to and different from either of the normal financial statements.

#29. **General Misunderstanding of Functional Differentiation.** The argument of #28 may seem to be analytical, purely abstract. Its conclusions are adverse to all accounting practices and proposals that use mixed rules or whose rules yield temporally mixed aggregates or differences. They are adverse to proposals that advance or condone the use of mixed valuations - amounts of present general purchasing power together with past costs, or unamortized past costs, or current replacement costs, or net (discounted) present values. The general case for the use of mixed valuations is that "different valuation bases are preferable for different assets and liabilities" (A.I.C.P.A. Study Group Report, 1973, 41). But preferable to whom? All parties having financial interests in a company will be concerned with its solvency, leverage and profitability, and no proof has been adduced to the effect that indicators of these features are improved by the use of different valuations for different components of the indicators. The study alluded to in #8 sought to discover whether respondents did in fact distinguish between differently dated types of information. In excess of 90 per cent of respondents would not associate the cost of an asset, or the depreciated cost of an asset with dated spending power or wealth. Over 60 per cent of respondents would not associate replacement prices with spending power, and over 80 per cent would not associate replacement prices with wealth or financial position. Over 85 per cent of respondents considered dated wealth and financial position to be independent of expectations. The majority responses in all these cases are consistent with the sharp identification of transactions and events with specific dates and periods that is characteristic of continuously contemporary accounting.

#30. **General Versatility.** The utility and serviceability of an accounting system are exemplified by the variety of commercial and financial conditions and problems with which it can readily cope. That variety includes growth and contraction, inflation and deflation, firms large and small, firms domestic and transnational, firms established and developmental, firms differentially organized and financed. It is notable that the specifications for styles of price-level adjusted historical cost accounting and current cost accounting contain very little by way of extension into varied settings. This "backwardness" or delay may be excused by proponents of those systems, for the recourse to multi-varietal accounting (main accounts plus supplementaries) may be said to leave the "hard cases" in no worse a position than they always were. But the excuse is also a cover for the complexities and difficulties of dealing, under those schemes, with foreign investment and foreign subsidiary accounting; with mining and other developmental ventures; with utilities which depend heavily on debt-finance; with group accounts and so on. Those difficulties may yet prove to be the rock on which indexed-cost and current cost styles of accounting will founder; for even in the "ordinary case" specification of rules and interpretation of their products has proved very difficult. Meanwhile solutions have already been developed for a variety of these more complex problems under continuously contemporary accounting.

----oOo----

Thirty reasons for CoCoA? It matters not what the number is; there are certainly other heads of argument. The principal point is that the rules and method and results of CoCoA satisfy simultaneously a variety of stipulations - general understanding and commonsense; expert opinion in the field of accounting itself and in related fields; technical simplicity and versatility; consistency with commercial contracts and exigencies; temporal pertinence; simultaneous serviceability for a variety of purposes; simultaneous serviceability to a variety of information users; and so on; and that in respect of no other style of accounting has consistency with those stipulations and conditions been demonstrated.

To be concerned with accounting standards is to be concerned with nothing less than the rationalization and standardization of a metrology. In other fields that step has been the precursor of significant advances in knowledge and technology. Men have done much with crude tools, crude instruments and crude measures. But they have never known how much progress lay before them until superior scales, instruments and controls became available to them. The tools now available in aid of financial administration are still crude tools, poorly articulated, never deliberately designed to deal effectively with any other matter than cash flows. But, as it seems to me, there is a vastly greater opportunity for the identification of varieties of financial and administrative malaise, and for their treatment, than has yet been imagined or explored. And it seems possible that financial accountability, business efficiency and the deployment of resources generally could be kept under more orderly and more exacting scrutiny than hitherto. It all depends on how soon a comprehensive, versatile, realistic, up-to-date and continuously up-to-date accounting comes to be adopted.

Given all the groups from which arguments in support of CoCoA can be drawn and have been drawn - why then does it remain ignored?

References

Note: Where two dates of publication are given, the first is usually the date of original publication, the second is the date of the edition, reprint or reproduction to which the page references relate.

A.I.A. Committee, Report of the Special Committee on Cooperation with Stock Exchanges of the American Institute of Accountants, 1932; reproduced in May. G.O., **Financial Accounting**, New York, 1943.

A.I.C.P.A. Study Group Report. **Objectives of Financial Statements**, New York, 1973.

Arthur Anderson & Co., **Objectives of Financial Statements for Business Enterprises**, 1972.

Bottini, P., "Financial Statements", **The Accountant**, 23 November 1929.

Chambers, R.J., **Securities and Obscurities**, Melbourne, 1973; republished as **Accounting in Disarray**, Garland Publishing Inc., New York, 1982.

Chambers, R.J., **The Design of Accounting Standards**, Monograph No 1, University of Sydney Accounting Research Centre, 1980.

Cournot, A., **Mathematical Principles of the Theory of Wealth**, New York, 1838/1960.

Dicksee, L.R., **Auditing**, London, 1909.

Dopuch, N., J.B. Birnberg and J. Demski, **Cost Accounting**, New York, 1969/1974.

Edwards, E.O. and P.W. Bell, **The Theory and Measurement of Business Income**, Berkeley, 1961.

Fawcett, H., **Manual of Political Economy**, London, 1863/1883.

Fisher, I., **The Nature of Capital and Income**, New York, 1906/1965.

Haig, R.M., "The Concept of Income - Economic and Legal Aspects", from R.M. Haig (ed.), **The Federal Income Tax**, New York, 1921, reproduced in R.B. Musgrave and C.S. Shoup, **Readings in the Economics of Taxation**, London, 1959.

Hayes, R., **The Gentleman's Complete Book-keeper**, London 1741.

Hicks, J.R., **Value and Capital**, Oxford, 1939/1953

Hobson, J.G., **The Science of Wealth**, London, 1911/1919.

Keynes, J.N., **The Scope and Method of Political Economy**, London, 1890/1930.

Ma, R. and R.D. Morris, "Disclosure and Bonding Practices of British and Australian Banks in the Nineteenth Century", 1980; subsequently published as monograph No.4, University of Sydney Accounting Research Centre,1982.

Marshall, A., **Principles of Economics**, London, 1890/1910.

Mill, J.S., **Principles of Political Economy**, London, 1848/1926.

von Mises, L., **Human Action**, London, 1949.

Montgomery, R.H. and others, **Montgomery's Auditing**, New York, 1949.

Morgenstern, O., **On the Accuracy of Economic Observations**, Princeton, 1950/1965.

Price Waterhouse International, **Accounting Principles and Reporting Practices**, 1973.

Rorem, C.R., **Accounting Method**, Chicago, 1928.

Sanders, T.H., H.R. Hatfield and W. Moore, **A Statement of Accounting Principles**, New York, 1938/1959.

Sands, J.E., **Wealth, Income and Intangibles**, Toronto, 1963.

Shackle, G.L.S., **Expectation, Enterprise and Profit**, London, 1970.

Sidgwick, H., **Principles of Political Economy**, London, 1883/1887.

Simons, H.C., **Personal Income Taxation**, Chicago, 1938.

Smith, A., **The Wealth of Nations**, London 1776/1937.

Stephens, H., **Italian Book-keeping**, London, 1735.

Financial Statements, Asset Valuation And The Neutrality Principle*

Professor Onida's interest in the development of accounting theory in non-European countries is attested by his surveys of work done, principally in North America, over the past several decades. The editors of the present volume invited me to deal with asset valuation principles with particular reference to the balance sheet and with the notion of the "neutrality" of information. I am pleased to have an opportunity in this way to pay tribute to one who has given close and careful attention to these matters, and whose critical observations have sought to bring to light things that were previously in the shadows.

The Legacy of the Past

When a manufacturer sets out to produce a serviceable product he has in mind the function which the product must serve. The sub-assemblies and parts which make up the product must be designed so that the end-product will do what it is expected to do. The end-product of accounting, likewise, must be specified if the components are to be designed to yield the service expected of it. We shall for the moment consider the end-product of the accounting process to be a balance sheet and a related profit or income statement. Later in this paper we shall consider some other information provided or calculations made by

---

* The text of this paper corresponds approximately with the pagination of the source.

132

accountants; but for the present we will concentrate on the design and production of periodical financial statements.

There have been many attempts to define or describe accounting - usually in terms of the provision of information that is serviceable in financial decision-making. But very little attention has been given to the specification of the ways in which the products of accounting enter into the decision-making process. If a balance sheet is to serve its users in some specific way, it should be capable of demonstration that its components are indeed serviceable. If a balance sheet is to represent the financial position of a company at a stated date, financial position must be defined; and once it is defined, the elements of any particular balance sheet must be consistent with that definition. Similarly, if an income account is to represent the net result of conducting the company's business, income must be defined; and the components of the income calculation must be such that the calculation yields an income amount consistent with the definition of income.

The twentieth century history of accounting thought is remarkable for its failure to proceed in this fashion. The American Institute of Accountants Special Committee on the Development of Accounting Principles, created in 1933 and renamed the Committee on Accounting Procedure in 1936, did not in its 26-year life specify what meaning should be given, or was intended by it to be given, to "financial position" and "profit" or "income". Neither did the Accounting Principles Board (which replaced the Committee on Accounting Procedure in 1959), nor the Financial Accounting Standards Board (which replaced the Accounting Principles Board in 1973). The Committee of the Institute of Chartered Accountants in England and Wales which was set up in 1942 and became responsible for the Institute's "Recommendations on Accounting Principles", published no definitions of the two terms. These committees and boards have published a vast amount on particular elements of accounts. But, in the absence of definitions of the key ideas in periodical accounting, in the absence of a specified framework with which the elements must be consistent, it is not surprising that they have had to cover the same ground - with varying recommendations from time to time – every decade or so, and still without resolution of many problems.

The academic literature has been equally lacking in definition and the discipline which definition imposes. It is well-known that, in the formulation of scientific theories, the definition of basic terms is essential. Definition is equally necessary in practical affairs; as, for example, in the framing of statutes. It is necessary because every proposition which makes use of any given term can then be interpreted, more or less exactly, by reference to the meaning of the term. The same applies to the discussion of accounting. If we do not know, and state explicitly, what financial position is, we cannot say whether one item or another constitutes part of it, or whether one magnitude or another (of any item) gives a better or poorer approximation to financial position. All of this should be well-known to accounting scholars; it is difficult indeed to understand why it is ignored.

The terms "profit" (or income) and "financial position" have been in widespread use for decades. Financial position has been used with reference to the aggregate contents of balance sheets in the United States for over fifty years, and is currently used with the same reference in the statutes of many jurisdictions following the United Kingdom pattern. It should be obvious to all accountants that, whatever else they may be, profit and financial position are aggregative in nature. Profit is the aggregate incremental consequence of the operations and events of a period. It is calculated by the processes of addition and subtraction. Financial position is a position of a company as a whole. The amounts of assets of the company and the equities of external parties in the aggregate amount of assets are obtained by addition; and the balance sheet is obviously aggregative.

Now, if aggregates are to be informative, their components must be capable of addition; and their sum must have some definite meaning in the context in which the aggregates are to be used. This is an elementary, logical and practical rule. It will be obvious that the sum of the height (in centimetres) and the weight (in kilograms) of any person can have no logical or practical meaning. Nor has the sum of the height and the waist-measurement of a man have any such meaning, even though both are measured in centimetres. But the elementary rule stated above is entirely overlooked if assets and equities are treated individually, each being valued on its own special basis.

At present, the recommendations, principles and standards of professional bodies around the world permit the inclusion in balance sheets of amounts which are quite different in kind and significance - amounts of cash (current purchasing power); inventories, sometimes at cost (an out-of-date price) and sometimes at market price (the equivalent of current purchasing power); plant at cost (an out-of-date price) less depreciation (an estimate based on expectations about the future); security investments at cost (an out-of-date price); and so on. Most textbooks and most of the theoretical discussion of accounting tolerate the same practices. The fallacy of adding such different amounts, each of quite different significance, was pointed out by Canning some fifty years ago[1].

The aggregation rule has significance in a further direction. We have pointed out that the amount of profit is an aggregate of the financial consequences of operations and events over a period. But when the commercial significance of the money unit changes over a period, the aggregation of the nominal amounts of the items of revenue and expense through the whole of the period is an improper aggregation. The fallacy of treating as identical all money amounts expressed in units of the same name when the economic significance of the money unit changes, has been pointed out repeatedly in the literature, both before and since Sweeney's work on the matter[2]. But there is yet no firm professional standard which deals systematically with the problem; and most of the periodical and textbook literature still deals only in a patchy way with the logic of aggregation.

In all other disciplines in which aggregate magnitudes are of importance the rules for proper aggregation are respected. If it is held that those rules do not apply in the construction of accounts, the burden of proof must be on

---
1. John B. Canning, **The Economics of Accountancy,** Ronald Press, 1929, pp. 319-20.
2. Henry W. Sweeney, **Stabilized Accounting,** Harper & Brothers, 1936.

those who make that claim. The proof lies in showing that a mixed aggregate has a definite and proper place in the deliberate calculations of users of financial information. It is not sufficient to assert that investors and others **do** in fact use the mixed aggregates that appear in balance sheets and income statements; for it is reasonable to suppose that users of financial statements **believe** that amounts which are in fact aggregated in those statements can properly be aggregated. It would be quite unreasonable of users to suppose that expert accountants would add amounts which have no common meaning.

No proof of the utility of mixed aggregates has been, or can be, advanced. One of the uses made of balance sheet information is to derive indications of solvency. The current ratio, the ratio of current assets to current liabilities, is commonly used as an indicator of short-run solvency. The extent to which current assets exceed current liabilities is significant as an indicator of solvency only if current assets are represented by amounts of money accessible at a given date (in cash, or from debtors, or by the sale of inventories). No indication of the money available or accessible to meet current liabilities can be obtained if the inventory component of current assets is shown at cost; for the cost price of a good does not represent the amount of cash accessible to its owner for any purpose, including the payment of debts. The same objection may be raised to the calculation of a debt to equity ratio, in which the aggregate amount of the equity is the difference between the amount of total assets (a mixed aggregate of current, out-of-date and calculated amounts) and the amount of liabilities (a sum of money owed). The same objection may be raised to the calculation of a rate of return, in which the profit (however calculated) is related to the mixed aggregate equity obtained by subtracting the amount of liabilities from the mixed aggregate of total assets mentioned in the previous sentence.

Financial Position

It may be supposed that, as so little has been said in the literature about financial position, knowledge of it has nothing to do with decision-making.

This view may have arisen from the treatment of output decisions in the economic theory of the firm. In expositions of that theory there is seldom any discussion of the resources available to the firm; the quantum of resources is either taken as a given amount or is supposed implicitly to be capable of being augmented without serious restraint. But in the world of commerce it is not the case that resources are of fixed amount or that their amount may readily be increased by any firm. The suppliers of funds are investors (through new investment and by profit retention) and creditors. The decisions of these parties are influenced by the solvencies, the debt burdens and the rates of profit of companies. Any indication of improvement or deterioration in the solvency or profits of a company may cause them to change their evaluations of the company's prospects, and hence to change their financial commitments to its affairs. For the same reasons, managers and financial analysts and advisers are interested in the same matters. Those indications cannot be provided otherwise than by periodical statements of financial position and profit.

It is said by some that financial position at a point of time is immaterial when the affairs of a company are continually changing by reason of its transactions and the impact on it of external influences. This too is mistaken. The changes that take place in the financial affairs of companies are often unplanned and often unwanted. Managers must take steps to counteract undesirable changes, or to take advantage of desirable changes. But what is meant by "change"? Change is a shift from one position to another; the two positions must be known if anyone is to judge whether the intervening events have improved or impaired the position.

It is said by some that the capacity of a company to pay its debts and buy its necessary services is not indicated by a balance sheet, but by a statement of its expected cash flows. This also is mistaken. Financial capacity to meet debts and other obligations through any period depends on the available cash and accessible cash at the beginning of the period as well as the cash flows during the period. If the financial capacity of a company to meet its debts at the beginning of a period is limited, the steps it takes during the period must be steps to improve that capacity.

The Neutrality Principle

It should be apparent that knowledge of financial position from time to time has much to do with the decisions made in the course of business. But what is financial position?

At any time a company is in a variety of "positions". It has a market position – it has so many orders on its order book, and so much inventory on hand or on order to meet the demands of customers. It has a technical or "engineering" position – it has a plant and machines and vehicles with certain physical capacities, each item of a certain age, and all of them arranged in a certain way. It has a staffing or personnel position – so many employees of specific skills engaged on specific tasks.

Ideally each of these "positions" would be consistent with one another, for inconsistencies entail sub-optimal employment of the total resources of a company. In fact, due to factor indivisibilities, all aspects of operations are seldom consistent. However, if a change in any aspect of a company's operations is to be considered, the present position of that aspect must be ascertained. The present position represents a capacity for doing certain things. Obviously it would be confusing and misleading to include in a statement of the **present** technical position some items of used plant stated at their **original** condition and capacity, some at their **present** capacity and some at a capacity based on an assumed programme of **future** maintenance.

Similarly, every company has a financial position from time to time. It has so much money on hand and claims to money; it has other assets which are convertible to money at their resale prices; it has liabilities to creditors, and there is a residual interest in the amount of the assets which is described as the shareholders equity. Just as the statement of a staffing or personnel position relates exclusively to numbers and kinds of employees, a statement of financial position relates exclusively to the financial aspects of a company. A statement of financial position represents the financial relationship of a company with the rest of the world; for its assets represent the wealth it commands by reason of their ownership, and its equities (liabilities and ownership) represent interests of other parties in the amount of the assets. Such a statement also represents the financial capacity of the company to meet its debts, pay its wages, purchase its supplies, extend or vary its investment in assets, borrow on the security of its assets and to do other things requiring money.

The physical characteristics of assets - the floor area of buildings, the ages of machines, the potential outputs of machines - have no necessary relation to financial position or financial capacity. Companies which have had enormous physical capacities by virtue of their possession of assets have become bankrupt. Likewise, the characteristics of employees and officers of a company have nothing to do with financial position. Any supposition that a balance sheet can be made to represent the whole of the features of a business is mistaken. And it is likely to lead to the misrepresentation of the very thing - financial capacity - on which the survival of business firms depends.

Further, just as we have said that technical capacity at a given date cannot be represented by a mixture of out-of-date, current and expectational statements, so also financial position cannot be represented by a mixture of past costs, current money amounts and expectations of future cash recoveries. For the avoidance of financial strain (and of bankruptcy) and for the planning of all future actions which entail the payment and receipt of money, knowledge of financial position from time to time is indispensable. And, as we have said above, knowledge of the current ratio, debt to equity ratio and rate of return of a company, and of changes in those ratios, is necessary to investors and creditors for the protection of their interests.

A balance sheet in which assets are stated at their current cash or money equivalents is the only kind of statement which represents a dated financial position. It is the only kind of statement which represents the aggregate financial consequences of the transactions of a company and of external events up to the date it bears. And it is the only kind of statement yielding ratios which may be proper tests of the propriety of future actions.

Some have argued that such a balance sheet is serviceable only for companies which are approaching or are at the point of liquidation - at which point, of course, the cash equivalents of assets are obviously relevant. This is not the case. Cash equivalents are relevant at the point of liquidation because claims against the company must be met by money payments. But the cash equivalents of assets are equally relevant **whenever** a change in the deployment of funds is under consideration, whether on the initiative of the management or under the pressure of other parties; for redeployment also entails money payments. However, it has been said, no company plans or intends to redeploy the whole of its funds at any time. Certainly. But, first, the achieved rate of return is one of the signals which prompt decisions to redeploy funds; and a genuine rate of return cannot be calculated without relating income to investment, both expressed in money or money equivalent terms. And, second, in choosing between alternative redeployments, the money equivalents of **any** combination of assets may be required.

The Neutrality of Balance Sheet Information

This is a convenient point for the introduction of the idea of the neutrality of balance sheet information. Money, being general purchasing power, is neutral with respect to all actions. That is one of its primary virtues; we can do with it what we choose. But the amount of money we have does limit our choices. We cannot reasonably plan to spend more than we have. However, there are still many ways of spending the money we have; and the future is where we will spend it.

The same applies to any asset convertible into money. **The asset itself is not neutral** with respect to future actions; it can only do specific things - transport goods, make screws, yield an income by way of interest, for example. **But the cash equivalent of the asset is neutral.** It can be taken into account in consideration of any future course of action for which money is required. A balance sheet in which assets are represented by their cash equivalents is exactly the same kind of balance sheet as a company would have when it initially raised its capital. At that time the whole of the assets is cash; at any later time the amounts of the assets would be cash and the cash equivalents of non-cash assets.

The point would not matter if original decisions about the use of cash were the very best possible decisions, and remained the best. But decisions on the use of money in business are made in the expectation of future events which may not occur or continue to occur in the way expected. The annual reports of companies and the financial press carry numerous accounts of the changes in products, processes and asset-holdings which changes in demand or changes in technology make necessary. Specific assets, even assets described as fixed assets, whole divisions, and whole subsidiaries are sold from time to time. There is no company which is free of the necessity of adapting itself to changes in its commercial environment, or to changes in its capacity to meet its ordinary operating outlays out of cash balances and cash inflows. Whether or not a company is able thus to adapt itself depends on the cash it can command, directly, or by the sale of non-cash assets. Financial position as we have defined it not only represents financial capacity; it also represents general capacity for adaptation.

The general capacity for adaptation has a direct bearing also on the prospects of investors and creditors. Investors and creditors have no special interest in the products or productive processes of companies which they finance. They expect to receive money by way of dividends and interest and repayments. They will put their money into companies from which money receipts can be expected, regardless of the specific processes and assets of those companies. They may know nothing about the specific effects of changes in demand and changes in technology on the operations of a company; but they may reasonably be supposed to know that any company must adapt itself to its circumstances, that the need to adapt may arise at any time, and that adaptation depends on the funds available to the company. Only a balance sheet which represents the funds available and accessible to a company at a given time will be indicative of the capacity of a company, by adaptation, to continue as a going concern through probable, but presently unpredictable, changes in its circumstances.

Income

In view of the emphasis that has been given to income or profit determination in the literature, it is of interest to explore the matter from that direction also. Like "financial position", "income" has been left undefined in the greater part of the accounting literature. Much ingenuity has been spent on distinguishing different kinds of income or gain - realized income, unrealized gains, operating income, money income, real income and so on. But these distinctions are not helpful unless the general term "income" is defined at the outset.

Some help may be obtained from the literature of economics. In accounting directed to the derivation of an account of the consequences of past transactions, we are concerned with computing income after the event, **ex post**. Hicks has given a definition of income **ex post**; it "equals the value of the individual's consumption **plus** the increment in the money value of his prospect which has accrued during the week; it equals consumption **plus** capital accumulation"[3]. If, says Hicks, we confine our attention to income from property (which is the kind of income we are concerned with when dealing with business firms), the above notion of income "is almost completely objective. The capital value of the individual's property at the beginning of the week is an assessable figure; so is the capital value of his property at the end of the week; thus, if we can assume that we can measure his consumption, his income **ex post** can be directly calculated". In the case of a business firm, the amount analogous to "consumption" is the amount paid out as dividends. It follows that the amount of income derived by the specification of Hicks is not "almost", but completely objective.

Meade and Stone have given a similar definition: "a man's money income in any period is equal to the money value of his consumption plus the increase in the money value of his capital assets. For the sum of these two is the amount which he could have spent on consumption **while maintaining the money value of**

---
3. John R. Hicks, **Value and Capital**, Oxford University Press, Second Edition, 1946, p. 179.

his capital stock intact"[4]. Similarly, Simons describes personal income as connoting "the exercise of control over the use of society's scarce resources". Its calculation "implies estimate . . . of the value of rights which [a man] might have exercised in consumption without altering the value of his store of rights. In other words, it implies estimate of consumption and accumulation"[5]. Similarly, Kaldor suggested that "under the postulate of perfect foresight", income **ex ante** is identical with income **ex post**, and "both can be written K_2-K_1, in other words, the actual appreciation in capital [or assets], as measured by market values"[6].

None of these notions of income is similar to the general cost-based method of calculation used in traditional accounting. The "money value of capital assets", "the value of a store of rights", and "the actual appreciation in capital" are all amounts which are determinable by observation at the beginning and end of a period, not simply by calculation based on traditional inventory valuation and depreciation rules. The point was made in a judgement of an English Court in 1911 where it was said that "profits" implies a "comparison between the state of a business at two specific dates", assets being stated at their "money values", or "market values" or "values in exchange"[7].

It should be clear that all of the views cited are consistent with the representation of a financial position by reference to the dated money equivalents of assets. They are all consistent with inclusion in the calculation of income of the amount of the rises or falls in the money equivalents of assets up to the date of a balance sheet. And some of the authors cited (Hicks and Kaldor, for example) make specific reference to the

---

4. J.E. Meade and J.R.N. Stone, "The Construction of Tables of National Income, Expenditure, Savings and Investment", **Economic Journal**, 1941, p. 219.
5. H.C. Simons, **Personal Income Taxation**, University of Chicago Press, 1938, pp. 49-50.
6. N. Kaldor, **An Expenditure Tax**, Allen and Unwin, 1955, p.63.
7. Fletcher Moulton L.J. in **Re Spanish Prospecting Co. Ltd.** (1911) 1 Ch. 92.

exclusion of "fictitious" gains, such as the extent to which the nominal amount of gains is offset by changes in the general level of prices (or in the general purchasing power of the money unit).

There has been much discussion of the meaning of "maintaining a capital". There are some who hold that provision for maintaining the physical capital of a firm must be made before a profit or income may be said to arise. The traditional process of accounting purports to be based on the maintenance of a nominal amount of capital. None of these ideas is consistent with the views of the economists cited above. The debates to which they have given rise will not be resolved as long as they are dependent on personal views of the propriety of one or other of the different notions of maintaining a capital.

But, as with financial position, so with income; a notion which yields an amount which is neutral as to the disposition of income is desirable. For income may be used to pay dividends, to repay debts, to extend or vary the investment of a firm in non-monetary assets, to pay taxes and so on; and how income may or shall be used should not be presumed when calculating its amount.

An Income Measurement Theorem

The threads of the argument may be drawn together by a formal demonstration[8].

Let U_1 and U_2 represent money units of the general purchasing power of the unit (lira, dollar, etc.) at dates t_1 and t_2, the opening and closing dates of a period;

Let $U_1 M_1$ and $U_2 M_2$ be the amounts of the net monetary assets (i.e. monetary assets less liabilities) at the two dates;

Let $U_1 N_1$ and $U_2 N_2$ be the sum of the money equivalents or net resale prices (values in exchange) of the non-monetary assets at the two dates;

---

8. The notation here used is a development of a less comprehensive exposition first published in 1961 and used in Chambers, **Accounting, Evaluation and Economic Behavior,** 1966.

Let U_1R_1 and U_2R_2 be the amounts of the net assets (which are equal to the amounts of the owners' equity) at the two dates;

Now, at t_1,

$$U_1M_1 + U_1N_1 = U_1R_1 \qquad [1]$$

and at t_2,

$$U_2M_2 + U_2N_2 = U_2R_2 \qquad [2]$$

Suppose the general purchasing power of the money unit falls, concurrently with a rise in the general level of prices by the proportion p.

Then, in terms of general purchasing power

$$U_1 = U_2(1 + p) \qquad [3]$$

At t_2, the only money units in circulation, the only money units that are therefore interpretable, and the only money units available for paying dividends and for other purposes are units U_2. Since income, Y, is the increment in the owners' equity (or net assets),

$$U_2Y_2 = U_2R_2 - U_1R_1 \qquad [4]$$

Substituting the value of U_1 from [3],

$$U_2Y_2 = U_2R_2 - U_2(1 + p)R_1 \qquad [5]$$

The expression now is wholly in terms of U_2. But we need a mode of expressing U_2Y_2 which indicates what shall be brought into the accounts by way of accounting for transactions. In respect of all non-monetary assets (inventories and other assets) **sold** during the period, let I represent the sum of the nominal differences between their selling prices and their actual purchase prices (or their recorded money equivalents at t_1, for non-monetary assets in possession at that date).

Let T represent the nominal amount of the aggregate net proceeds of all transactions (buying and selling) in non-monetary assets during the period.

The Neutrality Principle

Let E represent the aggregate nominal amount of all payments in the nature of expenses during the period (i.e. all payments which do not give rise to vendible non-monetary assets).

Let V represent the sum of the differences between the book values (before adjustment) of non-monetary assets at t_2 and their discovered money equivalents at that date; V thus includes depreciation (fall in price) of some assets and rises and falls in the money equivalents of other assets.

Then, in nominal amounts,

$$M_2 = M_1 + T - E$$

and

$$N_2 = N_1 + I + V - T$$

Since $M_1 + N_1 = R_1$; since $M_2 + N_2 = R_2$; and since the amounts of M^2 and N^2 are the amounts just previously indicated, make appropriate substitutions in expression [5]:

$$U_2Y_2 = U_2[(M_1+T-E)+(N_1+I+V-T)-U_2(1+p)(M_1+N_1)]$$
$$= U_2[(I-E)+V-p(M_1+N_1)] \qquad [6]$$

The absolute nominal increment in net assets in the period is $(I - E + V)$; but the component amounts are aggregates of money units of "mixed" general purchasing power. To obtain a valid increment in U_2, it is necessary to reduce the nominal increment by a nominal amount sufficient to increase R_1 to an equivalent number of units U_2 at R_2. The term $[- p(M_1 + N_1)]$ of expression [6], which is equal to $[- U_2pR_1]$ in expression [5], is that adjustment; it is charged against the nominal increment and corresponding credits are made proportionately to the opening balance of undivided profits and to other owners' equity balances. This adjustment may be called a capital maintenance adjustment since its object is to maintain in terms of general purchasing power the opening balance of owners' equity or net assets.

The term $(I - E)$ is the nominal amount of **realized gains** (or **net revenues**). Its amount results from the accumulation in the accounts of the opening balances and the amounts of transactions. The amount V may be described as a price variation adjustment; it represents **unrealized gains** or losses. It is similar to the usual adjustments made to accounts at the end of each period. It will be clear, therefore, that the accounting process is substantially similar to current practice - with the two exceptions (1) periodical valuation of assets at their dated money equivalents and (2) the "inflation" or capital maintenance adjustment.

The system thus described is complete, for it takes account of the only three possible causes of changes in the fortunes of companies - transactions, changes in asset prices, and changes in the general purchasing power of the money unit. Its elements are completely and systematically interlocked. All the "raw data" are, or are based directly on, experienced transactions or observed prices; they are therefore factual or objective. They are thus capable of independent verification by creditors, without recourse to calculations made for purely internal purposes. The balance sheet at any date represents the financial position of a company at that date in contemporary terms, which is the natural basis for making any judgement of the past and any estimation of the future. For those reasons the system is described as continuously contemporary accounting.

The above theorem yields accounts which are neutral with respect to all future actions and relevant to all calculations about the future. But at no point in the demonstration is any assumption made about future actions. And at no point is any assumption made about specific expectations of the management of the firm. It is this freedom from expectational elements and the concentration on a complete and factual record of the past which secures the neutrality of the resulting statements.

Decision-Making Calculations

As we have said earlier, there are other forms of financial calculation than those yielding balance sheets at stated dates and incomes earned up to those dates. We consider now some of those calculations.

The Neutrality Principle

A man may say: "I have so much money now, **and** I expect to do certain things with it which I expect to yield me so much money in the future". There are two propositions here. The first is a statement of position; the second is a statement of an expectation based on that position and certain other assumptions made about the future. If he did not know how much money he had at the time, he could not determine the "certain things" which are expected to yield "so much money in the future". The same man could **not** properly say: "I have so much money now **on the supposition** that certain things will happen in the future". That is a singular and hypothetical proposition. And it is absurd, since what a man has **now** is not contingent on what may happen in the future. This absurdity, of course, arises in conventional accounting wherever assets are valued or depreciation is provided on the basis of **expected** service life. It does not arise in an accounting where assets are valued at their money equivalents from time to time; for the amount of the money equivalent is accessible to a person or a company for any purpose in the same way as an amount of money in his possession is accessible.

How, then, are decisions made regarding the "certain things" which a man or a company may do in the future?

Suppose that at 31 December 19x5 a company had a net working capital (current assets less current liabilities) of U10,000; that it had three durable assets, A, B and C of which the net resale prices were U20,000, U30,000 and U40,000 respectively; and that in the year ended on that date the profit or income was U5,000.

Suppose that, in the light of current interest rates and the profits of other companies, the management of the company considered its profit to be inadequate, and that no greater profit could be obtained from the use of its existing assets. Suppose that, on investigation, two courses of action O(D) and O(E) are open to it; and that O(D) requires the sale of A and the purchase of D, another asset, for U20,000, and O(E) requires the sale of A and C and the purchase of E, another asset for U60,000. Suppose that no additional working capital is required; and that the profits from the proposed courses of action are, for O(D), using assets B, C and D, an expected profit of U6,000 per annum,

148

and for O(E), using assets B and E, an expected profit of U7,000 per annum. Clearly, the company should sell A and C and buy E.

The components of the calculations which yield this conclusion are:

(i) the money equivalents or net selling prices of the present assets
(ii) the purchase prices of the new assets, and
(iii) the expected net incomes from using (A + B + C), (B + C + D) and (B + E), all of which are mutually exclusive operations.

Notice that the **net selling prices** of existing assets are used in the calculations relating to **both** O(D) and O(E). In the same manner, the net selling prices of all assets or any sub-set of all assets enter into **every** calculation relating to a change in asset composition. Notice that the **purchase prices** of new assets enter **only** into the calculations based on the specific assumptions which entail their purchase. Similarly, the calculated income differentials apply **only** to the specific alternatives and the assumptions on which they are based. The same applies however large may be the number of alternative courses of action considered and however varied they may be.

There is thus one class of information which is serviceable in all calculations relating to the choice of one course of action from a number of alternatives. That class, the net selling prices of assets, may be described as neutral with respect to all alternatives. It has also been described as "generally relevant" information[9]. All other information is relevant to some specific course of action. It is "specifically relevant"; but only to the consideration of alternatives, not to the representation of financial position at a stated date. It is certainly not neutral with respect to all possible courses of action.

---

9. See Chambers, **Accounting, Evaluation and Economic Behavior**, pp. 154-6.

The above example has been simplified to the point where the calculation of the net present (discounted) values of the cash proceeds of the alternatives is unnecessary. But if, in the case of O(E), for example, the purchase price of E were U50,000 or U70,000, it would still be necessary to know the net selling prices of A and C in order to include in the present value calculation the proceeds of using the surplus cash or the cost of borrowing the deficiency.

Of course, the choice of one from several alternatives does not rest solely on the net present value calculations. It may rest also on the effects of each alternative on the liquidity of the company from time to time. This can be explored by setting up budgets of the consequences of the alternatives at dates intermediate between the hypothetical purchase and sale dates of the prospective assets. But, for this purpose, too, the money equivalents of assets are pertinent. For, any budgeting calculation, which is designed to indicate potential liquidity strains, must be based on money inflows and outflows and initial money equivalents of assets.

In any case, since profits and rates of profit, liquidity strains and debt burdens are features of the financial results and positions of a company as a whole, and since they are the principal indicators of the kinds of action which a company must take, it would be misleading to use any other basis of asset valuation than the money equivalents of assets in deriving financial statements which provide those indicators.

The above argument effectively dismisses the use of original costs or unamortized balances of the costs of assets in accounts which are intended to be serviceable in decision-making. It also dismisses the use of current costs or replacement costs, since any such cost is specific to an assumed course of action and provides no indication of the aggregate money amount accessible to a company for **any** of its present operations or for **any** variation in its operations.

Finally, we may consider the use of financial statements by managers or outsiders as indicators of results and prospects. In the first place, the rate of interest on relatively risk-free investments is one of the tests of the adequacy of company profits. A rate of interest is the relationship between a money return and a money investment, both amounts of money being expressed in a common denominator, and the money return being inclusive of rises or falls in the market value of the security. A rate of return calculated on the basis of accounts prepared in the manner described has exactly those characteristics; the changes in the market values of assets are included in the calculation of U_2Y_2; and U_2Y_2 may be related to $U_2(1 + p)R_1$ to obtain a valid rate of return.

Furthermore, since judgements of the results and positions of different companies are comparative judgements, their reliability is enhanced by a system which makes use of one rule for asset valuation, and relies on one source of data, the market at any particular time, for the valuations of assets of all companies.

Conclusion

For several generations it has been accepted that the opinions and estimates of accountants and managers should have a significant influence on the contents of financial statements. But experience under such a style of accounting has indicated that it has serious deficiencies. Companies which appeared to be financially strong have been found to be insolvent; others which have reported substantial profits have been found to be far less profitable. The above style of accounting, which I have described as continuously contemporary accounting, is designed to overcome these defects. It rests on the logical principle that only like magnitudes may be added, subtracted and related, and on the observable facts that the prices of assets change and the general purchasing power of the money unit changes. The derivation of a statement of financial position and the amount of profit or income becomes, then, a matter of observation and of direct and logical treatment of the observations. Its results are neutral and demonstrably relevant to the choices and judgements of managers and others, whatever they may choose to do. To be serviceable in that way surely, is what the products of a system of accounting are expected to be.

The Development of the Theory of Continuously Contemporary Accounting*

The method of accounting proposed in this book differs only in some, but important, respects from the traditional mode of accounting. It makes use of initial prices for all inputs. All buying and selling, stock and bond issues, loan repayments and lending, are accounted for in the same way as in traditional accounting. The system differs only in respect of the subsequent valuation of non-monetary assets and the calculation of income. It takes into the accounts the effects of changes in particular asset prices and changes in the general purchasing power of money. The statements that the system yields would give a continuous and complete historical account of the financial affairs of a firm, since at each balancing date the amounts of assets and equities are expressed in up-to-date terms at that date.

The manuscript of the book was completed in late 1964. The early 1960s was a high time for debate about accounting principles, postulates, concepts and theorizing - debate mostly in the abstract. Coming so soon afterwards, the book seems to have been considered by many as just another example of the same abstract theorizing. But its origins were otherwise and its intent was otherwise.

Early indications. In 1943-45, while working in the Australian Prices Commission, I was engaged in the analysis of the financial statements and cost calculations of firms. Prices were controlled by reference to both costs and profits. Ideally the figures supplied by firms should have been derived by the same rules, so that comparisons of firms and industries could be readily made. I had previously worked in two large manufacturing companies and had some idea of the rather crude ways in which cost calculations and asset valuations were made. Now, confronted by the accounts of many firms in many industries, all using their own combinations of accounting rules, the impression of disorder was intensified. The task of administering a public policy, of making

---

* The first version of this essay was prepared in 1971 for a Japanese readership. A second version was prepared for the Scholars Book reprint (1975) of **Accounting, Evaluation and Economic Behavior** (1966). This revised version was prepared in 1981 for the Japanese translation of the book, by Professor Ichiro Shiobara (1984). The object in each case was to link work antecedent and subsequent to the book to its main thesis, and to describe and explain some modifications since made to details of the style of accounting that the book sought to establish.

decisions which would be just and fair alike to companies and consumers of their products, in the face of idiosyncratic accounting, was very much a hit-or-miss affair. I faced the same difficulties on the other side of the fence, as a consultant for a trade association petitioning the Prices Commission, for some years in the late 1940s. This work on comparative analysis was similar to the work of security analysts, though for different purposes. It left a firm impression that the securities market was also hampered by individual differences in the accounting methods of companies.

Management studies. For nine years, from 1945, I was engaged in teaching aspects of management. I taught in all sections of the program, introducing a course in financial management in 1946 and courses in economics, statistics, organization theory and administrative theory from 1949 onwards. All this prevented me from taking too narrow a view of my own specialism. And, when dealing with financial planning and control, I was forced, as in 1943-45, to consider accounting from the user's point of view - both internal and external users. The traditional accounting textbook literature hinted at the use of accounts in financial analysis and budgeting. But it asked no pointed questions about the adequacy of the figures for these purposes. That such questions should be asked, and answered, was strongly suggested by the coexistence of different accounting rules yielding figures of greatly varying quality. How discriminating managers, investors and creditors could use such figures was at least puzzling.

On the management process itself, there was little good work at the time. We regarded Barnard's **The Functions of the Executive** and Simon's **Administrative Behavior** as the best. But they said relatively little about the economic objectives and constraints of managers. A theory of management, it seemed to me, should be based on a few key ideas - economic, legal, psychological and social - from which management rules and procedures might be deduced. The ubiquity of potential conflict suggested that one of the prime tasks of management was to maintain a workable equilibrium between the interests of "participants" in organizations. The ways in which interests were interlocked suggested that business behavior was necessarily adaptive in all respects - technical, economic, financial, social and political. For the viability of firms, Cannon's **The Wisdom of the Body,** and for the processes of management, Wiener's **Cybernetics**, were strongly suggestive. Cybernetics, or steersmanship, is what managing is about. And that depends on continuously up-to-date information. The track led back to accounting.

Early work in accounting. In 1947 I had published **Financial Management**, an attempt to link the financing of business with internal financial administration, and to link both with accounting. An occasion for greater concentration arose in 1949 when I was invited to give three lectures in Australian universities under the general title "Accounting and Financial Policy". The first of these [3]* argued that accounting rules and processes cannot properly be accepted unless their products aid directly the financial administration of business. Accounting is fact-finding; there could be no place in accounting for conservatism. The second lecture [5] dealt with the interest of external parties in financial information. It criticized traditional notions of the accounting entity, stewardship and the going concern. Contrary to widely expressed views, I held that the balance sheet and the income account were of equal importance to outsiders, and that the balance sheet should be equally serviceable for analysis of the past and consideration of the future.

The third lecture [11] dealt with the relation of accounting information to financial policy. The post-war inflation had for some years concerned businessmen. Under conventional accounting rules, reported profits were high. So were taxes and the prices of industrial goods. But the purchasing power of money was falling, and widespread fears were expressed about the erosion of capital and the maintenance of industrial capacity, with particular reference to the severity of taxes. Such complaints are an accepted part of the process of trying to influence governmental action and public opinion. But the defects of accounting gave businessmen cause for complaint, in my opinion. I had been collecting expressions of the views of company directors and examples of the devices they had adopted to cope with inflationary conditions - from Australia, the United Kingdom and the United States. I cited them in support of the conclusion that accounting information must be relevant to decision making and that "contemporary values, costs or prices are the relevant magnitudes".

---

* References at end of this essay.

These lectures and others of the same period [4, 6, 7] were the beginnings of much of what I have done since. In 1953 I had been appointed in the University of Sydney and was free to concentrate on accounting.

Accounting as communication. The notion of financial statements as messages to many interdependent parties, treated at some length in 1952 [5] was further developed at book length in 1955 [10], based on a study of the reports of 150 Australian, U.K. and U.S.A. companies. Many of the observed deviations in practice from avowed principle could have little justification otherwise than as yielding better messages; but the conflict of practice with principle seemed to justify the description of the state of accounting in Orwell's terms, "doublethink" and "doubletalk" [15]. Even when addressing colleagues and students – through articles and textbooks – accountants failed to convey clear messages [20, 24]. It was not surprising, therefore, that whereas the laws relating to accounts expected the truth to be reported, practice did not yield true and significant statements [13, 16, 19]. Of course, faulty communication and difficulties in communication are almost universal. I benefited and took some comfort later from Odgen and Richards' **The Meaning of Meaning**, Cherry's **On Human Communication**, Morris' **Foundations of the Theory of Signs** and other works on language and linguistics. My interest was not merely academic. I was concerned with the concrete or practical setting of accounting. I wished to know the conditions of effective communication, the information which was pertinent to recipients of messages, and the number and variety of the causes of failure of financial statements to inform users [22, 25, 26].

Observation of practice and of its consequences. The textbooks and much of the periodical literature of the fifties gave the impression that most writers were too fond of prescribing to spend time or energy in observing what was going on about them. The literature was dogmatic. Many of the things being done in practice were either disregarded or dismissed as improper. Some of the literature purported to be theoretical. But it was short on analysis, loose in argument and ambivalent in conclusion. I proceeded with two kinds of work in parallel; observing accounting practices and their consequences, and trying to put into some coherent order the general ideas which were held to constitute the theory of accounting.

The history of science and scientific ideas and the biographies of scientists of every type have long been of interest to me. They demonstrate that, although new ideas spring from the imagination, they are prompted by observables and are subsequently confirmed or rejected by reference to observables. It is impossible to experiment with the accounting of on-going firms in such a way that one or another method of accounting can be shown to be superior. But it is possible by observation to reach some conclusions about what is inferior or unserviceable. A study of inventory valuation methods in 1949 suggested the hazards of inter-company comparisons [2]. A later study of a larger sample, with some international comparisons, indicated the persistence of variety, and the difficulties of serious analysis [22]. An examination of asset revaluations and stock dividends of Australian companies over a ten-year period cast considerable doubt on the validity of some widely held accounting ideas [15]. A study of the general reporting practices of 150 companies in three countries has been mentioned above [10]. The inadequacies of the information available to investors was suggested by an examination of the antecedents of some mergers and defences against takeovers [15, 22], and by reference to litigation and reports of official investigations into company failures [13, 26]. I also drew on the histories of companies and on journalistic accounts of the activities of promoters, brokers and financiers of the recent and more distant past. Many of the then current practices are recurrent, and many of the practices of the day were understandable only by reference to events of the past.

One of the alternatives to experimentation is the observation of international differences. In all modern industrial countries, accounting serves substantially the same functions. As the study of other technologies has no national boundaries - basic physics, chemistry, engineering, mathematics, medicine and so on, are international - there was no good reason why there should be "national varieties" of accounting. But there were such differences. They must, it seemed, have arisen from particular local events, or the particular local development of laws and institutions, and were not necessary parts of a generally serviceable style of accounting. Beside the doctrines, laws and practices of Australia, the United Kingdom and the United States - which I could study intensively - I made more modest examination of some of the theory, laws and practices of a number of European countries. I found analogous but not identical reactions to the stress of inflation, and taxation, both where their effects were mild and where they were severe. And I found similar but not identical looseness in practice notwithstanding that the guiding principles were generally acceptable in themselves.

Much of what these local and international inquiries yielded was unusual; the whole corpus of practices was not explicable in terms of any consistent set of rules. Much also was anomalous, not to be expected in the light of the doctrines or principles avowed among accountants. But, so many of the variants and anomalies could be considered as responses to the same defects in conventional practice, that some general remedy seemed to be necessary and possible.

Accounting concepts. Concurrently with these explorations and inquiries, I was concerned with what purported to be accounting theory. Textbooks and articles are the common source of teaching material. But I found them very difficult to use. So often important ideas were undefined. Categorical statements were made without apparent reason. Links between the propositions of what was called accounting theory and the prescribed rules of the textbooks were obscure or missing altogether. There had been critics before. Paton (1922) had suggested the flimsiness of some of the "postulates" of accounting as it then was. Canning (1929) and Gilman (1939) had pointed out in graphic passages the inadequacy and inconsistency of some of the key ideas of traditional doctrine and practice. Sweeney (1936) had given critical attention to elementary but pervasive flaws in the basic arithmetic of conventional accounting. But, to judge from the textbook literature, a generation of teachers and researchers had eliminated none of the defects.

In a number of the articles already referred to, I dealt critically with all the main general ideas - the accounting entity, the accounting period, the going concern, stewardship, conservatism, consistency, the constant money-value assumption. Two summary articles in the early sixties [20, 24] were prompted by the fact that, although for about 15 years I had indicated faults in the conventional expositions of those ideas, they were still treated in the text books in the same inadequate way.

Criticism as such was not my object. I thought it should be

possible to teach accounting in a logical and principled way, each idea being clear itself and clearly linked to other ideas, and the whole giving a coherent prescription for practice. I formulated new connotations for some of the customary terms - new notions of the accounting entity, stewardship, the going concern, consistency. At an early stage I thought I was merely improving them singly, giving them some specific connection with business affairs. But if many such separate changes are made, the whole set of ideas becomes a different whole. New ideas, new terms must be introduced and explained; old terms which were undefined must be defined; and what survived of the old and what was new must be consistent and coherent, if teaching was to be by reason rather than by rote. I thought the reasoning should be explicit, in the nature of the theorems of geometry, for instance; and I developed theorems on periodical accounting [12] and neutrality [21] after that style.

Theory construction. By 1954 I believed it necessary, at least for myself, to set down the way in which a theory of accounting should be developed. In none of the important works on accounting was there a treatment of methodology. There was no pattern to follow except that of the well-developed sciences. And writers on accounting were following no pattern. My principal formal guides were Cohen and Nagel's **An Introduction to Logic and Scientific Method**, Larrabee's **Reliable Knowledge** and Robbins' **The Nature and Significance of Economic Science**. If the exercise was foolhardy and the result trifling, perhaps I would soon be told. I wrote "Blueprint for a Theory of Accounting" [8] in 1955 and two other pieces [9, 12] shortly afterwards in response to some criticism. I returned to the matter in the early sixties [17, 21] because no material change had occurred in the way in which accountants dealt with the construction and validation of their ideas.

The "Blueprint" paper was not simply a paper on method. It set out four substantive propositions which seemed to be necessary premises of an accounting theory. They were (i) organizations depend on the participation of many parties, (ii) organizations are managed rationally with the object of meeting the demands of those parties, (iii) financial statements facilitate rational management, (iv) accounting, the deriving of relevant financial information, is a service function. These ideas emerged from my work in the teaching of management. They seemed to some to have little to do with accounting. But they were the basis of all of my later work. They were developed and augmented in class notes and lectures over the next five years by ideas drawn from economics and other social sciences. Weber's **The Theory of Social and Economic Organization** and von Mises' **Human Action** were helpful - and interesting, since among other things, they both had some penetrating observations on monetary calculation and accounting.

In 1954, too, I developed a short accounting course for students of economics. Many students of economics would not undertake accounting courses. But they would encounter discussions of wealth, income, capital, profits, costs and benefits. They should know how these were calculated. The course dealt with accounting for households, small firms, large and complex firms, banks and other financial institutions, non-commercial institutions, governments, international dealings and national aggregate accounts. In each case the kinds of decision to be made were indicated. These decisions determined the kind of information which accounting should produce. The material developed for this purpose was published in book form in 1957 [14]. That it might be possible to construct a general theory of accounting emerged from this exercise. The relative scarcity of money and goods, the necessity of choosing, and the necessity of information for knowledgeable choice, are universals. Investors, managers, creditors, analysts, governmental regulators, all needed to know the past and present financial facts relating to domestic and commercial affairs. The differences between them were differences in detail, not differences in principle.

Visiting Britain, Europe and the United States in 1959 I hoped to encounter others who were working in a similar direction. The hope was disappointed. But I had for years talked and written enough about what accounting and accounting theory should be. It was time to attempt a comprehensive essay. The result was "Towards a General Theory of Accounting" [18, (1961)].

Towards a general theory. The paper dealt with accounting (1) under perfectly static conditions and (2) when changes occur in prices and in the general purchasing power of money between balance dates. The historical cost method was deemed to be satisfactory under perfectly static conditions. But if prices changed, non-monetary assets should be valued at balance date at replacement prices, in principle; if replacement prices were not available, they could be approximated by using an index of changes in the general level of prices. The amount of the net adjustment in asset values would be credited or charged to a residual equity adjustment account. It is not in the nature of income and its amount would not be available for dividends.

A substantial part of the paper was devoted to building up a set of foundations, assumptions or postulates. This seemed necessary if a firm case were to be made for any set of accounting principles or rules. The lack of it seemed to be the cause of the chaotic state of traditional accounting. Much of this part of the paper developed into the earlier chapters of **Accounting, Evaluation and Economic Behavior**. The "General Theory" paper also introduced the device of a highly simplified, transactionless, firm to work out the effects of changes in the level of prices. This simplification, an exercise in "comparative statics", was similar to those commonly used in scientific work and problem solving. I also rejected the old balance sheet notation, Assets = Liabilities + Proprietorship, for a notation which distinguished monetary and nonmonetary assets. The adoption of these two devices - since used by many others - was an important step in my work; they enabled me to experiment (on paper) with a wide variety of combinations of the variables. But the conclusions of the paper on a method of accounting I subsequently found to be far from satisfactory - in respects presently to be mentioned.

Measurement in accounting. The quantification of net income or profit is one of the tasks of accounting. From about the mid-thirties it was widely considered to be the principal task. The balance sheet, though described as a statement of financial position, was regarded as a mere by-product of the income calculation process. The prevalent historical cost doctrine made income calculation dependent on cost amortization (by ambivalent and varied rules) and the balance sheet, in respect of non-monetary assets, a repository of unamortized costs. This seemed quite at odds with the uses made of balance sheet figures; as much attention should be given to devising a realistic balance sheet as to devising a realistic income calculation [5, 11, 13].

The historical cost doctrine was not followed rigorously, in any case. Inventories were valued at the lower of cost and market; market selling prices were used where assets had readily determinable market values; assets were revalued downwards and upwards. The single justification for such deviants from the cost principle seemed to me to be the unrealistic consequences of using initial costs when current market prices came to differ significantly from those costs. There was a second problem. Balance sheet amounts for cash, receivables and payables were always in balance sheet-dated money units; unamortized cost balances could never be, even if the nominal prices of non-monetary assets remained unchanged. I would now describe these two problems as the price variation problem and the inflationary problem respectively. But during the fifties I did not distinguish them so clearly. In 1952 [5] I supported "superimposing on existing accounting technique machinery for taking into account by an index number correction the effects of changes in the purchasing power of money". In 1961 [18] I supported the use of replacement prices in principle, but the use of an index of changes in the general level of prices where replacement prices were not available. The possibility of an integral solution of the price variation and inflationary problems did not occur to me.

For some years in the late fifties I had been urged by Ernest Weinwurm (then of De Paul University) to give attention to measurement aspects of accounting. I delayed, thinking it wise first to be confident of what accounting was about. I turned to the literature of measurement in 1962. Campbell's **Foundations of Science**, Churchman's **Prediction and Optimal Decision**, Hempel's **Fundamentals of Concept Formation in Empirical Science**, Margenau's **The Nature of Physical Reality** and Stevens' paper "On the Theory of Scales of Measurement" were my main guides. This literature related principally to the physical sciences. But the parallels with financial matters were plentiful. The foot (or the meter), the pound (or the gram), the hour, the degree (of angle or temperature) - were neither more nor less "conventional" than the dollar or the pound. Measurements made with reference to these units were combined to yield derived measurements, such as density and velocity; there are analogous measurements in financial matters, such as rate of return and gearing or leverage. All measurements of change entailed observations of initial and terminal states; and if the conditions differed under which the two measurements were taken, adjustments were made of one or both measurements to measurements under a set of "standardized" conditions. On these last two points the practice of accounting differed from physical measurement; terminal states were obtained by calculation, not by observation; and no adjustment was made for the change in the conditions of measuring, changes in the significance of the unit and changes in the relativities of the measures (prices) of particular goods. Failure at these points seemed to be the reason for the variety of "accounting results" possible for the same set of events, and for the irrelevance of the figures to action at the terminal date. What should be done?

(1) The only observable financial magnitude of an asset at a given date is its price, and market prices are one of the key elements of choice. Dated financial positions should therefore be derived from market prices at stated dates. (All invented values, such as L.I.F.O. valuations, calculated depreciation figures, amounts of "deferred" charges and credits, were not measures of anything). (2) But which market prices - buying or selling? As accounts describe the accumulation of money-measurable wealth, market resale prices should be used for nonmonetary assets, for they alone represent the money equivalents of assets at any date. (3) Finally, as the increment in wealth (owners' equity) in a specific period was to be reported as part of the wealth of a firm at the end of the period, the opening amount of net wealth had to be adjusted for the change in the general significance of the monetary unit. The firm is not better off by the amount of this adjustment, since its effect is merely to secure the maintenance of the general purchasing power of the opening net wealth. I sketched the conclusions in "Measurement in Accounting" (1963) a redraft of which was published in 1965 [27].

This exercise cleared the air considerably. Replacement prices were rejected as they could not be regarded as elements of a dated financial position representing a firm's capacity to carry on or vary its mode of operation. The use of market resale prices for assets at balance dates would be merely a consistent application of the well-established accrual principle. The aggregate amount of financial capital (net assets or residual equity) could be adjusted for changes in the general purchasing power of the money unit; all of its components being dated money amounts, it could validly be adjusted for dated changes in a general price index. The resultant income calculation was inclusive of gains or losses from trading, from shifts in asset prices and from changes in the general purchasing power of the money unit.

The search for clear definitions of terms and clear enunciations of principles, in the interest of reduced diversity, and the search for a mathematically valid process of simultaneous calculation of positions and results, had been concurrent over some years. Changes in asset prices and in the general purchasing power of the money unit were regarded as inevitable elements of the environment and experience of firms, not as sporadic and occasional events. The prospect of a logical and practically serviceable accounting, consistent with the setting of financial judgement and choice, and free of ad hoc rules and auxiliary statements, seemed to be realizable.

The book. I commenced writing **Accounting, Evaluation and Economic Behavior** early in 1963 and finished the manuscript in December, 1964. It was published in February, 1966. It is one thing to see a desired end or conclusion; it is another to mount a coherent argument from elementary premises to that conclusion. I have seldom gone back over previous writing when setting out to write a new piece. I have tried to think about a matter before me as if it were new to me, without wondering whether my conclusions were consistent with what I had written before. Previous errors, in premise or argument, might thus be avoided. I have had no compunction about rejecting an idea I once espoused, if there were better argument or evidence for an alternative. In the late forties I had expounded traditional historical cost accounting in the absence of any systematic alternative. But by the early fifties it seemed to have so many flaws that some kind of price-level-adjusted historical cost accounting seemed preferable. By the early sixties the arguments for replacement price accounting seemed convincing, price-level-adjusted historical cost serving as an approximation - until it was discarded, as explained in the previous section. I had in fact spent some years working over, successively, each of the main types of actual and proposed accounting systems, on the way to the system proposed in this book.

It seemed that, in the general context of the book's title, some elements of every system must survive. Historical cost would be the first entry in any asset account; but it would not remain the basis of subsequent accounting for any asset. Replacement (or purchase) prices are necessary information whenever a replacement (or purchase) is under consideration; but only then. Present (discounted) values are necessary when choosing between alternative prospective projects or operations; but only then. It is necessary to use an index of the general level of prices whenever we wish to convert a quantity of money at one date into a quantity having equivalent purchasing power at another date; and that is necessary only for income calculation purposes. Market selling prices of non-monetary assets are necessary for the derivation of any dated statement of financial position. Each class of information thus had its proper place and function, if the whole course of **ex ante** analysis, accounting, and **ex post** judgement were considered.

To organize this account of the background of the book has not been easy. Over the whole period, many kinds of reading, searching and writing interacted - and interacted with educational and commercial experiences, for I was engaged as a consultant from time to time by firms large and small, in a variety of industries and by some governmental authorities. I was concerned persistently with the utility of financial information to those it served; technique had to be subordinate to this. The typical stance of others was just the reverse. Technique came first, the utility of the product being virtually an article of faith, and as such unanalyzed.

The work described was done over many years. This was important. It enabled me to observe many financial and commercial events - inflation and recession, increases and decreases in the severity of taxation, changes in company laws and regulations - and the influence they had on the accounting of many companies. It enabled me to study the successes and failures of many companies; reorganizations, reconstructions, mergers and litigation; and the connections between these things and accounting practices. And it gave me time to work intensively over the views of the proponents and critics of conventional and other forms of accounting, time to benefit from the stimulus of writers in a wide variety of other related fields.

* * * * * * *

The sequel. Towards the end of the book I wrote: "We have not come to the end of the road". This remark, intended to be merely descriptive, was unwittingly prophetic.

First, there were objections to the valuation of assets at resale prices. The idea had no respectable antecedent in the literature. MacNeal's **Truth in Accounting** came closest to it; but he proposed a mixed set of valuations, market prices, replacement prices and original prices. I had wished to avoid this mixture, on the ground that the sum of such prices could have no substantive meaning. But I also wished that my proposal should be workable, and palatable. Without abandoning resale prices in principle, I allowed that replacement prices and indexed calculations might be used as approximations or as "a matter of expedience, or of necessity, in the face of ignorance of the more pertinent price data" (**A.E.E.B.**, p. 248). Reviewers and critics saw this as inconsistency. But it seemed to me to be no different from the ways in which practising engineers, physicians and agronomists cope with practical difficulties. The theories which lie at the core of their technologies are idealizations; they guide, they do not dictate willy-nilly. Nevertheless, in the interest of logical rectitude, I have abandoned the use of replacement prices and indexed calculations "as approximations", in favor of their use "in deriving approximations" to the resale prices of assets - but only where there is a resale market. No statement of financial position is made the better by putting some figure other than an approximate resale price beside the asset. Some critics have expressed dismay at the rapid rate at which an asset value may fall, particularly in the initial years of its use. But they confuse user-value with exchange value, whereas only the latter has reference to financial position. Some have contended that both assets and liabilities should be valued at market prices if the proposed system were to be consistent; but this view presumes an unrealistic similarity or symmetry. These objections have been dealt with at length from time to time [53, 58, 59, 60, 80].

Competing systems. One is apt to be over-enthusiastic and credulous about his own work. But if it is to survive, either as a personal commitment or against the competition of other ideas, it must stand comparison, to its advantage, with all other actual or possible schemes. The first test of survival is frontal assault by others. Direct critical appraisals have provided occasion for working out in greater detail one facet or another of the theory [35, 39, 75]. Examination in depth of other proposals has generally confirmed the comparative advantage of continuously contemporary accounting; price-level-adjusted historical cost [31, 34, 74], present (discounted) value [39, 58, 59], and replacement price [29, 49, 60], theories and proposals have been so examined, singly (as indicated) or together [50, 83, 105]. And, of course, the accumulation of evidence and argument to the disadvantage of traditional accounting has continued [32, 46, 48, 56, 71, 95].

Piecemeal comparisons or judgements tend, however, to convey little impression of the comparative advantages of one proposal over the rest. I have argued that the goal of inquiry is the discovery of what is best [41]. Simultaneous analysis of the main types of system, using the same tests across the board, is a common way of ranking possibilities. Several exercises of this kind have been published [32, 50, 83, 105]. It has been alleged that these have demonstrated the superiority of continuously contemporary accounting – only to my satisfaction [67]; but there has been no attempt to demonstrate in a similar way the superiority of any other system.

It is still widely contended, of course, that it is not possible to judge what is best, most serviceable, as a style of periodical reporting. This professed inability to choose seems curious, coming from a class of persons who claim that the products of accounting assist in choosing or decision-making. The case for uniformity (**A.E.E.B.**, pp. 152ff.), restated at length [36], and the case against diversity of accounting as between firms [22, 30, 36] have never been rebutted. Unable or unwilling to choose what is best, some have supported supplementary financial statements, or multi-column accounting on a variety of bases in parallel. The case against these suggestions, based on overloading users with contradictory "information" [32, 34, 66, 67, 75] has not been answered.

The persistence of the debate about the merits of alternatives can be laid squarely on the failure to specify clearly the function of continuously generated information on the financial progress of a firm. That financial statements should be equally serviceable in making judgements about the past and decisions about the future was argued as far back as 1952 [5]. In the light of continuing confusion about the "objectives" or function of accounting, the argument has been restated [66, 75, 79, 86].

An improved notation. It was perhaps inevitable that the symbolic demonstration of the early part of Chapter 10 of the book would be used by others, who would assign different significances to its elements and conclusions. As I have already pointed out, I had myself misconstrued the result when I first developed it [18]. Other users of it seem to have overlooked the integral character of its elements; and though I gradually improved the notation to make those elements explicit [33, 40], others clung to the earlier form [96]. By 1969 I had developed a demonstration of the connection between opening and closing net assets of a period in the general case where there were net revenues, price variation adjustments and capital maintenance adjustments [50f, 54]. But only quite recently did I extend the demonstration to embrace all transactions and accruals. The latest form of it as given in [105] is set out below.

We proceed first to derive an expression for net income from the amount of assets and equities at the beginning and the end of a period, in the case where there were in the period no new capital contributions to the firm and no dividend payments.

Let $\$_1$ and $\$_2$ represent dollars of the general purchasing power of the dollar at dates t_1 and t_2, the opening and closing dates of a period.

Let $\$_1 M_1$ and $\$_2 M_2$ be the amounts of net monetary assets (cash and receivables less liabilities) at the two dates.

Let $\$_1 N_1$ and $\$_2 N_2$ be the sums of the money equivalents or net resale prices of non-monetary assets at the two dates.

Let $\$_1 R_1$ and $\$_2 R_2$ be the amounts of the residual equity (which are equal to the amounts of net assets) at the two dates.

Then, at t_1,
$$\$_1 M_1 + \$_1 N_1 = \$_1 R_1 \qquad (1)$$
and, at t_2,
$$\$_2 M_2 + \$_2 N_2 = \$_2 R_2 \qquad (2)$$

Let $\$_2 Y_2$ be the net income or profit of the period ended t_2; it is the amount of the increment in net assets:
$$\$_2 Y_2 = \$_2 (M_2 + N_2) - \$_1 (M_1 + N_1) \qquad (3)$$

Let p be the proportionate rise in the period in an index of the general level of prices, so that, in general purchasing power,
$$\$_1 = \$_2 (1 + p)$$

The amount $\$_2 Y_2$ may then be expressed wholly in $\$_2$ by substituting $\$_2 (1 + p)$ for $\$_1$ in (3):

$$\$_2Y_2 = \$_2(M_2 + N_2) - \$_2(1 + p)(M_1 + N_1) \qquad (4)$$
$$= \$_2(M_2 - M_1) + \$_2(N_2 - N_1) - \$_2p(M_1 + N_1)$$

Since all the amounts, including the value of p, are amounts observable or discoverable independently of any internal calculations of the firm, the amount of income is authenticated simply by authentication of the components of (4). We may now introduce the transactions and the effects of the changes in asset prices that occurred during the period.

Let T represent the nominal amount of the differences between the total sales proceeds (in cash or credit) of goods and services sold and the total purchase prices (for cash or on credit) of goods bought during the period; T thus includes transactions in trading inventories and transactions in all other non-monetary assets.

Let I represent, in respect of all non-monetary assets sold during the period, the sum of the nominal differences between their selling prices and their purchase prices, or, in respect of non-monetary assets in possession at t_1, the nominal differences between their selling prices and their recorded money equivalents at t_1.

Let E represent the aggregate nominal amounts of all purchases (for cash or credit) of services in the nature of expenses during the period (i.e., all payments which do not give rise directly to the possession of non-monetary assets).

Let V represent the sum of the nominal differences between the discovered money equivalents of all non-monetary assets at t_2 and their book values. V is thus the aggregate amount by which book values at t_2 will be written up or down to correspond with the discovered money equivalents of assets at t_2.

Then, in nominal amounts,
$$M_2 = M_1 + T - E$$
and $$N_2 = N_1 + I + V - T$$

Substituting these values of M_2 and N_2 in (4) above,
$$\$_2Y_2 = \$_2[(M_1 + T - E) + (N_1 + I + V - T) - (1 + p)(M_1 + N_1)]$$
$$= \$_2[(I - E) + V - p(M_1 + N_1)]$$
or, since $M_1 + N_1 = R_1$
$$\$_2Y_2 = \$_2[(I - E) + V - pR_1] \qquad (5)$$

The expression for net income in terms of changes in differently denominated ($_1$, $_2$) amounts of assets (3) has thus been converted, by a strict set of substitutions, to an equivalent expression in terms of transactions and accrued changes in the money equivalents of assets and a single denominator ($_2$). The terms of (5) are interpretable as follows.

The amount (I - E) is the realized net proceeds (in cash or receivables) of the period from all transactions in goods. It may be described as **net revenue**, in the sense of net inflow of cash and receivables. It is obtained by the usual process of accumulating the amounts of transactions in appropriate accounts. The amount V is the sum of particular price variation adjustments; it is the sum of "price adjustments" and "depreciation" in the pro forma income account given in Chapter 10 of the book. The third term is the capital maintenance adjustment, so described in the income account just mentioned. The components of (5) are the same as the elements of the income account in the book, though described slightly differently.

Note that although T, I, E and V are nominal amounts, the balance sheet at t_2 and the income $\$_2 Y_2$ are all expressed in $\$_2$. This indicates that the adjustments of the system (by recourse to discovered amounts and the general price index) fully compensate for the use of "nominal amounts" for certain of the components. It also confirms the propriety, within this system and not otherwise, of day-by-day accumulation of the amounts of transactions, regardless of their different purchasing power denominators through a period. The day-to-day accounting under continuously contemporary accounting (briefly described as CoCoA, since 1975) is the same as under traditional accounting; the difference between the systems lies only in what is "accrued" in the terminal adjustments for each period.

The generality of the income-calculation formula may be illustrated by some corollaries –

Corollary 1   If there were no transactions in a period,
$$\$_2 Y_2 = \$_2 [V - pR_1]$$

Corollary 2   If there are no asset price variations in respect of closing stocks of assets,
$$\$_2 Y_2 = \$_2 [(I - E) - pR_1]$$

Corollary 3   If there were no change in the general purchasing power of the money unit,

$$\$_2 Y_2 = \$_2[(I - E) + V]$$

Corollary 4 If dividends D were paid during the year
$$\$_2 Y_2 = \$_2[(I - E) + D + V - pR_1]$$
For, if D were paid during the year, in nominal terms
$$M_2 = M_1 + T - E - D$$
Substituting this value in (4), and proceeding as for the derivation of (5), $\$_2 Y_2$ becomes the above specified amount.

Corollary 5 If new capital $\$_a K_a$ was introduced at t_a, a date between t_1 and t_2,
$$\$_2 Y_2 = \$_2[(I - E) + V - (pR_1 + p_a K_a)]$$
where p_a is the proportionate change in an index of the general level of prices between t_a and t_2.

As before, the income of the period is the change in net assets otherwise than by new capital contributions:
$$\$_2 Y_2 = \$_2(M_2 + N_2) - \$_1(M_1 + N_1) - \$_a K_a$$
Converting all terms to the common denominator $\$_2$,
$$\$_2 Y_2 = \$_2(M_2 + N_2) - \$_2(1+p)(M_1+N_1) - \$_2(1+p_a)(K_a) \qquad (6)$$
It is immaterial whether $\$_a K_a$ was received in cash or goods or part in each way. Suppose it was received in cash. Then, in nominal amounts,
$$M_2 = M_1 + T - E + K$$
and $\qquad N_2 = N_1 + I + V - T$ (as before).

Substituting these values in (6), we obtain the amount specified in the above statement of the corollary.

Extensions. Group accounts were treated only briefly in the book. The notion of a group, for which consolidated accounts could be prepared, was accepted. But the whole drift of the book was away from invented fictions - and the "group" is a fiction. Legally, it owes nothing, owns nothing, has no stockholders, cannot sue or be sued. Financially, therefore, group accounts are meaningless. The function which consolidated accounts are expected to serve can be served far better by aggregative information on subsidiaries in parallel with the financial statements of the parent company [38, 95]. A comprehensive style of equity accounting has been suggested for the substantive (legal) accounts of holding companies [95]; but an equity accounting for incomes only of associated companies is open to serious objection [77].

Firms which have branches or subsidiaries in foreign countries are subject to several different influences which purely domestic firms escape. The specific prices of similar assets may differ between countries, the general levels of prices may vary at different rates, and the rates of exchange of domestic for foreign currencies may change from time to time. Continuously contemporary accounting is the only form of accounting by which account can readily be taken of these shifts, in such a way that the relative performances of sectors of multinational firms - as sectors in their own countries and as parts of the whole enterprise - may be assessed [65, 104, 105].

As occasion has arisen, the logic of tax allocation [43] and of the capitalization of mine exploration and development and similar outlays [72, 98] has been examined; both have been considered to yield misleading statements of periodical financial position. Means have been devised and suggested for dealing with these matters and with other prospective and contingent outlays in a manner consistent with the principles of continuously contemporary accounting [83, 95, 105]. Applications of the system in specific types of industry have been illustrated [81, 98]. And the propriety and equity of the system as a basis for business income taxation has been examined, to its advantage [92].

Economics and accounting. It seems to be widely believed that economists have long supported forms of accounting that entail the use of replacement prices or present (discounted) values for assets. In particular, "Hicks' definition" of income (**Value and Capital**, Ch. XIV) has been cited frequently, more frequently perhaps than all other economists together. But one wonders how many of those who cite Hicks have read the book, or indeed the chapter. Hicks gives six possible definitions, three **ex ante** and three **ex post**. As periodical accounting is a form of **ex post** calculation, it is of interest that the definition of income **ex post** that Hicks considers more favorably than others coincides with the notion of income under continuously contemporary accounting. Further, the definition of net wealth under that system coincides with the definitions of wealth by a long line of economists reaching as far back as Adam Smith [90, 105]. The economists on whose work the proponents of the use of replacement prices and net present values have relied, have been concerned with the pursuit of income and wealth, with choice **ex ante**, not with the measurement of income and wealth **ex post**. Advocacy of those valuation bases and objections to the use of resale prices in accounting thus appear to arise from inadequate discrimination between the different uses of different kinds of information [28, 62], and perhaps in some cases from misunderstandings of economists themselves [62, 99]. It has seemed necessary repeatedly to demonstrate that the principal ideas underlying continuously contemporary accounting are consistent with basic economic doctrine [37, 45, 67, 71, 105]. Sterling's **Theory of the Measurement of Enterprise Income** (published in 1970, but apparently written some ten years earlier) remains the only work similar to my own. Its derivation from substantially the same sources - economics and measurement theory - is some assurance of the consistency between those sources and our common conclusions.

Statutory and other standards. Laws and regulations in many countries prescribe some features of the financial reporting of business corporations. Most of the rules were introduced before accounting and its products became objects of analytical examination; and many specific rules are demonstrably inconsistent with the object of giving stockholders, creditors and others realistic indications of the periodical results and financial positions of companies. There has been extended debate over the intention of the statutes and regulations; but there can be little doubt that they never intended the users of financial statements to be misled. That the products of continuously contemporary accounting are consistent with the law, and that other systems are not, has been contended on a variety of grounds [48, 71, 73, 90, 95, 100].

During the sixties and seventies professional bodies gave increasing attention to the development of accounting standards on particular elements of accounting and accounts. Draft proposals were published for comment. Inflation accounting proposals in some countries gave rise to governmental inquiries. Submissions made to some of those professional bodies and governmental committees (American, Australian, Canadian and English) provided occasions for reconsidering the propriety of my own conclusions. Most of those comments and submissions were not published; but I later published critiques of a number of the standards and proposals that emerged [84, 88, 93, 95, 101, 105] and pointed out what seemed to be misunderstanding of continuously contemporary accounting on the part of its critics and the advocates of other schemes [91, 96]. In respect of those other schemes no attempt had been made to draft a general code or framework which might be incorporated in appropriate statutes or regulations; all were admittedly partial, incomplete. But I had published an inflation accounting draft that was quite general [82] and occasions arose for casting its principles in statutory or regulatory form [95, 102]. The principal issue in much of the discussion of statutory prescriptions was the meaning of "a true and fair view (or a fair presentation) of periodical results and financial position". A survey made of the ways in which specified financial magnitudes are applied to specified financial problem situations strongly suggested that respondents interpreted financial position in substantially the fashion that it would be represented under continuously contemporary accounting [106].

Method. In empirical science, method is the handmaid of substance - important on that account. Imagination is all that invention requires, but whether an invention is viable or serviceable is demonstrable only by recourse to the setting in which it is to serve [89, 95]. That accounting should be a signalling system of some sensitivity, the signals of which correspond with commercial and financial reality, seems incontestable. It is one of the key elements of continuously contemporary accounting. Yet the notion of correspondence continues to be ignored even by those who write of accounting as communication. Its neglect has prompted restatement in different settings on a number of occasions [47, 52, 55, 56, 70, 71, 86, 89].

That a signal shall correspond with some empirical fact, event or circumstance requires that the fact, event or circumstance be carefully observed. That a theory or a system of accounting shall correspond with the setting in which it is to be serviceable requires, in turn, that that setting shall be carefully observed. Imagination and invention are otherwise undisciplined. This has seemed to be characteristic of a great deal of accounting invention, on the part of professional associations and teachers alike. It has been counter-productive [63, 68, 70, 103]. The statistical analysis of stock market price behavior, to which some have resorted, and lines of argument which purport to link accounting information with the outcomes of selected courses of action, are unproductive of solutions to the problem of choosing between alternative accounting rules; for financial information is only one of the determinants of choice and, therefore, an even more remote determinant of the pay-off of a decision [78, 87].

The necessity of linking the observable with the theoretical I have tried repeatedly to stress [17, 42, 57, 64, 69, 76, 89, 103]. It has been one of the two main desiderata of my work. Observation of real world events cannot prove what it is right or best or most useful to do; but it can be suggestive. On the other hand, observation may reveal flaws and faults in what is currently done, and their particular forms. The imagination may thus proceed from both directions to a conclusion which is free (or freer) of the observed faults and which serves best (or better) those who expect to be well-served. The earlier part of this essay indicated that the method had long been followed. But the published pieces were spread over about 15 years and the examples used were only a small fraction of what had come under my notice. That I had not shown, adequately and in one place, its influence on the development of the theory was perhaps an impediment to wider sympathy with the theory. An outline of the "evidence for" the theory [56] was later developed into **Securities and Obscurities** [71]. That book makes reference to some of the accounting practices of over 250 named companies - American, English and Australian - and of many hundreds of others. Incidents in the lives of successful and failed companies; takeovers, litigated cases, official investigations; professional, official, judicial and scholarly dicta - from all these directions was drawn evidence of the inadequate and misleading nature of published financial information, or indications to the effect that financial calculations and statements based on market prices best serve managers, investors, creditors and others.

The second main desideratum of my work has been the pursuit of logical rigor. (I say "pursuit" advisedly. I have found myself in error too often to speak of the "attainment" of logical rigor). The most obvious example of this is the attempt to link all the main propositions (premises, assumptions, definitions and inferences) in **Accounting, Evaluation and Economic Behavior,** so that they are a progressive and coherent whole. Their numbering and their identification as premises or conclusions in the "Argument" section of each chapter is indicative of their association. The pursuit of rigor has prompted close examination of the arguments and conclusions of others, in respect of both substance and method [e.g., 20, 23, 29, 30, 74, 78, 103, 105, 106]; examination of the conditions of valid aggregation, relation and comparison [e.g., 35, 40, 46, 51, 85, 105]; examination of the quality of actual and potential accounting information as raw material for the inferences and judgements of users [46, 51, 55, 56, 61, 75, 86, 106].

The interplay of the observable, the logical and the imaginative is, as it seems to me, after the "circular" pattern of empirical science generally. To paraphrase Cohen and Nagel (**An Introduction to Logic and Scientific Method**, 1934, p. 396), evidence for principles has been obtained by appealing to empirical materials, to what is alleged to be "fact"; empirical material has been selected, analyzed and interpreted on the basis of principles. In virtue of this give and take between facts and principles, many things that were dubitable have fallen under careful scrutiny at one time or another.

The case for continuously contemporary accounting, thus, does not rest on any singular proposition in any singular discipline, and may not be dismissed by any such singular proposition. Its logical, empirical, legal, economic, financial, metrological and linguistic elements, reinforce one another. No such varied set of foundations has been identified for any other style of accounting. Observations and events since writing the book and the emergence of new evidence antedating the book have only served to strengthen my confidence in the validity of its main conclusion and in the logical and practical propriety of the method of accounting those conclusions entail.

March 1981

References

1. **Financial Management**, Sydney, The Law Book Co., 1947, 442 pp. Revised 1953, 432 pp. Revised 1967, 433 pp.
2. "The Spice of Accounting", **The Australian Accountant**, XIX (November 1949), 398-401.
3. "The Relationship between Accounting and Financial Management", **The Australian Accountant**, XX (September 1950), 333-55.
4. "Accounting and Inflation", **The Australian Accountant**, XXII (January 1952), 14-23.
5. "Accounting and Business Finance", **The Australian Accountant**, XXII (July and August 1952), 213-30, 262-6.
6. "Effects of Inflation on Financial Strategy", **The Australian Accountant**, XXII (September 1952), 304-11.
7. "Financial Practice and Fiscal Policy", **The Australian Accountant**, XXII (November 1952), 391-8.
8. "Blueprint for a Theory of Accounting", **Accounting Research**, 6 (January 1955), 17-25.
9. "A Scientific Pattern for Accounting Theory", **The Australain Accountant**, 25 (October 1955), 428-34.
10. **The Function and Design of Company Annual Reports**, Sydney, The Law Book Co., 1955, 322 pp.
11. "The Formal Basis of Business Decisions", **The Australian Accountant**, 26 (April 1956), 155-74.
12. "Detail for a Blueprint", **The Accounting Review**, XXXII (April 1957), 206-15.
13. "The Function of the Balance Sheet", **The Chartered Accountant in Australia**, XXVII (April 1957), 565-70.
14. **Accounting and Action**, The Law Book Co., 1957, 248 pp. Revised 1965, 287 pp.
15. "The Implications of Asset Revaluations and Bonus Share Issues", **The Australian Accountant**, 27 (November 1957), 507-31.
16. "Measurement and Misrepresentation", **Management Science**, 6 (January 1960), 141-8.
17. "The Conditions of Research in Accounting", **Journal of Accountancy**, 110 (December 1960), 33-9.
18. **Towards a General Theory of Accounting**, Australian Society of Accountants, 1962, booklet, 48 pp.
19. "Non-Comments on Non-Accounting", Meeting of the North Eastern Division of the American Accounting Association, Boston, October 1962, mimeo., 11 pp.
20. **The Resolution of Some Paradoxes in Accounting**, Faculty of Commerce and Business Administration, University of British Columbia, Occasional paper No.2, 1963, booklet, 33 pp.
21. "Why Bother with Postulates?", **Journal of Accounting Research**, 1 (Spring 1963), 3-15.
22. "Financial Information and the Securities Market", mimeographed 1963, 44 pp. **Abacus**, 1 (September 1965), 3-30.
23. "The Moonitz and Sprouse Studies on Postulates and Principles", **Proceedings** of Conference of the Australasian Association of University Teachers of Accounting, January 1964, 34-54.
24. "Conventions, Doctrines and Common Sense", **The Accountants' Journal** (N.Z.) 43 (February 1964), 182-7.

25. "The Role of Information Systems in Decision-Making", **Management Technology**, 4 (June 1964), 15-25.
26. "Company Losses - Safeguarding the Investor", **Current Affairs Bulletin**, 34 (October 1964), 162-76.
27. "Measurement in Accounting", **Journal of Accounting Research**, 3 (Spring 1965), 32-62.
28. "The Complementarity of Accounting and Economics", **Calculator Annual**, Singapore Polytechnic Society of Commerce, 1964-65, 78-86.
29. "Edwards and Bell on Business Income", **The Accounting Review**, XL (October 1965), 731-41.
30. "A Matter of Principle", **The Accounting Review**, XLI (July 1966), 443-57.
31. "A Study of a Price Level Study", **Abacus**, 2 (December 1966), 97-118.
32. "The Foundations of Financial Accounting", **Berkeley Symposium on the Foundations of Financial Accounting**, University of California, Berkeley, January 1967, 26-44.
33. "Price Variation Accounting - An Improved Representation", **Journal of Accounting Research**, 5 (Autumn 1967), 215-20.
34. "A Study of a Study of a Price Level Study", **Abacus**, 3 (August 1967), 62-73.
35. "Continuously Contemporary Accounting, Additivity and Action", **The Accounting Review**, XLII (October 1967), 751-7.
36. "Uniformity in Accounting", **The New York Certified Public Accountant**, XXXVII (October 1967), 747-54.
37. "Reality and Illusion in Accounting, Finance and Economics", **Michigan Business Review**, XX (January 1968), 1-9.
38. "Consolidated Statements are not really Necessary", **The Australian Accountant**, 38 (February 1968), 89-92.
39. "Measures and Values - A Reply to Professor Staubus", **The Accounting Review**, XLIII (April 1968), 239-47.
40. "New Pathways in Accounting Thought and Action", **The Accountants´ Journal** (N.Z.), 46 (July 1968), 434-41.
41. "Accepted, Better or Best? - The Goal of Inquiry in Accounting", **The Singapore Accountant**, 3 (1968), 27-33.
42. "The Linked Logics of Pedagogy and Practice", **Proceedings** of Conference of the Australasian Association of University Teachers of Accounting, August 1968.
43. "Tax Allocation and Financial Reporting", **Abacus**, 4 (December 1968), 99-123.
44. **Accounting, Finance and Management**, Arthur Andersen & Co., and Butterworth & Co (Australia), Sydney, 762 pp. Collection of 50 articles, 1948-68.
45. "Money and the Monetary Unit", **The Singapore Accountant**, 4 (1969), 79-85.
46. "What´s Wrong with Financial Statements?", August 1969; **The Australian Accountant**, 40 (February 1970), 19-28.
47. "Financial Information Systems", **The Australian Accountant**, 39 (August 1969), 364-8.
48. "The Missing Link in Supervision of the Securities Market", **Abacus**, 5 (September 1969), 16-36.
49. "Accounting and the Public Interest", in **Abram Mey Tachtig Jaar, Liber Amicorum**, Bussum, Netherlands, 1970, 44-53.

50. Methods of Accounting - a series, **The Accountant**, 1970
    a. "The Elements of Price Variation Accounting", 26 February, 299-303
    b. "Historical Cost Accounting and its Variants", 5 March, 341-45
    c. "Price Level Adjusted Accounting", 19 March, 408-13
    d. "Replacement Price Accounting", 2 April, 483-86
    e. "Present Value Accounting", 16 April, 551-55
    f. "Continuously Contemporary Accounting", 30 April, 643-47.
51. "Accounting - From a Logical Point of View", **The Singapore Accountant**, 5 (1970), 13-18.
52. "Financial Reporting and Administrative Accounting: Harmony or Conflict?", **Canadian Chartered Accountant**, 97 (August 1970), 114-20.
53. "Second Thoughts on Continuously Contemporary Accounting", **Abacus**, 6 (September 1970), 39-55.
54. "Towards a Theory of Business Accounting", in Roy Sidebotham, **Introduction to the Theory and Context of Accounting**, Second ed., 1970, 132-44.
55. "The Commercial Foundations of Accounting Theory" in Williard E. Stone (ed.), **Foundations of Accounting Theory**, University of Florida Press, Gainesville, 1971, 59-77.
56. "Evidence for a Market Selling Price Accounting System", in Robert R. Sterling (ed.), **Asset Valuation and Income Determination**, Scholars Book Co., Lawrence, Kansas, 1971, 74-96.
57. "Investigacion contable y tecnologica" ("Accounting Research and Technology"), **Revista Temas de Negocios**, Monterrey Institute of Technology, Second series, 1 (Spring 1971), 49-56 (Spanish language).
58. "Asset Measurement and Valuation", **Cost and Management**, 45 (March-April 1971), 30-35.
59. "Measurement and Valuation Again", **Cost and Management**, 45 (July-August 1971), 12-17.
60. "Value to the Owner", **Abacus**, 7 (June 1971), 62-72.
61. "Kaikeiriron Kesei no Hoho" ("Accounting Theory Construction"), **Kigyo Kaikei** (Accounting), 23 (August 1971, 16-21; September 1971, 21-26) (Japanese language); **Proceedings**, Third International Conference on Accounting Education, Sydney, 1972, 138-51.
62. "Income and Capital: Fisher's Legacy" (Irving Fisher, **The Nature of Capital and Income**, 1906), **Journal of Accounting Research**, 9 (Spring 1971), 137-49.
63. "The Anguish of Accountants", **Proceedings** of Annual Conference of Australasian Association of University Teachers of Accounting, Christchurch, August 1971; **Journal of Accountancy**, 133 (March 1972), 68-74; **The Australian Accountant**, 42 (May 1972), 154-61.
64. "The Validation of an Accounting Theory", **Waseda Business and Economic Studies**, 7 (1971), 1-21.
65. "Accounting in an International Economic Community", **Journal U.E.C.** (Dusseldorf), January 1972, 52-69 (English, French and reduced version in German); **Rivista dei Dottori Commercialisti**, XXII (1971), 1771-87.
66. "Multiple Column Accounting - Cui Bono?", **The Chartered Accountant in Australia**, 42 (March 1972), 4-8.
67. "Quo Vado?", **The Chartered Accountant in Australia**, 43 (August 1972), 13-15.

68. "Accounting Theory, Practice and Policy", **The Singapore Accountant**, 7 (1972), 39-43.
69. "Variedades de Investigacion Contable" ("Varieties of Accounting Research"), **Revista Temas de Negocios**, Monterrey Institute of Technology, Second series, 2 (Spring 1972), 353-60 (Spanish language).
70. "Accounting Principles or Accounting Policies?", **Journal of Accountancy**, May 1973, 48-53.
71. **Securities and Obscurities: A Case for Reform of the Law of Company Accounts**, Gower Press, Australia, 243 pp. May 1973; reprinted under the title, **Accounting in Disarray**, Garland Press, 1982; in Japanese translation by Professor Ichiro Shiobara, 1976.
72. "Mining, Taxing and Accounting", Australian Society of Accountants, State Convention, Mt. Isa, June 1973, **Convention Papers**, 23-32.
73. "Accounting Principles and the Law", **Australian Business Law Review**, 1 (June 1973), 112-29.
74. "General Purchasing Power Accounting - ED8 is not the Answer", **The Accountant**, 5 July 1973, 15-18.
75. "Misurazioni, Stime e Valutazioni nelle Decisioni Finanziarie" ("Measurement, Estimation and Valuation in Financial Decision Making",) **Rivista dei Dottori Commercialisti**, XXIV (1973), 1001-22.
76. "Observation as a Method of Inquiry - the Background of **Securities and Obscurities**", **Abacus**, 9 (December 1973), 156-75.
77. "The Use of the Equity Method in Accounting for Investments in Subsidiaries and Associated Companies", **The Australian Accountant**, 44 (February 1974), 40-44; **The Chartered Accountant in Australia**, 44 (February 1974), 18-22.
78. "Stock Market Prices and Accounting Research", **Abacus**, 10 (June 1974), 39-54.
79. "The Objectives of Accounting", **The Singapore Accountant**, 9 (1974), 39-45.
80. "Third Thoughts", **Abacus**, 10 (December 1974), 129-37.
81. "Inflation Accounting and its Implications for the Electricity Supply Industry", **Proceedings**, Conference of the Electricity Supply Association of Australia, Hobart, May 1975, 41-52.
82. **Accounting for Inflation**, Exposure Draft of a proposed accounting standard, University of Sydney, December 1975, 35 pp.
83. **Accounting for Inflation - Methods and Problems**, University of Sydney, December 1975, 120 pp.
84. "A Critical Examination of Australian Accounting Standards", **Abacus**, 11 (December 1975), 136-52.
85. "Whatever Happened to CCE?", **The Accounting Review**, LI (April 1976), 385-90.
86. "The Functions of Published Financial Statements", **Accounting and Business Research**, 22 (Spring 1976), 83-94.
87. "The Possibility of a Normative Accounting Standard", **The Accounting Review**, LI (July 1976), 646-56.
88. **Current Cost Accounting - A Critique of the Sandilands Report**, International Centre for Research in Accounting, Lancaster, August 1976, 80 pp.
89. "Accounting Principles and Practices - Negotiated or Dictated?", **Proceedings** of Accounting Research Convocation, University of Alabama, November 1976, 1-22.
90. "Fair Financial Reporting - in Law and Practice", in **The Emanuel Saxe Distinguished Lectures in Accounting, 1976-77**, City University of New York, 7-14.

91. "Continuously Contemporary Accounting: Misunderstandings and Misrepresentations", **Abacus**, 12 (December 1976), 137-51.
92. "Business Income Taxation and the Mathews Report", **Current Affairs Bulletin** (March 1977), University of Sydney, 24-31.
93. **Accounting for Inflation** (a critique of the Richardson Report, New Zealand), Invitation Lecture, Massey University, March 1977, 27 pp.
94. **An Autobibliography**, International Centre for Research in Accounting, Lancaster, May 1977, 70 pp (annotated bibliography of main books and articles, 1947-77).
95. **Company Accounting Standards** (with T. Sri Ramanathan and H.H. Rappaport), Report of the Accounting Standards Review Committee appointed by the New South Wales Attorney General, 1978, 170 pp.
96. "The Use and Abuse of a Notation: A History of an Idea", **Abacus**, 14 (December 1978), 122-44.
97. "The Taxi Company under CoCoA", in Robert R. Sterling and Arthur L. Thomas (eds), **Accounting for a Simplified Firm Owning Depreciating Assets**, Scholars Book Co., Houston, 1979, 183-203.
98. "Inflation Accounting in the Mining Industry", **Papers**, Australian Society of Accountants Convention, Broken Hill, September 1979, 18 pp.
99. "Canning's **The Economics of Accountancy** - After 50 years", **The Accounting Review**, LIV (October 1979), 764-75.
100. "Inflation Accounting, the Law and the Absurd", **The Accountants' Journal**, October 1979, 340-2.
101. "Usefulness - The Vanishing Premise in Accounting Standard Setting", **Abacus**, 15 (December 1979), 71-92.
102. Suggested Amendments to the Accounts and Audit Provisions and Schedule of the Companies Act of Sri Lanka, 1979, 34 pp (unpublished).
103. "The Myths and the Science of Accounting", **Accounting, Organizations and Society**, 5 (1980), 167-80.
104. "Accounting for Foreign Business", drafted 1980; **Abacus**, 19 (June 1983), 14-28.
105. **Price Variation and Inflation Accounting**, Sydney, 1980, 174 pp.
106. **The Design of Accounting Standards**, University of Sydney, Accounting Research Centre, 1980, 93 pp.

Accounting –
"One of the finest inventions of the human spirit"

Synopsis

> To commerce and to finance there can be
> great service given by accountancy.
> Its power, though, will not be fully known
> while bits and pieces stand apart, alone.
> To teach, to practise, to research, invent,
> is how the time of many has been spent.
> But cost of time and effort has been vain;
> for doubt, dispute, confusion still remain.
> A better prospect far there is in reach.
> If those who practise and research and teach
> were disciplined in such a way that each
> acknowledged that a common course of thought
> relates, for all men, to things sold and bought –
> Accounting, then, might do the job it ought.

451

Accounting as conspectus

> It lets us have a conspectus of the whole at any time without our needing to be confused by detail. What advantages are conferred on the trader by double-entry bookkeeping! It is one of the finest inventions of the human spirit, and every good manager should introduce it in his administration.

These words, put by Goethe into the mouth of one of his characters[1], epitomise a feature of accounting that is only vaguely sensed and given little deliberate notice by accountants. It is quite remarkable that the capacity of the products of accounting to focus attention on the affairs of a firm as a whole should have been captured so exquisitely by Goethe while its own exponents treat it otherwise. The words were uttered, let it be said, by an apprentice-merchant, young Werner, who had come to understand the virtue of ordered knowledge and disciplined action in business affairs. "Order and clarity", he said, "increase the pleasure in saving and earning. A man who is a bad manager no doubt feels at ease in darkness; he may well be not at all willing to reckon up the items that he owes. On the other hand, for a good manager there can be nothing more pleasant than to work out the balance of his growing happiness every day. Even a mishap, if it should surprise and irritate him, will not terrify him, for he knows at once what advantages he has acquired that are to be put in the other pan of the scales".

The business of doing business is a many-faceted affair. Good suppliers are to be sought, and good bargains struck. Customers are to be wooed, their trust and esteem to be nurtured. Workers of many kinds and many skills are to be induced to collaborate in productive and satisfying enterprise. Investors, financiers and creditors are to be persuaded to share in the outcome of risks they do not directly and by choice undertake. And the service and goodwill of a host of auxiliaries, entrepreneurial and governmental, are to be harnessed for the benefit of the firm in ways that are not inimical to the public interest. At every one of those points, acts of collaboration or cooperation and processes of coordination must be engineered, contrived, by informed negotiation. The information by which each facet of business is managed is appropriately diverse - sales, output, quality figures; plant and goods inventories; time worked and lost for various reasons; and financial information on the progress and state of the firm.

Whether that extensive and varied mass of information is qualitative or quantitative, physical or financial, it will not serve the purposes of decision-making, choice or negotiation unless it is self-consistent and consistent with the events and states it purports to represent. Stafford Beer has described the company as an exceedingly complex probabilistic system. "It must adapt itself to its economic, commercial, social and political surroundings, and it must learn from experience."[2] It can do none of these things well unless the information it uses is realistic and continuously up to date. Its financial affairs themselves are exceedingly complex. Managers and those who rely on them have not a thousand ears, a thousand eyes, a thousand hands. That is why they need, as young Werner said, "a conspectus of the whole at any time without needing to be confused by detail".

But what in fact do we have? Many minds and much labour have been devoted to developing the art of accounting. Many people have sensed the importance of realistic and up to date financial information. Jurists and eminent accountants, practising and academic, on both sides of the Atlantic and elsewhere, have held that financial statements should represent the truth about the dated state of affairs and results of companies, in up to date prices and money units. In 1887 Stirling, J. held that "It was the duty of the auditor....to see that (the balance sheet) was a true and accurate representation of the company's affairs".[3] In 1922, Paton wrote: ".... the periodic statement of financial position and the report (of income figures)...should consistently reflect true pictures of current business conditions and tendencies...if these statements are to form a basis for rational judgements".[4] And in 1938 Montgomery affirmed: "Accounting has but one purpose, to set forth the results of business operations accurately and truthfully...".[5] These are the words, respectively, of a judge, an academic and a practitioner. They seem clearly to promise a birds-eye view, or conspectus, of the financial consequences of business operations.

However, their intent is almost, if not altogether, circumvented by the detailed expositions and practices of accountants. If the financial position or state of affairs of a firm is to be represented by amounts assigned to a number of separate items, it might be expected, first, that financial position or state of affairs would be defined, and defined in such a way that it signifies the capacity of the firm to pay its debts and meet its necessary outgoings by virtue of what it possesses at a stated date. But position is seldom defined; and when it is, the definitions seldom indeed allude to financial capacity in the sense just mentioned.

In the second place, it might be expected that all of the separate elements of a statement of financial position would be assigned money amounts which are like amounts; for only like amounts may be aggregated to obtain a conspectus of the whole. But the literature of accounting endorses, and the practice of accounting proceeds by, the assignment of qualitatively different kinds of amounts to the separate elements. Initial costs, unamortized costs, replacement costs, realizable values, fictitious amounts and currently real amounts of money, money claims and money payable, may be and are commonly found in balance sheets - a heterogeneous jumble which can have no common significance, provide no conspectus whatever. It is reminiscent of M C Escher's drawings, particularly his "Relativity", in which a number of people are shown walking on the steps, the risers and the undersides of the risers of staircases.[6] There are sufficient familiar shapes - walls, floors, ceilings, archways, balustrades and human figures - to induce the viewer to believe he is looking at some comprehensible architecture; but a closer look reveals doorways that open into the floors, doorways whose thresholds are the junction of vertical walls, and human figures that are clearly defying gravity. Escher's art, of course, is intentionally a form of intellectual puzzle or diversion, confronting the viewer with elements which are all understandable if one chooses different viewpoints or perspectives successively, but are quite incompatible if one looks at the whole. It escapes any suspicion of deception because its incompatibilities are apparent.

I have not yet seen a bold and outright assertion that a balance sheet is just an intellectual puzzle or diversion. Yet it is. It has some signs that make it look real, descriptions of assets and debts, amounts of money, aggregates of those amounts. But the appearances are delusive, and there is nothing to tell the reader to what extent he may be misled. Imagine a person who, for quite practical reasons, wants to appraise the debt-dependence or the asset-composition of a firm - two things which a manager, an investor or a creditor might well wish to know. If he remembers the rule of common-sense arithmetic and notices that a variety of asset valuation rules are referred to in the firm's balance sheet, he should first wonder which of the rules is the appropriate rule for his purpose - that is the first aspect of the puzzle. Whatever rule he settles for, he must then ponder the potential difference between the valuation of each asset as shown in the balance sheet and the valuation that use of his chosen rule would yield. To master that aspect of the puzzle, for each "misvalued" asset he would have to discover or imagine or calculate a new value, an exercise bedevilled by his ignorance of the particular assets covered by a generic title in the balance sheet and fraught with multitudinous possibilities of error. Thirdly, since to appraise entails comparison of the features of one firm with those of another, he would have to go through the same process for each of the other firms he chose for comparison. The task is gargantuan. Of course, it is probably never undertaken. But the consequence is that any appraisal of debt-dependence and asset composition is inevitably astray, whether trivially or seriously no one knows. The same is true of every other feature of the financial affairs of firms where diverse valuation rules are employed; in particular, it is true of the rate of return, which is the prime indicator of the yield of a business venture and a prime element in the comparative appraisal of different ventures or investments.

How, then, has it happened that managers and outsiders are denied the conspectus that is commonly expected to be given by periodical accounts?

A lost ideal

Two contributories have already been identified - failure to define, or to be bound by the definition of, financial position or state of affairs; and failure to heed the arithmetical rule against the aggregation of incompatible quantities. Neither kind of dereliction is of recent origin. In 1683 Colinson contended that, by means of bookkeeping, a merchant could see "in an instant...his whole estate and in what posture it is in at any time".[7] Gordon (1787) claimed that "a faithful register of all (a merchant's) transactions, disposed and arranged in that order,...by which a real state of the whole, or any particular branch (of the business), may be at once discovered and laid open, for his own satisfaction or that of others, is absolutely necessary, not only to the welfare and prosperity, but to the very being of his trade".[8] There were other similar encomiums. But "whole estate", "posture" and "real state" were terms apparently regarded as self-explanatory. More recently, I know of no serious attempt to define financial position or state of affairs in the voluminous output of professional bodies and their committees over the last forty years.

And though writers on accounting from Pacioli onwards have included mathematicians, and bookkeeping or accounting was treated often as a branch of mathematics, no one before the 20th century seems to have given any attention to the rule against heterogeneous addition. With few exceptions, the treatises or handbooks supported the carrying forward of balances of cash (spending and debt-paying power) and merchandise and other inventories at cost (which is not spending or debt-paying power) and aggregating those unlike amounts, while contending that the results enable the merchant wisely to regulate his venturing, his expenses and his debts. Even today those accountants who show great versatility with statistical and mathematical styles of analysis pass over that mathematical solecism without the least discomposure.

Thus, long ago, the seeds were sown of that liberality (laxity) which today tolerates a wide range of different valuations of assets and debts, in doctrine and in practice. They were nurtured by 19th and early 20th century litigated cases on divisible profits. On the basis of a distinction between fixed and circulating capital drawn (for quite different purposes) by Adam Smith and other economists, it came to be held that circulating assets should be valued at unamortized initial prices. Ingenuity and indecision have since fostered a voluminous array of valuation rules based on initial purchase prices, current purchase princes, current selling prices and expected selling prices. Particular valuations may be derived by observation, by more or less arbitrary allocation, and by discounting expectations.

The professional and textbook literature has attempted to give some appearance of order to this array. Particular valuation rules have been held to be the appropriate or proper rules for particular kinds of assets or in certain (unspecified) circumstances. As each class of asset has its "own" function or style (for example, to make ongoing outlays, for early liquidation, for use but not for resale), it is held that each class should therefore have its "own-value". How the resulting jumble of valuations can yield the financial position of a firm, or serviceable representations of its debt-dependence, its asset-composition, and its rate of return is not explained.

This atomistic stance was not and is not deliberately chosen and consciously preferred. The intentions which seem to give rise to it emerge from apparently plausible considerations. First, there is the stewardship function. Taken in its pure form - that is, treating accounting as a means of assuring beneficiaries of the proper discharge of a simple custodial relation, every inflow is a part of all inflows and every outflow a part of all outflows. It is perfectly proper on that ground to set down and to aggregate all prices paid and received, whether the prices of identical goods were the same or different, and whether over time those prices had changed or not. A cash book would do it, and to this day does it. But the management of a firm is not a simple custodial job. It is a matter of taking optimal advantage of opportunities, given the means available or accessible to the firm. And that turns on actual market prices from time to time and the state of affairs of the firm, at any moment of potential action, in terms of those prices. It was not for nothing that the steward who returned exactly the sum entrusted to him was called "the unjust steward". Stewardship is not to be confused with simple custody. Only simple custody would justify the continued use in financial records (other than cash-books) of originally outlaid amounts as amounts for which managers are accountable.

A more deeply seated source and rationalization of the atomistic stance seems to be misunderstanding or misuse of the dictum: "different information is necessary for different purposes". The earliest enunciation of it that I know, in a setting related to accounting, is in the work of J M Clark: "there are different kinds of problem for which we need information about costs, and...the particular information we need differs from one problem to another".[9] Having said this, Clark proceeds at considerable length to relate specific costs or cost-clusters to specified problem-situations. Users of the same general dictum with reference to accounting generally have been far less circumspect. The AICPA Study Group on Objectives of Financial Statements will serve as an example. It held that"...the objectives of financial statements cannot be best served by the exclusive use of a single valuation basis...different valuation bases are preferable for different assets and liabilities. That means that financial statements might contain data based on a combination of valuation bases".[10] Now, a host of writers have claimed that the function of a balance sheet is to represent the financial position of a firm. How to do that is one of the "problems" confronting accountants. It is a singular problem, the solution of which serves a singular purpose in the first instance: to inform all who may wish to know the financial position of a firm. If "the particular information we need differs from one problem to another", there is presumably one particular kind of information that relates to this problem. The opinion of the Study Group, however, turns the "different information for different purposes" dictum on its head. In effect, it contends, without a shred of argument or evidence, that a heterogeneous mixture of different kinds of information serves the singular purpose of representing financial position!

It may be said, of course, that to describe the representation of financial position as a purpose or function of a balance sheet is too superficial a view; the "real" purpose is to aid the making of decisions or choices. Turn, then to that set of purposes. It is demonstratable that four quite different kinds of information are necessary in the course of decision-making, each in its own way.

Choice and information

(1) <u>Historical and presently dated information</u>

Consider first the managers of a firm. Among the choices of managers there are - to raise additional money or not; to raise additional money by share issue, borrowing or disposing of non-money assets; to borrow for long or short terms; to continue unchanged the existing complex of operations or to vary it in one or more ways; to pay dividends on one scale or another; and so on. For each of these, there is a variety of subsidiary or consequential options. Every such action will change one or more of the indicators of solvency, equity and debt composition, and asset composition; and every such action will be in contemplation of some calculable change in the rate of return.

We presume managers to be aware of the competition among firms for funds and for the resources that funds command, and of the pertinence to investors and others of the solvency, equity and debt composition, asset-composition and rate of return of the firms they may support financially. It follows that managers will be concerned from time to time with the mathematical values and trends in indicators of each of these features, and the compatibility of those values and trends with then present and prospective characteristics of the commercial and economic environment. And, given the competition among firms for funds and other resources, the managers of any firm will be concerned to know, as far as possible, the performances of other firms, in respect of each of the features mentioned, over similar periods and the circumstances of those periods.

The information on the financial performance of a firm, and on all features of that performance is derivable solely from its financial statements. The considerations of the previous paragraph lead to four general principles:

(i) Comparison of the financial features of firms will be valid only if all firms keep accounts in accordance with the same rules (the uniformity principle).

(ii) Inter-period comparisons (trends) of the financial features of any firm will be valid only if the rules of the firm are employed consistently in successive periods (the consistency principle).

(iii) Since all the named indicators are derived by relating aggregates (or aggregates and differences), the indicators themselves will be mathematically valid only if the elements of those aggregates are properly aggregable, that is, if the amounts of the elements

Accounting – "One of the finest inventions of the human spirit"

      represent the same financial feature of each element (the homogeneity principle).

(iv) Since financial statements relate to specified periods and specified dates, the amounts of their elements shall be amounts identified exclusively with those periods and dates (the temporality principle).

A fifth principle may be derived. Every balance sheet includes amounts of cash, receivables and payables – monetary items, the amounts of which at any date are the least problematical of all items. These amounts enter into the calculation of every indicator mentioned above. If the homogeneity and temporality principles are endorsed, the universal occurrence of monetary items strongly suggests that the financial feature of each element appearing in balance sheets should be its dated money or cash equivalent (for non-monetary goods, their net resale prices). That inference is reinforced by the facts (a) that the continuation of any current programme of activity entails changes in the amounts of one or more of the monetary items; (b) that one of the options at every "decision-point" is to vary the status quo; (c) that every variation is effected through a change in the amounts of one or more monetary items; and (d) that the investigative consideration of the potential outcome of every option is carried out (in budgets and DCF calculations) in terms of money amounts and money equivalents. It follows that:

(v) Financial progress to any date and the financial capacity of the firm to carry on or vary its operations is represented only if dated balances are amounts of cash, money owed and owing, and the money equivalents of non-monetary assets (the money equivalent principle).

This sketch is sufficient to identify most of the characteristics of a style of <u>ex post</u> accounting that is significant also as representing the position with which a firm faces its future. It represents the consequences of the past up to a dated present; it uses a singular valuation principle for a singular purpose. But already its utility for decision making purposes should be apparent. A firm with a "low" rate of return, a "low" current ratio and a "low" debt to equity ratio would be disposed to seek to improve its rate of return and its current ratio by business yielding higher margins and financed by long term debt, for example. Appropriate responses to other financial profiles may be imagined. But no financial profile dependent on fictitious, conjectural, arbitrary, outdated or prospective amounts can provide a firm foundation for judgements of performance or of potential.

(2) <u>Prospective discounted values</u>

Occasions for decisions may thus arise from discovery of an unsatisfactory feature of a firm's financial affairs. They may also arise from the emergence of new opportunities as they reveal themselves in the market place. New products, better processes, improved machines, more promising sales promotion devices, new ways of covering risks – the possibilities

are varied and numerous. We do not suppose that, when forced or induced
to consider emergent options, managers canvass <u>all</u> the possibilities.
We can suppose, rather, that officers closely concerned with processing,
buying, selling and financing will, in the ordinary course of events,
become aware of what seem to them to be the more promising of the
opportunities the market presents. We can suppose, further, that as the
outcome of every course of action is uncertain, the firm will seldom
change its style of operations in large chunks. It will proceed, therefore,
to consider the prospects of the more promising opportunities by formal
calculation.

This entails an entirely different kind of calculation from the determination of results and position <u>ex post</u>. It is <u>ex ante</u> calculation, all the components of which are conjectural. For the continuation of each segment of the existing style of operations that may be replaced by a new style, and for the prospective replacement or substitute style, DCF or NPV calculations will be made. Use will be made of the expected purchase or entry prices of factor inputs and the expected selling prices of product outputs. The calculations are wholly imaginative and exploratory, their object being to enable the firm's officers to rank prospective courses of action in terms of their aggregate prospective yields.

This is a second instance of a specific kind of information – discounted prospective cash inflows and outflows – serving a particular purpose. To enable managers to rank projects in terms of their expected net proceeds is the only function of discounted value calculations; no other class of information will perform that function where the net inflows from the projects under consideration fall at different rates at different times.

(3) <u>Prospective undiscounted information</u>

However, the time incidence of net flows and the contemplated means of funding new projects may differentially influence the solvency, the debt-dependence (financial flexibility) and asset composition (investment risk). To bring these features under scrutiny, exploratory budgets of operations and states for a number of future periods may be sketched. Based on the opening financial position, using the same hypothetical flow figures as in the NPV calculations, and estimating accruals, projected financial statements may be obtained for each of the highly ranked options or option-sets. That programme will be chosen which promises the optimal combination of rate of return and the other financial features mentioned.

This is a third instance of a particular kind of information – prospective net incomes and positions – serving a specific, identified function.

(4) <u>Four distinct kinds of information</u>

In all, then, there are four kinds of information, past experienced, recently dated, prospective discounted, and prospective periodical (undiscounted), each of which has a unique function, a function that is not performed by information of any one of the other kinds. Moreover the recently dated statement of financial position locks together the other three kinds of information, in formulation and in function. The ex post financial summaries and the accounts on which they are based encapsulate the financial experience of the firm, the consequences of its transactions and the effects on it of non-transaction events. They provide the basis for diagnostic inferences which may be of service in choosing courses or patterns of future action, and the position statement of latest date represents the financial capacities and constraints with which the firm faces its future. Their contents are entirely historical, historical revenues, historical costs, accrued historical gains and losses and balances of money and money equivalents at the closing date of the period which are themselves historical. The prospective calculations, straight and discounted are, except for the opening financial position, hypothetical, relating strictly to possibilities and expectations; expected purchase (entry or replacement) prices, expected selling prices and expected outcomes and balances.

It will be apparent that the principal kinds of valuation endorsed in the literature and in practice - historical cost, net realisable value, replacement cost and net present value - all have a place in this scheme. But they do not have the same place. I am disposed to think that the intuition of those who contend that all these valuations are pertinent in decision-making is not playing them false. Where error lies is in forcing all those valuations into a balance sheet purporting to represent a dated financial position; and the error stems from failure to analyse the functions of the differently dated and qualitatively different kinds of information which are the matrix of all emergent decisions.

(5) Investors' decisions

So much for management. The interests of external parties in financial information may be disposed of summarily. We will deal only with the situation of investors who are not substantial shareholders or investor-managers. We may suppose investors in shares to be interested in the yields of their investments from time to time. The periodical yield is dividend plus or minus the amount of the shift in the selling prices of the shares divided by the sum invested, or in the case of a continuing investment, divided by the selling price of the shares at the beginning of the period. Past share prices and dividends are discoverable independently of the accounts. Expected share prices and dividends, however, are the matters that are pertinent to the choice between holding, adding to a holding and reducing a holding. And expected prices and dividends are conjectural. As a first approximation to expected dividends, and since the profits of a firm are the source of dividends, the past rates of return of the firm may be used. Since the maintenance or growth of a rate of return depends in part on the continued solvency, the financial flexibility (debt-dependence) and the asset composition of a firm, the latest information on these features of the firm may reasonably be expected to influence investors' expectations. This is the same information on the firm's affairs as was said to be pertinent to managers.

Outsiders, however, can have little knowledge of the internal operations of firms or of the pressures that force them or the opportunities that enable them to vary their operations or their asset and equity compositions. Since the game of business is competitive, managers are loathe to release specific information on prospects or strategies which may benefit competitors more than it benefits the firm and its security-holders. Perforce, investors must rely on the releases of financial information by the firm, and such general information on developments that may influence future profits as they may discover from the news media. That makes it important that the financial statements of the firm shall correspond with its real states of affairs from time to time, that its profits shall be genuine increments in wealth represented in up-to-date money units, and that its balance sheet shall represent its dated capacity to carry on or vary its business by virtue of what it owns and owes, whatever its future plans or circumstances may be. In short, the same principles apply as were enunciated when dealing with the problem situations of managers. And for reasons there given, neither hypothetical replacement prices nor net present values are serviceable components of the aggregates used in calculations of the key indicators.

Investors have options, as do managers. But theirs are security or other property investment options. They may be supposed to seek that investment which, given their other investments, provides the prospect of an optimal combination of yields, convertibilities and asset holding risks. Their calculations of prospects are less complex than those of managers; but, in principle, they make use of the same kinds of information on the past and present and give consideration as well as they can to the prospects of firms in which they may invest, as managers do in their own setting. To that setting I now return.

(6) Decision models and practices

The managerial decision-making model I have sketched is a model of choice by elimination. "All choices are in fact largely negative; for every 'yes' implies a thousand 'noes' ".[11] Choice by elimination is not only plausible; it seems to be the only serviceable model where options are numerous and where expected or desired results are multi-faceted, two characteristics of all financial decisions. It is, however, a model. We do not hold that every choice necessarily proceeds by the formal steps outlined. Choices expected to have relatively trivial marginal consequences may be made simply on the basis of judgement without formal calculations. But even in such simple cases, analysis of the act of choice will reveal that the considerations of the formal model are in one way or another canvassed.

We do not even hold that the same formal process is followed for options of a non-trivial kind. One of the fruits of managerial experience is the capacity to comprehend, or to intuit, the consequences of complex sets of events or of single events having complex outcomes. Decisions and modifications of decisions come so fast on the heels one of another that there is often little time for the formal appraisal of options. And, indeed, little need; for one must live with the ever-changing moment, and what seemed promising must often be soon revoked as more promising or less damaging options arise anew. That being the case, what is significant for the survival and success of the firm is not the formal appraisal of every set of options when problem-situations arise, nor the formal evaluation after the event of every course of action deliberately set in train; it is the aggregate and cumulative consequences of many interdependent actions as they reveal themselves from time to time in periodical accounts ex post. The end of one financial year and the beginning of another is perhaps as good an occasion as any for review and major decision-making; but we do not exclude the possibility that crucial occasions may arise at any time.

That said, the function of the model is to indicate what kind of information is pertinent at what stage in the deliberative process. It emerges that at all stages aggregates of information of a specific kind are pertinent, one kind for each stage. No grounds whatever exist for mixed aggregates. Mixed (or "nonsense") aggregates arise from the use at one stage of information of a kind pertinent at another or others, confusing altogether the process of eliminating options.

(7) The meaning of financial position

Logic of choice apart, some inquiries of the last few years have yielded quite clear indications of what is widely understood by financial position and of the relationship between past and future. Surveys made in Australia, New Zealand, South Africa and the United States yielded a total of some 3,696 responses, of which 1,938 were responses of accountants and the rest were of people of other trades and professions.[12] Asked whether financial position would be best represented by valuing assets at their original costs, their replacement costs or what they would fetch if sold (their money equivalents), 82 per cent of all respondents and 81 per cent of accountants responding chose money equivalents. The responses of accountants were of special interest; for although by training and practice they may have been disposed to offer responses favouring original costs or replacement costs, they responded quite differently, and consistently with the rest of the respondents. Other questions asked whether the costs or the replacement costs of assets were associated with spending power, dated spending power being a significant aspect of financial position to managers and outsiders, whether a firm is to continue or to vary its operations and investments. Over 90 per cent of respondents - in total and accountants as a subclass - in the four countries denied any such association. Asked whether present wealth depends on future expectations, a proposition often advanced in support of accounting rules and practices, well over 80 per cent of all respondents and of the accounting subclass denied any such association. The responses reinforce the contention that, for the representation of financial position, any valuation other than a money equivalent valuation is irrelevant and potentially misleading.

Dogma and dialectic

These conclusions, so seriously at odds with the conventional wisdom, may not be palatable. Is it possible that so many exponents and practitioners could be so far in error? Yes, for reasons I shall give.

What we believe is to a very large extent dependent on what we learn when young, in our most impressionable age. It is sustained and supported by what our colleagues and acquaintances learn in the same fashion - often from the same books, teachers, study programmes, technical handbooks and so on that we ourselves encountered; but certainly from the conventional doctrines of our times. In those early years we are in no position to appraise what we are taught. And though in later years we may "learn by experience", that learning is conditioned by what we learned in the first place; we tend to learn "more of the same", to see things in the framework to which we have been or become accustomed. Dealing with scientific ideas, Butterfield observed:

> "...of all forms of mental activity, the most difficult to induce... is the art of handling the same bundle of data as before, but placing them in a new system of relations with one another by giving them a different framework...But the supreme paradox of the scientific revolution is the fact that things which we find easy to instil into boys at school...defeated the greatest intellects for centuries."[13]

Or, as Keynes, put it: "...there are not many who are influenced by new theories after they are twenty-five or thirty years of age."[14]

A second point. While learning a professional skill, we are generally incompetent to appraise, and even unaware of the existence of, the different styles and motivations of our mentors. Some of the works we study are directed to the solution of identified problems, some to exploration of the verbal and logical features of a field of study. Some to both. The distinction is captured by a mathematician writing of his field:

> "Dialectic mathematics is a rigorously logical science, where statements are either true or false, and where objects with specified properties either do or do not exist. Algorithmic mathematics is a tool for solving problems. Here we are concerned not only with the existence of a mathematical object, but also with the credentials of its existence... Dialectic mathematics invites contemplation. Algorithmic mathematics invites action. Dialectic mathematics generates insight. Algorithmic mathematics generates results...We never could have put a man on the moon if we had insisted that the trajectories should be computed with dialectic rigor."[15]

Dialectic is not, of course, to be despised. But it can be overdone, and poorly done. If the "objects" of a field of discourse are poorly identified, if the problems of the field are vaguely depicted, if the language of discourse is florid or heavily figurative, there may be much speculation and disputation but little elucidation. The three conditions just mentioned, and others like them, are common in accounting discourse. "Income" has given rise to seemingly interminable debate; "capital" and "wealth" only less so because they have been almost disregarded, though they are no less proper objects of discussion and definition.

Accounting — "One of the finest inventions of the human spirit"

The financial problems whose resolution may be aided by accounting information have been identified only sketchily, with such broad strokes that the linkages between decision-making and kinds of information are left altogether obscure.

Perhaps the classic success of pure dialectic has been the emergence, survival and prevalence of the so-called cost doctrine. Its elements were articulated in the mid-1930s, without any consideration of the functions of ex post financial information about firms in the commercial and financial context of the 20th century. It has been bolstered and buttressed by scores of supplementary ad hoc rules. That fact and the recurrent exposure of its flaws by the unexpected failures and successes of firms seem to have passed unnoticed. For allegiance to the doctrine persists in all the popular variations of accounting of the last couple of decades - current cost accounting, replacement cost accounting, indexed cost accounting. One algorithmic mathematician confronted with dialectic mathematics is reported to have said: "This is not mathematics, it is theology."[16] For even greater reason the remark applies to dialectic accounting.

The cult of dialectic accounting disparages the fruits of observation. It proceeds by decomposing aggregates into subclasses, about each of which different lines of argument are devised and to each of which different rules are applied. It invents such nonentities as "the lower of cost and market" and "sum of the years' digits depreciation". It fosters the belief that a more realistic income account can be produced by the same integral process as a less realistic balance sheet. It has generated taxonomies under which things are treated as assets and liabilities that are so regarded in no other setting and for no other purpose.

But for a real field day, the dialecticians have had nothing quite like the days of "inflation accounting". In the absence of inflation, a profit is commonly understood as an increment in net wealth, a sum that can be laid out as dividends or ploughed back (spent on other assets). And every householder knows that inflation reduces the quantum of goods and services in general at the command of every single pound's worth of his net wealth. In a nutshell, then, profit calculation is simply a matter of finding the nominal increment in net wealth in any period and reducing it by the effect of inflation on net wealth at the beginning of the period. But the metaphysicians of CCA scorn such a simple and understandable process. First they decided there is no such thing as inflation (or, if there is, it is unmentionable). Then they invented a whole menagerie of new creatures, which, like unicorns, have no real world counterpart. Tied as by a ball and chain to the cost doctrine, they have devised depreciation adjustments, cost of sales adjustments, monetary working capital adjustments current cost operating profits, gearing adjustments and current cost profits attributable to shareholders. They speak of the operating capability of a business, a term which has no unique meaning; and of the value to a business of its assets, a mixed magnitude that none of us would use in any problem-situation. And, consistently with the inward-looking nature of pure dialectic, they have offered no demonstration on the usefulness of the magnitudes of any of these inventions, or of the superiority of the resulting financial statements as indicators of solvency, gearing, asset and debt composition, and attained rate of return. At what time it will become clear that the scheme provides nothing by way of conspectus, only the future can tell.

A similar undeserved success has been the intrusion of net present values into balance sheet representations, As I have indicated, NPV is an ex ante motion, having no logical place in an ex post statement. And anyone who has observed the estimates of NPV made in the press from time to time will know how seriously they have diverged from subsequent reality. Some have written of net present value as the economist's notion of value. It is not; it is the economist's notion of ex ante valuation. Some have described NPV as the ideal valuation. It is not; it is the appropriate way of comparatively evaluating a set of prospects as seen by a specific person; it is not an apt way, it is no way at all, of discovering a firm's capacity to exploit any prospect. Some who have rejected NPV as a method of asset valuation have done so for the wrong reason. Valuations (a) by discounting prospective net receipts and (b) by recourse to some past or present price, have often been treated as alternatives, the latter being chosen because it is "more down-to-earth"[17], because it is less subject to "uncertainty and lack of objectivity"[18], and for like reasons. But the two modes of valuation are not alternatives. Those who have advanced ex ante valuation as an ideal for ex post accounting have quite misunderstood its setting in economics - as an element in the process of choosing between optional projects or investments. And that misunderstanding has been perpetuated by the device of identifying the value of an asset as one of the values, net replacement cost, net realisable value and net present value by Solomons[19], the Sandilands Committee[20], and numerous others. The upshot is an accounting that is a hybrid of conspectus and prospectus, which for practical purposes is a mule, dumb and sterile.

Some objections considered

There may well be a ground-swell of disbelief in my contentions. It may still be said, for example, that there can be no single asset value or valuation rule for accounting purposes. If the whole range of calculations, past, present and future, is made to fall within the compass of "accounting", there is, of course, no single value for all purposes. But such an all-inclusive usage is productive of confusion. If we follow it we may unwittingly invent sentences like "if it rains tomorrow, I was drenched yesterday". There are such sentences in accounting. Consider the entry in a conventional balance sheet - "Plant, at cost less depreciation, £100". This is shorthand for - "If the plant lasts three more years and then fetches £10 as scrap, its value at the end of last year was £100". To anyone respecting ordinary syntax or elementary logic, this is meaningless. I am convinced of the value of sharply distinguishing observations of the past and present from speculations about the future. The distinction has a long and respected lineage; only in the recent past has it been blurred, through failure to recognise that, though past, present and future data are used in decision-making, the processes of observation and conjecture are characteristically different.

Accounting – "One of the finest inventions of the human spirit"

Given the difference, there is only one kind of value indicative of dated financial positions, namely dated money equivalents.

A second class of objections is associated with replacement costs, or current costs, or, more generally, buying prices. Unquestionably at the point of deciding whether to purchase any good, the potential buyer attempts to relate the expected prices of acquiring it, and anything else its use or sale entails, to the expected proceeds of using or selling it. Currently expected costs (that is, outlays) are related to currently expected proceeds. The exercise is instantaneous. But if he buys the good he may not reasonably say thereafter that he paid more or less than the price of it, if the price at which he can buy subsequently rises or falls. He cannot rewrite history. But he can rethink prospects. As long as he possesses the good he can speculate on the wisdom of selling its product or of selling the good itself, and of selling it sooner or later. And when he sells it he is confronted anew with the relating of prospective outlays and prospective proceeds. This is not the same choice as before, for experience has been augmented and prospects will never be quite the same. He may buy the same good as before, a close substitute or an entirely different good. Only at the point of choice is a buying price pertinent; then, the buying price of every alternative good is as pertinent as the buying price of the "replacement" good. After purchase only selling prices are pertinent. The buyer (now the owner) must make the best of whatever comes his way as a consequence of his possession.

As all of this implies, there are two aspects to every choice – what is available as opportunity, and what means are available to exploit opportunities. What is available as opportunity is discoverable in the market place, never from accounts. What means are available is discoverable in the market place and expressed systematically only in accounting summaries. It is a curiosity that the replacement cost or current cost doctrine abandons altogether the systematic provision of information on the means available from time to time to exploit existing or new opportunities. Of course, information of that kind is unnecessary if we postulate "a continuing long-run firm with an established set of assets and an established production process",[21] - a firm whose commercial and financial processes are not liable to interruption or discord arising from changes in the tastes and exigencies of others or from changes in any of the technologies on which it relies. But it does not seem helpful to imagine such a stagnant firm in such a stagnant setting. Sir Alec Cairncross has cited a limerick that is apposite:

> A trend is a trend is a trend
> But the question is, will it bend?
> Will it alter its course
> Through some unforeseen force
> And come to a premature end?[22]

The perennially varying flux of business obliges firms actively to manage input and output mixes, stock levels, debt-commitments, cash-flows and so on, in the pursuit of profit, solvency and flexibility. Doing those things is what I understand by a going concern. Doing them well, coordinating them, is not imaginable without the conspectus of financial results and states from time to time that financial summaries based on money equivalents can give.

Which may give rise to a third class of objections. If accounting is as seriously inapt as I have suggested, how is it that so many business firms survive, succeed and grow? In the first place, there are ample sources of reliable and up-to-date information that managers can tap when necessary apart from accounting information, including, for market selling prices, second-hand dealers, trade publications, suppliers of new goods, and so on. Second, the ordinary conduct of business and many ameliorative changes may be financed out of the increments in working capital that arise from current trading profits; and changes in working capital may readily be kept under observation even under conventional accounting. Third, if all firms use similarly inapt accounting methods, methods which tolerate income-smoothing, the profit rates of none may appear to be out of kilter with the rest, except occasionally. Fourth, since all buying is done on immediately prior consideration of current buying and selling prices - and not at all by recourse to accounting values - the prospect of being misled by accounting values in the regular course of business is slight. Notwithstanding all this, some firms do get into difficulties, suffer occasional or disastrous losses and liquidity crises. Many cases of fraud and outright failure have been concealed for long periods through lax and cosmetic accounting, at great cost to investors and creditors. It could be overreaching to claim that these things could have been, or could in future be, avoided by a more realistic accounting. But by contrast it would be self-delusion to imagine that inapt accounting had or has nothing to do with them.

Time and space interfere with further forays among the objections. I have not yet found one objection that can withstand examination. But more important than piecemeal objections and retorts to them is the insidious influence of tolerance of nonsense numbers. A business system that produces and uses unrealistic and unreliable indicators of the progress and states of firms can inspire neither confidence, nor the pursuit of efficiency, nor respect for morality. Neither managers nor the rest of us can know how well firms and industries are managed. The figures and those that produce them may come under opprobrium, ranging from mild disdain to sheer contempt. Opportunists and adventurers may find lax accounting and those who support it convenient screens for venal schemes. Accountants themselves may come to doubt, to despise, to denigrate their art, choosing to side with those who would misuse and pervert it rather than to stand for thoroughly disciplined and self-disciplined practice. If we sow the wind, we shall reap the whirlwind. The art on which the business world depends and of which accountants are both the practitioners and the custodians deserves better than that.

Professional ideals and educational idealism

The history of every trade and profession has been marked by a long period of practice based on tradition, on trust by the present generation in the wisdom of the rules of thumb, conventions and doctrines of its forebears. In many fields, however, progressively superior knowledge and skill, new levels of excellence, have emerged, when the traditional wisdom has come seriously under question. To put the doctrines and practices of one's field under intensive scrutiny is not the duty or function of any specific sector of a profession. In accounting, as elsewhere, practitioners, outside observers, researchers, and teachers have had a hand in it. Their motivations may have ranged through the advancement of professional excellence, the better service of clients, the removal of rules or devices prejudicial to those who depend on accounts, the rationalisation of practice and doctrine, and the inculcation of respect for the systematic, coherent, realistic and service-orientated nature of what is taught. The distillate of these is professional excellence and intellectual discipline; together they constitute the legitimate aspirations of the practising and the educational arms of the profession.

There is, in principle, no conflict between professional excellence and intellectual discipline. Whitehead described a profession as "an avocation whose activities are subjected to theoretical analysis, and are modified by theoretical conclusions derived from that analysis".[23] Theoretical analysis of the beliefs and practices of professionals is a never-ending task. No doubt there are, in all professions, beliefs, doctrines and conventions still awaiting analysis. But only what can be observed, experienced and understood and what is consistent with other knowledge will carry each new generation of novice-professionals beyond the time-bound customs and conventions of their profession. Now, whereas there may appear to be no conflict between professional excellence and intellectual rigour, there may well seem to be conflict between what is practised and what is taught - indeed, between practitioners and teachers. It is a facet of the human condition that groups, of whatever kind, have a propensity for closing ranks against threats of interference with their established norms. If practitioners and teachers both react in that fashion we have a classical impasse, benefiting no one.

On the other hand, it is a feature of human social organisation that there are means of replacing old knowledge and old norms with new. The processes are research and education; the instruments are, generally, colleges and universities. Only in the last 30 years, perhaps only in the last decade, has the accountancy profession established anything like firm relations with the universities. That is too short a time to have developed the sense of shared concerns, the easy compatibility between profession and centres of learning, by which other professions have advanced. But it is long enough for some attitudes to have hardened against the notion of shared concerns.

In many places the professional organisations and their auxiliaries pay little attention to the capacities of the universities for research on practical matters. They have their own researchers "in house", removed from the atmosphere of independent inquiry of the universities and strongly conditioned by the conventional wisdom of their time. In many places, on the other hand, university researchers pay little attention to the application of theoretical analysis to the technical practices and problems of the profession. Their inquiries become abstruse, their publications readable by fewer and fewer. They turn to dialectic and shun problem-solving. Some profess to engage in what they do for its own sake, which is just another way of saying: do not ask us to be fruitful, collaborative or accountable. There is thus a closing of ranks on both sides.

I see no good reason for this intransigeance. The functions of the practising profession and the centres of learning can be better promoted by much closer collaboration, rather more respect on each side for the special skills and potentials of the other and rather more sympathy on each side for the difficulties of the other. If new ideas are to win support, it must be through the medium of the practising profession. If new ideas are to be worthy of support, they must go through the slow processes of conception, analysis, reformulation, evidence gathering, testing and so on, processes for which, in other professions, the independent centres of research and learning are recognised as properly equipped and competent.

If either or both sides lack the requisite patience and tolerance, they in their own generation will not suffer. The sufferers will be the young, those who at any present time are acquiring professional knowledge and skill and who will become the next generation of professionals. If we gloss over logical flaws and functional deficiencies in our art and its practice, they will rise again and again to bedevil our successors. We will not have prepared them to carry on the pursuit of excellence in directions where we have faltered. If we give them a narrow or atomistic view of their inheritance, we give them less than they, their profession and the business community at large deserve.

I give you some words of Jose Ortega y Gasset, Spanish publicist, teacher, philosopher, statesman, born 100 years ago this year:

> ...any age presents very disparate systems of convictions. Some are a drossy residue of other times. But there is always a system of live ideas which represents the superior level of the age, a system which is essentially characteristic of its times; and this system is the culture of the age. He who lives at a lower level, on archaic ideas, condemns himself to a lower life, more difficult, toilsome, unrefined... The man who lives on a plane beneath the enlightened level of his time is condemned, relatively, to the life of an infra-man... It is a life crippled, wrecked, false. The man who fails to live at the height of his time is living beneath what would constitute his right life. Or in other words, he is swindling himself out of his own life.[24]

The threat beneath Ortega's rhetoric is real; but those whose professional mentors and teachers have never given them a glimpse of the view from Pisgah will never know how much they have missed, will never know how much richer it is to live, work and think at the enlightened level of their times than to be chained to archaic ideas.

Accounting – "One of the finest inventions of the human spirit"

The prospect

What kind of view, then, may we have of the future? The wealth of nations, the living standards of us all, depend on the efficiency of business. And that depends on the prompt identification of potential sources of difficulty. It would, I imagine, be a ground for great professional satisfaction to be sure that accounting is playing its part in the pursuit of efficiency. But that is a satisfaction we yet have no right to claim.

Disciplined measurement of states and changes in state has been valued widely for the power it has given men over the variables that surround them and their enterprises. Modern medical diagnosis, means of navigation and the control of large scale or dangerous processes would have been impossible without well-designed measurement devices. Increasing ability to discriminate between symptoms and between sets of symptoms, for example, has been at the heart of the discovery of diseases not before identified and of therapies not before imagined.

The body commercial, the business firm, is far less well served. As I observed earlier, accounting is not the only device by which business affairs are managed and regulated. But it is the only way of obtaining systematic information on the progress and state of the whole – on profits, and on the exposure of the firm to the risks of trade variations, price variations, price-level variations, foreign exchange variations, liquidity variations and operating efficiency variations. The consequences of adverse variations in any of these directions may be countered by actions in one or more of the other directions. However, managers will not know the extent of experienced consequences nor the expected consequences of possible remedies while accounting fails to throw up signals that discriminate between the many possible, and deviously but systematically connected, sources of damage or advantage.

By way of illustration, a firm's rate of return is the compound product of its asset turnover, its mark up rate, its expense rate, its gearing and its tax rate. If a rate of return is to signify a genuine rate of increase in wealth, every numerator and every denominator of these rates must be a genuine money sum. No fiction will serve; every fiction will lead to misinformation on at least two of the key indicators or guides just mentioned. And contemporary practice and doctrine are loaded with fictions – hypothetical depreciation, "either-or" rules, lags and anticipations, omissions, and so on. Discriminating diagnosis and reasoned choice are seriously impeded, if not altogether aborted, by such undisciplined calculation. It is curious, but true, that none of the reports of official or professional inquiries into new styles of accounting has seriously noticed the many facets of the financial affairs of firms on which accounting could throw light. And it is demonstrable that the indicators which the old and many of the new styles of accounting yield may be suggestive of courses of action quite at odds with the remedial action appropriate to a firm's present state and style of operations.

Accounting can be a tightly disciplined art. I envisage the possibility, when it is so disciplined, of identifying many more potential difficulties - business maladies, if you will - than can now be identified; and more promptly. Accountants would no longer condemn themselves to "a lower life, more difficult, toilsome, unrefined"; for their labours would yield clear and positive benefit in the conduct of the complex business and financial arrangements that are characteristic of our times.

I return to my main theme. I attributed to others the view that a conspectus of business affairs from time to time is an indispensable aid to administration. I attributed to others the view that accounting processes can and should yield such a conspectus of financial matters. These are large and intellectually challenging ideas, worthy ideals of a profession bent on the pursuit of excellence. But they have been lost to sight through an almost mystical devotion to details in isolation, and beclouded by a cluster of eliminable arithmetical, syntactical and logical aberrations. It is high time that these false doctrines were cast out; high time that accounting was made what it is capable of being - the source of an invaluable conspectus of financial affairs, "one of the finest inventions of the human spirit".

Accounting – "One of the finest inventions of the human spirit"

References

1   J.W. von Goethe, <u>Wilhelm Meister's Years of Apprenticeship</u>, 1795, translation by H.M. Waidson, London, John Calder, 1977.

2   Stafford Beer, <u>Cybernetics and Management</u>, London, English Universities Press, 1959, p.17.

3   <u>Leeds Estate Building and Investment Society Ltd</u> v <u>Shepherd</u> (1887) 36 Ch.D. 787.

4   W.A. Paton, <u>Accounting Theory</u>, 1922; source cited, Accounting Studies Press reprint, 1962, p.425.

5   R.H. Montgomery, Foreword to E. Peragallo, <u>Origin and Evolution of Double Entry Bookkeeping</u>, New York, American Institute Publishing Company, 1938.

6   "Relativity" is reproduced in D.R. Hofstadter, <u>Gödel, Escher, Bach: An Eternal Golden Braid</u>, Penguin Books, 1980. Other works of the artist are reproduced in Hofstadter, and in M.C. Escher and others, <u>The World of M.C. Escher</u>, New York, Harry N. Abrams, 1972.

7   R. Colinson, <u>Idea Rationaria</u>, Edinburgh, David Lindsay & others, 1683; source of this and the following quotation, Yamey, Edey and Thomson, <u>Accounting in England and Scotland: 1543–1800</u>, London, Sweet & Maxwell, 1963, pp.8-9.

8   W. Gordon, <u>The Universal Accountant and Complete Merchant</u>..., Edinburgh, for A & J Donaldson, 1787.

9   J.M. Clark, <u>The Economics of Overhead Costs</u>, Chicago, University of Chicago Press, 1923, p.35.

10   Study Group on the Objectives of Financial Statements, <u>Objectives of Financial Statements</u>, New York, A.I.C.P.A., 1973, p.41.

11   G. Vickers, <u>Value Systems and Social Process</u>, Penguin Books, 1970, p.45.

12   The Australian survey was reported in R.J. Chambers, <u>The Design of Accounting Standards</u>, Monograph No.1, University of Sydney Accounting Research Centre, 1980. The South African survey was described briefly in <u>The South African Chartered Accountant</u> of December 1982 and January 1983. Results of the other two surveys have not yet been published. For carrying out the local surveys and analysing the results I have to thank Ron Peterson, University of Waikato; William Maguire, University of Cape Town; and William Hopwood and James McKeown, University of Illinois.

13   Herbert Butterfield, <u>The Origins of Modern Science, 1300-1800</u>, New York, The Free Press, 1966, pp. 13-14.

14 J.M. Keynes, <u>The General Theory of Employment, Interest and Money</u>, London, Macmillan, 1936, pp. 383-4.

15 Peter Henrici, "Computational Complex Analysis", <u>Proceedings</u> of Symposia in Applied Mathematics, Vol.20, 1974, p.80.

16 Attributed to Gordan in R.J. Davis and R. Hersh, <u>The Mathematical Experience</u>, Brighton, Harvester, 1981, p.184.

17 For example, W.T. Baxter, <u>Depreciation</u>, Sweet & Maxwell, 1971, p.28.

18 For example, D.A. Corbin, <u>Accounting and Economic Decisions</u>, New York, Dodd, Mead & Company, 1964, p.227.

19 D. Solomons, "Economic and Accounting Concepts of Cost and Value" in M. Backer (ed.), <u>Modern Accounting Theory</u>, Prentice-Hall, 1966, p.125.

20 Report of the Inflation Accounting Committee, <u>Inflation Accounting</u>, H.M.S.O., 1975, para 212ff.

21 E.O. Edwards and P.W. Bell, <u>The Theory and Measurement of Business Income</u>, University of California Press, 1961, p.275.

22 A. Cairncross, "Economic Forecasting", <u>The Economic Journal</u>, December 1969, p.797. The limerick was attributed to "Stein Age Forecaster"!.

23 A.N. Whitehead, <u>Adventures of Ideas</u>, 1933; cited from Mentor Book edition, 1964, p.64.

24 Jose Ortega y Gasset, <u>Mission of the University</u>, 1930; translation by H.L. Nostrand, London, Routledge & Kegan Paul, 1946, pp.65-67.

Accounting for Foreign Business

The currency translation problem is the same in kind as the inflation accounting problem. No demonstrable connection may be made between financial information and evaluation or choice unless the components of the information are derived uniformly in a dated setting. Proposals hitherto suffer in different degrees from heterotemporal aggregation and cross-temporal translation. By recourse to four examples of different relations between an investor company and foreign investees, an integral method is described for dealing with foreign transactions and investments, where prices and inflation rates are different and exchange rates may vary. The essence of the process is that the components of financial statements shall be made to correspond with their factual or factually based features from time to time.

Key words: Accounting theory; Foreign exchange translations (ACC); Inflation accounting.

Accounting for foreign operations, balances and interests does not seem to have attracted as much attention as the scale of international business suggests it deserves. Debate may have seemed unnecessary under the common U.K. practice of converting balances at the exchange rates of the closing dates of accounting periods. Those rates were appropriately dated, consistent with the dates of the statements so derived. There was, however, one anomaly to which no attention was paid. Accounts of foreign operations, where kept on traditional cost-based principles, would include amounts of heterogeneous significance — cash, an amount of current significance at the balance date; other assets, amounts having no necessary current commercial significance since they were determined at (and remained fixed since) their purchase dates. No economic or commercial significance can be assigned to the product of a price paid in 19x2 (or a depreciation-reduced residual of that price) and an exchange rate at the end of, say, 19x5.

METHODS IN DEBATE

The matter has become more complicated, however. Three alternatives (and perhaps variants of them) have been devised. The 'current/non current' method entails conversion of current assets and liabilities at closing rates and the conversion of non-current assets and liabilities at historical or initial exchange rates. The 'monetary/non-monetary' method entails conversion of monetary items at closing exchange rates and of non-monetary items at historical or initial rates. The 'temporal' method entails conversion of assets and liabilities on the same principles as the foreign subsidiary adopts in its own accounts. This method will accommodate any of the varieties of valuation method used by any or all subsidiaries.

Where there is any change in the exchange rate between the country of domicile of an investor company and the country of operation of a subsidiary, there will arise a 'gain' or 'loss' on the conversion (or translation). In principle, the different methods will yield different gains or losses. There were bound to be debates over the 'best' or the 'most appropriate'. Among recent surveys are Nobes (1980) and Flower (1981).

It is not intended to survey the debates. They arise, at bottom, from the fallacy of indiscriminate aggregation. If different assets are valued according to different principles — as they are under any form of accounting for non-monetary assets on a cost-base, historical, current or replacement — asset aggregates will be mathematically invalid and practically meaningless. Even a conversion by use of a common closing exchange rate does not remedy that, as noted already. The fallacy is compounded when different exchange rates are applied to different classes of asset and/or liability.

The fallacy seems to have passed unnoticed through the overlay of long-standing doctrine. There is good reason for sub-groupings of assets and liabilities into classes that are shortly to be converted to cash or liquidated and classes whose realization or liquidation is more distant; the reason lies in the sharpened appreciation the classification gives to the liquidity or solvency of a firm. But that provides no ground whatever for valuing the classes according to different rules. There is good reason why monetary assets may be distinguished from non-monetary assets; the reason lies in the differential risks to which the classes are subject, monetary assets being subject to the risk of inflation and non-monetary assets being subject to the risks both of changes in asset prices and of inflation. But that provides no ground whatever for valuing the classes according to different rules. So habitual has become the use of different rules, however, that their origins and validity are simply not questioned.

The currency translation problem is substantially the same in kind as the inflation accounting problem. When the money unit of a country becomes depreciated (able to buy less) through inflation, not a single unit of that money escapes; and not a single valuation in money units of any other good escapes. If, arbitrarily, we suppose that monetary assets alone are subject to the depreciation of the unit, we err. When the commercial significance, the value in exchange, of the dollar shifts, the whole frame of reference to which we relate anything denominated in dollars shifts. Likewise when the money unit of one country depreciates in terms of the money unit of another, not a single unit of the money investment or debt in one country of a person or firm in the other escapes that depreciation. The whole frame of reference, in which those in one country interpret what is denominated in the money units of the other, shifts.

As an instance of all this, I carry in my wallet a dated 1968 U.S. dollar bill, It would be pointless, indeed foolish, to expect that, when next I visit New York, I could demand at Macy's or Gimbel's goods to the 1968 value of a 1968 dollar in exchange for the dollar bill. And it would be pointless, indeed foolish, to tender that bill now to an Australian bank and to ask for the 1968 equivalent of a U.S. dollar in Australian dollars. Neither goods nor prices nor exchange rates in 1968 are pertinent to anything

I may now do, or to any inference I may draw from statements relating to present assets, debts or income.

ACCOUNTING UNDER CoCoA

Continuously contemporary accounting (CoCoA) gives effect to all these considerations. It rests on the notion that the managers of and investors in any firm may not effectively reason about the performance and prospects of the firm (and, having done so, choose whether to continue or to vary trivially or significantly, its present style and scale of business, or their investments in it) without knowing the factual consequences of working under the conditions that it actually worked under in the recent past. The 'consequences' of so working are, of course, the net income of the past period and the resulting financial position of the firm; and the rate of return, the debt to equity ratio and the asset and debt composition, which are derivatives of the statements of income and financial position.

The 'reasoning' of managers, investors and others about the past will have as its premises the ascertained facts of the past and the known or discoverable conditions that then prevailed. Nothing that is yet in the future is pertinent to the evaluation, appraisal or appreciation of past performance. Reasoning about prospects will take, as the common premises of every envisioned prospect, the state or financial position of the firm at the time of reasoning and the inferences drawn about past performance. Given these, each person must take, as additional premises, his or her own speculations about future conditions and about the potential reactions of the firm to those conditions. That is what budgeting and other imaginative or exploratory calculations are all about. In the context of the operations of foreign branches or subsidiaries, for example, the accounting should not give effect at any time to events that may afterwards occur or be brought about in the light of information on the past and present — such as dividend distributions, capital repatriation, new investment, expected changes in exchange rates. But in the (subsequent) context of choice, all of these things are proper subjects of additional premises.

Given these stipulations, a style of accounting for foreign operations may be devised in which all the necessary adjustments for experienced non-transaction events — changes in prices, in the purchasing powers of money units, and in exchange rates — are formally descriptive of the effects of those events. There will be no *ad hoc* stipulations; and each of the magnitudes derived will be derived by observation or as products of observables.

Such a style of accounting will be illustrated for several types of setting. We set up first some general features of CoCoA and of the foreign operations context of the illustrations to be given.

1. A statement of financial position at any time t_1 is represented by a balance sheet in which all assets are represented by their balance-sheet-dated money equivalents (for non-money assets, their current resale prices), and liabilities are represented by the amounts owing at the balance date.

2. Since all are identically dated money amounts, the aggregate amount of net assets (assets less liabilities) is equal to the amount of a company's equity in its assets. That

aggregate amount is the amount at the risk, at any time, of changes in the general purchasing power of the money unit of the company's country of domicile. It is sufficient in the example, then, to use a simplified balance sheet in which there appear only the amount of net assets and the amounts of equity, the latter being divided into 'capital and reserves' and 'undivided profits'.

3. For any currency unit M (e.g. marks) or F (e.g. francs), the domestic general purchasing power of M at t_1 may be represented by M_1 (likewise with other subscripts). There are no M_1 in circulation at t_2; there are only M_2. A balance sheet at t_1 is thus represented in M_1; and at t_2 in M_2. If in any period the general level of prices rises by p per cent (where p is represented by a decimal fraction) $M_1 = M_2(1 + p)$; that is to say, the general purchasing power of the unit M_1 is greater than that of M_2 by p per cent. Taking net profit (or income) to be the increase in general purchasing power in a period, if a company begins a period with net assets of $M_1 100$ and ends the period with net assets of $M_2 130$, and if p is 10 per cent in the period, the company would have to have $M_2 110$ to be in command of the same general purchasing power at the end as at the beginning. The amount M10 is described as a *capital maintenance adjustment*.[1] It is charged against the total increment (M130 − M100) to arrive at the net profit $M_2 20$; and it is credited to the opening nominal amount of equity, making that amount ($M_1 100$) equal to $M_2 110$. Where there are both 'capital and reserves' and 'undivided profits' at t_1, both figures are adjusted separately by the same proportion p.

4. The total increment (M30 in the example) will consist of *net revenues* (as derived in any pure trading account, as receipts less payments) and *price variation adjustments*. The latter are the adjustments at the end of a period necessary to raise or lower the then balance of any open account for assets (e.g. inventory or plant) to the money equivalent of those assets at t_2. The total of all price variation adjustments may be positive or negative. The net income of a period will then be the algebraic sum of net revenues, price variation adjustments and the capital maintenance adjustment.

5. Asset holdings and borrowings in foreign countries are subject to the price variations and inflation rates of those countries; and where those holdings and debts are expressed in the currencies of particular foreign countries, they are also subject to the effects of changes in the rate of exchange of the currency of that country for the currencies of each foreign country in which assets are held or debts are owed. If, then, the interests of a (domestic) company in assets abroad and the amounts of debt abroad are to be incorporated in the accounts of the company in units of the domestic currency, account must be taken of both the internal price changes and the inflation rates of each such country, and of the rates of exchange from time to time between the relevant currencies.

6. Since index numbers and exchange rates relate to specific dates, no conversion making use of them is valid unless the raw data (to be converted) relate to specific

---

[1] Where there are no subscripts, the amounts are nominal amounts of effects occurring through a period, even though the figures appear in the accounts at a specific date, or are nominal amounts that are not dated money equivalents (net selling prices).

dates. Hence the importance of deriving a proper set of money amounts and money equivalents as at balance dates.

7. While it is true that foreign subsidiaries may be incorporated in foreign countries, and that they are separate legal entities, it is customary to bring their affairs into the accounts of parent companies, usually in the form of the amounts 'invested' by parent companies. The financial significance of an investment in any asset changes as its selling price (money equivalent) changes. Initial amounts of investments are subsequently irrelevant. The money equivalents of assets on the other hand are relevant in one or more ways. They represent the amounts of money accessible to carry on or to change the style of a company's operations and assets; and even if no such change is in contemplation they represent the amounts invested from time to time as an up-to-date basis for calculating rates of return. The money equivalent of an investment in a foreign subsidiary serves the same function, both for managing the subsidiary in its country, and for managing the distribution of the resources between a holding company and any of its subsidiaries in however many foreign countries. Since the whole interest in a wholly owned subsidiary runs to its holding company, that interest may be represented by the money equivalent of the subsidiary's net assets; and it may be converted to the domestic currency of the holding company at any time at the rate of exchange effective at that time. The upshot is a complete equity accounting for any such subsidiary. In the examples to be used, the accounting for the holding company is such an accounting.

The examples will relate to an investor company in one country and a subsidiary in another, where during a period there are different domestic rates of inflation and different rates of change in particular prices. The rate of exchange of one currency for another will be supposed to change from an opening rate at the beginning of a period to a different closing rate. Changes in rates of inflation and rates of exchange during the period can be shown to be irrelevant to calculations of the results for a whole period (Chambers, 1980, pp. 48-9). The examples will thus provide for a number of the usual features of the affairs of companies operating in different countries, whether by way of branches or subsidiaries.

It is quite possible to set up the examples by recourse to a general symbolic notation. But it would be exceedingly complex, for the parameters, their values from time to time, and the operations on them, are numerous. It seems much easier to follow the accounting by recourse to numerical examples; and numerical examples should leave in no doubt the freedom of the process from *ad hoc* stipulations and its entire dependence on accessible data.

CASE 1: A WHOLLY OWNED SUBSIDIARY

Suppose Company A in M-land (currency M) owns all the shares of Company B in F-land (currency F). Suppose that the rate of exchange of M for F at t_1 is given by $M_1 1 = F_1 1.5$. Suppose that A and B conduct their businesses separately except for the investment of A in B, and that at t_1 and t_2 there were no debts between them. Suppose that the balance sheets of A and B at t_1 were as shown in Table 1.

ACCOUNTING FOR FOREIGN BUSINESS

TABLE 1
CASE 1 — BALANCE SHEETS AT t_1

	A		B	
Net assets (for A, excluding investment of A in B)	M_1	8,000	F_1	4,500
Investment in B	M_1	3,000		
	M_1	11,000	F_1	4,500
Equity — Capital and reserves	M_1	10,000	F_1	3,000
— Undivided profits	M_1	1,000	F_1	1,500
	M_1	11,000	F_1	4,500

Note: At the exchange rate at t_1, the investment of A in B is equal to the equity of B ($M_1 3000 = F_1 4500$).

Suppose that the companies traded for the period ended t_2; that during the period the rates of inflation in the two countries were in M-land 10 per cent (0.10), in F-land 12 per cent (0.12), and that the exchange rate changed so that at t_2 it was given by $M_2 1 = F_2 1.75$. The companies will have earned certain domestic net revenues, and will have suffered or gained from certain domestic price variations. In addition, the opening investment of A in B will have fallen in M-equivalents, since the rate of exchange is the price of F in M. The $F_1 4500$, equivalent at t_1 to $M_1 3000$, is equivalent at t_2 to $M_2 2571$ — a fall in the M-equivalent of M429. Given the figures for net revenues and domestic price variation adjustments in the two countries, the total outcome for the year (explained below) is given in Table 2.

TABLE 2
CASE 1 — INCOME ACCOUNTS FOR PERIOD ENDED t_2

		A		B	
(i)	Net revenues to t_2	M	3,500	F	2,000
(ii)	Price variation adjustments	−M	1,000	+F	400
(iii)	Capital maintenance and undivided profit adjustments (A, 8000 × 0.10; B, 4500 × 0.12)	−M	800	−F	540
(iv)	Trading profits	M_2	1,700	F_2	1,860
	Investment of A in B				
(v)	Exchange variation adjustment	−M	429		
(vi)	Profit of B (converted at $M_2 1 = F_2 1.75$)	+M	1,063		
(vii)	Equity in capital maintenance and undivided profit adjustments of B (converted at $M_2 1 = F_2 1.75$)	+M	309		
(viii)	Capital maintenance and undivided profits adjustment (3000 × 0.10)	−M	300		
(ix)	Total Profit of A	M_2	2,343		

The sum of the increments (i) and (ii) will have augmented the opening amounts of the net assets of A (excluding its investment in B) by 2500 to $M_2$10 500, and of

19

B by 2400 to $F_2 6900$. The specific amounts of (i) and (ii) will be functions of the conditions of trade, the asset compositions of the companies and the specific shifts in asset prices in the two countries.

The decrement (iii) is calculated on the basis of the opening net domestic assets of the two companies. In the case of A, the amount of the investment in B is excluded at this stage (but included under viii, see later) in order that a proper domestic rate of return (in units of equal purchasing power) may be calculated for A.

A company trading at home (e.g. A) and having subsidiaries abroad (such as B) would, it is presumed, wish to know the rates of return obtained in each of its countries of operations. It would want to know those rates of return on an inclusive basis; that is, inclusive of actual changes in the amounts of the net investments due to trading, and of price variations, and of the effects of the different rates of inflation in the countries of operation of subsidiaries.

A contrast may be instructive. Suppose that the trading assets of the two companies were cash and inventories; that both companies worked on a mark-up of 25 per cent on cost; that the inventories on a resale price basis at t_1 were $M_1 6000$ and $F_1 3600$ (so that on a cost basis they were M4800 and F2880); that the inventories were the same in amount, but not necessarily in composition, at t_1 and t_2. On a strict cost-based accounting, the net incomes of the two companies for the period ended t_2 would be the net revenues given in Table 2. The capitals employed at t_1 would be M6800 and F3780. The rates of return would thus be:

$$\begin{array}{lll} A & 3500/6800 = .515 & \text{or } 51.5 \text{ per cent} \\ B & 2000/3780 = .529 & \text{or } 52.9 \text{ per cent} \end{array}$$

(Note that the cost-based inventory values and capitals employed are expressed in M and F without subscripts, since they do not necessarily relate to prices at t_1).

Under the method of calculation of Table 2, the rates of return relate the inclusive trading profits (iv) to the opening net assets (capital employed) expressed in the same general purchasing power units, i.e., the opening net assets augmented by the capital maintenance adjustments. The rates of return on this footing would be:

$$\begin{array}{lll} A & 1700/8800 = .193 & \text{or } 19.3 \text{ per cent} \\ B & 1860/5040 = .369 & \text{or } 36.9 \text{ per cent} \end{array}$$

By contrast with the products of the conventional income calculation process, these rates of return are wholly realistic, since they are all-inclusive for each country, and mathematically valid, since they relate amounts with like purchasing power denominators. And the differences between A and B may be more instructive. We do not attach inordinate importance to the differences in any hypothetical example, but they are indicative of possibilities. In the present case, the conventional calculation suggests that A and B were not markedly different in outcome; on the other hand, the marked difference under the CoCoA calculation may lead to changes in expectations and policies in respect of the two companies. Argument to this effect was first presented in the context of the problems of administering the affairs of an international economic community (Chambers, 1972).

Turn now to the investment of A in B (Table 2). The exchange variation adjustment (v) takes account of the effect of the shift in the exchange rate on the amount of the opening investment. Since the rate of exchange is a price, the exchange variation adjustment is an example of a price variation adjustment. The investment at t_1 was $F_1 4500 = M_1 3000$, which at the exchange rate at t_2 is equal to $M_2 2571$. Hence the loss of M429 under (v).

The profit of B, item (vi), is simply the profit in F_2 converted to M_2 at the closing exchange rate ($F_2 1860 = M_2 1063$).

Item (vii) arises because, in calculating the profit of B, a certain part of the nominal increment in B's net assets was deducted to make up for the fall, due to inflation in F-land, in the general purchasing power of the opening amount of net assets. But that part nevertheless represents part of the nominal increment in the equity of A in B, and must be brought into the full account of changes in A's investment in B ($F_2 540 = M_2 309$).

Finally, there must be brought into account (viii), the capital maintenance adjustment in respect of the initial investment of A in B, which was excluded in the calculations of (iii) above. Since all the calculations of A are in M and the domicile of A is M-land, the inflation rate in M-land is the pertinent rate.

The total profit of A, item (ix), is then descriptive of the total change in the equity of A in its total net assets expressed in M_2. The rate of return of A for the period ended t_2 is the net profit, $M_2 2343$, divided by the opening total equity expressed in M_2 (i.e. $M_1 11\,000 \times 0.10 = M_2 12\,100$), 19.4 per cent.

Two points deserve further comment.

It will have been noticed that certain amounts in the profit calculation are designated simply by M and F, whereas the terminal amounts of profit and the terminal balance sheet (Table 3) have dated denominators, M_2 and F_2. The amounts having denominators with no subscripts are either sums of amounts expressed in the differently dated denominators through the period (as t_1 passes to t_2 and, say, M_1 gradually becomes M_2) or adjustments which give effect to changes experienced but not previously entered in the records (see Footnote 1). These adjustments are substantially analogous to the addition of 1.54 (nominal) to 1 (a measurement in inches) in order to obtain 2.54 (a measurement in centimetres). The arithmetical validity of the whole process is demonstrated elsewhere (Chambers, 1980, pp. 46-8).

It was pointed out in the section on the general principles of CoCoA that the inflation adjustments are apportioned between 'capital and reserves' and 'undivided profits'. This was not done in the above profit calculation, in the interest of simplicity. But the figures may be simply derived. Consider A. The total 'capital maintenance and undivided profits adjustments', (iii) plus (viii), amount to M1100. Corresponding with this debit there would be proportionate credits — a credit of M1000 to a capital maintenance reserve included in 'capital and reserves' and a credit of M100 to 'undivided profits'. By integrally related adjustments, the opening balances expressed in M_1 and F_1 come to be expressed in equivalent amounts in M_2 and F_2. The resulting balance sheets will be as shown in Table 3.

TABLE 3
CASE 1 – BALANCE SHEETS AT t_2

		A	B
Net assets (for A, excluding investment in B)		M_2 10,500	F_2 6,900
Investment in B		M_2 3,943	
[Capital and reserves	1,920		
[Undivided profit	2,023		
= Net assets ($F_2$6900 =)	3,943]		
		M_2 14,443	F_2 6,900
Equity – Capital and reserves		M_2 10,000	F_2 3,000
Capital maintenance reserve		M_2 1,000	F_2 360
Undivided profits		M_2 3,443	F_2 3,540
		M_2 14,443	F_2 6,900

The amounts of net assets were explained when dealing with items (i) and (ii) of the profit calculation. The investment of A in B corresponds with the equity of B (in B's balance sheet) at the exchange rate at t_2. The amounts of opening capital and reserves are shown at their nominal amounts, but in M_2 and F_2, and the capital maintenance reserves are shown separately; they may be merged. The undivided profits at t_2 are made up as follows:

Undivided profits	A	B
Opening balance (nominal)	1,000	1,500
Undivided profits adjustment	100	180
Profit of period ended t_2	2,343	1,860
	3,443	3,540

These accounts take systematic cognizance of all elements of the overall financial affairs of the companies and the group. They are up-to-date, expressed in money units of up-to-date general purchasing power, and self-consistent. The outcomes of the trading operations and events of the period are consistently calculated. The exchange loss on the initial amount of the investment in B for the period is identified; and if A wishes to calculate an inclusive rate of return for B (the aggregate outcome of its investment in B) on the same footing as the domestic business of A, it can readily do so. In the example the rate is $(-429 + 1063 + 309 - 300)/3300 = 19.5$ per cent. It is clear then that, although the operations of A and B were markedly different in result (19.3 per cent and 36.9 per cent; see above), the return on the investment in B, inclusive of the exchange rate loss, is only marginally different from the return on the domestic business of A. However, more important than the results in any given case is the fact that the contributories to them can be identified, and can serve as particular premises for judgements of the past and speculations about the future.

CASE 2 — PART HOLDING IN A FOREIGN COMPANY

Suppose now that at t_1 A held only two-thirds of the shares of B, and that in all other respects the assets, equities and transactions were as before. The investment of A in B will then appear in the opening balance sheet, corresponding to Table 1, as $M_1 2000$. The trading profits of A and B will be the same as in Table 2 (item iv). The amounts brought into account under A in Table 2 for the outcome of the investment of A in B will be two-thirds of the amounts shown in Table 2; their sum (v, vi, vii, viii) will be $M_2 429$; and the total profit of A will be $M_2 2129$. The return on A's investment in B, inclusive of the exchange rate loss, will, of course, be as before, 19.5 per cent.

CASE 3 — EQUITY IN AND LOAN TO A FOREIGN COMPANY

The demonstration can readily be extended to include debts between the companies and changes in debt. Those cases involve the same kinds of money equivalent calculation as in Case 1 and the same kind of gain or loss on shifts in the exchange rate.

Suppose that the interests of A in B at t_1, consisted of two-thirds of the shares of B, and a loan of $M_1 1000$ at 15 per cent per annum repayable at par in M-land. The balance sheets of the companies, corresponding to Table 1, would then be as in Table 4.

TABLE 4
CASE 3 — BALANCE SHEETS AT t_1

	A	B
Assets (for A, excluding interests of A in B)	M_1 8,000	F_1 6,000
Equity of A in B	M_1 2,000	
Loan of A to B	M_1 1,000	$-F_1$ 1,500
Net assets	M_1 11,000	F_1 4,500
Equity — Capital and reserves	M_1 10,000	F_1 3,000
— Undivided profits	M_1 1,000	F_1 1,500
	11,000	4,500

Suppose that the interest due at t_2 was then paid by B, and the debt to A was still outstanding; and suppose that all other transactions, events and conditions were as in the original example. The resulting income accounts and balance sheets are given in Table 5. Items corresponding to items in Table 2 are numbered correspondingly. Items (i), (ii), (iii) and (viii) are identical in both tables.

The interest paid by B (iia) corresponds with the interest received by A (va). The shift in the exchange rate gave rise to the exchange variation adjustment in respect of the loan to B (iib), and to the exchange variation adjustment for the opening equity of A in B (v). Balance sheet items (x) and (xa) correspond with the net assets figures of Table 3; they are shown separately for the purpose of explaining the differences between Case 1 and the present case. The net assets of B in Table 3 would have been

TABLE 5
CASE 3 — INCOME ACCOUNTS AND BALANCE SHEETS AT t_2

		A		B	
Income Accounts					
(i)	Net revenues to t_2 (as in Table 2)	M	3,500	F	2,000
(ii)	Price variation adjustments (as in Table 2)	$-$M	1,000	$+$F	400
(iia)	Interest paid: $M_2 1000 = F_2 1750$ at 15%			$-$F	263
(iib)	Exchange variation adjustment Loan: F1500 − F1750			$-$F	250
(iii)	Capital maintenance and undivided profits adjustments (as in Table 2)	$-$M	800	$-$F	540
(iv)	*Trading Profits*	M_2	1,700	F_2	1,347
Interests of A in B					
(va)	Loan interest received	$+$M	150		
(v)	Exchange variation adjustment on 2/3 of opening equity of B	$-$M	286		
(vi)	Profit of B: 2/3 converted at $M_2 = 1.75\ F_2$	$+$M	513		
(vii)	Equity in capital maintenance and undivided profits adjustments of B: 2/3 converted at $M_2 = 1.75\ F_2$	$+$M	206		
(viii)	Capital maintenance and undivided profits adjustment of A (for capital employed in B): $3,000 \times 0.10$	$-$M	300		
(ix)	*Total profit of A*	M_2	1,983		
Balance Sheets at t_2					
(x)	Assets of A less interests in B (as Table 3)	M_2	10,500		
(xa)	Gross assets of B			F_2	8,400
(xi)	Variation in assets from Table 3 — due to interest	M_2	150	$-F_2$	263
(xii)	Loan to B	M_2	1,000	$-F_2$	1,750
(xiii)	Equity in B: 2/3 of $F_2 6,387$ converted at $M_2 = 1.75\ F_2$	M_2	2,433		
		M_2	14,083	F_2	6,387
(xiv)	Opening capital and reserves	M_2	10,000	F_2	3,000
(xv)	Capital maintenance reserve	M_2	1,000	F_2	360
(xvi)	Opening undivided profits	M_2	1,000	F_2	1,500
(xvii)	Undivided profits adjustment	M_2	100	F_2	180
(xviii)	Profit of period	M_2	1,983	F_2	1,347
		M_2	14,083	F_2	6,387

net of liabilities. If, in the present case, the liabilities had been domestic to F-land, gross assets $F_2 8400$ and liabilities $F_2 1500$ would give the net assets $F_2 6900$ of Table 3. As the loan is payable in M-land, the closing amount is adjusted in the accounts of B for the exchange rate shift (xii). Item (xi) takes up the shift in aggregate assets of the companies due to the interest payment. All other items correspond (in kind, but not amount) with items in Table 3. It will be noted that the sum of (iii) and (viii) is equal to the sum of (xv) and (xvii).

CASE 4 — BORROWING ABROAD

The following example is devised to illustrate the case where a company borrows abroad and where the exchange rate shifts *against* the domicile of the borrowing company. Let all the assumptions of Case 1 hold with the following exceptions. (a) Suppose that, prior to t_1, B was not wholly owned by A, and that at t_1 A borrowed $F_1 1500$ in F-land for the purpose of buying up the outside interest on a 'net-assets basis'. The total equity of A at t_1 would thus be $M_1 1000$ less than in Case 1. (b) Suppose that the exchange rate shifted from $M_1 1 = F_1 1.5$ at t_1 to $M_2 1 = F_2 1.2$ at t_2, and that the inflation rates during the year were, in M-land 10 per cent and in F-land 6 per cent. After the transaction (a), the balance sheets at t_1 would be as in Table 6; and the income accounts and balance sheets for the period ended t_2 are given in Table 7.

The figures are derived by the same processes as those of the former example; items corresponding to items in Tables 2 and 5 are numbered correspondingly. Putting the whole exercise in its simplest form, the amount of the assets of the 'AB group' at t_1 was equivalent to $M_1 11\,000$ at t_1, against which there was a debt equivalent to $M_1 1000$ ($F_1 1500 = M_1 1000$). The net amount $M_1 10\,000$ is equivalent to $M_2 11\,000$. The amount of the assets at t_2 was equivalent to $M_2 16\,250$ ($M_2 10\,500 + F_2 6900$) against which there was a debt equivalent to $M_2 1250$; the net amount was $M_2 15\,000$. There was thus a profit of $M_2 4000$ as in Table 7.

INTEGRAL OR PIECEMEAL ACCOUNTING

The examples all illustrate the integral character of the accounting. The net revenues are pure transaction data, experienced and testable. The price variation adjustments are differences between book values at any time and the observed money equivalents at that time; they are observable and testable. The proportionate shifts in the general level of prices in each country are observables, as are the rates of exchange from time to time. No further inputs to the accounting are necessary; the data mentioned are sufficient to yield the statements of results and positions. The method is technically tight and self consistent. And it removes an anomaly.

The publication of standards, such as FAS8 (FASB, 1975) in the United States, and of exposure drafts in the United Kingdom and Australia, has provoked a variety of surveys, comments and agonized expostulations in the daily and periodical press. Underlying much of the anguish have been the consequences of accounting for many assets by conversion of costs at purchase-date exchange rates, and conversion of debt at closing-date exchange rates, when exchange rates have moved 'adversely'. And underlying the standards and drafts has been the belief that it is possible to resolve accounting problems by piecemeal edicts unrelated to business realities.

It is a standard conclusion of analytical economics, and a generally observable phenomenon where imposed constraints do not interfere, that if the rate of inflation in one country is greater than in another through some period, the rate of exchange of the currency of the former for that of the latter will tend to fall. The examples are consistent with this general proposition. In Case 4, in particular, the rate of

TABLE 6
CASE 4 — BALANCE SHEETS AT t_1

			A		B	
Net assets (for A, excluding investment of A in B)			M_1	8,000	F_1	4,500
Investment in B	M_1	3000				
Less debt of A in F-land	M_1	1000	M_1	2,000		
			M_1	10,000	F_1	4,500
Equity — Capital and reserves			M_1	9,000	F_1	3,000
— Undivided profits			M_1	1,000	F_1	1,500
			M_1	10,000	F_1	4,500

TABLE 7
CASE 4 — INCOME ACCOUNTS AND BALANCE SHEETS AT t_2

				A		B	
Income Accounts							
(i)	Net revenues to t_2 (as in Table 2)			M	3,500	F	2,000
(ii)	Price variation adjustments			−M	1,000	+F	400
(iii)	Capital maintenance and undivided profits adjustment (A, 8000 × 0.10; B 4500 × 0.06)			−M	800	−F	270
(iv)	Trading profits			M_2	1,700	F_2	2,130
Investment of A in B							
(v)	Exchange variation adjustment at t_2 (on equity of A in B at t_1)			+M	750		
(va)	Exchange variation adjustment at t_2 (on loan raised at t_1 in F-land)			−M	250		
(vi)	Profit of B (converted at $M_2 1 = F_2 1.2$)			+M	1,775		
(vii)	Equity in capital maintenance and undivided profit adjustments of B (converted at $M_2 1 = F_2 1.2$)			+M	225		
(viii)	Capital maintenance and undivided profits adjustment (2000 × 0.10)			−M	200		
(ix)	*Total profits of A*			M_2	4,000		
Balance Sheets at t_2							
Net assets (for A, excl. investment in B)				M_2	10,500	F_2	6,900
Investment in B		M_2	5750				
Less debt in F-land		M_2	1250	M_2	4,500		
				M_2	15,000	F_2	6,900
Equity — Capital and reserves				M_2	9,000	F_2	3,180
— Capital maintenance reserve				M_2	900	F_2	1,590
— Undivided profits				M_2	5,100	F_2	2,130
				M_2	15,000	F_2	6,900

inflation was supposed to be higher in M-land than F-land, and the exchange rate was supposed to have moved against M-land. The M-equivalent of the debt in F-land thus increased by M250, and A will have lower profits and assets as a consequence (item (va) of Table 7). But, at the same time and for the same reason, the nominal M-equivalent of the equity of A in B will have risen from M3000 to M3750 (item (v) of Table 7). It should be clear that, in every such (or opposite) case, the amount of one of these changes will offset to some extent the amount of the other. No great score should be set on the absolute magnitudes that occur in the examples. What the examples show is that the whole set of conditions, in the two companies and in the two countries, is interlocked, and that accounts of them, all of them, may be correspondingly interlocked. It is partial, and therefore improper, accounting to bring into account only the effect of the shift in the exchange rate on the amount of debt.

Of course, it is equally improper to apply a dated exchange rate to any price, amount of money or money aggregate that is not of the same temporal framework as the exchange rate. (The so-called 'temporal' method of accounting for foreign business does not satisfy this condition. Strictly it is a multitemporal or heterotemporal method, and disregards altogether the unique temporal setting to which and as at which periodical statements are drawn). Accounting under CoCoA avoids that solecism by the use of discovered and uniformly dated money amounts and money equivalents.

EQUITY ACCOUNTING AND STATISTICAL REPORTING

The method illustrated is a form of equity accounting in respect of the investor company A. To represent the investment of A in B by the initial or augmented outlay by A is generally recognized to be inadequate representation. Hence the traditional consolidation process. But the results of that process purport to represent the whole of the business of the 'AB group', which is not in law nor for many practical purposes an identifiable entity having assets and liabilities and earning profits. An alternative process for giving substance to whatever is shown as an investment or an interest of an investor company in other companies seems called for; and an alternative has been devised (Chambers, Ramanathan and Rappaport, 1978, Ch. 9).

In the simple case of two companies, the parallel display of the income statements and balance sheets of both — as in the examples, but properly extended in detail — will serve. Where there are many foreign investee companies, the components of the income statements and the balance sheets of those companies may be converted to the currency of the investor company's country and aggregated and shown in the second column (the B column of the examples). The proportionate interests of the investor company in the investees may then be calculated severally, aggregated, and shown as the aggregate interest of the investor company in investees in the balance sheet column of the investor company. The treatment of the contents of the statements of investees as a statistical aggregation avoids the impression, given by a single consolidated statement, that all the assets, debts and profits attach to or are derived by an identifiable legal entity. The whole suggestion is operable, and its products are instructive, only to the extent that the basic figures for all companies are balance-sheet-dated money amounts.

IN SUM

The mode of accounting illustrated proceeds from the suppositions (i) that no party may evaluate a past performance or a future prospect without knowledge of the present state of a firm in a present temporal and market setting; (ii) that a foreign investee company must be managed in the context of its own market and financial setting; and (iii) that, even if it is managed locally, its investor company (in another country) will want to assess both the investee's performance of itself, and the impact of that performance on the whole group of companies of which it is a part. Unless the periodical information on progress and state corresponds with and embraces the effects of the course of actual financial affairs — as CoCoA attempts to do — the association between financial information and choice or judgement must remain tenuous. None of the other foreign business accounting proposals escapes that cloud — for all involve heterotemporal aggregations and cross-temporal 'translations'. Both are logical solecisms yielding non-measurements. That being the case, their products will almost inevitably provide cause for dispute and complaint as the experienced effects of drifts in prices and exchange rates fall out of step with the ways in which accounts portray them.

We have held it to be a general characteristic of continuously contemporary accounting that it embraces the consequences of all the risks assumed — the risks of shifts in the composition of a firm's trading, the risk of shifts in prices and the risk of inflation; and that the consequences portrayed correspond with the consequences experienced. The present demonstration shows that similar claims may be made for representation of the consequences of those risks in more countries than one, and the consequence of shifts in exchange rates.

It may reasonably be expected that any present or proposed accounting system would be able to cope with these variables completely and systematically. For if the accountants of a firm cannot or do not quantify the effects of shifts in its environment, its management is forced to rely on inadequate information, or on its intuition of the upshot of complex and deviously interacting phenomena. It may properly be considered a point in favour of any newly proposed scheme or system that it can deal with such a common, if complex, set of problems as arise from foreign business. The point may be claimed for CoCoA. For no other proposal has a systematic and inclusive scheme for foreign business accounting emerged.

REFERENCES

Chambers, R. J., 'Accounting in an International Economic Community', *Journal UEC,* January 1972.

———, T. Sri Ramanathan and H. H. Rappaport, *Company Accounting Standards,* N.S.W. Government Printer, 1978.

———, *Price Variation and Inflation Accounting,* McGraw-Hill Australia, 1980.

Financial Accounting Standards, Board (FASB), *Accounting for the translation of foreign currency transactions and foreign currency financial statements,* (FAS8) 1975.

Flower, John, 'Foreign Currency Translation' in Christopher Nobes and Robert Parker (eds), *Comparative International Accounting,* Philip Allan, 1981.

Nobes, C. W., 'A Review of the Translation Debate', *Accounting and Business Research,* Autumn 1980.

The Functional Utility of Resale Price Accounting

This paper presents the outcome of inquiries made in the expectation of clarifying the relationship to judgement and action of some ideas and magnitudes common in accounting discourse and practice. It is commonly held that the information yielded or to be yielded by accounting processes should be useful. Beyond that point, however, there has been widespread debate about the money amounts representing assets that are useful as elements of periodical balance sheets and income statements; and in what ways the individual amounts and aggregates of them are useful has generally been left in doubt.

The inquiries were made by mailed questionnaire. Substantially similar questionnaires were used in Australia, Canada, New Zealand, South Africa and the United States, through 1980-1982. They yielded 4932 usable responses. The authors, dates of surveys, and places of publication of the results were as follows:

    Chambers (Australia, 1980), **The Design of Accounting Standards**, University of Sydney Accounting Research Centre, 1980.

    Chambers and W.A.A. Maguire (South Africa, 1981), "Responses to Financial Information: A South African Study", **The South African Chartered Accountant**, December 1982, January 1983.

    Chambers, W.S. Hopwood and James C. McKeown, (U.S.A., 1981-82), "The Relevance of Varieties of Accounting Information: A U.S.A. Survey", **Abacus**, December 1984.

    Chambers and H. Falk (Canada, 1982), **The Serviceability of Financial Information: A Survey**, The Canadian Certified and General Accountants Research Foundation, 1985.

    Chambers and R. Peterson (New Zealand, 1982), tabulations only; unpublished.

I am indebted to the named collaborators for assistance in funding the inquiries; for devising local questionnaires; for selecting potential samples; for mailing and processing responses; and for aid in preparing the separate reports.

Background

The prices of goods and services are signals to consumers, merchants and producers of the existence and prospect of opportunities for trade. Whether a person as consumer or a business firm as producer or trader can take advantage of any such opportunity depends on command from time to time of cash and things convertible to cash by sale, and the extent of debts to others. Persons and firms having a variety of possessions - money, goods and rights to receive money - may, as new prospects attract their attention, consider selectively the money they owe, the money they possess and the non-money possessions they could sell to avail themselves of singular opportunities. Only on rare occasions may they consider the **aggregate** of the money equivalents of their assets, the money they possess and what other possessions would fetch if sold; for example, when a major change in asset holdings is in contemplation, or when substantial debt (in relation to asset holdings) has been or is about to be incurred. However, since any one or any combination of non-cash assets may be sold to make any change in asset holdings, knowledge of the values in exchange of those assets is, in principle, a prerequisite to choice from among the opportunities available.

The relationship between the aggregate amounts of assets, debts and residual interests in assets of any party may be described as financial position. The balance sheets of business firms have the appearance of representing those assets and interests. A long line of practitioners, academics and judges have held that balance sheets do, or should, represent financial positions; and balance sheets are commonly described as, or accepted as, representing financial positions. However, seldom do textbooks and the more scholarly literature of accounting or finance develop well-formed concepts of financial position, wealth and income. Consequently many ways of determining the amounts by which assets and equities are represented in balance sheets have been used in practice or advanced by proponents of systems claimed to be superior to traditional practice. The values in exchange or money equivalents have been accepted in all these cases for cash, receivables and payables. But only under one proposal - continuously contemporary accounting, CoCoA for short - has the consistent and systematic use of those values been upheld.

A symposium organized by Professor R Sterling, held at Rice University in 1978, was intended to explore the possibility of reaching "agreement on a core theory of accounting". The participants included advocates of all the main modes of periodical asset valuation. The brief to participants stipulated that they should deal with the accounting for a simplified company having only two classes of assets, cash and depreciable taxicabs. Attention would thus be focused on the accounting for cash, on which there is widespread agreement, and on the accounting for a representative non-cash asset, on which there is equally widespread disagreement. Ross Skinner, who provided the closing "synthesis", found that there was little in common among the contributions as a whole. My paper advanced the use of values in exchange or dated money equivalents as the general principle of periodical asset valuation. Of that paper, "The Taxi Company under CoCoA", Skinner said: "...we still need empirical substantiation of the Chambers premise. In fact, I suspect that the reason Chambers' model has not won widespread acceptance is the lack of intuitive appeal of his premise" (Sterling and Thomas, eds, 1979, p.359). I had supposed, to the contrary, that the use of resale prices for the representation of financial position would have immediate intuitive appeal to all who buy and sell and borrow and lend, for the choice that gives rise to every such action is predicated on the cash available, or accessible by the sale of non-cash assets, to the actor. The premise seemed to be "empirically substantiated" by the most common experiences of a money economy. However my supposition may have been mistaken. Many things taken for granted are in need of questioning now and then.

I have always preferred observation at a distance from what is observed to the use of contrived experiments and questionnaires as sources of evidence in support or refutation of beliefs. In **Securities and Obscurities** (Chambers, 1973) a large number of observed and reported events and dicta were held to be supportive of the functional utility of the products of continuously contemporary accounting. However, if commercial, financial and accounting events were not acceptable as "empirical substantiation", perhaps inquiry by questionnaire would clarify the matter, one way or the other.

Certain conditions would have to be met. Whether any rule for quantifying assets yields serviceable information is made most clearly evident in commonly experienced circumstances. Some use should therefore be made of simple but common problem situations as test devices. Terms descriptive of accounting ideas, processes or systems may evoke vocationally conditioned responses. Their use should be minimized. A number of methods of quantifying assets should be put under test, separately and comparatively; but a limited variety to avoid confusion at the points of response and analysis. Attention would therefore be confined to asset valuation on the historical cost, replacement or current cost, and resale price or value in exchange, rules. Ambiguity in test material and ambivalence in responses are not altogether avoidable in one-shot questionnaire inquiries. Some questions of similar purport, phrased in slightly different terms, could be used as checks on their occurrence. Experiments and surveys are expected by their designers to throw some light on matters in doubt or debate. But test material should be devised to avoid leading respondents in any one of the directions in debate. Some balance in question content and haphazard arrangement of questions through the questionnaire might achieve this. As the matter at issue was the usefulness of information, in bits and in aggregates, questions dealing with components and with aggregates should be included. In case knowledge of my association with the inquiries might influence responses, the source and return destination of questionnaires was identified as a research or educational establishment in all cases.

A series of questions along these lines was given a test-run at a small academic conference in Los Angeles in July 1979. It revealed a tendency to give responses qualified by caveats and provisos. Any simple question can be made to be complicated, and its object may be aborted, by the introduction of conditions or additional premises at the respondent's option. The questionnaire used in the principal studies therefore directed respondents to make no assumptions other than those stated in the questions. The pilot run also revealed internal inconsistencies in individual responses. Members of a group of persons having different theoretical commitments might be expected to respond quite differently to some of the questions. But it was not expected that members of this group would give logically contradictory responses to related questions. On the other hand, both the literature and the practice of accounting tolerate inconsistencies; adding an amount of cash (balance-dated general purchasing power) to the price of a non-cash asset (differently dated general purchasing power) in a dated balance sheet is an example. Whether a larger and different sample of respondents would exhibit similar inconsistencies was not known. To discover that would be an interesting by-product of the exercise. The general style of the pilot questions was retained.

The Australian survey, intended initially to be the only one, was made in early 1980. The questions were cast in such a general form, however, that they could be answered alike by accountants and non-accountants; and, with minor alterations, by respondents in any economy having commercial practices and financial publicity laws similar in purport to those in Australia. In the middle of 1980, and in the light of the Australian results, steps were taken to replicate the survey in Canada, New Zealand, South Africa, the United Kingdom and the United States. The U.K. proposal was later abandoned for lack of financial support.

Sample composition

A "fairly large" sample was sought of persons qualified as accountants and of other persons who, by profession or occupation or other experience, might be expected to make use of financial magnitudes appearing in the products of accounting processes. It was thought that the two major groups might give similar responses on the usefulness of singular bits of information, but might entertain different ideas about such aggregates as income or profit, financial position and wealth. The professional training of accountants, their vocational preoccupation with traditional accounting rules, and their familiarity with the debate over alternative styles of accounting, may give rise to some such differences. The sample should therefore include a substantial number of qualified accountants and of other people. Among the others were practitioners in the finance, legal, medical, veterinary and engineering professions, business executives, and in two countries a number of workers' union officials.

Mailing lists were stratified to secure fairly large subsamples of accountants and others. Use was made of professional and other directories. Names were selected haphazardly; but as directories are usually selective, as what could be used depended on what was available, and as the willingness of addressees to cooperate could not be known, the mailing lists could not be described as random samples or as representative of specific professions, trades or callings. At best, it could be said that the mailing lists and the responses extend across the broad spectrum of people who, as business people or investors on their own account, would have some practical knowledge of financial matters. That would suffice; the inquiry was to be exploratory of common understandings, not exploratory of the differences between the understandings of different classes of person. By "fairly large", used above with reference to samples and subsamples, nothing stronger was or is intended than that the respondents should be a non-trivial number of persons having some of the diversity of the population of the community at large. The compositions of the samples and of the aggregate of samples is given in Table 1.

Table 1 - Sample Compositions - Five Countries

	Australia	Canada	New Zealand	South Africa	U.S.A.	Total
Effective mailing	1944	2251	1000	2017	1835	9047
Usable responses	1126	1236	677	1065	828	4932
Response rate - per cent	58	55	68	53	45	55
Composition of respondents - per cent.						
Accountants	66	52	69	48	26	49
Banking and finance	9	7	9	12	-	8
Economists	-	-	-	-	20	3
Legal practitioners	7	8	8	6	16	9
Others	18	33	14	34	38	31
	100	100	100	100	100	100

Response rates varied, as between countries and subsamples in each country. For each country they were at least as good as, and in some cases better than, response rates reported for other inquiries conducted in the same manner. There seemed to be nothing specific in the questionnaire that would turn recipients against responding. As mild inducement, the Canadian inquiry offered respondents a summary of the raw results; the response rate was no better than the average of the other surveys. The general indifference of many people to inquiries by mail is all that can be offered as explanation of failure to respond.

The Questionnaire

Some of the questions detailed simple problem situations in which knowledge of some money amount is necessary and certain kinds of amounts were given. Others sought to elicit what respondents would regard as, or include in the calculation of, wealth, financial position and income; some gave quantified examples, others gave verbal options. On advice from a specialist in sample surveys, respondents were provided with two options (yes:no) in most cases. The following are examples; the identifying symbols correspond with those used in Table 2.

W1 If you have $1000 in the bank and 100 company shares for which you paid $1500 three years ago, and you have no other property, would the sum of these amounts ($2500) indicate how much money is at your disposal now?

Yes 1
No 2

W8 Do you think your financial position would be best represented by the relationship between:

(a) what you owe (your debts), and the total of all your money and the amount your other possessions would fetch if they were sold? 1

or (b) what you owe (your debts), and the total of all your money and the prices paid for your other possessions? 2

or (c) what you owe (your debts), and the total of all your money and what you would have to pay to buy your possessions if you did not already have them? 3

Collaborators in the replications were given a modest amount of freedom to vary the details of the questions, to be consistent with local currencies and prices; to vary the composition of the questionnaire; and to vary the composition of the sample. Some questions were included in only some of the surveys; hence the blanks in Tables 2 and 4. But the key questions, on wealth and financial position, and significant words were used throughout, and the general coverage of the questionnaires was substantially the same in all cases.

The questions fell almost equally into two groups, one relating to wealth, financial position and spending power, the other to income and changes in wealth. The terms "wealth", "financial position", "spending power", "gain", "loss" and "better off" were used, as having more or less common interpretations. If this assumption was in error, the error would become apparent through responses. The word "value" was not used at all; its many possible meanings would have been a source of vexatious ambiguity. Likewise "worth" was used sparingly. "Assets" was used only once. As indicated earlier, the object of using terms that might be readily and commonly interpreted was to avoid the possibility of confusion that might arise from the use of terms of art. The wealth-oriented and income-oriented questions were spread haphazardly through the questionnaire, so that respondents would be obliged to think afresh in answering each question.

Interpretation

In the absence of a coherent set of ideas linking financial magnitudes with judgement and action, responses to each of the questions would stand in isolation. Responses to a question relating to spending power could not be connected in any way with responses to a question on wealth, or financial position, or income, for example. However, a coherent set of ideas may be developed around spending power. In a market economy, the capacity of any party to engage in transactions with others depends on access to spending power. Spending power is signified by holdings of money and of other things having value in exchange. In a credit economy, it depends also on the debts of the party from time to time; for the liquidation of debts is a commitment of spending power. Spending power is augmented by income-earning operations, the sale of services by persons or the trade in goods and services by firms. Every party whose means are scarce relative to wants will choose, between optional transactions within accessible spending power, that or those expected to yield the greatest advantage or the least disadvantage at some subsequent time. Expected advantage includes expected spending power. To choose to advantage depends, among other things, on knowledge of accessible spending power and debts from time to time, and the rate at which net spending power has increased or diminished between such times.

In this scheme, spending power (the values in exchange of possessions), financial position (the capacity to engage in transactions by virtue of exchangeable possessions and debts), wealth (the spending power represented by exchangeable possessions net of debt) and income (the periodical increment or decrement in wealth) are integrally related ideas. And the amounts that represent them are integrally related amounts. Given the conditions stipulated - interpersonal exchange at money prices, credit and scarcity of means - to any notion of wealth there is a corresponding notion of income.

In setting up the questionnaire, there could not be, and there was not, any presumption that respondents would adopt or endorse any specific notion of wealth. That was to be discovered. Whether to the notion of wealth endorsed by any respondent there would be a corresponding notion of income was also to be discovered. But in analyzing responses it would be convenient to have a self-consistent set of ideas that might be used as a standard or yardstick. It was supposed to be intuitively obvious that spending depends on spending power. The above set of ideas linking spending power with financial position, wealth and income could serve as a means of analyzing responses. To every question of substance, then, there corresponds a response that may be described as "expected on analytical grounds", a unique response that can be shown to be a necessary premise of choice on grounds related to the logic of choice in financial matters. The raw data would thus yield distributions of responses, the frequency of analytically expected responses, and, by cross-tabulation of responses to similar or related questions, an indication of the consistency of ideas entertained by respondents or deducible from responses.

The results are set up in Tables 2 and 4. In those tables the forms of the questions are digests representing closely the purport of the questions used. The words and phrases emphasized in the tables identify the principal reference of each question. Generally those exact words were used in the questions, but of course without the emphasis. The arrangement of the questions is orderly; the arrangement in the questionnaires was haphazard.

Wealth, Financial Position and Spending Power (Table 2)

The questions provided opportunity for considering a variety of ways of estimating wealth, financial position and spending power - past costs, replacement costs, expected proceeds of use, and the selling prices, of assets. The substantial proportions of negative responses to questions W1, W2, W3, W5 and W6 signified general rejection of initial costs, replacement costs and expected proceeds, taken singly, as estimators of spending power and wealth. When, in questions W7 and W8, relating to aggregate wealth and financial position, three optional values for assets were offered, substantial proportions of respondents indicated that the

Table 2 Wealth, Financial Position and Spending Power
Percentages of analytically expected responses (A.E.R.)

		A.E.R.	Aust.	Can.	N.Z.	S.Afr.	U.S.
W1	Is **spending power** indicated by the cost of an asset?	No	97	96	96	96	97
W2	Is **spending power** indicated by the replacement cost of an asset?	No	62*	84	95	90	90
W3	Is **wealth** indicated by the unamortized cost of an asset?	No	95	91	96	94	93
W4	Are amounts of assets indicative of **debt paying or spending power**?	Yes	23*	56	59	56	46
W5	Does present **wealth** include expected proceeds of the use of assets?	No	97	97	–	–	–
W6	Does present **wealth** depend on expectations of the future?	No	85	–	80	90	79
W7	Is **wealth** indicated by the sum of cash holdings and (a) the cost of assets? or (b) the selling prices of liquid assets and the buying prices of durable assets? or (c) the selling prices of non-cash assets?	(c)	93	91	91	90	89
W8	Is **financial position** best indicated by using for assets (a) what possessions would fetch if sold? or (b) the prices paid for non-cash assets? or (c) the purchase prices of non-cash assets?	(a)	83	82	83	78	83
W9	Is a person insolvent whose immediate debts exceed the **worth** of assets?	Yes	69	62	86	71	60

* The Australian (earliest) form of the question was subsequently made more precise.

selling prices of assets were the appropriate means of quantifying assets. The conjunction of these two sets of responses gives grounds for supposing that the money equivalents of assets - the amount of cash and the selling prices of non-cash assets - are considered to be magnitudes relevant to financial choices and judgements as against other magnitudes for possessions at a given date.

It is of interest, futhermore, that these majority responses corresponded in all cases with the analytically expected responses. In effect this is confirmation of the suppositions on which the analytically expected responses were based. The responses to questions W4 and W9 were, in aggregate, in line with the analytically expected responses, but to a less decisive extent. The word "assets" was used only in W4 and "worth" was used only in W9: both questions alluded to the relationship between amounts of assets and amounts of debt.

However, the substantial majorities of analytically expected responses to the other questions taken singly mask some anomalies. Of the five exercises, the Australian and Canadian data were the most intensively examined; but from the general similarity of responses there seems to be no necessity for expecting the other surveys to differ. Questions W7 ("wealth") and W8 ("financial position") were intended as cross-checks. Both yielded substantial majorities in favour of the use of resale prices or money equivalents. But for the two questions together quite a number of individuals gave inconsistent responses (see Table 3). Other anomalies are apparent from the data of Table 2. Spending power was said to be associated with asset costs by 3 to 4 percent of respondents (W1): replacement cost was said to be associated with spending power by a non-negligible minority.

Table 3 Wealth and Financial Position: Money Equivalent Responses

	Australia		Canada	
	Number	Percent	Number	Percent
Wealth (W7)	1041	93	1121	91
Financial Position (W8)	935	83	1009	82
Both (i.e. consistent)	889	79	955	77
Total responses	1126	100	1236	100

Income and Changes in Wealth (Table 4)

The questions on income and changes in wealth were expected to indicate what is commonly understood by income and whether the common understanding is consistent with what is understood by wealth. As the greater part of accounting practice deals with **business** income, and as the greater part of accounting debate is concerned with what shall be included in business income calculation, questions were framed principally with reference to one class of investment for income, company shares. It seems likely that the classes of person who would be respondents would have had some experience of investing in securities or of dealing with the security investments of others. Further, there is a known source of share prices, so that accrued gains or losses on share holdings could be readily determined.

As indicated earlier, under the scheme by which the analytically expected responses were determined, wealth and income are integrally related. That income is an increment in wealth has been explicitly endorsed by many writers on accounting. Further, it is implicit in the processes of double-entry bookkeeping; for whether income is computed as a difference between dated wealths, or balance sheet figures are residuals consequential on calculation of income in other ways, the derivation of one entails the magnitude of the other. Under the conditions stipulated - interpersonal exchange of money prices, credit, and scarcity of means - it might therefore have been expected that responses to the questions digested in Table 4 would exhibit the same (high or low) degree of correspondence with analytically expected responses as those of Table 2.

It turned not to be the case. In the earlier surveys (Australia, South Africa, United States) it was taken for granted that a realized difference between a purchase price and a selling price would be regarded as a gain or a loss. When such questions were later asked (Y1 and Y2 of Table 4), unexpected minorities responded otherwise. If wealth is properly estimated by reference to what assets would fetch if sold (see the large majority response to question W7 of Table 2), rises and falls in the prices of assets still in possession might be expected to be included, by a corresponding majority, as gains or losses in income calculation. The responses to questions Y3, Y4 and Y5 showed no such

Table 4 – Income and Changes in Wealth
Percentages of analytically expected responses (A.E.R.)

		A.E.R.	Aust.	Can.	N.Z.	S.Afr.	U.S.
Y1	Is the difference between a purchase price and a higher price obtained on sale of an asset a **gain**?	Yes	–	77	66	–	–
Y2	Is the difference between a purchase price and a lower price obtained on sale a **loss**?	Yes	–	80	–	–	–
Y3	Does a fall in the price of an asset represent a **loss**?	Yes	33	56	53	37	49
Y4	Is **income from an investment** the difference between dividends received and a fall in the selling price of an asset held?	Yes	–	–	35	24	37
Y5	Is one **better off** by the amount of a rise in the price of an asset held?	Yes	–	58	61	49	66
Y6	Does **wealth** decrease by the amount of a fall in the price of an asset held?	Yes	–	–	91	84	88
Y7	Does **profit** imply a corresponding increase in wealth?	Yes	–	60	–	–	–
Y8	Does **profit** imply a corresponding increase in **spending power**?	Yes	16	–	21	25	25
Y9	Is the effect of inflation on a fixed nominal amount of assets to **reduce wealth**?	Yes	92	93	92	93	87
Y10	Is one **better off** consequent upon using a less costly rather than a more costly unit of a homogeneous stock?	No	98	96	97	97	94

majority. The result was materially better when a fall in price was related to wealth (Y6). Responses to questions relating profit to wealth and spending power (Y7, Y8) were widely divergent from expectations.

Two other rather different questions made up the set. A large proportion of respondents considered the effect of inflation on asset holdings to be a reduction in wealth (Y9). Question Y10 was expected to indicate whether respondents had any common response to a situation in which cost-flow assumptions (such as F.I.F.O. and L.I.F.O.) are widely used in accounting. In the case of a homogeneous stock, which unit is used first, of units bought at different prices, has no bearing on subsequent well-offness. A large proportion of respondents was of that opinion.

Some General Inferences

The substantial similarity of responses, across five countries in many cases, may have been expected. The countries surveyed have substantially similar laws, understandings and practices in commercial and financial matters; and the classes of person whose responses were sought would be likely to have had substantially similar experience of personal and commercial financial arrangements. It was initially supposed, as indicated earlier, that accountants as a class may have responded differently to some questions than other persons, due to their training and vocational conditioning. But that supposition seems to have been mistaken. Table 5 gives the responses of accountants to certain questions. By inspection, it will be seen that these percentages are of approximately the same order of magnitude as those for the whole samples given in Tables 2 and 4. It appears then, that confronted with problem situations or with questions that made no allusion to accounting practices, accountants differed in no substantial way from the rest of the samples. In particular, for the five countries, there was the same general rejection of replacement cost (W2) and unamortized cost (W3), and endorsement of selling prices (W8), in the situations specified, contrary to widely held opinions and practices.

Table 5 – Percentage of Analytically Expected Responses of Accountants to Selected Questions

		Australia	Canada	New Zealand	South Africa	U.S.A.
Number of respondents		748	641	468	510	212
Question	W2	62*	86	93	89	92
	W3	96	94	97	95	91
	W6	87	–	80	90	82
	W8	82	80	81	81	81
	W9	71	64	89	73	66
	Y3	32	51	55	38	42

* Earliest form of a question later made more precise.

Some general features of the questionnaires and responses deserve closer attention.

Almost all the questions that made specific use of the terms "wealth", "financial position", and "spending power", yielded high proportions of analytically expected responses (W1, W2, W3, W5, W6, W7, W8, Y6, Y9, Y10). Almost all of the questions that made use of the terms "gain", "loss", "income" and "profit", yielded lower, and in some cases much lower, proportions of analytically expected responses (Y1, Y2, Y3, Y4, Y7, Y8). As well, in all surveys there were minorities, both of accountants and non-accountants, who entertained such notions as: the cost of a security 3 years ago is indicative of present spending power: the difference between the purchase price and the realized sale price of an asset is not a gain or a loss, as the case may be; inflation has no bearing on the wealth represented by an earlier dated money sum.

These minor oddities, and the marked difference in responses to wealth-oriented and income-oriented questions, suggest that respondents do not entertain as clear and systematic a notion of the relationship between wealth and income as may be necessary for analytical or prescriptive rigor. That may have been anticipated. Accounting textbooks, handbooks, standards and practice display great tolerance for diversity and inconsistency in what is represented as wealth and income. Non-accountants having experience of accounting and its products would have been subject to influence in the same direction.

The high proportions of analytically expected responses to wealth-oriented questions are not explicable in the same terms. The traditional way of representing financial position and wealth ("shareholders´ funds" is the common description) is by a balance sheet in which non-monetary assets are valued at their costs or unamortized costs; and most of the discussion of alternatives has focused on some variety of replacement costs or discounted proceeds of use and sale. All of these modes of asset quantification were rejected by large majorities of respondents; and large majorities endorsed "what possessions would fetch if sold" (resale prices or money equivalents). For accountants and non-accountants those majorities were of the same order of magnitude, what is more. The responses suggest, further, that wealth, financial position and spending power are considered to be closely related notions, for questions using each of those terms generally yielded high percentages of analytically expected responses. It appears, then, that respondents held clearer and more exact ideas about wealth and changes in wealth than about gain, loss, profit and income.

There is a plausible explanation. Buying and selling and borrowing and lending are much more frequent experiences than income calculation. Any party contemplating one or more of these actions on a non-trivial scale must ask himself: "how much money do I now have access to by nature of my present possessions and debts?" The same question would be asked by any party considering whether present income is or is not adequate to make feasible some future course of action, and by any party who wishes to know on what scale a present rate of income must be augmented or may be reduced. The answer to the question is necessarily a spendable sum, of cash in hand and what could be raised by disposing of non-cash assets. Far less frequently is income of a period calculated; and hence, far less frequently does the possibility of a connection between income and wealth come to be considered by individuals. The most common experience of income calculation by individuals is for the purpose of income tax assessment, and for that purpose accrued gains and losses (the subject of questions Y3 and Y4) are disregarded. Further, to the question, "what is my income?", asked at any other time, the answer will inevitably be vague. People of the kind who were respondents commonly have more than one source of income. Some income may be subject to deductions at the source. Income from property may be auxiliary income for which no finer estimate is necessary than is given by cash received. In short, a cash-flow notion of income may often be convenient and sufficient, even to those who would accrue shifts in the prices of assets when estimating wealth.

In the circumstances, indeed, the third of the conditions under which observation would be expected to correspond with the model of informed action - namely scarcity of means - is not satisfied. A person, whose stock of means or whose income provides a buffer against want, is not impelled to keep the employment of the stock and the income it yields under anxious scrutiny. The classes of person who made up the samples in these surveys are likely to have fallen within the description. To professional and salaried incomes, income from property may be a welcome supplement, not an economic necessity. Investment in securities or other property may be chosen on the maximizing principle; but by reason of the uncertainity of investment outcomes, the costs of transactions and the auxiliary nature of property incomes, those investments may be subjected to only occasional reconsideration.

Some Conclusions

On the basis of figures such as those of Table 3, it may be said that at least 3 out of 4, and possibly a much higher proportion, of the respondents would **not** be misled by a statement of wealth or financial position in terms of the values in exchange of assets, and **would** be misled by a statement that quantified assets in other ways. There is no such clear indication in respect of income or income calculation from the responses. Though the previous section offered some speculative explanation of the inconsistencies found in individual responses, and of the mass divergence of some responses from what was analytically expected, responses to income-oriented questions give no direct guidance to an ideally informative notion or magnitude of income. Respondents may have entertained loose or ambiguous ideas about the relationship between dated income and dated wealth in respect of personal affairs. Recall that most of the problem situations specified in the questions were in the nature of personal problem situations. No such vagueness is tolerable, however, in the accounting for business firms or for the information of parties financially interested in them.

Business firms are perennially at the risk of the impact, on spending power, financial position and income, of innovation, obsolescence, competition and changes in tastes. The impact on any firm is no different in principle or effect whether it arises from trading gains and losses or from changes in the money equivalents of durable or other goods while in a firm's possession. To actual or prospective changes in the prices of assets, senior executives and subordinate buying, selling and processing executives may react, remedially or aggressively; but only if the means of doing so are, and are known to be, at the firm's disposal, and only to the extent that doing so will not adversely affect the firm's financial position in other ways. Prompt and coordinated action to sustain profits and maintain solvency depends, then, on sensitive and up-to-date indicators of the firm's access to spending and debt-paying power, and the rate of growth of net spending power, from time to time. Unless the rate of return - a key indicator of financial success - is the ratio of a dated increment in net spending power to a dated amount of net spending power, it bears no relationship to the grounds and circumstances of a firm's decisions and actions.

Substantially the same reasoning applies to external parties entitled to receive periodical financial statements. The laws relating to financial publicity are intended to enable outsiders to judge in their own interests, the amount and the reliability of the spending power they may receive by way of interest or dividends. That judgement cannot reasonably be made unless what is reported as a periodical result is the periodical increment in spending power. Nor can judgements reasonably be made of a firm's solvency, leverage, asset composition and debt-dependence from time to time unless the components of these indicators are expressed in dated amounts of spending or debt paying power. Apart from the laws relating to corporate financial publicity, no contractual provision for the supply of financial information to creditors and their agents or trustees is of value, as signal to lenders or constraint on borrowers, unless that information is of the same kind. Further still, since investors and creditors may or must choose between the firms whose operations they will support, no comparative judgement can properly be made unless the results and positions of business firms generally are determined by recourse to the (externally ascertained) values in exchange of their assets from time to time.

Although the surveys gave no unequivocal indication of wide endorsement of a particular way of calculating income, such a way is entailed in the large majority responses to wealth-oriented questions. Of course, under any mode of double-entry accounting, what is represented as income and what is represented by a balance sheet are simultaneously determined or mutually entailed. But under systems using asset values other than dated money equivalents, there is no specifiable and intelligible relationship between periodical aggregates and the determinants of judgement and action.

It is curious that, despite the universal bearing of financial position on choice and action, its practical significance has been largely disregarded. Textbooks may mention it briefly. Formal inquiries and professional directives over the whole of their history have not attempted to elucidate it. The whole of commercial operations and much of the business of individual persons are directed to the acquisition and disposal of spending power. But the income amounts and balance sheet aggregates of systems using original cost, replacement cost and discounted proceeds as asset valuation bases, have no ostensible connection with spending power.

For the future, there is no reason to suppose that it will be proper to use asset valuation rules which, in some obvious information-use situations, are analytically irrelevant and so generally rejected by respondents to these inquiries. If accounting is to provide serviceable information in a large variety of circumstances to a large variety of information-users, the evidence and argument in favour of valuing assets in financial statements at their resale prices, strongly suggest its superiority to other modes of valuation.

REFERENCES

Chambers, R.J., **Securities and Obscurities**, 1973; republished under the title **Accounting in Disarray**, by Garland Publishing Inc., New York, 1982.

Sterling, Robert R. and Arthur L. Thomas (eds), **Accounting for a Simplified Firm Owning Depreciable Assets**, Scholars Book Co., Houston, 1979.

Accounting Books Published by Garland

New Books

Ashton, Robert H., ed. *The Evolution of Behavioral Accounting Research: An Overview.* New York, 1984.

Ashton, Robert H., ed. *Some Early Contributions to the Study of Audit Judgment.* New York, 1984.

*Brief, Richard P., ed. *Corporate Financial Reporting and Analysis in the Early 1900s.* New York, 1986.

Brief, Richard P., ed. *Depreciation and Capital Maintenance.* New York, 1984.

*Brief, Richard P., ed. *Estimating the Economic Rate of Return from Accounting Data.* New York, 1986.

Brief, Richard P., ed. *Four Classics on the Theory of Double-Entry Bookkeeping.* New York, 1982.

*Chambers, R. J., and G. W. Dean, eds. *Chambers on Accounting.* New York, 1986.
Volume I: Accounting, Management and Finance.
Volume II: Accounting Practice and Education.
Volume III: Accounting Theory and Research.
Volume IV: Price Variation Accounting.
Volume V: Continuously Contemporary Accounting.

Clarke, F. L. *The Tangled Web of Price Variation Accounting: The Development of Ideas Underlying Professional Prescriptions in Six Countries.* New York, 1982.

Coopers & Lybrand. *The Early History of Coopers & Lybrand.* New York, 1984.

---

*Included in the Garland series Accounting Thought and Practice Through the Years.

*Craswell, Allen. *Audit Qualifications in Australia 1950 to 1979*. New York, 1986.

Dean, G. W., and M. C. Wells, eds. *The Case for Continuously Contemporary Accounting*. New York, 1984.

Dean, G. W., and M. C. Wells, eds. *Forerunners of Realizable Values Accounting in Financial Reporting*. New York, 1982.

Edey, Harold C. *Accounting Queries*. New York, 1982.

*Edwards, J. R., ed. *Legal Regulation of British Company Accounts 1836–1900*. New York, 1986.

*Edwards, J. R., ed. *Reporting Fixed Assets in Nineteenth-Century Company Accounts*. New York, 1986.

Edwards, J. R., ed. *Studies of Company Records: 1830–1974*. New York, 1984.

Fabricant, Solomon. *Studies in Social and Private Accounting*. New York, 1982.

Gaffikin, Michael, and Michael Aitken, eds. *The Development of Accounting Theory: Significant Contributors to Accounting Thought in the 20th Century*. New York, 1982.

Hawawini, Gabriel A., ed. *Bond Duration and Immunization: Early Developments and Recent Contributions*. New York, 1982.

Hawawini, Gabriel, and Pierre Michel, eds. *European Equity Markets: Risk, Return, and Efficiency*. New York, 1984.

*Hawawini, Gabriel, and Pierre A. Michel. *Mandatory Financial Information and Capital Market Equilibrium in Belgium*. New York, 1986.

*Hawkins, David F. *Corporate Financial Disclosure, 1900–1933: A Study of Management Inertia within a Rapidly Changing Environment*. New York, 1986.

*Johnson, H. Thomas. *A New Approach to Management Accounting History* New York, 1986.

*Kinney, William R., Jr., ed. *Fifty Years of Statistical Auditing*. New York, 1986.

Klemstine, Charles E., and Michael W. Maher. *Management Accounting Research: A Review and Annotated Bibliography.* New York, 1984.

*Lee, T. A., ed. *A Scottish Contribution to Accounting History.* New York, 1986.

*Lee, T. A. *Towards a Theory and Practice of Cash Flow Accounting.* New York, 1986.

Lee, Thomas A., ed. *Transactions of the Chartered Accountants Students' Societies of Edinburgh and Glasgow: A Selection of Writings, 1886–1958.* New York, 1984.

*McKinnon, Jill L. *The Historical Development and Operational Form of Corporate Reporting Regulation in Japan.* New York, 1986.

Nobes, Christopher, ed. *The Development of Double Entry: Selected Essays.* New York, 1984.

*Nobes, Christopher. *Issues in International Accounting.* New York, 1986.

*Parker, Lee D. *Developing Control Concepts in the 20th Century.* New York, 1986.

Parker, R. H. *Papers on Accounting History.* New York, 1984.

*Previts, Gary John, and Alfred R. Roberts, eds. *Federal Securities Law and Accounting 1933–1970; Selected Addresses.* New York, 1986.

*Reid, Jean Margo, ed. *Law and Accounting: Pre-1889 British Legal Cases.* New York, 1986.

Sheldahl, Terry K. *Beta Alpha Psi, from Alpha to Omega: Pursuing a Vision of Professional Education for Accountants, 1919–1945.* New York, 1982.

*Sheldahl, Terry K. *Beta Alpha Psi, from Omega to Zeta Omega: The Making of a Comprehensive Accounting Fraternity, 1946–1984.* New York, 1986.

Solomons, David. *Collected Papers on Accounting and Accounting Education.* New York, 1984.

Sprague, Charles F. *The General Principles of the Science of Accounts and the Accountancy of Investment.* New York, 1984.

Stamp, Edward. *Selected Papers on Accounting, Auditing, and Professional Problems.* New York, 1984.

*Storrar, Colin, ed. *The Accountant's Magazine—An Anthology.* New York, 1986.

Tantral, Panadda. *Accounting Literature in Non-Accounting Journals: An Annotated Bibliography.* New York, 1984.

*Vangermeersch, Richard, ed. *The Contributions of Alexander Hamilton Church to Accounting and Management.* New York, 1986.

*Vangermeersch, Richard, ed. *Financial Accounting Milestones in the Annual Reports of United States Steel Corporation—The First Seven Decades.* New York, 1986.

Whitmore, John. *Factory Accounts.* New York, 1984.

Yamey, Basil S. *Further Essays on the History of Accounting.* New York, 1982.

Zeff, Stephen A., ed. *The Accounting Postulates and Principles Controversy of the 1960s.* New York, 1982.

Zeff, Stephen A., ed. *Accounting Principles Through the Years: The Views of Professional and Academic Leaders 1938–1954.* New York, 1982.

Zeff, Stephen A., and Maurice Moonitz, eds. *Sourcebook on Accounting Principles and Auditing Procedures: 1917–1953 (in two volumes).* New York, 1984.

Reprinted Titles

American Institute of Accountants. *Fiftieth Anniversary Celebration.* Chicago, 1963 (Garland reprint, 1982).

American Institute of Accountants. *Library Catalogue.* New York, 1937 (Garland reprint, 1982).

Arthur Andersen Company. *The First Fifty Years 1913–1963.* Chicago, 1963 (Garland reprint, 1984).

*Bevis, Herman W. *Corporate Financial Reporting in a Competitive Economy.* New York, 1965 (Garland reprint, 1986).

*Bonini, Charles P., Robert K. Jaedicke, and Harvey M. Wagner, eds. *Management Controls: New Directions in Basic Research.* New York, 1964 (Garland reprint, 1986).

Bray, F. Sewell. *Four Essays in Accounting Theory.* London, 1953. *Bound with* Institute of Chartered Accountants in England and Wales and the National Institute of Economic and Social Research. *Some Accounting Terms and Concepts.* Cambridge, 1951 (Garland reprint, 1982).

Brown, R. Gene, and Kenneth S. Johnston. *Paciolo on Accounting.* New York, 1963 (Garland reprint, 1984).

*Carey, John L., and William O. Doherty, eds. *Ethical Standards of the Accounting Profession.* New York, 1966 (Garland reprint, 1986).

Chambers, R. J. *Accounting in Disarray.* Melbourne, 1973 (Garland reprint, 1982).

Cooper, Ernest. *Fifty-seven Years in an Accountant's Office. See* Sir Russell Kettle.

Couchman, Charles B. *The Balance-Sheet.* New York, 1924 (Garland reprint, 1982).

Couper, Charles Tennant. *Report of the Trial . . . Against the Directors and Manager of the City of Glasgow Bank.* Edinburgh, 1879 (Garland reprint, 1984).

Cutforth, Arthur E. *Audits.* London, 1906 (Garland reprint, 1982).

Cutforth, Arthur E. *Methods of Amalgamation.* London, 1926 (Garland reprint, 1982).

Deinzer, Harvey T. *Development of Accounting Thought.* New York, 1965 (Garland reprint, 1984).

De Paula, F.R.M. *The Principles of Auditing.* London, 1915 (Garland reprint, 1984).

Dickerson, R. W. *Accountants and the Law of Negligence.* Toronto, 1966 (Garland reprint, 1982).

Dodson, James. *The Accountant, or, the Method of Bookkeeping Deduced from Clear Principles, and Illustrated by a Variety of Examples.* London, 1750 (Garland reprint, 1984).

Dyer, S. *A Common Sense Method of Double Entry Bookkeeping, on First Principles, as Suggested by De Morgan. Part I, Theoretical.* London, 1897 (Garland reprint, 1984).

*The Fifth International Congress on Accounting, 1938 {Kongress-Archiv 1938 des V. Internationalen Prüfungs- und Treuhand-Kongresses}. Berlin, 1938 (Garland reprint, 1986).

Finney, H. A. *Consolidated Statements*. New York, 1922 (Garland reprint, 1982).

Fisher, Irving. *The Rate of Interest*. New York, 1907 (Garland reprint, 1982).

Florence, P. Sargant. *Economics of Fatigue of Unrest and the Efficiency of Labour in English and American Industry*. London, 1923 (Garland reprint, 1984).

Fourth International Congress on Accounting 1933. London, 1933 (Garland reprint, 1982).

Foye, Arthur B. *Haskins & Sells: Our First Seventy-Five Years*. New York, 1970 (Garland reprint, 1984).

Garnsey, Sir Gilbert. *Holding Companies and Their Published Accounts*. London, 1923. Bound with Sir Gilbert Garnsey. *Limitations of a Balance Sheet*. London, 1928 (Garland reprint, 1982).

Garrett, A. A. *The History of the Society of Incorporated Accountants, 1885–1957*. Oxford, 1961 (Garland reprint, 1984).

Gilman, Stephen. *Accounting Concepts of Profit*. New York, 1939 (Garland reprint, 1982).

*Gordon, William. *The Universal Accountant, and Complete Merchant . . . [Volume II]*. Edinburgh, 1765 (Garland reprint, 1986).

*Green, Wilmer. *History and Survey of Accountancy*. Brooklyn, 1930 (Garland reprint, 1986).

Hamilton, Robert. *An Introduction to Merchandise, Parts IV and V (Italian Bookkeeping and Practical Bookkeeping)*. Edinburgh, 1788 (Garland reprint, 1982).

Hatton, Edward. *The Merchant's Magazine: or, Trades-man's Treasury*. London, 1695 (Garland reprint, 1982).

Hills, George S. *The Law of Accounting and Financial Statements*. Boston, 1957 (Garland reprint, 1982).

A History of Cooper Brothers & Co. 1854 to 1954. London, 1954 (Garland reprint, 1986).

Hofstede, Geert. *The Game of Budget Control.* Assen, 1967 (Garland reprint, 1984).

Howitt, Sir Harold. *The History of The Institute of Chartered Accountants in England and Wales 1880–1965, and of Its Founder Accountancy Bodies 1870–1880.* London, 1966 (Garland reprint, 1984).

Institute of Chartered Accountants in England and Wales and The National Institute of Economic and Social Research. *Some Accounting Terms and Concepts. See* F. Sewell Bray.

Institute of Chartered Accountants of Scotland. *History of the Chartered Accountants of Scotland from the Earliest Times to 1954.* Edinburgh, 1954 (Garland reprint, 1984).

International Congress on Accounting 1929. New York, 1930 (Garland reprint, 1982).

*Jaedicke, Robert K., Yuji Ijiri, and Oswald Nielsen, eds. *Research in Accounting Measurement.* American Accounting Association, 1966 (Garland reprint, 1986).

Keats, Charles. *Magnificent Masquerade.* New York, 1964 (Garland reprint, 1982).

Kettle, Sir Russell. *Deloitte & Co. 1845–1956.* Oxford, 1958. *Bound with* Ernest Cooper. *Fifty-seven Years in an Accountant's Office.* London, 1921 (Garland reprint, 1982).

Kitchen, J., and R. H. Parker. *Accounting Thought and Education: Six English Pioneers.* London, 1980 (Garland reprint, 1984).

Lacey, Kenneth. *Profit Measurement and Price Changes.* London, 1952 (Garland reprint, 1982).

Lee, Chauncey. *The American Accomptant.* Lansingburgh, 1797 (Garland reprint, 1982).

Lee, T. A., and R. H. Parker. *The Evolution of Corporate Financial Reporting.* Middlesex, 1979 (Garland reprint, 1984).

*Malcolm, Alexander. *A Treatise of Book-Keeping, or, Merchants Accounts; In *the Italian Method of Debtor and Creditor; Wherein the Fundamental Principles of That Curious and Approved Method Are Clearly and Fully Explained and Demonstrated . . . To Which Are Added, Instructions for Gentlemen of Land Estates, and Their Stewards or Factors: With Directions Also for Retailers, and Other More Private Persons.* London, 1731 (Garland reprint, 1986).

*Meij, J. L., ed. *Depreciation and Replacement Policy.* Chicago, 1961 (Garland reprint, 1986).

Newlove, George Hills. *Consolidated Balance Sheets.* New York, 1926 (Garland reprint, 1982).

*North, Roger. *The Gentleman Accomptant; or, An Essay to Unfold the Mystery of Accompts; By Way of Debtor and Creditor, Commonly Called Merchants Accompts, and Applying the Same to the Concerns of the Nobility and Gentry of England.* London, 1714 (Garland reprint, 1986).

Pryce-Jones, Janet E., and R. H. Parker. *Accounting in Scotland: A Historical Bibliography.* Edinburgh, 1976 (Garland reprint, 1984).

Robinson, H. W. *A History of Accountants in Ireland.* Dublin, 1964 (Garland reprint, 1984).

Robson, T. B. *Consolidated and Other Group Accounts.* London, 1950 (Garland reprint, 1982).

Rorem, C. Rufus. *Accounting Method.* Chicago, 1928 (Garland reprint, 1982).

*Saliers, Earl A., ed. *Accountants' Handbook.* New York, 1923 (Garland reprint, 1986).

Samuel, Horace B. *Shareholder's Money.* London, 1933 (Garland reprint, 1982).

The Securities and Exchange Commission in the Matter of McKesson & Robbins, Inc. Report on Investigation. Washington, D.C., 1940 (Garland reprint, 1982).

The Securities and Exchange Commission in the Matter of McKesson & Robbins, Inc. Testimony of Expert Witnesses. Washington, D.C., 1939 (Garland reprint, 1982).

*Shaplen, Robert. *Kreuger: Genius and Swindler.* New York, 1960 (Garland reprint, 1986).

Singer, H. W. *Standardized Accountancy in Germany. (With a new appendix.)* Cambridge, 1943 (Garland reprint, 1982).

The Sixth International Congress on Accounting. London, 1952 (Garland reprint, 1984).

*Stewart, Jas. C. (with a new introductory note by T. A. Lee). *Pioneers of a Profession: Chartered Accountants to 1879.* Edinburgh, 1977 (Garland reprint, 1986).

Thompson, Wardhaugh. *The Accomptant's Oracle: or, Key to Science, Being a Compleat Practical System of Book-keeping.* York, 1777 (Garland reprint, 1984).

*Vatter, William J. *Managerial Accounting.* New York, 1950 (Garland reprint, 1986).

*Woolf, Arthur H. *A Short History of Accountants and Accountancy.* London, 1912 (Garland reprint, 1986).

Yamey, B. S., H. C. Edey, and Hugh W. Thomson. *Accounting in England and Scotland: 1543–1800.* London, 1963 (Garland reprint, 1982).